Library Automation in Transitional Societies

LIBRARY AUTOMATION IN TRANSITIONAL SOCIETIES

Lessons from Eastern Europe

Edited by

Andrew Lass & Richard E. Quandt

ANDREW W. MELLON FOUNDATION

New York   Oxford   •   Oxford University Press   2000

Oxford University Press

Oxford   New York
Athens   Auckland   Bangkok   Bogotá   Buenos Aires   Calcutta
Cape Town   Chennai   Dar es Salaam   Delhi   Florence   Hong Kong   Istanbul
Karachi   Kuala Lumpur   Madrid   Melbourne   Mexico City   Mumbai
Nairobi   Paris   São Paulo   Singapore   Taipei   Tokyo   Toronto   Warsaw

and associated companies in
Berlin   Ibadan

Copyright © 2000 by Oxford University Press

Published by Oxford University Press, Inc.,
198 Madison Avenue, New York, New York 10016
http://www.oup-usa.org

Oxford is a registered trademark of Oxford University Press

All rights reserved. No part of this publication may be reproduced,
stored in a retrieval system, or transmitted, in any form or by any means,
electronic, mechanical, photocopying, recording, or otherwise,
without the prior permission of Oxford University Press.

Library of Congress Cataloging-in-Publication Data
Library automation in transitional societies : lessons from Eastern Europe / [compiled by] Andrew Lass,
Richard E. Quandt.
   p. cm.
Includes bibliographical references.
ISBN 0-19-513262-9
1. Research libraries—Europe, Eastern—Data processing. 2. Academic libraries—Europe, Eastern—
Data processing. 3. Research libraries—Data processing—Social aspects—Europe, Eastern. 4. Academic
libraries—Data processing—Social aspects—Europe, Eastern. 5. Post-communism—Europe, Eastern. I. Lass,
Andrew. II. Quandt, Richard E. III. Andrew W. Mellon Foundation.
Z675.R45L537   1999
027.7'0947—dc21   98-50384

9 8 7 6 5 4 3 2 1

Printed in the United States of America
on acid-free paper

Foreword

In recent years, staff members of The Andrew W. Mellon Foundation, often working in collaboration with others, have conducted a number of research projects. The objective has been to contribute ideas on issues important well beyond the walls of the Foundation, while simultaneously increasing our own understanding of fields in which the Foundation provides significant financial support.

Much of this research has focused on higher education. With data drawn primarily from their experience in the United States, various scholars have investigated such subjects as the factors behind the rising costs of higher education,[1] the state of the humanities,[2] admissions practices and policies at selected liberal arts colleges,[3] and student aid at the national level.[4] Extensive research is now underway on race-sensitive admissions policies and on other questions of diversity.

Libraries occupy a central place in both the research and teaching areas. For this reason, the Foundation has had a long-standing commitment to the ensuring of the health of libraries and of the other channels of scholarly communication. It has assisted, in various ways, the great independent research libraries in the United States and scores of university libraries. In the last few decades, in particular, the adverse economic forces affecting libraries, which were analyzed in detail in a volume prepared by Foundation staff,[5] persuaded the Foundation to start a more systematic program of grant-making in the area of electronic and digital libraries, with the objective of shedding light on the question of whether electronic libraries might ultimately slow down or even arrest the apparently inexorable cost squeeze in which research libraries have found themselves for the past 20–30 years. The first scholarly results of grant-making in this area are a set of research papers, written mostly by grantees of the Foundation, which were presented at a conference in Atlanta in April 1997 and have been published by the University of California Press.

---

1. Charles T. Clotfelter, *Buying the Best: Cost Escalation of Elite Higher Education* (Princeton, N.J.: Princeton University Press, 1996).

2. Alvin B. Kernan, *What's Happened to the Humanities* (Princeton, N.J.: Princeton University Press, 1997).

3. Elizabeth A. Duffy and Idana Goldberg, *Crafting a Class, College Admissions and Financial Aid, 1955-1994* (Princeton, N.J.: Princeton University Press, 1998).

4. Michael McPherson and Morton O. Shapiro, *The Student Aid Game: Meeting Need and Rewarding Talent in American Higher Education* (Princeton, N.J.: Princeton University Press, 1998).

5. Anthony M. Cummings, Marcia L. Witte, William G. Bowen, Laura O. Lazarus, and Richard H. Ekman, *University Libraries and Scholarly Communications* (Washington, D.C.: Association of Research Libraries, 1992).

Quite independently of these efforts, the dramatic political changes in Central and Eastern Europe that started in 1989 convinced the Foundation that higher education, and, in particular, research libraries, were a much-neglected resource in the region. It seemed reasonable, as well as consistent with the Foundation's long-term policy of seeking coherent rather than episodic interventions, to concentrate resources on libraries and, in particular, on library automation. This area, neglected during the Communist period for various reasons, was ripe for massive intervention. After eight very active years of support for library automation in the region, it seemed desirable to sum up the accomplishments of the Central and East European libraries. This assessment was undertaken within the framework of a Conference on Library Automation, held in Warsaw, October 16–18, 1997, under Foundation auspices, and with the active and indispensable help and participation of the National Library of Poland. The present volume contains the papers that were presented at that conference. It is a valuable study of technology transfer and transitional societies.

In reading this volume, one cannot help being impressed by the range and depth of expertise exhibited in it and by the concrete achievements that have taken place in so many libraries. Within a scant eight years, many libraries in the region have attained West European and American standards, and in some cases have leapfrogged them for the well-known reason that latecomers can often gain an advantage by immediately adopting the latest technology. But perhaps most important, library standards and protocols in Eastern Europe now largely conform to proven models, the quality of librarianship has risen enormously, and librarians of the region face the future with a new sense of confidence and professionalism.

The present volume has been edited by two people who have been at the center of the library changes in Eastern Europe: Richard E. Quandt, Hughes-Rogers Professor Emeritus at Princeton University, and Senior Advisor for the Mellon Foundation, has directed the Foundation's East European program since 1990, codirects our activities in the electronic and digital library field, and participates in library projects in South Africa. And Andrew Lass, Professor of Anthropology at Mount Holyoke College, has been the general manager and organizer of the Foundation's library projects in the Czech Republic and in Slovakia, and also participates in the South African projects.

These two stalwarts have contributed enormously to the transformation that has occurred in Eastern European libraries. Beyond that, they have been committed friends and mentors to so many talented individuals in Eastern Europe, who have sought to take advantage of what has been learned in other parts of the world, and who have demonstrated anew that so much can be accomplished through the combination of ability, hard work, and determination. It is a privilege for me to add these words of endorsement to a volume that records the results achieved by a series of projects that speak for themselves.

William G. Bowen
April 6, 1998

Contents

Contributors, xi

Introduction, 3
ANDREW LASS & RICHARD E. QUANDT

PART I. Library Policy and the State

1. *Library Automation:* Fortunes and Miseries in Poland, 23
   ADAM MANIKOWSKI

2. *Developing National Information Infrastructures in Central and Eastern Europe:* The Content-versus-Conduit Debate, 28
   CHRISTINE L. BORGMAN AND NADIA CAIDI

3. *A Coordinator's View of the Impact of Policy on the Financing and the Managing of Library Automation,* 45
   JURAND B. CZERMIŃSKI

4. *Libraries of Central and Eastern Europe:* Basic Dilemmas, 59
   JELA STEINEROVÁ

5. *The Changes in the Functions of University Libraries and of Educational Policy in Poland After 1989,* 74
   KRZYSZTOF ZAMORSKI

6. *In Search of an Optimum Model of Development,* 83
   MIROSŁAW GÓRNY, BOGDAN MARUSZEWSKI, AND JAN ANDRZEJ NIKISCH

PART II. Case Histories

7. *Automation and Academic Libraries in Hungary:* Theory and Practice in a Period of New Challenges, 93
   BÉLA MADER

8. *Automation in the National Library in Warsaw:* From an In-House System to INNOPAC, 104
   JADWIGA SADOWSKA

9. *The Retrospective Conversion of the Catalog in the Library of the American Studies Center, Warsaw University,* 113
   EWA PALUSZKIEWICZ

10. *CASLIN, Priorities of the Czech National Library, and Government Policy on Information and Libraries,* 120
    VOJTĚCH BALÍK

11. *Cooperation, Consortia, Compatibility, Connectivity:* The Case of CASLIN, 134
    MARTIN SVOBODA

12. *Some Problems with Library Automation in the KOLIN Library Consortium,* 141
    DARINA KOŽUCHOVÁ AND ĽUBOMÍRA ŠOLTÉSOVÁ

13. *Realization of the CASLIN Project in the Slovak National Library and Its Impact on the Automation of Libraries in Slovakia,* 153
    IGOR PROKOP, MILAN RAKÚS, AND DANIELA SLÍŽOVÁ

14. *The Aleph Implementation at the National Library of the Czech Republic,* 168
    IVA PŘÍBRAMSKÁ

PART III. Cataloging, Authority Control, Retroconversion, Subject Headings, Search, and Union Catalogues

15. *A Retrospective Conversion:* The Case of Debrecen, 183
    OLGA GOMBA

16. *The Retrospective Conversion in Czech Libraries,* 196
    BOHDANA STOKLASOVÁ

17. *The Implementation of an Automated System at the University Library in Bratislava, Slovakia,* 204
    ZUZANA ŘEPIŠOVÁ

18. *Cataloging Standards in Czech Libraries,* 219
    BOHDANA STOKLASOVÁ

19. *Evolution of Authority File Work in Poland,* 224
    ANNA PALUSZKIEWICZ

20. *The Union Catalog:* Different Library Systems, Different Solutions, 235
   BŁAŻEJ FERET

21. *New Possibilities for Information Retrieval*, 251
   GÉZA BAKONYI

22. *Why, and How to, Translate a Subject Heading System:* Authority Control Provides a Solution, 267
   KLÁRA KOLTAY

23. *Integrating Internet Resources into the Library Catalog*, 284
   PÉTER GYÜRE

24. *Knowledge and Information Processing*, 293
   TIBOR CSÍK AND KATALIN VARGA

25. *The Dissemination and Archival Storage of Old Materials as Electronic Documents*, 313
   ADOLF KNOLL

26. *The Automation of Special Collections:* General Issues, 327
   JOANNA PASZTALENIEC-JARZYŃSKA

PART IV. Management Issues

27. *The Sequencing of Automation in Central and East European Research Libraries*, 335
   HENRYK HOLLENDER

28. *Managing Delays:* The Micropolitics of Time in the Czech and Slovak Automation Projects, 345
   ANDREW LASS

29. *The Kraków Project:* Problems of Management, 360
   EWA DOBRZYŃSKA-LANKOSZ

30. *Staffing Patterns for Academic Libraries of Central and Eastern Europe, Russia, and the CIS Countries*, 374
   ROBERT M. HAYES

31. *Staff Preparation for Automation*, 399
   MARIA ŚLIWIŃSKA

32. *Interactions Between Library Automation and Staff and Patron Training*, 407
    EWA KRYSIAK

33. *The Special Role of the Hungarian National Library in the Formation and Management of Consortia*, 420
    MIKLÓS FOGARASSY

34. *The Human Aspects of Library Automation*, 427
    MÁRTA VIRÁGOS

35. *The Contribution of Integrated Library Services to the Ensuring of Quality Services*, 443
    JUDIT SKALICZKI AND ÉVA ZALAI-KOVÁCS

Contributors

VOJTĚCH BALÍK is Director of the National Library of the Czech Republic and in 1992–1996 was Chairman of the Board of Library Directors for the CASLIN Project. E-mail: vojtech.balik@nkp.cz.

GÉZA BAKONYI is Deputy Director and System Librarian in the Main Library of József Attila University in Szeged, Hungary, where his duties include supervision of the integrated library system. He also participates in teaching in the department of Library and Information Science at the University and at the Juhász Gyula Teacher's Training College. E-mail: bakonyi@bibl.u-szeged.hu.

CHRISTINE L. BORGMAN holds the Presidential Chair in Information Studies at the University of California, Los Angeles, where she is a Professor in the Graduate School of Education and Information Studies and in the Communication Studies Program. She is also Visiting Professor in the Department of Information and Library Studies at Loughborough University in England. E-mail: cborgman@ucla.edu.

NADIA CAIDI is a doctoral student in the Department of Library and Information Science at the Graduate School of Education and Information Studies, University of California, Los Angeles. Her dissertation research is on the development of national information infrastructures in Central and Eastern Europe and its implications for libraries. E-mail: ncaidi@ucla.edu.

JURAND B. CZERMIŃSKI has been the Rector's Plenipotentiary for computerization at the University of Gdańsk since 1988. He has also headed the University of Gdańsk Automation Project during the same period, and was (from 1993 to 1997) the Chairman of the Interuniversity Coordinating Committee for the implementation of the VTLS. E-mail: jurand@chemik.chem.univ.gda.pl.

TIBOR CSÍK is the Head of the Reference Section in the National Education Library and Museum in Budapest. He is presently working on his Ph.D. thesis and lecturing on classification, indexing, and abstracting at different schools of library and information science. E-mail: h10259csi@ella.hu.

EWA DOBRŻYŃSKA-LANKOSZ is Deputy Director of the Main Library of the University of Mining and Metallurgy in Kraków, Project Manager of the Kraków Library group, and is also the chairperson of the VTLS Coordinating Group in Poland. E-mail: lankosz@libnvl.biblio.agh.edu.pl.

BŁAŻEJ FERET is Deputy Director of the Main Library of the Technical University of Łódź, Poland and is head of the Łódź Consortium of Academic Libraries and the manager for the automation project of the ten libraries using the Horizon system. E-mail: blzferet@sunlib.p.lodz.pl.

MIKLÓS FOGARASSY is Senior Advisor of the National Széchényi Library at the Center for Library and Information Science. He was responsible for creating and managing three library consortia in Hungary that were funded by The Andrew W. Mellon Foundation. E-mail: fogaras@oszk.hu.

OLGA GOMBA has worked in the library of Lajos Kossuth University from 1962 to 1995, serving as its Director for the last 15 years of that period. She has a PhD in library science and currently teaches library management at the University. E-mail: ogomba@libware.lib.klte.hu.

MIROSŁAW GÓRNY is a Senior Lecturer at Adam Mickiewicz University in Poznań and teaches in the fields of library and information science. He is also Vice President of the Board of the Poznań Foundation of Scientific Libraries. E-mail: mgorny@hum.amu.edu.pl.

PETER GYÜRE is former Head of IT department of Lajos Kossuth University Library in Hungary. He introduced one of the earliest integrated library systems in Hungary and coordinated several library automation projects. He is currently software development director at Dataware. E-mail: gyp@dataware.hu.

ROBERT M. HAYES is Professor Emeritus in Library and Information Science at the University of California, Los Angeles. He continues to serve UCLA on a recall appointment as Principal Investigator for CELCEE, an ERIC Adjunct Clearinghouse on Entrepreneurship Education funded by the Ewing Marion Kauffman Foundation. E-mail: rhayes@ucla.edu.

HENRYK HOLLENDER is Director of the Warsaw University Library. Formerly at the Institute of Library and Information Science, Warsaw University, he continues to teach about academic libraries and library management at the university. E-mail: hhol@plearn.edu.pl.

ADOLF KNOLL is Deputy Director of the National Library of the Czech Republic. He is also member of the UNESCO Memory of the World International Advisory Committee and its Sub-Committee on Technology. E-mail: adolf.knoll@nkp.cz.

KLÁRA KOLTAY is Deputy Director of the Lajos Kossuth University Library, Debrecen, Hungary. She has been engaged in the automation and subject heading translation projects of the library as well as in the VOCAL cooperative cataloging project of 21 Hungarian libraries. E-mail: kkoltay@giant.lib.klte.hu.

DARINA KOŽUCHOVÁ is Director of the University Library, P. J. Šafárik University in Košice, Slovak Republic. She is also the Director of the Košice Library Information Network (KOLIN). E-mail: kozuchov@kosice.upjs.sk.

EWA KRYSIAK, specialist in electronic user services and library automation, works at the National Library in Warsaw, Poland, where she manages union catalogues. She is also active in the Polish Librarians Association as the President of the Warsaw Region and of the Library Automation Commission. E-mail: ekrysiak@bn.org.pl.

ANDREW LASS is Professor of Anthropology at Mount Holyoke College. He has been actively involved in assisting the Czech National Library since 1990 and, starting in 1993, has been project manager and grants administrator of the CASLIN projects funded by The Andrew W. Mellon Foundation. E-mail: alass@mtholyoke.edu.

BÉLA MADER is Director of the University Library of the Attila József University in Szeged, Hungary. E-mail: mader@bibl.u-szeged.hu.

ADAM MANIKOWSKI is Professor of Early Modern History at the University of Białystok and was General Director of the National Library in Warsaw from 1993 to 1997. He is also a member of the European Commission on Preservation and Access. E-mail: hmanik@obta.uw.edu.pl.

BOGDAN T. MARUSZEWSKI is Full Professor at the Poznań University of Technology and his research interests are in continuum physics, thermodynamics and thermomechanics, and geometrical properties and waves in solids. He is involved in library automation through his position as Chairman of the Council of the Poznań Foundation of Scientific Libraries. E-mail: Bogdan.Maruszewski@sol.put.poznan.pl.

JAN ANDRZEJ NIKISCH graduated from the Technical University Poznań in 1972 (automation systems) and received his PhD in 1981 in computer controlled systems. He then became assistant professor at the Institute of Computer Engineering. His research interests include wide area control systems, system optimisation and currently digital library systems. Since 1996 he has been the President of the Board of Poznan Foundation of Scientific Libraries. E-mail: nikisch@pfsl.poznan.pl

ANNA PALUSZKIEWICZ is the head of the Section for Formats and Name Authority Files at the Center for Formats and Authority Files, Warsaw University. E-mail: pania@plearn.edu.pl.

EWA PALUSZKIEWICZ is former Head Librarian of the American Studies Center Library at Warsaw University. E-mail: paluszk@plearn.edu.pl and ewa@bluemarble.net.

JOANNA PASZTALENIEC-JARZYŃSKA is Deputy Director of the National Library in Warsaw and is also the research secretary responsible for international and public relations and special collections. She is a Member of the Board of the Polish Librarians' Association. E-mail: bnjpjarz@bn.org.pl.

IGOR PROKOP is the CASLIN manager at the Slovak National Library and the Deputy Director for information science and technology at the library. E-mail: prokop@esix.matica.sk

IVA PŘÍBRAMSKÁ is a system librarian at the National Library of the Czech Republic, where she is responsible for library information system implementation. E-mail: iva.pribramska@nkp.cz

RICHARD E. QUANDT is Emeritus Professor of Economics at Princeton University, and Senior Advisor at The Andrew W. Mellon Foundation, where he directs the East European Program and codirects the Electronic and Digital Libraries Program. E-mail: req@quandt.com.

MILAN RÁKUS is the system librarian at the Slovak National Library where he is responsible for the implementation of the Aleph software system and the realization of the CASLIN project. E-mail: rakus@esix.matica.sk.

ZUZANA ŘEPIŠOVÁ is a program analyst at the Institute of Computer Science at Masaryk University in Brno, in the Czech Republic, and has been responsible for library automation since December, 1996. Previously, she was system librarian at the University Library in Bratislava, in the Slovak Republic. E-mail: zure@ics.muni.cz.

JADWIGA SADOWSKA is the Deputy Director of the National Library in Warsaw, and at present is responsible for library automation. She also directs the Bibliographic Institute, which is a national bibliographic agency. E-mail: sadowska@biblnar.bn.org.pl.

DANIELA SLÍŽOVÁ was the acting director of the Slovak National Library from 1994 to 1997 and now heads the union catalogue division of the library. E-mail: slizova@esix.matica.sk.

MARIA ŚLIWIŃSKA is Deputy Director of the Nicholas Copernicus University Library in Torun, Poland, and is responsible for library modernization and computerization. E-mail: m.sliwinska@bu.uni.torun.pl.

ĽUBOMÍRA ŠOLTESOVÁ was Chief Librarian at the Medical Library of the University Library of P. J. Šafárik University in Košice, in the Slovak Republic. She is Manager of the Košice Library Information Network (KOLIN). E-mail: soltesova@kimex.sk.

JELA STEINEROVÁ is associate professor of Library and Information Science at Comenius University, Bratislava, in the Slovak Republic. She has been involved with research and teaching in knowledge organization and information retrieval. Since 1983 she has worked in library and information institutions in Slovakia as a specialist in library automation and information services. E-mail: steinerova@fphil.uniba.sk.

BOHDANA STOKLASOVÁ is Director for Cataloguing and National Bibliography at the National Library of the Czech Republic. She is responsible for introducing the international standards (UNIMARC, AACR2, LCSH) during the recent implementation of the ALEPH system. E-mail: bohdana.stoklasova@nkp.cz.

MARTIN SVOBODA was the Manager of CASLIN and is now Director of the State Technical Library in Prague. He is a member of the Open Society Institute Network Library Program Board and of the European Libraries Automation Group Board. E-mail: m.svoboda@stk.cz.

KATALIN VARGA is the head of the Library Department in the National Educational Library and Museum in Budapest. She is also teaching an introduction to library works at Janus Pannonius University. E-mail: h8921var@ella.hu.

MARTA VIRÁGOS is the Chief Librarian of the Central Medical Library of the Medical University, Debrecen, Hungary. She holds a PhD in Library and Information Sciences and has supervised research and a number of projects in library automation. She has a leading role in Hungarian and international organizations of health librarians. E-mail: marta@lib.dote.hu.

ÉVA ZALAI-KOVÁCS is head of the Central Library of the University of Horticulture and Food and President of the Alliance of Libraries and Information Institutes in Hungary. E-mail: ekovacs@hoya.kee.hu.

KRZYSZTOF ZAMORSKI is a social and economic historian, currently serving as the Director of the Jagiellonian Library in Kraków. He is also an Associate Professor and actively participates in the University's Institute of History. E-mail: zamorski@if.uj.edu.pl.

Library Automation in Transitional Societies

Introduction

ANDREW LASS
RICHARD E. QUANDT

In 1990, The Andrew W. Mellon Foundation initiated a program of support in Hungary, Poland, the Czech Republic, and Slovakia (the latter two being Czechoslovakia at that time). While the initial functional objectives of the support were somewhat more limited, at present they include economics and management training; the development of market economies; support for higher education, in the form of assistance to research libraries and universities; agricultural-technology transfer; and a substantial program of short-term research fellowships for scholars in the humanities and social sciences.

While assistance to higher education could, in principle, have taken various useful forms, research libraries appeared, for several reasons, to be prime targets for systematic and substantial support. First, libraries under the Communist system were largely passive repositories of knowledge, characterized by efforts at user-friendliness that were pale imitations of the patterns that evolved in the West. Second, while during the 1950s there was some attempt at a central design for unified library protocols within the Soviet bloc, it took the form of minor changes in cataloging rules, with the aim of bringing them closer to those of the Soviet system. And these were never carried out systematically, nor were they considered with a view of other international developments. Even individual countries' libraries were characterized by substantial disparities in library standards. It was not until the early 1980s that some national libraries took the initiative of developing a national standard for a catalog record exchange format.[1] For the most part, national libraries focused on maintaining a national bibliography and on housing the legal deposit copies of domestically produced library material. Third, the scarcity of funds allocated to libraries by the state made libraries lag far behind their Western counterparts in acquisitions of library materials

---

We are indebted, for encouragement, advice, and help, to more people than we can acknowledge here, but we would like to mention especially William G. Bowen, Richard Ekman, and Thomas Nygren of The Andrew W. Mellon Foundation; Adam Manikowski and Ewa Krysiak of the National Library of Poland; Patricia Kuc of Mount Holyoke College; and Phyllis Durepos of Princeton University. We are deeply grateful for their contributions.

1. See the chapters by Prokop et al., and by Svoboda, in this volume.

and of computing equipment and software.[2] Fourth, as is well known, the organization of the East European societies was a classically hierarchical and top-down one, which discouraged both the collaboration among similarly placed institutions and the taking of initiatives. Finally, the Foundation appeared to be nearly the only one of the U.S.-based, as well as the West European, foundations that had an interest in providing substantial support for research libraries, and it was fairly clear—at least in 1990 and 1991—that, absent Mellon Foundation support, East European libraries were not going to receive massive support from either foundations or the East European governments.[3] It is a happy coincidence that the Foundation's decision to provide library support coincided with the beginning of the massive development of information infrastructures, the Internet, and the general revolution in scholarly communication.

There was a great temptation to funnel all support in the direction of acquisitions, so as to start to undo the many years of neglect during the Communist period. And, indeed, the Foundation did provide a total of about $1 million for acquisitions in places where these appeared to be particularly effective, such as at the National Library of Poland, the Agricultural University in Gödöllő (Hungary), the Attila József University in Szeged (Hungary), and the Sabre Foundation, a U.S.-based organization that provided journals and books for a large variety of East European libraries. But it was clear that at a time when journal and monograph costs were rising at such a rate that even relatively rich American research libraries were facing significant financial pressures and were beginning to cancel subscriptions,[4] achieving "catch-up" in East European library acquisitions was a Sisyphean task. It appeared much more important to provide assistance for the renovating of library infrastructure (broadly speaking), by providing assistance for the introduction of integrated library automation.

From 1990 through 1997, the Foundation in fact provided assistance for the introduction or further development of library automation in over 80 research libraries.[5] These initiatives took perceptibly different courses in the various countries that received assistance, mostly because of the experience acquired by the Foundation over time and because of more or less accidental circumstances. Thus, libraries in Hungary basically automated, or improved the state of their library automation, individually. All automation initiatives in the Czech Republic and Slovakia were carried out, at the urging of the Foundation, on a consortial basis, with each step or stage representing a joint effort by a set of libraries, but with each stage being (loosely) coor-

---

2. It should be said that the acquisition of library materials in the humanities and social sciences was also unfavorably affected by the regimes' ideological opposition to Western materials.

3. In retrospect, there are notable exceptions to this bleakness of this picture; we note the support provided by the Pew Charitable Trusts and the Soros Foundation(s), particularly the Regional Library Program.

4. See A. M. Cummings, M. L. Witte, W. G. Bowen, L. O. Lazarus, and R. H. Ekman, *University Libraries and Scholarly Communication* (Washington, D.C.: Association of Research Libraries, 1992).

5. While the core countries for this type of support still included Hungary, Poland, the Czech Republic, and Slovakia, in 1996 an Estonian consortium of seven libraries and a Latvian consortium of eight were added to the program of support. A full listing of libraries receiving substantial support is in the appendix.

dinated with all preceding stages.⁶ In Poland, automation efforts started with individual libraries, and some of the initial libraries involved in these efforts happened to choose the identical integrated software—the Virginia Tech Library System (VTLS) —and formed an informal alliance. After that, the Foundation recognized the advantages of the consortium-based approach and largely insisted that further automation efforts be undertaken by consortia.⁷ The automation efforts in Estonia and Latvia are being undertaken by one consortium in each country.

The Foundation increasingly insisted on the consortium-based arrangements because they seemed to promise several distinct advantages over the piecemeal approach. In designing consortia, the Foundation required that consortium members commit themselves to using identical software, identical hardware, and identical library protocols. The promise of this approach was that (1) more favorable prices could be obtained from vendors who—as a result of dealing with a consortium— would gain larger orders from purchasers; (2) the training and learning needed by library staffs and by patrons would be less expensive as well as faster than would otherwise be the case; (3) less time, money, and effort would have to be wasted in "localizing" a large number of different systems to East European circumstances and languages; (4) the larger number of users of a given system or of a given type of hardware, due to the consortium-based approach, might make it profitable for vendors to establish local representation and technical support; (5) the resulting citywide (and we hope, eventually, countrywide) union catalogs and on-line public access catalogs (OPACs) would be more easily created and would have more uniform standards, thus enhancing user-friendliness, and usefulness for scholarly communication; and (6) joint initiatives by several or many libraries would encourage the growth of joint collection development and other joint actions benefiting the libraries and their patrons.

As a result of these initiatives, a great deal of experience was gained in the 1990–1997 period in regard to the problems of automating libraries in the post-Communist world, in different countries, and in different organizational contexts. The autumn of 1997 seemed to be an opportune time to pool the experience that has been gained, and this was accomplished at the Conference on Library Automation, organized by the Foundation and hosted by the National Library of Poland, on October 16–18, 1997, in Warsaw.⁸ The first drafts of the chapters in this volume were prepared for and

---

6. All libraries supported in the Czech Republic and Slovakia are part of CASLIN (Czech and Slovak Library Information Network), the identifiable subparts of which are the original CASLIN group; MOLIN (Moravian Library Information Network); KOLIN (Košice Library Information Network); and LINCA (Library Information Network of the Czech Academy of Sciences). The latter three are sometimes referred to as CASLIN Plus.

7. In addition to the original VTLS group (Warsaw University, Jagiellonian University, the University of Gdańsk, and the University of Mining and Metallurgy,) VTLS-based groups came into existence in Kraków, Lublin, and Wrocław, and Dynix/Horizon-based groups came into existence in the cities of Poznań, Łódź, and Toruń. The National Library—a relative latecomer in making a software decision—chose INNOPAC and is not part of a formal consortium.

8. This is by no means the first such conference. See, for example, *International Conference on Library Automation in Central and Eastern Europe*, edited by Monika Segbert, Katarina Steinwachs, Peter Burnett

presented at that conference. The principal motifs of the conference, which correspond to the organization of this volume, were (1) library policy and the impact of the state; (2) historical data and case studies; (3) technical considerations, including both library protocols and standards, as well as issues of computer implementation, retrospective conversion, and search questions; and (4) management and human resource development issues.

Policy Issues

A fundamental obstacle to developing and automating libraries in Eastern Europe was the societal and political environment in which they operated at the beginning of the transition in the years 1989–1990.[9] There is an unsurprising amount of agreement about the basic factors. Manikowski notes (in chapter 1 of this book) that the first fundamental obstacle is the awkward organizational control that the state exercises over libraries. Typically, national libraries report to the Ministry of Culture; libraries in universities devoted to the arts and sciences nominally report to the Ministry of Education; agricultural libraries, to the Ministry of Agriculture;[10] medical libraries, to the Ministry of Health; libraries in higher educational institutions of the military, to the Ministry of Defense. (In contrast, as Borgman and Caidi note [in chapter 2], the national computer network in each country tends to be managed by a small number of people and reports to a single ministry.) None of the libraries tends to have budgetary autonomy, and the formation of consortia among libraries reporting to different state agencies is often not an easy process. In fact, as Balík (in chapter 10) and Kožuchová and Šoltesová (in chapter 12) point out, in the CASLIN projects, this regulatory and budgetary dependency of libraries on governing institutions has continued to have a dampening effect on the ability of libraries to implement change, including the new technologies, up until the present time. Manikowski notes, as a second obstacle, the lack of a constructive attitude of university administrators toward their own libraries, probably derived from the Communist legacy of considering information to be only for the privileged few—hence libraries were somewhat dangerous institutions and did not deserve the degree of attention that, say, science laboratories received. A final point, strongly echoed by Śliwińska (in chapter 31) and by Steinerová (in chapter 4), is the fact that, by modern standards, the library staff tended to be not well trained and inward, rather than outward, looking; conservative

---

(Luxembourg: European Commission, DG XIII/E-4, 1997) (ISBN 92-828-0305-8). For related material, see also, *Library Development in Central and Eastern Europe from Assistance to Cooperation: An Investment in the Future*, compiled by Rachel Roberts (Luxembourg: European Commission, DG XIII, 1994) (ISBN 92-826-2657-1); *Library Networking in Europe*, edited by H. P. Geh and M. Walckiers, London and Washington, D.C.: TFPL Publishing, 1995) (ISBN 1-870889-58-4); *Library Management: East-West Relations*, edited by Ian R. Mowat and Maria Śliwińska, (Toruń: Nicholas Copernicus University, 1955) (ISBN 83-231-0671-1); and Vladimir Zaitzev, "Problems of Russian Libraries in an Age of Social Change," *Daedalus* (Fall 1996), pp. 293–306.
    9. Fortunately, this environment has been improving year by year.
    10. Poland is an exception here in that agricultural universities there report to the Ministry of Education.

in their approach, and resistant to innovation. The training of librarians was inadequate, and even today it is often difficult to find the right number of well-trained librarians if a particular job is needed to be done. After 1989 both libraries and computer networks started to develop at an uncharacteristically rapid pace for the Communist period. It is clear that the computer networks at the beginning of the post-Communist period were totally inadequate for the tasks of information content delivery that were deemed necessary for the last decade of the century. Borgman and Caidi show that the content-versus-conduit debate in the region has some parallels with that debate in the United States: Libraries wished to be the primary content providers, computer network representatives were most concerned with providing high-quality conduits, and government agencies wished to coordinate and promote the interests of libraries or networks for which they were responsible. But the networks have grown and improved and most large cities by now have high-speed fiber-optic connections within the city, permitting library consortia to operate effectively, at least as far as the conduit is concerned.

Sources of funding for libraries and computer systems and networks started to become available, both from state sources (initially in rather small amounts) and from foreign foundations, and while various—often home-grown—automation efforts existed before 1989, libraries had, for the first time, the opportunity to purchase modern, integrated library automation systems from Western vendors. Czermiński (in chapter 3) illustrates the perils inherent in decision-making by state agencies, analyzes the trade-offs in designing communication highways, and discusses the distilled wisdom of how to deal with vendors and what to do or not to do, as well as possible "models" of library automation. Zamorski, in chapter 5, discusses the impact of broad changes in the functions of universities and library systems, with reference to Poland, although it is clear that many of the changes experienced there were also occurring in other countries. One of the most striking changes was caused by the conscious policy of increasing the student body in higher education; the number of such students doubled in Poland between 1989 and 1994, during a period in which real expenditures on higher education were falling—by 7.2 percent in 1993 and by 3.1 percent in the subsequent year.[11] While total library acquisitions grew during this period, the cataloging backlog increased enormously, at least in part because so much time was taken up by instructing staff on how to operate with new computer systems and because financial constraints made staff additions impossible. At the same time, and on a much more positive note, the qualifications of staff have increased and financial constraints have become less binding during this period, and investment in libraries has increased. In particular, libraries, which have mostly been housed in historical buildings not designed as libraries, are now beginning to get new homes: The National Library of Poland has moved into a large modern addition to its old building; Warsaw University is constructing a brand new library; Jagiellonian University is undertaking a major addition; the National Library of the Czech Republic has constructed a new library annex; and the Attila József University in Hungary will build a new library.

---

11. In the following year, real expenditures rose 4.3 percent, but the student body increased by 11 percent.

History and Case Studies

Automation, as Mader points out (in chapter 7) in his survey of its history in Hungary, represents but a brief interval in the many centuries during which libraries have existed. As soon as it was recognized that a machine-readable bibliographic record could be used many times and for many purposes, and could be shared among libraries, the advancement of automation was inevitable. Mader distinguishes three distinct periods: pre-1970, the period from the mid-1970s to the late 1980s, and the 1990s. It was an important characteristic of the Communist period that information was restricted; hence Eastern Europe could not participate freely in the technological developments that were occurring in Western libraries prior to 1989. He points out that the changes in higher education, which started to take place in 1990 in Hungary and had some parallels in other East European countries, were based on certain key principles that led, pari passu, to the requirement that libraries be modernized. These principles consisted of the newly established freedom of learning, education, and research; the commitment to substantially increase the number of students; the creation of regional, multi-faculty universities;[12] the creation of new, integrated management systems; and the return to universities of the historic right to grant advanced degrees, which they had lost during the Communist period to academies of science—institutions that were favored by the Communist system both financially and in terms of prestige. While some libraries had taken some minor steps toward automation before 1989, the real push began alongside the political transformation of the late 1980s.

Of course, integrated automated library systems from the West were not really available to East European libraries in the pre-1989 period, if for no other reasons than financial ones. As a result, home-grown systems made their appearance and, as Sadowska notes, for example (in chapter 8), the National Library of Poland embarked on the development of the system MAK in 1986, designed primarily for small libraries. The National Library actually started to use this system in 1991 and it worked well enough to permit the creation of a database for the Polish National Bibliography. MAK was a DOS-based system, installed in a Novell network, and can currently accommodate over 100 simultaneous users. While it does handle MARC formats, it is not a complete system and has, for example, no acquisitions or circulation modules. In 1996, the National Library purchased INNOPAC, which is being implemented at present.

In the Czech Republic and Slovakia, the development rested on a conscious creation of a consortium. A historic meeting took place at the Mellon Foundation's offices in New York, on October 18, 1991, which was attended by the following: the respective directors of the National Library of (then) Czechoslovakia, the Brno State Library, the Bratislava University Library, and the Slovak National Library (arguably the

---

12. The Communist period was characterized by the substantial fragmentation of universities and by the creation of institutions of higher learning that had a single mission: Most of these institutions were either created *ex nihilo*, like the University of Transport and Communications in Žilina, Slovakia, and the University of Veszprém in Hungary—which was devoted, in the beginning, largely to chemical engineering—or created by carving up existing universities.

four most important research libraries in the country); the authors of this introductory essay; representatives of other U.S. foundations; library experts; and others. It was agreed that a consortial approach was likely to be more effective than a piecemeal approach and the creation of the Czech and Slovak Library Information Network was the ultimate outcome. Other subnetworks joined CASLIN in subsequent years, such as KOLIN, MOLIN, and LINCA.[13] With minor exceptions, all of them selected Ex Libris's Aleph as the integrated library system. The history of the installation of Aleph and the creation of CASLIN are chronicled in the chapters by Balík, Svoboda, Prokop et al., Příbramská, and Kožuchová and Šoltésová, from a variety of points of view.

The Czech and Slovak libraries also developed home-grown automation products of various types in the 1970s and 1980s. In Slovakia, an automation project was created for the benefit of the Slovak National Bibliography, from 1972 to 1985. Attempts at integrated systems were undertaken in the late 1980s: MAKS in the Czech Republic and IKIS in Slovakia, both being based on CDS/ISIS. They employed the Czech-Slovak Exchange Format, which was not quite like UNIMARC, but its subsequent conversion to UNIMARC did not prove to be difficult.[14] As Svoboda argues, the creators of CASLIN realized that the principal advantage of a consortium is its ability to exploit human, financial, and technical resources more effectively than individual institutions can. The price that has to be paid for this is a partial surrender of each institution's own identity and objectives, but the gain tends to far outweigh the cost. Consortial approaches permit shared cataloging and other shared activities, which enhance efficiency, and services to users.

Selecting a system has, in all cases, been an arduous process, and it would be instructive to be able to figure out the total number of person-hours invested by system purchasers in designing their requests for proposals (RFPs) and evaluating vendor replies, as well as the person-hours invested by vendors in replying to RFPs. But selecting the system is only the first chapter of the story. The system has to be "localized," which means that system and help messages as well as manuals have to be translated into the appropriate East European language[15]—which in turn means that the software system must be able to produce the appropriate diacritical characters and must also obey the appropriate sort sequence (for example, in Polish, "l" precedes "ł"; "o" precedes "ó"). While this may seem to be a minor problem, it has, in fact, dogged the installation of systems throughout Eastern Europe. In addition to localizing the system, it frequently also had to be customized to the local library's needs in ways which were not automatically taken care of by the system as originally installed. Příbramská notes that this was particularly the case with respect to the system table that defines database structures, since the one that CASLIN members wished to use was substantially more complex than the one that Aleph automatically provided.

13. See note 6.
14. See, respectively, the chapters by Balík, by Svoboda, and by Prokop et al., in this volume.
15. One should not overestimate the extent to which English-speaking librarians are present in the libraries of the region.

Negotiating with vendors has not been as easy and smooth as it might have been and the promised functionality did not always appear as promised.[16] On occasion, the precontract negotiations with vendors were exceptionally arduous and time-consuming.[17] Local representation of vendors was not always adequate and the vendor might, at times, have been represented by a local firm on an agency basis; such firms may be overextended, may experience conflicting demands on their resources, and may therefore service particular clients only inadequately. Software patches have often introduced new errors, although anyone who is familiar with the evolution of software knows that this is a common problem. In all of these matters some of the difficulties may be attributed to the various libraries' inexperience in dealing and negotiating with Western vendors and, generally, in acting as autonomous agents in a marketplace.

Problems in training require special mentioning. In some instances, training was retarded because of language problems. In other cases, the rate at which training could be absorbed had to be tailored to the rate at which modules could be introduced in libraries. In still other instances, librarians may have been fearful of new computer systems or library protocols. In nearly all cases the requisite personnel power was not made available and librarians, in addition to learning and operating a new system, had to continue to discharge their customary functions. Nevertheless, after many hurdles, setbacks, and frustrations, integrated library systems are increasingly in place and functioning.

Technical Issues

It is quite evident that the arrival of integrated library automation in Eastern Europe gave the librarians of the region a massive impetus to rethink every aspect of managing libraries. The shift in emphasis from considering libraries to be passive repositories of knowledge to regarding them as active conduits of scholarly information focused much attention on making libraries user-friendly—for example, on use of union catalogs and OPACs; on effective searching; on training library patrons, and not only library staff; and on a whole set of related problems. The possibility of collaborating with other libraries underscored the need to have common standards, so that information could be accurately and broadly exchanged. The sense that the world of libraries in Eastern Europe was on the move required that librarians think about issues of macro-implementation and problems of sequencing—for example, what steps have such high priority that they need to be taken immediately and what steps may be deferred.[18] And finally, what is the proper rate at which databases should be built? Should one sacrifice accuracy and completeness in the keeping of records for the sake of increasing the number of records as quickly as possible, or should one go

---

16. See, in this volume, the chapter by Příbramská.
17. See, for example, in this volume, the chapter by Kožuchová and by Šoltésová.
18. See, in this volume, the chapter by Hollender.

more slowly, but ensure that records are complete and error-free?[19] All of these questions involve complex materials and difficult choices, on many of which reasonable people may often disagree.

Cataloging Standards and Authority Files

It is clear that the arrival of automation caused many libraries and library systems to rethink issues of standards; and much fundamental work in this area has been accomplished by the Czech National Library and by the Polish VTLS-based libraries. Stoklasová (in chapter 18) illustrates the fundamental changes by noting that in the initial CDS/ISIS and MAKS periods it was not even clear whether UNIMARC would have any practical use or whether it would remain merely an attractive theory. The Czech National Library did not initially feel that it could accept the use of AACR-2,[20] because of its inherent Anglo-American bias, although ISBD recommendations had been in use, without modification, since 1989. As long as databases were small, there appeared to be no need for authority control and working with keywords was deemed sufficient; certainly, Library of Congress subject headings (LCSHs) were suspect because of their American bias. By the mid-1990s, the National Library had published a translation of AACR-2; the translation of UNIMARC is now complete; and keywords are no longer used for subject access, but LCSHs are used in areas relevant to the collections. As a result of the careful work done in the National Library, it has become the first East European library to supply records to OCLC. Fundamental work on authority files has been done at Warsaw University. And in this regard, A. Paluszkiewicz notes (in chapter 19) that headings are the basic access points of a catalog; that effective searches require uniform headings; and that a union authority file is the proper source of such headings—this avoids much duplication if it is used by many libraries.

The Warsaw University Library not only prepared guidelines in Polish for authority files (based on the relevant International Federation of Library Associations [IFLA] publications), but also prepared Polish manuals for USMARC, the format subsequently adopted for Poland by the Polish National Library. The ongoing work in this area is undertaken by the Center for Formats and Authority Files, while the union authority files are maintained on a Warsaw University Library server, and serve all Polish libraries. The center is responsible for union authority file maintenance, coordination of library cooperation with respect to the creation of authority files, work on the methodology of formats, and training.[21] The authority files are created by librarians from several libraries and are, in turn, used in many local databases. The original participating libraries were all VTLS-using libraries, but recently, the Copernicus

---

19. There is nothing new about the dilemma of quick-and-dirty cataloging versus slow-and-accurate cataloging: The debate about the trade-offs in this area will continue as long as there are librarians.

20. *Anglo-American Cataloguing Rules*, 2d ed. (Chicago: American Library Association, 1998).

21. The subject authority files are primarily based on RAMEAU, with some reliance on LCSHs and the Canadian RVM.

University Library, which uses Dynix/Horizon, also joined the common effort. There is no doubt that the work accomplished by these libraries will have a profound effect on the development of careful library work in Poland.

Very much in the same spirit is the work of Koltay, who (in chapter 22) considers the importance of authority control for translating subject headings. This, of course, has a profound impact on the efficiency of searches, and if catalog records do not contain subject headings, the efficiency of keyword searches will be impaired. Authority files help to keep the database clean. In the light of these considerations, Lajos Kossuth University, in Debrecen, Hungary, decided to rely on Library of Congress subject headings—which appeared to be a particularly sensible decision in the light of the fact that no general Hungarian subject list was available for adoption. As a practical matter, LCSHs are translated as they are required and the authority records will continue to contain the original English headings.

Retrospective Conversion

Retroconversion is an important activity that is being undertaken in many libraries by the use of different methodologies. The differential difficulties of retroconversion are illustrated by a comparison of this effort at the American Studies Center of Warsaw University—which has a small library consisting overwhelmingly of American materials—with the efforts at the National Library of the Czech Republic, at the Bratislava University Library, and at the Lajos Kossuth University Library (in Debrecen).[22] In the case of the American Studies Center, it was possible to use CAT CD450, a microcomputer-based system based on the OCLC On-line Union Catalog. In the case of the National Library of the Czech Republic, the number of matches in OCLC proved to be small, and many of those appeared to be of dubious quality; hence, the library decided to undertake a semiautomatic conversion from catalog cards employing the COMDAT technology, which starts with the scanning of records, and after OCR produces editable ASCII records in the MARC format. At the Bratislava University Library, the conversion had to be undertaken from the Israeli system called "MAGIC," which was done by a customized MAGIC-to-Aleph conversion program provided by Ex Libris.[23] At Lajos Kossuth University, alternative methods were carefully costed out, and the most cost-effective procedure appeared to be the manual creation of MARC records from catalog cards; it is interesting that, irrespective of the methodology employed, the cost of creating a retrospective MARC record at this university appeared to hover near $1 per record. It is even more interesting if we compare this cost to the experience of other libraries, knowing full well that retroconversion

---

22. See, respectively, the chapters, in this volume, by E. Paluszkiewicz, by Stoklasová, by Řepišová, and by Gomba.

23. Difficulties, of course, were plentiful. Some mandatory UNIMARC fields are missing in the MAGIC structure, other fields are useful to keep but have no UNIMARC equivalent, and still other fields are necessary for the functioning of Aleph but are outside the scope of UNIMARC.

means different things in different places, and thus a direct comparison is not wholly meaningful. But, at the American Studies Library of Warsaw University, the per-record cost of conversion ranged from $0.61 to $0.90,[24] whereas at the Czech National Library the retrospective creation of a detailed bibliographic record cost about $1.50.[25] It is somewhat comforting that these figures are of at least comparable orders of magnitude. We should also note that the conversion of special collections raises some additional problems, such as whether the USMARC format allows for appropriate identification of data elements of all types of documents, in accordance with Polish users' normal expectations, and whether indexes of a common type, which are to be used in searches of the automated catalog, will be sufficient for the needs of special collections.[26] We should also note that the need to deal with rare materials in special collections is not restricted to methods of cataloging and searching, but reaches into the realm of preservation, in which the National Library in Prague has made major steps forward.[27]

Development Issues on the Macro Level

Górny, Maruszewski, and Nikisch (in chapter 6) first treat the question of how to speed up computerization, which in their view is proceeding, but too slowly. Their recommendation is twofold: first, to centralize the preparation of bibliographic descriptions in the National Library (of Poland), and second, to accept, at least for purposes of local libraries, simplified catalog descriptions—for example, incomplete records—so that books can be lent immediately after their arrival. They also wish to place increasing emphasis on electronic library resources. They deplore Polish libraries' limited ability (mostly for financial reasons) to provide access to electronic databases, and express the hope that ultimately electronic libraries will prove to be money-savers.

Feret (in chapter 20) examines the trade-offs between union catalogs that are based on a single database and those that rely on distributed search. He undertakes an examination of a variety of software vendors, with a view toward determining the vendor's ability to provide union catalog services for a consortium. He notes that most OPACs currently in existence are based on a centralized database, and that although a distributed-search mechanism is easy to implement, it is rarely implemented because the current version of Z39.50 does not allow the retrieval of holdings information from the server. It is also clear that a distributed search depends on network quality, a matter of continuing importance in Eastern Europe, but that libraries using different automation systems should consider the distributed approach.

---

24. See, in this volume, the chapter by E. Paluszkiewicz.
25. See "Retrospective Conversion in Czech Libraries," by B. Stoklasová, in this volume.
26. See, in this volume, the chapter by Pasztaleniec-Jarzyńska.
27. See, in this volume, the chapter by Knoll.

14   *Introduction*

Search and Information Processing

Three chapters address the vexing problem of how the library patron finds what he/she is looking for in an environment in which there is an explosive growth of at least certain parts of collections, and in which browsing among stacks is less important that using computer technology. Gyüre (in chapter 23) concentrates on integrating Internet resources directly into library catalogs, an integration that is being successfully carried out at Lajos Kossuth University in Hungary. Csik and Varga (in chapter 24) discuss knowledge representation, the impact of computerization on the segmentation of knowledge, search engines; and they examine a large sample of databases with respect to the number of subject-representing criteria they employ. Bakonyi (in chapter 2) deals with a very practical problem—that is, readers often find it difficult to formulate their search terms. He reviews various European Union projects for information access and retrieval and discusses various types of searches and solutions adopted, such as the multidatabase search, catalog navigation, context-sensitive help, graphical user interfaces, as well as searches in full-text databases. He concludes that the more specialized and technical the work becomes, the more important it becomes for people to collaborate and to exchange knowledge and information.

Managerial Issues

The transformation of a library system from a traditional and mostly manual system —relying on historically rooted standards and having no commitment to the providing of efficient user access, locally or globally—into a modern system that uses universal standards and is integrated into the worldwide community of librarians and patrons is a truly daunting task even if it takes place in a single library. The work becomes ever more demanding if it involves a consortium of several libraries. Characteristic of the library's state before the decision to automate is taken is (1) the lack of hardware, (2) the lack of software, (3) the lack of networks, (4) the lack of modern library standards, (5) the lack of training, and, perhaps most important, (6) the lack of a clearly articulated mission for the library.

As a minimum, it involves, from the preparation phase to the completed implementation, the following tasks.

1. assessment of the library's needs and short and long-term objectives;
2. assignment of personnel to various tasks and the establishment of a hierarchy for automation personnel, with clearly defined responsibilities;
3. preparation of requests for proposals involving software and hardware;
4. evaluation of proposals and selection of hardware and software systems;
5. preparation of, and negotiations with vendors over, contracts; performance and acceptance testing; and payment schedules;
6. preparation of the physical space for equipment, training, administration;
7. constructions of LANs;
8. training of personnel and more general consideration of human resource management issues;
9. installation and testing of hardware;

10. installation and testing of software;
11. acceptance of appropriate library standards (bibliographic, cataloging, authority)
12. preparation of manuals and handbooks;
13. customization and localization of an integrated automated system;
14. start-up of system modules in an operational setting;
15. assessment of alternatives for retroconversion;
16. start-up of retroconversion; and, in the event of automation within a consortium,
17. establishment of an overall structure of governance, including a system for conflict resolution.

While the above is surely only a partial list of steps that need to be taken, it is likely that, with a few exceptions, in most instances of library automation the librarians who were to implement the project became aware of the need to pay attention to these issues only after the process had begun. Furthermore, while there is also a general agreement on the importance of appropriate management in the achievement of a successful library transition to the new technologies, a familiarity with modern methods of management was gained from literature rather than from experience. We need to keep in mind that all the library automation projects discussed in the present volume arrived at the doorsteps of libraries that were in the process of changing their top management and facing new challenges from the larger social, political, and economic order of their respective countries. In other words, the transformation of libraries was, and continues to be, but a part of an all-encompassing transition. And insofar as the automation projects could be identified as the wedge that helped transform the libraries from the inside out, it is important to recognize that the ability of the libraries to meet this welcome challenge was affected directly by an essentially unstable environment. This became particularly obvious to the project managers, the first to realize that their success and, ultimately, the success of the project as a whole had more to do with the limitations of human, rather than technical, resources: the poorly qualified staff; the continuous brain drain of talented individuals who moved to the more lucrative jobs in the private sector; and the degree to which the quality of the workforce also depended on a badly needed improvement in the quality of library schools.

Project Management

The preparation of the project proposal, the selection of vendors, and the process of implementation—all these required coordination and, with a consortium as the final goal, forms of cooperation empowered with decision-making authority that crossed the established organizational hierarchies of separate institutions. But, as Dobrzyńska-Lankosz points out in chapter 29—which compares the strategies of several Polish projects—the approaches to management differ quite widely. In the case of Kraków, three consecutive management plans were developed to (a) prepare the project and submit it for funding, (b) manage its implementation, and (c) run the new library system. From the beginning it was clear that library automation must fit into the larger plans for a metropolitan network, must be accepted as an integral part of the university administration, and must formalize ties between the participating libraries.

Only by having the relevant parties on board, and by having clearly defined procedural rules, could it be possible to come to a consensus on technical matters and actually carry out the project in a responsible way. The key in this case is the founding of a "Kraków Library Group" as the core, with a signed agreement that defines procedural matters, and with a three-tier divisional setup involving the technical expert groups, the project management, and a steering committee. Except for the case of the Lublin libraries, whose organizational structure appears to be less clearly defined, all the other projects reviewed by the author follow the same basic logic. The difference seems to lie mostly in how actual decision-making authority is assigned.

All the CASLIN automation projects evolved similar management structures, with one important difference: A general project manager and grants administrator designated by the Mellon Foundation (with a residence in the United States) worked to (a) coordinate the initial preparation of the projects and (b) provide general guidance and administer the funds. The chapters by Balík, by Svoboda and by Prokop et al. point to the central role played by the different expert groups that involved members of different libraries in cooperative decision making. They also point to the difficulties that such interlibrary cooperation entails as individual library representatives may or may not have the authority to make decisions on behalf of their home institution. As Svoboda argues, while the agreement on the adoption or the development of shared and internationally compatible standards is one of CASLIN's unqualified successes, the traditional tendency of institutions toward pursuing individual interests worked against a true consortial association. This suggests that consortia develop in response to clearly perceived needs rather than during the anticipation stage. Kožuchová and Šoltésová, after describing the KOLIN system of project management and placing the implementation process in the context of the larger picture, further reinforce the observation that the project's success is ultimately dependent on the social, political, and economic well-being of the country. A similar argument is made by Balík in his review of the CASLIN project as a whole and of the Czech National Library, in particular. On the other hand, the chapter by Lass looks at the manner in which the interplay of factors mentioned above, ranging from the macroeconomic to the micropolitical, directly affects delays in the implementation process and, as a result, reinforces poor time management habits and has a negative effect on the results.

In the Hungarian context, Skaliczki and Zalai-Kovács look at the deliberate use of management methods as a means of managing change. They believe that library automation software can be understood as a key tool of total quality management (TQM) and ask a series of questions—in a survey sent out to a group of libraries using major integrated systems—that address the relationship between library automation and the qualitative improvement in both technical and public services. In this context, Virágos's discussion of the implementation process at the Debrecen Library Consortium is particularly instructive since she is able to demonstrate the importance of strategic planning, systems analysis, and feasibility studies in both helping the library reengineer its work patterns (the analysis of the cataloging of work flows is particularly instructive) and getting the library staff as well as the reading public on board by keeping everyone informed of the progress being made.

Finally, it is the expectation that the new system will fulfill certain needs, rather than others, that plays a significant role in the whole process of convergence. These ideas inform the system selection process, the implementation process, and the varied attitude toward the outcome. Most important, they reflect the library's traditional mandate rather than a full understanding or appreciation of other approaches to librarianship, especially not those (such as the Anglo-American tradition) that are reflected in much of the library automation software. Hollander's analysis of module sequencing in the East-European projects makes this point very clear. While his survey data indicate a wide variety of approaches to the implementation process, they also highlight a continuing traditionalism (with cataloging and circulation given top priority over some of the potential fruits of automation, such as interlibrary loan, document delivery, orientation toward digital libraries, among others).[28] The question then remains—and only time will provide the answer—whether library traditionalists will learn from the new technologies that they themselves have chosen.

Staffing and Library Education

The quality of the staff and, by extension, the education of the future generation of librarians are, without doubt, among the most pressing concerns of the library's management. Interesting data on library staffing and workload in Eastern Europe emerge from the chapter by Hays. While workloads in both technical and public services are about half of those found in typical U.S. libraries, the professional librarians outnumber the supporting staff by a large margin (compared to the United States where the opposite is the case). This raises some serious questions regarding the impact of automation on staffing: The dramatic reduction in the need for professionals in technical services is matched by a dramatic increase in the need for professionals in public services—with new and different qualifications—and for the nonprofessional support staff. These and other changes in human-resources policy may be quite difficult to implement without an overall shift in library philosophy and without the support of library education programs. This concern is reaffirmed by Śliwińska, who takes a closer look at the state of the profession in Poland at the end of the 1980s, as it faced the challenge of the library automation projects. The gist of it is that it was unprepared for the transition. But, neither were the library schools, the universities' administrations, or, for that matter, the users. The results of her extensive survey indicate that the majority of librarians received their first professional exposure to the new technologies through the vendor training programs and that, as recently as 1996, library schools were still not providing instruction on automation projects and vendor negotiations, and were only beginning to move from a traditional view of library science—mostly historically and theoretically oriented—to an intensive, hands-on

---

28. It is noteworthy that acquisitions modules may, in fact, never get properly implemented in some libraries, because of different accounting conventions in Eastern Europe, and because many acquisitions modules designed for Western users do not have as rich a menu for the provenance of books as the menu desired in some East European contexts, a point also discussed in chapter 14 by Příbramská.

exposure to modern library standards and technologies. Of course—to return to a point made earlier—only when the libraries' image improves (together with the salaries) will it be possible to attract and retain a new generation of library professionals and halt the present brain-drain that has plagued all the Mellon-funded library projects discussed in this volume. This concern is echoed in Steinerová's chapter as well. As she points out, where the new management has now identified with the changing mission of the library, and the project managers and system librarians are clear about what their positions entail, the bulk of the library staff still faces this hurdle. Not only must the education of librarians better reflect real needs but, she argues, libraries need to play a more active role in helping to change the way knowledge is managed in the educational system as a whole. Libraries in the region need to be better integrated into the life of the university (a point also echoed by Manikowski) and, more important, information management methodologies need to become integral parts of the education of individuals in any field. Only then can libraries come together and cooperate in fulfilling their newfound mission of offering both traditional services and a gateway to the global information society.

Appendix: Major Supported University and Other Libraries

The Czech Republic and Slovakia

Czech National Library
Moravian Regional Library
Library of the Czech Academy of
　Sciences
Masaryk University
Palacký University
State Library of Olomouc
Slovak National Library
University Library of Bratislava
Šafárika University
University of Prešov
State Library of Košice
Technical University of Košice

Hungary

National Library
Agricultural University of Gödöllő
Agricultural University of
　Debrecen
Medical Univerity of Debrecen
Attila József University
Budapest University of Economic
　Sciences
Lajos Kossuth University

University of Miskolc
Janus Pannonius University

Poland

National Library
Warsaw University
University of Gdańsk
University of Wrocław
Ossolineum Library
Nicolas Copernicus University
Jagiellonian University
University of Mining and Metallurgy
Kraków Polytechnical University
Kraków Agricultural University
Kraków Academy of Economics
Marie Curie Skłodowska University
Catholic University of Lublin
Agricultural University of Lublin
Technical University of Lublin
Catholic University of Lublin
Lopaciński Library of Lublin
Adam Mickiewicz University
Agricultural University of Poznań
Academy of Economics of Poznań
Technical University of Poznań

Library of the Poznań Society of Friends
   of Arts and Sciences
Raczyński City Public Library of Poznań
University of Łódź
Technical University of Łódź
Piłsudski Regional Library of Łódź

Estonia
National Library
Library of the Academy of Sciences
Tartu University
Tallinn Technical University
Estonian Agricultural University
Estonian Literary Museum Archival
   Library
Tallinn Pedagogical University

Latvia
National Library
Academy Library
University of Latvia
Technical University
Patent and Technology Library
Fundamental Library of the Latvian
   University of Agriculture
Library of the Medical Academy
Research Medical Library

PART I

Library Policy and the State

CHAPTER 1

Library Automation
Fortunes and Miseries in Poland

ADAM MANIKOWSKI

Historians like to wonder, "What if . . . ?," never answering the question. One of the most famous questions of this type is, "What would have happened if General Blücher had not arrived in time to help the Duke of Wellington?" Of course, no serious historian dares to discuss what would have been the history of Europe if the battle at Waterloo had ended with the opposite result. But the real problem lies in the fact that the help of the Prussian army during this battle could have been, or could not have been, extended. That is, the historian is dealing here with an event that did help a great deal, but which need not necessarily have happened.

I think that—while keeping our sense of proportions—in the case of the assistance The Andrew W. Mellon Foundation provided for the provoking and accelerating of the processes of automation at the big research libraries in Poland, we are dealing with the same type of phenomenon. The more than 15 million dollars given to Polish libraries during the last eight years represents a level of support that has never before been provided, apart from state support. One could discuss whether the progress of the supported projects is satisfactory or whether all the funds have been used in the most economical manner, but one has to confess that there would be very little to discuss if, in fact, this assistance had not been provided at all. Under the circumstances, one thing may be taken for granted—namely, that after a few years the Mellon Foundation support completely changed the way of life of a major portion of Polish research libraries.

In other words, sooner or later, the automation of Polish libraries would have taken place anyway; however, it is also clear that without Mellon Foundation support the automation would have been postponed and would have been driven by an entirely different process. This support does not only mean that very substantial capital has been injected into Polish research libraries, but even more important, that the conditions attached to the grants have stimulated the directions of computerization and provoked staff members to demonstrate self-reliance and initiative, often forcing them into active cooperation with counterparts in other libraries.

On the basis of several years of experience in managing the National Library, I feel that the support given to this institution by American donors, similar to that given to other big research libraries, was not limited to providing financial assistance only in the name of some unspoken higher objectives, but forced upgrades in management on the sponsored institutions and encouraged their openness toward cooperation with other libraries. The Foundation's pattern of grant-making has shown a rare form of awareness of the constraints that impeded the development of automation, constraints that have been deeply embedded in three spheres:

1. The system of subordination of libraries to various administrative agencies of the state—which have exhibited inaction, and concerns about their own narrow interests—has impeded and sometimes prevented joint activities in the field of automation;
2. The undervaluing, or even the neglect, of the development of libraries by universities and research institution, which should act as their natural sponsors and donors;
3. The tightness of library circles and their conservatism were factors that turned out to be major obstacles to innovation, with the result that libraries, with only some exceptions, have not manifested their own initiatives.

Some four years ago, when I became the director of the National Library, the Mellon Foundation had already had contact with the library for over a year. However, at that time, proposals to computerize it were imagined to be nothing more than some vague promises to the effect that, upon receipt of considerable funds, computer specialists and Warsaw librarians would quickly introduce automation based on the MAK system, which may have been well suited for the needs of a small library, and which, when suitably developed, could constitute the rudiments of a new, home-grown library system. It is fair to say that such a proposal would not have given automation a good chance to succeed, and even in the case of partial success, it would have been extremely expensive both in terms of routine maintenance and future enhancements. This bears some resemblance to the attempts, which persisted for a number of years, to develop an original Polish motor vehicle, which—according to the dreams of consecutive generations of designers and engineers—would be a comparably modern, but much less expensive, vehicle than its Western European counterparts. Its designers had completely forgotten that the reengineering, from scratch, of such a technologically complicated product would turn out to be extremely expensive, with only a minimal chance for success.

In the case of selecting a library system, the situation seems far more obvious. The motor vehicle industry, by virtue of its size and its revenues, could at least compete in the market and achieve some standing in industry if the state were willing to assume the risk of creating the home-grown product. But in the library's case, considering the limited mobility of library systems, their technical character, and the need for continual investments in their development, the attempt, by even the biggest libraries, to create a system for their own use and needs seems a priori absurd in the light of their well-known lack of financing.

Realizing this, the National Library approached a second call for computerization proposals by the Mellon Foundation, in 1993, with the understanding that the sponsor would be prepared to fund the realization of a complex library automation project only if its creators could demonstrate a credible and convincing vision of automation, one based on the use of a system currently in operation in other big libraries, and could guarantee the completion of the project in a timely fashion.

These conditions seemed very reasonable, but also forced the National Library to prepare a long-overdue detailed analysis of its own needs as well as potentialities. This analysis was finally formulated in a "Request for a Grant." Frankly, in the beginning this whole matter seemed, to me and my colleagues, an unnecessary waste of time. We had thought that if we selected one of the systems that was operating successfully somewhere else, its overdetailed analysis would not have yielded much benefit. I also shared that view and only now, with a few years of perspective, can one suitably appreciate how sensible that procedure was. Its most important result was that for many months some dozens of people—managers and other staff—had been intensively thinking about the library's needs in the field of automation and, what is perhaps even more important, about the library's new organizational structure that would replace old structures developed since the creation of the National Library. It also turned out that even the biggest Polish library cannot carry out such an analysis without some outside academic experts, and the participation of Dr. Jurand Czermiński, Dr. Zdzisław Dobrowolski, and Dr. Krzysztof Heller proved that automation is more often successful if it is jointly carried out by many libraries.

I shall largely skip the next stage of the automation team's work, although it had its interesting ups and downs—namely, the selection procedure for choosing from among American and Western European library systems that already had a track record; the purchase of the various system modules; the maintenance arrangements for the configuration of the system selected for the National Library; and the complicated construction of a local area network. At the moment, the National Library is poised to start what it hopes will be a successful operation of the system.

Many of the details of this process are presented in this volume by my colleagues in a more precise and expert manner. Not being an automation expert, I shall concentrate on the factors I mentioned at the outset, which strongly affected the automation process—and, to my regret, mostly negatively—not only at the National Library, but at other libraries throughout the country as well.

What, then, was the meaning of the Mellon Foundation grant for the automation processes of the National Library? The grant received from the Foundation, nearly $1 million, not only meant financial support on a very large scale; but also, the conditions of the donor required a rapid pace of implementation. Coming back to the question posed in the beginning of this chapter, namely, "What if . . .?," we have to conclude that automation would have been possible on the basis of the National Library's own budget. The grant of $1 million is about 10 percent of the library's annual budget and less than 40 percent of its annual expenditures on investment. Given that automation expenditures acquire goods with a lifetime of several years, it is not unreasonable to claim that if a high priority were assigned to automation, the National Library could have carried it out on its own, and, in all likelihood, so could some university libraries. However, I do not think that such a decision could have been taken in the early 1990s, and even now it is very difficult to obtain funds for automation; indeed, the real constraints that prevent automation from occurring more rapidly than what we now observe are the factors cited at the beginning of this chapter.

The first constraint cited is that the libraries are subordinated to various administrative agencies of the state: Most university libraries report to the Ministry of National Education, a sizable proportion of other types of research libraries to the Polish Academy of Sciences, and the National Library to the Ministry of Culture and Art.

The public libraries are governed by local authorities, and other big libraries report to still other agencies of the state. None of them, except for the National Library, has budgetary autonomy. The characteristic of Polish bureaucratic structures is that, given the multiple administrative controls, the acquisition of funds from state agencies for joint automation projects has almost no chance of succeeding.

There were attempts to create a State Library Council—with the inclusion of representatives from the big libraries and academic institutions—that would have had funds from the state budget for the initiating of joint automation projects by several libraries. Unfortunately, the "political will" of the governing coalition voted it down in 1997, even though it would not have resulted in the creation of a new bureaucracy, but would only have given libraries subordinated to different state agencies an opportunity to be modernized in a rational approach that economized on financial and human resources.

The second significant obstacle turned out to be the economic policy of universities and scientific research institutions toward their libraries. It is true that the financial condition of science and higher education has been a critical one for many years. But it is also true that when further cuts have to be imposed, libraries are often the first to suffer. Most recently, this situation has changed, as attested by the construction of a new library building for the Warsaw University Library and by the construction of an extension for the Jagiellonian Library. But this is far too little if we consider that none of the three recently created universities (in Szczecin, Opole, and Białystok) are equipped with a decent library and nothing has been done to date to improve this situation.

The third factor, the most painful to speak about, is the one that pertains to our own library environment. This factor is the tightly knit character of library circles and, in addition, the exceptional reluctance of libraries to engage in innovative activities of any kind. Perhaps we can justify this to some extent by noting that libraries, like other institutions devoted to the preservation and conservation of the national heritage, ought to exercise exceptional precautions when introducing changes of a revolutionary character.

However, the attitudes of librarians toward automation must be radically changed. Thus, librarians have to be aware of the fact that library-organization policies will have to be changed, organizational divisions between units will become outdated, and work flows will have to be restructured; but along with these changes, the work will become more interesting and demand more self-reliance. The problem is that these changes cannot be carried out in a gradualist or incremental manner if a stringent time schedule is to be adhered to.

In spite of some of these less-than-inviting circumstances, Polish libraries have not much to be ashamed of in the field of automation. Library consortia that have been created as a result of the influence of the Mellon Foundation, such as the VTLS group and other intracity agreements among libraries, prove that libraries are able to jointly realize automation projects, and it is likely that university authorities will soon realize that it is rational and profitable to support such initiatives. It is also the case that the attitudes of librarians toward automation, especially in university environments, are also changing, although not as fast as might be desired.

The least likely to undertake reforms are the state agencies, although I have to point out that the Ministry of Education has given some support to joint action by university libraries. The commendable exception to our criticism is the Committee of Scientific Research (KBN), which is the only ministry controlled not only by political forces but also by representatives of the scientific communities elected in a democratic manner.

I can conclude that, in spite of some general complaints about financial stringency, a lack of state-of-the-art equipment, and some pervasive pessimism, a large portion of the big research libraries are so far advanced in automation that the process must be considered irreversible. No doubt, a substantial role has been played in this by the Mellon Foundation's sponsorship of libraries: It has provided a "first push," and the conditions of the grants forced the libraries, and their parent institutions in some cases, to cooperate and to integrate their automation processes. Now it is the libraries' turn to take the initiative and to further develop the changes that have been initiated and to deepen the integration that has begun. In order to achieve this as soon as possible, it will be necessary to convince the political elite, as well as the Polish society at large, that these endeavors are important and worthwhile. Poland is a country in which one cannot expect private sponsorship in the near future, and the support of the Batory Foundation (the local Soros Foundation) and the Foundation for Polish Science (Fundacja na Rzecz Nauki Polskiej), with the long-term nature of its wise policy of library support, will not be sufficient to ensure adequate library automation throughout the country. The best way to achieve this goal is to demonstrate the efficiency and social usefulness of the modern libraries, to explain to the outside world what library automation is, and what benefits accrue from easy access to information—not only for the man on the street, but to scientists and politicians. Clearly, this should be accomplished as expeditiously as possible, although communication skills are not the forte of librarians. But that is another story.

CHAPTER 2

Developing National Information Infrastructures in Central and Eastern Europe
The Content-versus-Conduit Debate

Christine L. Borgman and Nadia Caidi

The continuing convergence of telecommunications, computing, and broadcasting technologies is fueling debates over the future of an information society. Central to these debates are issues surrounding the technology and policy for the development of information infrastructures on the national and global levels. Information infrastructures are social and technological systems that interact with their environments (Hughes, 1989; Law, 1989). We can study multiple aspects of such systems, including institutional factors—players and stakes, technology and industrial policies, and the regulation of telecommunications on the national and international levels; technical factors—network development and architecture, equipment choices, and standards, including their influence on usability, flexibility, functionality, and compatibility; and societal factors—general attitudes of users toward technology and innovations, adoption and implementation strategies, privacy, consumer rights, equity of access, universal service, and values.

In this chapter, we focus on the institutional factors involved in the development of information infrastructures in six Central and Eastern European countries: Croatia,

---

Support for research in Central and Eastern Europe in 1993–1994 was provided to us by the Office of International Studies and Overseas Programs, the Academic Senate, the Center for European and Russian Studies, and the Graduate School of Education and Information Studies—all of which are located at the University of California, Los Angeles. Support for our 1994 interviews in Hungary was provided by the Hungarian Ministry of Culture and Education, under a World Bank project, and the ministry granted permission to use the data in this research. Additional support for travel in Central and Eastern Europe in 1993 was provided by the Hungarian-American Fulbright Commission, the U.S. Embassy in Slovenia, and the Ministry of Science, Technology, and Information Science, in Croatia. Support for writing portions of this research was provided by the Rockefeller Foundation, and the Bellagio Study Center, Bellagio, Italy. The Andrew W. Mellon Foundation provided support for presenting this work as a paper at the Conference on Library Automation in Warsaw. Marianne Afifi, Eva Fodor, Aniko Halverson, Agnes Koreny, and Katalin Radics provided superlative research assistance in multiple languages. Thanks are due to these people and many others who discussed ideas with us and who commented on our drafts of related essays, but we acknowledge that any errors and interpretations are ours.

the Czech Republic, Hungary, Poland, Slovakia, and Slovenia. While these countries are grappling with all of these factors and more, the institutional factors are among the most pressing, and we were able to obtain data on them. Specifically, we address the "content-versus-conduit" aspects of the debate over the development of information infrastructure in this region. These issues were debated in the United States in the early 1990s, and similar discussions began at about the same time in Central and Eastern Europe (CEE). Sometimes characterized as "product versus pipes," this debate is over the primacy of the content, or product (the information) versus the primacy of the conduit, or pipes (the infrastructure) in the development of a national information infrastructure. The relationship among traditional content and conduit players will change as the information infrastructure is being developed, and new players are likely to emerge. Creating a technological system on both a national and an international scale is not likely to be a "zero-sum game"; hence the concern of all players about their stakes in the game of building a national information infrastructure.

Our data are drawn from interviews we conducted in the region, in 1993 and 1994, with more than 300 administrators or professional staff members of libraries, computer networks, and government agencies. The interviews were conducted at an early stage in the development of an information infrastructure in the region, at a time when these and other issues were being actively debated. These are not the only players with stakes in the development process, but each of these groups has stakes in the content, the conduit, or both. We analyze the perspective of each of these three groups, the consistencies or disagreements within each, and we make comparisons between them.

A Review of the Infrastructure Literature

The development of a global information infrastructure (GII) creates incentives for countries to cooperate and incentives for them to compete. Countries cooperate because no single player can develop and maintain the entire infrastructure, either technically or economically (Levy, 1997). Competition creates new markets for the products and services of the GII. Some forms of national and international regulation are required to enable fair competition, while encouraging cooperation (Lin, 1994; Mansell, 1993).

"Content" (or products) refers to the information that flows through the conduits. While much of the electronically produced content available today is conduit-specific, the convergence of technologies in a GII promises to carry content in multiple forms (text, voices, graphics, sound, video, images), whether alone or as multimedia. The many players involved in the production and distribution of content (for example, entertainment industries, publishers, software and computer games producers) each take different perspectives on the content-versus-conduit discussions. From the perspective of these players, the conduits are of little value if no content is flowing through them (Gordon and McKenzie, 1994; Press, 1993; Rebello, 1992).

The term "conduit" (or pipes) usually refers to the physical networks involved and to the technical platform on which a network is based. However, the variety of technologies and services available for delivering content leads to multiple frameworks that reflect the stakes of each of the players. Telecommunications companies, cable companies, Internet service providers, and broadcast radio and television networks may each employ a mix of wired and wireless technology, for example, yet each may apply a different metaphor to frame the content-versus-conduit debate (Schon and Rein, 1994). From the perspective of these players, conduits are a necessary condition for the development of national and global information infrastructures; without an adequate conduit, electronic content such as video-on-demand, WebTV, and on-line shopping cannot be delivered.

Content and conduits are therefore complementary components of the information infrastructures, and they will evolve together: Improvements in conduits lead to new forms of content, which places new demands on the conduit; and new content leads to new forms of conduits to deliver it.

Our focus is on the stakes that national and global information infrastructure players have in content, conduits, or both. Because the debate was most advanced in the United States, we briefly review the players in this debate and their stakes in the United States, then analyze the components of the debate from the perspective of institutional players in Central and Eastern Europe. Because our interviews in CEE were conducted in 1993 and 1994, we emphasize research and policy reports from this period.

The Content-versus-Conduit Debate from a U.S. Perspective

Information infrastructures integrate multiple technologies, applications, and services that previously were separate. In this process, new relationships emerge between players, each of whom has a stake in the new social-technical system being created (Caidi and Lievrouw, 1997). The U.S. debate over content versus conduits was dominated by two big players: telephone (both local and long-distance) companies and cable television companies. Each had a large installed base of computing technology and was politically active. These players had a stake in deregulation, which they claimed would make them more competitive, and thus reduce costs and improve services (Pelton, 1993; Irwin and Walsh, 1993; Schiller, 1995).

In communications regulation, universal service is the principle that everyone should have access to the communications network and that access should be priced at the same rate, regardless of the cost to the provider, thus ensuring that those in rural or otherwise expensive-to-serve areas are supported equally with those in cities and other high-concentration areas. Universal service takes on new meaning in the national information infrastructure (NII) and the GII, as it can imply access to the network (the conduit) or access to the content that flows through the network (Anderson et al., 1995; Harasim, 1993; Kahin and Keller, 1995; Keller, 1995; Lynch, 1993).

The open-systems principle, also known as open architecture or open interfaces, is that networks are required to implement technical standards in their hardware and software that enable competitors to interconnect with their systems, and that competitors should be allowed to interconnect (Branscomb & Kahin, 1995; Mansell, 1993). The open systems principle is fundamental to the architecture of the (NII) and the GII because systems must be interoperable to achieve global interconnections (Libicki, 1995).

The Content-versus-Conduit Debate from a Central and Eastern European Perspective

The countries we are studying in Central and Eastern Europe entered the 1990s with a minimal telecommunications infrastructure and a minimal installed base about computing technology. They were immediately faced with complex choices about where to invest their resources. After the political changes of 1989, the new governments in CEE recognized that their underdeveloped telecommunications infrastructure was a barrier to economic growth (Kelly, 1991). They invested in computing networks that would parallel the improvements in basic telecommunications capacity, with the help of supplemental funding support and cooperation from the European Union, and from U.S. and other sources. By late 1994, Central and Eastern Europe was the fastest-growing region on the Internet (Internet Society, January 1995), with a 40 percent growth rate in the number of host computers there, compared to a 26 percent overall increase internationally in Internet hosts. The six countries studied are now investing over 40 percent of their telecommunications revenues in "expenditures associated with acquiring ownership of property and plant used for telecommunication services," with the Czech Republic, Croatia, and Hungary reinvesting close to 70 percent of their telecommunications revenues (ITU, 1997, p. A-87).

In each of the countries we studied, one government ministry is responsible for regulating telecommunications, although the scope of responsibility and the name of the agency varies by country. The CEE countries' typical telecommunications organization is more similar to the traditional European PTT (postal-telephone-telegraph) model than to the U.S. model. The computer networks and libraries may or may not be overseen by the same government ministry, as we explain later when introducing each of the results sections.

A Parallel between U.S. and CEE Conditions. We see a parallel between the conditions under which the content-versus-conduit debate arose in the United States and in Central and Eastern Europe. Computing and communications technologies were converging to create new services and new relationships among players. Changes in the government regulation of communications provided new growth opportunities, while changing the relationship among players, and changing the stakes for each. However, the political economy of the region is much different than that of the United States, and the computer networks were in their infancy at the time of our interviews, so we might expect different paths for development.

We addressed the question of how content and conduit issues are interpreted by the three institutional players we studied: What do they view as their stakes? To what extent do their stakes reflect those in the U.S. debate? In what ways do the three players have similar concerns and to what extent do they have contrasting concerns?

A Two-Year Study: Research Methods

Over a two-year period, one of us conducted two waves of interviews and a mail survey in six countries in Central and Eastern Europe. The countries chosen for the study were Croatia, the Czech Republic, Hungary, Poland, Slovakia, and Slovenia. Interviewees included library directors, heads of library automation programs and other senior library staff members, computer network administrators, and government policymakers. Interviews were conducted in English, either directly or through translators familiar with the issues being addressed. The 1993 interview questions were general and open-ended, seeking to establish a baseline for the growth of library automation and computing networks, the motivations and goals of those involved, and the use of international standards for document description and representation.

We returned in 1994 with a set of specific interview questions about planning and priorities for library automation and computing networks, conducting 33 interviews and 14 group meetings with a total of 139 people. The 1994 interviews and meetings were held with senior administrators of computing networks, government policymakers, and senior management officials of national and state libraries. Altogether, 300 persons (counting those who were interviewed twice) in six countries were interviewed in two years.

Concurrent with the 1994 interviews, we sent a mail survey to a 50 percent sample of all the research libraries in these six countries. The survey provides quantitative data on the implementation of automated library systems and on the use of computing networks, complementing the qualitative results from the interviews. We originally reported the survey data in a journal article (Borgman, 1996a); in the next section of this chapter we report and further discuss data from the interviews. Library automation in the region is compared to developments in automation in other parts of the world in a related article (Borgman, 1997), and is set in a larger policy context in an earlier article (Borgman, 1996b).

Players and Stakes

In this section we present our survey data for each of the three players we studied: computer networks, libraries, and government agencies. We first provide background on the situation of each player, including that player's stake in the development of national and global information infrastructures; we then report the results of the interviews. We found a substantial degree of consistency within the group of network representatives interviewed and within the group of library representatives interviewed. The government representatives were drawn from agencies that oversee computer networks, libraries, or both. Their interests tended to be aligned with the interests of those players they manage, but with perspectives that reflected their governmental role as well.

Computer Networks in Central and Eastern Europe

Background. Until the dissolution of the Soviet bloc in 1989, modern information technologies were either difficult to obtain in Central and Eastern Europe due to embargoes on Western products and the limited production of domestic technology; or expensive when they were available, especially if hard currency was required; or otherwise hindered, whether due to restrictions on information flows or resistance to change (Becker and Szecsko, 1989; Behr and Lippman, 1994; *Finding Common*

Ground, 1991; Heinz, 1991; Mastanduno, 1992; Molnár, Rózsa, and Tamás, 1990; Poznański, 1987; Rudka, 1991). Access to information technologies varied among countries and among types of institutions within countries as well.

Computer networks were begun in the region in the mid-1980s, and were often developed by departments of computer science, physics, or engineering, either in universities or national academies of science. Once the embargoes that had prevented international connections were lifted, and once domestic and foreign resources became available for growth, most of the networks were taken over by government ministries. In some cases the same personnel who had created the networks continued to manage them; in other cases new personnel were appointed to manage these larger operations. Ministries of science and technology typically are responsible for network funding and oversight, whether directly or indirectly, through the delegating of responsibility to a unit of the academy of sciences, a university computing center, or an academic department. We interviewed the heads of the national computer networks in each of the countries we studied. These were the administrators responsible for managing the operations and for representing the network in international network governance organizations.

At the time of the interviews, network access was available to universities, academies, government agencies, and the libraries affiliated with them. Minimal access was available to the blossoming private sector, although the networks hoped to expand to support broader economic sectors, once the network foundations were laid.

Content-versus-Conduit Issues. Computer network agencies are responsible for the conduit aspects of their national information organizations: telecommunications lines and transmission technology, including communication protocols and national and international switching. These agencies typically did not have direct responsibility for the content carried by the networks, although they were responsible for maintaining relationships with their users, who provided the content and made use of it.

Findings on Content. Our respondents' accounts revealed that the communications capabilities of computer networks are viewed as being more important than the delivery of content. In the words of one network director: "A good communications system is better than the information itself." Most of the networking people interviewed disassociated themselves from the content, or the applications side, sometimes referred to as "higher level services."

Nevertheless, network administrators generally acknowledged the importance of providing content and developing applications and services (such as databases, online catalogs) for their countries. Another network director noted, "Infrastructure is easily developed and is penetrating to the users. Where market economy should fit is in the services." Content and information services (and especially domestic information) in the CEE region were viewed by our informants as being underdeveloped.

Questioned about their perception of the role of libraries as content providers, our informants expressed mixed reactions. One respondent reported a feeling of skepticism toward the ability of libraries to provide content through the network, because of the lack of local production of information resources in electronic forms. Another respondent noted that libraries were not active enough in this area. One felt that libraries had not "the least technological grounding to allow for or improve services."

Several respondents remarked that a functioning market economy was necessary for the development of information services and for the increased availability of content on the networks. One network head worried that "the services part of [the country's] economy is completely virginal." The situation in regard to domestic information in one country was characterized as "anarchic" by a network administrator, who saw a lack of shared vision and goals among the countries of the region.

Findings on the Conduit. The highest priority of networking people interviewed was to improve the existing telecommunications and computing infrastructures of their countries. They are eager to replace the old switching technology with digital transmission systems; some mentioned specific technologies, such as those involving the upgrading of telecommunications lines from twisted pairs to fiber optics and of switches from mechanical ones to ATM technology. One respondent noted that "access was so slow that everybody was thinking it makes no sense to [have] a common or shared system." Saturation of network capacity and inadequate bandwidth were concerns raised frequently by network administrators. Some addressed these problems by cooperating with their national telecommunications providers, while others pursued independent networking initiatives.

Despite the recognition by most governments of the importance of developing a technological infrastructure, several respondents emphasized the lack of adequate funding for purchases of technical equipment, for the development of computing centers, or for conducting research. "Technology changes so fast" that it is difficult to "plan ahead," one respondent said. Other respondents expressed concerns about whether those who were funding computer networks had an adequate understanding of technology issues. Networking people often find themselves caught in debates on technology-policy issues, such as the protocol wars between OSI and TCP/IP that were under way at the time. One respondent remarked that networking people have difficulty doing long-term strategic planning because of the number of players involved in the development of computer networks in the region.

Despite the focus of the respondents on the communications infrastructure, network directors are aware of the necessity of "bringing computer networking [to the point where it will] become a common service." Initiatives to increase public awareness on the value of telecommunications and computer networks remain scarce, but as one respondent mentioned, "We realize the importance of it."

Libraries in Central and Eastern Europe

Background. Library services in the region are based on a mix of European library traditions and communication principles from the Communist system (Clavell, 1983; Krzys, Litton, and Hewitt, 1983; Mader, 1995; Nabatova, 1983; Simsova, 1968). Library policymakers recognize that substantial changes in management and services will be required if these libraries are to play a central role in the new political and social structure, whether or not they agree on what those changes might be (Balík, 1992; Molnár, Rózsa, and Tamás, 1990; Tóth, 1990; Wołosz, 1991).

We found a few large collections and thousands of small collections within each country, all of which were managed under a complex mix of centralized and decentralized control. Although national library laws under the previous system created national networks and specified some cooperative activities, they also created structural barriers to cooperation, such as the organizing of subcommunities of libraries that reported to different government ministries, and that were divided both by type of library and by the subject area of the library's collections (Davies, 1992; Rózsa, 1992; Segbert, 1996). CEE countries often established scientific and technical information centers independent from libraries, so as to provide information in strategic areas. Most of our interviews were conducted at the larger university, academy, national, and special research libraries, as these were the first to have access to computer networks.

Content-versus-Conduit Issues. Libraries are responsible for selecting, collecting, organizing, preserving, conserving, and providing access to information, whether it is in print, electronic, or other forms. These institutions are the traditional content providers for their countries, although the many different types of libraries (national, academic, university, special, public) all have their own constituencies and missions. The national libraries are responsible for maintaining the national bibliographies that represent the social, cultural, and scientific history of their countries.

The notion of the conduit changes considerably in the shift from the print form to the electronic delivery of information. In a print environment, libraries exchange records and materials with each other through the postal system, and deliver their resources to their users in person, requiring that users visit the library buildings. In an electronic environment, libraries can exchange records and other content with other libraries via the conduit provided by computer networks, and can deliver content directly to users. The scope of their clientele expands from those with access to the library building to those who have access to the computer network, either domestically or internationally. Until the political changes of 1989, CEE libraries functioned with a minimal level of computing or communications technology. They concentrated on building and maintaining collections for their local clientele, rather than on providing access for a general audience. The collections and services were usually tailored to a small and well-defined clientele, instead of focusing on the creation of unified resources for institutions or countries (Borgman, 1996a).

Findings on Content. The librarians we interviewed clearly view libraries as the primary social institution responsible for providing information services in their countries. They emphasized the value of computer networks for content delivery and for cooperation among libraries. The most common assertion of library directors in all the countries studied is that libraries' catalogs and collections are very important information resources that should be accessible on their national networks. Respondents frequently mentioned the richness of the national heritage contained in their collections, using terms such as "old, very old collections," "valuable information"; they spoke of "opening our libraries to the world," and "promoting our libraries." Librarians also mentioned the value of computer networks and technology for disseminating information about their national and cultural heritage.

These libraries wish to make more effective use of their collections, and thus the attainment of wider, better content delivery appears to be the primary motivation for implementing technology. By automating their catalogs and other databases, they can make them available on their national networks and thus provide better services to their user communities. Computer networks are viewed by some librarians as a means for allowing for libraries to make a transition from a "just in case" model (building great collections) to a "just in time" model (providing access to information regardless of location or ownership); or, as one respondent put it, "Physical location should become a secondary concern."

Cooperation among libraries was viewed by many as essential to the improvement of content delivery. Of central concern was the electronic provision of cataloging records by national libraries. However, many of our respondents expressed concern about the priorities of their national libraries and about the rate at which they were proceeding with automation and with creating electronic content resources that could be shared. Some commented that their country's libraries put too much emphasis on collections and on the "rigor put into cataloging records," and not enough resources into technology: "If [the national library] had to choose between putting two people in networking or two people in the library, [they] would put the people in the library."

Findings on the Conduit. Our respondents expressed the hope that technology would improve cooperation among libraries at a local (university, city), national, or regional level through the sharing of resources and the exchanging of catalog records with regional and foreign institutions. Some respondents were more optimistic than others. One noted that "the libraries are willing to cooperate, but not all conditions are ready yet for [promoting] this cooperation." Another commented that the governments of CEE countries are so focused on creating new national identities, and on maintaining political and economic stability, that cooperation is not among their top priorities. Others emphasized the potential role that computer networks have in unifying the libraries into a structured system by linking together scattered library collections.

Affordable access to the networks is a major concern within the library community. Concerns expressed by many of our respondents are captured in this quote: "There are many problems, but everybody, I think, has the same problem: financing."

Government Agencies in Central and Eastern Europe

Background. Governments continue to play a central role in the mass media and in the development of technologies in Central and Eastern Europe and in other formerly-Communist countries (Gross Schaffer, 1995). The situation of government agencies is difficult to summarize because it varies greatly among the six countries studied, and because the structure of government agencies is in a state of flux in this period of political and economic transition. We selected government agencies and individuals for interviews on the basis of their role in overseeing computer networks or libraries.

Content-versus-Conduit Issues. In this region, responsibility for telecommunications, computer networks, libraries, and other aspects of the information infrastructure is divided among many government agencies. Contradictions in vision and competing priorities among ministries were concerns often cited by our respondents in government agencies, as well as by those in computer networks and libraries.

The national computer network in each country is managed by a small number of persons and reports to a single ministry. In contrast, each country has thousands of individual libraries, with varying missions, and responsibility for them is divided among a large number of ministries. We mostly interviewed administrators in ministries of culture, education, or science and technology who were responsible for national libraries, other major research libraries, or computer networks. To simplify the reporting of our results below, we discuss our interviews with administrators responsible for libraries in the section on content and our interviews with those responsible for computer networks under the section on conduits, unless otherwise noted.

Findings on Content. The government administrators who oversee libraries recognize the importance of libraries as content providers and as keepers of the national cultural heritage. Most want to see a greater development of electronic resources by libraries and by other agencies. The production of domestic information was characterized as "underdeveloped" by many respondents, who said we need to "create our own databases," "handle images," and create information-handling tools to search databases. Potential users of the electronic form of information include not only librarians ("if they see benefits, then they will use information in the electronic form"), but also the business sector, which is being encouraged to utilize computer networks for access to information resources.

Content-related concerns of government administrators focused on the coordination of libraries' activities. To varying degrees, they wish that libraries in their countries could share resources, reduce the duplication of efforts in cataloging and automation, and thus provide better national services, presumably at a lower overall cost. One respondent indicated that [my ministry's] goal is to "make some order for the future of libraries." A number of respondents noted that the interest in building a structure for library cooperation is not a new idea, but at the advent of computer networks in these countries makes cooperative content provision practical for the first time.

Discussions of the role of government ministries in the coordination of library activities quickly unearthed the tension between central planning, viewed by many as a remnant of the old political system, and a decentralization program, viewed by many others as a key element of a democratic future. Some administrators feel that a clear vision presented and implemented by the government is essential to the coordination of library services, although at least one stated that "[central] planning is a waste of time." Yet other government officials interviewed think that computer networks will make it possible to coordinate decentralized information services, thus achieving a balance of power.

The tension of the centralization-decentralization debate was apparent in administrators' views of librarians and in librarians' views of government agencies. Some administrators doubted librarians' eagerness to cooperate with each other. As one put it, [Some libraries] "still don't see quite well the value of this plan [of integrating library resources and information activities with technology]." Another respondent said that while some librarians "answered [the call for a collaboration] in very competent ways, there were also some who feel threatened." Similarly, some librarians doubted their parent agencies' ability to facilitate cooperation. One library respondent observed that government ministries find it hard to "let go of the old habits of controlling cultural institutions." Both ministry staff members and librarians expressed concern about the future role of national libraries; some feel that a strong national library, with centralized powers, will be essential for the coordination of services, and others feel that their national library is too powerful, too conservative, and is slowing progress toward an effective decentralized library network.

While some librarians said that their governing ministries would not allow them to pursue technology initiatives without explicit consent, some in the ministries felt that too many librarians were waiting for "somebody from above to tell them what to do and provide the environment [for them]." These ministers were hoping for "more grassroots initiatives" from the libraries. Other librarians saw direct funding, with minimal government intervention, as the fastest path to growth: "When there is money, there is progress; we don't need policy, we need money."

These tensions are also being played out in the national legislatures of the countries we studied. At the time of the interviews, laws that defined library services were under review for the first time in several decades, as part of the political and economic transition from socialism and central planning toward democracy and open markets. Typically, respondents discussed the legal issues as follows: "[The system needs a] radical change of environment"; "the decision-making system asks for another environment [and for] changes in the configuration of institutions"; the "legal ground is still foggy"; "[the people involved need to] agree upon guidelines and a clear vision of the goals" before establishing the details.

The outcome of these debates has a direct effect on cooperative activities and on the delivery of content over computer networks. The governance of library institutions influences factors such as the ownership of local data and systems, standards for sharing bibliographic records, and the interoperability of systems.

Since government agency administrators are responsible for the planning, policy, and coordination processes, much of the interviewing addressed these issues. Many viewed cooperation among the libraries under the control of their ministry as a necessary first step. Although some were concerned that constructing cooperative networks organized within the control of a single ministry might inhibit later cross-ministry cooperation, others were not optimistic about the idea that cross-ministry cooperation was even possible, and viewed the creation of multiple library networks as better than having no networks at all. And others viewed a national network that would serve all types of libraries as the top priority for cooperative activities. One country formed a commission for the study of library cooperation, which included representatives of the primary government agencies in charge of libraries. Specific objectives expressed by government officials included the "enhancement of the cooperation between university and state scientific libraries," the need to "coordinate core collections for public libraries," the improvement of "access to library catalogs," the "creation of union catalogs," and the "introduction of shared cataloging."

Some government officials recognized that plans and policies alone are insufficient: "If you want to do something new, something creative, you need people liking it and motivated to do it"; hence the importance of "talking, explaining, marketing."

Some of these officials emphasized the need for people with marketing, management, or public relations skills, who would act as agents of change. One expressed the need to motivate and to change people's attitudes, while saying that "we don't know how to do it." Others viewed the market economy and the private sector (businesses, other information providers) as potential catalysts for the development of information activities. Although there are "not [yet] much data on information markets and new uses," many hope that these initiatives will result in "open[ing] the door for everyone to this world of information."

Findings on the Conduit. The government ministries or other agencies responsible for computer networks are charged with developing and deploying the technical framework for the information infrastructure in their countries; hence, managing the conduit is their primary role. The centralization-decentralization debate exists here as well, but appears to be manifested as the tension between wanting to establish a computing and communications conduit versus a comprehensive information infrastructure that includes content and services.

Respondents frequently mentioned the neglect of the infrastructure and services sectors under centralized planning, and the high priority the new governments are placing on rebuilding the technological infrastructure. At least one respondent indicated that "the computing and communications infrastructure has priority number one [at the Ministry of Science and Technology]. We'll have it because we realize the importance of it." They are concerned, in like manner, with international connectivity: "We are following very closely what is happening with the information highway in the European Union and elsewhere."

We did find that communication services, such as electronic mail, were more likely to be centralized than were information services, such as database access. Multiple government agencies were involved in creating electronic resources, with the use of minimal national coordination. To some, having a variety of independent projects was "more profitable," "useful," or "necessary" for the development of an information infrastructure, and was better than centralized planning. Others were concerned about the lack of coordination among government agencies, viewing it as evidence of the failure to achieve a common vision for a national information infrastructure.

Yet others viewed the present situation as a necessary step toward a common vision that would support the goals of networks, libraries, and other information providers. As one respondent reported, "We were confronted with a situation of having librarians on one side and the information scientists or technologists on the other. We had to find a way to bring them together, to integrate the library functions and the functions of the specialized information centers and integrated systems by using an up-to-date, modern technology." Some see the presence of a "wide government network that is [available] for each one who is interested," as a means of motivating libraries to automate and to synchronize their procedures and equipment.

Conclusions

The content-versus-conduit debates were active in the United States in the early-to-mid-1990s, having been fueled by telecommunications deregulation, the growth of the Internet, and the formulation of broad policies for national information infrastructures. Similar developments and discussions were under way in Central and Eastern Europe, but they were built upon very different histories of telecommunications, technology policy, and library services. The political changes of 1989 that led to new forms of government and new economic policies also led consequently to substantial investments in technologically based information infrastructures for these countries.

In the six countries we studied in Central and Eastern Europe, we focused on how the debates were framed within the computer networks, the libraries, and the government ministries that oversee them. These groups were concerned with establishing foundations for the information infrastructures of their countries, and with assuring that their stakes would be protected as conduits and content services matured. Most of our respondents who were involved with networks were scientists or technologists, and most were more concerned with the science and technology of computer networks than with policy issues.

The librarians we interviewed were eager to stake their claim as primary content providers in the electronic world of computer networks, as well as in traditional areas of library services. Our respondents were the early adopters of technology, eager to move forward, and often concerned that their colleagues in other libraries were moving too slowly. This group saw computer networks as offering an excellent opportunity to expand the services and influence of libraries in the new social order that was evolving.

For the most part, the government ministry staff people we interviewed took a broad view, saying they wanted to coordinate the activities of libraries to improve content services, and wanted the networks to provide affordable, quality service to support libraries and their users. As the policymakers and planners, they were caught in the middle of the political tensions created by the centralization-decentralization debate.

Comparison of the Players

Each of the three institutional players involved is protecting its respective stakes, as would be expected. Computer network administrators care most about providing a high-quality conduit; content is important to them, but they view its delivery as the role of others. Libraries care most about delivering content; they want an inexpensive, reliable network available for their use. Some people in each of these two groups expressed stereotypical views of the other: Some network administrators doubt the libraries' ability to adapt to the electronic age; some librarians doubt the networks' ability to recognize the significance of their role as content providers, saying that networks instead view libraries only as users of the networks. The average is somewhere between these views, with each group respecting the role of the other, even if one does not claim to completely understand the other's perspective.

The government ministry representatives interviewed were concerned with promoting the interests of the libraries or the computer networks for which they were responsible, and for coordinating the work of those within their purview. Ministries responsible for libraries were mixed in their opinion of the libraries' ability or willingness to work together, while libraries often were skeptical of ministries' ability to effectively coordinate services. Some government administrators focused on developing workable coordination plans, whether within or among ministries, while others encouraged innovative grass-roots efforts from libraries. Similarly, some libraries awaited direction from their ministries, while others sought minimal interference in their plans and policies.

We found less divergent views among government ministries that oversee networks and the networks themselves. However, computer networks are much smaller and more unified organizations than are libraries, and are more tightly coupled with the ministries that oversee them. These administrators have the common goal of developing and deploying a high-quality, reliable network, as quickly as possible, and all are faced with the competing needs of the multiple constituencies eager to use the network.

Content versus Conduit. In the United States, the content-versus-conduit debate began in the telecommunications industry, as new players entered the fray, and as proposed changes in government regulation shifted the relationships between traditional players. Libraries and other organizations concerned with the public interest became involved in the issues of universal service and open systems.

The content-versus-conduit debate was being conducted in Central and Eastern Europe in the early 1990s, in parallel with the debate under way in the United States. The debates began from different starting points, however. The United States pioneered in the telecommunications industry, and now has one of the world's most advanced national networks; and having established the Internet, it has by far the world's most advanced national computer network, with the greatest penetration of network access. Cable television, electronic publishing, and other higher-order services were maturing in the early 1990s, and library automation had been under way for more than 30 years (Borgman, 1997). In contrast, Central and Eastern Europe was emerging from 40 years of socialist governance during which most of the innovations in information technology were unavailable, unaffordable, or discouraged (Borgman, 1996a). At the time of our interviews, these countries were in the process of rapidly shifting from a minimal telecommunications infrastructure to the most modern technologies. Libraries were in the early stages of automating their catalog data, bringing local databases on-line, and obtaining basic connectivity services, such as electronic mail and access to remote information services.

Centralization versus Decentralization. To some of the ministers, librarians, and network directors we interviewed, a common vision promulgated, managed, and funded by the government was considered essential for achieving an effective information infrastructure; to others, this approach was viewed as a continuation of socialist centralized planning. To some others of those interviewed, decentralization was considered essential for promoting grass-roots, innovative, and entrepreneurial approaches that exemplify the transition to a democratic, market economy; and to others, this approach represented chaos, lack of a common vision, and a recipe for disaster. This variety of opinions is evidence of the early stages of the debates, of the establishment of stakes and positions, and of the emergence of new players.

Next Steps. In the content-versus-conduit debate—among computer networks, libraries, and government ministries—that was being played out in Central and Eastern Europe in the early 1990s, we could see a microcosm of the political, economic, and social tensions that have characterized the transition to a new political economy for the region. All involved want to contribute to the new social order, and they want to be assured of an important role in that order. Those in the forefront are frustrated with those moving more slowly. All are some stereotypical views of other players. These debates will continue, and they will mature as the technology advances, as legal and economic matters are sorted out, and as more of the players gain experience, domestically and internationally. What is most important to all concerned is that they keep talking to each other and hearing each other's concerns, which hopefully will lead to balanced solutions that serve the public interest.

References

Anderson, R. H.; Bikson, T.; Law, S. A.; and Mitchell, B. M. 1995. *Universal Access to E-mail: Feasibility and Societal Implications.* Santa Monica, CA: Rand. Available at http://www.rand.org/publications/MR/MR650/

Balík, V. 1992. Challenges and possibilities for developing research libraries in former socialist countries. *The Liber Quarterly* 2(3): 305–312.

Becker, J., and Szecsko, T. (eds.). 1989. *Europe Speaks to Europe. International Information Flows between Eastern and Western Europe.* London: Pergamon Press.

Behr, P., and Lippman, T. W. 1994; March 31. U.S. lifts cold war sales curbs. Move opens markets for communications, computer companies. *The Washington Post,* p. A1.

Branscomb, L. M., and Kahin, B. 1995. Standards processes and objectives for the national information infrastructure. In B. Kahin and J. Abbate (eds.), *Standards Policy for Information Infrastructure.* Cambridge: MIT Press, 3–34.

Borgman, C. L. 1997. From acting locally to thinking globally: a brief history of library automation. *Library Quarterly* 67(3), 215–249.

Borgman, C. L. 1996a. Automation is the answer, but what is the question? Progress and prospects for Central and Eastern European Libraries. *Journal of Documentation* 52(3), 252–295.

Borgman, C. L. 1996b. Will the global information infrastructure be the library of the future? Central and Eastern Europe as a case example. *IFLA [International Federation of Library Associations] Journal* 22(2), 121–127.

Caidi, N., and Lievrouw, L. A. 1997. *Momentum, resistance and the construction of the information superhighways: A case study using socio-technical analysis.* Paper presented at the International Communications Association's 47th Annual Conference, Montreal, May 22–26, 1997.

Clavell, J-P. 1983. Western European librarianship: Its background, emergence, and development. In Krzys, R., Litton, G., & Hewitt, A. *World Librarianship: A Comparative Study.* New York: Marcel Dekker, 67–72.

Davies, R. 1992. Libraries in the former socialist countries: A new situation. *The Liber Quarterly* 2(2), 215–226.

Finding Common Ground: U.S. Export Controls in a Changed Global Environment. Panel on the Future Design and Implementation of U.S. National Security Export Controls. 1991. Committee on science, engineering, and public policy, National Academy of Sciences, National

Academy of Engineering, Institute of Medicine. Washington: National Academy Press.
Gordon, M. L. and Mckenzie, D. J. P. 1994. From county roads to superhighway: keeping pace with the new business and legal turns on the information superhighway. *Illinois Libraries* 76(3), 124–148.
Gross Schaffer, L. 1995. *The International World of Electronic media*. New York: McGraw-Hill.
Harasim, L.M. (ed.). 1993. *Global Networks: Computers and International Communication*. Cambridge: MIT Press. (First MIT Press paperback edition, 1994.)
Heinz, J. 1991. *U. S. Strategic Trade: An Export Control System for the 1990s*. Boulder: Westview Press.
Hughes, T. P. 1989. The evolution of large technological systems. In Bijker, W. E.; Hughes, T.P.; and Pinch, T. (eds.). *The Social Construction of Technological Systems: new Directions in the Sociology and History of Technology* (pp. 51–81). Boston: MIT Press.
International Telecommunication Union (ITU). 1997. *The World Telecommunication Development Report 1996-1997*. 3rd ed. Geneva: United Nations Press.
Internet Society. (January 1995). Latest Internet host survey available: The Internet is growing faster than ever. URL: http://www.nw.com/zone/WWW/isoc-pr-9501.txt
Irwin, D. A., and Walsh, K. 1993. Understanding the FCC's forbearance policy. *Telecommunications* 27(9), 41–42.
Kahin, B., and Keller, J. (eds.). 1995. *Public Access to the Internet*, Cambridge: MIT Press.
Keller, J. 1995. Public access issues: An introduction. In B. Kahin and J. Keller (eds.). *Public Access to the Internet*. Cambridge: MIT Press, pp. 34–45.
Kelly, T. 1991. Telecommunications in the Rebirth of Eastern Europe. *The OECD Observer, 167* (December/January), 19-22.
Kryzs, R.; Litton, G.; and Hewitt, A. 1983. *World Librarianship: A Comparative Study*. New York: Marcel Dekker.
Law, J. 1989. Technology and heterogeneous engineering: The case of Portuguese expansion. In Bijker, W.E.; Hughes, T. P.; and Pinch, T. (eds.), *The Social Construction of Technological Systems: New Directions in the Sociology and History of Technology*, (pp. 111–134). Boston: MIT Press.
Levy, J. 1997. *Towards a new global technology order for a global society?* Electronic Newsletter, *FYI France* (edited by Jack Kessler), January. URL: http://www.fyifrance.com
Libicki, M.C. 1995. Standards: The rough road to the common byte. In B. Kahin and J. Abbate (eds), *Standards Policy for Information Infrastructure*. Cambridge: MIT Press, 35–78.
Lin, C.A. 1994. Audience Fragmentation in a Competitive Video Marketplace. *Journal of Advertising Research*, 34(6), 1-17.
Lynch, C. 1993. Interoperability: The standards challenge for the '90s. *Wilson Library Bulletin*, March, 38–42.
Mader, B. 1995. Library automation systems in academic libraries in Hungary. *Program* 29 (3), 285–293.
Mansell, R. (1993). *The New Telecommunications: A Political Economy of Network Evolution*. London: Sage.
Mastanduno, M. 1992. *Economic Containment: CoCom and the Politics of East-West Trade*. Ithaca: Cornell University Press.
Molnár, I.; Rózsa, G.; and Tamás, P. 1990. An approach to a computer-based information economy model. *International Journal of Information and Library Research* 2(3), 141–158.
Nabatova, M.B. 1983. Eastern Europe. In R. Kryzs; G. Litton; and A. Hewitt (eds.), *World Librarianship: A Comparative Study*. New York: Marcel Dekker, 133–135.

Pelton, J. N. 1993. Toward a new national vision: A blueprint for America's information highways. *Telecommunications* 27(9), 25–32.

Poznański, K. 1987. *Technology, Competition and the Soviet Bloc in the World Market.* Berkeley: Institute of International Studies, University of California.

Press, L. 1993. The Internet and interactive television. *Communications of the ACM* 36(12), 19–23.

Rebello, K. 1992. Your digital future. *Business Week,* No. 3282, Sep. 7, 57–64.

Rózsa, G. 1992. Hungarian research libraries: Their contribution to the European culture and cultural heritage. *The Liber Quarterly* 2(2), 33–40.

Rudka, A. 1991. Western Export Controls: An East European View. In D. M. Kemme (ed.), *Technology Markets and Export Controls in the 1990s.* New York: New York University Press, 1991.

Schiller, H. 1995. The global information highway: Project for an ungovernable world. In James Brook, and Iain A. Boal. *Resisting the Virtual Life: The Culture and Politics of Information.* San Francisco: City Lights, 17–33.

Schon, Donald A., and Rein, Martin. 1994. *Frame Reflections: Toward the Resolution of Intractable Policy Controversies.* New York: Basic Books.

Segbert, M. 1996. *Library co-operation with Central and Eastern Europe. Reports of Country Visits, Version 2.0.* Luxembourg: Commission of the European Communities, Directorate General XIII, Telecommunications, Information Market and Exploitation of Research, Libraries Program (DG XIII/E-4).

Segbert, M., and Burnett, P. (eds.). 1997. *Proceedings of the Conference on Library Automation in Central and Eastern Europe,* Budapest, April 10–13, 1996. Soros Foundation Open Society Institute Regional Library Program, and Commission of the European Communities, Directorate General XIII, Telecommunications, Information Market and Exploitation of Research, Libraries Program (DG XIII/E-4). Budapest: Open Society Institute.

Simsova, S. 1968. *Lenin, Krupskaia, and Libraries.* G. Peacock and L. Prescott (trans.). London: Clive Bingley.

Tóth, G. 1990. Problems in Hungarian library policy. *Libri* 40(4), 336–349.

Wołosz, J. 1991. The role of national libraries and the centralized management system in the countries of Eastern Europe. *Alexandria* 3(3), 131–148.

CHAPTER 3

A Coordinator's View of the Impact of Policy on the Financing and the Managing of Library Automation

JURAND B. CZERMIŃSKI

This chapter should be understood as a record of the author's reminiscences during his long term as Chair of the Coordinating Committee for VTLS implementation.[1] It was originally planned as an analysis of Polish state policy, but as the writing of it progressed, greater attention was paid to other policies, as well as to their mutual relationship. Policy in Poland is widely known for its peculiar character. Inevitably, everyone wants someone else to disclose some policy to him/her, while at the same time attempting to hide his/her own policy. Therefore, any task that targets such a matter might be perceived as requiring a kind of mixed behavior: a spy's and an engineer's investigation of the contents or structure of a "black box" that has only input and output channels and no information about its type of, say, proprietary query language. By the nature of the matter discussed, the resulting opinions can be very subjective, incomplete, and often unjustified. Some of the problems we faced from 1993 to 1998 may look different today, especially those concerning the export of high-level technology.

European Perspective

Before discussing the impact of policy on the process of the computerization of Polish libraries, it is valuable to briefly recall some European demographic data concerning the subject under discussion. If Russia is recognized as the only large European country, then, accordingly, Poland, by its size and population (*Demographic Yearbook 1996*) can be included among the medium-size European countries, such as Germany, France, and Spain. If, on the other hand, the "development path" model is being considered (Jarosiński and Rajewski 1992), then Poland belongs with Spain, Portugal, Greece, and Turkey, and far below such countries as Denmark, Belgium, and Austria. In 1990 The Andrew W. Mellon Foundation initiated a program of assistance

---

1. http://www.bg.univ.gda.pl/~jurand

to Poland and thereby founded, on a politically somewhat unstable basis, a new axis—the beginning of a new bridge between old friends and partners dramatically divided by past fate. Thus the United States has again proved able to offer international help more readily than have wealthy neighboring European countries. But the European countries, despite their official declarations about a free flow of personnel and capital, are still very suspicious of the possible "undeclared" hidden agendas of big projects. Is this an example of investment in the most promising country or a second-level human Solidarity? Is it a well-calculated anticipation of a new Europe's "Drang nach Osten," or a deep faith in the immortality of personal and organizational sacrifice? Or both?

Polish University Libraries: A Perhaps Risky Choice for Aid

The Mellon Foundation first targeted its primary efforts toward the automation of Polish university libraries. The choice was appropriate, but perhaps somewhat risky. Polish university staffs employed in science departments were reasonably experienced in the use of computers and rather experienced in networking, but this was not the case for the average technical library staff. The prevailing number of, let us call them *first-generation* library directors, recruited from university staffs graduated from history and literature departments with no tradition of computer use or understanding of modern technology at all. An even more desperate situation existed during the writing, and then the managing, of advanced, multilevel, technical projects with a strictly defined beginning and end. To add to this cup of bitterness, I should note a lack of commonly accepted standards at the national level and the number of different cataloging rules applied through previous decades—all that had been left untouched without regard for the future. And last, but not least, I have to mention the very low quality, state-owned telecommunication system, with its very expensive telephone rates and a new public-packet switched digital network. Simply speaking, it is nothing to be proud of. In official verbal declarations, the organizational abilities of libraries were excellent, staff qualifications were high, and the ability to absorb funds practically limitless. Everything appeared much better than in reality. One thing is certain: No one was thinking of promising quick, spectacular results.

With this burden, whether known or unknown, conscious or unconscious, the first three Polish universities—Warsaw University, Jagiellonian University, and the University of Gdańsk—were invited to submit their historical proposals.

Surprising Approval of Grant Requests

One could interpret the approval of grant requests at levels exceeding, in some cases, the recommended project budget by a factor of nearly two as a kind of miracle. The strong injection of a large amount of U.S. dollars and the short period of time required to report on the projects' accounts rapidly changed the usual approach, causing a sort of adrenaline shock. Universities traditionally competing for funds and publicly demonstrating their independent, unique way of thinking unified their efforts and formed strong local project teams consisting of well-known, countrywide specialists. Furthermore, they agreed to use common standards and were soon joined by yet another university (the University of Mining and Metallurgy in Kraków), the first member that contributed to the newly born community from its own funds. In a short time, top university authorities (rectors and prorectors) signed an agreement to found the first consortium-based structure in Poland. The initiative to organize a legalized form of cooperation came from project team heads from Gdańsk, Warsaw, and Kraków, while the form of the agreement was recommended by Director S. Madej of the Ministry of National Education. It took less than one year to add the next valuable members to the project—the University of Wrocław and the first Polish subconsortium in Lublin—all due to a funding policy that became increasingly open. It may be appropriate here to say a few words about this policy, as seen through the project coordinator's eyes. My experience resulted from the designing and managing of thirteen projects during the last six years, with grants being received from five sources and totaling $1,800,000; in table 3.1 I present the rankings of grant providers in which the following abbreviations are used:

LG: Large grant
SG: Small grant
MEL: Andrew W. Mellon Foundation (United States)
OSI: Open Society Institute, a subsidiary of the Soros Foundation; the grant was recommended to the Higher Education Support Program (HESP) by the Batory Foundation (Poland)
EC: European Community funds; the ranking is based on the coordinator's experience with the PHARE program subproject of the Central Statistical Library in Warsaw
KBN: State Committee for Scientific Research (Poland) (Komitet Badań Naukowych)
ME: Ministry of National Education (Poland)
EC: European Community funds; ranking is based on the coordinator's experience with the TEMPUS (1994) and PHARE/FIESTA II (1997) projects

Table 3.1. Coordinator's Rankings of Grant Providers

	Types and Providers of Grants						
Aspects of Grants	LG MEL	LG OSI	LG EC	LG KBN	LG ME	SG MEL	SG EC
Grant level	5	4	5	4	4	5	5
Instructions—simple	3	4	1	5	5	—	3
Application documents—simple	4	3	1	5	5	5	2
Grant-approval duration	5	4	1	2	5	5	4
Budget flexibility	5	1	2	3	4	5	3
Budget modification procedure	5	3	2	2	4	5	—
Project manageability	5	5	2	3	5	5	3
Net budget dissolution	5	2	2	2	3	5	2
Constraints	5	5	1	3	3	5	1
Total	42	31	17	29	38	—*	—

Rankings are: 5 = superb; 4 = very good; 3 = good; 2 = satisfactory; 1 = unsatisfactory
*No data are provided in cases of insufficient information.

48 *Library Policy and the State*

The Mellon Foundation proved to be an excellent grant provider within the class ranked. Colloquially put, its policy appeared to be "grant recipient friendly." The grant recipients' pleasure of cooperating with the Mellon Foundation could not be matched by any other grant provider ranked above. In terms of the matter under discussion, its policy can be characterized as fast-acting, open, trusting, understandable, flexible, and judicious. Lack of bureaucratic complexities and its remarkable speed in approving budget modifications indicate a more personal, rather than collegial, character of the project foundation's supervisory role.

All of the above may look like a commendation for The Mellon Foundation. In fact, however, the purpose of the table is to instruct grant applicants concerning the importance of management methods and recommendations concerning the good practices required by grant providers. Grant applicants often, it seems, disregard these recommendations, prompting dire consequences for themselves.

The Problems of Importing Electronic Technology

The world is broken into pieces that form a puzzle, with some pieces missing. These days it is impossible to assemble it into one complete picture. Instead, one can distinguish a few apparently consistent structures. In terms of the control policy of the Co-ordinating Committee for Export to Communist Areas (COCOM), between 1989 and 1994, Poland migrated across at least three different categories of high-technology importers.

Starting in the late 1980s, some Polish experts, later invited to join the library teams, received their initial experience in understanding the terms of importing modern electronic technology within the interministerial project RRI-14, a creation of the National Academic and Research Network (KASK). In 1989 it was not even possible to officially purchase the SCO Xenix package for legal use in Poland.[2] Later, the experts were involved in IBM's Academic Initiative and additionally the Gdańsk experts with negotiations with ICL and Hewlett-Packard and Kraków experts with IBM and Sun Microsystems. Additional legal experience in the preparation of Polish international trade contracts was acquired, between 1989 and 1991, at the National Commission of the independent union Solidarity. The contracts proposed were not always "on the level," and it is understandable that this produced a defensive reaction, which influenced Polish policy and resulted in the following conclusions being drawn from it:

---

2. Letters and orders sent by the RRI-14 Project coordinator (Wrocław Technical University) were completely ignored and remained unanswered. In November 1991, the situation was still similar, when, out of 43 leading automated-library-software vendors invited by the University of Gdansk to offer their products, just a small fraction answered. Further bidding procedures carried out in Kraków by Jagiellonian University and the University of Gdańsk showed that only two vendors (VTLS and GEAC) were ready to come with fully preconfigured equipment to demonstrate their systems. It is worth noting that COMECON (Council for Mutual Economic Assistance) countries were widely recognized as sites famous for the illegal copying of software and serious deficiencies in respecting authors' rights. The Polish consumer had to wait a few additional years until Parliament approved a bill on intellectual property and authors' rights in 1994, one and a half years after a corresponding bill was enacted in Hungary.

- A strong, known system producer is more reliable than a young, dynamic company offering low-priced products.
- It is desirable not to buy remarketed hardware, as it is likely to be technologically outdated and soon may have no support and no replacement parts.
- The customer must be aware of the total power consumption of the hardware, air-conditioning, and ventilation systems. Furthermore, he or she must analyze total room space requirements for servers, disks, magnetic backup, and telecommunication equipment.[3]
- The purchase of large mainframe systems for library purposes is definitely discouraged.
- Separate analysis must concern ownership of the hardware and software. It is unacceptable to purchase the system featuring a single subsystem or even one critical part owned by the vendor or any other company/agency.
- If part of the system is imported on the basis of COCOM restrictions, then the customer must agree to accept inspections from appropriate authorities (including a 24-hour-per-day accessibility to logfiles).
- The importing of RISC technology is strictly controlled and the availability of the technology depends not only on system performance but also on many externally unknown factors, some of which may reflect, for instance, the usage of a particular system in the vendor's country.
- Vendors of telecommunication equipment are allergically sensitive to any declaration of future use of the equipment over the wide area network (WAN). It is wise to speak and write about only the local area network (LAN) connection, even if the hardware is fully capable of operating over the WAN.
- It is recommended that more expensive, but reliable PC computers be purchased, which are not only assembled but also tested and certified.
- Special attention must be paid to any software license agreement. A right-to-use (RTU) clause for an *unlimited period of time* must be included. It is totally unacceptable to have to sign a license agreement, which specifies any form of renewal of license and its subsequent costs.
- Any draft agreement is prepared by the vendor and reflects *only* his priorities. The end user must add to the agreement all necessary clauses important from his point of view. It is advisable that the end user demand ownership of the data or software files produced with the use of licensed software. In particular, libraries must remember that the catalogs and other computer files produced by licensed software must be owned by the licensee.

---

3. An unacceptable library director policy at the University of Gdańsk Library led to the adaptation of a small part of a narrow corridor for placing, in a space of a mere 7.2 m^2, the following: three departmental servers with a total of 19 SCSI units connected, two jukeboxes, nine telecommunication processors (one router, two switches, FDDI, and ATM), four access switches, a repeater, an HP DTC Communication Server, ARPA Telnet, a KA9Q IP Router, a 19" modem panel, UPS, and a network printer. The equipment was extremely difficult to service and there was practically no room for system development. At the same time, catalogers obtained premises that satisfied very good international standards of 12 m^2 per person, while the computer staff had half of that (6.4 m^2 per head). This is in great contrast to other libraries famous for their productivity, which have a much smaller space occupied by catalogers and have more space for computer hardware and staff (for example, Warsaw University). All these factors are undesirable sources of invidious comparisons, comments, and dissatisfaction.

- Up to the day the license agreement is signed, the vendor must not be certain that his offer is the only acceptable offer and the end user has already decided to purchase his software. The customer must be ready to cease negotiations at any moment. It is advisable to engage in contract negotiations with 2-3 vendors in tandem and work simultaneously with all corresponding draft agreements.
- The system purchase-priority scheme should be as follows: (1) telecommunications equipment, (2) application software, (3) computer hardware and system software. With some constraints imposed on the last two types of goods, the order of items purchased from the first group may well dictate purchases the remaining ones. It is safer to purchase a system which is exactly the same as the one recommended by the application-software vendor; otherwise, the vendor can blame user-configured hardware and/or system software as being responsible for the application's malfunctions.

Preparation for Future Communication Highways

From the very beginning of the common project it was clear that reliable interlibrary communication over the WAN would be critical for the success of the project. When designing the University of Gdańsk's project, I was fully conscious of the following facts.

First, the Gdańsk University Library should have at least one partner using the same technology (both network and library).

Second, since American WAN technology for reliable data transmission was strongly controlled in all of the former COMECON countries, the university project must be able to internally test the system over the WAN before another university library partner for cooperation is found. The following strategies surrounding the issue were considered: First, if no U.S. export license for telecommunication equipment is received, then pure domestic, home-grown, low-speed X.25 technology for WAN communication will be used. Second, the University of Gdańsk may receive a U.S. export license, but telecommunication equipment will be delivered with some protocols or functions disabled or deleted in order to limit the use of it to the LAN.[4] Such a situation is unacceptable for the University of Gdańsk, since it is the only Polish University with its departments located throughout the tri-city area of Gdańsk, Sopot, and Gdynia, and any one part of its system must communicate with the rest over the WAN. The University of Gdańsk is ready to face such an unwanted situation and is prepared for negotiations in order to receive its equipment as fully operational over the WAN for its internal, purely civil purposes. Once received, it could be easily delivered to other Polish cities. Third, if both the IP and X.25 technologies are available, then the IP is considered the preferable one due to the higher speed it offers to the end

---

4. Such a situation occurred at the University of Mining and Metallurgy, Kraków, where IBM delivered early model RS/6000 workstations with the TCP/IP protocol deleted. This was due to the vendor's policy rather than to the U.S. government (Department of Commerce or Department of Defense) policy or COCOM policy, since at almost the same time the University of Gdańsk received its Hewlett-Packard (HP) 9000 server and workstations fully supporting TCP/IP.

user.[5] This preference was decided on the assumption that the reliability of telecommunication lines will gradually improve, diminishing the role of the bandwidth-consuming X.25 transmission error control mechanism. In reality, this assumption turned out to be much better than what had been anticipated.[6] Fortunately, Poland's foreign policy successfully met the requirements of U.S. government security policy (which was always counterbalanced by its commerce policy) and resulted in the most successful 2(c) variant. The correct choice of a vendor for the routers (Cisco was chosen over HP and DEC) was made after a long, detailed examination of European IP centers (Copenhagen, Stockholm, Vienna, Trieste, Geneva) and of the results of router tests that were available from Harvard University (Bradner 1991). It allowed the University of Gdańsk and most other Polish universities to connect to the global Internet without any complications.[7] It is remarkable that all these selections were made on the basis of our own experts' experience, and that all were correct.

A Clash between Divergent Viewpoints on Library Collections

With all the technical selections completed, all hardware successfully delivered and installed, the application software parameterized, and the text of the application-software license agreement carefully reviewed, negotiated, and signed, it seemed to project staffs that a market-oriented, faceless and soul-less humbug—let's call it "frenemy" (friend plus enemy)—had been left far behind. All systems delivered were useful only for start-up work, mostly in an autonomous, off-line mode, and required a rapid upgrade. The exhaustion of smaller grants in Warsaw and Wrocław eliminated 50 percent of the consortium from the planned cooperation because of network hardware and software deficiencies. Additional funds were urgently needed, but the Mellon funds directed to the libraries produced widespread envy.

---

5. Cisco routers offered up to 10 mbps over the LAN and 4 mbps over the WAN (serial-synchronous) while the market's fastest X.25 adapter for an HP 9000 server offered 384 kbps over synchronous lines; and the Polish PTT-owned X.25 Public Packet Switched Network (POLPAK), offered, to end users in a few major Polish cities, a 19.2-kbps committed bit rate (CBR).

6. In the next few years, Polish academic and research institutions using funds from the State Committee for Scientific Research formed 11 strong metropolitan centers (including 5 supercomputer centers) and built their private, fiber-optic metropolitan area network (MAN) backbones. Most of them supported mixed ATM/FDDI technology and some MANs (for example, Gdańsk and Wrocław) offer ATM OC-12 622-mbps backbones. With full support from the State Committee, a newly born initiative to receive better intercity 34-mbps ATM (E-3) transmission over fiber-optic lines broke a nationwide monopoly by the Polish Academic and Research Network. A new academic network initiative is being coordinated by the Poznań Network and Supercomputer Center (PCSS) and provides 34-mbps ATM links between Poznań, Gdańsk, Łódź, Katowice, and Warsaw.

7. An improper choice was made in Poznań: The DEC router there was unable to communicate with Cisco routers with the WAN synchronous serial port. On the other hand, our firm persuasion must have influenced Hewlett-Packard's policy, and after a few years, HP started to sell its first routers, marked "Cisco compatible." Similarly, our perpetual-pressure policy led HP to a fundamental change in the specification of its old and excellent Avista Flow Control Protocol (AFCP), from a nonrouteable version to the routeable version.

Libraries are commonly recognized as "service units," "support units," or "infrastructure units." The less time that the research staff in certain fields spends in reading rooms, the less attention that the staff pays to library problems. Due to this fact, chemists, physicists, biologists, and computer engineers often consider a library as a sort of expensive, inefficient structure with unnecessary, overstaffed units. For this reason, most libraries serving science or engineering-oriented institutes that belong to either the Polish Academy of Science or industry have a minimal staff (one to three) and open-shelf access to their collections.

This is not the case in institutions devoted to literature or history, where patrons are accustomed to spending most of their research time in libraries and consider them to be milestones toward the development of any modern society. And to demonstrate their gratitude, most libraries reserve their highest, management-level positions for history and literature professors.

These two lobby groups also have divergent viewpoints on the importance of library collections. Whereas scientists demand more expensive, imported journals, literature professors wish to have more books. This causes an apparently unexpected phenomenon: Academic staffs from humanities departments quickly recognize the power and usefulness of on-line public access catalogs (OPACs), and related on-line services like interlibrary loans (ILLs), and begin supporting library automation. At the same time, a professor of physics may oppose an upgrading of the library server in favor of benefits for his lab, like buying a new workstation for his graduate students.[8]

In some cases a new group of library staff members may cause an imbalance within the local situation and create intrinsic enemies. Usually library automation is carried using the following models:

1. The library server is owned by the library.
2. The library shares computer resources in a departmental, corporate, or metropolitan center.

Both models have advantages and disadvantages. It seems that the second model is better suited to a library, if the corporate computer center is large and rich. Such a center should be able to manage a separate database server alongside its computing and general-purpose servers and to do frequent upgrades of its systems. If for some reason, either political or organizational (for example, the lack of an institutional computer center), the library is forced to organize its own computer center, then a number of problems may soon arise. Apart from the necessity of instituting a permanent, large-scale fund-raising activity for the system, the library director might intro-

---

8. This example is not far from reality. Amazingly, most collision situations in library automation projects were caused by physicists. These situations occurred on the local, metropolitan, and national levels and were directed toward freezing library computerization. In two cases created by physicists in Kraków and Wrocław, mediation by the Interuniversity Coordinating Committee chairman proved the usefulness of the interuniversity agreement. In Gdańsk the "cold war" initiated by the Institute of Theoretical Physics and Astrophysics did not reach the library project even on the metropolitan level.

duce a new and very powerful group consisting of computer-system and network administrators and operators. Just like flight controllers at an airport, this group has strong opinions about its power and its market value. In Polish budgetary institutions, it is impossible to keep permanent computer-system administrators without allowing them to receive a high-paid part-time job in a private company (a salary can be as much as 10 times higher in private enterprise than the one earned in a comparable position in a library!). Librarians soon recognize the group as favored, and begin disinformation campaigns directed against programmers and the computer staff, claiming they are unfriendly and do not like to do some things that are within their competence. On the other hand, system operators claim that their qualifications are very high and that they have much more important things to do than replace librarians' paper in printer trays. In Poland, this is still a very serious problem and a number of system administrators have already left their positions at university libraries. Its solution has a local character and depends on the library director's competence and on the library board's policy, but may significantly disturb cooperation between libraries.

To complicate the picture, many technical and arts-oriented universities were developing their own, specialized automated library software. All their combined efforts aim to convince governmental sponsors that they should support domestic products only because of technical (simplicity) and economical (low-price) reasons.

All these issues involve top-, middle-, and low-ranking library staff and drive them into endless discussions and explanations with different lobbying groups, making work less effective and resulting in a diminished share of the library's influence on the institutional and regional level.

State and State-Backed Finance Sources

The Ministries

The majority of Polish libraries are financed from the state budget. During the last five decades, Poland has changed its governmental structure only a few times. Currently, not a single ministry exists that is charged with subsidizing all types of schools. This means that academic libraries have their statutory activities subsidized by several sources. While general and engineering schools are subordinated to the Ministry of National Education, medical schools are subordinated to the Ministry of Health; different types of military schools, to the Ministry of Defense; agricultural schools, to the Ministry of Agriculture; theatre, music, and fine arts schools, to the Ministry of Culture. In the more distant past, most of these specialized universities, with the exception of military schools, were departments of more comprehensive universities, which simplified the management of education. Nowadays, we notice that some of the first steps are being taken to reconsider the previous structure: Jagiellonian University, for example, incorporated the Medical Academy in Kraków as its Medical College. Our experience from the last three decades suggests that the core-ministerial subsidy policy is carried out mainly by a strong, permanent administrative staff, with little or no influence from top-rank political officials (ministers, deputy ministers), or by occasionally created advisory teams, and the staff processes application materials very competently. Ministerial structures are more conservative than governmental agencies and implement modern network technology.

The State Committee for Scientific Research

In order to solve the problem of financing noneducational research institutions, such as the Polish Academy of Sciences or similar bodies, the State Committee for Scientific Research (KBN) was established in 1991, as a sort of governmental agency with ministerial competence. Undoubtedly, the KBN is the largest domestic project supporter and grant provider. Its organizational structure is based on the following:

1. a permanent, administrative staff featuring a somewhat political flavor;
2. an elected committee, consisting of 60 professors, that was assembled in 1997 into 12 commissions (the number of elected members increased from 28 in 1991 to 60 in 1997)—among them, humanities and social sciences account for 15 percent of the seats, with the rest being held by natural and engineering scientists;
3. a number of supporting advisory task teams comprising invited scientists.

The committee is dominated by scientists, as defined in the Western sense of the word. There was not a single literature or history professor among the authors of the reference book *Society-Science-Government*. The book was published as part of the KBN Science and Government Series, which could serve as a sort of creed for the KBN founders. Can the current committee build a uniform strategy for financing research libraries? I suspect not, at the moment. Both the geography of the membership, and the fields of research for respective KBN commissions, are hard to explain or accept. Among the five KBN members in the H-1 Commission of Humanities Research (Frąckowiak 1997), there are two professors representing the small community of the History of Art, and not a single professor representing the most popular fields, such as the History of Polish Literature or Polish History. The H-2 Commission of Humanities Research, encompassing Sociology, Economy, and Law, includes one sociologist, four economists, and not one lawyer. Of these five representatives of (supposedly) the whole country, three come from one university (the University of (Łódź). Fortunately, this is the worst case. Nothing similar to this has happened in the P-4, P-5, and P-6 Commissions. But the system, publicly known for its dubious practices in preelection periods, allows us to conclude that it is not healthy and needs basic restructuring.

In contrast to the elected committee, the new term of invited advisory commissions seems to be more promising.

The Foundation for Polish Science

The third important source of the domestic funds for the support of different library programs is the Foundation for Polish Science, established in 1991 on the basis of the funds left by the Central Fund for Scientific and Technological Development (which had been dissolved in 1990). The foundation is managed by a three-member board and supervised by a seven-member foundation council, among which four were KBN members in 1997.

Types of Policy

All the units described above, being a peculiar mixture of both elected or appointed decision-makers, moderators, and lobbyists, occasionally publish their policy. The *published policy* can emerge from the work of invited experts and, therefore, is a combination of goodwill and dreams about how the policy should look (see for example, Hollender 1996). It is reasonable to call it the *advised policy*. On the other hand, the published policy might come from a top-rank executive at the ministerial level (see, for example, Madej 1998), and thus its lifetime depends on the durability of the particular executive post rather than on the lifetime of the actual cabinet ministry. We can call it the *declared policy*.

The other half of the issue can be called the *executed policy*. In many cases the latter one seems to be much more obscure than the published policy. Sometimes it is difficult to understand what exactly are the actual rules concerning the approval of grants, and it is almost certain that there is no true coordination of the library projects on the national level. Numerous facts demonstrate that a library can receive funds for its collection development and, at the same time, significantly reduce the number of library posts, its funds for books, and budget for shelving. It appears certain that the initiative to build a plan of nationwide coordination of different library projects must be created at the libraries' level. On the other hand, all grant providers still have important means to force libraries to unify their efforts. Some steps have already been taken, but some are still to come for ministries, committees, and foundations. Now the solution has to be achieved at the national level and may possibly require some financial arguments.

A Review of Particular Finance Policies. Out of these three sources executing their policies, appropriate ministries create a permanent flow of funds for academic libraries. The ministerial funds cover the statutory activity of libraries, including collection development, staff salaries, and hardware purchases. These funds are not limited by product category and allow greater flexibility for library grant applications. For obvious reasons, there are the usual limits on the level of approved subsidies. Ministerial funds usually do not require a cofinancing scheme and are highly appreciated due to the ministries' tolerant, understanding grant supervision.

KBN's grant subsidiary policy is derived from the balance of the advisory teams' project rankings and from elected committee approvals and revisions, with the final decision belonging to the latter. This is difficult to analyze and sometimes seems inconsistent. For instance, in 1996 there were two groups of funds directed to libraries —they focused on the following:

- large library systems
- contents of library databases

In fact, in the first group, two different kinds of categories were combined: the purchase of application software licenses (usually handled by the KBN in the other class of grants), and the costs of retrocataloging. In the second group, retrocataloging and system support were also combined. A truly unfortunate fact is that these types of grant categories were not published before, and were possibly arranged ad hoc during the ZII Commission or Committee (Zespół ds Infrastruktury Informatycznej—Team for Information Infrastructure) meeting. It is likely that the reality is far too complex to fathom for current committee advisers and that the committee needs some additional years of experience.

The third source, the foundation, has only one permanent library program, LIBRARIUS, which is oriented toward supporting library-premises development and supplying noncomputer equipment. In 1996, over 20 percent of the annual foundation budget was directed to libraries.

In early 1990s, the State Committee for Scientific Research was dominated by physicists, computer specialists, and engineers. This most powerful lobby controlled a significant portion of the budget subsidies through the ZII advisory task team for the development of the information technology (IT) infrastructure of R&D. An unprecedented stream of funds was targeted at forming strong metropolitan area networks (MANs), and metropolitan computer centers. This policy has continued to date and, among other benefits, has had a great impact on the development of our countrywide, networked library system. One year after the IT infrastructure of R&D had been initiated, the committee decided to dedicate a portion of its budget for the development of networked databases. This created an excellent basis for initiating the process of financing retrocataloging and retroconversion. A new KBN policy with respect to cofinancing grants is also widely accepted by the grantees, at least in the case of database development. Grants received for purchasing computer software require that at least 10 percent of a grant be paid by the grantee, while the grants for development of databases need to have at least 50 percent of the total project cost covered by the grantee. In this case, however, the committee allows grantees to contribute their share in kind: A grantee may produce on his own at least the same number of records as the number paid for by the committee. To complete this description, it is worth noting that the cofinancing of software purchases turned out to be much more flexible and understanding than it appears from the official documents. To summarize, the KBN proved to be an excellent governmental agency, which created the correct hierarchy of budgetary investments for building a modern IT infrastructure. The most impressive feature of the committee is its antimonopolistic character, with its great ability to rapidly change the status of a particular grantee.

The KBN's great achievements in the area of building the IT infrastructure should not overshadow the fact that the automation projects of the Polish academic and research libraries still do not have a competent and effective advisory commission within the KBN structure. The Polish academic and research community needs a quick solution of this issue. It is important to recall the fact that, for instance, the Virginia Tech Library System (VTLS) is the largest on-line application running on a nationwide scale with a well-documented daily production. This system is worthy of recognition as a separate project with a separate fund that covers its maintenance within the SPUB subsystem (special projects and research devices), but the same applies to the other organized systems. All of them should be coordinated as a special governmental library automation project, possibly by the National Library.

Tax and Customs-Duty Exemption Policies

Foreign donors do not accept the imposition of any type of tax on expenditures related to their grants. Since minor services (for example, travel costs) or goods (for example, books) may be purchased without paying VAT, most grants must deal with two possible ways of handling the issue: a tax exemption procedure or a tax refund procedure. For educational or research institutions in Poland, the direct import is the best way to avoid tax payments and lower the costs. But the Polish VAT-level-setting policy causes our educational institutions to prefer the direct importing of finished products to the purchase of equivalent domestic products for economic reasons. It is surprising that Polish authorities still refuse to protect their own job market. In many cases, however, large Western vendors (3Com, Cisco) allow only conditional direct-export schemes for end users where the entire contract value must exceed a certain threshold—usually $100,000. In such a case, an end user can have the final invoice issued in a foreign country. This requirement is usually hard to meet these days. Understanding this situation, many dealers in Poland worked out a new type of facility with Western vendors and now offer a direct-import facility to academic or research institutions. In order to do so, they open a company branch office in Western Europe and open an account in a foreign bank. This allows Polish universities to make an appropriate remittance in a foreign currency directly to the foreign bank; and to receive an invoice from the original vendor with two names on it—it says, "Send to: (name of end-user institution), bill to: (name of importing company/Polish dealer)." This entire procedure is in full compliance with Polish financial regulations. In general, it is a good solution. However, there is no rigid scheme to indicate whether a particular imported item will be charged a customs duty and/or VAT. Many dealers and resellers rely nowadays on specialized customs agencies experienced in establishing the detailed characteristics of the imported goods, which may lead to defining the product classification number as corresponding to a class which is tax-exempt. Many of our projects run in the 1990s clearly demonstrated that this remains more or less an art rather than a science. A particular contract evaluated by one dealer as unavoidably taxable can be accepted and successfully handled by another dealer as tax-exempt.[9]

In many cases, decisions or facilities reveal the influence of some proximity effect. NATO and the European Community (EC) members were central targets of Poland's foreign policy during the 1990s. Both offered Poland strategic adaptation programs, supported from the Polish side by the corresponding parliamentary acts and decrees.

---

9. In one particular contract, the University of Gdańsk needed a Panasonic NV-W1E videoplayer with the NTSC/PAL/SECAM conversion facility. If the apparatus is simply classified as a videoplayer, then it must be subject to tax. If, however, it is classified as a "device or signal processor with magnetic storage" or an "analogue signal converter," then the item may be tax-exempt. Acceptance of the classification depends only on the decision of a particular customs officer.

The latter are EC-oriented, facilitating financial operations in cases of intergovernmental agreements. This means that when private foundations offer informal but effective help they get no special facilities. In vain did our consortium attempt to lobby the deputy finance minister (who was also a professor at Warsaw University) to extend the decree originally prepared to facilitate grants received from the EC to grants received from The A. W. Mellon Foundation. Fortunately, a large number of other grants successfully met the requirements and gradually caused local treasuries to treat nongovernmental grants as tax-exempt.

Individualized Policies. With the advent of the production phase of the Polish VTLS library automation projects (the opening of the first circulation modules), the libraries involved tend to have more individualized policies than at the beginning of their automation projects. At the same time, the influx of foreign funds and Western influence diminished while funding from domestic sources increased from 3% of total spending in 1994 to more than 40% in 1997.

References

Bradner, S. 1991. *Router Tests* Version 4, Benchmarking Methodology Working Group/IETF Tech. Report. Cambridge: Harvard University.
Demographic Yearbook. 1996. New York: United Nations.
Frąckowiak, J. K., 1997. *Sprawy Nauki*, 2(34), p. 21.
Hollender, H. 1996. "Wybrane problemy automatyzacji bibliotek" (Selected issues of library automation) in *Komputeryzacja bibliotek naukowych w kontekście standardów oprogramowania bibliotecznego*. Ed. by J. B. Czermiński. Published by Wydawnictwo Uniwersytetu Gdańskiego, Gdańsk.
Jarosiński, W., and Z. Rajewski. 1992. "The Level of Expenditures on Scientific Research in Poland and in Some Selected Countries." in *Science and Government Series, Vol. 2: Society-Science-Government*. Edited by A. Kukliński, State Committee for Scientific Research, Republic of Poland, Warsaw.
Madej, S. 1998. "Welcoming remarks by Stanisław Madej" in: *Proceedings of the 21st International Conference, ELAG '97*. Edited by J. B. Czermiński. University of Gdańsk, Gdańsk.
1993 Statistical Yearbook. New York: United Nations.

CHAPTER 4

Libraries of Central and Eastern Europe
Basic Dilemmas

JELA STEINEROVÁ

The aim of this chapter is to identify the basic dilemmas that plague the development of libraries in Central and Eastern Europe, as evidenced by the Slovak library system and by the results of a 1996 manpower survey of library and information-market needs. The survey was conducted by the Department of Library and Information Science (DLIS), Comenius University, Bratislava. My discussion here considers library automation within its broader social and economic context and looks at future developments in light of some basic practical and theoretical needs. In the first section of the chapter the rather poor conditions of library and information work are related to several key dilemmas that characterize this region. I then present the details of a survey of Slovak libraries (including references to two appendixes), together with a discussion of the survey's methodology and of some conclusions drawn from it. Finally, I present some remarks on library integration, intellectual power, and education.

What Dilemmas?

The Double-Transition Dilemma

Once we regard library and information work as integral parts of society, then it becomes apparent that the technology impact has both positive and negative consequences. In this double-transition dilemma, established institutional structures are breaking down, while new social and communication structures are being formed. Libraries are seeking a new position within a changing society. Like so many institutions, they are a bit behind the aggressive and rapid technological changes. Such is the trend all over the world.

Libraries in Central and Eastern Europe are affected by the transition to the information society more than are libraries in the United States and in Western Europe. In spite of the significant help and support from abroad, the state of the libraries is far from satisfactory. On the one hand, libraries have to enter the changing electronic space and try to reformulate their digital library functions (which might be quite different from their traditional tasks). On the other hand, libraries have to struggle for their survival within the changing social and economic environment.

But it is mostly people who carry the burden of these transitions. Do we know enough about their needs, views, capabilities, possibilities, feelings, and fears? I believe there might be something specific, or common, to a region, for example, Central Europe (Hungary, Poland, the Czech Republic, and the Slovak Republic), with respect to people in libraries. This specificity is connected with social relationships beyond institutions or technologies (because libraries are so institutionalized, and technologies so impersonal). That is why I will concentrate on these opaque, broader issues of the human and social contexts of library and information work.

It is through these contexts that some of the most salient features of library work in Central Europe are best revealed. Although the internal isolation (institutional, managerial, or professional) has been overcome, the quality of products and services offered needs more attention (user-orientation and efficiency, desirability of professional success). The strategic objectives of library work are not always clearly defined and organizational structures are often too complicated, affected by too many emotions and by problematic human communication (between management and staff, management and authorities, or the library management and that of the larger organization, agency, or university). Meanwhile, the support of young professionals who work in libraries is now rather weak, in spite of significant improvements over the previous era. These concerns make the dilemma of double pressure on our library workers all the more apparent.

The Dilemma of Library Management versus Qualified Staff

Sophisticated automated library systems need well-trained and educated people, but it is almost impossible for our libraries to get and keep such new professionals. That is why it is essential that more attention be paid not only to the education and training of people who work in the libraries of Central and Eastern Europe, but also to their professional status, which is rather low.

The DLIS manpower survey (discussed below) showed that in most cases library managers have been aware of the changing environment, including the new directions that information technology (IT) offers to library work. But problems connected with rather traditional organizational issues and, of course, with people, remain. The ability of library workers to respond to changes can vary significantly, as does their motivational level, which is also rather low (for example, concerning continuing education and quality of work).

The paradox is that library managers need new professionals (for the new information professions), but they can find them neither within their own libraries nor in library schools. Library school graduates look for more attractive jobs outside traditional institutional settings. That is why most managers have to do a lot of professional work (in those new jobs for which they do not have the proper person).

We indeed need to acknowledge that managerial change is no longer the key problem of Central European libraries. Rather, the challenge is presented by the professional changes and by the corresponding lack of experts for the new (technological) responsibilities. Take the situation at Slovak libraries and in library education as an example: There are a number of important projects (supported from abroad) such as, for example, CASLIN, KOLIN, and HUSLONET, but it is extremely difficult to find qualified professionals who would be able to further develop these systems. The older generation is not willing to learn new methods of work, while the younger generation leaves for other jobs. And the state support for these projects is very weak, if there is any at all. That is why it is important to question what the future will bring to Slovak library systems.

A new image of the library in the post-Communist society and a new status for the institutionally independent information professionals are essential parts of that future. The problem is that the once secure value systems have been seriously undermined and that it will take time to agree upon new ones. Slovakia is a good example of the struggle of traditions and principles with many cultural, educational, communication, and cognitive issues. This struggle includes libraries as well. Librarians in Slovakia and in Central Europe still need time to reflect on their profession's new situation and on the management of change in which traditional institutions grow to become more flexible information and communication structures. Finding ways to handle change in the libraries of Central Europe requires a willingness to engage in self-reflection and to understand people who now work, and who will work, in the new library and information professions (as documented in the DLIS survey).

The Technology-versus-Culture Dilemma

Another dilemma is caused by the false idea of what automated library systems have to offer ("They will solve every problem, when we have the systems; we have already achieved our goals"). In many of our libraries the digitization is thought of only in terms of secondary (bibliographic) information. World developments, however, show a more crucial change represented by the universe of electronic knowledge. Library workers in Central Europe are still at the very early stage of reflection about these processes.

They need to understand the depth of change that traditional library processing is facing, as becomes an organization devoted to knowledge management. Traditional patterns of professional work (experience) have been seriously questioned and it takes time and effort to try to build new professional values. Technological optimists in our libraries are not always the best at seeking these values while the day-to-day practices somehow eliminate the need for the professional value-making process. Even in library education there is a danger of confusing training in technological skills and learning the nature of communication and the processes of knowledge management. In the future, technological literacy will more generally spread in Central Europe and library and information professionals will be taught mainly knowledge management principles.

Technological development requires a natural interaction between information management systems that, in turn, assume an open social structure. Again, in Central European libraries there is a need for a new culture of cooperation. The global technological partnership in knowledge management should inspire new attitudes toward standards and unification as librarians overcome their fear of being too technical and too global. The question is how to find a balance between the global character of knowledge and communication and the local needs for its retrieval and use, and also to find ways of incorporating specific local cultures into global knowledge.

As shown in the DLIS survey, the expectations and visions of library and information managers are clearer than everyday practices, which are limited in several ways—for example, with respect to funding, management, staff recruitment, and training. In some cases rigid, centralized traditions may be very strong (Slovakia is a good example of some of these problems that might also be latent in other Central European countries).

All these and other interrelated factors make the situation of librarians in Central Europe more and more complex. The principles and directions are generally accepted, but the time for realization requires much patience and the work of generations.

The Education Dilemma

We are now redesigning the curriculum of our schools. Whereas previously the content of courses was ideologically dependent, historically oriented, and quite academic and theoretical, we are now looking toward more integrated and global principles of knowledge management. This is in contrast to the traditional approach, which emphasizes the difference between information analysts and information managers, where the former focus more on content description and the latter on issues surrounding access. However, changes in this area are rather slow to develop, mostly due to the limiting conditions of the educational system in particular countries.

The problems connected with education in library and information science result in a search for a new balance between theory and practice, between general and specialized education, and in the overcoming of institutional barriers in an effort to move beyond the bibliographic approach to content-driven approaches and to new user-integrated paradigms. Moreover, Central European library schools have to struggle with a generally low appreciation of the social value of education and knowledge.

In fact, a new field has been emerging from library and information science. But courses in IT cover a topic that is rather different than that of information science and management. The university education should deal more with (and reflect upon) the principles of knowledge management.

Pedagogy—the question of the proper methodology (which used to be more passive than participatory)—is another dilemma of library education in Central Europe. There needs to be more flexibility in the use of interactive learning software (courseware) that offers the possibility of adaptation to individual needs and learning styles.

Fostering new patterns of partnerships (between students and teachers) and new patterns of learning in the information society will change traditional library education in Central Europe. A broader knowledge base within information science education (including the understanding of social systems and services, critical thinking, and a professional understanding of knowledge management) will be required by the job market. The core of this modern education is directed at a critical analysis and interpretation of received knowledge that comes in a variety of forms and from different sources. Creative principles are linked not only to technologies, but also to an emphasis on the methodological components of information science education, which should develop people's abilities in independent, lifelong learning. Of course, technological and interpersonal communication skills should be a part of this education, but the use of acquired information and its transformation into knowledge and decision-making mean a real challenge to information science education in Central Europe.

Since the institutional aspect of this education is still a rather traditional one in Central Europe, change is really dependent on the teacher. The support of transformation of teaching methods and teaching aids in library and information science could help speed up the needed change. New technologies suggest the possibility of a more open learning process and of a different organizational model for education in Central Europe, one with more complex interactions between many components (including students, teachers, programmers, managers, technicians, advisers, multimedia courseware, conceptual mapping, case studies, etc.). Supportive and modular development of integrated knowledge should get more attention in our teaching methodologies (and more funding).

The situation in libraries demonstrates that retraining goes hand in hand with the education of a new generation of young people. Since there is a sort of gap between the thinking of the young and of the old, we can see the need for new courses. At the DLIS, we have developed several postdiploma courses and although people are interested in attending them, there was not money enough to teach them on a larger scale.

To deal with the thinking gap, we could start with a dialogue—situated in the multicultural setting of Central Europe—on the restructuring of library and information science education, and on other educational challenges that we all share. The International Center for Information Management, Systems, and Services (ICIMSS), at Copernicus University, in Toruń, Poland, is a good starting point for such a dialogue.

There are many other problems that could be identified in regard to the development of Central and Eastern European libraries. The four dilemmas discussed above have been identified as the ones most visible at the present time. They are the results of the economic, technological, social, and political contexts of library and information work. As we look to the future, they could serve as the main issues for a future discussion of libraries in Central Europe.

The Case of Slovak Libraries—A Survey of Future Manpower Needs

Methodology

The Department of Library and Information Science carried out its survey in 1996. We used questionnaires in combination with personal interviews conducted in selected libraries. The number of participating libraries whose managers filled out the questionnaires was 38 (out of the total of 50 questionnaires that were sent to managers). This sample, however, included not only various types of libraries—research libraries, academic libraries, and public libraries, but also some special (private and state) information institutions that work with information on a larger scale. The numbers and types of libraries surveyed are included in table 4.1 (see appendix 4.2).

The survey included two parts: The first one shows the present state of information professions in libraries and information institutions, and the second part concentrated on institutional requirements and needs for future education.

The first part of the survey was aimed at eliciting information in regard to the present-day description of several hypothetical information and library professions: information analyst, reference librarian (information adviser), information manager, information broker, library manager, and systems librarian. The model for these professions, including job descriptions (see appendix 1), was presented to library and information managers. They were asked to indicate which of these are matched at their institution, which portions of these jobs are performed at present, what education and experience these workers presently have, and how many workers will be required for these jobs in the future development of their institution.

In the second part the survey, the respondents were asked to indicate the types of knowledge and the disciplines (subjects) that they felt would be essential for entering these professions in the future, as well as the information technologies they thought relevant at various levels (from the basic level, and that of office automation, to database systems and to the Internet). The disciplines included the present and prospective courses in library and information science as taught by the staff at the DLIS.

Results

Tables 4.2–4.5 (in appendix 4.2) show the numbers of workers and their present educational background for two model professions: information analyst and information manager. For the purpose of this chapter I have selected these two professions as examples (the other professions are analyzed elsewhere in this book). In fact, all of these professions are in real life very close to one another, as they include many overlapping activities. But we have used the model only as a starting point, since the titles of professions vary for different libraries. The existence of different types of libraries (they vary by size, types of users, staff background) has been another limitation. It was clear that librarians presently perform these jobs mostly part-time (because of different, traditional job divisions), which is why respondents had the option of indicating the percentage or portion of a person's time taken up by the described activities. In our results we have taken into account those answers that indicated more than a 30 percent correspondence with our model definition of each profession.

The educational background of those working as information analysts and as information managers (in some cases they may represent the same person) is rather similar. Secondary education is predominant at public libraries. As for information analysts, only about 30 percent in research and academic libraries have a university-level education in library and information science. The number is rather low in public and specialized libraries. The situation is somewhat better in the case of information managers. University degrees in LIS have been noted among more than 40 percent of those working in research and public libraries. It is also interesting that in special libraries a university education other than in LIS is predominant for both professions. Indirectly, we note a tendency toward a transition from traditional library activities to special information management services (in special library or information centers) and this should, over time, be reflected in an increase in those with LIS education.

The second part of the survey is even more interesting, since it reflects the opinions of present library managers as they look to the future (see tables 4.6–4.13). As far as the information analyst is concerned, more than 50 percent of managers require LIS education for this profession with an emphasis on experience in information analysis, general services and information services. In the case of IT skills, managers expect experience with office automation and networks, in particular, and, of course, a knowledge of English. LIS education as well as other specialized university degrees are required for information managers. In practice, information services are most required. Again, knowledge of English and familiarity with office automation are taken for granted.

If we compare tables 4.14 and 4.15, we can see, in the top ten disciplines, different requirements for information analysts and for information managers, respectively. While an information analyst should be more resource-oriented, information managers are supposed to concentrate on the Internet. The tables also show a rather traditional and not always clear knowledge of the conceptual structures of Information Science among library managers in Slovakia. It would be interesting to ask, in a follow-up survey, what they mean by "information analysis" and by "information management." The common disciplines for both professions include Information Resources, Information Analysis, the Internet, the Language of Information Technology, and Multimedia. Apart from Information Analysis, information analysts should concentrate on such specific subjects as Text Analysis, Document Processing, Users of Information, Social Communication, and Knowledge Organization. For information managers the specific disciplines include Psychology, Legal Issues, Management, and Information Policy.[1]

Although we are aware of the potential problems with interpreting the survey data (for example, overlapping concepts of "users" and "psychology," of "information analysis" and "knowledge organization," and of "document processing"), and also of the influence of the existing educational stereotypes, we are nevertheless able to infer several interesting conclusions.

First, while information analysts will have a tendency to be more concerned with resources and their content (their detailed description and organization), managers should be more aware of the way resources are accessed. They should take in the whole system, including the human side (psychology) and the conditions under which information is used (for example, legal and information policies).

---

1. The analysis of the response percentage for all of the six professions included shows that managers require the following courses for future professionals: the Internet, Information Resources, Users of Information, Information Analysis, Information Languages, Psychology, Social Communication, and Knowledge Organization (Kimlička, 1997b).

Second, analytical skills clearly define the key qualities of the information analyst (such as the knowledge of data processing or of working with texts or multimedia formats). There is, however, a need to go further, beyond the formal methods that touch but the surface of information. We need to train people for the appreciation of the deeper qualities of human thought, whether in the organization of knowledge or in the ability to understand the psychological and social rules of using information.

Third, the particular skills of information managers are linked to a variety of needs, with a focus on facilitating the interaction between different information resources and users (involving Psychology, Legal Issues, and Information Policy). Of course, general management issues are also keys to this job.

Fourth, for the future planning of LIS education it is necessary to go beyond the distinction discussed above, between methods that address issues of access and other public services, on the one hand, and resource-oriented disciplines, on the other hand. In fact, the borders between the two are disappearing and integration is evident. For example, the Internet discipline includes both resources and services, means of communication and use of information, and yet, it remains primarily a technology. Similarly, the differences between Information Resources and Multimedia involve very different levels of description and they should not be mixed (for example, a general category and a special object form). It is clear that integrated access to the LIS disciplines is required (including resources, services, methods of access, technologies).

Fifth, although the job descriptions for information analysts and information managers have been rather hypothetical, education for them should be integrated (as common disciplines) with the prospect that they could be combined into one specialty.

Other details about our survey have been, and will be, published in Slovak professional journals and proceedings.[2]

What Can We Expect in the Future?

Integration

In the future we should concentrate more on an integrated view of our profession, which should include more library partnerships and cooperation. Due to the historical development of our societies many past stereotypes persist. In the Slovak environment, one can see many different paradigms of social systems that confront the world of logic with that of emotions, as well as much uncertainty and irregularity. However, in contrast to this environment, the automated library and information systems require a basic model of ordered and integrated logical processes and relationships. That is why it is not so easy to transfer technological know-how to our settings.

We need to understand integration as the new model that lies beneath the surface of library automation. This can include new approaches to library partnerships within the region and at the international and global levels; new models for the inte-

---

2. *CSONLINE '97,* Infos '97, *Bulletin CVTI '97,* Acta Universitas Comeniana—Library and Information Science 17, forthcoming.

gration of the social sciences, humanities, and technical sciences; new models for integrated, versatile professionals. The principles of global communication lead to the integration of sources and services, and to a transcending of the restrictions of time and space. In library work, these changes are reflected in the move from the traditional approaches to acquisition and storage toward the access and use of knowledge based on integrated technologies. The pattern of bibliographic research is moving toward service-, process-, and product-oriented information work.

Integration means that information sources are becoming more and more global, access is becoming rather virtual, and use of knowledge is facilitated by tailor-made and value-added information products. In these terms integration is hidden behind more visible automated and housekeeping processes and would need special support in the libraries of Central Europe (even from abroad).

Intellectual Power

We should realize that the foundations for automated libraries in our region have already been created, but continuous development should not end with bibliographic systems. Successive reduction of intermediary activities becomes a fact. For transition to an electronic universe of knowledge, we need not only technology, but also, especially, intellectual power (the content and meaning of information, information analysis and consultancy, and reformulation of the roles of libraries in the information society). In fact, intellectual access to knowledge becomes more important than technological access only.

But the intellectual principles underlying library and information systems are not as transparent as basic library management principles. Therefore, from start to finish, work on library and information systems demand increased attention to proper communication of an intellectual framework. Here the importance of local knowledge is underestimated. Thus the principles of sharing local cultural values within a global context should also be more clearly understood and presented. In contrast to automation projects, there is little evidence of any support for these important principles for the Central European library and information environment.

Education

Since education is linked to changes in our field, we might want to offer a new perspective, one based on the identification of our main difficulties as well as of the common principles that all of us in our region share. This could not only improve our understanding of the regional spirit, but also suggest some new ideas that go beyond the established library education ideas in developed countries. Taking into the account the development of an information society, we might assume that basic technological and information literacy (including information retrieval skills) would be taught as part of a general education at primary and secondary school levels. One of the possible solutions for university education might be the integration of library and information science with social sciences and humanities (psychology, philosophy, theory of general science, sociology, general linguistics and semiotics, economics, and management).

Considering the close links to education and scholarly communication, knowledge management in the region cannot be seen as a predominantly commercial activity. Some of the new electronic or multimedia information products have a very short life span (they are only "information moments") and it is extremely difficult to calculate their costs (e.g., electronic journals, knowledge base, and search engine). In some cases tailor-made information products could be seen as a project offering a particular perspective and as items designed by an individual for a special moment of use (as being "modules" of knowledge composed by the user-creator himself).

All the dilemmas and contexts cited here show that new educational patterns should be sought. Within the region, these patterns will probably be typical of a reasonable coexistence between traditional (print-based publication, library) principles and new (electronic) ways of knowledge management in terms of new social communication patterns. Among the new qualities of products and services the human being still stands at the heart of the transformed library and information work. New professionals should be able to make knowledge and information comprehensible through their human intervention, which comprises analytic and synthetic capabilities, interpretation, and creativity.

References

Kimlička, Š. 1997a. Knižnično-informačné profesie pre informačnú spoločnosť. [Library and information professions for information society.] In *CSONLINE '97*, International conference, Vyhne, 10.-12.6.1997. Bratislava: Slovnaft.

Kimlička, Š. 1997b. Knižničná informačná veda—teória a metodológia pre praxiu. [Library and information science—theory and methodology for practice.] In *INFOS '97*, 5-14. Bratislava: SSK—Slovak Association of Librarians.

Kimlička, Š. 1997d. Profesia súčasnosti a budúcnosti–systémový knihovník. [Profession of present and future systems librarian.] *In Bulletin CVTI* vol. 1 (1997), no. 1, pp. 12–16.

Kimlička, Š. et al. 1997c. Analýza potrieb informačných profesií na trhu práce v SR: Hodnotenie vedeckého projektu—fakultný grant FiFUK č. 16. [Needs analysis of information professions in the labor market of the Slovak Republic: Evaluation of a research project], Faculty grant FiFUK, no. 16. Bratislava: FiFUK, suppl., tables.

Kimlička, Š. 1998. Systémový knihovník—profesia 90.tých rokov. [Systems Librarian—the profession of the 1990s.] In *Knižničná a informačná veda XVII. [Library and Information Science.]* Zborník FiFUK. Bratislava: Comenius University 1998, pp. 5–21.

Steinerová, J. 1997. *Vzdelávanie v budúcnosti a informačná veda* (Future learning and information science). Paper presented at 4th Iternational Organization of Information Specialists Meeting, 3–6 June 1997, Štrbské Pleso.

Appendix 4.1

Prospective Information Professions (Job Responsibilities and Skills)

Information analyst: analysis of information needs, analysis of documents and information sources, indexing, search-queries formulation, retrieval in local and external (Internet) information resources, text analysis, conceptual analysis, information modeling, information and information-sources evaluation, consolidation of information, preparation of analytical reports.

Reference worker (information adviser): analysis of information needs, search-queries formulation, users' navigation in internal and external resources (Internet) and institutions, retrieval in local and external information resources, knowledge of legal guidelines for the use of information resources.

Information manager: analysis of information needs, analysis of documents and other information resources, retrieval in local and external (Internet) information resources, information modeling, evaluation of information and information resources, consolidation of information, organization of information resources, information-resource management in organizations, information provision for projects, legal background in the use of information and information resources.

Information broker: analysis of information needs and requirements, formulation of search queries of users, retrieval in local and external information sources, development of information products, financial analysis and information-services projects, information and information-services brokering.

Library manager: library strategy and planning, economic and financial scheduling for library, marketing scheduling for library, marketing of single library services, library public relations; financial, organizational, operational and personal management of library; legal background in the operation and use of library services.

Systems librarian — library and information systems (LIS) manager: analysis of information needs and requirements, systems analysis and LIS design, project management of LIS, strategy and planning of LIS and organizations, information policy of library and society; standardization, unification, and legislation for LIS at the library level and its environment; organizational and personal management, LIS databases management, management of network, maintenance of and innovation in LIS.

Source: Š. Kimlička, et al. 1997. "Analýza potrieb informačných profesií na trhu práce v SR : Hodnotenie vedeckého projektu–fakultný grant FiFUK č. 16." [Needs analysis of information professions in the labor market of the Slovale Republic: Evaluation of a research project, Faculty grant FiFUK, No. 16] Bratislava: FiFUK, nestr., príl., tab.

Appendix 4.2

First Part of the Survey: Present State of Information Professions in Libraries

50 questionnaires were sent to managers, 38 were returned (76%).
Types of libraries: research, academic, public, special
Univ.—LIS: number of workers with university education—library and information science
Univ.—other: number of workers with university education (other than in LIS)
Sec. educ—number of workers with secondary education

Table 4.1 Overview of Types of Libraries Participating in the Survey

Research	%	Academic	%	Public	%	Special	%	Total	%
8	21	10	26	12	31	8	21	38	100

Table 4.2 Information Analyst (Present State) - Number of Workers according to Educational Background

Workers	Libraries (number responding)				
	Research (8)	Academic (10)	Public (12)	Special (8)	Total (38)
Univ.—LIS	16	4	4	2	26
Univ.—other	24	8	3	12	47
Sec. educ.	11	—	13	—	24
All	51	12	20	14	97

Table 4.3 Information Analyst (Present State) - Educational Background (%)

Workers	Libraries				
	Research	Academic	Public	Special	Total
Univ.—LIS	31.3%	66.6%	20%	14.2%	26.8%
Univ.—other	47.05%	33.3%	15%	85.7%	48.4%
Sec. educ.	21.5%	—	65%	—	24.7%

Table 4.4 Information Manager (Present State) - Number of Workers according to Educational Background

	Research	Academic	Public	Special	Total
Libraries	8	10	12	8	38
Workers	28	19	7	9	63
Univ.—LIS	12	7	3	3	25
Univ.—other	13	11	1	6	31
Sec.educ.	3	1	3	—	7

Table 4.5 Information Manager (Present State) — Educational Background (%)

Workers	Libraries				
	Research	Academic	Public	Special	Total
Univ.—LIS	42.8%	36.8%	42.8%	33.3%	39.6%
Univ.—other	46.4%	57.8%	14.2%	66.6%	49.2%
Sec. educ.	10.7%	0.05%	42.8%	—	11.1%

Second Part of the Survey: Requirements for the Future

Education requirements
N. resp.—number of positive responses

%—proportion of positive responses
LIS—university education, library and information science
AIS—university education, applied information science (within another major subject)
EIS—university education, information economics
OU—other universities
OUB—other universities + LIS bachelor degree
LISIT—university education, library and information science + information technologies, bachelor degree
Total — total number of respondents for the profession (different for different questions)

Table 4.6 Information Analyst: Education

	LIS	AIS	EIS	OU	OUB	LISIT	Total
N. resp.	21	11	4	8	4	5	38
%	55.26	28.9	10.5	21.05	10.5	13.1	

Requirements for practice
HW—experience in hardware and information technologies
SW—experience in software and information technologies
CT—experience in cataloging
IS—experience in information services
IA—experience in information analysis
GS—experience in general services
MA—experience in management

Table 4.7 Information Analyst: Experience

	HW	SW	CT	IS	IA	GS	Total
N. resp.	4	8	10	14	24	15	38
%	10.5	21.05	26.3	36.8	63.1	39.1	

Foreign Language Requirement
Eng.— English; Ger.— German; Fr.— French; Russ.— Russian; other (Spanish and other)

Table 4.8 Information Analyst: Languages

Lang.	Eng.	Ger.	Fr.	Russ.	Other	Total
N. resp.	34	14	3	6	3	36
%	94.4	38.8	8.3	16.6	8.3	

72 Library Policy and the State

IT Skills Requirements (at User Level)
Basic—basic knowledge of HW, SW, DOS, Windows
Office automation (e.g., MS office)
DBS—database systems
Net—Unix, Novell, Internet

Table 4.9 Information Analyst: IT Skills (User Level)

	Basic	Office automation	DBS	Net
Total	33	23	32	30
N. resp.	22	22	20	22
%	66.6	95	62.5	73.3

Table 4.10 Information Manager: Education

	LIS	AIS	EIS	OU	OUB	LISIT	Total
N. resp.	16	13	6	5	5	4	31
%	51.6	41.9	19.3	16.12	16.12	12.9	

Table 4.11 Information Manager: Experience

	HW	SW	MA	IS	IA	GS	Total
N. resp.	4	9	14	21	16	14	32
%	12.5	28.1	43.7	65.6	50	43.7	

Table 4.12 Information Manager: Languages

Lang.	Eng.	Ger.	Fr.	Ru.	Spanish	Total
N. resp.	29	12	11	4	1	30
%	96.6	40	3.3	13.3	3.3	

Table 4.13 Information Manager: IT Skills (User Level)

	Basic	Office automation	DBS	Net
Total	28	18	26	27
N. resp.	18	17	13	19
%	64.2	94.4	50	70.3

Top Ten Disciplines Required for LIS Education

Table 4.14 Information Analyst—Top Ten Disciplines

Discipline	Number	%
Total	36	
Information Resources	34	94.4
Information Analysis	33	91.6
Text Analysis	33	91.6
Document Processing	31	86.1
Internet	31	86.1
Users	28	77.7
Information Languages	27	75
Multimedia	26	72.2
Social Communication	26	72.2
Knowledge Organization	26	72.2

Table 4.15 Information Manager—Top Ten Disciplines

Discipline	Number	%
Total	30	
Internet	29	96.6
Information Resources	28	93.3
Psychology	28	93.3
Information Management	26	86.6
Information Languages	26	86.6
Legal Issues	26	86.6
Management	25	83.3
Information Policy	25	83.3
Information Analysis	25	83.3
Multimedia	25	83.3

Types of Libraries Participating in the Survey

Research: major libraries in the country, known also as "scientific" libraries, formerly central libraries for special networks of libraries (e.g., technical, medical, pedagogical) and regional state scientific libraries.

Academic: libraries of major universities (economic, agricultural, technical) in different regions (reflects the situation in Sept.–Dec.1996, prior to administrative-regional transformation); new universities formed in 1997 have not been included.

Public: major public libraries serving populations of former counties of different regions in Slovakia.

Special: libraries of major enterprises, other companies, and special private and state institutions.

CHAPTER 5

The Changes in the Functions of University Libraries and of Educational Policy in Poland after 1989

KRZYSZTOF ZAMORSKI

The objectives of the national educational policy, and the changes that it is bringing about, have an immediate impact on libraries, which are one of the bases of scholarship and higher education. The assessments made in this chapter are those of a director of a library—to be sure, the oldest library, and one of the largest, in Poland—who will, at some point, again be only a library patron.

The assistance Polish libraries received from The Andrew W. Mellon Foundation came at the right moment and was generally sensible and effective. Librarians welcomed the changes that were now being made possible, and worked toward them; and Polish sources of funds, such as the State Committee for Scientific Research and the Polish universities themselves, contributed substantially. The road to reform was neither easy nor straight, and while we made our own share of mistakes, a great deal has been accomplished since 1989.

Real Dimensions and Strategic Aims

All close observers of the discussions about the strategic aims of the development of higher education in Poland can easily describe the basic trends for the foreseeable future. The progress of reforms in Poland is at a sufficiently advanced stage so that we may now assign a higher priority to the expansion of the economy than to drastic methods of stabilizing it. We clearly need to steer a middle course between emphasizing stabilization mechanisms and encouraging the growth of consumption. However, in our efforts to develop higher education, the problem is that in many cases we still think of scholarship more as a beneficial result of economic growth than as one of its basic stimulants.

The conflict between the more-or-less wishful thinking of a librarian/economic historian and the ideas contained in some important essays[1] leads me to anticipate the

---

1. See, for example, G. Kołodko, "Strategia dla Polski" (Strategy for Poland), Warsaw, 1995; "Szkolnictwo wyższe i nauka: Stan—perspektywy, zamierzenia" (Higher education and science—perspectives,

following strategic trends in the development of scholarship and the educational system in Poland:

1. a full adjustment of the higher educational system in Poland to the European standards, in anticipation of Poland's joining the European Community;
2. more active and effective incorporation of universities and of scholarship into the process of economic transformation in Poland than has occurred so far. This is desirable in order to accelerate the rate of GDP growth from 5 percent to 8 percent per year. Higher education and scholarship may contribute to the accelerated growth, by, for example:

   - training young, competent, and efficient managers and employees for private and state institutions;
   - training specialists who can work effectively with broad ranges of future technologies, both foreign and domestic;
   - training university graduates so as to reduce unemployment through the provision of varied skills by elastic educational programs;
   - intensifying research and higher education, thereby stimulating markets by creating a demand for the latest technical solutions;

3. a decided increase in the educational level of the society, which is a condition needed for the consolidation of the democratic system in our country.

If these trends materialize, even if only on a modest scale, libraries, and university libraries in particular, will be substantially affected. The efficient attainment of trends 1 and 3 should result in a university population that accounts for 28–30 percent of all 19-year-olds. If one tried to achieve this by 2002, as had been assumed some time ago, on the verge of the economic transformation, one would need to increase enrollments in Polish universities by 1,450,000, which would be twice the level of enrollment in 1994–95. This increase would take place under very unfavorable demographic conditions. We are still feeling the demographic effect of World War II: The peak of the impact of the postwar period's demographic boom will occur in 2002. In other words, up to the year 2002, the number of 19-year-old undergraduate candidates will grow at the rate of 2–3 percent a year. This will occur even if we assume that we will not create new places for university students, nor increase the fraction of the potential student population that is enrolled. In 2005, the number of 19-year-olds will be the same as the number in 1994. The plan for higher education anticipates that the desired 28–30 percent rate of enrollment for 19-year-olds can be reached only in 2007.

When Poland regained its independence and began to form a new democratic order, it was soon realized how important it was to change, improve, and regulate higher education. While the reforms in this area that had been promised by politicians have not yet been effectively carried out, it would be unfair to claim that noth-

---

plans), Warsaw, 1995; "Założenia długofalowej polityki edukacyjnej państwa szczególnym uwzględnieniem programu rozwoju na poziomie wyższym" (Foundations of the long-term educational policy of the state with particular regard to the program of development of higher education), Warsaw, 1996.

ing has been changed in this respect. But it is also fair to say that the changes that will be discussed here occurred within the framework of the reforms of the political and economic system; these reforms left a marked imprint on Polish universities. The economic system has indeed completely changed and so has the functioning of a majority of Polish universities.

The analysis of the structural changes that occurred after 1989 is based on the changes in the laws governing the activities of libraries, particularly of academic libraries. There are three sets of acts that laid the legal foundations for the activities of university-level institutions in Poland:

1. The set of acts that defines the scope of scholarship and higher education, including:

    - the Act of Higher Education, of September 12, 1990, and the accompanying Act of Scientific Degrees and Titles;
    - the act of January 12, 1991, which created the Committee for Scientific Research;
    - the broad amendment, of February 22, 1991, to the act on research and development;

2. The set of acts defining the scope of libraries' functions, including:

    - the Act of the Legal Deposit Copy, of November 7, 1997;
    - the Act of Libraries, of June 27, 1997;

3. The set of acts regulating the use of library materials (copyrights), passed on February 4, 1994 — the Act of Copyright and acts concerning related rights.

It may not be a well-remembered fact, but one of the first parliamentary acts of the so-called "Contract Seym" (the name comes from the political contract between the democratic opposition and the ruling Communist Party — the so-called Round Table — which initiated the series of democratic changes) was the new Act on Higher Education and the accompanying Act on Scientific Degrees and Titles, passed on September 12, 1990. However we may interpret this act, it still expressed the attitude of the new authorities toward scholarship and higher education. It is certainly far from perfect and it is difficult to consider it an effective means for solving the basic problems of scholarship and higher education. However, it is essential for librarianship, because it very generally delineates the scope within which university libraries may act — which subsequently led to the definition of university statutes and library regulations. This act regulates two important matters in a rather controversial way. First, it defines the status of the librarian's profession in the academic community in a manner that does not correspond to the needs of a changing reality; second, it incorrectly defines the demands imposed on directors of academic libraries.

The amendment of February 22, 1991, changed the structural location of research units in the new system of scholarship in Poland and this decided the fate of the libraries owned by these units. Those that survived (employment in these institutions diminished by 27 percent in 1991–1993, but it is still at a very high level) have developed library activities according to their needs. They may be potential partners for academic libraries in terms of their access to literature and to databases.

The situation of the libraries of the Polish Academy of Sciences, the intended coryphaeus of science, is much worse. The new act for the Polish Academy of Sciences has not yet been passed. In Kraków, the activities of the Polish Academy of Sciences have been revived and it has attempted to regain a property it formerly owned, which contains a library with interesting collections. The libraries of the Polish Academy of Sciences, with incomparably more difficult problems than university libraries, have embarked upon the process of automation. The unsettled legal status of the academy's institutes causes financial problems that are more serious than they are in other types of institutes, and this affects libraries as well. While the fall in employment in these institute, particularly in 1991–1993 (by 9.5 percent), impeded their education activities, since 1994, there has been an increase in their employment levels and their educational activities appear to be reviving as well. Therefore, the functions of these institute libraries will gradually change. These libraries, initially intended only for research purposes, must, and are likely to, relieve the infrastructure of university libraries. It is only a question of when and how this will occur.

However, the most important change that occurred in Polish science after the fall of communism was the creation of the State Committee for Scientific Research. The essence of the changes that this institution introduced is as follows:

1. Decisions about the purchase of equipment, and about other investments and the allocation of financial resources for scientific research, are based on the advice of independent experts.
2. Open and uniform criteria for the evaluation of projects were introduced.
3. Elements of competition have appeared in the process of allocating funds to scholars and institutions.
4. At present, the committee is probably the only body in Poland that is able to look at the needs of the state from a perspective other than that of a government department.
5. Annual rankings of research institutes have been introduced.

Although one could have many reservations about it, one cannot deny the positive role that this government institution played in financing the development of science in the Third Polish Republic. As far as libraries are concerned, they profited in two ways.

First, it became possible to computerize academic libraries, thanks to the substantial funds provided by the Committee for Scientific Research. This also led to the creation of a modern computer network in Poland—an infrastructure that was absent in the era of communism. And although one may surely have doubts about the standard of work of the National Academic Computer Network (NASK) and about its character, and one may see an urgent need for an alternative network operator, the fact that huge financial support was received, at the moment of the greatest economic collapse, for building a computer infrastructure shows that the Committee for Scientific Research had gotten its priorities right, and we should be justly proud of it.

Second, the moment Jagiellonian University received assistance from the Mellon Foundation, the Committee for Scientific Research earmarked a part of its own funds for the support of the Mellon projects. While this support might not have been as great as we would have liked, and did not allow for a systematic upgrading of terminals and an enhancement of existing local area networks in Polish libraries, it was thanks to these funds, among others, that many internal networks were established at Polish universities. These changes made it obvious that a library is not confined by its walls and that the ideal objective of the computerized library is to offer service at the reader's desk.

It is very significant for the Jagiellonian University Library that the Committee for Scientific Research seriously committed itself to the improvement of this library—which is the oldest Polish library—and made a major contribution to it. Finally, I also need to cite the important role of the Foundation for Polish Science. It is a pity that it is practically the only organization outside the government that has a perceptibly beneficial effect on everybody in the fields of science and culture.

The most important legal acts regulating the activities of university libraries are the work of the present Parliament and are embodied in the Act of the Legal Deposit Copy, of November 7, 1997, and the Act of Libraries, of June 27, 1997. These acts are likely to have substantial influence on the evolution of Polish librarianship.

It may be premature to make firm predictions about the probable changes in Polish librarianship. However, the effects of the Act of Legal Deposit Copy are likely to be largely beneficial for librarianship, and the act is also likely to have favorable effects on the book market. If the executive regulations that inevitably get attached to acts of Parliament are compatible with the objectives of the Ministry of Culture, the legislation will potentially—

1. encourage the development of the book market, particularly in cases of books that have small print runs;
2. encourage the application of bibliographic controls and the registration of multimedia publications;
3. create a national system for the protection of the Polish cultural heritage;
4. create additional mechanisms for stimulating the development of the book market and libraries.

Unfortunately, thus far the executive regulations attached to the act are more reminiscent of regulations in the Communist era. The number of libraries that receive obligatory copies is now 15, but the only libraries that are capable of managing this task are the National Library, and perhaps Jagiellonian's Main Library—that is, once the physical addition to it is completed and 4–6 full-time employees are added to its staff. Once again, some libraries will donate less useful books to other libraries—which is prohibited by law in the case of legal deposit copies. It is nevertheless true that only those university libraries flourished that had access to legal deposit copies. The multiplicity of legal deposit copies that publishers are required to provide is inflicting substantial costs on the system: The Polish Post Office must provide free shipping for legal deposit copies and publishers cover the costs of providing free deposit copies by charging higher prices than they would if there were no legal deposit requirement, thus raising the costs of education. Access to books will remain at a relatively low level and the system of book distribution will be inefficient. Acquisitions departments in academic libraries will have little incentive to change their behavior.

It would be reasonable to act on the advice of the Polish Chamber of Books and transfer some of the publishers' subsidies to libraries for the purchase of books. The number of publishers in Poland is very large and many of them have little or no experience in the business.[2] In 1995, there were only 65 publishers who published more than 23 titles per year, and 93 published between 10 and 22 titles. Among the rest, the majority published only a single title per year.[3]

Contrary to the Act of the Legal Deposit Copy, the Act of Libraries (1997) is not a practical piece of legislation. Its merit is that it strengthens the position of public libraries—a step that was long overdue. However, the act simply does not cope imaginatively with the need to encourage library development in the future. It does not reshape the functions of libraries and does not create a place for libraries in a national information system. The libraries remain under the jurisdiction of various ministries, and no effective method has been proposed for coordinating their development. The influence of the State Library Council is likely to remain limited in an environment in which, for example, public libraries report to the Ministry of Culture; academic libraries, to the Ministry of Education; and prison libraries, to the Ministry of Justice.[4]

However, human resources are all-important. And the most favorable situation in this regard is that of the academic libraries. No doubt, the National Library is also in a favorable position with respect to human resources, as well as to funds. The National Library ought to collaborate with the academic libraries, but is under no obligation to do so. On the basis of past experience, one must wonder whether the academic libraries, the special research libraries, the public libraries, and the National Library will be able to develop an effective system for the exchange of knowledge and skills among themselves, or whether several, nonoverlapping centers of librarianship will develop. Even if there were some arguments for the latter solution, I should note that only academic and research libraries are likely to become deeply involved in computerization, and that they are therefore natural allies of the National Library, provided that it is willing to accept some of the accomplishments of the academic libraries and not insist on creating its own system of library standards and bibliographic descriptions. But it is clear that the cost of a dual system of libraries is too high, and that the primary responsibility for carrying changes in the Polish library system will fall upon academic and research libraries.

The Problem of Changes in the Functions of University Libraries

In 1996, the portion of the gross domestic product spent on Polish education was still below the level it had attained in 1991. Given the national educational aspirations de-

---

2. According to the Bibliographic Institute of the National Library, 7,000 organizations are engaged in book publishing. See *Ruch wydawniczy w liczbach* (Polish publishing in figures) 41 (1995), National Library, Bibliographic Institute, Warsaw, 1996, p. 6.

3. This is in stark contrast to, say, Oxford University Press, which published 521 titles in 1995.

4. See chapter 1 (by Manikowski) in this volume.

scribed earlier, and the harsh realities of financing education, many universities spontaneously began to reform the content and profile of educational programs. The Ministry of Education, which is aiming at increasing the percentage of the university-age population who attend universities, made the budgets of institutions within its jurisdiction depend on enrollments. This took place in an environment in which aggregate expenditures on education were diminishing and in which it is unconstitutional to charge full-time students for tuition. The obvious consequence of this was an exaggerated development of part-time (extramural) studies, which may affect the overall quality of education, since programs for part-time students may not be on the same level as those for full-time, residential students. More beneficial effects of the budget crunch are that some universities were forced to reform their systems of budgeting and financial control; and that the introduction of a three-tiered system of education not only increases the number of students but also provides a richer menu of choices.

The political changes also led to the rapid emergence of private universities.[5] While this development is largely beneficial, it also poses some serious dangers, because it creates the wrong incentives. Since private institutions are permitted to charge tuition, they are sufficiently well-off to be able to hire full-time academics, who are employed at public universities, for part-time positions, thus permitting these academics to supplement their meager salaries. Regular staff members at state universities often have multiple positions, and the attendant increase in their aggregate teaching loads clearly diminishes their opportunities for scholarly research. Many of the private universities have a poor infrastructure and libraries with only minimal levels of collections, hardly suited for providing a quality education, although some of them have been able to develop an adequate infrastructure so as to effectively compete against state universities. As a result of all these changes, the number of university students doubled between 1989 and 1994, in spite of the fact that higher-educational expenditures decreased by 7.2 percent in 1993 and by 3.1 percent in 1994; and while they increased by 4.3 percent in 1995, the number of students in that year increased by 11 percent.

The impact of the macro-level changes on the Jagiellonian University Library during 1990–1995 was to clearly diminish the rate of growth of the collection. This agrees very well with what happened in the book market during that period: The decline in the rate of growth is evident, first, in 1992–1993 and 1993–1994 and pertains to books. In spite of a budget crunch, there was no decline in the collection of serials, which were deemed essential for preserving the infrastructure of scholarship at Jagiellonian University.

It is a curious and serendipitous fact that the introduction of an integrated automated system at the Jagiellonian Library coincided with the decline in acquisitions. It is certain that the need to train librarians, many of whom had never been exposed to computers, in the new system would have resulted in a diminution of the number of items cataloged and processed in the library. Fortunately, this occurred at a time when the total number of acquisitions was smaller, anyway. Two years later, when acquisitions substantially increased as a result of the new Act of the Legal Deposit Copy,

---

5. By 1993, there were 32 such private universities in Poland.

the backlog would have massively increased and the library would have had to substantially increase expenditures to catch up with the backlog.

There is a continuing conflict between the growth of the Jagiellonian student body and the resulting growth in the number of items that require processing by the library's Circulation Department and the limited funds at the disposal of the library. The best estimate is that the student body between 1988–1989 and 1996–1997 grew from 10,429 to 19,358, while the number of items charged to users for in-library use grew from 307,000 to 385,000 and the number of books circulated outside the library increased from 108,000 to 195,000. At the same time, there were no funds available to increase the size of the library staff; hiring an additional person would have meant that the salaries of the existing staff members would have had to be reduced. There are only two potential short-term remedies for this situation: outside sources of funds, and the rationalization of the structure of employment and of the table of organization within the library.[6] However, the latter remedy is not an easy one, partly because the distribution of professional qualifications among librarians is such that it makes personnel reassignments difficult, and partly because of an irrational resistance to the employment of student labor, which is maintained on the grounds that only librarians are competent to work in the library.[7]

Much of the circulation activity at Jagiellonian University takes place in branch libraries. In the Main Library, there are still queues at cloakrooms and computer terminals and it will be difficult to alleviate all the current problems if the university has to reach the European standard of education by 2007. However, on the whole, librarians are reasonably content with the state of circulation, in spite of the heavy demands that come not only from the students at Jagiellonian University, but also from those at the other 12 institutions of higher learning in Kraków. In any event, the longer-term future is promising: A sizable extension is being built for the Main Library at Jagiellonian, which will increase the stack area and provide additional reading rooms and will generally improve the quality of circulation.

Conclusion

The purpose of this chapter was to describe the realization of the strategic objectives of higher education in Poland within the framework of the Jagiellonian Library. The comparison between the macro-level developments and the micro-scale ones at Jagiellonian University are not completely unambiguous. The dangers that are inherent in these developments include:

1. the lack of a sensible and an effective legal framework for libraries that would guide their development;
2. the continuing dispersal of libraries among a number of different jurisdictions;

---

6. See chapter 30 (by Hayes) in the present volume.
7. But note that in North American libraries as much as 25 percent of the work is performed by student employees.

3. the general exhaustion of resources that results from efforts to make existing university structures more effective;
4. the meagerness of funds specifically allocated to libraries by the agencies responsible for the development of scholarship.

At the same time, there are some positive and promising developments:

1. A group of libraries exists in Poland, mostly in the academic sector, that has shown itself able to respond to the challenges posed by the new higher-educational aspirations of a post-Communist Poland.
2. Highly qualified, expert library staffs are being built throughout Poland.
3. Elements of competition have appeared in the allocation of funds, creating the hope that the best projects will be rewarded with funding.

CHAPTER 6

In Search of an Optimum Model of Development

MIROSŁAW GÓRNY
BOGDAN MARUSZEWSKI
JAN ANDRZEJ NIKISCH

The situation of research libraries in Poland is a very complex one, due to rapid developments in information technology and to a substantial delay in the computerization process in the country. Consequently, three problems overlap. The first problem is related to the fact that Polish libraries are only in the initial stage of computerization; the delay has indeed been a very long one, having lasted for more than 20 years. The present process of computerization is not only incredibly slow but also costly, which disrupts the normal operations of libraries; and its effects have only marginally improved their operations. The second problem is related to the emergence and rapid growth of scientific information resources in the electronic form. Providing effective access to these resources requires an appropriate technological and organizational infrastructure—what is currently in place in Polish libraries does not answer the needs. The third problem arises from the need to convert some part of the printed resources of Polish libraries into the electronic form. This is related to the growing tendency to digitize information resources throughout the world. If digitizing does not begin in Poland, the effectiveness of accessing scientific information through its libraries will decline even more in comparison to the situation of the libraries in developed countries. There are thus three concurrent technological and organizational problems that must be solved at the same time. And the situation is aggravated by very poor cooperation among libraries, and by the fact that Poland lacks specialists in library computerization, including both librarians who are well versed in the MARC format and specialists in information technologies in general. In addition, the finances of libraries are very meager. Finally, it seems that library computerization has, in a sense, become a goal in itself. Therefore, the question arises as to what steps should be taken in the next few years to successfully cope with these problems.

Problem 1: Speeding Up the Benefits of Computerization

Today there are a few dozen libraries in various stages of computerization in Poland. They have several hundred thousand bibliographic descriptions (although some of them are not in the MARC format). The number of bibliographic descriptions grows slowly but surely, as do the expertise and experience of librarians. A central authority file is in place, at least with respect to names. If we maintain the status quo, we may start experiencing major effects from computerization only in four to five years. Academic libraries need a database of national printed resources and an efficient system for tracking their usage. Other research libraries (for example, libraries of the Polish Academy of Sciences or of research institutes) are greatly interested in a database of national resources. Therefore, efforts should be focused on building a central catalog for the whole country, encompassing Polish printed resources.

In developed countries, libraries prepare their own bibliographic descriptions for about 5 percent of their acquisitions. For the remaining acquisitions, descriptions are downloaded from central catalogs. How can a similar situation be achieved in Poland? The main obstacle is the slow tempo for preparing bibliographic descriptions. It seems, therefore, that collection cataloging must be included in a nationwide shared cataloging program. For this, two solutions come to mind: (1) have all libraries catalog their collection resources using a central authority file, and prepare bibliographic descriptions that they would make available to each other; and (2) have only central libraries and the National Library develop bibliographic descriptions and make them available for free to all state research libraries in Poland. If the second solution were adopted, an extensive training program in the USMARC format for at least a few hundred people could be avoided. It seems that with this solution it would be easier to make the descriptions uniform. Besides, the accuracy of descriptions would be much higher than with the first solution. A serious technical problem is posed by the manner of retrieving and copying descriptions. If the second solution were adopted, the search will be confined to central subject catalogs. This would facilitate the downloading of catalog descriptions and the making of interlibrary loans. In libraries where there are few outside users, it might be possible to get rid of the local computer catalog entirely by exclusively using descriptions located in a central catalog, which would also contain a local call number. Also, it would be easier then, for organizational reasons, to produce subject catalogs on CDROMs or on DVDs. Such catalogs might be very popular with libraries without access to wide area networks (WANs), for example, some public or school libraries. These catalogs might turn out to be an inexpensive solution when charges are introduced for using WANs.

The solution involving central subject catalogs would make it necessary to accept the introduction into local catalogs of simplified catalog descriptions of books, so that they could be lent out immediately. Writing a description containing only the name of the author, the title, the year of publication, and at best a few subject headings (in 90 percent of cases the reader is satisfied with that) takes 5–6 times less time than writing a full description. To make a book available for lending, it is enough to assign a call number to the book and paste a bar code on it. Immediately after the book is returned, an attempt would be made to replace a simplified description with a full one retrieved from a central catalog. For example, in the Horizon system, books with a simplified description belong to the special handling group of sources and the system sends them for cataloging after readers return them. Naturally, details of the suggested solution would have to be worked out. The introduction of simplified cataloging of acquisitions—in particular, Polish ones—and the confining of the development of full bibliographic descriptions to central libraries would allow us to substantially shorten the time needed to build a local database (for example, a reference catalog). A drawback is the appearance in some databases of headings that are not related to any bibliographic descriptions and are difficult to remove. By the way, a good database management system should allow for quick removal of such headings. After all, the existence of such "empty" headings does not disable the system.

The use of central subject cataloging might also help find a solution to the problem of retrospective conversion of Polish printed resources. Central libraries would simply add descriptions of older items to their catalogs. Descriptions of foreign-language publications, however, should be taken mainly from foreign central catalogs (any charges could be covered by the Committee for Scientific Research). Translation of subject headings into Polish does not seem to be necessary. There are no translations into Polish of the bibliographic descriptions, keywords, or abstracts contained in dozens of bibliographic databases that have been used in our libraries for many years. It seems that the present situation, where everybody does everything and decides about everything, considerably slows down the progress of computerization. Libraries, particularly small ones employing fewer than 40 people, face problems which most of them cannot cope with. It is nonsense to expect each of the 200 research libraries to search for strategic solutions on their own. Almost none of them are prepared for that and the majority of them should not get involved in it. If the computerization of Polish research libraries is to bring about quick and palpable effects, an effective system of creating bibliographic descriptions of Polish publications and of distributing them to local catalogs should be put in place as soon as possible. Otherwise the whole process will degenerate into a laborious and costly endeavor that will result in the frustration of the librarian profession and in a move by many libraries toward accessing commercial resources in the electronic form, which is much easier and more spectacular.

Problem 2: Electronic Resources

In 1995, the number of titles of sources published on CD-ROMs was 9,691 and the number of databases made available (both on CD-ROMs and on line) was 8,525.[1] Already, the *CD-ROM Directory 1996*, published by TFPL Inc., records 13,000 titles of sources on CD-ROMs that are available around the world. The directory also lists 4,000 publishers of sources on CD-ROMs. The *Multimedia Yearbook 1996*, also published by TFPL, lists 10,000 companies that are involved in the production of CD-ROMs and of multimedia. In 1995, about 700 journals in electronic form were recorded.[2] In 1994, British university libraries spent about £7 million on electronic information, with the remaining academic libraries spending about £2 million.[3] British producers of information in the electronic form earned profits in the range of £2,881 million in 1994, while British publishers of printed sources earned only £2,142

---

1. Claire Creaser, *Electronic Publishing. Statistics of Supply and Library Use* (Loughborough Univ.: Loughborough, Eng.:, 1996), p. 21.
2. Ibid., p. 22.
3. *Library and Information Statistics Tables* (Loughborough Univ.: Loughborough: 1996).

million.[4] British university libraries spent £2.4 million on efforts to access on-line databases (about 31,000 sessions) in the 1994–1995 fiscal year, with global expenditures amounting to £272.3 million (including £38.2 million for purchasing books and £50.4 million for purchasing journals).[5]

The numbers cited here illustrate the growing importance of information in the electronic form. Polish libraries fully appreciate this tendency and try to make available for their users as many such resources as they can. However, their funds are meager. In 1995, the average Polish university library bought library materials in other-than-traditional print formats for 17,550 PLN (the smallest sum was 2,000 PLN while the highest was 33,800 PLN). In total, all Polish university libraries bought 44 titles.[6] At the same time, British university libraries bought 2,090 titles of sources on CD-ROMs.[7] Even after taking into account that there are 5 times as many universities in Britain than there are in Poland, the difference is considerable. It is even more so in that some titles recur in all libraries. The remaining Polish academic libraries (42 libraries reported giving access to nontraditional sources; 7 libraries did not provide such access at all) bought 90 titles of sources on CD-ROMs (on the average, a single library had 6 titles, while the largest number of titles was 23). A single library spent on that on the average 24,300 PLN (about $10,000) per annum.[8] Special libraries (mainly libraries of the research institutes at the Polish Academy of Sciences) spent on the abovementioned sources, on the average, 6,200 PLN per annum ($2,000 to $3,000). The smallest reported amount was 1,500 PLN, while the largest was 20,000 PLN. In total, 15 titles were bought by 25 libraries. The remaining 28 libraries that answered the questionnaire discussed in the citation in footnote 6 did not have any computer equipment.[9]

In fact, Polish libraries virtually do not provide access to commercial databases on-line. By comparison, the library of Augsburg University (with 1,840,000 books, 6,500 titles of journals, and 113 employees) provides access to 42 such databases.[10] In 1994, the libraries of Washington University spent $107,330 only on access to on-line databases (for the sake of comparison, the whole collection development budget, from which access to databases is paid for, was $2,718,850).[11] Providing access to nonprint materials is rarely done through a network in Polish libraries. Admittedly, in 1995, all Polish university libraries had a local network and access to the Internet. However,

4. Ibid.
5. *Library and Information Statistics Unit Annual Library Statistics 1996*, ed. By John Sumsion, Claire Creaser, Catherine Hanratty; (Loughborough Univ.: Loughborough: 1996), p. 121.
6. Mirosław Górny and Arthur Jazdon, "Wykorzystanie techniki informatycznej w polskich bibliotekach naukowych," [The Implementation of Information Technology Projects in Polish Research and Academic Libraries] *Przegląd Biblioteczny*, nos. 5/6 (1997), pp. 280–285.
7. *Library and Information Statistics*, op. cit.
8. Górny and Jazdon, op. cit., p. 136.
9. Ibid., p. 138.
10. Data are from the WWW page of the library at Augsburg University (Germany).
11. B. J. Johnston and V. Witte, "Electronic Resources and Budgeting: Funding at the Edge," in *Electronic Resources: Implications for Collection Management*, ed. G. Owens (Binghamton, N.Y.: Haworth Press, 1996), p. 12.

these were usually much smaller networks than analogous installations in Western European and American libraries. The average size of a network used in a Polish university library was about 70 workstations in 1995 (the smallest network had 15 workstations and the largest had 100). Four libraries provided access to CD-ROMs through a network (having, on the average, at 9 stations, with one library having 20). And one library was making preparations for that.[12] Having no such detailed statistical data for foreign libraries, let us use just a few random examples:

- The library of the University of Sussex (in Brighton, Eng., with 750,000 books, 40 databases, about 750,000 loans per annum, 98 fulltime employees) has 83 terminals for the staff (34 are also available for users), 60 workstations for the staff, and 12 stations for users. Besides, there are 77 stations for users, served by the Computing Service.
- The library of Uppsala University (Uppsala, Swed., with 227 employees and a collection with 133,000 meters of shelves) has 450 workstations, terminals, and servers.
- The library of Roskilde University (Roskilde, Den., with 500,000 books, 49 employees) makes use of a library network comprising 100 workstations. The network, through which 37 CD-ROM titles can be accessed, comprises two servers and two jukeboxes (served by 2 people occupying a room of 10 square meters). Over 500 workstations on the campus are connected to the network.
- The library of Smith College (Northampton, Mass., with 1,176,000 books, 4,600 titles of journals and serials, 65 employees) works with a network comprising four servers and 164 terminals.[13]

In this case the solution to the problem seems to be relatively the easiest: Polish libraries must extend their networks at least twofold or in some cases even threefold. This would call for a onetime expenditure of roughly $150,000 to $200,000. In addition, they would have to raise funds to employ computer engineers and find premises to put in an appropriate number of workstations. Unfortunately, the majority of Polish research libraries not only do not have funds to purchase so much hardware, but also do not have sufficient working space to put the hardware in, even if they received the equipment for free. Nevertheless, efforts to extend computer infrastructure in the libraries seem to be absolutely necessary. They would greatly contribute to solving the other two problems discussed here. Besides, the extension of networks would make it possible to concentrate the purchase of nonprint sources in one place and to distribute them over a national computer network, which is surely a less expensive solution than the purchasing of several, or over a dozen, copies of the same database by individual libraries around the country.

Problem 3: Modernize Today or Delay As Usual?

"Electronic libraries, virtual libraries, digitization"—these terms mean not only quicker access to information but also lower costs. If only for that reason, conversion of printed resources into the electronic form is an attractive solution for Polish libraries, which are indeed constantly short of funds. The maintenance of printed

---

12. Górny and Jazdon, op.cit., p. 134.
13. Information is from staff members of the libraries, and was obtained in 1997.

resources is very expensive (involving purchasing, cataloging, storage, providing access). All of these call for a large staff, the upkeep of large buildings, and the maintenance of the collection. According to the calculations made at the Library of the Academy of Medicine in Poznań, the maintenance of one meter of shelf space costs 3.70 PLN per annum. The cost of supporting subscriptions to foreign journals (286 titles in one year only) amounted in this library to about 23,000 PLN in 1996; the collection for 1992–1996 cost 46,000 PLN. Additionally, the salaries that were assigned to the servicing of the whole collection of foreign journals amounted to 100,000 PLN.[14] Electronic resources do not take up so much space, call for fewer staff persons, and allow access around the clock, including weekends and holidays. Moreover, electronic resources allow a large number of users to access them at the same time (for example, EBSCO usually sells licenses for 20 simultaneous users). Another advantage is the elimination of losses due to damage or theft. Finally, electronic resources are far easier to scan (for example, there is the possibility of using keywords).

Unfortunately, electronic resources also have disadvantages. First, sources published by recognized publishers are more expensive than printed ones, despite the fact that their production is cheaper. However, the monopoly of publishers allows them to impose high prices. On the other hand, if noncommercial institutions attempt to digitize printed resources, they run into copyright problems. Nevertheless, there are dozens of programs of resource digitizing now being carried out.[15] Among the best known are the programs implemented at the Columbia University Law School Library and at the Library of the Chicago Kent School of Law at the Illinois Institute of Technology. At these libraries, books from the basic collection are being converted into the digital form. At Columbia University the program encompasses 10,000 books. The cost of scanning one book is about $100. But in this way one can save $20 million that otherwise would have to be spent on the construction of a new storage facility.[16] Michael Lesk estimates the cost of scanning a 300-page book at $30.00. According to him, the cost of building storage space for such a book is similar.[17] Among the projects strongly stressing the economic aspect of the problem is the Journal Storage Project (JSTOR), originally, funded by The Andrew W. Mellon Foundation. The project encompasses 117 journal titles about 4 million pages of text. Thanks to JSTOR, the journal *Ecology* in the electronic form (back issues are available from 1921 to 1994; 77,000 pages in total) could be obtained by a library for a sum not exceeding $1,500.[18] Electronic libraries are costly projects, but eventually their operation is less expensive than that of libraries with printed resources. With the develop-

---

14. Przemysław Magdziarski, "Analiza kosztów utrzymania czasopism w wersji drukowanej i elektronicznej na przykladzie Biblioteki Głównej Akademii Medycznej w Poznaniu I bazy ADNIS." [Analysis of Maintenance Costs of Printed and Electronic Journals in the Medical University Library in Poznań], Adam Mickiewicz University: (M.A. thesis, Poznań, 1997).

15. In Australia alone there are 18 such project being carried out. http://www.dlib.org/dlib/

16. S. Michael Malinconico and Jane C. Warth; "Electronic Libraries: How Soon?" *Program 1996*, no. 2, p. 138.

17. Michael Lesk, "Substituting Images for Books: the Economics for Libraries" (1996). http://community.bellcore.com/lesk/unlv.html

18. http://www.mellon.org/jsesc.html

ment of technology, the costs of maintenance for electronic libraries will drop. The costs of maintenance for traditional libraries, however, will rise (prices of paper, costs of energy that is necessary to maintain buildings, and prices of parcels of land for development are all on the increase). Don Waters judged that the costs for the traditional library would rise about 4 percent per year while the computer costs declined 50 percent every five years.[19] Between 1986 and 1996, American research libraries increased their expenditures on serials every year by 8.4 percent. However, the number of purchased titles declined in the same period by 7 percent. The number of purchased monographs dropped by 21 percent between 1986 and 1996. However, outlays to purchase them increased each year by 2.6 percent. The price of a journal in the United States increases annually by about 9.5 percent and that of a monograph by 5 percent. This represents a sharper increase than the rate of inflation.[20] Another, equally, or even more, important argument for digitizing is the far greater efficiency of work with electronic resources. All scholars and students who work with a large number of texts, using many auxiliary sources (for example, dictionaries) and, at the same time, using their personal databases and a text editor, soon come to appreciate the advantages of an electronic office. Searching great numbers of information sources in a short period of time without moving away from the desk, the easy transferring of texts between documents, and the simultaneous use of specialist software are the advantages that printed sources can never offer. However, taking into consideration relatively high initial costs, should we not postpone these costs until later and concentrate all efforts on traditional computerization? We believe not. Electronic libraries involve many legal, technical, organizational, and standardization issues. In many respects this is a far more complex issue than the introduction of integrated library systems. Therefore, we have to begin our first trials with electronic libraries to prevent another delay. Besides, we have to remember that the future belongs to electronic libraries, if for no other reason than the fact that we are approaching a generation that has been brought up in front of a monitor.[21] After all, we are too poor to afford delays in the implementation of electronic libraries.

Conclusions

A hard task, quite naturally is, faced by anybody who would attempt, absent an in-depth analysis, to determine the plan of development for the system of information science in Poland for the next 4 to 5 years. Nevertheless, we are convinced that the

---

19. John Garrett and Don Waters, "Archival Roles and Responsibilities, Managing Costs and Finance," in *Preserving Digital Information*, 1996, http://www.rlg. org./ArchTF/tfadi.randr.htm#costs.

20. *ARL Statistics 1995–96*, ed. Martha Kyrillidou, Ken Rodriguez, and Kendon Stubbs Association of Research Libraries: (Washington, D.C. 1997), p. 9.

21. Richard P. Widdicombe writes that he has seen students who preferred to use a fulltext access system to journals for a fee, rather than climbing stairs in order to get the same journal in printed form for free. Widdicombe, "Eliminating all Journal Subscriptions Has Freed our Customers To Seek the Information They Really Want and Need," *Science and Technology Libraries* 14 (1993), p. 9.

most attention should now be paid to the three problems we mentioned in this chapter. We urge that the following steps be taken:

1. A national program of shared cataloging should be implemented as soon as possible, assigning the task of creating bibliographic descriptions, in the first place, to large central libraries and the National Library. The problems of retroconversion should also be left to these libraries.
2. As far as it is possible, the purchasing of foreign databases, both on local carriers and accessible on-line ones, should be centralized and the necessary computer infrastructure in all the research libraries should be expanded.
3. The work on digitizing should be started. It should first include teaching collections and journals. There are a few programs of digitization in the European Union that we could join.

PART II

Case Histories

CHAPTER 7

Automation and Academic Libraries in Hungary
Theory and Practice in the Period of New Challenges

BÉLA MADER

Only a few people would dispute the idea that our beautiful new world has become the world of information. Indeed, in this information society more and more people produce and provide information of different kinds and value—both information of great value and information with no reasonable value. And more and more people are accustomed to regularly consuming information. But mass production and mass consumption are impossible to achieve through manual methods alone. They need automation. Neither the term "mass" nor the term "automation" is taken to be pejorative in this context. "Mass" symbolizes the spreading of democracy and the strengthening of the competitive market economy, while automation proved to be the only way to satisfy the ever-increasing demand for information.

Libraries have always been key elements in the information-providing process. For a couple of thousand years, the majority of their activities has been almost completely confined to collecting documents that contain information. For a couple of hundred years, increasingly sophisticated cataloging has broadened the access to information and libraries nowadays have more or less become information producers. At universities, students and professors have required more and more information for teaching, for learning, and for research.

A Brief History of Library Automation

The history of library automation spans not more than 30 years. This period seems to have been a very short one and, at the same time, a very long one. After the slow but unique steps taken in the first 20 years, the last 10 (the 1990s) represented a tremendous acceleration of the automation process. The result was the introduction of a new quality standard. After automating single library activities previously done manually,

---

It was a great help for me to study the works of Hungarian librarians, written in Hungarian and accessible mainly as manuscripts. Special thanks to Géza Bakonyi, Péter Gyüre, Károly Kókas, and others, for their indirect contribution to this chapter.

libraries have now arrived at the point where they have the ability to implement the digital library in the twenty-first century.

From the Hungarian point of view, in particular, it would be interesting to remember how it all began. After the simple data processing solutions applied in circulation activities, the first generation of automated cataloging systems were introduced in the United States at the end of the 1960s. The key element of library automation was the recognition of the importance of automated bibliographic records, or, even more so, the recognition that once a bibliographic record has been created in machine-readable form, that record can be used repeatedly and for different purposes. The standard for doing this was the MARC standard, on the basis of which the mass production of bibliographic data began. As the next step, the libraries that were employing the MARC standard were able to realize a further idea. This idea later proved to be one of the most useful ones for modern libraries: to share bibliographic records and to create shared cataloging systems and union catalogs.

Second-generation automated library systems emerged in the middle of the 1970s. They were built on the basis of a standard bibliographic record, with the advantages of multiple uses in the library and in information-using processes. Once a record had been entered, it could also be used in different modules of the same system. An important development on the hardware side also enlarged possibilities for libraries: The minicomputer revolution had simultaneously taken place, and since machines were relatively inexpensive, libraries could afford to buy their own integrated automated system. But the systems they bought were not very reliable when used on mainframes with mainframe operating systems; they were designed to use data management software that hardly improved over time; and the "turn-key" systems offered only limited possibilities for the librarians to intervene. These automated library systems, however, convinced the libraries that their cataloging, circulation, and acquisition activities not only could be automated but would *have to be* automated. The third generation of automated integrated library systems evolved in the late 1980s. A dramatically accelerated development of hardware resulted in not only very powerful computers, but also inexpensive ones, coming on the market. Open operating systems, especially UNIX, eliminated the dependency on special hardware, which previously had been a serious problem. The basis of the integrated system software has become the relational database management software in almost every case. Accepted worldwide standards determined the processes as well as the procedures and the sophisticated solutions that needed to be considered—for example, the support of SQL, the Z39.50 protocol, and others. Librarians became familiar with the client-server architecture. Dramatic changes had taken place in the development of user interfaces. Both the librarian and the end user could delight in an electronic world that featured graphics, color, icons and wastebaskets, and a dozen windows on every screen.

This immense development could not have been achieved without the most rapid progress in network technologies. By the end of the 1980s, a sizable part of the world could enjoy the benefits of a very high-speed transfer of huge quantities of texts and, what is more, of sounds and images as well. The development of wide area networks was one of the priorities of this period, and the opportunities provided by this development had a great impact on the development of local networks. The very rapid progress in this field initiated cooperation among all the information providers. As with the simple bibliographic record used earlier, now information could be shared. The end user began to be accustomed to the existence of the virtual library where the accessibility to information became more important than its ownership.

The development of new attitudes of the virtual library leads our institutions into the era of the fourth generation of systems. The requirement of the information society is nothing less than access to global information. The revolution and dramatic progress achieved through the Internet over almost the entire world is increasing the role of libraries in the information-producing-and-consuming procedure. It also requires the libraries to introduce several activities in which they never engaged before and forces them to properly use their traditional collections and sources in a new information environment. Library activities in the building of databases, the use of CD-ROMs and the networked CD-ROM, multimedia solutions in the library, and other information activities are not simply side-effects. They will be cited below in my description of Hungarian developments.

Hungary's Response to the Challenges of the Information World

Hungary is in an ambivalent situation concerning library automation (as well as in many other instances). The suppression and control of information were characteristic features during an almost 50-year period (until the end of the 1980s) in Hungary, as well as in the other countries of the Eastern bloc. While fundamental changes resulted from the utilization of new technologies in the libraries of the Western Hemisphere, most of the users (among them, many students and professors) of Hungarian libraries could not take advantage of browsing in open stacks, enjoy the benefits of union catalogs and shared resources, as well as the benefits of on-line access and special catalog databases. Ideology and, in the latter part of the period, the economic situation controlled information and access to it. Information was considered by the ruling party to be more important from the philosophical point of view than from the economic one. This reveals that information was almost without economic value (nobody was willing to pay for information in a library), but at the same time it remained a dangerous thing that needed to be firmly controlled. It is my view that the libraries, the universities, and, a fortiori, the academic libraries suffered a great deal from the control of information. On the other hand, the demand for information has always existed and the technology developments in Western libraries were familiar to the Hungarian librarians. Moreover, seeking and finding the holes in the control mechanisms, they made enormous efforts to adapt the new theories and technologies in spite of the budget shortages they faced and the dramatic cuts in their acquisitions of journals and monographs. Hungarian librarians who were working in the academic, national, and special libraries not only became familiar with the theories and practices of library automation, but some of them also had conceptions and plans about how to improve them.

In these circumstances, library automation could be described as a revolutionary, rather than an evolutionary procedure. While we can find almost all the elements of the abovementioned world developments in our own case, the normal steps from an earlier generation to a later and more developed one can barely be identified. There is a sharp demarcation line in this development. The accelerator in Hungary was not the technological development but the change in the political system.

It was the libraries that began to take advantage of the new possibilities provided by the young democracy for the very first time. In all types of libraries, a core of appropriate personnel began to discuss the new tasks. Because they had recognized most of these earlier, it was only a matter of time before they realized them. In spite of high inflation, uncertain funding, and the traditional library structure, which was not adequately responsive to changes, they tried to exploit the opportunities for strengthening and modernizing libraries by means of new sources and new alliances. The immediate and favorable reaction of libraries to the demands that could be freely manifested, and to the opportunities that offered different kinds of supporting sources, had two results that were equally important for users and librarians. First, during these 6–7 years of freedom, a development had taken place in Hungarian libraries that afforded them the ability to catch up with Europe. The second result is perhaps of somewhat more importance and may be more properly understood by our companions in the former Eastern bloc. While surrounded by almost all of the disadvantages experienced by a society in a state of transition, the libraries survived. This is the story I will tell here, concentrating on the academic libraries.

Hungarian Universities and the Need for Developing Academic Libraries

After the change in the political system in Hungary, the most important objective was to establish a new, democratic, and more efficient relationship between society and the economy. Both political and economical analyses of the new situation considered the development of higher education to be among the priorities for achieving that aim. A development strategy had been worked out at the very beginning of the new era, and its principles more or less determine the current procedures as well. A development concept called "Higher Education in Hungary until the Year 2000" pointed to the need to create the university of the twenty-first century.

The Development Concept in Higher Education

The development concept at the beginning of 1992, having been based on an analysis of both international educational trends and the current situation, laid special emphasis on the following priorities and objectives: (1) to realize the freedom of learning, education, research, and competition guaranteed by the constitution; (2) to considerably increase the number of students (by 50-60 percent), while preserving the quality of education at the same time; (3) to set up regional universities with several faculties, as well as university alliances (contrary to the small vocational universities of the socialist system), that would be the most important elements in renewing higher education; (4) to establish a consolidated and integrated new management system that would replace the fragmented activities of the old centralized direction; and (5) to return the right of granting scientific degrees (Ph.D.'s) to universities to strengthen their scientific autonomy.

As a consequence, the system of higher education underwent fundamental changes. Institutional democracy was stabilized, and curricula were changed. The credit system is in the process of being introduced at almost all universities, a new and adequate harmony between diplomas and degrees has evolved, and the preconditions for diploma equivalencies are being created.

As the basis of the newborn higher education system, new forms of financing higher education institutions were also established. The state subsidizes the universities on a normative basis for which the determining factor is the number of students enrolled. Tuition fees were introduced, and elements of nonstate financing, as well as grants from foundations and different funds, became more important.

These objectives and regulations were the ones that determined the roles of academic libraries in the new, democratic environment. Academic libraries have traditionally been basic parts of the higher education institutions in Hungary. The general change in higher education demanded the immediate response of these libraries, because the objectives generated rapidly increasing demands for library and information services, both as to quality and quantity.

Increasing Demands. Among the qualitative aspects, libraries had to face the following ones: (1) the freedom of education, learning, and research increased, both in range and depth, the demand for literature of many kinds; (2) the new subjects at the universities required a more extensive library background and continuous development of services; (3) the students' increasingly greater command over foreign languages multiplied the demand for literature written in foreign languages; (4) the new techniques of collecting and providing information created a greatly increased demand for new types of nontraditional services.

As to the quantitative aspects of the demands, the academic libraries met the impacts of the substantial increase in the number of students; of the growing number of library users who were attending courses at the faculties of the universities; of the relative but remarkable growth in the number of library users that was due to the change in the educational structure; of the emergence of postgraduate education and also postsecondary training; and of the appearance of the elements of lifelong learning.

The qualitative and the quantitative aspects affected each other and intensified each other's effects. Nevertheless, even the most developed and best-prepared academic libraries were not able to satisfy the local needs. The first surveys completed just after the change in the political system indicated that in most university libraries the space for accommodating users was insufficient. Storage space for the already-existing holdings was also insufficient. Even the basic conditions for developing a modern, open-stack library structure were lacking. No acquisition standards existed, and statistical data indicated that the library expenditures per student in the developed countries were orders of magnitude greater than in Hungary. The methods of funding academic libraries were not (and have not yet been) formulated. Library infrastructure in academic libraries, as compared to general university infrastructure, proved to be poor. The answer to the question which arose in the early 1990s—namely, whether academic libraries could perform their functions as modern libraries—was in the negative. Although, as a result of several successful applications for grants, steps were taken toward developing library automation and stopping the decline in acquisitions, it was crucial to concentrate on strategically planned development.

The Objectives of the Development Strategy

The strategic-planning efforts of academic libraries were organized by the Ministry of Education and Culture under the title of the Textbook and Higher Education Libraries Program (THEL) and were supported by special assistance from Japan. The program's priorities concentrated on four interrelated fields: increasing collections, implementing library automation, restructuring the library's management, and staff retraining. These have been of equal importance, but library automation has been in a position of being primus inter pares. The activities of this program of strategic planning (in which not only Hungarian, but also numerous foreign experts, were involved) were later synchronized with a similar, but nationwide strategy (the National Specialized Literature Information System in Hungary, initiated by the government), which also considered the academic libraries as determining elements of the national information system. The surveys, analyses, and studies done by experts or expert groups of librarians resulted in a comprehensive strategic development plan, known in Hungary as the "Neal Report." This 1995 report determined the most important elements of future action in library automation, as follows:

1. A shared cataloging system should be implemented based upon widely accepted standards and providing a union database of library holdings. Hungarian academic libraries cannot continue to invest limited resources in duplicative cataloging activities. Such a system will also serve as the basis for an expanding interlibrary loan program and enhanced access to centrally managed, high-use electronic databases. A consortium board should be established to coordinate and implement the full cooperative program and to direct the shared cataloging agency.
2. Higher education libraries should develop plans for local system acquisition, implementation and development, and funding should be provided from World Bank and government sources for hardware, software, and in-library network support. These systems should adhere to widely accepted standards, including telecommunications linking (Z39.50), and provide integrated functionality.
3. Higher education libraries should develop plans for converting local holdings into their online catalog databases and contribute these records into the national union database. The consortium board should manage this retrospective conversion program working initially with the national library for Hungarian materials and 3 to 5 large libraries for foreign materials.
4. A program of demonstration projects should be implemented for Hungarian-specific national databases and for electronic and networked information services in individual libraries and groups of libraries.
5. Library automation is central to efficient operations and quality services, and it is recommended that appropriate funding be made available through World Bank and government funding.[1]

---

1. James G. Neal, "Summary Report," THEL Program, Libraries Subproject (Budapest, 1995), p. 10

The principles of participation were also determined by the strategic plan. While it was considered to be essential that all Hungarian academic libraries have opportunities to participate in and benefit from this program, it was of equal importance that participating libraries should agree to a set of important principles, as follows:

> participate in a shared cataloging/union database program; adhere to established bibliographic standards; adhere to established telecommunication standards; adhere to established system user interface standards; adhere to established data exchange format standards; commitment to automation of operations and services; commitment to retrospective conversion of local collections; commitment to a program of expanded information services.[2]

The objectives of THEL (and those of the national development strategy) were precise, modern, and worth following, but neither the one set of objectives nor the other were implemented as official strategy. And we have a very simple explanation for why this happened: Both sets of objectives were also strategies, more or less, in 1995 for getting a substantial World Bank loan or government funding. But after 1995 the chances were better than at the end of 1994, or in the beginning of 1995, for applying for substantial loans and funding for library development purposes.

It is interesting that while the strategic plans described above have never been approved by the authorities, their most important details became well known not only to the libraries but also to the authorities and to several organizations influencing decision-making. The development plan as a whole has never received the required substantial moneys, but most of the important objectives found sources of funds, such as state funding, or grants from foundations.

Hungarian Library Automation Objectives: from Planning to Implementation

The Early Period of Automation in Academic Libraries

In the middle of the 1970s only a few academic libraries expressed serious interest in automation of library work. The main field of its application was cataloging and its main purpose there was to eliminate manual work with catalog cards and card catalogs. Computers did not appear in the libraries, which relied on the capabilities and the assistance of the computer centers at the universities. This period was followed by the spread of personal computers (PCs) in the libraries (mostly IBM PCs, or IBM-compatible ones) in the early 1980s. Apart from word processing software for PCs, the most widespread software was that for database management. With such software, the construction of databases began in several libraries. The era of stand-alone personal computers lasted for a relatively long time in the libraries. The librarians thus had time to learn how to create a bibliographic record but they had to wait a few years for its appropriate use. However, an important achievement was the fact that most of the

2. Ibid.

records created during this period were suitable for later conversion. As a result of this development, the OPACs of the later integrated systems could usually start up with a considerable number of records. One more important thing should be mentioned: This early automation period determined the attitude of librarians as being one that was not against, but was definitively favorable toward, library automation in most of the academic libraries.

The Period of Catching Up with the Rest of the World

At the end of the 1980s, the opportunity arose for the use of network versions of certain library software. Local networks were built in more and more libraries. The server was usually provided not by the library but by the computer center of the university. Moreover, during this period, the Information Infrastructure Development Program (IID) had an indirect but determining impact on the academic libraries. The IID was founded as a national institution to develop the information infrastructure of the fields of education, research, technical development, and culture. With IID support, a national computer network was established that connected, besides education and research centers, several public institutions, including libraries. Within this program, the libraries received IID support to enable them to provide their already-existing services and databases to the overall academic community. A national backbone network of information processing (IP) technology and leased lines was established under the coordination of the IID. This Hungarian backbone was connected to the international backbone network.

The opportunity for cooperation among libraries and for the sharing of information appeared on the basis of the development of both local and wider area networks. The demands for the providing of electronic information services influenced almost all of the traditional fields of library work. As a result of this influence, the first integrated automated systems appeared at the beginning of the 1990s in some of the Hungarian academic libraries. These systems belonged to the second- and third-generation groups of systems, indicating that the 30-year-long history of library automation elsewhere has been remarkably shortened in Hungary.

The results of this first period of development in Hungary (it lasted, in my opinion, from the end of 1989 till the end of 1993) were shown by two surveys conducted in 1993 and 1994 by the IID to provide preliminary data for the development of academic libraries and to establish a national system for providing scientific and special-literature information (this period was not long ago, but these years seem to represent a long historical period). It is interesting to compare the situation of the country's twenty-six academic libraries from the point of view of library automation. For example, the surveys showed that the few personal computers (mainly XTs) that were almost the only devices at the end of the 1980s had by now almost entirely disappeared. The first servers of medium capacity now appeared in the libraries, the most common ones being VAX and SUN devices. The number of AT PCs increased remarkably and some of them already directly served users' needs. According to the statistical data of the surveys that related to the hardware facilities of the academic libraries, the situation was as follows (the total number of units in operation is given for each type of equipment):

Middle-capacity server (for example, VAX 3500, VAX 6410, Sun Sparc Classic, Sun Sparc 10): 19
PC-286: 117
PC-386: 107
PC-486: 41
Multimedia workstation: 29
PC with single CD-driver: 23

The surveys produced data on the number of integrated automated library systems in academic libraries: Among the twenty-six academic libraries, only eight had integrated systems at this time. The eight systems include five different kinds of integrated ones (TinLib, Oracle LIB, Aleph, Voyager, and Dynix). The use of five competing systems points to a special feature of Hungarian library automation, which caused problems in establishing the shared cataloging system. Considering that twenty-six universities and about 120,000 students are involved, these numbers seem to be unbelievably low. On the other hand, this development required substantial support from sources that were not traditional ones or were not present under the socialist system. Indeed, it was foreign and domestic funds and foundations that helped the libraries to develop library automation. Without the helping hands of the funds and foundations, the steps necessary for library automation development would never have been taken in these libraries. Besides the support of the CEF (Catching up with Europe Fund), PHARE, TEMPUS, and several other funds, it was the Mellon Foundation that played an extraordinarily important role in the automation of academic libraries in Hungary. The phrase "just in time" is the most useful way to characterize the contributions of the Mellon Foundation. Academic libraries could now purchase their first servers, could provide a couple more workstations for users. They were able to subscribe to their first CD-ROM databases.

This first period of development can also be considered an experimental one. The strategic plans were only being developed, and the coordination of common activities was weak in regard to fund raising. The libraries had to follow several rules related to stipulations made by the funds and foundations. On hardware side the result was a satisfying one, but as to integrated automated library software, the independent applications involved resulted in future problems. The competition among the different integrated systems made the road to the achievement of a shared cataloging system a bit rough. On the other hand, the developmental elements in this period multiplied the demands for complex and comprehensive solutions to problems in library automation.

Further Development Steps toward Better Information Services

The strategic plan for academic libraries that was based on the developments cited above emphasized that it was time to establish comprehensive national plans for library automation and networks. A decision needed to be made to establish an information infrastructure that would make the most effective use of Hungary's information and financial resources and provide the best services. All the studies conducted within the framework of strategic planning found the library automation situation in Hungary to be appropriate for taking the next steps. One of the most important tasks was to implement a shared cataloging system and to convert the records of major collections into the system. On the initiative of the academic libraries, the major Hungarian libraries, which also included special libraries and the National Library, worked out a draft plan for implementing the shared cataloging system in the middle of 1996. An application to the Soros Foundation and to the Open Society Institute Regional Library Program succeeded in raising funds for this purpose. After detailed studies were done and discussions of committees of experts were held, both on cataloging and on automation, the "Request for Proposal" for the system software was issued in 1996. Meanwhile, a lot of work that needed to be done and agreements that had to be reached were in fact completed or about to be completed. The cataloging standards, classification issues, character sets, user interface standards, as well as the type of MARC record format for the system, were discussed. The Hungarian National Shared Cataloging System (in Hungarian its acronym is MOKKA)—a consortium of fifteen major Hungarian libraries—began its activities. Other nationwide services were also introduced in 1996, and were initiated as a program by the academic libraries but are available for all types of libraries—this program, called KözElKat, provides a common interface for connecting different library OPACs for information retrieval. A third initiative on the national level also came from academic libraries, which do the work for it: It is the MEK (Magyar Elektronikus Könyvtár, meaning Hungarian Electronic Library); it collects the digitized texts and provides access to them.

The development in library automation undertaken locally in the academic libraries served as a foundation for these nationwide developments. At the end of 1997, all the academic libraries had their integrated automated library systems. The systems are: Aleph, Dynix/Horizon, OLIB, TinLib, and Voyager. There are differences involved in the installation and operation of all the modules. The most commonly used ones are the cataloging, OPAC, and circulation modules. Enormous efforts were made to accelerate retrospective conversions (the academic libraries were also supported by a national foundation in this effort). All the academic libraries can be accessed on the Internet. They produce information at a top level and their home pages offer many kinds of electronic services. The digitizing of very valuable and unique library materials has already begun and worldwide access to special collections through the Internet is being offered.

The number of CD-ROM databases has rapidly increased. Most of the academic libraries could provide these databases in their local networks using so called CD-ROM-towers. The new solution for CD-ROM networking, the CD/HD system, also appeared in some of them.

There is a shortage of terminals, and of workstations for librarians as well as for users. The demand for student clusters became very strong; students want comprehensive electronic services in the libraries and they have a right to these. But most parts of the development plan for library automation are the results of special funding. And the paths to funds and foundations are becoming increasingly narrow. Maintaining and operating the facilities and services require regular subsidies. The most recent task of academic libraries has been to persuade the state to include expenses in the library budget that have never before been there.

The picture describing the state of library automation in Hungary would not be a complete one without mentioning the role of librarians. Some of them function at the highest international level. Most of them are devoted to electronic work, and are willing to be trained and retrained. In fact, training and retraining became an almost everyday procedure. The librarians are instrumental in creating interfaces that can be very easily used. This is the work of several librarians devoted to democracy, libraries, and automation, which resulted in a situation in which the differences between Hungarian academic libraries and those of the developed part of the world are now only quantitative ones. Hungarian academic libraries can indeed provide the same quality and types of services as the libraries of the Western Hemisphere. These services are based on the providing of less special literature, fewer journals, only a few special databases, and are accessible sometimes only on a small number of devices. There are only a few electronic journal subscriptions, but users can order interlibrary loans through e-mail. The academic libraries, of course, also have some common problems. The lack of coordination leads to parallel developments in certain areas. The libraries are facing an interesting contradiction: the lack of information in an information society. Our libraries have to participate in more European and worldwide projects. They must increase the efficiency of their services, and contribute to the solving of a couple of additional but important problems, for example, the issue of the electronic copyright. In this situation it seems to be encouraging that these libraries behave as if they represented the leading edge in Hungary. They are user oriented and, last but not least, they seem to be surviving in the present transition period of the society.

References

Bajza János, Martos Balázs, Nagy Miklós, Springer Ferenc, Tóth Beatrix. "Implementation of the Computer Network System for Hungarian Higher Education Libraries: Proposed Plan." In "Automation of Libraries of Hungarian Higher Education Institutions," Budapest, 1994.
Borgman, Christine L. "Final Report to the Hungarian Ministry of Culture and Education." World Bank Project, Module 1.3: Library Automation and Networks. Budapest, 1994.
Heseltine, Richard. "Library Automation Outlook." Hull, Eng., 1995.
Mader, Béla. "Library Automation Systems in Academic Libraries in Hungary." *Program: Automated Library and Information Systems* 29, no. 3 (1995): 285–293.
"National Specialized Literature Information System Implementation. Initial System Design." Budapest, 1994.
Neal, James G., "Summary Report," Textbook and Higher Education Libraries (THEL) Program. Hungary. Libraries Subproject. Budapest, 1995.
Roth, L. E.; Griffiths, J.-M.; Drabenstott, K. M., Hensley, R. D.; Jacob, M. E. L.; Luker, I. K.; and Rousseau, G. J. "East European Information System Development: Basis for Educational Reform and Democracy Building." A final report on Grant USIP-91F-117, from the U.S. Institute of Peace to the University of Tennessee. November 3, 1992.
Sóron László; Mader Béla; Dömötör Anna; Virágos Márta; and Darányi Sándor. "Textbook and Higher Education Libraries (THEL) Program," Hungary. Libraries Subproject. Budapest, 1994.
"The Development of Higher Education in Hungary until the Year 2000." Summary: Decision Support Suggestions. Budapest, 1992.
"The Development of Higher Education in Hungary until the Year 2000." Theses and Proposals. Budapest, 1992.

CHAPTER 8

Automation in the National Library in Warsaw
From an In-House System to INNOPAC

JADWIGA SADOWSKA

The National Library (NL) in Warsaw is the main library in Poland and the biggest one. It was established by a decree issued by the president of the Republic of Poland on February 24, 1928. The staff consists of over 900, including about 450 people who are directly involved in library work. It is situated in two buildings, five kilometers apart. Its collections comprise about five million volumes, covering mainly the humanities.

Since the beginning of its existence, it has been the national bibliographic agency. On the basis of the legal deposit of Polish publications, it has been compiling the current national bibliography of monographs,[1] and that of serials.[2] For over forty years the National Library has been preparing the bibliography of foreign polonica,[3] and the index to the Polish serials.[4] The NL has also been compiling the retrospective national bibliographies of monographs since 1901 and of serials since 1946. Besides, it maintains the union catalogs of foreign books and Polish and foreign serials held in Polish libraries. The National Library is also (1) the bibliographic and library standardization center; (2) the preservation and conservation center for rare prints and other library materials; (3) an information center that publishes statistics; (4) a research center, conducting studies in the fields of bibliography, history of books, and readership; and (5) a publishing house, specializing in the publication of works in the fields of bibliography, librarianship, and information science.

But first of all, the NL is a big research library visited every day by 500–600 users—students and research workers. There are almost 500 seats in 7 reading rooms.

For many years the NL has cooperated with international information systems like ISSN (International Standard Serials Numbering), in Paris; ISBN (International Stan-

---

1. *Bibliographic Guide. Official List of Printed matter in the Polish Republic.* 1946–. National Library. Bibliographic Institute. Continuation of *The Official Index of Prints* published in 1928–1939.
2. *Bibliography of Serial Publications.* National Library. Bibliographic Institute. Published since 1958, primarily under the title *Bibliography of Periodicals and Complete Editions.*
3. *Foreign Polonica. Bibliography.* National Library. Bibliographic Institute. Published since 1956.
4. *Index to Periodicals.* National Library. Bibliographic Institute. Published since 1947.

dard Book Numbering), in Berlin; the Index Translationum in Paris, published under the auspices of UNESCO; and EROMM (European Register of Microform Masters), in Göttingen, Germany. The NL has also cooperated with a great number of Polish libraries.

Beginnings of Automation at the National Library

The NL has been working on the automation of its functions for over 15 years. However, it should be said that in the beginning of the 1980s we did not have the opportunities to use adequate computer technology, neither hardware nor software. We used a leased IBM mainframe computer and very simple software, which permitted data input. The only accessible foreign library system we knew was CDS/ISIS, distributed for free by UNESCO in East European countries. The NL did not use that system since at that time we were working on creating our own.

In the beginning, automation at the NL was concerned with the union catalog of Polish serials and of foreign monographs and serials held at the Polish libraries. For many years we entered data and printed them in a paper edition.[5] Unfortunately, those records were created in a non-MARC format and because of that, we have had to carry out a conversion to prepare them for a loading into the INNOPAC database.

In the middle of the 1980s, software designers from the NL started to create in-house library systems for mainframe computers and microcomputers. The mainframe system was never completed, although the cataloging module was used for some time. Finally, work on it was stopped in 1993. The work on a microcomputer system was successfully completed.

In 1986 we bought several very simple PCs and started to edit the national bibliography of monographs using in-house software. Data were prepared in the MARC-BN format.[6] At first, we worked without a proper computer network. The network was temporary and connected to only some parts of the buildings. A structural computer network was built only in 1996.

The year 1990, though, can be regarded as the turning point for the NL and other Polish libraries, owing to economic and political transformations. Opportunities to buy some hardware opened up for many libraries. Foreign companies became interested in Poland as a market for hardware and library software. Polish library staff members began to more frequently visit Western countries to look at library systems there.

To show the progress in the hardware conditions at the NL between the years 1986 and 1996, we may note that the number of PCs grew from 10 to 300 and the network grew from 20 to 600 potential users. Since 1992, we have been able to use e-mail. All these changes brought us closer to the libraries of the developed world.

---

5. *Union Catalog of Foreign Serials in Polish Libraries.* National Library. Union Catalog Department.
6. *SABINA System. Format for Monographs.* Prep. By Zofia Moszczyńska-Pętkowska. Warsaw, National Library, 1982; *SABINA System. Format for Serials.* Prep. By Zofia Moszczyńska-Pętkowska, Warsaw, National Library, 1983.

MAK—Computer Library System for Small Libraries

As indicated before, in 1987 the NL started to create a microcomputer system for small libraries. In 1991 the system, called MAK, was able to carry out various library functions and the NL began to use it to create the database for the national bibliography of monographs. Basically, the system contained two modules: cataloging and OPAC. Later, the circulation module was added. Soon, many libraries, especially ecclesiastical libraries, became interested in testing its functions. They suggested many changes and improvements. Over the few next years, the NL used MAK for other functions as well. In 1992, the system was operational in about 50 Polish libraries. In every single year since then, it was implemented by about 70 additional libraries. At present, it is used by over 400 Polish libraries, especially public libraries.

MAK is a DOS-based system and was installed in a Novell network. At the NL, it worked at first with 20 simultaneous users, and at present it works with over 100 simultaneous users. The NL uses it to create all parts of the national bibliography: monographs, serials, polonica, and the index to serials, and also to catalog other kinds of documents. We use it in the union catalog of foreign books, Polish serials, and special collections. Unfortunately, in the past, due to the lack of an adequate computer network, our databases were created separately and they were not integrated. Consequently, there are several databases in the NL that have to be unified in one database in the INNOPAC system.

MAK is a very flexible system that is able to handle all kinds of MARC formats—every user can create and modify the structure of the database and indexes. Unfortunately, it has no acquisitions and serials-control modules. It was unable to access the data on the Internet, but fortunately, this problem has already been solved. MAK is installed on our CD-ROMs. It also permits us to test the INNOPAC system that was bought by the NL.

Assistance from the Andrew W. Mellon Foundation

In 1992, the NL hosted the visit of a consultant from the United States.[7] His task was to offer consulting advice on library automation. During his stay, several vendors of integrated library systems were invited to the NL to demonstrate their products. They were mainly American companies: VTLS, Dynix, Endeavor Information Systems, GEAC Computer, and an Israeli company, Ex Libris. At that time we also learned how to prepare a "Request for Proposal." In 1991, the NL received a grant from The Andrew W. Mellon Foundation for staff training and development. Toward the end of 1992, a group of five staff members of the NL and our U.S. consultant went on a 30-day study tour to visit American libraries and to examine their automated systems. The group visited the Library of Congress and the OCLC (Online Computer Library Center) in Dublin, Ohio, as well as several large libraries—among others, the Kent State University Library (Ohio), the Western Waldo Library in Kalamazoo, the West-

---

7. Stan Elman from the USA was the National Library consultant in 1992.

ern University Michigan Library, the Princeton University Library, the National Agricultural Library in Beltsville (Md.), and the New York Public Library. That tour gave us an opportunity to see several computer software systems in operation. These were VTLS, Dynix, Cuadra Star, Aleph, Notis, GEAC, and INNOPAC. The U.S. tour enabled us to also assess to some extent the previous automation achievements of our library.

At that time, four Polish research libraries in Warsaw, Kraków, and Gdańsk received grants from Mellon Foundation for the purchase of integrated library systems. The NL also planned to apply for a grant for automation to the Mellon Foundation. In January 1994, after almost a year of preparations, the NL submitted a "Request for Grant" addressed to Mellon Foundation.

The application for the grant consisted of three parts, plus enclosures: (1) general information about the NL (its history, organization, functions, legal and financial basis, the size of the collection, catalogs); (2) the current status of its automation (databases, hardware, software, automation plans, the approximate costs of automation); (3) the "Request for Grant" (financial needs for software, hardware, and the computer network).

Our approximate calculations indicated that we would need almost $900,000 to start a composite automation of library operations. We planned to earmark one-third of this sum for software, and about a quarter for the network hardware. We planned to spend about one-third on the purchase of a server, terminals, and PCs. The rest of the total was to be spent on two years' worth of maintenance fees.

In June 1994, we were notified by Mellon Foundation that our request had been approved and that we would receive $880,000. In August 1994, this sum of money was transferred to the NL's bank account.

Our "Request for Proposal," to be sent to vendors, was almost ready at that time. We also started active preparations for building a local structural computer network.

The first expenditures that came from the Mellon grant were made at the beginning of 1996. In March 1996, we bought a DEC Alpha 2100 server and DEC Campus Licenses. In April 1996 we paid the first installment of our bill for software to Innovative Interfaces. From April to August 1996, we bought the server and other hardware for the computer network. In October 1996 we bought 70 PCs. In February 1997 we paid the second installment of our bill for INNOPAC. Our expenditures basically follow the plan submitted in the "Request for Grant." Only software turned out to be more expensive than we had originally assumed. This was due, among other things, to the purchase of additional software functions, beyond the standard package.

I think that so far we have managed the Mellon fund well. Thanks to this fund, we have bought the necessary hardware, built a structural computer network for almost 600 stations, and bought the INNOPAC integrated library system.

Why INNOPAC?

On October 20, 1994, the NL sent "Request for Proposal" to each of the following 14 integrated library systems vendors:

1. Best-Seller Library System Inc. (United States)—Best-Seller system
2. BIBSYS (Norway)—BIBSYS system
3. BLCMP (England)—TALIS system
4. Cuadra Associates (United States)—CUADRA STAR system
5. Dabis Gesselschaft (Germany)—DABIS system
6. Dynix (USA)—Marquis system (now called Horizon)
7. Endeavor Information Systems (United States)—VOYAGER system
8. Ex Libris Ltd (Israel)—Aleph system
9. GEAC Computers (United States)—GEAC Plus system
10. IME (England)—TinLib system
11. Innovative Interfaces (USA)—INNOPAC system
12. Max Elektronik S.A. (Poland)—PROLIB system
13. Pica Centrum (Holland)—PICA system
14. VTLS Inc. (United States)—VTLS system

January 20, 1995, was the deadline by which all proposals were to be received. We received 10 offers. Four companies did not reply: Best-Seller, BIBSYS, BLCMP, and Dabis Gesselschaft.

In February 1995, the general director of the NL set up an Evaluation Group on Integrated Library Systems. The proposals were evaluated by the same people who had prepared the "Request for Proposal." Before making the final decision, the Evaluation Group visited Polish libraries where the integrated systems were implemented. The systems included Aleph, at the Parliamentary Library in Warsaw; Horizon, at the University Library in Toruń; TinLib, at the University of Technology's Main Library in Kraków; and VTLS, at the University Libraries in Kraków and Warsaw. The opinion about those systems was very important for us, because the systems operated under Polish conditions.

The final decision was made on July 28, 1995: The INNOPAC system of Innovative Interfaces was chosen. In choosing the system for the NL, we first took into account the vendors' replies to the "Request for Proposal" and how these replies were prepared. We also considered the vendors' approach to our request, the reliability of the replies (we added a checklist of questions). Moreover, we took into account the potential workload for the NL during the implementation of the system—we looked for a turnkey, state-of-the-art system that would also be stable. We were afraid of systems that were too modern in the sense that their vendors announced many upgrades over a short period of time, and of those that intended to implement some functions only in the future. We wanted to have a system that would be well prepared to handle the USMARC format for bibliographic, holdings, and authority records. The size of the libraries where the systems were installed was also taken into consideration. Of course, financial conditions were also important, but not crucial. We realized that first-class products cannot be cheap.

We have to say that the systems were comparable, and all companies submitted good customer references, so the choice was not easy. After a careful examining of the received proposals, we chose INNOPAC, fully confident that we made the right choice.

The Implementation of INNOPAC

On March 18, 1996, the contract between the NL and Innovative Interfaces, for the purchase of the INNOPAC system, was signed. We bought the following modules: cataloging, OPAC, circulation, acquisitions, and serials control. We also bought the alternate database software for the union catalog and 150 user licenses.

The original schedule for the INNOPAC implementation assumed that the system would become operational and be accepted by the end of 1996. In March 1996, the parameters of files, indexes, the structure of bibliographic records, and holdings records were to be defined. The installation of the software was planned to take place in May, and the TESTPAC installation, in June. In September 1996, we planned to sign the TESTPAC approval document and, in October, to load the real data to the INNOPAC database. It turned out, however, that we could accept TESTPAC only in January 1997, mainly because of erroneous displays, and the keying and sorting of Polish and foreign diacritical marks. Also, we did not sign off on the keyword index, because in our opinion it was unable to properly play its role—first, because the words contained only 12 characters, which are not enough for inflected languages. The second reason that the keyword index was not accepted was that the way it was sorted did not agree with the tradition of sorting in Polish. The problem of increasing the number of characters in the keyword index has already been solved by the vendor, but the company is still working on changing the sorting method and we do hope that the problem will be solved soon in a manner that meets our expectations.

The other problem was posed by the diacritical characters. They ought to have been compatible with the ISO 6937 standard, because this is the standard that was accepted by Polish libraries. Concerning screen displays, we decided to use characters in accordance with Page Code 1250. Unfortunately, we had some difficulties with characters that have no image in this standard. The proper way of coding diacritical marks is very important for us, because of our data export and import program (we cooperate with almost 500 Polish libraries), and because of the production of the national bibliography on the basis of our data. I should point out that the NL does 100-percent original cataloging of Polish publications and, we estimate, over 50 percent of foreign publications. This is the reason why keying is so crucial for us.

Location codes were also the source of certain problems. The NL uses over 150 location codes. In our case, the codes refer both to item and bibliographic records, contrary to the case of regular libraries, where the problem is less complicated.

An important thing for us was the method of inputting and displaying serials holdings. We wanted it to be fully compatible with USMARC for holdings. Finding a solution to this problem took us several months, but it was finally solved to our satisfaction.

For some time we discussed the issue of authority records. It is an important problem for us, because the NL creates authority records and because the national bibliographic agency is responsible for them throughout the country. On the basis of these records, the NL has also been publishing "National Library Subject Headings"

(*Słownik Języka Haseł Przedmiotowych Biblioteki Narodowej*).[8] At first, some of the implementation problems were probably the result of our poor understanding of some INNOPAC functions. Every training session improved our knowledge about the system. We are constantly exploring the system, but of course we do not know it as well as the INNOPAC staff knows it. At the beginning, many other problems occurred, almost certainly due to the vendor's imperfect understanding of the specific functions of the National Library and of the national bibliographic agency. Our project was not typical, in the sense that the NL is a library that mainly creates data and transfers them to other libraries and does not import much from others. We believe the implementation of INNOPAC in a national library, such as the National Library of Poland, is a new and difficult task for the company. However, we hope that it can be very informative for the vendor and stimulate further developments.

The next problem involved formats and the fact that the NL did not start its automation process from scratch. We had over 600,000 records in our own MARC-BN format, and in non-MARC formats that we did not want to lose. A portion of these records seemed ready to be loaded. For INNOPAC we decided to use the USMARC format.[9] We had to produce MARC-BN/USMARC conversion software. We have successfully completed this task. In the course of our work on the conversion, it turned out that our data are not unified, because they were created in separate files and record structures were different. We also had diacritical marks coded in our own way. That was the reason that we could not promptly prepare for the loading of the database. While we were preparing the conversion to USMARC, we introduced many corrections to the records.

The next cause of the delay was the fact that the NL, as the national bibliographic agency that publishes the weekly national bibliography, cannot stop its current work even for a few days. Consequently, the implementation of INNOPAC is carried out simultaneously with the current activities of the NL.

INNOPAC is being implemented and modified via the Internet. To illustrate the extent of the interaction with the vendor, I should note that during the time of the implementation, we exchanged over 200 letters with Innovative Interfaces. I will add that the vendor carried out three training sessions (17 days), and in July 1997, we started the polonization of the OPAC. From the technical point of view the task is quite easy, since INNOPAC has a very efficient editor for this purpose. Of course we have difficulties with Polish terminology, but this is a different kind of issue. Unfortunately, we have not yet started working on the alternative database for the union catalog, and we have no experience with the alternative database.

The next problem is that of the bar codes. There are no bar codes on our documents. Assigning them remains our responsibility.

The implementation of the system has missed the original deadlines by several months. At the time of this writing, the understandings with the company presume

---

8. *National Library Subject Headings*. Prep. By Ewa Stepniakowa and Janina Trzcińska, 3rd ed., Warsaw, National Library.

9. *USMARC Format for Authority Data*.

that the system will be approved and that we shall begin to use it in our everyday work in February 1998.

Prospects of Cooperation with Libraries in Poland

According to our estimates, over 1,200 Polish libraries use computer systems. There are about 20 systems in use, including several Polish systems and several foreign ones. The most frequently encountered are (1) MAK, designed and distributed by the National Library and used in over 400 libraries, particularly public libraries; (2) SOWA, designed and distributed by the Sokrates company of Poznań, used in about 200 libraries of various types; (3) MOL, designed and distributed by the MOL, a Gdyni company, used in about 300 libraries, particularly school libraries; (4) foreign computer systems, of which the most frequently used ones are two American systems—namely, VTLS, sold by VTLS, and Horizon, sold by Ameritech—and TinLib, sold by IME (England), and Aleph, sold by Ex Libris (Israel).

The NL, as the national bibliographic agency registering all publications with a Polish imprint, considers it important to cooperate with all libraries and computer systems. We hope that this cooperation will be possible and will run smoothly, thanks, we hope, to the application of the same standards for bibliographic descriptions, document description formats, character coding, and data transmission.

Bibliographic records at the NL and in other Polish libraries are created according to the ISBD standards for particular types of documents. Libraries use Polish equivalents of these standards. Bibliographic records created at the NL are the basis for the creation of electronic catalogs. The main partners in this are public libraries, in whose collections Polish publications account for 95 percent of the holdings. Academic libraries also use them, though in these libraries Polish publications account for only about 50-60 percent of the holdings.

It should be emphasized that since 1994, the NL has been working on the retroconversion of the national bibliography. Results of this can be seen on CD-ROMs edited annually by the Bibliographic Institute. Since then we have been retroconverting bibliographic descriptions of Polish books published in 1985–1981 (about 50,000 records).

As stated before, at the beginning of the 1980s, NL developed a format called MARC-BN, which is used today by the NL and, in fact, by the predominant majority of Polish libraries. In 1992, academic libraries, which bought the VTLS system, decided to use the USMARC format. They were joined by the NL in this decision. Thus, at present two formats are used in Poland: MARC-BN and USMARC. Probably in the future only one format will be used, namely, USMARC. This will, however, take place no sooner than in several years' time. In the meantime, the NL prepared software for the conversion from MARC-BN to USMARC. In doing this, we were mindful of our own data, but we are also preparing USMARC/MARC-BN conversion software, keeping in mind those libraries in Poland that, for so many years, have used the National Library data and will not switch to USMARC immediately. As a rule, libraries implementing new integrated library systems begin their work in the USMARC format. So far, there are less than 100 such libraries. The USMARC format has been implemented in INNOPAC as well.

Authority files of personal, corporate, and geographical headings and uniform titles represent an important aspect of automated systems. The National Library and other academic libraries are working on this. As regards names headings, both the NL and other academic libraries follow the same principles, but we differ on subject headings. The NL continues to work on its subject headings, which have been used in the national bibliography and the NL catalog for over 50 years.

The next issue that has an impact on effective cooperation is character coding. Polish libraries implementing computer systems, and the NL, use the ISO 6937 standard. Data exchanges among the libraries are done according to the ISO 2709 standard. We thus hope that by using uniform standards we shall be able to effectively cooperate with all libraries, irrespective of the computer systems they use.

References

Przewodnik Bibliograficzny. Urzędowy Wykaz Druków Wydanych w Rzeczypospolitej Polskiej. [Bibliographic Guide. Official List of Printed matter in the Polish Republic]. 1946–. Warsaw: Biblioteka Narodowa. Instytut Bibliograficzny. It is the continuation of *Urzędowy Wykaz Druków [The Official Index of Prints]* published in 1928–39.

Bibliografia Wydawnictw Ciągłych. [Bibliography of Serial Publications], Warsaw: Biblioteka Narodowa, Instytut Bibliograficzny. It has been published since 1958, primarily under the title *Bibliographia Czasopism i Wydawnictw Zbiorowych [Bibliography of Periodicals and Complete Editions].*

Polonica Zagraniczne. Bibliografia [Foreign Polonica. Bibliography]. Warsaw Biblioteka Narodowa. Instytut Bibliograficzny. Published since 1956.

Bibliografia Zawartości Czasopism [Index to Periodicals]. Warsaw: Biblioteka Narodowa. Instytut Bibliograficzny. Published since 1947.

Centralny Katalog Zagranicznych Wydawnictw Ciągłych w Bibliotekach Polskich [Union Catalog of Foreign Serials in Polish Libraries]. Warsaw: Biblioteka Narodowa. Zakład Katalogów Centralnych.

Słownik Języka Haseł Przedmiotowych Biblioteki Narodowej [National Library Subject Headings]. Prep. by Ewa Stępniakowa i Janina Trzcińska, 3rd ed. Warsaw: Biblioteka Narodowa, 1997.

System SABINA. Opis druków zwartych SABINA System [Format for Monographs]. Prep. by Zofia Moszczyńska-Pętkowska. Warsaw: Biblioteka Narodowa, 1982.

System SABINA. Opis wydawnictw ciągłych [SABINA System. Format for Serials]. Prep. by Zofia Moszczyńska-Pętkowska. Warsaw: Biblioteka Narodowa, 1983.

USMARC Format for Authority Data. Prep. by Network Develoment and MARC Standards Office. Washington, DC, 1993.

USMARC Format for Bibliographic Data. Prep by Network Development and MARC Standards Office. Washington, DC, 1994.

USMARC Format for Holding Data. Prep. by Network Development and MARC Standards Office. Washington, DC, 1989.

CHAPTER 9

The Retrospective Conversion of the Catalog in the Library of the American Studies Center, Warsaw University

EWA PALUSZKIEWICZ

The American Studies Center (ASC) at Warsaw University was founded in 1975 as the result of an exchange agreement signed by Warsaw University and Indiana University (in Bloomington). It was one of the first Eastern European centers established for the study of American culture and politics.

The aim of its activities was the promotion of research in American Studies and the overseeing of academic exchanges with several American universities. In 1992, a five-semester M.A. program in American Studies was established in the center. Currently, 400 students are enrolled in it.

The library at the ASC is an integral part of the center, serving research, academic, and educational purposes. Its collection consists of books, journals, magazines, and microforms, all dealing primarily with the United States in areas that include the humanities (mostly literature), history, social sciences, and economics. Since May 1996, when the United States Information Service (USIS) libraries in Warsaw, Kraków, and Poznań were closed, the ASC library has become the largest of its kind in Poland and, indeed, in all of Eastern Europe. It now holds 20,000 volumes of books, including 5,000 that were moved from the former USIS library in Warsaw, and serves the academic community of the Warsaw University as well as other academic institutions in Poland.

The Automation Project for the ASC Library

The automation project for the ASC library was designed in cooperation with library and computer specialists at Indiana University during the ASC' head librarian's visit there in 1991. Both the visit to Indiana University and further purchases of computer hardware and software for the ASC library would not have been possible without generous financial support from the Andrew W. Mellon Foundation.

The project anticipated the creation of the library's on-line catalog, which would be accessible to patrons through the local computer network, and the automation of circulation procedures. The on-line catalog would provide library patrons with new search possibilities.

The first move toward the automation of the library was the selection of an integrated library system. After considering various options, we decided to follow in the steps of Warsaw University's Main Library, which had just selected the Virginia Tech Library System (VTLS), and to purchase Micro-VTLS, a system designed for smaller collections. The center is located far away from the main campus, so it seemed reasonable to get separate software for the center's library and to proceed with the automation project, rather than waiting for the implementation of VTLS in the Main Library and the possibility of joining its network. Another reason for choosing this option was the unique character of the ASC collection, 98 percent of which consists of books written in English and published mostly in the United States.

Knowledge of the English language is a prerequisite for library users; consequently, it was not necessary to translate system commands, help screens, the language of cataloging, or subject headings from English to Polish. This fact has also determined the method of retrospective conversion of the catalog, giving the ATC the opportunity of using the already existing English databases. In-house, full data entry with the use of the OCLC product CAT CD450 has been selected as the best method for the ATC's purposes.

OCLC Services: CAT CD450

CAT CD450 is a microcomputer-based compact disc cataloging system that uses subsets of bibliographical records extended from the OCLC On-line Union Catalog (OLUC) on a compact disc (CD). It allows the user to find bibliographic records needed for cataloging; to edit records derived from a CD; to prepare original records; to export bibliographic records for transfer to a local system; and to print catalog cards and spine labels. Bibliographic records on CD-ROM can be searched by name, title, various publication parameters, ISBN, ISSN, LCCN (Library of Congress control number), subject headings, and other entry points, either by individual fields or in combination using Boolean Logic. OCLC offers the following databases on CD-ROM, which, since June 1996, have been available in a Windows version:

- Recent Books Cataloging Collection,
- Older Books Cataloging Collection (formerly the Older Books and Most-Used Nonbook Collection),
- Law Cataloging Collection,
- Medical Cataloging Collection,
- Music Cataloging Collection,
- Hispanic Cataloging Collection,
- Library of Congress Authorities Collection.

The American Studies Center Library subscribes to the first two databases cited above, thanks to funding provided by the Andrew W. Mellon Foundation and by the United States Information Service, which made a multiyear subscription possible. The Recent Books Cataloging Collection includes the Library of Congress records and OCLC member-input records in the books format, restricted, by an imprint date, to the last six years. The Older Books Cataloging Collection consists of the records for books published since 1900. With the change from DOS to Windows, this collection has been converted to a 100 percent book format; formerly, it was 85 percent books and 15 percent nonbook material. Both of these collections consist of two CDs each, with all files being arranged alphabetically by title and updated semiannually. The change from quarterly to semiannual updates, which occurred with the introduction of the Windows version, was enacted in order to avoid approximately a 98 percent overlap of data. The number of records in the database was also expected to increase considerably. The CAT CD450 is a very versatile and user-friendly system. Its only disadvantage is a rather high cost, which increases each year, bringing the ASC's initial cost of 1,958 GBP in 1994 up to 3,278 GBP by 1996.

Procedures of the Retrospective Conversion for the ASC Collection

At the ASC library, the retrospective conversion of the catalog was conducted in two ways for the ASC collection (which contained proximately 15,000 volumes)—all the bibliographic records were searched on CD-ROMs, edited, and downloaded to the local system; for the former USIS library collection (approximately 5,000 volumes), records in the MARC format were imported from the DataTrek library system (this system had been used in the USIS library) to the local system.

Usually, the card catalog is a primary source for the retrospective conversion. However, several factors made the ASC card catalog an eclectic and sometimes unreliable source of conversion information. Over the past 20 years, ASC books have been cataloged by various catalogers, according to two sets of Polish cataloging rules. Occasionally, new acquisitions were presupplied with sets of cards, printed in the United States, according to the Anglo-American Cataloging Rules. These cards made their way into the library catalog, too. Also, after moving the library to our new location in 1992, we could not be sure if all the books listed in the card catalog could really be found on the shelves. Unfortunately, due to circumstances and the lack of time, it was impossible to check this before starting the retrospective conversion.

Therefore, for a consistent and reliable source of information on the library holdings for retrospective conversion purposes, it was necessary to refer directly to the books on the shelves. The library has open stacks, and books are arranged according to the Dewey Decimal Classification system. They had to be cataloged in a shelf-by-shelf manner, with no more than a hundred books unavailable for patrons at a time. Such an arrangement made it possible to avoid too much chaos in the library, with limited access to books, and made it easier for both patrons and librarians to survive this transformation.

Each of the cataloging collections that was accessed is contained on a 2-CD set, but the cataloger's workstation has only one CD-ROM drive. In order to avoid a continual switching of CDs, books had first to be divided into two groups according to the date of publication (recent versus older books) and then further divided according to whether they would occur on the first or the second CD of the set.

Searching for bibliographic records is usually most effective when done according to the LCCN. On the full-screen display of the record it is necessary to check if the information in the following fields exactly matches what appears in the book:

245—title and subtitle
100—author's name
260—place of publication, name of publisher, date of publication
020—ISBN

Then field 092—for the locally assigned Dewey call number—is added. In the ASC library, the local call number consists of the Dewey Decimal Classification symbol and the first three letters of the author's name or the title of the book. Most of the records in the OCLC databases already include symbols of both the Library of Congress and the Dewey Decimal Classifications. It is not always possible for the cataloger to find a record that exactly matches what is in the book in the library collection, but often a record for a different edition of the book can be found and modified. All editing procedures like copying, moving text, deleting text within a record, or transferring text between records can be very easily done on-screen. When all the necessary revisions have been made, the record is ready for validation. The system checks the MARC structure of the record and verifies that all fields, subfields, indicators, and coded values are valid. Validated records are stored in the local save file, and they are marked as ready to be exported. They can now be loaded into the local system. In the local system, the book's bar code number is added to the appropriate record, along with additional information, such as the copy number, the volume number, or the book's location in the library (for example, reference collection).

At the ASC library, retrospective conversion of 50 bibliographic records takes approximately 6–12 hours, requiring 2–10 minutes to do searching, editing, verification of one record in the CAT CD system; it takes 20 minutes to export the batch of records from the CAT CD system to the Micro-VTLS; and 5 minutes to retrieve a single record in the Micro-VTLS, add the bar code number and additional information, and double-check the record's correctness. The OCLC databases provided us with almost all the bibliographic records necessary for the retrospective conversion. Only for approximately 1 percent of the ASC books were the matching records not found. This does not include publications in Polish, although records for some of them are available in the CAT CD system. So far, retrospective conversion of this part of the collection has been postponed due to the lack of Polish characters in the Micro-VTLS system.

Every book that comes into the library is registered in an inventory book. These huge inventory books, considered by many people to be old-fashioned, turned out to be an excellent tool for keeping track of the retrospective conversion. A copy of a label, with a bar code number, is placed next to the entry for the corresponding book in the inventory. After the main part of the retrospective conversion is finished, this inventory will enable librarians to track books that, for various reasons (they have been checked out, misplaced), have been omitted.

Procedures of the Retrospective Conversion for the USIS Collection

The retrospective conversion of the part of the collection that was transferred from the former USIS library required different procedures. From the entire USIS collection, only 80 percent of it was selected for relocation to the ASC. All the bibliographic records were copied, in the MARC format, from the local system (DataTrek) onto floppy discs and downloaded into the Micro-VTLS. There was not enough time, however, to individually select bibliographic records and carefully compare the records' contents before copying them onto discs. As a result of this, the number of bibliographic records added to the Micro-VTLS was greater than the number of books transferred to the library.

A part-time helper (a student at the Institute of Library and Information Science) joined the ASC librarians in matching every book that came to the library with a proper bibliographic record. Although the transfer of the records from one system to another was an easy operation, several unexpected problems appeared after the librarians took a closer look at the new records. The contents of the records transferred from DataTrek differed from the ones downloaded from the CAT CD450, in terms of punctuation, subfield codes, indicators, and authority control. In consequence, the ASC database turned into a "dirty database." All new records required some modification; certain characters had to be added in order to make the records look consistent when displayed. Some of the corrections—the ones that were easy to spot and didn't require cataloger experience—were promptly made by the student helper. The records for those books that were twin copies of the ones already in the ASC collection were written over the records for the latter. Despite being twin copies the books would not necessarily have identical call numbers, due to an admissible variation in the assigning of the Dewey Decimal Classification symbols in both libraries. It was necessary to determine whether the call number on the book spine matched the one in the catalog. For each volume of a multivolume publication, a separate item ID should be contained in the bibliographic record. Mysteriously, when these records were retrieved in the Micro-VTLS, only the first volume's item ID could be found, and the missing ones had to be reentered.

Improving the accuracy of the bibliographic records demanded extremely close attention. It was also a time-consuming procedure, yet it had to be performed in a hurry in order to have the books available for the anxiously waiting library patrons. Books that entered the ASC collection were marked on the printout of the shelf list from the USIS library. This list leaves out all the books that were not transferred and will help determine the records to be deleted.

Catalogs in the ASC Library

The CAT CD system provides an option for producing catalog cards but it requires a specific kind of card (with the American format), different from the ones that were available in Poland. For some time, new acquisitions were cataloged in the traditional way (cards were typed and printed out on an electronic typewriter) as well as in the on-line catalog. Cards were added to both the alphabetical catalog and the so-called subject catalog, which in fact was, rather, a shelf list. It was, however, a time-consuming procedure, and in 1996 the card catalog was closed and replaced by the on-line catalog accessible through three computer terminals. In the past, the computer catalog contained insufficient data for library patrons to conduct searches. At this point, the local data base contained enough records to make the use of it more effective than confusing. Only cards for publications in Polish are still being added to the card catalog.

118 *Case Histories*

Cost of the Retrospective Conversion

The following is the total breakdown of expenses that had to be covered in the 3-year period of the carrying out of the retrospective conversion of the ASC catalog:

Hardware (a minimal configuration)	
1 file server	$ 2,050.00
1 cataloger workstation	$ 1,290.00
1 OPAC terminal	$ 630.00
Total	$ 3,970.00
Software	
Micro-VTLS (license, installation, maintenance fee)	$ 17,085.00
OCLC databases	$ 4,862.00
Total	$ 21,947.00

Labor cost: $ 2.40 per hour

The total cost per record depended on the time required for searching, editing, and verifying a single bibliographic record in the CAT CD system. That time ranged from 2 to 10 minutes (as noted earlier). Consequently, the cost of one record ranged from $ 0.61 to $0.90. This calculation was based on the software (only OCLC databases) and labor expenses necessary for the conversion of 15,000 records.

Conclusions

It took 3 years to carry out the retrospective conversion of the catalog in the American Studies Center. It probably could have been done in less time, had the circumstances been different. When the whole process was started in 1994, there were only 2 librarians working at the ASC, and, except for the summer break, the library was open to the public all year. Consequently, only one librarian was assigned to carry out the retrospective conversion, with occasional help from the other librarian. In the following years, two more people joined the library staff, but the library kept expanding and the number of users increased, so the situation improved only slightly. Unexpected problems with the local system were another obstacle. Then, when the librarian responsible for doing the retrospective conversion quit in 1996, training for the person who replaced her also temporarily slowed down the work.

Although it may seem that the retrospective conversion, as it was carried out at the ASC library, was expensive, one has to be aware of the unquestionable advantages of this method. It is far less time consuming to transfer the bibliographic records from CD-ROM than to do the original cataloging. Records derived from CD-ROM already contain subject headings (which again saves an enormous amount of the cataloger's time) and names are consistent with the authority files.

By June 1997, most of the work in the retrospective conversion had been completed. Library patrons now have access to the on-line catalog, which provides them with new search options (title, subject, word). The librarians are concentrating on identifying and cataloging books that were omitted, and on correcting inconsistencies in the bibliographic records. They are also working on creating the patrons' database in order to utilize the Micro-VTLS circulation module. Fully automated check-out and check-in were expected to be introduced at the beginning of the 1997–1998 academic year, to the great relief of librarians and library patrons alike.

References

Grudziewska, Elżbieta. "Retrokonwersja katalogów w Bibliotece Ośrodka Studiów Amerikańskych" [Retroconversion of Catalogs at the American Studies Library] *Przegląd Biblioteczny* 64, no. 4 (1996), 337–345.

Nakamure, Margaret. "Retrospective Conversion Using a Combination of Choices. A Case Study of the Hawaii School Library Network Project," *School Library Media Quarterly* (Fall 1991), 24–29.

Ogonowska, Anna. "Retrokonwersja katalogów bibliotecznych" [Retroconversion of Library Catalogs] *Przegląd Biblioteczny* 64, no. 4 (1996), 265–279.

Sadowska, Jadwiga. "Retrokonwersja zbiorów bibliotecznych w Polsce. Stan prac, potrzeby I zamierzenia" [Retroconversion of Library Collections in Poland] *Zagadnienia Informacji Naukowej* 2 (68), (1996), 3–10.

CHAPTER 10

CASLIN, Priorities of the Czech National Library, and Government Policy on Information and Libraries

VOJTĚCH BALÍK

Goals and Achievements

The aims of the Czech and Slovak Library Information Network (CASLIN) project were to connect Czech and Slovak libraries of any type and size to each other, so that they could share the Union Catalog, coordinate their acquisitions or substantially improve loan services, and to guarantee that any user, no matter where he is located, is at once able to communicate with the Union Catalog on-line. The participants undertook (as quoted from the "Statement of Intent," the launching document of the CASLIN project) "to lay a solid foundation of a nationwide library network providing both home and foreign users with easy, fast, and unrestricted access to the information stored in or mediated by the libraries and information centers."

The structure of the network was intended as a bipolar (corresponding to the Czech Republic and Slovakia), yet symmetrical, integrated, and cooperative system based on shared cataloguing, and with two national centers and two union catalogs, and a corresponding network of satellite libraries on each side. The goal was to build the core of an open network, which any library in both countries and abroad could join and, thereby, make its information services available to everybody. This, of course, also meant an adherence to international standards.[1]

The project's first initiative came from The Andrew W. Mellon Foundation, which showed an interest in increasing the level of library services in the former Czechoslovakia. Between 1990 and 1991, American specialists explored the state of library cooperation at the time and, in October 1991, the representatives of the Foundation in New York informed the directors of the four largest Czech and Slovak libraries of

---

1. The Czech and Slovak Library Information network initially involved the following four libraries: the National Library in Prague, the Moravian Scientific Library in Brno, the Slovak National Library in Martin and the University Library in Bratislava. See also *Statement of Intent* at http://www.nkp.cz/caslin/.

their intention to support a project of library cooperation.[2] An earlier agreement,[3] among the four library directors, to join efforts and to cooperate in solving major questions of library development, led, in November 1991, to a second agreement that laid the foundation for a national library network as expressed in the signed "Statement of Intent."

Then, in March 1992, the abovementioned American specialists organized a seminar in Prague to promote the role of the Czech National Library and of libraries in general, and to encourage the concept of library cooperation among the representatives of both government ministries and the Parliament.

The CASLIN project was prepared, and was then presented to The Andrew W. Mellon Foundation, along with a request for funding, in June 1992. Meanwhile, a decision was made at the government level (effective from January 1, 1993) to split the Czechoslovak Federation into two independent republics, so that, by default, the CASLIN project became an international one. In December 1992 the Mellon Foundation's Board of Trustees approved a 1.1 million grant. This amount would make it possible to purchase the necessary components (both library automation software and the main parts of the hardware) for the four libraries involved. In January 1993 the Aleph system (created by ExLibris, of Israel) was selected—as a result of a tender sent to eight system vendors—since the ExLibris system proved to best comply with the consortium's requirements. A few months later a $200,000 grant from the Pew Charitable Trusts (Philadelphia) was approved to help with the training and the educational aspects of the CASLIN project. Early in the spring of 1993, the Digital Equipment Corporation was selected as the hardware supplier, and in May 1993 the agreements for the project's implementation with ExLibris were signed; with that the projected three-year period for the project's implementation commenced.[4]

---

2. See *Ročenka Národní knihovny v Praze* [Annual Report of the National Library in Prague], 1989–1991.

3. See e.g., Vojtěch Balík, Jaromír Kubíček, "Rada ředitelů hlavních knihoven ČSFR: česko-slovenská spolupráce v knihovnictví" [The board of directors of central libraries of the CSFR: Czech-Slovak cooperation in library sector], *Národní knihovna* 2 (1991), 2, pp. 90–93.

4. See e.g., Adolf Knoll, "Američtí experti v Národní knihovně v Praze" [American experts in the National Library in Prague], *Národní knihovna* 2 (1991), pp. 94–96; *CASLIN (Czech And Slovak Library Information Network): automation and preservation project proposal presented to The Andrew W. Mellon Foundation and The Pew Charitable Trusts*/documentation prep. by members of the CASLIN Group; submitted in their behalf by Andrew Lass, Mount Holyoke: Mount Holyoke College, 1992; *Výroční zpráva Národní knihovny v Praze* [Annual Report of the National Library in Prague], 1992; 1993. English summaries; "Jednání o novém knihovnickém informačním systému" [Negotiations about a new library information system], *Národní knihovna* 3 (1992), 5, pp. 214–215; "CASLIN," *Národní knihovna* 4, 2 (1993), pp. 102–104; *CASLIN: Czech and Slovak Library Information Network: Česká a slovenská knihovní informačnís ít': vznik, principy a předpoklady realizace* [CASLIN—origin, principles, and prerequisites of realisation], Prague: Národní knihovna, 1993; Martin Svoboda, "CASLIN—Česká a slovenská knihovní informační sít'" [CASLIN: Czech and Slovak Library Information Network], *I'93*, 35 (6), 1993, pp. 150–161; Martin Svoboda, "CASLIN—Česká a slovenská knihovní informační sít'" [CASLIN: Czech and Slovak Library Information Network], *Automatizace knihovnických proces IV.—Ústí nad Labem:* Dům techniky, 1993, pp. 12–26; *CASLIN: Czech and Slovak Library Information Network: 1993 status report*, Prague: Národní knihovna, 1994, 6 pp.; Martin Svoboda, "CASLIN: A project for library cooperation," *Library*

Since then, a number of key goals have been attained and several important decisions that were made have resulted in rules that are binding for all participants.[5]

- The Aleph system is now running on Digital Alpha servers. It is fully localized, so that at least the core data processing flow is now working on a routine basis in each of the four libraries.
- The local catalogues in the four libraries are being continuously filled with records coming from three main resources: machine-readable records from already existing automated data pools; records resulting from the cataloging process for new accessions; and records resulting from the retrospective conversion process.
- A decision was made to introduce, and firmly adhere to, international cataloging rules, recommendations, and standards. UNIMARC was chosen as the standard exchange format, and AACR2 (*Anglo-American Cataloging Rules*, 2d edition) as the cataloging standard; ISBD (International Bibliographic Standard Description) recommendations were adopted together with the LCSHs (Library of Congress subject headings) as the leading principles of subject cataloging. Finally, UDC (Universal Decimal Classification—Master Reference File) *Hague Consortium* was adopted as the subject indexing code (available on CD-ROM).[6]
- CASLIN union catalogs are being developed in both countries. So far, in the case of the Czech CASLIN Union Catalog, run by the National Library, fifteen libraries have joined the agreement on sharing data with the Union Catalog. They are all ready to meet the National Library's data structure recommendations, that is, the obligatory minimal-records format. [7]

Technology News (13) Jun/Jul 94, pp. 5–7; Martin Svoboda. "CASLIN v roce nula" [CASLIN in the year zero], *I'94*, 36 (6), 1994, pp. 152–154; "*CASLIN 1994*", *I'94*, 36, 12 (1994), insert. 4/1994; *Automatizace našich knihoven na postupu* [Progress of the automation of Czech libraries] [report from the seminar], *I'94*. 36 (2), 1994, pp. 50–51; Daniela Slížová, Igor Prokop, "Koncepčné otázky a hlavné problémy informatizácie v Matici Slovenskej" [The concept and major issues of the Slovak Library automation programme], *Knižnice a informácie*. 26 (10), 1994, pp. 412–416; Martin Svoboda, "CASLIN: souborný katalog či něco víc?" [CASLIN—union catalogue or something more?], *Infocus*, 1, 5 (1995), pp. 136–138; Iva Přibramská, *Automatizovaný knihovnický systém ALEPH* [Automated library system Aleph], *Národní knihovna*, 6 (1995), 6, pp. 211–212, Dušan Katušťák, "New developments in librarianship and bibliographic control in Slovakia", *International Cataloguing and Bibliographic Control*, 25 (1), Jan/Mar 96, pp. 16–18. Also see http://www.nkp.cz/caslin/.

5. For general survey of events, decisions, and achievements see e.g., Martin Svoboda, "Stručný projekt automatizace NK pro rok 1994" [A brief project of automation in the National Library in 1994], *Informační bulletin Národní knihovny*, (1994), 4, pp. 19–23; *Výroční zpráva Národní knihovny ČR* [Annual Report of the National Library of the Czech Republic], 1994; 1995. English summaries; Vojtěch Balík, "Zhodnocení projektu CASLIN a výhledy" [CASLIN Project—assessment of the realisation and outlook for the future], *Knihovny současnosti '95*, Brno: Sdružení knihoven ČR, 1995, pp. 34–44; Martin Svoboda, "CASLIN: from project to consortium." Paper presented at the International Conference on Library Automation in Central and Eastern Europe, Budapest, Hungary, April 10–13, 1996; see also http://www.nkp.cz/caslin/.

6. See e.g., Bohdana Stoklasová, "Od ISISu k ALEPHu aneb Od Výměnného formátu k UNIMARCu" [From ISIS to ALEPH or from Czech-Slovak Exchange Format to UNIMARC], *Informační bulletin Národní knihovny* (1994), 4, pp. 9–18, English summary. Bohdana Stoklasová, *International cataloging standards: Their implementation in Czech libraries*, Prague: Národní knihovna ČR 1995, 39 pp.

7. See Gabriela K Krčmařová, "Souborný katalog CASLIN" [CASLIN uniuon catalog], DUHA: *informace o knihách a knihovnách z Moravy*, 11 (Summer 1997), 2, pp. 3–7. See also http://www.nkp.cz/caslin/

- Both the Czech and Slovak national bibliographies contain data recorded in UNIMARC. In addition to the traditional printed format, they are now available in both countries on CD-ROM as well as on websites. The Czech National Bibliography operates within a standard framework identical with that of CASLIN, for example, UNIMARC, AACR2, ISBD, and LCSH's, Czech version.[8] More recently, the 1996 Czech National Bibliography's records set has also been downloaded into the Online Computer Library Center (OCLC) WorldCat, as a result of a collaboration agreed upon in 1995. The Czech National Library served as a testing site for the OCLC UNIMARC>USMARC conversion program development.
- A special CASLIN program in micrographic preservation has been launched with the aim of joining the international micrographic programs (European Register of Microform Masters—EROMM). [9]
- The CASLIN system's training program has been successfully completed and several special management seminars were held.[10]

Management, Procedure, Institutional Form

The form of cooperation established by CASLIN members, for example, cooperation between the abovementioned four libraries, was that of a consortium bound de facto by the agreement on a shared realization of the project as financed by The Andrew W. Mellon Foundation and the Pew Charitable Trusts. This involved three kinds of ties and responsibilities:

1. The "Statement of Intent," for example, is an agreement binding all of them to each other;
2. An obligation of the four-member group toward the two foundations—the expenditure of the awarded funds was bound by the terms of the project as approved by the donors;
3. Contractual obligations between each of the four members and the primary vendor (the Ex Libris Co.), even though in the vendor agreement, CASLIN is treated as a single organizational body.

The mechanism of decision-making within CASLIN developed gradually. The "Statement of Intent" itself addresses this issue only to the extent that it emphasizes a fair selection of the system, the obligation of the members both to proceed jointly in

---

8. See http://www.nkp.cz
9. Jiří Polišenský, "CASLIN—pracovní skupina pro ochranné mikrofilmování" [CASLIN—working group on protective microfilming], *Národní knihovna*, 7 (1996), 6, pp. 212–214; *Výroční zpráva Národní knihovny ČR* [Annual Reports of the National Library of the Czech Republic], 1993; 1994; 1995; 1996. English summaries.
10. See *CASLIN '93: Management training: sborník příspěvků ze semináře: Rožnov pod Radhoštěm, Czech Republic 5.-9.9.1993* [proceedings of the seminar], edited by Jaromír Kubíček, Brno: Státní vědecká knihovna, 1993, 58 p; *CASLIN '94: Management training II: zborník príspevkov zo seminára: Liptovský Ján, Slovakia 19.-23.6.1994* [Proceedings of the seminar], Martin: Slovenská národná, knižnica, 1996, 94 pp.; *CASLIN '95 Seminar Proceedings: [Consortia]: Smolenice, Slovakia 27.-31.8.1995*, Bratislava: University Library, 1995; *CASLIN '97: Libraries of the Future: Dlouhé Stráně, Czech Republic 8.-12.6.1997*, Brno: MOLIN, 1997. 136 pp.

all matters and to establish a library association with the objective of coordinating the joint use of the network.

Initially, in 1992-93, the four-member CASLIN board of library directors was the final, decision-making body. An eight-member Advisory Expert Group, consisting of project managers and system librarians from each library, had, as its main objective, the selection of the system that best complied with the requirements of the project. In January 1993, after the board of directors approved a system recommended by the expert group, the activities of the latter body were expected to increase immensely in volume and content, and, therefore, the structure of the project's management changed accordingly. A new, larger board of directors and managers was established to collectively discuss and make decisions in all matters. In addition, special expert working groups were established to inquire into different aspects of both the implementation of the system and the realization of the project itself and to recommend proper solutions.

Good progress in the original CASLIN project led The Mellon Foundation to lend its support to other projects of cooperation in automated networks (under the general title of CASLIN+). As had already been agreed upon, and in adhering to the principles and rules of CASLIN, the CASLIN board and working groups were opened up to representatives and experts from the new projects so that cooperation became much more extensive. The additional projects include LINCA (Library Information Network of the Czech Academy of Sciences),[11] MOLIN (MOravian Library Information Network),[12] KOLIN (KOšice Library Information Network)[13] and, finally, RETROCON, a retrospective conversion project of the Czech National Library.[14]

More recently, there has been a growing general interest, among a wider group of libraries, in cooperation and in joining CASLIN. After the initial, four-member CASLIN period came to an official close (the awarded funds had been spent), representatives of more than twenty libraries met in mid-1996 to declare their wish to cooperate in the spirit of principles and rules laid out by CASLIN. An attempt followed to prepare a common project for broad library cooperation in automated networks.[15]

---

11. See e.g., Anežka Bad'urová, Antonín Vítek, Ivana Kadlecová, Jan Hartman, "Knihovna Akademie věd České republiky na cestě do CASLIN Plus" [The Library of the Academy of Sciences of the Czech Republic works towards joining CASLIN Plus], *I '94*, 36 (12), 1994, pp. 306-308; Jan Hartman, "LINCA— projekt automatizace Knihovny AV ČR" [LINCA—project of automation in the Library of the Academy of Sciences of the Czech Republic], *Národní knihovna*, 6 (1995), 3, pp. 113-115; *LINCA-INFO* [bulletin], Prague, Knihovna Akademie věd ČR, 1995; see also http://www.nkp.cz/caslin/.

12. See e.g., Marie Nádvorníková, "MOLIN—záměry a realizace" [MOLIN – purpose and realisation], *Infocus*, 1, 2 (1995), p. 34-36; "Grant projektu MOLIN" [The MOLIN Project awarded with a grant], *I '96*, 38, 6 (1996), p. 162-164; see also http://www.ics.muni.cz.

13. See http://www2.tuke.sk/tu/library/kolin-e.html.

14. See e.g. Bohdana Stoklasová, Miroslav Bareš, *Restrospective Conversion in Czech Libraries*, Prague: Národní knihovna ČR, 1995, 39 p; *Výroční zpráva Národní knihovny ČR* [Annual Report of the National Library of the Czech Republic], 1996, English summaries; Bohdana Stoklasová, "Retrospektivní konverze katalogů Národní knihovny České republiky" [Retrospective conversion of catalogs at the National Library of the Czech Republic], *Národní knihovna*, 8 (1997), 3, p. 111-116.

15. See e.g. "Jednání o CASLIN 2" [CASLIN 2 meeting], *Národní knihovna*, 7 (1996), 4, p. 116-118; Gabriela Krčmařová, "Souborný katalog CASLIN – katalog České virtuální knihovny" [CASLIN Union

While CASLIN has the potential of becoming a really open network for all those who accept its principles and goals, it is presently understood in terms of the following:

- goals set out by the "Statement of Intent" of the four directors in 1991;
- principles and rules, whether provided by the "Statement of Intent" or agreed upon during the subsequent implementation process;
- tools, for example, rules of procedure, standards, and technology; and
- individual projects as ways of realizing the principles and goals of CASLIN.

In fact, there is no institution or body bearing the name CASLIN at the present time. The 1996 agreement between the Slovak and the Czech national libraries that stipulates the ground rules for cooperation in developing the CASLIN union catalogs, or the agreement between the Czech National Library and a number of other libraries on sharing data with the Czech Union Catalog, as well as some other agreements, should be seen as isolated cases.

Indeed, there is something missing that would help the existing, but rather idealized and abstract reality of CASLIN turn into a reality more visible, material, and enduring. It could be the following:

- the codification and definition of CASLIN as a system of principles, goals, standards, and tools;
- an association as a formally established group of bodies adhering to, cooperating within, and realizing the CASLIN project; or
- the adoption of a project as a general model of network cooperation to be achieved, including the planning of all the required steps, such as a financial analysis, as well as the time schedule. [16]

The reason for the lack of institutional form and representation in the CASLIN project may be found in the rather low degree of willingness of the institutions involved to enter into any bond when it is not necessary for some very specified and visible goal. It is true to say that the whole idea of the CASLIN project has been perceived with ambivalence. Some tended to understand it as a name for a very practical project which was tied to a grant awarded in order to procure the software and hardware for some of the Czech and Slovak libraries and enabling a mutual linkup. Others took it as a more general program for the transformation and improvement of the whole concept and mission of libraries in the two countries. Different attitudes of this kind—for example, the more pragmatic versus the more political—influenced the management and decision-making processes in the CASLIN group. The group did succeed in agreeing on a common system, as well as on standards—for example, on international standards that would become obligatory for those cooperating within the CASLIN network—because such unification proved to be the necessary precon-

---

Catalog – catalog of the Czech virtual library], *Automatizace knihovnických systémů 1996*, Prague, SKIP, 1996, p. 21–29.

16. See e.g. Vojtěch Balík, "Projekt CASLIN", *DUHA: informace o knihách a knihovnách z Moravy*, 11 (léto 1997), 2, p. 2–3; Gabriela Krčmařová, *Projekt CASLIN dnes* [CASLIN Project today], http://www.nkp.cz/caslin/.

dition for the proper functioning of the network. On the other hand, members of the CASLIN group failed to agree on the establishing of an institutional form of cooperation of any kind. So, the shared system and standards became the only common basis and bond for the four CASLIN libraries, apart from the three kinds of ad hoc bonds and obligations mentioned above. In general, libraries are yet to be fully convinced of any benefit that would stem from cooperation based on some more general and strategic goals and principles and, therefore, they do not feel the need to join associations or consortia of this kind. Instead, a library prefers to focus on its own benefits, which seem more easily attainable by way of individual steps than through cooperation, common projects, and policies with long-term effects. To some extent, such an approach can be considered realistic, especially if one considers the environment within which libraries are trying to develop.

CASLIN and State Information Policy

To understand the environment that the CASLIN project entered into, a brief introduction to the general background and current picture of the cooperation of Czech libraries may be useful.

The library sector of the former Czechoslovakia is going through a period of transition from a system based on central regulation to a new, integrated, and cooperative system. Since the current situation is still frequently changing, it is not easy to provide a clear general picture of the situation.

In the period of so-called First Czechoslovak Republic (1918–1939), the decentralized British and American public library system became the model for the first Library Law of 1919, which obliged all municipalities to provide for their local public libraries, so that they could ensure open access for the public-at-large. In addition, the number of various university, special, and technical libraries, as well as of documentation centers, grew at that time.

During the socialist period (1948–1989), an extensive institutional library and information infrastructure was built. Two, mutually connected systems (so-called networks) were decreed by law.

First, the so-called Unified Library System was, according to the second Library Law (1959), designed to include all libraries but actually the public libraries were predominantly represented in it. The socialist regime adopted the principle of guaranteeing the existence of the local and municipal libraries that were operated in the previous political period, while also demanding that public libraries play a political and ideological role in educating the population.

The second system, the so-called Czechoslovak System of Scientific, Technical, and Economic Information, comprised a hierarchically organized structure including thousands of document centers that provided the fields of science, technology, and industry with specialized information.

Neither of the systems represented a truly cooperative network, since neither on-line interlibrary communication nor shared universal union catalogs were in place. However, there were a few good examples of library cooperation; for example, the *National Register of Foreign Books* (i.e., a union card catalog) was developed at the former State (now National) Library in Prague. A similar catalog of foreign periodicals was located in Bratislava. The international interlibrary loan services, or access to foreign databases, despite being available only from one center, also deserve mention. There were also several good examples of library coordination within regional frameworks.

The political changes of 1989, when the radical democratic transformation took place, had obvious consequences for thinking about the role and place of libraries and information services in the newly emerging democracy. A proposal for a revised library law immediately arose out of mutual discussions but the library community appeared to be divided along substantive lines on its main principles. Meanwhile, the government's politically conservative tendency, which worked against any state regulation, resulted in an indifferent approach to efforts, wherever they were undertaken, at establishing mechanisms for coordination and cooperation among libraries. Until recently, the key political players have remained unconvinced either about the fundamental role that libraries play in society and of their assistance in education policy and social development, or about the economic benefits of efficient interlibrary coordination.

As a consequence, the mechanism of library funding remains unsettled and will most likely continue to change for some time. At present, the library system that is publicly funded could be described as follows.

In addition to the National Library, the Ministry of Culture is directly responsible for the funding of nine regional state research libraries. In the past these libraries played a coordinating role for district and municipal libraries within their own administrative region (actually a large territory comprising several districts). Another part of their mission was to direct their library services to more special audiences including the academic community located in the region. Since the former regional division of the country is no longer valid and the future redistricting (with its administrative responsibilities) is not yet in place, the nature of the future budgetary and administrative oversight is not clear at present. In any case, oversight possibilities and methods are being considered to enable regional universities as well as scientific institutions to use the library services provided by the state research libraries in a more effective way.

So-called district libraries come under the administrative oversight of each district. Those libraries are, one by one, being taken over by the municipal governments and as a result, their prevailing tendency is to no longer support broader-based, rather than locally focused, library activities. As a result, library coordinating and cooperative systems that were formerly active within some regions for many years are disintegrating. In addition, the number of municipal and local libraries has declined steadily over the past few years.

The Ministry of Culture has lost its direct administrative authority over district and municipal libraries and so it tries to use indirect efforts to control their development, mostly through its ministerial recommendations addressed to local authorities.

Meanwhile, and as a consequence of the development of the private sector, the whole structure and the content of the need for information by organizations and companies have fundamentally changed. The System of Scientific, Technical, and Economic Information, mentioned above, has been entirely dissolved as thousands of information centers have changed their profile. Many of them have closed down, while some have been absorbed into technical libraries and a number of them have transformed themselves into commercial organizations.

There are also areas where the level of demand for scientific information has continued to grow, while these areas are retaining almost the same organizational structure. Good examples of these are the areas of public health and medicine, covered by the National Library of Medicine, which coordinates special bibliographical services. Another is the area of agriculture, with its Central Library of Agriculture and Forestry and an extensive network of information centers. And finally, there are the many scientific-research activities located at universities or at the Academy of Sciences.

There is a great difference between the situation of libraries providing for the information needs of universities in the Czech Republic and that of standard university libraries elsewhere. Since almost no true campus-type universities were built in the Czech Republic, and certainly none after World War II, there are consequently almost no central university libraries there. Nearly all of the universities depend on their information needs being fulfilled either by the faculty libraries of the individual schools or by the state research libraries of the respective town or region in which a university is located. As a result, the large number of independently operated faculty libraries, together with the small departmental libraries, do not represent a single cooperating system when, in fact, their collective holdings, if made accessible, could be quite helpful to the educational and research purposes of the schools. But, for the most part, libraries face space and technical problems as well as a shortage of personnel. Nevertheless, both university and ministerial authorities are now aware of these different issue and appropriate legislative as well as financial solutions are gradually being prepared.

Although the government in 1992 approved a document addressing the development of a public information services policy, the role of libraries occupies but a marginal place in it. Subsequently, a law regulating the state information system was passed. This law presupposes an extensive and systematically conceived infrastructure that will consist of specialized information centers run by the state administration (and not by libraries), with the aim of coordinating the production of predominantly administrative and economic information.

Presently, there is still no governmental project designed to formulate an information policy in the Czech Republic. Plans to meet the needs and requirements of a future information society are not part of any current political programs, nor are such plans in any overarching, government-funded project, be it for the improvement of the communications infrastructure or for the development of library and information services. The manner in which library institutions are funded—and the daily problems that this gives rise to—only reflects this lack of policy. Following the general political trend to cut public fund expenditures, primarily in the nonprofit sector, the government and those responsible for library funding, respectively, tend to focus only on the economic aspects of running libraries and look to short-term results that can be attained mostly by means of budgetary cuts. A strategy for any long-term savings that could be achieved from library cooperation is missing. As a result, the government's overall library budget is not being effectively allocated. Furthermore, no library governing mechanism—such as a board of trustees—has been put in place to assist the director in decision-making. Instead, all strategic decisions regarding future goals, such as they are, rest entirely with the library director, who alone has to convince the funding administration of their importance.

In such an environment, the ideas and principles of the CASLIN project that emphasize library cooperation were not met by real appreciation or enough interest, nor by matching moves on the part of the government administration, for quite a long time. The CASLIN project was simply taken as yet another case of support coming from abroad for a few domestic libraries who had come up with this initiative on their own. If anything, the ideas that it promoted were simply taken as the conditions of the grant that had to be met in order to receive the funds. In effect, the government administration, at least in the first phase of the CASLIN project's implementation, remained rather closed to any change in their attitude toward the principles of library cooperation.

Promoting the important role that libraries and the whole information sector play in social development still rests with libraries themselves. Nothing but actual progress in library cooperation, if possible, appears to be convincing enough to change the attitude of politicians as well as of the public toward these institutions. This was also the case with the CASLIN project: The successful progress of its implementation, and the information activities and public-relations efforts that were integral parts of the project, gradually brought it recognition.

Today CASLIN, with its principles, goals, and standards, has become a model of library cooperation. As a result:

- CASLIN, as a model of library cooperation, has been incorporated into the legal statutes of the National Library of the Czech Republic.
- A matching fund, to meet the challenge of the grant from The Andrew W. Mellon Foundation, was awarded to the Czech CASLIN members by the Czech Ministry of Culture in 1995. This made it possible to fulfill the planned, as well as additional, hardware and software needs.
- The Ministry of Culture provided funds to cover a group internet-access license for the project's first two years (1995–1996) to the ten libraries that come under its purview.
- The CASLIN principles and its current achievements have served as models for a program initiated by the Ministry of Culture to support the development of a library network: The program for the development of libraries in the context of the development of information superhighways was first submitted to the Czech government in 1995; but it failed to gain support and therefore failed to pass. [17] The same thing happened to the second version of the program, called "information services of libraries in a networked environment," in the following year. Finally, at the end of 1996 a similar initiative of the Parliament was successful in promoting the program of the development of an infor-

---

17. The original Czech title is: *Program rozvoje knihoven jako součást rozvoje informačních dálnic ČR;* see e.g.: Jaroslav Císař, Eva Sedláková, "Program rozvoje informačních dálnic České republiky" [Program of the development of information superhighways in the Czech Republic], *Infocus*, 1, 6/7 (1995), pp. 167–168.

mation network of public libraries.[18] The 1997 funding was administered by the Ministry of Culture and assigned to those projects that aim at contributing to the development of the library network and to common data resources, provided they generally comply with the main principles and standards of CASLIN (some of the projects were mentioned above). The problem is that the funding for the programs sponsored by the ministry, as mentioned above, is allocated only on a yearly basis. It is important to introduce a long-term funding scheme so that the CASLIN programs can be continued.
- Finally, some financial resources have been made available from other ministerial programs supporting education and research, with some of them having been earmarked for library cooperation projects. This has made it possible to pursue the goals of CASLIN through additional special projects.

CASLIN and the Czech National Library

The National Library has been involved with automation for quite some time. Nevertheless, due to a lack of capital, the necessary hardware and software were for years unavailable. For this reason, most of the library's attention was focused on analysis, planning, standards, learning from the experiences of others, education, and training. For this reason, too, the core members of the library staff were in a position to master complex integrated systems, which, considering the circumstances, were the most productive ways of using these resources.

Prior to the CASLIN period, the Czech National Library focused its R&D in automation on a number of cooperative initiatives and on the development of effective tools for such cooperation. For one, the so-called Czech-Slovak exchange format was a common exchange format developed in late 1980s and agreed upon for two national projects prepared by the national libraries. MAKS (Modular Automated Library System) on the Czech side and IKIS (Integrated Library Information System) on the Slovak side were both based on CDS/ISIS. Though not exactly UNIMARC, it was, nevertheless, rigorously grounded in ISBD so that its conversion to the UNIMARC format, which would be undertaken some years later, proved to be relatively easy. This exchange format was, and still is, widely used by hundreds of Czech and Slovak libraries that work with CDS/ISIS. It has also been adopted as an exchange format for most of the locally developed software packages.[19]

---

18. See *Program rozvoje informační sítě veřejných knihoven*; for information on projects submitted see list of projects and grantees at http://www.nkp.cz/caslin/.

19. See e.g., Ivana Geltnerová, "Informace o spolupráci knihoven v oblasti automatizace" [Information on the cooperation of libraries in automation], *Národní knihovna*, 2 (1991), 4, pp. 231-233; Martin Svoboda, "Československá knihovní síť': stav a výhledy" [Czechoslovak library network: state of the art and outlook for the future], *INFOS '92*, 22. Information Science seminar, Bratislava: Alfa, 1992.; Martin Svoboda, "Koncepční hlediska automatizace knihoven" [Conceptual issues of the library automation], *Automatizace knihovnických systém*, Prague, SKIP, 1992, pp. 10–15; *Ročenka Národní knihovny v Praze* [Annual Report of the National Library in Prague], 1989–1991; *Výroční zpráva Národní knihovny v Praze* [Annual Report of the National Library in Prague], 1992; 1993, English summaries; *MAKS – Modulární automatizovaný knihovnický systém* [MAKS – modular automated library system], Prague, SK ČSR, 1989, 7 vol.

The National Library has for a long time been aware of its singular responsibility for the various tasks resulting from the IFLA core programs, UAP and UBC-IM. The library's decision to move away from the Czech and Slovak exchange format only a couple of years after its introduction was, therefore, only a logical step. The adherence to internationally accepted standards and recommendations, in spite of their low appeal to smaller libraries, is considered a top priority. Such an attitude is naturally in congruence with that of CASLIN since the Czech National Library (as well as the Slovak National Library) is charged with being the national center and seat of the CASLIN Union Catalog.

Apart from the problems surrounding the implementation of the new integrated system, the process of implementing the CASLIN project—including the acceptance of new standards—also faced problems. For quite a long time, parts of the staff of the National Library thought of CASLIN more as a political program having little to do with solving internal needs and problems of the library. They preferred to focus their efforts on the latter especially when, by the beginning of the 1990s and after decades of neglect, the core functions and services of the library were on the verge of collapsing and a recovery and transformation of the institution were of critical importance. The management of the library had to face a very complex problem as it tried, at one and the same time, to work on interlibrary cooperation; introduce a new integrated system; and resolve a number of very elementary issues such as the critical lack of storage space, the bad condition of the majority of collections, the low quality of public services, and the staff's insufficient qualifications. The process of changing people's working habits, as well as the requirements for new skills and qualifications, was altogether quite taxing, and the appearance of contradictory opinions and misunderstandings inevitable. In addition, there is at times a slightly negative, perhaps subconscious, attitude toward foreign influences in the Czech Republic and that includes the National Library as well. Some members of the staff may have viewed the CASLIN project, with its principles and international standards, as something strange, coming from the outside, and not complying with domestic habits, traditions, and the language. All this together created a complex of obstacles of various kinds inside the library, while delays and complicated misunderstandings on the part of the system vendor only added to this situation and made the atmosphere even worse. In order to manage it, it was necessary for the libraries to develop their own programs for training and improved intralibrary public relations, which were based upon the CASLIN management seminars organized for CASLIN group members.

There was also a pressing need to change and improve both the organizational structure and the system of responsibilities at the National Library. For example, soon after the CASLIN project had been launched, it became apparent to all libraries involved that the special duties and the working agenda of the system librarian needed to be defined. At the Czech National Library, after the system librarian was appointed, a special department was established for this purpose, initially as part of the Department of Library Automation as it existed at the time. Later on this division was turned into a separate Department of Library Systems.

The same holds for cataloging standards. The application of new international cataloging standards had originally been considered a matter of library automation as well. Only later on was this activity moved to the Division of Cataloging and National Bibliography, where it truly belongs.

As a model of library cooperation, CASLIN was given legal standing when it was included in the 1995 statutes of the National Library. The wording for this is as follows: "[the National Library is] the national center of CASLIN (Czech and Slovak Library Information Network) and the coordinating body for the uniform application of its respective standards and norms."[20]

A special department in the National Library was established (once again, by detaching its functions from the Department of Automation), with the task of coordinating the realization of the CASLIN project on the Czech side, while also maintaining contacts with the Slovak part of the project. The department functioned for the rest of the initial CASLIN time period (as covered by the Mellon grant) and for some time thereafter. More recently, specific departments at the National Library have absorbed its remaining duties (for example, those of the system librarian, the Department of Automation, or the Union Catalog) and the CASLIN department was closed.

Finally, a new Union Catalog Department has developed out of the abovementioned *National Register of Foreign Books*, (for example, the union card catalog)—a register of books, acquired by Czech and Slovak libraries, that had been hitherto part of the Loan Department.

All those libraries pertinent to building the Union Catalog have joined a Union Catalog Interlibrary Working Group. Appropriate rules of collaboration have been agreed upon and set down in the bilateral agreement, signed by each of the libraries (fifteen so far) and the National Library. A time limit of one year has been designated to test the viability of this initiative. In order to govern this group more effectively, a smaller Union Catalog board was elected.

In addition to the Union Catalog initiative, there are other cooperative projects between the National Library and other libraries (presently funded by grants from the Ministry of Culture) that further the achievement of many of the CASLIN goals. These are, for example:

- The shared retroconversion of the Czech National Bibliography as well as other bibliographical resources has as its goal the inclusion of the whole Czech book production of the twentieth century (a total of about 500,000 records, to be completed by the year 2000). The records will be available in UNIMARC both on-line and on CD-ROM. The participants include the National Library working together with nine regional state research libraries.
- The shared cataloging of current Czech books published, with the purpose of having as complete a Czech national bibliography as possible. Regional publication records that are exclusive to the respective state research libraries are used for this purpose. Participants include the National Library and nine regional state research libraries.
- The analytical cataloging of Czech periodicals has as its purpose the improvement of existing cooperative efforts to compile the bibliographical database of articles as well

---

20. See "Statut Národní knihovny České republiky" [The Statutes of the National Library of the Czech Republic], *Národní knihovna*, 6 (1995), 2, pp. 74–76. See also http://www.nkp.cz/caslin/.

as to set up links to full texts, if possible. Participants include the National Library, regional libraries, and several special research libraries.
- Microfilm preservation of newspaper collections involves eighteen of the rarest and, at the same time, most endangered, if not already damaged, titles. The purpose is to use this opportunity to bring improvements in microfilming technology and methods to other libraries, as well as to lay the foundations of the union archive of microcopies that complies with EROMM standards. Participants include the National Library and two regional State Research libraries.

All the collective activities listed above, as well as several others (such as the application of international standards), need both an organizational grounding and a platform for opinion sharing. For this reason the National Library has organized specialized consortia and interlibrary work groups, some of which are bound by contractual agreements. But the entire administrative and organizational responsibilities, as well as the initiative itself, still rest with the National Library alone, for example, its appropriate departments and staff. Undoubtedly, this simple setup works quite nicely and could be beneficial to the libraries involved, provided, however, that the appropriate funding will be forthcoming in the years to come, most of all for the Union Catalog initiative. But, perhaps most important, it is the principle of sharing data, opinions, responsibility, and decision-making—for example, that of partnership—that must be strongly emphasized as the precondition for true cooperation. This is quite different from the established model, in which the National Library is merely the service provider while other libraries are merely the service recipients.

CHAPTER 11

Cooperation, Consortia, Compatibility, Connectivity
The Case of CASLIN

MARTIN SVOBODA

The Library Automation Scene

In the early sixties, while the Czech and Slovak libraries were correctly perceived as a danger to the establishment, government and party officials developed and supported systems of scientific and technological information, according to the Soviet model, in a vain effort to slow down the increase of the technological lag behind the West. At that time central information offices—the IINTE in Warsaw, the CINTI in Sofia, the OMIKK in Budapest, the UVTEI in Prague, and the MCNTI in Moscow— were thriving, while the majority of libraries made no progress.[1] After 1968, the isolation from developments abroad was almost impermeable. The first signs of a real introduction of modern technologies did not appear in the Czech National (then State) Library until 1982 and were limited to the production of a phototypeset national bibliography of books. The situation was quite similar in Slovakia (then part of Czechoslovakia), although the Slovak National Library lived in a somewhat more relaxed atmosphere and received somewhat better support: The production of the Slovak national bibliography had started eight years earlier and gradually covered all document types including articles in Slovak periodicals. Only the final years of Communist rule in Czechoslovakia saw some real support for several state-operated libraries. The very last Communist five-year plan (1985–1989) provided the Czech

---

I owe the idea for this chapter to Professor Andrew Lass of Mount Holyoke College, South Hadley, Mass., our longtime grants manager, adviser, and friend. He suggested that instead of doing a plain narration— "we did this and that"—I should discuss the crossroads we encountered and try to explain why we made the decisions we made.

1. The acronyms indeed stand for the states' central offices of scientific, technical, (and sometimes) economic information. A whole system was organized by industry branches: There were national institutes of information for chemistry, for mechanical engineering, for the nuclear industry, for forestry and agriculture; they were loosely supervised by the national head office, and closely cooperated with partner branch information institutes from other COMECON countries. At the top of pyramid sat the MCNTI/ICSTI (Mezhdunarodnyi centr nauchnoi i tekhnicheskoi informacii/International Center of Scientific and Technical Information). Most of this structure vanished after 1990; some professionals trained in these systems found their new mission in libraries.

National Library and three state research libraries with some funds to begin modernization; there was also a parallel plan in Slovakia. But this progress involved a very thin layer of libraries and it was coming from above, not from those whom it should have served.

System Principles: Crossroads Number One

Two parallel projects were devised in the late eighties and their implementation then began in earnest. These were the MAKS project in the Czech Republic and the IKIS project in Slovakia. Both projects were aimed at building a unified nationwide system based upon a hierarchical concept, as was expected in those days. Unlike IKIS, the Czech MAKS project was never worked out down to the lowest level of technical detail. Nevertheless, the ability to communicate from the center down to the local library, as well as in the opposite direction, was considered the main issue.

We were thus confronted with several questions about how to try to attain the ability to communicate in the future. Clearly, question number one involved the data compatibility warranted by a unified structure or format of bibliographic records. The second question was how to transfer data between network nodes and the final question was what hardware and software to use. No system in Czechoslovakia at that time used a data structure compatible with world standards. The exposure of librarians to such standards in the Czech Republic was limited to ISBD (International Standard Bibliographic Description), used exclusively for the national bibliography of books (since 1982). All other bibliographies and catalogs were using a native format based on the so-called Prussian instruction, with an added Soviet flavor. Knowledge of the UNIMARC standard (USMARC was out of the question, anyway for political reasons before 1990) was rather superficial. Finally, the available software, UNESCO's CDS/ISIS, was unable to support such delicacies of UNIMARC as indicators and repeatable subfields. Considering all these factors, it should not be too surprising that we developed our own Czech and Slovak Exchange Format, following the ISBD block structure to the letter. This format, though neither USMARC nor UNIMARC, was atomized enough to make a future conversion possible.

As far as data communication between libraries is concerned, leased lines via modems were viewed as the appropriate method; due to the poor state of the telecommunications infrastructure and poor equipment in libraries, this concept never came to life and the manual transfer of floppies was the highest level of interconnection achieved.

As to technology, we were confronted with the decision about whether to stay with (unreliable) mainframes or whether to bet on the future development of PC technology. Luckily enough, we opted for the latter. As to the software, we decided to build the system around the database system called CDS/ISIS,[2] available for free, from UNESCO. This decision made it possible to make better use of resources that had been previously earmarked for the unproductive mainframe technology.

---

2. I believe all the post-Communist countries should pay tribute to the creators and distributors of this wonderful and flexible starter tool.

System Considerations: Crossroads Number Two

Some time after the "velvet revolution," the state provided very limited funds to further develop the system. This gave us time to do missionary work among the district and smaller libraries—fear of computers and a feeling that automation was avoidable were quite strong there. We did our best to "overcome these persisting attitudes"[3] and to explain the importance of standards for future cooperation.

In 1991, we identified three possible development paths: "minimum growth"; a "mature system"; and "bargains" for the National Library as a hub of the future library network. The minimum-growth path represented the conservative option of slowly increasing the number of isolated or possibly LAN-connected PCs and of broadening the scope of the already accepted and tuned-up CDS/ISIS-MAKS. This solution was provoking no resistance among the staff, it was rather cheap, and still allowed us to make the best use of a system already known to the staff. Both the hardware and the data were applicable in the future system; hence no resources would be wasted. The disadvantage of it was the lack of authority checking, but more important, the lack of public access to catalogs. This option was quite easy to follow, it was the least stressful one, but it could not provide a desired outreach from behind the walls of the library.

A mature system, that is, a procurement of a carefully selected, suitable, integrated modular library system working in an "industry standard" environment was desired for at least two reasons. At the practical level, we wanted to introduce the knowledge of modern library technologies in order to improve service, to climb over the library walls; at the micropolitical level, we considered the new technology a wedge to break the petrified behavioral patterns and to introduce new dynamics. The high cost was an obstacle for this option, but we were sure that this was the only way we could go if we really wanted to make "a great leap" and get in contact with the rest of the world.

We mentioned the third option—"bargains" for the National Library—for the sake of completeness, not because we ever seriously considered it: Several vendors had proposed to us cheap, outdated systems, incompatible with any standards. Though such proposals often look very attractive, they have at least two big disadvantages: No new change-inspiring technology is introduced and the low initial cost is soon outweighed by steeply rising maintenance costs, not to mention an increasing dependency on the supplier.

Our obvious choice was the mature-system option. However, we had to follow the minimum-growth option for some time, because the funds at our disposal did not permit the mature-system option. This had negative consequences that we had not immediately realized: As the automation remained hidden behind the walls of the library, the involvement of other libraries was weakened and delayed. They did not consider the efforts of the National Library, efforts directed at the users at all levels, to be their business.

---

3. See chapter 4 of this volume.

Birth of CASLIN

The preceding discussion supports the view that the possibility of obtaining funding from The Andrew W. Mellon Foundation for the further development of the library's networks arose in an environment quite well prepared for the introduction of substantial changes in technology. The Mellon Foundation's representatives insisted on supporting a joint project of a group or a consortium rather than of isolated libraries. The standing committee of four directors of the largest Czech and Slovak libraries provided such a base and the four directors signed the "Statement of Intent," the launching document of CASLIN (the Czech and Slovak Library Information Network). The key issue of the statement was "to lay a ... foundation of a ... library network providing users with easy, fast, and unrestricted access to the information ..." The objectives were:

- to improve public services—through improved access to catalogs, we planned to make more effective use of primary resources;
- to improve cooperation, and, by introducing the shared-cataloging concept also improve the economy of the library system as a whole;
- to achieve coordination of library acquisitions and other activities as a side effect.

Such objectives are noble and nobody would hesitate to sign their name to them—in particular, when funding is in sight. The future would show that though we were ready to accept a change in technology, we were not so ready or willing to change our habits.

CASLIN's Achievements and Failures

The development of the organizational structure of CASLIN can be divided into three phases related to the available funding. In the "pre-Mellon-funding" period, the conduct of libraries and their activities were subordinated to the objective of carefully and effectively preparing the project so as to obtain the funding for it. All the different opinions and attitudes were subordinated to the common goal. The simple structure of the board of (four) directors and the eight-member Experts' Group was adequate. The technical principles were already established at this phase as necessary components of the system selection process.[4] These were widely publicized, and remarkably influenced the library automation scene.

The CASLIN group exhibited an instrumental behavior aimed at securing and reasonably allocating the funds in the project's funding phase. It became apparent that the Experts' Group, which had been adequate for preparing the project, handling the tender, and commence the project's implementation, was no longer adequate for the growing tasks. The CASLIN working groups (WGs), which would report to the CASLIN board, were established to take care of different aspects of the project. The idea was that besides controlling the development of the project from their point of view, the WGs would prepare guidelines that would, after approval of the CASLIN

---

4. These included UNIMARC, ISO/CCI, UNIX, TCP/IP, Z39.50, and ISO character sets.

board, become mandatory for all CASLIN members and, it was hoped, for the whole library community, wherever applicable.

The most efficient of these groups was the WG for Standards and Bibliographic Description, which prepared the extremely important documents required, the set of CASLIN standards, and the minimal requirements for the preparation of the CASLIN union catalog. These documents confirmed and enhanced the recommendations of the Experts' Group and introduced the use of the *Anglo-American Cataloguing Rules.* The board of directors approved the whole set of documents as CASLIN standards. We can now say that the majority of both the Czech and Slovak library community and local library systems producers accepted it. Should the CASLIN project have no other effects, we have to be grateful for this one. It enabled an unprecedented development of very different systems that were still able to communicate with each other in the network, and thus fulfilling the idea of a multicolored open network.

On the other hand, the new organizational structure of CASLIN, including the board, working groups, and other bodies, and their relationships and responsibilities, did not have enough time to settle in. Czechoslovakia broke up into two countries, the end of funding was quite rapidly approaching and local interests began outweighing the idea of common goals. There was never a sufficient push for the board of directors to approve the "rules of the game" in writing. Some of the working groups did not work well, and their inability to make decisive decisions affected other, dependent decisions and caused delays in implementation, yet there was no formal power that could have corrected this inactivity. The original idea of stimulating a greater involvement of libraries outside CASLIN in tasks of common interest was not fully accomplished.

The "post-Mellon-funding" phase saw a further decline in the drive for real, democratic, and majority-controlled cooperation; the pursuit of local objectives became stronger than that of common goals. The division of the state apparently influenced this process. Different groups met different fates. The Standardization and Bibliographic Description WG was transformed into a cataloging advisory board to the director of the Czech National Library. The Retro-conversion Group met twice and its second meeting was exemplary: It voted to dissolve itself because of the lack of willingness to cooperate; each participant considered his or her problems so unique that the group found no purpose in the exchange of experience and opinions. The CASLIN Union Catalog Group vanished, only to be revived as the "CASLIN–Union Catalog of the Czech Republic." As far as I know, only the Microfilm Preservation Group keeps working on an international, Czech-Slovak level.

The last pitch to establish CASLIN as a consortium, which we made in the final year of the Mellon funding, failed. The participants did not see a sufficient reason to sign up for cooperation, without the existence of a list of specific tasks, just to keep the group formally together in case an opportunity or a need arose. Creation of a platform for negotiating and approving agreements and standards of general interest, for discussing future intentions, and eventually for running the union catalog was not seen to be compelling enough to establish yet another body; the pursuit of individual objectives prevailed. The running of the CASLIN union catalog remained and still is the statutory task of the National Library.

This in no way means that the spirit of cooperation is forever dead, but, rather, that the scheme of things looks a bit different now. What does remain of CASLIN, then?

- There is the set of CASLIN standards—for example, the minimal CASLIN union-catalog record requirements, including AACR2, UNIMARC, and ISO character sets;
- The agreement between the Czech and Slovak national libraries guarantees any user of one national union catalog access to the other union catalog under the same provisions that hold for her/his home national catalog.
- The "CASLIN–Union Catalog of Czech Republic" has an active work group or, rather, a steering committee. As of 1997, 15 libraries had signed an agreement on cooperation.
- All the CASLIN libraries are linked to the national academic subnets of Internet and most of their OPACs are therefore accessible from all over the world.
- The Czech Parliament increased the 1997 budget of the Ministry of Culture by more than $1 million to support the networking and shareable-data production in the public libraries;[5] the funding continued in 1998, though cut to one-third of the first year's budget.
- Last and most important, the arrangement of the CASLIN Plus consortia is doing much better.

We can definitely conclude that the CASLIN project was not managed as well as it could have been. The success of consortia, however, depends strongly on people and on their willingness to work together.

Summary

No doubt, the CASLIN project helped the Czech and Slovak libraries catch up with library developments in the rest of the world. To summarize, the legal deposit is electronically processed; the retrospective conversions are under way in several large libraries (there are many smaller ones that already have their full catalog in an electronic format); the operation of the union catalog is gaining momentum; the electronic document delivery system is operational in some libraries; the rules of digitization for preservation were specified and this method is used in several programs; the microfilming for preservation is coordinated on an international level; and the map of Web access points in libraries is getting quite dense.

Weak Points

On the other hand, there are still some weak points that need to be dealt with. The preparation of the legal deposit records is so delayed that they cannot be used for shared cataloging, which would save funds for many libraries. There are insufficient resources to begin the processing of those electronic documents that should be considered part of the national heritage but are, instead, vanishing like old daguerreo-

---

5. More than 100 projects received a grant. The map of grantees can be seen at: http://alpha.nkp.cz/caslin/map-e.html.

types. And there is not enough goodwill to agree on a shared user profile or to give top priority to a shared acquisition policy that would, in turn, help ease the budget without impairing the quality of service to users. Each one of these problems illustrates that it is possible to be wasteful even under a situation of a shortage.

CASLIN indeed managed to create an environment where, thanks to adopted standards, many tasks can be solved locally, without the need for central authorities. This allows the players on the automation scene to behave with greater freedom. But there are still many tasks that are beyond the abilities of any single institution. But "clubs" of those who are ready to sacrifice a small part of their freedom for the sake of jointly achieving much more are appearing only slowly.

The moral of the story is, as one might have expected, nothing new: It is much easier to introduce a new technology than to change the habits and attitudes of people. The former can be accomplished within months while the latter will take years, if not generations. But this does not mean that we may give up.

References

Svoboda, Martin. "Automation in libraries—how to proceed?" In *LIBER '92: International Conference*. Budapest : Széchényi Könyvtár, 1992.
Svoboda, Martin. "CASLIN: from project to consortium." In *EUR 17551—International Conference on Library Automation in Central and Eastern Europe*, pp. 263–271. Luxembourg: Office for Official Publications of the European Communities, 1997.
Svoboda, Martin, and Stoklasová, Bohdana. "Computerization of Czech Libraries: History, Present, and Future. In *NIT '91: Fourth International Conference: New Information Technology*, pp. 217–221. West Newton, Mass.: MicroUse Information, 1991.

CHAPTER 12

Some Problems with Library Automation in the KOLIN Library Consortium

DARINA KOŽUCHOVÁ AND Ľ'UBOMÍRA ŠOLTÉSOVÁ

Although libraries have been important institutions of society for ages, automation is a modern phenomenon designed to make their work more effective and to provide faster, higher quality services. The new age of library automation in Slovakia commenced in the early 1990s when The Andrew W. Mellon Foundation arrived in the Czechoslovak library environment with support for the CASLIN project. In contrast to the previous, mostly independent automation efforts, the new approach stressed networks and cooperative access to library automation, while insisting on international standards aimed at mutual compatibility on the national and worldwide levels. These criteria are respected also by KOLIN (Košice Library Information Network), a consortium which, as part of the CASLIN-plus-consortia projects, contributes to the expansion of national networks of interconnected libraries. A special feature of KOLIN is its reliance on the cooperative principles that normally characterize consortia. The automation of KOLIN libraries, under the conditions of a consortium, is therefore a multidimensional process that is influenced by many factors, all of which play their part in determining the final result.

The Genesis of KOLIN

The beginnings of the project go back to 1992, when the library of the P. J. Šafárik University and, later, the library of the Technical University first prepared separate projects to essentially automate all library processes and submitted the plans to the Mellon Foundation. However, the latter preferred projects of a wider scope, one that would go beyond the solving of problems of separate libraries. At the same time, the four biggest Czechoslovak libraries announced their common intention to cooperate in building the Czech and Slovak Library and Information Network (CASLIN). These facts provided a decisive impetus in the origin of the Consortium of Academic Libraries of Eastern Slovakia (CALES), which was founded in 1993 by the university libraries of the P. J. Šafárik University and of the Technical University as a voluntary and open association of academic and other scientific libraries.

The intentions of CALES were to support existing library cooperation and to help raise its quality as well as to foster it in all areas where such cooperation was desirable for the mutual and beneficial unification of the intellectual, material, and financial resources of its members. Some other academic and research libraries in Košice also joined the consortium—among them, the Regional State Library, the biggest research library in the region.[1] And the ideal means for reaching the goals of CALES was the common project of building KOLIN. Although some library processes had already been automated in each of the participating libraries, these were largely isolated attempts that lacked cohesive integration. The intention of KOLIN was the systematic, gradual, and complete automation and integration of basic library processes, both at the level of individual libraries and at the level of the consortium as a whole.

The following objectives of KOLIN were given priority: (1) the substantial raising of the quality of library and information services; (2) the elimination of the acquisition of duplicate works, the transfer of routine procedures to computers, and rationalizing work flows and making them more transparent; (3) participation in building a national library and information network and helping in the creation of a union catalog of documents—in cooperation with other CASLIN libraries—by observing common cataloging rules and exchange formats; and finally, (4) building databases and establishing the principles of managing a regional library and information network. The basic means for achieving the objectives of the project would be the establishment of an integrated library information system, implemented gradually in the KOLIN libraries, module by module, with due regard to systemwide solutions. The system that was finally selected—because it was the most suitable one—was Aleph, sold by the Israeli firm Ex Libris. The final choice of the system was a critical moment for the project and tested the will and ability of libraries to cooperate.

Starting in October 1995, when the grant for the KOLIN project was approved by the Mellon Foundation, intensive work was undertaken in connection with writing a contract and signing it with the vendor of Aleph—Ex Libris. The process became a very complicated and prolonged one, because of the problematic departure of the director of Ex Libris's Prague office. The management of Ex Libris did not feel it had to honor the agreements that had been made by the Prague agency and therefore refused to deal with requests for system testing, acceptance, and guarantees. After an unsuccessful joint meeting, KOLIN's communications with Ex Libris were handed over to an intermediary—a representative of the Mellon Foundation, who, after long and arduous exchanges of individual claims on both sides, succeeded in forging an agreement. The contract regarding an integrated library information system between Ex Libris and KOLIN was signed by all the contracting parties (three KOLIN libraries, the software vendor, the hardware vendor, and the Mellon-appointed grant administrator) in September 1996. The signing of this contract made it possible to finally order and schedule the delivery of the hardware and software. The usual process of obtaining

---

1. The Regional State Library (formerly the State Scientific Library) is an independent legal entity and after the tranformation of territorial and administrative divisions of the Slovak Republic in 1996, its administration came under the purview of the Regional Office instead of the Ministry of Culture.

VAT and import duty exemptions for the equipment preceded the actual delivery. And, since some of the delivered equipment had the wrong components installed and had to be exchanged, the acceptance of equipment for the first phase of the KOLIN project had to wait until February 1997. This was immediately followed by the installation of the localized Slovak version of Aleph 3.2–5.14, which ended in April 1997 with the delivery of Slovak manuals and DAT-tapes.[2] Between February and May 1997 the first training sessions took place—most notably, system training for system librarians and system administrators and two training sessions for catalogers. Gradually, training covering the UNIX system, the UNIMARC format, and new cataloging rules was taking place. Recently, the parameters of the Aleph system have been adjusted to match the requirements of the KOLIN libraries, while the technical, personnel, and organizational conditions for implementing the cataloging module and OPAC have been put in place. While the plan foresees all the KOLIN libraries working with a single, shared protocol, many of the parameters must first be unified, and the experience with the use of the Aleph functions, which may be based on different conditions and different stages in the implementation of the system, must be shared. The common intention was to implement at least two modules annually: cataloging (including authority control), OPAC, and acquisitions in 1997; circulation and serials control in 1998; interlibrary loans and other functions in 1999. To some, this rate of progress might seem slow. However, taking into account the conditions characterized below, this is a realistic objective. The next task is to finish the conversion of data created in the pre-Aleph systems (CDS/ISIS, Dataflex, Ingres) into the UNIMARC format and to secure the delivery of hardware for phase two of project, without which it is impossible to begin the implementation of the next modules. A longer-term objective is the transfer from the old version of Aleph to a new one based on the ORACLE database.

Institutional Conditions

Automation of the library has been part of the strategic development plan of all KOLIN member libraries. Reaching that strategic goal involves a long-term process that consists of finding methods for surmounting different barriers created by outside problems (which may be insoluble by the library itself) and by internal problems that may be surmounted by suitable management techniques. The complicated social and macroeconomic environment in which the libraries work was greatly affected by the far-reaching changes in the country's political climate and by the turn to market economies after 1989. Inevitably, they influenced all the KOLIN libraries regardless of whether they act as independent legal entities or are part of the academic environment. Institutional-level problems in the automation of individual libraries are determined by several fac-

---

2. A necessary condition for the systematic installation of Aleph in the KOLIN libraries was the development of the Košice computer network, CANET. At the beginning of 1997, the fourth phase of CANET was completed, in which the fiberoptic connection of all KOLIN libraries in Košice was achieved. An important landmark in joining the Prešov library to the rest of KOLIN occurred when the transmission speed of the Košice-Prešov line was increased from 14.4 kb/sec to 64 kb/sec.

tors. Key among them are (1) the absence of appropriate economic safeguards for the development of library activities; (2) the dependence that libraries have on their governing bodies; (3) the level of the strategic thinking of the library's managers, its ability to conceive strategic objectives, to undertake a program of cooperation, to adapt to changes in the environment, and to look for optimal solutions; and (4) the extent of the application of modern technologies and the quality of the infrastructure.

Specifically, one can speak of at least three crucial areas in which the abovementioned points play a decisive role: the economic situation, the low status of libraries and their lack of administrative independence, and personnel problems.

The Economic Situation

The steady decline in funding for libraries is a general phenomenon in Slovakia. It is manifested by an ever-decreasing budget, which, in the environment of KOLIN libraries, is essentially the only source of financing. Yet, in contrast to the times when library work was done in the traditional way, automation may raise costs associated with hardware and software, due to the use of new information technologies, computer maintenance, and license fees. Lower budgets and higher prices for books may force the KOLIN libraries to reduce the allocations of funds for automation. The KOLIN library managers attempt to persuade their superiors (university managers) to set budgets, which would, at least minimally, reflect the growth in prices of library materials and of the expenses associated with automating library processes. The reasons for the permanent financial crisis are directly related to the unsatisfactory performance of the state's economy and to the government's priorities, which do not encourage library managers to pursue alternative sources of income and funding. For example, any income from library services, the potential for which could be positively affected by a library's activities, cannot be used by and for the library itself—this income is defined as part of the state's budget and it has to be transferred to it under the penalty of a law. In fact, exceeding the library's projected annual income does not raise budgetary allocations for the next budgetary period. The library's budget allocations by the university's administration are not really open to creative solutions, since the overall university budget, allocated by the Ministry of Education, is so insufficient that the university has a hard time covering its other needs. Budgetary expenditures are supervised monthly, and unreasonable regulations often hinder its effective and creative use. In such a complicated economic situation, when a university fights for its survival, it is very difficult to have objective criteria for dividing the budget among competing university needs. Even if a high priority were assigned to library automation, it would be difficult to imagine how this could be done, given the current budget.

The lack of funding also affects the librarians' wages. Their inferior salary brackets and the inability to pay them bonuses are the main reasons that librarians leave for better-paid occupations.[3] Other sources of funding (for example, from sponsors),

---

3. Salary conditions of the employees in budgetary organizations are determined by a law from 1992, according to which the librarians are put into salary brackets according to their work activity.

considered common abroad, are very difficult to obtain in the environment of Slovak libraries. Libraries are not held in high esteem and the public knows neither the nature nor the importance of library work. Private donations are also of limited importance, for legal reasons, and it is not realistic to regularly count on such financing. Changes in legislation pertaining to business practices and the application of marketing techniques in libraries may partially improve their financial situation. Setting up library consortia, or other forms of interlibrary cooperation that aim for a common development strategy, can result in advantageous prices from the software and information media vendors, in the sharing of equipment, and in sharing the use of experts and of other services. Some predictability of the state's financial support however, is necessary for the realization of an extensive, financially and conceptually demanding library automation project. Special grant funds, in addition to the library budget, could help libraries reach these goals.

The Low Status of Libraries and Their Lack of Administrative Independence

These factors are both closely tied to the social standing of libraries. In spite of the fact that much of what library automation has to offer is now (more or less) up and running in most libraries, the majority of the state and local government officials, as well as the majority of the public, perceive libraries as cumbersome institutions incapable of answering society's needs. Until now, libraries have failed to find their place as the new knowledge and information-service providers. This situation negatively affects their standing in society as well as the conditions that society provides them in order that they may fulfill their function. This situation is very much the result of practices inherited from the past and is characterized by the eradication of self-governance by experts and the reliance, instead, on centralized administrative and bureaucratic methods of management. The functions and tasks of the KOLIN university libraries are indeed determined by orders issued by their superiors, the university administrations themselves—for these are self-governing bodies and the state has no impact on their activities.

Compared to the past (the years prior to 1989), their present position could be considered appropriate to the tasks and needs at hand.[4] In practice, though, things are a bit more complicated: The centralized allocation of funds to higher education; the overall concentration of procedural, economic, and personnel issues at the highest levels of the university's administration (the rectorate); and the lack of experience with modern organizational structures in our settings—these have contributed to the fact that at present, not a single university library in Slovakia enjoys legal independence. As a re-

---

Division of the activities in the salary brackets is unacceptable and often does not correspond to the character of the work. In the libraries the average salary used to be, and even today is, well below the Slovak average.

4. Prior to 1989 the majority of university libraries were listed among special university work places, together with campuses, publishing houses, and administrative units of the rectorate. Despite the changes, there remains the negative fact that the last amendment of the Law of Universities does not mention the term "library."

sult there are fewer and fewer openings for independent decision-making on matters that pertain to the budget, on personnel issues, or even on issues that are, specifically, library ones. There are often problems in determining and enacting jurisdiction over the management of university libraries and in maintaining clear communication lines between the university's management and the libraries.

With the specialized knowledge of library science being underestimated by the administration, the library's management is left to its own devices as it makes decisions about the direction of automation, about the position the library should take vis-à-vis other organizations, and about how it is to uphold standards. Seldom is the library director a member of the rector's advisory council, and he or she therefore has limited possibilities for effectively presenting the library's interests to the university's management. Under these conditions, it is very difficult to realize long-term automation projects that require not only the financial aid but also the full moral support of the university's management. This is particularly hard felt in those subsystems (such as circulation) that deal with the public, since they are the last ones to make it onto the board's agenda. Moreover, cooperation of the library with other units of the university may also be problematic. Such is the case, for example, with the computer center, where the cooperative interest and the will of the management and staff of these other units does not translate into any procedural rules or clear delineation of responsibilities for the project of automation (for example, the building of the network infrastructure that connects the individual schools and the university to the information network). In this context it is necessary to use modern information technologies to present the library's activities and intentions, to seek new methods of communication with the administration and the public.

Personnel Problems

The absence of marketing methods in library management, a lack of knowledge of related areas, and a poor presentation of library activities to the outside world are all reasons for the isolation of libraries, and for the unwillingness to invest in their operations, development, and personnel support. The library's management is quite often forced to concentrate on immediate problems and on defending the library's very existence. The reasons are often found in the poor level of its strategic thinking, its inability to cooperate, the minimal effort made by both the management and the staff to adapt to changes and to look for new, optimal solutions to problems of library organization and management, not to mention the conservatism and psychological inertia of the library's staff.

The personnel situation at the KOLIN libraries is made more complicated by the fact that there is a lack, in the number as much as the degree, of qualified individuals. This lack of qualified librarians in the labor market translates into the inappropriate accumulation of assigned administrative and professional tasks and, consequently, into a situation of overburdened librarians with less time to attend to managerial and conceptual work (such as the automation project). It is naive to expect that automation will quickly solve all existing problems. On the contrary, it will demand many changes, which could cause a lot of problems in the beginning. New working procedures also require a change in the internal organization of the library, including the management's style and the relationships between separate departments. Library automation may require the formation of new departments responsible for running and maintaining the system (including networks, hardware, and the library system itself), and, with a library participating in a consortium, departments, which focus on issues that deal with the consortium as a whole (such as public relations or the union catalog department). Additionally, there is a need for temporary work groups that come together in order to resolve specific issues that deal with the process of automation. Of course, one also needs a positive response to the library's personnel needs from those in charge (such as the regional office or the university Administrators). The problem of the lack of qualified librarians has to be solved, sooner rather than later, by hiring people who may not be ideally qualified (and may not hold appropriate degrees) but who are open to gradual retraining by means of postgraduate courses and training programs.[5]

Consortium Issues for the Management

As mentioned above, the Consortium of Academic Libraries of Eastern Slovakia was established in 1993 when the two founding members signed its charter. This charter specified the nature of the CALES consortium, including its mission, the areas for cooperation, and the means of reaching common goals. The founding of the consortium was not grounded in any legal documents but, rather, came out of the pragmatic need for a mutual agreement on cooperation. Common activities during the preparation of the KOLIN project made it clear that further rules of cooperation needed to be defined. These rules help cover matters that involve the sharing of financial resources, the use and ownership of purchased equipment and distinguish the KOLIN project libraries from the rest of the CALES group. An interim agreement on shared financing was signed in 1995. Finally, it is the KOLIN consortium contract of 1996 that appears to resolve all seeming inconsistencies associated with the earlier agreements. It simply defines as the parties to the contract only those libraries that are directly involved in the KOLIN project. Though the term "consortium" is not reflected in Slovak legislation, the term "library consortium" is well known in foreign library practices. Participation in a consortium has, no doubt, many advantages: (1) the pooling of expertise in the resolving of complicated tasks, as, for example, in the implementation of modern network applications; (2) the saving of precious personnel by the centralization of some of the common activities, (3) the realization of financial savings through joint acquisitions and the dissemination of document databases, as well as in administrative and managerial work; and (4) a stronger position vis-à-vis vendors, whether in price negotiations or in other business dealings. But it also has its problems.

---

5. The Department of Library Science and Scientific Information at Comenius University, in Bratislava, has carried out a complex investigation in libraries of different types, with the aim of finding out the interest of libraries in new types of professional qualifications. Evaluation of the investigation may create the basis for forming new library profiles. See Kimlička (1997).

The KOLIN project is an extraordinarily complicated one, not only from the conceptual standpoint but also from a purely organizational one. It involves finding solutions to entirely new and complex problems—which involves major changes in work flow or raising the overall quality at all twelve individual libraries that come under the consortium of four KOLIN libraries. The placing of these twelve libraries in two cities, Košice and Prešov, complicates the situation even further since the cities are about 35 km apart.[6] Maintaining good connections and a clear information flow between separate, geographically scattered libraries is fraught with complications. In such cases, gathering, analyzing, and disseminating data are slower and the same holds for decision-making. They are affected by the ability to think and behave in terms of the consortium—for example, to learn to consider and prefer the needs of the whole over the needs of individual libraries. Since the libraries are not on an equal footing, some feel that they would develop faster on their own and that the attitude—advocated by the consortium—of bringing all the libraries to the same level is really a hindrance to them. And even as libraries demonstrate that they can work together as a consortium, the individualistic attitude of experts (of whom many find it difficult to share their knowledge for the benefit of the whole) remains a serious problem. Though, on paper, all members of the consortium are equal, not all of them are equally active in pursuing individual goals, in looking for new solutions, or in focusing on the project's development. The frustrations of overextended librarians may ultimately mean that they assign less priority to the consortium and begin to underestimate the responsibilities that are held by every member in regard to the consortium.

It should be clear, from what has been said so far, that in such an unsettled environment it is not easy to achieve an agreement. The situation is made all the more complicated by the need to involve other areas of the home institutions in the project's implementation, such as computer science centers, lawyers, or controllers, and then to achieve their mutual agreement. And the problems do not end when an agreement is reached. For after all, the essential point is that these agreements and rules of engagement should be upheld, that compromise solutions should not be questioned, and that the decisions of the consortium's representatives, whether or not they are members of one's own institution, should be respected. There may be different solutions for particular problems, but their character must fit into a single system. In looking for solutions, one needs to go beyond a problem's observable surface and try to comprehend its essence (usually hidden), the reasons for the problem; and, only then, should one propose necessary steps.

The following structural elements and rules of KOLIN's management attempt to both respect these complications and resolve them in a systematic way.

---

6. On January 1, 1997, an important organizational change occurred when the P. J. Šafárik University was divided into two separate entities by the Parliament of the Slovak Republic, namely, the Košice part and Prešov University, in Prešov. Paradoxically, this did not have a particularly negative effect on the KOLIN project, since from the very beginning, the more or less individual status of the Prešov branch of the university library of the original P. J. Šafárik University was respected in technical and organizational matters.

The Executive Board. The Executive Board of KOLIN oversees the project's development; while keeping one eye on the project's aims, it devotes the other to making basic decisions that pertain to the implementation process. It also represents the project to the outside world. The composition of the Executive Board was agreed upon and confirmed by the university's rectors and by the representative of the Ministry of Culture. It consists of the following members: the project manager; the directors of each of the participating libraries (one of whom is elected as the director of the whole project); and the CASLIN project's coordinator and grants administrator, an external and temporary member representing the Mellon Foundation.

The Implementation Group. To realize concrete goals and solve particular problems, the Executive Board appoints an Implementation Group, the members of which are involved with the implementation at their own libraries. The Implementation Group consists of its chair and an agreed-upon number (two to three) of specialists from each local library. Communication between the Executive Board and the Implementation Group is maintained by the project manager and by the chair, as well as through the latter's participation at the meetings of the Executive Board. In addition to the Implementation Group, the Executive Board can establish short- or long-term work groups that consist of experts who focus on narrowly defined tasks or problems. The majority of KOLIN's work groups correspond to the equivalent groups established within the larger CASLIN framework. In this manner the Executive Board and the Implementation Group attempt to make the individual tasks and responsibilities of workers more transparent. This also promotes efficiency by permitting a suitable specialization of labor.

The Advisory Board. Overseeing the Executive Board and the Implementation Group is an Advisory Board, the highest decision-making unit, which keeps an eye on the project's overall philosophy as well as its practical implications. It assists the Executive Board in making decisions that require the attention and participation of the larger community. This board has both internal and external members. The former represent the interests of cooperating organizations (such as the rectors and the controllers), while the latter represent the interests and opinions of the wider community of users. Everyday practices and new problems require an optimization of the organizational and management structure, a current evaluation of its functionality, the creation of immediate communication channels (for example, by means of "mailing lists"), and the unambiguous definition of responsibilities, along with the maintaining of a fair distribution of work at all levels.

The Future of KOLIN: Two Lines of Development

One can predict the future development of libraries with only a relative degree of certainty. Developments in information technologies as well as in other areas of society correspond to changes in readers' needs and, by necessity, in the very character and role of libraries. The traditional library, with its document collection neatly arranged, is being transformed into a digital library without walls. Under these circumstances new opportunities are opening up for librarians as multifaceted specialists, as knowledge brokers who are capable of analyzing, organizing, managing, filtering, and elaborating on different types of traditional and digital information. These new librarians should play a key role in supporting and educating the new and future users. The future offers librarians many possibilities—the point, however, is to accept worldwide trends and try to work them into the world of libraries. It would be naive to think that librarians alone could manage such fundamental changes. After all, libraries do not exist in a vacuum but in a concrete economic and social environment. And the fact is that governmental support of libraries is fundamentally greater in the more advanced democracies than in the countries of Central and Eastern Europe, where, it appears, the importance of libraries to education and culture remains grossly underestimated. We are looking at different degrees of support, at different financial and material conditions, and a different level of application of advanced technologies and methods. Because of these differences, the solution for the same particular task in Central and Eastern Europe and in the more advanced democracies may yield very different results. It follows from the overall lower standards of the organization of work in Slovakia that the same results are attained at much higher costs. With this in mind, it is possible to understand the Mellon Foundation's projects as positive incentives for librarians to aim for higher goals, to learn new ways of accomplishing tasks, to accept the worldwide trends toward solving problems through cooperation, and to gain new knowledge and experience.

The future of KOLIN should follow two lines of development: New, IT-informed services should be offered within the existing KOLIN network in a routine way, and the network itself should be broadened to accept new members. Their level would be gradually brought up to the prevailing standard without any loss of special services or of targeted users. From Aleph we expect more than just the fulfillment of the predefined system parameters. Together with other new information technologies, we look forward to the creation of a user-friendly, intelligent environment in which it will be possible to integrate public services—in both the traditional (printed) and the digital (on-line) sense—with local and distant electronic sources (such as the WWW). The development of a "learning-resource center" with an integrated library, and computer and media services, is a long-term aim. Achieving these aims requires that changes in thinking and in the organization of work take place at least at the institutional level. A change in the organizational structure of the library, one that would permit the establishment of new departments or divisions that would be responsible for many of the new functions (often IT-related), of new channels of communication and new work relationships that enable the introduction of innovative work flows, would help accomplish such a change.

Changing the thinking habits of librarians is a long-term process, one which is closely connected to the complex system of social relations in the whole society. More attention needs to be given to the use of existing contacts with the public, with the media, and with the university's administration. At present, libraries fulfill many complicated tasks by using new approaches and new technologies. Their activities, however, seem not to be fully appreciated; and public relations offices could become the means of overcoming this communication barrier, by providing a clear picture of library activities, of its services, resources, and public events. It is necessary to stress, in addition to the influence of new work methods (stemming from the new information technologies) and of the qualitative aspects of the new relationships with foreign partners, the importance of the continued training of the library staff. Up-to-date libraries need more experts—qualified, flexible, independent people able to think and work in a creative manner. The development of a new relationship between the librarian and the user demands an education in ethics and psychology, in addition to laborious training in library and computer sciences and in languages. While not often mentioned, in the end it is the user—his comfort in accessing complex and integrated sources of knowledge and information—that stands in the background of all the efforts at cooperation and development.

References

CASLIN PEW '95: *Seminar Proceedings, Smolenice, August 27–31, 1995.* Bratislava: University Library 1995.
CASLIN PEW IV: *Libraries of the Future: Seminar Proceedings, Dlouhé Stráně, Czech Republic, June 8–12, 1997.* Brno, and Olomouc: Vydavatelství Univerzity Palackého, 1997.
Ehnová, Marta and Terézia Miškovičová. "Legislatívné otázky slovenského knihovníctva. In *Východiská transformácie slovenského knihovníctva: Zborník z konferencie Slovenské knihovníctvo v čase spoločenských premien a do roku 2000, Bratislava, Október 15, 1994.* ["The Legislative Issues of Slovak Libraries," in: *Proceedings From the Conference on Slovak Libraries in The Time of Social Change and Up To The Year 2000, Bratislava, October 15, 1994.*] Bratislava: Slovenská asociácia knižníc, 1994.
Jensen, David P. "Vplyv automatizácie na organizáciu práce. In *CASLIN '94: Zborník príspevkov zo seminára CASLIN Management Training, Liptovský Ján, Slovenská republika, Jún 19–23, 1994* ["The Influence of Automation on the Organization of Work" in: *CASLIN'94: Proceedings from the CASLIN Management Training Seminar, Liptovský Ján, Slovak republic, June 19–23, 1994*], Martin: Slovenská národná knižnica v Matici slovenskej, 1997.
Katuščák, Dušan. Aktuálne otázky postavenia knižníc, knihovníctva a informatizácie na Slovensku. In *INFOS '97 : informatický seminár, Jasná pod Chopkom, Apríl 14–17, 1997.* ["The Present Issues in the Status of Libraries, Librarians and Automation in Slovakia" In *INFOS'97: Information Science Seminar, Jasná pod Chopkom, April 14–17, 1997*], Bratislava: Centrum vedecko-technických informácií SR, 1997.
Kimlička, Štefan. "Knižničná a informačná veda—teória a metodológia pre praxiu," In *INFOS'97: 27. Informatický seminár, Jasná pod Chopkom, Apríl 14–17, 1997.* ["Library and Information Science—theory and methodology in practice," in: *INFOS'97: Information Science Seminar, Jasná pod Chopkom, April 14–17, 1997.*] Bratislava: Centrum vedecko-technických informácií, 1997.
KOLIN (Košice Library Information Network): *A CASLIN Plus library automation project: A proposal presented to The Andrew W. Mellon Foundation.* Andrew Lass (ed.), South Hadley: Mount Holyoke College, September, 1995.
Kramárová, Alžbeta. *Vysokoškolské knižnice, ich postavenie a úlohy vo vyspelých štátoch sveta a v Slovenskej republike.* [*University Libraries, Their Place and Role in Developed Countries and in Slovakia.*] Bratislava: Slovenská technická knižnica—Centrum VTI SR, 1995.
Lábsky, Ondrej, and Zuzana Kaffanová. *Stav, pripravenosť a plány akademických knižníc SR na automatizáciu: Štúdia.* [*The Present State, Readiness and Plans of Academic Libraries in Slovakia for Automation: A Study.*] Bratislava: Slovenská technická knižnica—Centrum VTI SR, 1995.

Sakálová, Elena. "Knižničný manažment a transformácia spoločnosti." In *INFOS '96: 26. Informatický seminár, Jasná pod Chopkom, Apríl 15–18, 1996.* ["Library Management and the Transformation of Society," in: *INFOS'97: Information Science Seminar, Jasná pod Chopkom, April 14–17, 1997.*] Bratislava: Slovenská technická knižnica—Centrum VTI SR, 1996.

Sompel, Herbert Van de, and Guido Van Hooydonk. *Technology and collaboration: creating and effective electronic information environment in an academic context: Proceedings of the 18th International Online Information Meeting, London, December 6–8 , 1994.*

Šiška, Vladimír. "Automatizácia v knižnici. In *Štátna vedecká knižnica v Košiciach 1946–1996: Jubilejný zborník* ["Library Automation," in: *State scientific library in Kosice 1946 to 1996: A jubilee volume.*] E. Kundrátová (ed.), Košice: Štátna vedecká knižnica, 1996.

Šoltésová, Ľubomíra. "KOLIN," In *INFOS '96: 26. Informatický seminár, Jasná pod Chopkom, Apríl 15–18, 1996.* ["KOLIN," In: *INFOS'97: Information Science Seminar, Jasná pod Chopkom, April 14–17, 1997.*] Bratislava: Slovenská technická knižnica—Centrum VTI SR, 1996.

Trgiňa, Tibor, and Nataša Beláčiková. "Odborné vzdělávanie a sociálné postavenie knihovnikov." In *Východiská transformácie slovenského knihovníctva: Zborník z konferencie Slovenské knihovníctvo v čase spoločenských premien a do roku 2000, Bratislava, Október 15, 1994.* [*Proceedings From the Conference on Slovak Libraries in The Time of Social Change and Up To The Year 2000, Bratislava, October 15, 1994.*] Bratislava: Slovenská asociácia knižníc, 1994.

CHAPTER 13

Realization of the CASLIN Project in the Slovak National Library and Its Impact on the Automation of Libraries in Slovakia

IGOR PROKOP
MILAN RAKÚS
DANIELA SLÍŽOVÁ

The Introduction and the History of Automation
in the Slovak National Library

The Slovak National Library (SNK), in Martin, is the national library of the Slovak Republic. Historically, it is a part of the oldest, and a more comprehensive, national cultural institution called Matica slovenská and is governed by the latter.

The Slovak National Library is among the first libraries in Slovakia to automate library information processes. The efforts of SNK in the automation of bibliographic and library processes fall into three periods:

   1972–1985: the project to automate the Slovak National Bibliography,

   1985–1992: the project to create the Integrated Library Information System (IKIS)

   1993–1997: the project to create the Czech and Slovak Library Information Network (CASLIN).

The history of automation of bibliographic and library processes in SNK goes back to the beginning of the 1970s, when SNK undertook the project of the Automated Information System of the Slovak National Bibliography (AIS SNB). This system worked sequentially and only in a batch mode. The system provided for the creation and storage of bibliographic records and for the searching and the production of printed bibliographic outputs, photographically or by a printer. SNK began the routine processing of SNB in 1976. The AIS SNB was on the level of other European systems and satisfied all the requirements of that time. Some other large libraries in Slovakia began to use computers at the beginning of the 1980s.

In the second half of the 1980s, SNK recognized that if it wanted to keep pace with world trends and improve its services to users, it would have to adopt integrated library information processes and systems. Project IKIS [22] was undertaken in the years

1985–1989 and it should have been completed by 1992. The main goals of the project were to create a library computer network, a union catalog, shared cataloging, and new standards. The emphasis was on cooperation among libraries. In addition to SNK, practically all significant libraries in Slovakia were included in the project. Within its framework, extensive analyses of library processes were carried out and standard library automation projects for three basic types of libraries were prepared. The first stage of the project was formally completed by the final evaluation of project documentation.

Hardware purchases for the project were restricted to Central and Eastern Europe. As to the software, for various reasons it was decided to use the system CDS/ISIS. However, while this system did not provide ready solutions for library applications, it still enabled libraries to define and create searchable databases. In spite of many problems, the system was finally more or less successfully put together and implemented in SNK. However, we did not manage to connect the EC computer to the then existing computer network based on the X.25 protocol. The features and technical parameters of the available hardware and software made the realization of the project impossible. The implementation of the basic idea of shared cooperative cataloging throughout the country was slowly being postponed. A difficult conversion of 350,000 records into an exchange format for bibliographic and catalog records (VF IKIS) was necessary to make them compatible with the internal structure of CDS/ISIS and to create a database on the EC computer. This enabled significantly faster searching in the on-line mode at the library.

One of the main results of the IKIS project was the creation and dissemination of the so-called exchange format based on MARC formats, and although its form still had a very national character, it was a first step toward standardization in the exchange of bibliographic records. This format was then disseminated to practically all libraries and to systems that were being developed in Slovakia. The exchange format VF IKIS was prepared in close coordination with experts from the National Library in Prague, and thus a practically identical exchange format was introduced in both parts of Czechoslovakia. Cooperation between the two national libraries was already ongoing.

The distribution of printed catalog cards was terminated and subscribers could get records on diskettes in exchange format IKIS and ISO 2709. Thus, experiments with the downloading of records began. Some libraries imported these records directly into their own local systems; others created special stand-alone databases for searching.

The conceptual solution should have been followed by its implementation in the years 1989–1992, but the developments after the political changes in 1989 had an important influence—some of it was positive and some of it negative—on the process. Since currently installed technology was inadequate for the needs of the project, a reevaluation was undertaken, which led to the implementation of schemes based on PCs in most libraries. SNK installed its local area network (LAN) based on PCs and on Novell Netware. We had developed application support for the OPAC and cataloging, and partially for acquisitions and for full bibliographic processing. These processes started to work in an on-line mode.

As databases began to grow (to more than 100,000 records) and network traffic increased, the inadequacy of this solution became evident. It was apparent that this solution could only be temporary and that the large databases of the National Library required another solution. We began to examine various possibilities for funding the automation of the library from nonstate resources, mostly from abroad. At that time, The Andrew W. Mellon Foundation invited the directors of the four most prestigious and largest libraries in Czechoslovakia—SNK, in Martin; the University Library in Bratislava (UKB); the National Library in Prague (NKP); and the State Research Library, now the Moravian Library, in Brno—for a visit to the United States. The result was that the Mellon Foundation expressed its willingness to support the libraries after the submission and approval of a project proposal, which would set up principles of cooperation and contain a joint agreement expressed in a "Statement of Intent" by those four directors. Thus CASLIN began.[1]

Realization of CASLIN in SNK

The SNK staff had identified the basic systems issues of library automation, which were then addressed by work groups that were created and disssolved as needed. Their composition, operating methods, and period of existence depended on the character and complexity of the tasks and problems. The most important group was the Board of Directors and Managers (of the participating libraries); and it is regrettable that after the Mellon grant was expended, the Board of Directors of CASLIN was dissolved, which was due to its failure to formally establish CASLIN as an institutional consortium or association.

Funding. The Mellon grant was used for purchasing the main servers, the software system Aleph, some PCs, and accessories, as well as equipment for two work sites for micrography. Later, CASLIN also managed to get a complementary grant from the Pew Charitable Trusts. This grant was exclusively for funding training, education, seminars, some travel costs, but also for the setting up of two DTP work sites in the national libraries to support public relations work by CASLIN and the national libraries.

In retrospect, it turns out to have been a far-sighted decision to have the grant administered by the independent administrator appointed by the Mellon Foundation, who was responsible for disbursements. Grant funds were kept in the United States and the libraries received only goods and services. This was important because, according to current legislation, it exempted the goods and services from a VAT and customs duties. It was also very useful in a case such as ours, in which the grantee is a subsidiary of another entity (Matica slovenská), and in which financial flows are not transparent and financial discipline is questionable. Thanks to the independent administrator, conflicts among CASLIN members were minimized. It also turned out to be important that the grantee was an institution, and not the state, which might allocate resources in a manner responsive to the current political situation. The Slovak state agency in charge of the libraries participating in CASLIN—for example, the Ministry of Culture—has not provided additional financing to complement the grants of American foundations and for further development. The libraries obtained

---

1. For a general description of its aims, principles, and history, see the chapter by V. Balík in this volume [27].

only normal budgets, not sufficient for the further needs of the project. Although the project has the highest priority inside SNK, the top management of its parent institution, Matica slovenská, gradually began to move priorities from the national library to some other functions and activities. Practically the only significant investment ($165,000) was the construction of a LAN in Matica slovenská. We managed to pay for the cost of maintenance of hardware, software, and the operation of the system out of the SNK budget. Unfortunately, the state administration did not show an appropriate interest in the project and has not yet financially supported it.

We recommend that, in the case of such a large and significant project, the private donor require a matching grant from the appropriate government agency to ensure its further development.

Selection of the System. The successful implementation of any automation project depends on the selection of suitable software, which may also determine the hardware platform. For the selection of library software, a working group of experts from the CASLIN libraries was set up. This group started to work even before the grant was approved. The group's knowledge was based on previous experience, printed materials, presentations of systems, and visits abroad. A very detailed questionnaire, comprising more than 1,000 questions, was prepared for vendors. It became a part of the "Request for Proposal." CASLIN also hired an independent consultant from abroad, who shared in the preparation of the tender and its evaluation, and CASLIN greatly benefited from his work and experience. Although it takes time to acquire full knowledge of a system, it appears to be the case that the final selection proved appropriate: Digital Equipment Corporation (DEC) was selected as the hardware supplier, on the advice of Ex Libris.

The Supplier. Good relations with a supplier, his seriousness and reliability, and precisely written contract language, as well as contract adherence, are the other conditions for a successful implementation. Ex Libris became the software and hardware supplier for CASLIN. The preparation of the contract was a very salutary experience. Though CASLIN had been trying to design as detailed an agreement as possible, we could not avoid some ambiguity in the text of the main agreement and in the annexes. This experience enriched the know-how of working-group members, who could subsequently use this in advising other libraries.

Relations with, and support by, Ex Libris were good at the beginning, but gradually deteriorated. The reasons for this were the stringent requirements of CASLIN, some lack of effort and a diminishing interest on the part of Ex Libris, and a gradual deterioration in communications, for which both parties are probably responsible. Discussions are being held with the support office of Ex Libris in Budapest, regarding measures to improve the situation. Visits by Ex Libris people are not frequent, even though there are still quite a few problems to be solved. Often, the response of Ex Libris to a perceived problem referred to a future version of the system, even though the installation of that version was not immediately possible because it required some other changes and additional payments.

Hardware. SNK installed a DEC 3000/500 AXP with 256 MB of memory and 24 GB of disc capacity, with a UPS V30 NB. Additional DEC equipment is used in the LAN with 450 outlets.

The delivery time for, and the implementation of, the system were affected by the CASLIN decision to acquire a state-of-the-art DEC Alpha-chip computer, which still required at that time a U.S. export license. In addition, some of the required software (COBOL) was not ready in time for the planned delivery. The practical solution to this problem consisted of an initial delivery of demo computers, then a delivery of some intermediate machines, and, finally, of the desired DEC Alpha computers. It soon turned out that the original configurations were inadequate, especially with respect to the RAM and disk space, but subsequent enhancements improved this situation. It is gratifying that equipment reliability is very high.

Software. CASLIN installed version 3.2.5_11 of Aleph, operating under Digital Unix V. 3.2C. The increased disk capacity permitted mirroring, which contributes to a higher level of reliability and security for the whole system.

As Aleph migrated from demo computers to intermediate computers and production computers, the operating system also changed from ULTRIX to DEC OSF/1 and ultimately to DEC UNIX. Aleph itself was also gradually changing from version 3.2.3 to 3.2.4 and to the present 3.2.5, and each had several patches, which placed great burdens on computer people, and required periodic modifications in the Slovak-language localization of the system.

It became apparent both in the implementation phase and in the subsequent full-scale operations that not all of the promised features really worked or existed. Problems arose from the very beginning in the implementation of UNIMARC in Aleph. UNIMARC features were being implemented in new versions of Aleph only step-by-step. Several unexpected problems emerged that had to be solved mostly by ourselves —for example, printed outputs, because the standard printouts provided by Aleph did not meet our requirements. This finally led to problems with system acceptance. The above problems taxed our capacities and caused delays in the implementation of the system (see also, the chapter by Lass in this volume [28]).

The system is relatively difficult to prepare for use and to maintain, but is very flexible. Aleph, as used at SNK, proved very reliable and stable from the technical point of view and rarely crashes without good reason. In spite of all the drawbacks, it is a system that fulfills our essential requirements and is still developing. Ultimately, however, satisfaction, depends to the great extent on the proper configuring of the system and this, in turn, depends on a solid familiarity with it.

Standardization. CASLIN emphasized standardization in order to meet the requirements of the international exchange of bibliographic records and to achieve compatibility with international systems. The CASLIN libraries decided to use UNIMARC as the exchange format, the International Bibliographic Standard Description (IBSD), and the Anglo-American Cataloguing Rules (AACR-2)—which was an important transition from national standards to international ones. These decisions were based on extensive study, and also required the translation into Slovak and the publication of numerous items (1–9), so they would be available to all librarians in the Slovak Republic. We created a new publication series, "Standardization and Methodological Materials" (see 10–12).

After long negotiations among the CASLIN libraries, the content and the form of records for the CASLIN union catalog were agreed on and this material was published, too. All these changes caused problems because the libraries had approached their tasks without being aware that decisions would influence librarianship in both republics for many years. It was therefore necessary to find compromises for the sake of present and future partners, which slowed down the pace of Aleph implementation. We also agreed on a document typology according to the UNIMARC scheme, as well as on the use of the UDC for classification. The National Library in Prague translated and published a new edition of the UDC on CD-ROM, and SNK is doing the same task so that the updated edition is available for catalogers as soon as possible. CASLIN libraries use the character set LATIN 2 ISO 8859-2 with the so-called gizmo notation enhancement for characters not included in ISO LATIN-2. We expect to use UNICODE in the future. The use of protocols Z39.50 and http is supported for access and both protocols are implemented in Aleph.

SNK started to publish the Slovak National Bibliography on CD-ROM in 1997. The CD-ROM contains records in UNIMARC. The use of the internationally recognized standards will enable an exchange of records with OCLC and other foreign partners. We provided OCLC samples of records for testing in August 1997.

Legislation. lthough the Board of Directors of CASLIN paid remarkable attention to formalizing CASLIN's existence, this was finally not achieved because of the rather complicated interplay of laws, the models of control over participating libraries, funding issues, and issues of decision-making in the proposed consortium. The situation got particularly complicated when Czechoslovakia split into the independent Slovak and Czech republics and CASLIN became international, because the legal environments in the two republics gradually began to differ. Finally, we gave up on establishing CASLIN as a formal consortium and cooperation in the future will be covered by bilateral agreements between national libraries and their partners. An agreement on cooperation between the national libraries has been signed (13). SNK is preparing the text of an agreement on cooperation with partner libraries on the union catalog. SNK is also attempting to introduce provisions into a new bill on libraries, which would recognize the existence and operation of CASLIN, and which would replace the present, inadequate 1959 law on libraries.

The Conversion. The conversion of library data is usually difficult. Learning from past experience, we gradually carried out three conversions. The first conversion of about 1,000 records served for debugging. In the second conversion, we converted about 80,000 records. It was necessary to do this conversion quickly in order to be able to test Aleph and to provide access to the catalog of SNK in Aleph as soon as possible. Only after all necessary issues of the conversion were clarified was it possible to perform the final conversion and load the catalog of SNK. All three conversions employed a converter that consists of SNK's own proprietary software produced as an enhancement to CDS/ISIS.

Technical Processes. The opportunity of introducing new technologies led the management of SNK to an analysis of existing technical procedures, their optimization, and adaptation to new conditions. The fundamental processes are the processing of documents, the storage of documents, and the use of documents. Currently, all types of documents are being processed in Aleph, with the exception of serials and analytical bibliographical records.

The basic modules of every system are the OPAC and the cataloging modules. The OPAC is fully functional and at present there are five PCs available for users in the catalog area near the circulation desk—which appears to be sufficient up to now.

One can search the computerized catalogue of SNK (more than 250,000 records) and the catalogs of the other three CASLIN libraries, as well as the local database of SNB articles (more than 650,000 records). The number of records in the catalog increases daily by about 100 records from the current processing of acquisitions, the retroconversion, and the so-called short cataloging of items in the "live" collection. Access to the OPAC using a WWW browser is in an experimental stage but already available for outside users via the Internet, although this application needs to be improved. Because the Aleph GUI OPAC as well as WWW browsers are running under Windows, this user-friendlier access requires more powerful PCs that are not available at the moment, and thus public users in SNK can use only the standard OPAC.

Almost from the very beginning of the CASLIN implementation, the OPAC was also available to remote users from the Internet—from 1994, only through telnet, but from 1996, also via WWW. We consider the connection of our Aleph database server to the Internet as one of the main benefits of the Mellon Foundation grant. The ability to provide remote services is of vital importance to SNK, because it is not located in the capital of the Slovak Republic, nor in one of the other five large cities or academic centers. We believe that if other libraries started to provide access to our databases, interlibrary loans would increase.

Cataloging is also fully functional. SNK has processed all the documents in Aleph and UNIMARC since 1996, and books since 1995. At present, the transition to Aleph for processing the bibliography of articles in periodicals is being prepared.

The acquisitions module is being used only partially. This module was relegated to the background for a lack of staff capacity and because a lower priority was assigned to it by the national library, which acquires most items through legal deposit and purchases fewer items due to insufficient funds and higher prices.

Circulation is considered to be rather complicated and very visible by library users, and therefore a sensitive issue. Its automation is even more complicated if a library, such as SNK, holds millions of volumes, only part of which is included in the computer catalog, and documents are stored in closed stacks. Study of the issues revealed that it would not be efficient, even in a transitional period, to have a dual (manual as well as automated) circulation system. The management of SNK decided that after automated circulation is placed in operation, all documents must be lent through the automated system. Running the automated circulation system would require special measures, because only about 20 percent of holdings were in a machine-readable format at that time, and the system would require documents to be registered in it before they might be lent.

Thus, there arose a need for fast computer cataloging of documents frequently lent (the "live" part of the collection) that have no records in the computer catalog. Special work shifts had to be instituted for fast short cataloging, which placed much stress on the staff. Short-catalog records are to be completed later in the process of retroconversion. Input of the "live" part of the collection was done in two stages: before and after the start of automated circulation. The first preparatory stage differed from the second stage in that documents in the first were inputted after being returned to the library by borrowers, while in the second stage they are inputted before the loan is executed in the automated system. Both stages required the establishment of temporary work sites and we are unable to estimate how long they will be needed.

The new rules for circulation [20] went into effect on October 30, 1996, and users were required to reregister, which provided a new database of users. Readers may search the documents in the local catalog of SNK through the OPAC module by using PCs located near the circulation desk, and may place an order or a hold or a photocopy request through the system. They need not write down anything, as in a classic circulation system. The module seems to be working very well and reliably. Bar codes are used to identify books as well as readers, who have been issued plastic readers' cards.

The implementation of circulation was very difficult and demanding, but the increasingly positive responses of readers seem sufficient compensation. In any event, real time savings will become manifest only after most of the "live" collection has been computer cataloged. The library also seemed to benefit from the automatic generation of overdue notices, which brought in substantial fine revenue, although this is likely to decline in the future. But loans will continue to increase, as will user satisfaction.

Serials control has not yet been implemented. We also postponed work on the integration of the National Agency of ISBN processes into the system until some location and management issues are decided by competent authorities.

Work on the preparation of a union catalog continues, although the minister of culture assigned the task of operating the union catalog to the University Library in its Charter. Some authorities have attempted, without apparent reason, to discredit the union catalog in SNK.

Organizational Changes. SNK did not undertake as sweeping a set of organizational changes as the National Library did in Prague. We intend to make incremental changes as required by the development of Aleph. The most significant change in organization was a change in the document flow and processing such that all documents from the acquisitions department first come through the cataloging department and only then proceed to the National Bibliographic Institute for full bibliographic processing and the completion of records. This system has been in effect for three years and needs to be evaluated soon.

Bar codes. The unique identification of objects using bar codes speeds up and improves the quality of operations. We have used bar codes for identification of documents and readers since 1996. Bar-code labels are placed on all newly acquired documents and on all documents entering the automated circulation system. SNK uses double labels that are 50 x 30 mm. The handling and use of bar codes in SNK is described in references 16–18. Bar codes do not represent the acquisition number, call number, content, format, or any other aspect of the document, and are thus completely independent. Similarly, bar codes on readers' cards are just an identification number and do not include any other information. Our experience showed that the strategy of assigning independent bar codes is very advantageous. Appropriate links between bar-code numbers and records containing relevant data are maintained by the system.

SNK produces the labels itself. Since a bar code is an independent number, it is possible to produce labels in advance, using specialized autonomous software. The plastic readers' cards are also produced in the library. The bar code is printed on a card, together with the name of a user, at the moment of registration and the cards are issued immediately.

We use coding system CODE 39 with 10 alphanumerical positions. The decision to use this code was not by chance. It seems to be more suitable for libraries than, for example, European Article Numbering (EAN), since it avoids paying for EAN membership. Slovak and Czech libraries designed and agreed on the coding system for libraries that uniquely allows them to identify the document or user in all libraries participating in the system. The first two parts of the code comprise the code of the library and the interpretation of the other positions of the code is an internal matter for each library. Aleph supports the identification of documents and readers via the bar code.

A Retrospective Conversion. A retrospective conversion is a very expensive and time-consuming process, requiring either the use of advanced technology or a lot of manpower. The solution to this problem at SNK significantly lags behind the state of the art not only in advanced countries but even in Central European countries. SNK is aware of the urgency of this task, but up to now its possibilities have been very limited. Unlike the National Library (NKP) in Prague, SNK did not receive an additional grant from the Mellon Foundation for this task. Though the technology developed in NKP looks promising and might be used also in SNK,[2] we do not have sufficient funds to apply it. In addition, the aim of SNK is not only to provide access to scanned images of catalog cards but also to load the structured UNIMARC records into Aleph, which is much more time-consuming work for catalogers. Thus, we are proceeding in a classic way by the keyboard entry of records from cards into Aleph. For this, we have received funds for 10 positions from the Ministry of Work and Social Affairs, through the Office of Work in Martin. It would be helpful for the retroconversion at SNK if the National Library in Prague were to provide access to the records of the Czech National Bibliography and of its catalog in UNIMARC. We also expect significant benefits from our cooperation with other libraries in Slovakia.

Staff. The main problem of SNK in the area of automation was the lack of suitable technology until the Mellon Foundation provided the grant. After buying hardware and software, and achieving a certain level of installed equipment, it began to be clear that the main problem was the lack of a highly qualified staff. The problem was not so much in the training of librarians for routine work, but it was and still is the insufficient capacity for the development and preparation of new applications in automation, and for the solution of the technical problems in those parts of the CASLIN project that had not yet been automated or did not even exist in SNK at all. SNK has highly qualified staff members but their number is insufficient and they also have to perform routine duties. To some extent there is also a problem of an inadequate knowledge of foreign languages, especially of English. Unfortunately, the management of SNK has only a limited authority to determine its own personnel policy. We only recently managed to create significant financial incentives for key persons in the CASLIN project.

---

2. See B. Stoklasová, "The Retrospective Conversion in Czech Libraries," in this volume.

162 *Case Histories*

The relatively long time required to bring CASLIN on-line also had negative effects through personnel changes due to promotions, resignations, and other reasons. These changes were considerable and systems librarians and systems programmers have changed in all the CASLIN libraries during CASLIN's lifetime.

Training.   Training for Aleph started very intensively and succesfully in the summer of 1993. The approach of Ex Libris and of CASLIN was very constructive and progressive, full of responsibility and enthusiasm. The level of the training sessions was very good. However, when the staff started to get involved in the real-life operations of Aleph, staff members had to solve a lot of problems when Ex Libris was not able to solve them promptly, and the tempo of training gradually slowed down. It would be useful in such projects if the vendor's staff could stay at the library site for a longer period or at least provide regular visits to the site.

The four CASLIN seminars that were sponsored by the Pew Charitable Trusts and other sponsors were extremely useful. The seminars contributed considerably to a broadening of the horizons and knowledge of the CASLIN librarians and library managements.

Microfilming.   The CASLIN project was focused not only on automation but also included support for microfilming. A part of the Mellon Foundation grant ($200,000) was dedicated to the creation of microfilm laboratories in both national libraries.

The task of the working group for microfilming was to select and purchase hardware and microfilming facilities. This was originally a two-member-group and was gradually enlarged by representatives of other libraries of CASLIN+.[3] The activities of the working group were focused on designing the concept for the preservation of microfilming, on establishing rules and standards, setting up the rules for cataloging, and registering micromedia in the Aleph environment. The key problem for the working group was to meet the high quality level of microfilm production prescribed by international standards. In 1996, the group split into two national commissions, one in each republic. The priority of the new commissions is to establish cooperation on the project, called the "national program of preservation through microfilming documents."

The grant permitted the purchase of micrographic technology for SNK, which led to a reorganization of this department in Matica slovenská and to its incorporation in the structure of SNK. The new equipment is powerful and allows us to attain the quality required by the international standards.

Union Catalog.   One of the main ideas of CASLIN was the idea of a cooperative, shared cataloging and bibliography. For realizing this idea, a union catalog for CASLIN was needed. The union catalog should consist of three parts: (1) the CASLIN union catalog, Czech part, located at NKP in Prague; (2) the CASLIN union catalog, Slovak part, located at SNK in Martin; and (3) the union catalog, Slovak part, for foreign periodicals, located at UKB in Bratislava.

The union catalog should be (1) informative; (2) methodical, cooperative, and standardized; and (3) controlled with respect to data entry. It should include titles re-

---

3. This constitutes an expansion of CASLIN beyond the original four members.

ported to the National Agency of the ISBN. These records would allow better control of acquisitions in libraries and improve publishing activities, effectiveness, and publishers' policy.

An important element in building the union catalog will be the retroconversion of the catalog in SNK. SNK also maintains a card union catalog of the Slovak research libraries that contains some 3 million titles. In addition, catalogs of other libraries contain other thousands of records, some of them in machine-readable form.

Through the union catalog and the transparent interconnection of automated systems of particular libraries, users should be able to get current information about the status of each copy of a requested document in the system. A standard record of the union catalog will also contain data on subject description, such as UDC and subject headings. This will allow universal searches on any topic. The system will also include various working databases, such as directories of publishers, booksellers, libraries, and various controlled dictionaries and code lists. The union catalog will adhere to the standards mentioned earlier. The basic principles for creating and operating and maintaining the union catalog are given in a 1994 article (14). SNK organized a meeting of 38 libraries on union catalog issues in May 1997 and the participants agreed with the concept of a union catalogue that was presented without major comments.

A new organizational unit of SNK, for the management of the union catalog, will be created. The manager of the union catalog will organize cooperation based on bilateral agreements with other libraries. The board for the union catalog will determine the principles of the cataloging policy and of cooperation, and outline future developments. Although this board will be separate from the Czech participants in CASLIN, both national libraries agreed on participation (13). The union catalog management unit will coordinate activities inside and outside SNK. In cooperation with various SNK departments and divisions, it will coordinate work on the retroconversion, the maintenance and creation of authority files, the methods of bibliographic description, and the structuring the databases. The basic principles of cooperation are given in a 1996 document (1/1).

International Collaboration and Cooperation. CASLIN became an international project when, on January 1, 1993, Czechoslovakia split into the Slovak Republic and the Czech Republic. Even though some minor problems arose, the political changes did not harm the cooperation between Slovak and Czech librarians in the CASLIN project. On the contrary, we felt that mutual respect for each other as equal partners improved our relations. Alhough recently the level of communication between Czech and Slovak librarians has become attenuated, we believe that our cooperation will continue on a high level.

We feel that a very important aspect of international cooperation is to exchange records of material called "patriotica." Political, historical, and demographic developments caused significant groups of Czechs and Slovaks to live in other countries. The intellectual output of these groups is part of Czech and Slovak culture. It is important that the records of relevant authors, languages, or content in other countries be marked with special codes and regularly exchanged between national bibliographies. We had such cooperation with the National Library of Hungary and we are ready to continue this cooperation.

The Impact of CASLIN on Library Automation in Slovakia

The impact of CASLIN is felt in three areas: (1) standardization; (2) the introduction and use of information technology in libraries; (3) the introduction of electronic technologies to foster the development of information networks in the Slovak Republic.

Standardization. At present, SNK is very much involved in the dissemination of the UNIMARC format to as many libraries as possible and in supporting its use by them. SNK is preparing the library community for the use of these standards. SNK published a Slovak translation of the UNIMARC Manual (1, 2), all manuals of ISBD (3–9), and also prepared and published some other methodological materials necessary for shared cataloging and creating a union catalog (10–12). SNK organizes workshops, seminars, training, and other educational events and provides consultations on these issues for librarians from various libraries.

SNK also cooperates with system vendors and users of other systems (VTLS, Rapid Library, Libris) and is making efforts so that all libraries may accept and use the new library standards as soon as possible. The transition to UNIMARC will take some time but we believe that it will gradually be accepted in all the libraries of Slovakia.

Impact on Information Technology in Libraries. The results of CASLIN promoted its expansion to CASLIN+ and resulted in other grants from the Mellon Foundation —in particular, to the consortium of libraries in Košice (see the chapter by Darina Kožuchová and Ĺubomíra Šoltésová in this volume [29]).

The results achieved by SNK promote automation and the introduction of IT to other, smaller libraries, and the offer of services by SNK (the OPAC via the Internet; e-mail; the Slovak National Bibliography on CD-ROM; the electronic transmission of files of bibliographic and cataloging records; a WWW server) creates a supportive environment for other libraries.

The Program for Electronic Libraries. SNK is responsible for library development and is keenly aware that there is no state policy on automation and that funding is inadequate. It therefore prepared a proposal for the electronic modernization of libraries as part of the information network development program in the Slovak Republic. The program would involve all significant research and regional public libraries (about 50 libraries). The proposal is described in a 1996 document (21) and was submitted to the Ministry of Culture in 1996. Although it has received much support in the press, no government support has been provided so far and the outlook is not promising.

The Future. The future of CASLIN in Slovakia and of the program to make libraries electronic depends on the future position of SNK. The Parliament passed a new law regarding Matica slovenská (24), in which Matica slovenská is defined as a public body, similar to that of state TV and state radio, and SNK as an independent legal entity but a daughter institution of Matica slovenská. This created a conflict between Matica slovenská and the Ministry of Culture. The minister of culture decided to transfer some of the functions of the National Library to the University Library of Bratislava (UKB). Unfortunately, an explicit formulation of the functions of the SNK was not included in the law and the management of UKB supports the transfer. The new Charter of UKB (23) issued by the minister of culture defines this library as the central state library and it assigns it functions that SNK has been fulfilling for more than 40 years. This is in conflict with all previous agreements and also with the understandings with CASLIN.

The government decided that in spite of the prevailing views of the library community, UKB will fulfill the essential parts of the national library's tasks. If this really happens, it will be a significant step backward and will have a negative influence on the development of Slovak librarianship in the coming years.

The Ministry of Culture is unable or unwilling to listen to the library community: the libraries, the Slovak Association of Libraries, and the Slovak Association of Librarians. It seems that the Ministry of Culture intends to use the new law as a tool of political enforcement and not for the improvement of libraries. Unfortunately, the government's approach make one fear for the future development of libraries in Slovakia.

Conclusion

CASLIN represents a continuation of previous projects by SNK toward the full automation of our own library and of the whole library system in Slovakia. The grant from the Mellon Foundation enabled the continuation of this project, but on a much higher technological level. SNK could not have achieved this technological level without substantial financial support, which would not have materialized from Slovak government sources because of the lack of development funds in general, and because of the pervasive lack of interest and ignorance about libraries that government agencies, but particularly the Ministry of Culture, have exhibited during the period of the Mečiar government (1993–98).

The Mellon grant enabled SNK to acquire modern, powerful hardware and a professional library software system, which gave considerable encouragement to librarians. As a result, the SNK staff approached the CASLIN project responsibly and with enthusiasm. While the system is not completely operational, much of it is up and running. In future years, SNK intends to focus on cooperation with other libraries to build and operate a union catalog. In spite of the fact we did not manage to institutionalize the CASLIN consortium, we believe that cooperation among libraries and the union catalog may work on the basis of bilateral agreements. While CASLIN may have been delayed, it will achieve its objectives.

References

Dušan Katuščák, *UNIMARC manuál: Slovenská verzia*. [The UNIMARC manual: Slovak version], Martin: Matica slovenská, 1994.

UNIMARC/AUTORITY: Univerzálny formát pre autority [UNIMARC/AUTHORITIES: A Universal Format for Authorities], Jarmila Majerová (transl.) Martin: Matica slovenská – Slovenská národná knižnica, 1996.

ISBD(G): Všeobecný medzinárodný štandardný bibliografický popis; anotovaný text [ISBD(G): The Universal standard bibliographic description: annotated text], Translated and edited by Dušan Katuščák, Martin: Matica slovenská, 1994.

ISBD(M): Medzinárodný štandardný bibliografický popis pre monografie [ISBD(M): International Standard for the bibliographic description of monographs], Introduction by Dušan Katuščák, translated and edited by Jarmila Majerová; Martin: Matica slovenská, 1994.

ISBD(CM): Medzinárodný štandardný bibliografický popis pre kartografické materiály, [ISBD (CM): International standard for the bibliographic description of cartographic materials], Translated and edited by Eleonóra Janšová, Introduction by Dušan Katuščák, Martin: Matica slovenská, 1995.

ISBD(CF): Medzinárodný štandardný bibliografický popis počítačových súborov [ISBD(CF) International standard for the bibliographic description of computer files], Translated and edited by Juraj Hauptvogl, Introduction by Dušan Katuščák, Martin: Matica slovenská, 1994.

ISBD(S): Medzinárodný štandardný bibliografický popis pre seriály [ISBD(A): International standard for the bibliographic description of periodicals]. Translated and edited by Jarmila Majerová; Introduction by Dušan Katuščák. Martin: Matica slovenská, 1995.

ISBD(A): Medzinárodný štandardný bibliografický popis pre staré tlače (antikvária) [ISBD(A): International standard for the bibliographic description of old prints (Antiquarian)], Translated and edited by Dušan Katuščák. Martin: Matica slovenská, 1995.

ISBD(CP): Pravidlá aplikácie ISBD na popis článkov [ISBD (CP): The ISBD application rules for articles description], Translated and edited by Dušan Katuščák and Martina Vargová, Martin: Matica slovenská, 1994.

Eleonóra Janšová, Anna Kucianová, Jarmila Majerová, Viera Matejíčková, and Mária Okálová, *Metodika popisu kníh vo formáte UNIMARC v systéme Aleph: Príručka používateľa: Verzia V 1.1* [Methodology of book description in the UNIMARC format and the Aleph system: User's Handbook version V 1.1], Štandardizačné a metodické materiály, vol.1, Martin: Matica slovenská – Slovenská národná knižnica, November 1995.

Záznam pre Súborný katalóg CASLIN. [The CASLIN Union Catalogue record], Štandardizačné a metodické materiály, vol. 2, Martin: Matica slovenská – Slovenská národná knižnica, 1996.

Eleonóra Janšová, Anna Kucianová, Katerina Chovanová, Ľudmila Rohoňová, *Metodika popisu článkov vo formáte UNIMARC v systéme Aleph: Príručka používateľa: Verzia V 1.0* [Methodology of periodicals' description in the UNIMARC format and the Aleph system: User's Handbook version V 1.0], Štandardizačné a metodické materiály, vol.14, Martin: Matica slovenská – Slovenská národná knižnica, October 1996.

Zmluva o spolupráci pro rozvoji CASLIN medzi Maticou slovenskou – Slovenskou národnou knižnicou a Národní knihovnou České republiky. [Agreement on cooperation in the development of CASLIN between the Matica Slovenska – The Slovak National Library and the National Library of the Czech Republic], Internal material.

Daniela Slížová, "Súborný katalóg CASLIN," [The CASLIN Union Catalogue] In: *Infos 95: Zborník z jubilejného 25. Informatického seminára konaného v dňoch 3.-6. apríla v Jasnej pod Chopkom* [Infos 95: Proceedings from the 25th, jubelie seminar in information science in Jasna pod Chopkom, April 3–6, 1995], Spolok slovenských knihovníkov, April 1995.

Statement of Intent of CASLIN libraries' Directors. Internal material of CASLIN. See: http://www.nkp.cz/caslin/texty/stmint.html

Milan Rakús, "Implementácia programového systému ALEPH v Slovenskej národnej knižnici Matice slovenskej," in: *Infos 95: Zborník z jubilejného 25. informatického seminára konaného v dňoch 3.-6. apríla 1995 v Jasnej pod Chopkom* ["The Implementation of the Aleph system in the Slovak National Library of The Matica Slovenska," in Infos 95: Proceedings from the 25th, jubelie seminar in information science in Jasna pod Chopkom, April 3–6, 1995], Spolok slovenských knihovníkov, April 1995.

Milan Rakús, "Ďalšie skúsenosti s implementáciou programového systému ALEPH v Slovenskej národnej knižnici Matice slovenskej" in: *Infos 96: Zborník z 26. Informatického seminára konaného v doch 15.-18. apríla 1996 v Jasnej pod Chopkom* "Further experiences with the Aleph system in the Slovak National Library of The Matica Slovenska" in: Infos 96:

Proceedings from the 26th seminar in information science in Jasna pod Chopkom, April 15-18, 1996]. Spolok slovenských knihovníkov, April 1996.

Rakús, Milan "Implementácia programového systému ALEPH v Slovenskej národnej knižnici Matice slovenskej (rok 1996)" in: *Infos 97: Zborník z 27. Informatického seminára konaného v dňoch 14.-17. apríla 1997 v Jasnej pod Chopkom* ["The Implementation of the Aleph system in the Slovak National Library of The Matica Slovenska (in the year 1996)" in Inos 97: Proceedings from the 27th seminar in information science in Jasna pod Chopkom, April 14-17, 1997], Spolok slovenských knihovníkov, April 1997.

Tibor Takács, "Automatická identifikace v knihovnách: Využití čárového kódu a automatizované zabezpečení knihovního fondu" ["Automatic identification in libraries: The use of the bar code and of computerized security in Libraries"] in: *Information sources* Vol. 1., Brno: Sdružení knihoven České republiky, 1993.

Knižničný poriadok Slovenskej národnej knižnice Matice slovenskej v Martine. [Library rules of the Slovak National Library, Matica Slovenska], Martin: Matica slovenská, 1996. See: http://www.matica.sk/snk/sluzby/knipor.html

Slížová, Daniela and Prokop, Igor *Program elektronizácie knižníc ako súčasť' rozvoja informačných sietí SR* [Library Automation Projects as Part of the Development of Information Networks in the Slovak Republic], Martin: Matica slovenská – Slovenská národná knižnica, May 1996. See: http://www.matica.sk/snk/progel0.html

Dušan Katuščák, Miroslav Bielik, Štefan Ďurovčík, Igor Prokop, L'udmila Repková and Daniela Slížová, *Integrovaný knižnično-informačný systém na báze elektronizácie* [The electronic basis of the Integrated library-information system], Martin: Matica slovenská, 1985.

Zriad'ovacia listina Univerzitnej knižnice [The Constitutional Document of the University Library], see http://www.ulib.sk/listina.htm

Zákon NR SR z 13. februára 1997 o Matici slovenskej, in: *Zbierka zákonov*, 68/ 1997 [The National Parliament of the Slovak Republic Law on the Matica Slovenska from February 13, 1997], See http://www.matica.sk/texty_html/zakon.html

Miloš Kovačka, Daniela Slížová, and Igor Prokop, *Národný program retrokonverzie a konverzie generálnej bázy slovacikálnych bibliografických údajov a klasických slovacikálnych knižničných dokumentov* [The National Program for the retroconversion and conversion of the general catalogue of bibliographic records and of classical book documents pertaining to Slovakia.], Martin: Slovenská národná knižnica v Matici slovenskej, March-June, 1996. See http://www.matica.sk/snk/ret_1.html

Štandardy pre Štátny informačný systém Slovenskej republiky [State Information System Standards of the Slovak Republic], Bratislava: Štatistický úrad Slovenskej republiky, July 1993.

Vojtěch Balík, "Caslin, Priorities of the Czech National Library, and Government Policy on Information and Libraries," see chapter 10 in present volume.

Lass, Andrew, "Managing Delay: The Micropolitics of Time in the Czech and Slovak Automation Projects" see chapter 28 in present volume.

Darina Kožuchová and L'ubomíra Šoltésová, "Problems of Library Automation," see chapter 12 in present volume.

CHAPTER 14

The Aleph Implementation at the National Library of the Czech Republic

IVA PŘÍBRAMSKÁ

The purpose of this chapter is to warn libraries about the mistakes we made at the National Library of the Czech Republic, rather than celebrating our successes. I hope that other libraries can learn from them, as we did.

The Agreement between Vendor and Customer

The basic document involved not only in negotiations with a library system vendor, but also in the implementation of a system, is an agreement between a vendor and a customer. In our case, the customers were the four Czech and Slovak libraries that joined in a consortium called CASLIN (Czech and Slovak Library Information Network).[1] These libraries decided to buy Aleph, an integrated library information system produced by Ex Libris, of Israel.

The basis for this decision was Ex Libris's response to the CASLIN "Request for Proposal" (RFP). The RFP, distributed to the potential vendors, was very detailed and was based on the model for some American RFPs. The detailed nature of the RFP permitted some inconsistencies to creep in: (1) Although the main intention of CASLIN was to buy an integrated system (for example, a system in which different modules share the same data), the RFP asked for the capability of searching bibliographic data at more places of the material in almost all modules—which seems to indicate that we were prepared to accept more bibliographic databases; (2) some U.S.-specific items were not removed; (3) some items of great importance were listed, but not sufficiently specified and explained (the most troublesome of these pertained to UNIMARC functionalities).

It is not the case that everything could have been done in a much better way. At the time of RFP's preparation, there was almost no accumulated experience about how to do this, not only in the National Library (NL) but also in the entire Czech and Slovak Republics, since there was only one integrated library information system in use there

---

1. The National Library of the Czech Republic, the National Library of Slovakia, the Brno State Library, and the Bratislava University Library.

—TinLib. With a little information from leaflets and foreign journals, and almost no practical experience, neither systems analysts nor librarians had enough knowledge about what functionality should be expected or demanded. We had clear ideas only about the OPAC and cataloging modules, since for some six years we had used CDS/ISIS, a system produced by UNESCO for the constructing and searching of databases of different types.

The agreement between the CASLIN libraries and Ex Libris, which was signed in May 1993, consists of different parts and appendixes, most of which had a great impact on the Aleph implementation. The agreement in fact consisted of four separate agreements, signed separately:

1. Software License and Services Agreement
2. Training Agreement
3. Software Maintenance Agreement
4. Hardware Supply Agreement

Software License and Services Agreement

This part specified the rights and commitments of both parties. In addition to other important provisions, the system's acceptance procedure is discussed here, with further reference to one of the appendixes.

The acceptance of the system was divided into three parts, covering all modules in the order in which they were supposed to be implemented. The system's functionality was required to be checked against the Aleph specifications (as delivered by Ex Libris) and Ex Libris's responses to the CASLIN RFP, which had been marked as already implemented, and which were related to the localization of the system (which we promised to do ourselves). The main condition for beginning the acceptance procedure was that the CASLIN staff had to receive relevant training. By that time we were expected to have enough experience to recognize which functions were really supported by the system. We believed that, in case of discrepancies between Ex Libris's declaration and our experience, we would be able to demand and get the entire promised functionality.

As we found out after two days of negotiations concerning the first acceptance benchmark, Ex Libris's attitude was quite different. We were told that the customary procedure for satisfying the Aleph acceptance test was to demonstrate what Aleph could do. Anyway, during the negotiations it became clear how important every word of an agreement, and especially of an RFP, is.

Although the whole system had already been paid for, the state-of-the-art of acceptance procedures was rather poor in the autumn of 1993, which was the time of the first Aleph installation. In the first installation phase, the acquisitions, OPAC, cataloging, and the authority and holdings maintenance modules were accepted with various objections.[2] In the second phase, the circulation module was accepted (with objections) and

---

2. About these there is a substantial correspondence.

also the serials module. The third phase deals with the union catalog model and with ILL and selective dissemination of information (SDI). We should add that for a long time we were not prepared to undertake and complete all the necessary training, and only in 1997 did the CASLIN libraries agree to the continuation of the training process.

Training

The time schedule for the basic training cycle for systems people and for librarians was described in the appendix of the agreement. Because funds were scarce (in spite of the grants from The Andrew W. Mellon Foundation and the Pew Charitable Trusts), a model for two-tier training for librarians was adopted. First, selected librarians were trained (usually four from the two national libraries and three from the two "satellite" libraries). The librarians who participated in training activities changed according to the topic of the particular training course (only system librarians had to attend all courses). The professional level of the Ex Libris trainers was very high, and their knowledge of the system's behavior and their teaching abilities were quite good.

The duty of the system's "superusers" was to train their colleagues. Most of them fulfilled this obligation. Trainers, especially for the OPAC and cataloging modules, were quite busy and showed a great deal of devotion since, besides teaching the training courses, they usually had to do all their regular work. We gradually worked out a system of cyclical training for library staff, which included not only Aleph training for the different categories of librarians working with different modules, but also basic UNIMARC training for most of the participants.

The main problem was that the implementation of different modules was (and still is) occurring at a slower pace than had been expected, so that there was no point in undertaking some of the Ex Libris training, because we would not be able to apply the knowledge acquired.

Software Maintenance

Support services. The history of our ongoing support is rather complex. In the beginning, the Ex Libris staff from Israel was responsible for it. It gave rise to various problems, ranging from misunderstandings because of the language barrier to problems with slow Internet connections, which complicated remote on-line maintenance. At the time, we appreciated the opportunities for the direct negotiations, especially training lessons and occasional visits. The situation did not change even after Ex Libris established a branch office in Prague, since that office was more business- than implementation-oriented. A remarkable improvement was achieved after a competent programmer and librarian started to work for Ex Libris in Prague. The communication with the new team became much easier (although only one team member was Czech), and the team helped with the installation of new versions, and took on the burden of the system testing. The team did its best, but in the case of more complex issues, it was in almost the same situation that we had been in before: Although the team reported to Israel, it often did not receive any advice or answers to questions. Unfortunately, for various reasons this support ended.

Currently, we are supported by a Hungarian company that cooperates with Ex Libris. The company's staff members are agreeable and capable people, but they are too busy, since they have to cover too large a region, one with many installations; hence our reports and questions often seem to fall between the cracks. Once again, the only opportunity for moving things forward is via on-site visits, which were promised as a quarterly occurrence. Unfortunately, this form of support, on a regular basis, is not covered by the agreement and thus appears to depend entirely on Ex Libris's goodwill.

The problem with the agreement is that, although it specifies how Ex Libris should act when various system failures appear, such failures are not clearly defined. The category of "minor problems" is too broad. The agreement ought to distinguish between minor problems that affect the librarians' work and problems that prevent borrowers from using some Aleph functions, since in the latter case a malfunction can result in the library's losing credibility (in the NL, it concerns especially WWW interface issues and, recently, problems with the basic search command FIND). No definition of the primary Aleph functions is included in the agreement, although they are mentioned as an important category.

Distribution of new versions and patches, and the documentation. The agreement included a promise that we would receive a new version of the system each year. In addition, too many patches are distributed not only with corrections of mistakes but also with a description of new and improved functions. Since the system is being developed in a very dynamic way, it is not easy to follow and test all modifications. We have the printed documentation for each version, the electronic documentation for each version and patch, and a list of changes for each patch. The quantity of documentation is sufficient, but the quality is rather poor. In the users' part of the documentation there is a mixture of information for librarians and for systems people. The systems part of the manual is not carefully updated, and it is often the case that the manual is one or two steps behind actual system behavior. The supporting company is, in part, trying to solve this problem. It tests all patches and promised to release only such patches as will solve some of the major problems. The accumulation of these corrections helps in the localization of the system but delays the effective use of various new functions.

Suggestions concerning system maintenance. Is there a way to prevent some of the maintenance problems? First, one might not pay for functions that the vendor said would work (in some particular manner requested by us) but do not. It would be very useful to obtain from experienced libraries some model(s) (at least) for the maintenance part of the agreement. Our experience in this field does not seem sufficient even for our next attempt to buy a system, should we wish to do so in the future. It seems that the most important thing for success is the goodwill on the part of both the vendor and the customer and it is not clear that this is at an optimal level.

Hardware Supply

Even before our first contacts with suppliers, we felt it important to negotiate with only one entity, which would supply both the library information system and the basic hardware on which the system should run. The reason was to avoid a situation in which different suppliers could blame each other for possible problems. As we required a library information system that would run under the UNIX operating system, Ex Libris suggested that we choose between Digital Equipment (DEC) and IBM. Our choice was DEC. Since I was not involved in negotiations with DEC, I will omit further discussion of this subject.

Localization of the System

Since the CASLIN libraries were the first customers of Ex Libris in the former Czech and Slovak federative republic, they agreed that their employees would do all the necessary translations: the users' part of the Aleph manual, and all system tools for communication with the user (screens and system messages). Here "users" include librarians, so we translated not only the OPAC but other modules as well: the acquisitions, serials, circulation, cataloging, holdings, and authority maintenance modules, plus the SDI and ILL functions—altogether, about 1,000 different screens. Since many librarians did not have adequate English-language skills, all the translating had to be done prior to the first installation. To shorten the delay caused by this, the CASLIN libraries shared all the work in the first stage of implementation; thus, for a time, Aleph communicated with librarians partly in Czech and partly in Slovak. Only later did we complete both language versions. It is impossible to exaggerate the difficulty of making translations without knowing how the system works.

Communication, Cooperation

Although some of us had learned English at school, before 1989 there were not many opportunities to use it. Thus, when the political situation changed, we had many communication problems. Unfortunately, the main documents (the agreement and the RFP) exist only in an English version. Since every word is important in such materials, there were only a few people in the CASLIN libraries who were able to correctly understand everything (at least we thought so). In particular, the legal language of the agreement is too complicated. For libraries that buy a system from a foreign vendor, I would suggest that they make sure that they have both language versions. Although only one is necessary for negotiating with the vendor, the version in the local language is very important for all librarians.

We had the greatest language problems during the Ex Libris training courses. It was often impossible to find librarians with a good knowledge of all the processes that a particular module contained and with at least a basic knowledge of English. As a result, nearly all training courses for librarians had to be translated by one or two system librarians. This was clearly at the expense of the actual time that could be devoted to the gaining of practical experience with the system. And what is worse, not even all CASLIN system people were able to discuss problems in English, which prevented them from asking questions and led to the loss of important information.

Communication with the vendor was also influenced by the real difficulty posed by the exchanging and sharing of information among the four CASLIN libraries. The influence of a common climate in the society can be noticed.

Implementation

Definition of the System Tables, UNIMARC

After the system was installed and localized, the work for system librarians and system managers started in earnest. Since Aleph is really open to different kinds of modifications, the setting up of various system tables was sometimes complicated and very time-consuming. The most complex table defines the database structure, since we definitely did not want to use the simple structure that is being used in Israel.

The decision to use UNIMARC as an internal structure, in order to avoid loss of information during conversions, was made even before the system was selected. We expected our request for UNIMARC, which was unfortunately not clear and precise enough, to be fulfilled. However, as a standard, commercial library information system, Aleph does not include some essential features; some data have to be entered not only in the form required by UNIMARC, but also in the form in which it can be used for searching and displaying. Some data even have to be stored in three different forms.

The difficulties of incorporating UNIMARC as an internal format lead to some more general comments. UNIMARC was originally designed as a format for exchanges between libraries in countries in which a special national format had already been developed, and which were often supported by some national cataloging rules. In both the Czech and Slovak republics, we also used a national exchange format, built under the auspices of CDS/ISIS. We had no corresponding system of cataloging rules, and we tried to merge nearly-30-year-old rules with ISBD recommendations. After contemplating the preparation of something that could be called CZMARC—based on UNIMARC—we decided to adopt a more generally used exchange format. The intention behind the implementation of such a commonly used format as an internal format was to avoid the loss of information during conversions.

Under the influence of other national libraries in Europe, we decided on UNIMARC. But UNIMARC, primarily an exchange format, is not supported by any special cataloging rules that we might also have needed. Although we tried to follow ISBD recommendations, these cannot replace cataloging rules. Only one (unsuccessful) attempt to create our own, completely new, cataloging rules was made, and we ultimately decided to use AACR2. After a few years we daresay that this is a feasible combination.

In 1993, when we bought a new library information system, we did not want to keep our national exchange format as an internal format. We did not have corresponding cataloging rules, and we definitely did not want to develop and maintain them. We were willing to change everything in order to communicate with the rest of the world—on the basis of bibliographic data—as easily as possible. I believe that many other libraries in Central and Eastern Europe that started to use their first truly integrated library information system were (and some still are) in the same situation. One can only hope that the willingness to adopt something that is already in use is no longer considered suspect in Europe, in which many countries would like to maintain their specific identities—which is the main obstacle to the carrying out of certain international projects, such as building the multinational and multilingual CERL HPB database.

At that time, we chose UNIMARC in the belief that future cooperation with other European national libraries would be achieved. We did not expect that our cooperation with OCLC would become more intensive and fruitful. As a result, we lost two years while waiting for OCLC's program for conversion from USMARC to UNIMARC, which we would not have needed if we had been using USMARC.

I do not want to compare USMARC and UNIMARC as to, for example, the granularity, content of the fields. Thinking of standard (i.e., not homemade) library information systems, I see the following advantages of USMARC:

- USMARC is a practice-checked internal format with a rounded-off system of rules (although successful "format harmonization" can change the situation).
- The feature of embedded (linking-entry) fields is implemented in USMARC in a more pragmatic manner.
- There are many more library information systems that support USMARC (even Ex Libris started to pay more attention to it, because it is expanding in North and South America). Only several local systems are able to provide full support for UNIMARC.

Finally, a very personal comment: The enormous support for UNIMARC in Europe is explained, apart from other reasons, by a fear of things from America, and mainly from the United States.

In 1993, when the CASLIN libraries decided to use UNIMARC, we were the first Ex Libris customer who wanted to implement UNIMARC with all its features. Special modifications were made to Aleph to enable it to adopt indicators and differentiate them from simple text, but there is still no acceptable way of handling (displaying and searching) linking-entry fields and fixed fields. Since UNIMARC data are mostly entered without punctuation marks, it is not possible to follow ISBD recommendations in their entirety in the Aleph formatting language. There was a time when we were in despair, thinking about slightly changing the internal structure. Now, the smaller modifications,[3] and the duplication of some data in a different form, especially for searching or instead displaying forms dynamically generated according to special indicators, seem sufficient. Analytical records are the only exception. The addition of some non-MARC fields appears to be necessary for solving our problems. Are we too exacting?

Instructions for using Aleph in the NL. To remind librarians of the most important system functions, to present the information about Aleph that cannot be found in the Aleph manual, and to disseminate information about the special local setup of the system,[4] the systems librarian department publishes a type of user manual. At present, we are already using its sixth version, which not only exists in a printed form but is also accessible as HTML files.

---

3. Such as using the nine digits devoted to national use, together with additional subfields.
4. This included a list of statuses, a description of special local non-MARC fields, information about the content of access files, instructions about how to enter diacritical characters, how to invoke special homemade programs.

The Timetable for the Implementation

The initial installation of Aleph did not have the guaranteed functionality we wanted and we decided to start the actual implementation only after the next version was delivered. In the meantime, we participated in most of the Ex Libris training courses, and continued with the training in our library.

Another enormous task had to be accomplished: Since, for some years before the installation of Aleph, we had been working with CDS/ISIS,[5] we had a relatively large number of bibliographic records in the national exchange format. The total amounted to about 100,000 records in different databases. These records had to be converted into UNIMARC and we decided to do it ourselves. As our catalogers tend to be precise, we spent a long time analyzing and comparing both structures and testing the CDS/ISIS reformatting tools that, supplemented by moderate-sized, homemade programs, were used for the conversion.

This greatly delayed the whole implementation process because the conversion of records created for the national bibliography was the principal precondition for using Aleph in our library in a real production mode. The lack of workstations for the librarians also contributed to the delay, so that at the beginning of 1995, when we started to catalog foreign books that were new arrivals at the library, processing could not begin in the acquisitions department, but only later in the cataloging department.

The processing of Czech books began in September 1995. We continued to use the same work flow for creating bibliographic records as we had used for the description of Czech books in CDS/ISIS. But CDS/ISIS is not an integrated library automation system, which means that acquisitions librarians could only begin the processing by creating a short bibliographic description, and hence all acquisitions data were processed in the traditional way. Although CDS/ISIS was very important for the Czech librarians—because it allowed them to become familiar with modern information technology and gave them the chance to start catching up with a world advanced in information processing (in terms of numbers of bibliographic records processed)—it could not help librarians become familiar with the other important functions of automation, such as acquisitions and circulation. This fact is largely responsible for the delay in the implementation of Aleph.

The processing of most of the other types of documents started in 1996. Some of these had already been processed in CDS/ISIS, and during the first half of 1998, we succeeded in converting old records into UNIMARC and Aleph, primarily the records of graphic and cartographic materials, theses, musical scores, and sound recordings. AV materials and computer files (CD-ROMs) will be recatalogued in Aleph. The processing of micromedia for monographic materials has begun in 1997. The delay in serials processing, which was the most painful, was caused by problems with the conversion program as well as with cleaning the database of Czech periodicals, which had been maintained in CDS/ISIS until the beginning of 1998. The conversion of records of foreign serials from ISSN Compact was finished at the end of 1997. The loading of

---

5. Note that the beginnings of the "automation" of the National Bibliography date back to 1983.

electronic records into the database has already begun—which therefore allows us to implement the serials module.

We have many difficulties with analytical records. The most important Czech newspapers and journals are excerpted in our library and in other cooperating libraries. Since the most complicated structure of UNIMARC linking-entry fields is used for analytical descriptions, we had to find an alternative solution for the internal structure of some fields in analytical records. The conversion of almost 400,000 analytical records was completed in 1998, and this enables transferring this material from CDS/ISIS to Aleph. Thanks to a grant from the Ministry of Culture of the Czech Republic, we were be able to buy some additional licenses for Aleph, and some programs have been developed for creating and checking hyperlinks to the primary documents (usually to the electronic version of the issue) that are in the public domain.

For the description of rare books, we would like to use the same nice Aleph feature that supports links between records in a database and external files. Images of important pages can complete the description and, unlike language-dependent notes, they are understandable to more users and scholars.

Of course, every borrower is interested in the implementation of the circulation module. Circulation has been automated in the Slavonic Library, a branch of the NL, since September 1997. The NL itself started online registration of loans and returns in September 1998. Unfortunately, users are still not allowed to place hold requests online on their own. The reason is very simple: we do not have enough bibliographic and especially holdings records in our on-line catalog. The OPAC of the NL contains now about 450,000 bibliographic records. Many of these were originally created only to be published in the national bibliography, so they did not contain information about copies that can be loaned out (only the shelf mark of the archive collection).[6] In addition, since CDS/ISIS did not work with any special holdings records (as Aleph does), all location information was included in bibliographic records. A few years ago, a lot of library staff from different divisions and departments participated in searching out location information for records already entered into the database and entering them into bibliographic records. Programs for this data validation and for holdings records creation had to be prepared. The final stage of the whole process will be completed in the summer of 1999 and thus the main condition for the implementation of the full circulation module will be fulfilled.

To speed up the enlargement of the NL on-line catalogue, we designed a project that will link the results of the great retroconversion project (see chapter 16 by B. Stoklasová) to a short bibliographic description, which will be done prior to loaning the document. This will help us to identify images of scanned cataloging cards that have the highest priority for conversion into text form and UNIMARC structure.

There are some records for which retroconversion using this technology is not efficient. These are especially serials records where the bibliographic record is followed by much detail about library holdings. We prefer to enter basic bibliographic information manually and to link these records to images of catalogue cards, stored

---

6. They contain only the shelf mark in the archive collection.

on a disk array. The development of the technology started on the end of 1998 and will continue in 1999, thanks to the additional funding from the Czech Ministry of Culture.

Printing Issues

Although Aleph can produce basic printouts (cataloging cards, inventory lists), our needs were too special to rely exclusively on those functions—the national bibliography as well as catalog cards, which we decided to print for books published before 1996 and for special documents published before 1997, needed to be formatted according to ISBD recommendations. Since we do not use the acquisition module for all documents processed in Aleph (see the discussion below), we cannot use standard printouts and we had to design our own programs to meet our needs.

Internal Implementation Issues

I have already mentioned the decision to use UNIMARC as an internal format. This caused difficulties for the system and for the staff as well. Since our old cataloging rules for creating the content of particular data elements could not be used, the decision to adopt the AACR2 was accepted. Old, long, previously coordinated subject headings were not suitable for computer searches. Therefore, it seemed necessary to make their form more similar to the Library of Congress Subject Headings. As a result, librarians had to change not only the technology, but also the format and the rules, all at once. We are still fighting the consequences of this "Big Bang," since we need too much time for processing of documents and the national bibliography is not up-to-date.

Another problem arose from the way in which holdings information is entered and maintained in the system. There are various pieces of information that have to be entered, because of circulation status (copy status, bar code, sublibrary, and location), which have never been used before. Although there was some kind of consensus concerning who will enter these data, when, and how these data will be entered, most of the staff taking part in the processing did not wholeheartedly adopt the decisions.

This is a result of lack of integration among the strongly specialized divisions. Sometimes they seem to work for themselves, and not on behalf of the NL and for the borrowers, the patrons. Even though the automation system makes them cooperate in principle, some librarians seem unwilling to understand their colleagues' problems, and it sometimes even results in antagonism, which is difficult to overcome. It is difficult to find a solution to this problem in a library that has more than 400 employees.

What will have to be solved very soon is the question of how to integrate copy cataloging into our "processing line." This issue became more urgent after some union catalogs began to be built in the Czech Republic, which means that we now have relatively easily accessible sources and it would be an error not to use them. In fact, we are not prepared for working in the mode that is common in developed countries. People still would rather create a record by themselves, from scratch, than use different sources of records. Some people jealously guard their records or the data they enter into them. They would be happy to have their own database, which would relieve them from having to share the data or from discussing their content and form with their colleagues in different departments.

In large libraries such as ours, there are still two specialized groups of librarians—acquisition librarians and catalogers, both of which work with computers, but often with traditional attitudes. Acquisitions librarians concentrate on finding relevant documents, and to them, a bibliographic description is only a tool for identifying them. It is very difficult to convince them that they should also look for a source of bibliographic information. The situation is a little better for foreign documents, since important sources of information about them have been in the electronic form, which has supported the downloading of records for a long time. Unfortunately, these records usually need a conversion. It seems that the most valuable source of records for foreign documents will be the WorldCat (OCLC), since OCLC recently completed its own program for the conversion from USMARC to UNIMARC. We already started to upload records from it as of the end of 1997.

We have to analyze the work flow in acquisitions departments to find a way of incorporating copy cataloging into the initial stage of processing. Unfortunately, it is already clear that in case one cannot upload bibliographic records on-line from different sources, the delay of off-line processing is not acceptable for acquisitions librarians. This means that catalogers have to sometimes be involved in searching different sources of records and merging records they find with those created by acquisitions librarians.

These problems are probably the consequences of the fact that in the preproject phase, and during the project, communications in the library were or are far from ideal. There are communication barriers between different levels of management, and many staff members are not willing to read instructions or announcements.

The CASLIN Union Catalog

The NL also started to use Aleph for the Czech part of the CASLIN Union Catalog. Although the system offers two models for building some kind of union catalog, or of union list, neither of them is sufficient—we need a more sophisticated mechanism for excluding duplicate records during the uploading to the database. The CASLIN Union Catalog needs to cooperate not only with Aleph libraries but also with libraries with TinLib, BIBIS, CDS/ISIS, and with different systems produced in the Czech Republic. Since we could not afford to pay for additional system development, we tried to find alternative ways. The situation changed, recently, thanks to an additional grant from The A.W. Mellon Foundation, and a completely new solution is being developed at the moment.

Conclusions

Aleph—a Dynamic System

Reflecting on some of the critical things I have said, it is important to emphasize the positives and to say that not everything is bad in regard to Aleph or to Ex Libris. We are quite happy to have a system that is dynamic, and with new progressive features being implemented (such as WWW access to the databases, the Z39.50 protocol, and self-service for circulation). Sometimes the Ex Libris people are even willing do more for us than they ought to according to our agreement. Our main problem is that through our inexperience in negotiations and because of a lack of clarity in both the RFP and the agreement, we gave Ex Libris too much leeway, which Ex Libris used. It is now clear how important good project management is. Czech librarians have had inadequate opportunities to learn it. They need more information about TQM and/or ISO 9000 in libraries, and at least a few need to be trained in the modern methods of management in order to be more effective in relations with partners such as system vendors.

Aleph shares with other systems the characteristic that it is not a special system for a national library—it does not permit easy handling of many documents acquired through the acquisitions module, such as legal deposits and various kinds of gifts, and there is no easy way to register a document exchange (in both directions). Aleph is a system for a library with open stacks rather than closed ones, the latter being more common in Central and Eastern Europe.[7] It does not differentiate, in a desirable manner, between loans in reading rooms and loans outside the library.

Librarians versus Library Information Systems. In general, we are trying to bend the system to our needs, sometimes perhaps unnecessarily, but librarians should not be subserviced to the system. It is the great responsibility of a project manager and a systems librarian to maintain a balance between some nonstandard requirements and a system's functionality.

---

7. However, Ex Libris is trying to overcome this and to at least partially solve related problems.

PART III

Cataloging, Authority Control, Retroconversion, Subject Headings, Search, and Union Catalogues

CHAPTER 15

A Retrospective Conversion
The Case of Debrecen

OLGA GOMBA

The establishment of the Universitas of Debrecen—the association of five Hungarian institutions of higher education—required some way of unifying the libraries of the member institutions. The most important step toward this end was automation—the introduction of the Voyager integrated library system.

After the introduction of the computer-based system and cataloging method, a new problem arose: Should the member institutions convert their existing catalogs into a machine-readable format? Quite early in the process of automation, it turned out that one of the most important tasks was the establishment of a database—for example, the creation of bibliographic files that represent the very essence of automation.

As early as the mid-1980s, there were some attempts to introduce machine-readable cataloging, but with not much success. Nevertheless, we cannot ignore their role in the preparation of library computerization and the acquisition of experience.

Since 1992, the Voyager integrated library system,[1] which was originally developed in the United States, has been available for the libraries of the Debrecen Universitas. The Debrecen libraries acquired their computerized integrated system at a time when it was in a relatively well-developed stage for such systems. The OPAC of the system offered some previously unknown possibilities: fast and accurate retrieval of bibliographic records in various ways; searches in collections stored in different media; displays of the records in short, normal, long, and MARC formats; and access to a series of external databases. This has placed at our disposal a new system, a new method that supports searches for bibliographic and various other items. The need to utilize the system and to persuade the users to accept the idea that the considerable sum of money at our disposal was productively spent on the automated library system, and the recognition that the sense and the basic value of the computer-based system lie in the bibliographic database, encouraged us to search for new, up-to date solutions and to undertake further tasks. We further accept the recognition that "well-designed databases . . . will outlive several generations of systems and equipment."[2]

Thanks are due to Susan Orosz-Milicz, head of the Cataloging Department at the Lajos Kossuth University Library, for much useful information.

1. Olga Gomba, "The Integrated Library System of the Universitas," *Könyv és Könyvtár* 17 (1994): 13–29.
2. Marlene Clayton and Chriss Batt, *Managing Library Automation*, 2d ed. (Brookfield, VT: 1992), 175.

We finished the retraining of the staff, and, following the system's short introductory stage, we decided to close down our card catalogs. We did so because the given staffing conditions and the economic position of the institutions did not allow us to choose the safest, but most expensive, solution: building, in parallel, the traditional catalogs and the new computer-based database. And so, parallel with the closing down of the card catalogs, the new type of work began, with a cataloging module that involved authority control. In the case of the Lajos Kossuth University Library, this meant the processing of 20,000–25,000 documents per year (including about 18,000 that are book-format items).

Given this rate of increase in the database—although the regular yearly acquisitions themselves cannot be regarded as negligible in its growth—it was clear that we had to do our best to accelerate the building of the database.

In consequence, for the libraries in Debrecen concerned with designing and implementing computer-based cataloging systems, it was inevitable that they would convert their card catalogs to machine-readable records, perform a retrospective conversion, and find solutions for a whole host of other problems.

It was found that the working hours of the regular staff were completely taken up by the day-to-day loading of the bibliographic database with current data. So a fund had to be created for the beginning and then for the continuation of the retroconversion. The problem was solved by a number of successful applications for funds: Support was given by the Hungarian National Technological Development Committee, the National Information Infrastructure Developing Program, the Fund for the Development of Higher Education, the National Cultural Fund, and the Mellon Foundation.

Before starting the actual work, further decisions had to be made. As a first step, we had to convert the machine-readable records produced in the experimental period. We also had to estimate the number of traditional formats that were to be transformed into machine-readable records. It was also important to determine how much time the whole process would take, and at what cost. So initially, we had to determine the time and cost involved in the creation of one new record with the various possible methods.

Considering that the staff of the library was not very experienced in the field of retrospective conversion, there were some questions to be answered. The answers to these questions are no longer issues today. However, since the librarians were used to the traditional cataloging methods, analyses had to be made before each decision. The decisions involved the following aspects:

- The existing titles are not to be processed again—for example, it is not necessary to take the book itself in hand, instead of the catalog cards, when preparing records.
- We have to be satisfied with working on the basis of the catalog cards.
- The preparation of records must be supported by the deriving of records from external databases; these derived records can be reedited to comply with the Hungarian standards for the bibliographic descriptions, or with the inside rules and practices of the library, but only if it is reasonable to do so.

After the decision was made on the retrospective conversion, it was imperative to analyze the work process for the retroconversion and to determine, step by step, the consecutive elements of the process. It not only was of interest for the library from the point of view of work organization, but it also helped to determine the conversion cost per record completed. Thoroughly examining how much is to be paid for the constituent parts of the process performed by the librarians or students greatly helped us to determine the total price of a record, because the total cost per record was calculated from these partial data. The separation of the constituent parts of the work process was very useful since the complete record was frequently prepared by more than one person, due to the division of labor that was used. The phases determined were the following:

- the management and organization of the work;
- the preparation of data entry;
- descriptions in the MARC format, according to the cataloging cards; or,
- the derivation of records from an external database, including editing them, in case of need, and the completion of these records with local data;
- control sampling;
- authority control, and the preparation of authority records;
- computerized database management.

At the beginning of the retrospective conversion we noted that various amounts of worktime were necessary for the preparation of different types of records. The most economical method is to derive records from other existing databases and supplement them with the local data, without a great deal of modification. Somewhat more time is required for the preparation of the new record from the card catalog. Considering that the library carried out retrospective conversion, and not recataloging, it was not necessary to prepare original records unless the quantity and quality of the data available on the card catalogs were below the acceptable minimum. We had to accept the fact that retroconversion cannot involve the reprocessing of the collection. The quantity of data on the old catalog cards generally falls below the ideal one, as compared to the desirable quantity utilizable in computer-based library systems. Experience showed that, fairly often, we had to go back to the original documents to acquire more data or to correct them. During the retrospective conversion, the estimated proportion of cases in which an item was not identifiable by information from the cataloging cards was as high as 3 percent. In these cases the records had to be completed with data from the volumes that were taken in hand, with the help of the shelf numbers.

The measurements performed during the record-processing work in the Library of Lajos Kossuth University gave the following results:

- Preparing the bibliographic record for one item, together with the authority records, takes about 30 minutes.
- On average, 4–7 authority records are necessary for a title.
- Giving class marks and subject headings for an item, and preparing the desirable number of authority records for them, takes about 30 minutes, and during this process 4–5 subject headings per record are entered.
- About 10 authority records are to be prepared for a bibliographic record, considering all formal and content elements.

One must count on an increase in the time taken for record preparation if an extra person does the record description, another one does the authority records, and a third one supplies the subject headings. As an example of the time increase, one notes that in the next step of the work process one must identify the records, take them from the OPAC to the workfile for editing, and give them subject headings. A further factor in the time increase during the processing is the case in which the librarian adds to the local subject headings the versions from the Library of Congress (LC) database with their Hungarian translation.

Reediting of records derived from an external database is frequently inevitable and takes much time. Some examples for derived LC records are the following:

- One has to add the volume data.
- There are notes in the record that must be translated for the Hungarian records.
- One has to translate the supplementary data.

Another example, taken from the Hungarian National Bibliography (HNB), is the case in which we have to edit the whole record of omnibus editions, to put them into the library's own database.

After a time, the progress of database processing will become faster because the increase in authority records will reduce the number of them necessary for one bibliographic record. This means, for example, that today one might have to prepare six authority records for one bibliographic record, but in the future the number of such authority records corresponding to one bibliographic record might be no more than two or three. The time saved in this way can be used to maintain the authority file, to draw similar items together, or to complete records. In the Lajos Kossuth University Library such types of work are in progress.

The expense involved in data processing was determined by taking into account the various possibilities available in the methods of record preparation. The cost per record has closely followed the Hungarian rate of inflation ever since the beginning of the work. Table 15.1 presents the current charges for the various tasks involved in record preparation. The total cost for one bibliographic record (plus authority records) can vary but one can generally calculate a cost of $2.00 per record, on the basis of the current official rate of exchange. The wages are to be paid for the tasks detailed in the table. Included in the wages specified is a 39 percent social insurance tax required by Hungarian regulations, so the librarians' wages are reduced by this 39 percent and also by the personal income tax. The net income for each person is different, depending on one's level of private income and of private taxes, so net incomes are not detailed here.

We tried to calculate, on the basis of the whole collection, how much time and cost would be necessary, to prepare new machine-readable records. Given the size of the collection, the work would indeed have been enormous and very costly. To illustrate this statement, we estimate that it would take two million U.S. dollars (at 1997 price levels) to process the rest of the collection (1,250,000 volumes) of the Lajos Kossuth University Library. The basis of the estimation was the average price per record, together with the authority records: $2.00, of which $1.20 is the gross wage and $0.78 is the amount of the compulsory social insurance. As far as the whole collection of the Universitas (that is, of the five university libraries) is concerned, the total cost would

Table 15.1 Charges for Various Record-Preparation Tasks

Type of Task	Payment to Cataloger (gross wage per record)
Preparing a new bibliographic record, including authority records	$1.64
Deriving a bibliographic record from an external database, including the preparation of authority records	$1.23
New bibliographic record without authority records (prepared from a cataloging card or derived from an external database)	$0.82
Preparing authority records for one bibliographic record	$0.82
Reediting of a bibliographic record derived from an external database without authority records	$0.66
Fitting bibliographic record, derived from our own database, into the workfile and adding holdings data to it	$0.40
Preparation of data processing per record	$0.10
Computer processing per record	$0.10
Management and organization per record	$0.10
Financial work per record	$0.07

be twice as large. Considering the necessary costs for the collection of the Lajos Kossuth University Library, 10 persons could finish the retroconversion work in 32 years if we took 240 workdays per year and did 16 records per day.

We are aware of the fact that such calculations cannot be accurate. Nevertheless, they indicate an order of magnitude. Thus, the choice of which parts of the collection to subject to retroconversion becomes even more important. Making a decision in this case was quite difficult since the number of library items affected was nearly six million in the five Universitas libraries and over four million in the central and departmental libraries of Lajos Kossuth University (including 1,400,000 books and periodical materials in the central library).

Because of the changes made in bibliographic descriptions in 1986, a new catalog was started that divided the old catalog into two parts; it seemed feasible to start the retroconversion with the recent records and go backward in time toward 1986. Anyway, this part of the catalog is the most frequently used one, so the retroconversion also assisted computer-based circulation.

Our original concept (the basis of which were the publication data of the books) had to be altered, because the Hungarian National Cultural Foundation announced a competition for funds for the retroconversion; and the specifications for participating in this competition prescribed our choice of a specialized field. So, according to this new concept, we had to concentrate on choosing a specialized field for the competition—our choice was mathematics. Thus, we began the retroconversion of the library of the Institute of Mathematics and Information Science at Lajos Kossuth University, and of the mathematics field of the central library. For some years this field has constituted a national collection offering national services. Processing this part of the collection is not only of local, but also of national, interest. The work was begun with the most recent materials.

It should be noted that building a database according to specialized fields needs to be approached with caution, so as to reduce the possibility of an overlap with other institutions before a nationwide, shared cataloging system is established.

A precondition for the support by the National Cultural Foundation (NCF) was the use of a unified format for the work—HUNMARC. On the other hand, HUNMARC was not ready when the automation of the library system began—so, for example, in the Voyager library system, USMARC is used; and neither do the other systems in Hungary use the Hungarian MARC as their entry format. This is why support was given to systems that can later be converted to HUNMARC, and vice versa. In this way the NCF greatly contributed to the acceptance of a unified Hungarian exchange format.

While preparing for the retroconversion, we had to decide which of the three main options should be used for the process:

1. use of the services of a vendor;
2. in-house conversion;
3. derivation of records from outside databases and from a particular type of database.

Out of these three possibilities, in-house conversion is predominant, although we also derive records from other sources. However, this latter activity is carried out from background databases on CD-ROM.

The retroconversion program of the Lajos Kossuth University Library was supported by the funds won in the competition, and it was this financial support that allowed us to start. The retroconversion was carried out by expert staff members and mostly by the university students trained for this work. They began the processing work with catalog cards that were selected according to the previously mentioned criteria. The person in charge of the retroconversion process was the head of the processing department. This person continuously oversaw the work. The students were mostly library science or information science majors. The background knowledge necessary for the work included a familiarity with the computer and the software, knowledge of the MARC format, and basic information on the processing of library documents. So work was not simply of a technical nature. It was important to make this perfectly clear because some members of the university staff—in particular, at the beginning of the work—tended to underestimate it.

The cards were distributed in packages of 50–100, on which records were kept by the librarian in charge, and the operators were responsible to her. In a retroconversion using the Voyager system, the bibliographic records are prepared in two stages: record entry from the cards, and authority control. The latter task was performed mostly by expert librarians. Before authority control is performed, the records go to workfiles, and the new record becomes accessible in the OPAC after the authority control stage.

To make work easier, outside databases were purchased. In the acquisition program of the Universitas, the libraries' interest was focused on outside databases on CD-ROM, for example, on different bibliographies, library catalogs, which—once purchased—could be background databases for the work process of the retrospective conversion. The first such database was the CD-ROM edition of the Hungarian National Bibliography—first the material between 1975 and 1991, and then its recent edition (1975–1995). With the help of some conversion software, we could derive the records of the Hungarian publications of the given period. The individual records were supplied with the necessary local codes and then they were accepted unchanged, while we ignored the possible differences, apart from the abovementioned exceptions. In this way, we could save some time and extra expenses, in spite of the fact that larger storage capacity was needed, but as it was not possible to save all the time we wanted to save in this regard, it was necessary to complete the records using some local standards (see figure 15.1).

Work was furthered by the purchase of the Library of Congress's CD-ROMs. As mentioned earlier in connection with the records derived from the Library of Congress database, here, too, there are some problems, because some parts must be reedited and translated before being loaded into the Hungarian database (see Figure 15.2).

At the same time, during the in-house retrospective conversion we obtained some information from, among others, the Dutch DMP (Direct Marketing Press, b.v. Afd. Direct Marketing Services), and the European Center of OCLC. Even using an outside service, there would be a lot of extra work—which means extra costs—in the library. The expenses would be increased by the preparation of the entry, and the use of authority control; and one cannot fail to consider two other facts that increase the costs:

- value-added tax;
- the profit-oriented nature of the vendor—for example, in 1995 the vendor's offer was: $1.07 per bibliographic record, without authority records; the cost of a similar record is only $0.82 with the use of in-house processing.

In addition, when negotiations with the external suppliers began, serious pressure inside the library was exerted on the management. The engagement of any external service would have been perceived as being against the interests of the library staff and the enrolled workers (students). The librarians, having relatively low salaries, took this work upon themselves not only for professional motives but also for financial reasons, just as in the case of the university students. So, as the use of vendors' services would have been contrary to the interests of our own staff and the university students, and as the in-house process was found satisfactory, we did not avail ourselves of the outside services. Even if we had chosen a vendor for the retroconversion, we would have had to do part of the work—such as the preparing of authority records—by ourselves. Cooperation with a vendor would have meant higher expenses because of the extra work inside the library, and so, again, we did not avail ourselves of this possibility. From the three main options (cited earlier), Lajos Kossuth University Library chose in-house database building on the basis of the use of traditional cataloging cards and the simultaneous use of the outside databases, not by deriving records from the Internet but by buying CD-ROMs. Most libraries, not only in Debrecen, but also in other places in the country, chose in-house retroconversion, probably for similar reasons.

The format for processing is the MARC—which is the format for the process of international exchange—so among the most important specifications for the purchase of the new integrated library system was MARC compatibility. So the question of format was decided before automated cataloging was begun.

In the Lajos Kossuth University Library a thorough examination preceded the

Figure 15.1 Derived MARC record from the Hungarian National Bibliography on CD-ROMs

000	01490aam 2200421 i 4500
001	963 10 3762 2
005	19960711090304.0
008	810409s1981 hu 00000 hun d
020	$a963 10 3762 2(kötött)$c423,- Ft
020	$a963 10 4278 2
020	$a963 10 4277 4
040	$aMNB$cHUN$dHuDeKLEK
080	$a621.37/.39(035)
130	$aElectronics engineer's handbook$l(magyar)
	245 00 $aElektronikai kézikönyv /$cfőszerkesztő Donald G. Fink ; szerkesztő Alexander A. McKenzie ; [a magyar kiadás főszerkesztője Solymosi János] ; [szerkesztők Szücs Péter, Tabéry Gábor, Nagy Borbála] ; [szerzők Anderson, Byron S. et al.]
260	$aBudapest. :$bMûszaki Kvk.,$c1981$e(Debrecen :$fAlföldi Ny.)
300	$a2 db (1743 p.) ;$c26 cm
503	$a1. köt. . - 61 p. : ill.
503	$a2. köt. - . 875-1743. : ill.
504	$aBibliogr. a fejezetek végén
700 1	$aMcKenzie, Alexander A.
700 1	$aSolymosi János
700 1	$aSzücs Péter
700 1	$aTabéry Gábor
700 1	$aNagy Borbála
700 1	$aAnderson, Byron S.
949	$a12.769 I$lD1/20tmev1$z09078703
949	$a12.769 II$lD1/20tmev2$z09078697
999	$aDEBR$bD1/20$g12.769 I$aDEBR$bD1/20$g12.769 II

choice of the appropriate MARC elements for in-house processing, and so MARC was made an adequate processing format for the new library system.[3] In choosing the MARC tags, it was important to find the suitable fields for the catalog of the Lajos Kossuth University Library and to assure ourselves of getting as many data as possible for exact and correct searches.

For the practices of the Lajos Kossuth University Library, the most frequently used fields for the different types of documents are fixed, but when it is necessary, one can create further fields and subfields. In the cataloging module of the system there are various input possibilities in the MARC format for the data of different types of library materials, for example, books, serials, scores, audiovisual materials, computer files, CD-ROMs, Internet documents. There are many more fields fixed in the Lajos Kossuth University Library than the minimum level determined by the MARC Stan-

---

3. Voyager integrated library system, is described in USMARC reference manual prepared for internal use by a librarian of the Lajos Kossuth University Library in 1997.

Figure 15.2 Derived MARC record from the LC CD-ROMs

000		00672pam 2200229 i 4500
001		87034622
003		DLC
005		19970617104914.0
008		871207s1988 nyua b 00110 eng d
010		$a 87034622
020		$a0 471 85391 7
050	0	$aQA331.5$b.D46 1988
082	0	$a515.8$219
100	10	$aDePree, John D.$d(1933-)
245	10	$aIntroduction to real analysis /$cJohn DePree, Charles Swartz
260		$aNew York :$bWiley,$cc1988
300		$axi, 355 p. :$bill. ;$c24 cm
504		$aBibliogr.: p. 347-348.
500		$aIndexek
583		$xTK
650	0	$aFunctions of real variables.
650	0	$aMathematical analysis.
700	1	$aSwartz, Charles$d(1938-)
949		$a21.390$lD1/20tmkz09163430
999		$aDEBR$bD1/20$g21.390

dards Office.[4] In spite of this difference, the minimum concept of the MARC Standards Office is important in the retroconversion process. Nevertheless, I should mention that the minimum concept of the MARC Standards Office concerning the retroconversion process is acceptable both from the professional and the economic points of view. During the performance of the retroconversion one cannot avoid having at least some minimum level of interest in achieving smoother everyday work among both management and the library staff. Why is it necessary to decide this on a minimum level? The cards in the card catalogs were prepared in different periods and thus they are inconsistent. The quantity of the data, and the "architecture" of the cards prepared in different periods of the library's history, comply with different standards and are consequently different. Once we accept this minimum level, it can be easier to find solutions to problems emerging in our everyday work, especially at the beginning of the retroconversion. The main point of this is to determine how many concessions the librarian doing the retroconversion can make in the light of the right extent and quality of a record. The experience of the Lajos Kossuth University Library shows the need for an agreement about the minimum level of work among the librarian and the catalogers, or, rather, the work group doing the retroconversion. Situations exist in which such an agreement can be useful. For example, in the Lajos Kossuth University Li-

---

4. USMARC. *Format for Bibliographic Data. Including Guidelines for Content Designation*, 1994 ed. (Washington, D.C.: Network Development and MARC Standard Office, Cataloging Distribution Service, Library of Congress).

Figure 15.3 MARC record with the letter X

000	00409nam 2200277 4504
001	bibKLT00137973
005	19970418112235.0
008	970418 1989 xx 00010 eng
245	00 $aSocial antropology and the politics of language /$cEd. by Ralph Grillo
260	$bRoutledge,$c1989
695	$aX
949	$a565.387$lD1$n15.212/1989$tkf$z02450629
999	$aDEBR$bD1$g565.387

brary, a portion of the old catalog cards have no subject heading. By accepting the minimum level of the MARC Standards Office, the library can prepare new records without subject headings. If the library later decides to add subject headings to these records, they may be added. As a reminder, the cataloger preparing records during the retroconversion process can insert a sign—for example, the letter X (see figure 15.3). With the help of this sign, one can find these reconds and supplement them. As a result, taking the original material in hand is reasonable only when the data on the cataloging cards are not enough, as compared to the MARC minimum. The retroconversion process is very expensive and time-consuming; hence, especially in the first period of the retroconversion, our principal aim should be to increase the number of records and not to augment the richness of the data. It is necessary and reasonable to make this compromise, but it is not so easy to do that in the world of computer systems, where the number of hits depends on the sufficient quantity and the good quality of the data.

At the time of the choosing of the computer-based library system and, later, in the cataloging work, with the help of the Voyager system, authority control was very important.[5] The use of authority records ensures the consistency of the elements of the records. Authority control is important if one is to implement the consistency of, for example, the names of authors, institutions, conferences, subject headings, the titles of series, as well as the unified titles. This procedure enabled one-step searching of all records on an author, a series, or a subject heading.[6] We did not want to have a bibliographic database without authority control, when the answers to the search would not be consistent and full, in which case the system would be unable to find every record for the particular search. Besides the advantages there are disadvantages. The use of authority control raises expenses due to the cost of the control work done after the preparing of records and the work of data unification, but its advantages are well worth this extra cost.

---

5. On the importance of authority control for an automated library system, see *Retrospective Conversion: History, Approaches, Considerations*, ed. Brian Schottlaender (New York: Haworth Press; London: Norwood. 1992), 167; and *Cataloguing and Classification Quarterly* 14, nos. 3–4 (1992).

6. Klára Koltay, chapter 22 in this volume.

Table 15.2 Funds Granted to 5 Debrecan Libraries, and The Number of Records They Prepared

Institution	Collection (number of documents)	Funds Granted($)	Planned Records (number)	Number of Records Prepared	Cost per Record
Lajos Kossuth University, Central Library	1,300,000 (books and serials)	52,297	49,160	35,005	2.20
Library of Medical School	140,000	26,148	24,580	23,481	1.10
Library of Agricultural University	120,000	20,919	19,664	18,573	1.10
Reformed Theological Academy	630,000	31,378	29,496	31,015	1.00
Institute of Nuclear Research	56,000	8,889	8,355	9,109	0.97
Total data	2,750,000	139,631	131,255	117,183	1.27

In 1993 the five libraries of the Debrecen Universitas submitted a tender for funds for database building, and for the purchase and installation of security systems, to the World Bank's Fund for Catching up with European Higher Education (hereafter cited as the CEHEF), during Round 3 of the Higher Education Development Program. In December 1993, the Universitas was informed that the tender was successful; however, the World Bank provided, for both purposes, a smaller amount of funds than originally requested. The entry of data was then done by the libraries of the Universitas in 1994–1995.

Specifically, in this tender submitted to the CEHEF, the five members of the Universitas requested $283,687. After the acceptance of the proposal, the CEHEF granted the Universitas, for the data entry program, funds that amounted to 50.84 percent less than the figure requested. And the funds given were divided into smaller parts for each of the libraries, according to the function and the size of each collection; each library's share was not proportional to the number of records it entered. Table 15.2 presents a breakdown of the funds granted to each of the five libraries. During this significant database-building process, within the framework of this project, 117,183 machine-readable records were prepared by the libraries of the Universitas. Each library built its database in accordance with its collections' needs and its own priorities. The planned quantity of records was reduced because of the cuts in the funds allotted. The number of records prepared was smaller than planned by 14,668 records. The reasons for this reduction were as follows:

- the large amount of work to be done;
- difficulties in planning, and the different levels of processing work, for each library; and
- an increase in the wages paid.

I have to note that, compared to the other libraries of the Universitas, for the Lajos Kossuth University Library—as the second national library collecting deposit copies—a higher level for the processing was important, including the preparation of authority records for the bibliographic ones. This is another reason for the differences between the numbers for the planned records and for the actually prepared records.

The budget available for processing work was also reduced by a 5.66 percent VAT, a figure of 6 percent for university overhead costs, and a 2 percent handling charge.

The instructions for preparing bibliographic records and authority records were identical for the participating libraries. The databases established in the individual institutions are the bases of a common, unified catalog system and promote cooperation that is based on the local network of the Universitas.

In the Lajos Kossuth University Library, as a result of the retrospective conversion, bibliographic records were prepared for 75 percent of the books published after 1986. And 30 percent of the books published between 1978 and 1986 were processed within the automated library system. One can also search 90 percent of the periodicals with holdings data from the year 1986. The Reformed Theological Academy brought into the new system the most frequently used data of its collection. The Institute of Nuclear Research processed Roman alphabet book formats and various conference documents. The Agricultural University Library processed Hungarian and foreign books published after 1985. The Library of the Medical School brought into the system 50 percent of the data on Hungarian and foreign specialized books and 25 percent of its bound periodicals.

The developing database of the actual automated library system offers more and more information, on a fairly large part of the library collections, to the students, professors, and scientists of the Universitas; and, moreover, to users outside the Universitas through the Internet, as a part of the actual virtual library of our new world. One can access the databases by local, national, and international networks. This database building, assisted by the abovementioned automation project, has become very significant in the development of these libraries, by increasing the quantity of information accessible through the libraries' automated systems. The value of the computer-based system was increased by the developing databases, which indeed give precious and rich information through the abovementioned networks.

The library cooperation among the members of the Universitas was systematically organized in the form of consultations. Typical of the process was a permanent form of cooperation—on the basis of an agreement, the dividing of the common budget and the whole process of retrospective conversion could be implemented.

A great help during the performing of the retrospective conversion was the opportunity to visit libraries abroad, using the funds provided by the World Bank for this purpose. These study tours were instructive not only for the exchanging of experiences but also for the opportunity to study the more recent methods of database building, for example, use of bibliographic networks. The most important result of these instructive trips was a cooperative data exchange between the Library of Congress in Washington, D.C., and the Lajos Kossuth University Library. The Library of Congress agreed to translate its subject headings into Hungarian for use in the Library. The Lajos

Kossuth University Library sends its own records of Hungarian books to the Library of Congress in return for a license for use of LC subject headings.

The collections of the Universitas libraries complement each other with respect to subject fields and through cooperation in the development of common software and hardware. This joint database is continually growing richer; a significant portion of the traditional card catalogs is being converted to the machine-readable database and it is getting better and better to use. This database-building work is continuing, but its pace depends on the financial situation of the libraries. Further significant and continuous efforts are necessary to automate this huge data collection. The sizes of the collections in relation to the financial situation did not provide an opportunity for libraries to finish the retrospective database building—which, in fact, no one could aim at. Considering the existing financial sources, the libraries must choose only parts of their collection for the retrospective processing. In the project referred to, the most important principle for the retroconversion was to process the relatively latest items, so we moved backward in time. One therefore cannot predict the completion date for the retroconversion in the Universitas libraries because of the sizes of the collections and the limited financing. A continuous effort at these institutions is being made to get money for the continuation of the retroconversion in the Universitas libraries, by taking part in various competitions for funds.

CHAPTER 16

The Retrospective Conversion in Czech Libraries

BOHDANA STOKLASOVÁ

One of the basic conditions of "open" libraries is that they make their catalogs, the key to their collections (not only the new ones), widely and freely available. Today, the retrospective conversion of catalogs belongs to the highest priorities of the National Library (NL) of the Czech Republic. There are some five million catalog cards awaiting conversion, cards of various provenance and character, including hand-written cards from early nineteenth century. Considering the quantity that is to be converted and the special features of these cards, the retrospective conversion of the NL catalog is very costly and requires a substantial commitment of time on our part.

Primarily thanks to grants in the 1990s from the Mellon Foundation, together with help from the Prague firm Comdat, the NL developed a conversion methodology that met with a warm response both at home and abroad. In fact, initially it was exclusively foreign grants that enabled us to start the conversion, since at home there was a lack of any sustained interest in this activity and thus even financial support was minimal. The library's budget was too limited to include any implementation of this process: for a long time, all we could afford to do was just develop and experiment.

The situation changed somewhat in 1996 and 1997—top-level technology and the incredible amount of work that went into the development and improvement of this system were finally recognized, and the Ministry of Culture awarded us specific funds; and local grants, too, started coming in.

History

Having in mind preservation rather than conversion, we made a few segments of the catalog—specifically, those of the Music Division and of the Slavonic Division—available on microfiche. Because of financial limitations, however, it was not possible to film the largest catalog at the Library, that is, the General Catalog of the complete collection. Our analysis of various databases, particularly OCLC, showed that there is a surprisingly small number of matches and even the few that were found were of dubious quality. Besides, at the time of our initial searching, we were not yet equipped to convert even the good matches into UNIMARC.

We had no choice but to give up the thought of exporting at least the foreign-imprints matches, and so we started considering a manual transcription of the catalog. Our discussions with SAZTEC (a Eugene, Oreg., vendor) were promising as far as a time framework was concerned, but the firm's price of $4.00 per record was prohibitive. Eventually, in 1992, the NL contracted a local company to convert catalog cards. Although the price per record was considerably lower than what SAZTEC wanted, the quality of the final product was regrettably quite low. We spent lot of time in the preparatory phases as well as in the follow-up and cleanup. In 1994, only about two years into the project, we abandoned it and started exploring new ways.

The environment and the conditions have in fact not changed much since 1990: The number of matches in OCLC remained pretty low; there was no good USMARC/UNIMARC conversion protocol; SAZTEC increased its price to almost $6.00. However, from 1991 to 1994, high-quality scanners and new powerful software were developed, thus increasing the speed and quality of the ICR/OCR process. Especially the latter condition, together with the willingness of the firm Comdat to invest time and energy in research and development (without much promised revenue), was instrumental in our quest—a three-phase modular approach to the retrospective conversion was developed; it was tested, and eventually we were gradually able to put it into production at the NL.

RETROCON Technology

The whole process indeed consists of several phases, and its modularity was conscientiously thought through, with the goal being that of eliminating duplication and prioritizing the conversion of the most heavily used sections of the catalog (for more details, see Stoklasová and Bareš, 1995).

- *Step 1—scanning:* The catalog cards (or pages from the printed bibliographies) are scanned by state-of-the-art equipment that guarantees a high-quality image, essential for subsequent processing. Thanks to a specially developed software KATALOG, both the library staff and the users can start browsing this auxiliary catalog right after scanning.
- *Step 2—transcription:* The scanned images are converted from a pictorial (TIFF) image into ASCII characters (on unstructured text). In the case of high-quality images this process is done automatically, using OCR, while images that are fuzzy, or unclear in other respects, are manually converted.
- *Step 3—structuring (tagging):* In this final phase the unstructured records are converted into a UNIMARC (but it can be any MARC or non-MARC) record. Again, depending on the degree of clarity of the record, tagging can be done automatically, whenever it is feasible to use a specific algorithm, or manually—that is, staff analyzes the record and tags each field as needed. The special software helps to create, in a short period, high-quality records (see figure 16.1).

The most salient feature of this approach is its applicability in the full system or in modules, depending on an institution's needs and means. The RETROCON technology has been used, up to now, at the National Library for the creation of bibliographic

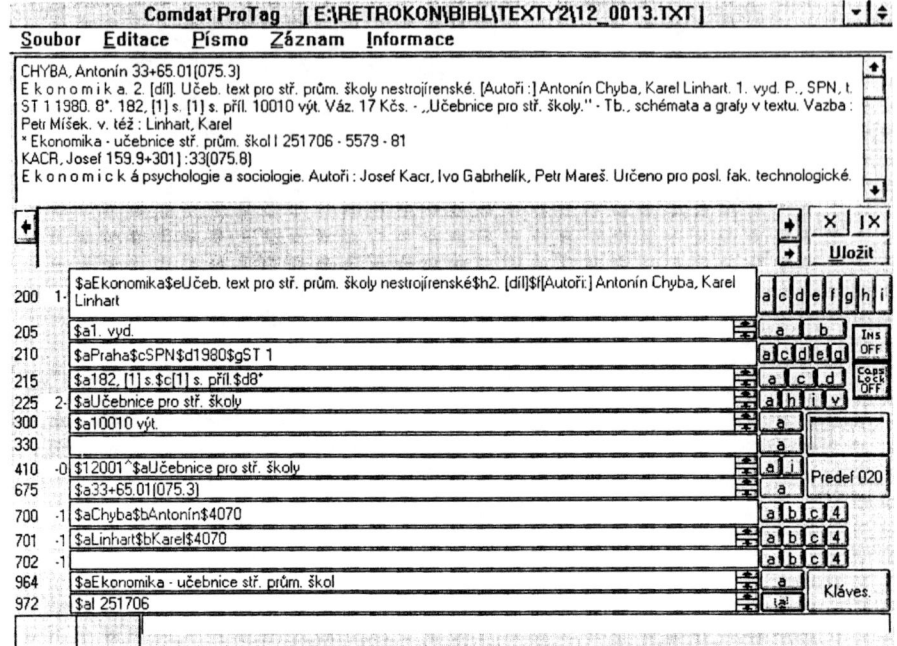

Figure 16.1 Tagging a Record

records, and, using the basic tenets of this technology, we also started creating authority records.

Running Projects

RETROCON-SF (Retrospective Conversion of the Research Catalog)

The catalog of the research collections contains mainly the cards of the circulating collection—that is, the collection used most heavily, serving primarily the needs of university students. It consists mainly of Czech books that are frequently requested, and we fortunately have on-line records available for these that go back to 1983, when we started automated cataloging. Obviously, it would also be desirable to convert the older part of the catalog—cards representing foreign imprints and some special categories, all totaling some 40,000 records, none of which are included in the yearly cumulation of the printed catalog of the Czech National Bibliography. Because of their heavy usage the first phase of this project was to convert these cards into UNIMARC; today it is fully available in our Aleph-based OPAC. I should point out that this goal was achieved with the help of many university students, who assisted during the scanning/tagging process in a "students for themselves" action.

RETROCON-BKCK (Conversion of the Bibliographic Catalogue: Czech Books)

The *Bibliographic Catalogue: Czech Books* is the main focus of the "Making Czech Production of the twentieth Century Available" project, whose results will be accessible via the Internet as well as on CD-ROM. Most of the approximately half-million records, covering Czech imprints from as far back as 1922, are included in the Bibliographic Catalog. However, there are also records contained in a few other bibliographies, from the early part of the twentieth century, that we aim to convert. Most entries are in fact detailed citations, also containing added entries and subject headings, UDC symbols, and, frequently, annotations. From the international viewpoint, this will provide a great enrichment of projects such as UBC-IM, UAP, and COBRA, and even OCLC has expressed interest in these records.[1] And of course, on the national level, the on-line availability of these records will allow a less-demanding and cheaper conversion at many institutions in the Czech Republic. In fact, many Czech libraries and research institutions are participating in this collaborative effort—each cooperating institution converts specific sections of the paper version of the Bibliographic Catalog, which then decreases the number of cards they have to convert from their own catalog.

Thanks to this project, by the end of 1998, some 230,000 records had been added to the on-line database. I should mention that this collaborative effort had the blessing and financial support of our own Ministry of Culture, without which this phase would not have been possible. All records will be included in the CASLIN union catalog and, as I mentioned earlier, they will be loaded into OCLC; a CD-ROM version is now also available. We anticipate that by the end of the decade, the entire Czech book production of the twentieth century will be on-line. This achievement will put us into the group of the bibliographically developed countries, who have the majority of their national production on-line. This effort is also greatly admired abroad because of our success in persuading individual institutions to join this project. This is especially noteworthy since our libraries, for almost half a century, were lingering in a decentralized and individualized climate, rather than enjoying the rewards of centralization and cooperation.

RETROCON-GC (Retrospective Conversion of the General Catalogue)

The main source of our vast holdings of some three million titles is the General Catalog, whose catalog cards themselves are historical artifacts and, as such, must be preserved. A curious amalgam of an official catalog and a shelf list, the GC is located in a crowded space and, for historical as well as practical reasons, is not open to the public. We are in the process of moving it to the new Hostivar central depository. Since we had no time, personnel, or funds to fully convert it (the cost estimate was more than one hundred million Czech crowns), and since we needed to preserve it and make it widely available (for the first time), we were able, in a six-month period in 1966, prior

---

1. Our most recent cataloged records of current Czech book production are now available in OCLC.

to the move, to at least scan the General Catalog for only a fraction of the total cost, some nine million Czech crowns.

Thanks to the Comdat-developed Katalog software package, it can now be browsed on-line as easily as paper catalog cards can be read. It is regrettable that the jukebox we use is somewhat limited, since it can service only four workstations at any given time, and thus this historical artifact, despite the most modern technology, is not yet fully available to the user. We eliminated this shortcoming—with the help of donations from Hewlett-Packard and funds from the Czech Ministry of Culture—by making the catalog available to the public, in 1998, through the use of powerful memory storage devices. We will also combine the very short UNIMARC records in Aleph with these images, especially for the old, hand-written cards and serials with a long history. These are the parts of the catalog that will have to wait, for a very long time, for a full retrospective conversion, or they may never be converted into UNIMARC. The first results seem to be very promising. To facilitate the extremely time-consuming retrospective conversion itself, we are phasing this approach so that first there will be sort of a circulation-driven RECON; next, we will start converting foreign imprints; and lastly, after the completion of the RETROCON-BKCK, we will convert the remainder of the Czech imprints that might have been missed in that project. Of course, future conversions will depend on available funding.

RETROCON-AUTHORITIES (Retrospective Conversion of National Authority Files)

Up until 1995, the concept of authority control was almost nonexistent in Czech libraries. However, with the growth of on-line records, it became imperative to at least start thinking about this feature. In the past few years we have given more attention to this topic and, at the end of 1996, we established a National Authority Records Control Department, which will, in addition to the NL main database, name access points; maintain, monitor, and create authority records of Czech names; and be responsible for cooperation with the IFLA and the EC in this area. In fact, the established RETROCON method is also being used in the conversion of individual institutions' paper catalogs of their "authority files," which only remotely resemble a true authority file. *Other Catalogs That Are to be Converted.* The catalogs discussed above are, by far, not all that we have to convert in order to avoid the costly maintenance of traditional paper catalogs and to satisfy our users. Altogether, there are an additional two million cards in the Serials General Catalog, the Catalog of nineteenth-Century Czech Book Production, the Catalog of the Library of Library Science, and the portions of the catalogs of the Music Division and the Slavonic Division that have, at least, been microfiched. The sequence of timing and the level of completion of each project will depend on the outcome of the various grant proposals that we submitted in 1997 and that we plan to submit in the future.

Each of these projects requires specific variations on previously used conversion methods—for example, extended cooperation with other institutions will be needed; RETROCON- GC will have to be coordinated with Aleph specifications; and circulation-driven RETROCON will require cooperation among the Circulation Department, the

Cataloging Division, and the Systems Office. However, in their final version, most records will have to be in the UNIMARC format, be they bibliographic records or authority records.

Prices

It is extremely difficult to discuss and compare prices for retrospective conversions. Of course, the prices are different for a short "standard" catalog record and for our very detailed bibliographic record. The "standard" catalog record can be very different in different countries and libraries—and even within one catalog (if different rules were applied at different times).

Our price for the retrospective conversion of the "standard" catalogue record is $1, which includes the selection and the marking of records not available in machine-readable form from other sources; scanning; transcription; tagging and editing for compliance with ISBD conventions; adding and checking the missing data, such as a country's code and language; checking, archiving, distributing records to, and collecting records from, participating people; transportation; and the price for equipment, management, and invoicing. The source of the data below is the catalog card and the result is the record in UNIMARC, which is then ready to be imported to the Aleph system:

```
LAB       -----nam0^22-----1i^450^
001       gk61160149
005       19980102
100       $a19980102d1989^^^^u^^y0czey0103^^^^ba
101 0     $ager
102       $aDD
200 1     $aChaos in dissipativen Systemen$fRonald W. Leven, Bernd-Peter Koch, Bernd Pompe
210       $aBerlin$cAkademie-Verl.$d1989
215       $a189 s.$cil.
225 2     $aWissenschaftliche Taschenbücher$iMathematik-Physik$vBd. 304
300       $aMit 29 Abb. und 1 Tb.
300       $aBibliogr. na s. 175-187
675       $a530.162(035)=30
700 -1    $aLeven$bRonald W.$4070
701 -1    $aKoch$bBernd-Peter$4070
701 -1    $aPompe$bBernd$4070
801 -0    $aCZ$bABA001
801 -1    $aCZ$bABA001$c19980102
801 -2    $aCZ$bABA001$c19980102
964       $aSystémy disipativní - neuspořádanost - příručky
971       $aH 92268
```

Our price for retrospective conversion of the detailed bibliographic record is $1.50 (including scanning; OCR; tagging; adding and checking the missing data, such as country code and language; checking, archiving, distributing records to, and collecting records from, participating libraries; transportation; and the price for equipment, management, and invoicing). The source of the data below is the bibliographic record from the printed Czech National Bibliography and the result is the record in UNIMARC, then ready to be imported to the Aleph system and to be included in the Czech National Bibliography on CD-ROM:

```
LAB      -----nam0^22-----1i^450^
001      bk197800020
005      19970106
020      $aCZ$bbk197800020
100      $a19970106d1977^^^^u^^y0czey0103^^^^ba
101 0    $acze
102      $aCS
200 1    $aStarověký Egypt$fMilada Vilímková$g[Fot.:] Bedřich Forman, Milan Zemina,
         Philip Goldman$gMapka Egypta: B. Forman
205      $a1. vyd.
210      $aPraha$cMF$d1977$gSvoboda 1
215      $a339, [2] s.$c[32] s. barev. fot. Příl.$d8°
225 2    $aVelké epochy kultury$vSv. 2
300      $a25000 výt.
300      $aBibliogr.
300      $aPřehl. Egyptských dějin a světových kultur
300      $aEgyptská božstva
300      $aJmenný, místní a věcný rejstřík
300      $aZkr.
300      $aFrontispice
300      $aObálka a vazba: B. Forman
330      $aV rozsáhlém výběru fotografií, opatřených komentářem a úvodními texty, představuje autorka bohatou kulturu starověkého Egypta. Zachycuje počátky kultury v údolí Nilu, politické dějiny Egypta, státní a společenskou organizaci, soukromý život obyvatel, náboženské představy, jazyk, písmo a literaturu, vědu, techniku a výtvarné umění.
410 -0   $12001^$aVelké epochy kultury
675      $a779:932
700 -1   $aVilímková$bMilada$4070
801 -0   $aCS$bABA001$c19780000
801 -1   $aCZ$bCBA001$c19970106
801 -2   $aCZ$bABA001$c19970106
964      $aEgypt starověký – dějiny a kultura – výklady populární
972      $aII 78418
998      $aKoldová$bhaku
```

Conclusion

Several years ago, the retrospective conversion of our catalogs was my nightmare. The presence of millions of catalog cards waiting for conversion, and extremely limited financial resources, resulting from low government support, are not a very good combination, but there is always some hope. Our RETROCON projects, supported only by the Mellon Foundation at the very beginning, are now firmly supported by the

Ministry of Culture. As a result, these projects opened a substantial portion of our library to our local and distant users. We strongly believe we will soon be able to open the whole National Library and other libraries. Parliament decided to support the retrospective conversion of the Parliamentary Library catalog in 1997 and 1998, using the technology described in this chapter. Support for RETROCON activities is indeed finally coming from the most important source.

Reference

Stoklasová, Bohdana, and Miroslav Bareš. 1995. "Retrospective Conversion in Czech Libraries." Prague: Národní knihovna České republiky.

CHAPTER 17

The Implementation of an Automated System at the University Library in Bratislava, Slovakia

ZUZANA ŘEPIŠOVÁ

This chapter discusses the process of implementation for an automated system in a large scientific library. It does not cover all the details but, rather, focuses on the crucial processes of analysis, data conversion, the database setup, and the gradual introduction of the system into the library's operations. Library automation is a complex matter and this chapter describes the range of activities that one system librarian was involved in.

The University Library (UL) in Bratislava is the oldest and largest academic library in the Slovak Republic. Established in 1919 as the Comenius University Library, it was, by 1954, serving as a national library, along with maintaining its academic mission. In 1954, it became an independent research library serving the broad public. The UL has played a significant role as the Slovak copyright library (since 1919); as a conservation library for Slovak dissertations (since 1978); a UN (since 1950) and UNESCO (since 1957) depository library; a center for international ILLs (since 1964); a center for union catalogs of foreign literature acquired in Czechoslovak libraries (since 1965); and an International Publications Exchange Center (since 1984). In the period 1947–1992, the UL was entitled to the legal deposit of publications in the Czech Republic.[1] The total number of volumes in the library amounted to 2,207,324 in March 1997.[2]

In June 1997, the Ministry of Culture promulgated a new constitutional charter,[3] and the organizational structure of the library underwent several significant changes. The University Library's National Library Center was established, and it took over several nationwide functions provided until then by the Slovak National Library in Martin. However, negotiations between these two institutions are just starting.

---

1. http://www.ulib.sk/english/history.htm
2. "Štatistika výkonov za 1. štvrt'rok 1997." Interný materiál Univerzitnej knižnice v Bratislave [Statistics report for the first quarter of 1997. Internal document of the University Library in Bratislava].
3. http://www.ulib.sk/listina.htm

The first attempts at automation had begun around 1970, when a database of foreign serials was experimentally processed on IBM 7040 and IBM 360/20 computers.[4] However, after two years, insurmountable obstacles put an end to this activity. In 1981 the UL, as one of four Slovak scientific libraries, started to store bibliographic records of monographs on an RPP16S computer that was originally designed for industrial process control. Although the only computer output in these early years involved the production of catalog cards, it represented, nevertheless, the beginnings of gradual library automation. In 1989, the cataloging module of the PC-based Israeli Magic system was introduced. A network version of this and the implementation of other modules were planned for the beginning of the 1990s. The data structure did not follow international standards and was even incompatible with the local exchange format widely used by the largest Czechoslovak libraries. When the UL adopted the idea of global library automation and networking, which culminated in the CASLIN project,[5] it was decided not to continue with the implementation of Magic. In 1993, an integrated library automation system, Aleph, was chosen, and since 1995 it has been used for document processing at the UL.[6]

Data Conversion

The library had begun to use computers for data storage in 1981. When the Aleph system arrived, approximately 200,000 bibliographic records were ready for conversion. By the time the switch from Magic to Aleph was contemplated, RPP16S bibliographic records had already been converted to the Magic structure. In other words, two files of records of different quality levels were available. For 1981–1988, the RPP16S records were without diacritics and only in capital letters, while for 1989–1994, the less problematic Magic data were available.

Since the library did not have programmers with the appropriate qualifications, and since the data structure was unique, part of the agreement with the vendor of Aleph, Ex Libris, was that it would provide a customized Magic-to-Aleph conversion program. The other three CASLIN libraries converted their CDS-ISIS data themselves.[7] After a preliminary analysis of the Magic data structure, it became obvious that a completely successful conversion was impossible: The UNIMARC structure was new to the region, and many of the required fields simply did not exist and had to be globally created, while for several Magic fields it was problematic to find an appropriate UNIMARC equivalent.

---

4. Kristína Kollárová, "Prípravné obdobie pre vlastnú prevádzku výpočtového strediska v Univerzitnej knižnici Bratislava," in *INFOS '81. Zborník z 11. Informatického seminára*, konaného v dňoch 30.marca– 2.apríla 1981, v Starom Smokovci, Bratislava, 1981, pp. 179–185 [Preparatory period for the real operating of the computer center in the university library in Bratislava, in INFOS '81: proceedings from the eleventh Informatics Seminar, held on March 30–April 2, 1981, in Star Smokovec].
    5. For all important CASLIN materials, see http://www.nkp.cz/caslin/Welcome.eng.html
    6. See appendix 17.1 for the chronology of the Aleph implementation.
    7. The three are the National Library of the Czech Republic, in Prague, the Slovak National Library in Martin, and the Moravian Regional Library in Brno.

The following patterns were found:

- "perfect match" fields;
- fields mandatory in UNIMARC and missing in MAGIC;
- fields useful to keep but with no UNIMARC equivalent;
- fields containing holdings, acquisitions, or other information;
- fields necessary for Aleph functions and not in UNIMARC;
- fields that could be generated from other fields or parts of other fields;
- useless fields not needed for the future.

Magic data were in six separate files linked by a unique document number. Appendix 17.2 gives a description of the Magic export-files structure that was supported by UNIMARC field equivalents. Besides the UNIMARC fields several local fields, such as OSYS (old system numbers) and KAT (including information for catalog card printing), were maintained in Magic, but quite a few of these were considered useless and, therefore, candidates for deletion. The conversion table and a Magic data sample were sent to Israel, which led to the discovery of some serious problems. While fields had not undergone any further reallocation, several changes had been introduced on the subfield level. However, no method was found for unraveling several fields, such as the note field and the subject-heading field. During the period in which cataloging was done by Magic, the note field was filled with different types of information (the note itself, a formal descriptor, additional inventory numbers). Since the 3XX UNIMARC (note) field was not indexed and, therefore, not searchable in Aleph, it was decided to keep this field without significant changes. Only the inventory numbers were removed for creating holdings records.

In the Magic structure, it was impossible to distinguish the general subject heading, the personal name SH, or the conference or meeting name SH, or the corporate name SH, because only two fields were devoted to what in UNIMARC is the whole 6XX group. Therefore, it was decided to create the repeatable 606 field, which stands for the general subject heading with only two possible subfields: $a for a topical heading and $x for a general subdivision. The first heading from the Magic SH string was taken as the topical one ($a), and everything that followed was converted to the general subdivision ($x). These two cases only illustrate the complexity of the conversion; in reality, there were many more complications. The whole conversion was done in three steps and negotiations with Ex Libris took approximately one year. After the library agreed that no other corrections were required, Ex Libris provided a source conversion program. The conversion itself was done in the library.

The mandatory fields for a union catalog minimal-data record, as determined by the National Library in Prague, are described in table 17.1.[8] All four CASLIN libraries agreed to follow these recommendations and they are also mandatory for all other libraries that wish to join the union catalog in the future.

A full bibliographic (BIB) record is created from 3 kinds of fields:

---

8. "Záznam pro souborný katalog: Unimarc" [Record for union catalog: UNIMARC] (Prague, 1996).

Table 17.1 Minimal-Data Record (Monographs) for the CASLIN Union Catalog

Field	Description	Conversion Status
000	Label	newly created field
001	Record ID number	newly created, partially generated
005	Last update date	newly generated
010	ISBN number	$a,$d match
100	General coded data	newly created, partially generated
101	Document language	match, conversion of language codes
102	Country of publication	match, conversion of country codes
200	Title statement	$a match, $e,$f generated from another field
205	Edition statement	$a generated from another field
210	Publication	$a,$c,$d match
215	Physical description	$a match
225	Series	$a,$h,$v partial match
300	Note	$a partial match
675	UDC number	$a match
700	Primary intellectual responsibility	$a,$b match
701	Alternative intellectual responsibility	$a,$b generated from another field (partial success)
702	Secondary intellectual responsibility	$a,$b generated from another field (partial success)
710	Corporation—primary responsibility	nonexisting field and data in Magic
711	Corporation—alternative responsibility	nonexisting field and data in Magic
712	Corporation—secondary responsibility	nonexisting field and data in Magic
801	Source of cataloging	newly created, partially generated from another field
910	Ownership	$a,$s,$t not yet implemented

1. 0XX-9XX UNIMARC fields
2. fields for library use (data from conversion and internal information)
3. Aleph function fields (such as LN and YR, for language and year of publication filtering; BASE, for logical base assignments).

The next step in the data conversion was the creation of holdings records. After an analysis of the holding-file structure and a determination of the fields that could be used as the basis, the library carried out the conversion program. The holdings file and the BIB records file were separate files linked by the system number. Fields that were generated from BIB records or were assigned globally were as follows:

- sublibrary code—the sublibrary code for all records was UK1;
- item status—two item statuses for loans, generated on the base is of the shelf-mark value;
- shelf mark—taken from the bibliographic record;
- inventory number—taken from the bibliographic record.

The remaining 32 holding record fields were either left blank or were assigned a default value as required by the system. However, this problem was not completely solvable either. As mentioned, some of the inventory numbers were relocated to the note field. This was a valid procedure mostly in those cases in which more than two inventory numbers occurred per BIB record, but was not applicable for the whole database. For not very clear reasons, an unknown quantity of inventory numbers never entered the database and was kept in the paper form. Since the inventory number is an item-unique number important for circulation, the Department of Stacks faces the crucial task of checking and manually adding all missing numbers. This is currently being done.

The UL has, since 1984, operated a union catalog of foreign serials purchased in Slovakia.[9] A part of the database is also a directory of over 1,000 contributors to the catalog, 400 of whom are active. Since the database has existed, several systems and formats have changed, the latest change, occurring prior to the conversion to Aleph, being the addition of the CDS/ISIS exchange format structure. The National Library in Prague contributed to the conversion by providing a CDS/ISIS-Aleph conversion program. However, several local improvements and data reallocations were needed, mainly for the location field, which had undergone the most significant structural changes. Below are examples of both CDS/ISIS and Aleph location fields (BAA001 and LME301, for example, are institutional codes maintained centrally by the National Library, and +/− stands for permanent/temporary storage of material):

CDS/ISIS structure

910:^r1990^bBAA001+,LME301+,BAB002+,BAB019-
910:^r1991^bBAA001+,LME301+,BAB019-
910:^r1992^bBAA001+,LME301+,BAB002+,BAB019-
910:^r1993^bBAA001+,LME301+,BAB002+

Aleph structure

KZP 0000001 910 L $$aBAA001$$u+$$r1990-1993
KZP 0000001 910 L $$aBAB002$$u+$$r1990,1992-1993
KZP 0000001 910 L $$aBAB019$$u-$$r1990-1992
KZP 0000001 910 L $$aLME301$$u+$$r1990-1993

In 1996, the CDS/ISIS exchange format data were converted to CDS/ISIS UNIMARC and this became the real working database updated on daily bases. Such a temporary solution was the most harmless, since CDS/ISIS allowed for a number of outputs and printouts that Aleph had not yet been "taught." It is only a question of time and of use of programmers' skills before this problem will be solved. The union catalog of serials is displayed on-line in Aleph and updated quarterly.[10]

Analysis of Document Flow

The library attempted to determine the greatest possible simplification of its document flow, no matter how complex it might be, in order to find a basic level of overall document flow and to determine its main components and links expressing mu-

---

9. Lydia Sedláčková, "KZP—súborný katalóg zahraničných periodík CASLIN," in *INFOS '97. Zborník z 27. Informatického seminára*, konaného v dňoch 14.–17. apríla 1997 (Bratislava, 1997), pp. 121–125 [KZP–A union catalog of foreign serials, CASLIN. In INFOS '97: proceedings from the Twenty-seventh Informatics Seminar held on April 14–17 1997].

10. Access to Aleph databases: telnet omega.ulib.sk, login: opac; http://www.ulib.sk

tual relationships. The analysis was done with the new Aleph integrated system in mind and reflected the various features that the system offered. However, the analysis is not yet complete, and this is one of the obstacles that has prevented the implementation of the circulation and serials-control modules and of budget control in the acquisitions module.

Figure 17.1 shows the document flow throughout the whole library—the purpose of this figure is to find the simplest way of treating all the stages of a monograph's flow. Since the way in which a document enters the library affects how it is handled, the pattern for this was followed during the entire analysis. Documents in fact enter the library in seven different ways:

- legal deposit, to which the library has been entitled since its founding;
- purchase, mostly of foreign literature but, since 1993, also of Czech publications;
- gift received from various donors, divided, in the follow-up, into valuable material entering the database and into books that may not stay in the library in the future for various reasons (offered as gifts to another institution, multiple copies, nonprofile documents);
- exchange of material with various (domestic and foreign) institutions and libraries;
- depositing of UN and UNESCO materials;
- replacement of lost material
- recataloging of books once processed in the library and later deleted from the list of holdings.

The big rectangles stand for the three main points the document passes through during processing. After an initial identification, description, and the assignment in the Acquisitions Department, it proceeds to the Descriptive Cataloging Department, and, finally, the BIB record is finished in the Bibliographic-Information Department, where the subject classification is done. The Closed Stacks Department, where physical documents end up for final processing, supports all kinds of interactions either within the library or with the outside world, as indicated in the chart. The only exception in this model is the literature provided by the UN and, specifically, by UNESCO, which is kept and treated individually. This material bypasses the Acquisitions Department and rejoins the flow of documents in the cataloging process.

Acquisitions. The processes in Acquisitions reveal, more precisely and in detail, the complex relationships involved. All incoming material is sorted and initially identified. Then librarians search the database for already-existing bibliographic records or browse card catalogs for duplicates. Legal deposits (LD), gifts (G), and exchanges (E) enter the library from the outside and books designated as replacements (REP) and for recataloging (REC) enter from other departments within the library. Exchanges (E) are of two kinds: materials sent by an exchange partner at the library's request (E1), and materials that are purchased for an exchange partner (E2). The former undergoes the regular procedure while the latter is treated separately. The Circulation Department delivers replacements (REP) for lost books. Since the university library is a deposit library, patrons are obliged to replace lost materials with either the same items or similar ones. The book is then processed in the normal way. Materials that need recataloging (REC) arrive from Stacks Maintenance, where they are also responsible for

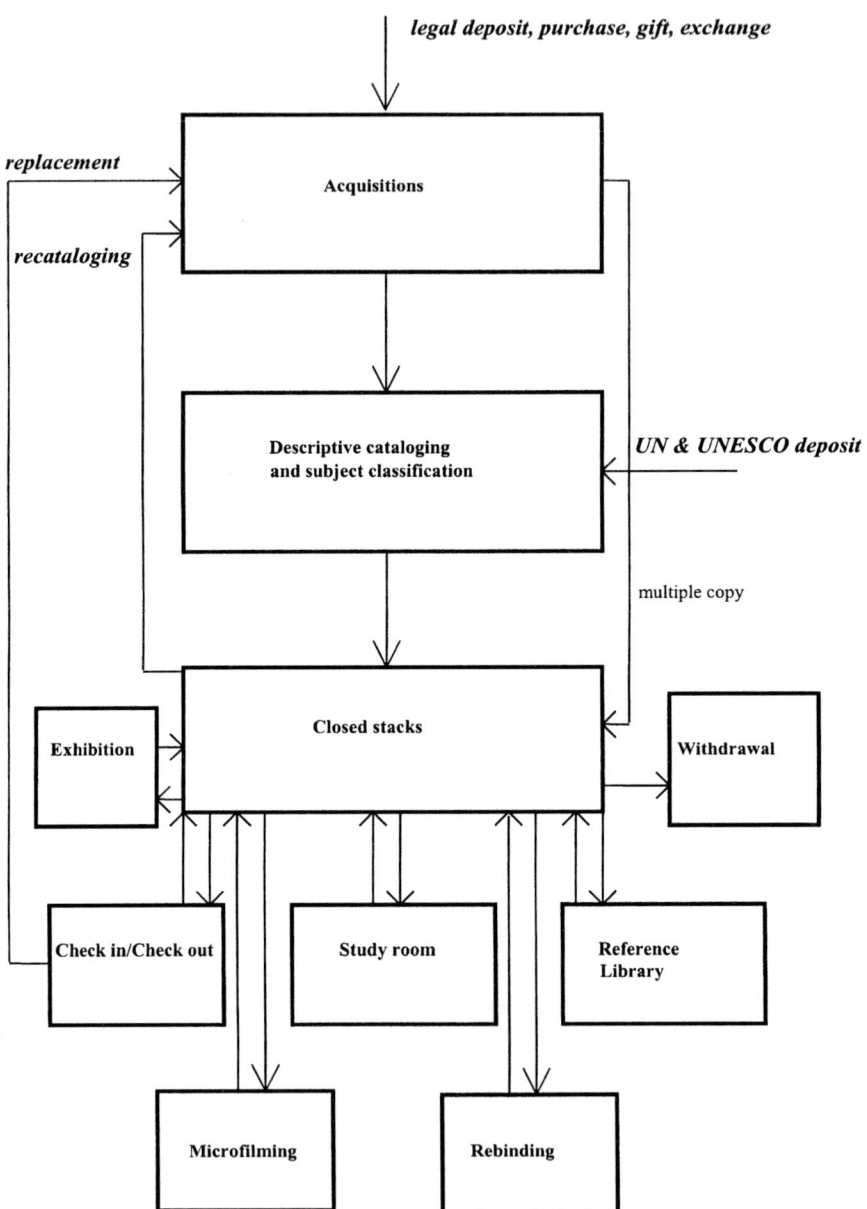

Figure 17.1 Document Flow throughout a Whole Library

regular checks on library holdings. In most cases, when a book is not available for a long time (and not on loan), its record is removed from the on-line or the card catalog and deleted from the inventory list. Then, if it is later found, it is processed anew and the procedure starts in the Acquisitions Department. The acquisitions board meets once a week and makes the decision on the final location of the book and also on titles and number of items that are to be purchased. It also evaluates books received as gifts (G), and determines what matches the library profile and will then be accepted (G1) and what material does not match and will then be offered to other libraries and institutions (G2). The final step in the book procedure in Acquisitions is the creation of a holding record that contains information about loan status, the inventory number (a unique number for each item), the shelf mark, and the library division classification. One copy then goes to the Cataloging Department for descriptive cataloging and all multiple copies head straight for the closed stacks. Once the book is processed in Acquisitions, the library database will receive either an originally created, new, and short bibliographic record, or a full bibliographic record converted from previous systems, with an appended-holdings record for incoming material.

Descriptive Cataloging and Subject Classification. After leaving Acquisitions, books proceed to the Cataloging Department. A descriptive cataloger, with a book in hand, either finishes the bibliographic record or makes checks on the converted record. Similar processing is done in the UN & UNESCO Information Center, which takes responsibility for the depository materials held separately from other library holdings. The last stage involves subject analysis and classification. All material is transferred to the Bibliographic-Information Department, where subject catalogers fill in the appropriate subject fields and the bibliographic record is completed. After that, books end up in the stacks.

Closed Stacks. After their arrival, all documents are labeled with a shelf mark and are sorted according to holding information. The majority are located in adjacent closed stacks, and books whose destination is a particular reading room are put aside and a notice is sent to the Public Services Department. The Central Book Registry, a subdivision of the Stack Maintenance Department, plays a key role in organizing and registering the document flow. Up to now, information about a document's status and location, if it is outside the stacks, is provided mostly by manual methods. The Registry keeps track of material that each of ten study rooms has on a permanent loan, and also registers loans to the reference libraries. Library stacks and cooperating departments have mostly two-way relations. When material leaves for, or returns from, an exhibition, rebinding, and microfilming, it passes through this registration point. A withdrawal is the only case in which a document flows in one direction—out of the library. Material for loans to patrons is treated differently: It leaves the stacks without a centralized registration and the responsibility for keeping updated information on loans rests with the Public Services Department, namely, the Circulation Desk.

Database Structure

The Global Library (GBL) occupies the highest level in the database structure (see figure 17.2). It has a separate set of program tables, screens and system-messages files,

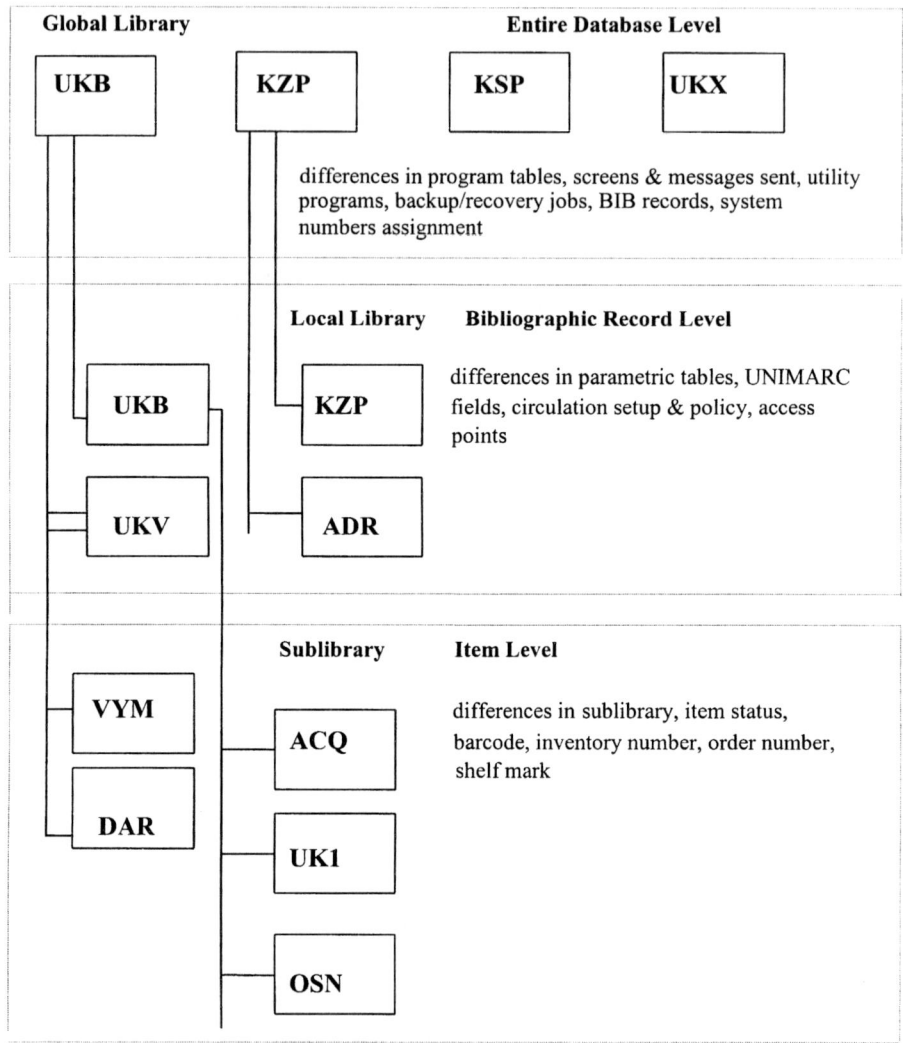

Figure 17.2 Aleph Database Structure in the University Library, Bratislava

utility programs, and backup/recovery jobs. System numbers for bibliographic records are also allocated on this level. Each GBL must have at least one local library (LL) defined within it, and the pattern of a GBL-and-one-LL assignment is usually followed. Individual local libraries within one GBL can be, but are not necessarily, differentiated within parametric tables, screens, access points, and circulation policies. The sublibrary definition operates on the item level. All the databases itemized below are LL databases.

- The UKB database of monographs contains 225,110 bibliographic records.[11] It includes records originally created in Aleph (since February 1995) and all data converted between 1981 and 1994.[12] There were also 6,424 bibliographic records of Slovak theses downloaded in 1997.
- The UKV database is devoted to temporary material that is either sent to exchange partners at their request, or is given as a gift. This environment has already been set up, but is not currently operating.
- The KZP database is a union catalog of foreign serials purchased by libraries and other institutions in Slovakia. After the latest update, the number of records was 14,064.
- The ADR database is a directory of contributors to the KZP union catalog. The number of non-UNIMARC records is 1,153; however, not all registered institutions are active. Information stored here includes the name of the institution, and its code, full address, contact person, e-mail data, changed data, and date of the last update.
- The KSP database will be for serial control within the University Library. After the decision was made to keep serials separate from monographs, a new GBL-and-LL assignment was created to accommodate data.
- The UKX is a test database with the LL UKX and UKY, and its structure and length vary according to the problem being tested.

The Implementation of Aleph

Aleph is an integrated modular system. It was clear from the beginning that a complete switch and automation of all manual procedures at once was hardly feasible. An implementation by modules seemed to be the optimal solution. All CASLIN libraries agreed to a particular sequence for the gradual introduction of the cataloging module, authority-files maintenance, the OPAC, the acquisitions module, and circulation and serials-control modules. In February 1995, the on-line cataloging of monographs in Aleph started. However, this did not mean the end of Magic. Aleph could not support several kinds of printouts that turned out to be crucial, such as inventory lists and catalog cards. This led to parallel processing activities in the two systems for all of 1995. Librarians in the Acquisitions Department created a bibliographic record in the cataloging module for all incoming material and entered a basic description and holding information. Processing followed in descriptive and subject cataloging. At the outset, the introduction of Aleph slowed down cataloging, the main features of which included work on duplicates, with the use of the same number of librarians; a new system; the new UNIMARC format; new AACR2 cataloging rules; and entirely new activities, such as the maintenance of name and subject-authority files. Nevertheless, 1995 was a successful year in which a huge amount of work was done. Programs for inventory lists were set up; the LAN in the building was finished and the library was connected to the Internet; data conversion was carried out; the OPAC was introduced to the public; and the first attempts with WWW Aleph were initiated.

---

11. All data here were as of September 13, 1997.
12. There were originally databases of two local libraries, a UKM containing converted Magic data (1989–1994) and a UKN RPP16S conversion (1981–1988), that were, after corrections, eventually merged with the Aleph UKB database.

The following year, 1996, saw the closing of Magic. Cataloging became more or less routine and the backlog diminished. The problem of the printing of catalog cards was solved. A new KZP database (a union catalog of foreign serials) was put on-line. All incoming material began to be bar-coded. WWW access to the databases was made available. For all intents and purposes, the cataloging, maintenance, and OPAC modules were fully implemented. In 1997 a new global library was established for a future database of serials. The serials-control module seems to be one of the user-friendliest modules. Its implementation was scheduled for the end of 1997 or, at worst, early in 1998. Circulation, on the other hand, is the weakest aspect of library automation at the UKB. This, unfortunately, is the library's Achilles' heel. Some preparatory work has begun, but the most important preliminary step, a detailed analysis of document flow, and of interactions between Public Services and Stack Maintenance, has not been completed. A database of users is currently being created. As for the acquisitions module, the principal operations (orders, invoices, and claims) are still being manually carried out, in spite of the analysis of procedures that has been completed and the solutions that have been proposed. Thus far, all efforts to bring the acquisitions module on-line have completely failed.

Conclusions

Thanks to the CASLIN Project, indisputable achievements on both the nationwide and local levels were attained. Among these, the adherence to international bibliographic standards was the most valuable. In the library, automated catalogs were made available to the public and made accessible from remote sites. The implementation of the new system also accelerated data conversion and permitted the enlargement of the on-line database.

Automation also exhibited some weaknesses. Several particular problems are analyzed in other chapters in this volume.[13] Besides general problems, every institution had its own specific failures. The biggest problem of the University Library was that it underestimated the human aspects of the CASLIN Project's implementation. From 1994 to 1997, the personnel in the key positions of systems librarian, systems programmer, and project manager changed ten times. It is important to stress that at no time in the library's history of Aleph's implementation was there a full-time programmer employed by the library. In addition, five of the so-called superusers who underwent training provided by the software vendor Ex Libris, and were intended to be future trainers for the whole library staff, have left the library, with no provision having been made for their successors. A very long time has passed since trained staff members had the opportunity for the kind of hands-on experience with the system that would allow them to extend their knowledge. This has led to a reluctant and distrustful attitude toward even the smallest system changes off the beaten track. The main driving force, the feeling of commitment to the idea of a far better automated future that worked perfectly at the beginning, has faded away.

---

13. For a discussion of contractual problems with vendors, and for software and hardware problems, see the chapter by Iva Příbramská. Implementation delays are the topic of Andrew Lass's chapter.

Communication among departments, library management, and the implementation group was not easy and straightforward, and problems arose because solutions were often ad hoc ones rather than systematic ones. All this confirms the earlier observation that it is important to remember that automation is done by humans and not by computers.

Appendix 17.1. Chronology of CASLIN Events

1991

November 11, 1991	CASLIN "Statement of Intent"

1992

December 14, 1992	Funding granted by the Mellon Foundation

1993

January 23, 1993	Library system vendor Ex Libris—its Aleph—selected
May 31, 1993	Agreements signed
June 1993	First High Level Training, Israel
August 1993	First System Training, Diviaky
	Data conversion negotiations with Ex Libris, localization, UNIMARC implementation started
September 5–9, 1993	CASLIN-Pew, first seminar (Roznov pod Radhostem)
November 1993	First users' training, Brno
November 16, 1993	Demo machine installed in the library

1994

January 1994	Training room opened in the library
February 3–4, 1994	First seminar for system librarians and system programmers, Prague
April 27–May 5, 1994	Second Aleph system seminar, Israel
May 1994	LAN building started
June 19–23, 1994	CASLIN-Pew second seminar, Liptovsky Jan
August 22–23, 1994	Acceptance number 1 (OPAC, Cataloging, Acquisitions)
August 30, 1994	DEC Alpha server and Aleph 32_4 version installed in the library
November 11, 1994	Second system seminar for system librarians
November 29, 1994	Aleph version 32_4.8 upgrade

1995

January 1995	Database structure and tables definition
February 1995	All books cataloged in Aleph system, but simultaneously running on old system
March 1995	External programs for inventory lists and other protocols assigned

April 1995	Analysis of final data conversion done by Ex Libris
June 1995	Merging of two conversion files, database of 190,000 bibliographic records created (1981–1994)
July 1995	Inventory-list printouts available
August 27–31, 1995	CASLIN-Pew third seminar, Smolenice
September 1995	LAN finished, the library on the Internet
October 1995	7 OPAC terminals introduced to users
November 1995	Cataloging-card printouts from Aleph (conversion to Magic)
December 1995	Aleph version 32_4.17 upgrade WWW Aleph setup
Dec 1995–January 1996	Merging of the current data (1995) and conversion database (1981–1994); UKB database consists of over 200,000 BIB records
1996	
January 1996	Bar-code assignment of incoming documents Closing of the Magic system (the end of parallel processing)
April 15–19, 1996	MARC-AACR2 training, Prague
May 1996	WWW access to the database opened
June 1996	Creation of a new database, KZP, a union catalogue of foreign serials; conversion from CDS-ISIS to Aleph
June 18–19, 1996	Aleph 32_5.11 version upgrade
June 25, 1996	Networking a demonstration of data exchange with the Slovak National Library in Martin
July 1996	Global corrections of databases UKB and KZP
August 1996	Access-points definition for WWW
1997	
permanent task	Holdings check-out
March 12, 1997	Global library KSP created for serials
May 1997	Last update of KZP and ADR local libraries
August 1997	Slovak dissertations downloaded to UKB database

Appendix 17.2. Magic Files Structure

KAFIL002.TXT file

Number	Field	Length	UNIMARC Conversion
1	Internal book number	9	OSYS
2	Record number on tape	3	REC-NO
3	Means of acquisition	5	ACQ data
4	Shelf number 1	20	972 $a
5	Shelf number 2	20	972 $a
6	Author 1	42	700 $a,$b
7	Author 2	42	701 $a,$b
8	Number of lines of title	2	useless information
9	Collective title	42	useless information
10	Place of publication	42	210 $a
11	Publisher	42	210 $c
12	Year of publication	42	210 $d
13	Pages	42	215 $a
14	Series	42	225 $a
15	Volume	42	225 $v
16	Number of lines of note	2	useless information
17	Inventory number 1	20	973 $a
18	Inventory number 2	20	973 $a
19	Price 1	9	010 $d
20	Price 2	9	010 $d
21	Currency	1	ACQ data
22	ISBN 1	20	010 $a
23	ISBN 2	20	010 $a
24	Single/multi volume item	1	LBL pos. 8
25	Number of copies	1	holding information
26	Country of publication	4	102 $a
27	Language	2	101 $a
28	Vendor	8	ACQ information
29	Number of lines of references	2	useless information
30	Number of lines of UDC	2	useless information
31	Number of lines of subject headings	2	useless information
32	Field of science	2	useless information
33	Catalog	42	KAT
34	Date of cataloging	10	801 $c

KAFIL003.TXT file

Number	Field	Length	UNIMARC Conversion
1	Internal book number	9	OSYS
2	Line number of title	2	useless information
3	Title	Unlimited	200 $a

KAFIL004.TXT file

Number	Field	Length	UNIMARC Conversion
1	Internal book number	9	OSYS
2	Line number of note	2	useless information
3	Library note	unlimited	300 $a

KAFIL005.TXT file

Number	Field	Length	UNIMARC Conversion
1	Internal book number	9	OSYS
2	Line number of reference	2	useless information
3	References	42	702 $a, $b

KAFIL006.TXT file

Number	Field	Length	UNIMARC Conversion
1	Internal book number	9	OSYS
2	Line number of UDC	2	useless information
3	UDC	42	675 $a

KAFIL007.TXT file

Number	Field	Length	UNIMARC Conversion
1	Internal book number	9	OSYS
2	Line number of subject heading	2	useless information
3	Subject heading	84	606 $a, $x

References

Kollárová, Kristína. "Prípravné obdobie pre vlastnú prevádzku výpočtového strediska v Univerzitnej knižnici Bratislava." In *INFOS '81: zborník z 11. Informatického seminára*, konaného v dňoch 30.marca–2.apríla 1981 v Starom Smokovci. Bratislava 1981, pp. 179–185 [Preparatory period for the real operating of the computer center in the University Library in Bratislava. In INFOS '81: proceedings from the eleventh Informatics Seminar, held in March 30–April 2, 1981, in Stary Smokovec].

Sedláčková, Lýdia. "KZP"—súborný katalóg zahraničných periodík CASLIN." In *INFOS '97: Zborník z 27. Informatického seminára*, konaného v dňoch 14.–17. apríla 1997, Bratislava 1997, pp. 121–125 [KZP —Union catalog of serials, CASLIN. In INFOS '97: proceedings from the twenty-seventh Informatics seminar held in April 14–17, 1997].

"Štatistika výkonov za 1. štvrťrok 1997." Interný materiál Univerzitnej knižnice v Bratislave [Statistics report for the first quarter of 1997: internal document of the University Library in Bratislava].

"Záznam pro souborný katalog: Unimarc." Tištěné monografie [Record for Union Catalog: Unimarc. Printed monographs]. Prague, 1996.

CHAPTER 18

Cataloging Standards in Czech Libraries

BOHDANA STOKLASOVÁ

When Frederick Kilgour, the founder of the Online Computer Library Center (OCLC), visited the National Library in Prague in 1992, he was most favorably impressed with the results of our automation program at the library, the quality of our records, and especially by the attention we pay to adherence to international standards. At the end of his visit he expressed the hope that our records might enrich the OCLC database in the near future. I took these words more as an encouragement of our efforts than as an imminent reality. Yet, his words proved providential: the National Library in Prague became the first library in a post-Communist country whose records were accepted by OCLC; further, the library is now one of the most important foreign institutions cooperating with OCLC on the UNIMARC-to-USMARC and USMARC to UNIMARC conversion.

In this chapter I describe the background for these successes, which were nevertheless accompanied by many periods of trials and error.

History of the Implementation of International Standards

In the Czech libraries, the implementation of international standards in cataloging was closely related to the beginnings of automation during the 1980s. Despite our growing belief that standards are crucial, the acceptance of these standards was not without obstacles. Our experience may help other institutions in Eastern European countries in their standardization efforts.

When considering the implementation of international standards, it is important to decide about two basic issues:

- which standards to choose;
- whether to implement the selected standards without major changes or with sweeping changes that reflect the national cataloging tradition.

Perhaps the main stumbling block in our decision-making process was our decades-long isolation from the West and our stubborn adherence to stifling rules from the past, even after the exposure to new and better ways.

The National Library in Prague took some time to decide on the right course. After many vacillations, our post-1989 exposure to international standards contributed to our belief that if we accepted international standards, we would improve our daily work and render our records more acceptable to the rest of the world. The implementation of international standards in Czech libraries can be described as having occurred in several phases, as follows.

CDS/ISIS and MAKS: The 1980s Trial Period

In the early 1980s, interestingly enough, it was not catalogers, but the people in the Systems Division, who perceived that automated cataloging without international standards is futile. Initially, all their proposals and experiments were viewed either with suspicion or with amused skepticism by their colleagues in the Cataloging Division. The main reason for this attitude was our lack of experience with automation, with machine-readable records, and of course even with routine international cooperation.

The Systems Division staff, however, had considerable knowledge of, and by now experience with, automation since they had to tailor CDS/ISIS to our needs.[1] This bare-bones system needed a library module, which took all the skill of the Systems Division to develop. In order to hasten the introduction of automation, not even the Systems staff paid much attention to international cataloguing standards during that phase of the project. However, the experience they gained during the development period fostered our awareness of the need for standardization.

Automation indeed started in Czech libraries on a larger scale in the second half of the 1980s, when the National Library started to implement some international standards, following an extensive period of evaluation, selection, and modification of these standards—which included the following:

- ISBD. The International Standard Bibliographic Description (ISBD) has been used since 1989 without modification, initially for the production of the Czech National Bibliography (beginning with the 1982 edition).
- UNIMARC. It was not clear at the outset whether UNIMARC would remain just an attractive theory or whether it would also have practical use. Besides, the format did not appear to be compatible with CDS/ISIS. While our lack of experience led to some improvements in our own Czech (and Slovak) Exchange Format, these improvements were not in the spirit of UNIMARC, which we frankly did not completely understand. The Czech Exchange Format is essentially a simplified version of UNIMARC. For instance, objective limitations such as the availability of only 99 fields, or the inability to utilize indicators, were embedded in CDS/ISIS and so we had to conform to these limitations. We removed fixed fields, and we eliminated the "duplicated" recording of authorship (found in the 200$f,$g and 7XX fields). We even felt that the recording of authorship only once in each record was a definite improvement, only to find out later that this feature was a major flaw of our system, making conversion of these records to UNIMARC rather difficult. Let me warn others who may be contemplating following the same route: Modification of standards is always dangerous, since valid objections and obstacles become easily supplemented by subjective ones. The result is something

---

1. CDS/ISIS is available from UNESCO for free.

far removed from the initial international standard. Yet, although we did not pay much heed to our foreign colleagues' advice to accept UNIMARC as is, we have, unwittingly, built into the Czech Exchange Format a high degree of "granularity," which overcame the other defects during the conversion.
- AACR2. At the outset, we felt that we could not accept the use of AACR2 (*Anglo-American Cataloging Rules*, 2d edition) because the Anglo-American bias of these rules made them unsuitable for Czech cataloging. However, it already became clear to us toward the end of the 1980s that we needed new rules, since the existing ones (published in the 1960s) provided no guidance or answers for our contemporary cataloging problems. Unlike the machine-readable format, however, the new cataloging rules, which were being developed on the basis of ISBD, with some lip service being paid to AACR2, were never completed: The numerous omissions and exceptions embedded in the proposed new rules convinced us that accepting AACR2 was the only right course to take.
- LCSH. As long as we worked with small databases that did not require any kind of authority control, we saw free keywords as being the ideal way to present the subject matter. Further, subject headings were viewed by us as an undesirable vestige of the paper catalogs, although we had to use them in the published National Bibliography. Because of the inherent North American bias of LCSH, we rejected this thesaurus a priori, without doing an in-depth analysis or evaluation of its principles.
- UDC. The University Decimal Classification (UDC) scheme is used extensively in Czech libraries; its role has not been diminished in any way by the implementation of automation.

The Current Situation

In the mid-1990s, the National Library in Prague and several other institutions in the Czech Republic ceased to use CDS/ISIS and started to use various integrated systems, but with the same old questions being posed: Which standards should be chosen, and how do we implement them?

Our road toward accepting standards was influenced by many "nonstandard" circumstances, whether it was our politically influenced isolation from our Western colleagues, or the inherent need to further develop existing models, rather than accept them.

By the mid-1990s, the National Library in Prague had gained enough valuable experience with automation and standardization. The cataloging staff started working together with the Systems Division staff, and we now have a number of highly trained professionals who are versed in both areas. There are now several databases, some of which also try to support authority control.

Our attitude toward standardization in the area of description as well as in that of subject analysis has substantially changed: Without it, we could not cooperate with OCLC. We continue to make the various standards available by translating them into Czech. Finally, most of these standards play a substantial role in our CASLIN union catalog. The current situation is as follows:

- ISBD. All formats are now available in Czech translation.
- AACR2. The Czech translation of the rules has now been published. We have decided to accept the rules in full and we have prepared Czech interpretations of several points.

We lean toward AACR2 whenever there is a conflict between AACR2 and ISBD. The adoption of AACR2 also brought many new features into our cataloging, such as uniform titles and corporate names. Despite our initial aversion to AACR2, our catalogers now see their clarity and feel comfortable with their principles. Regardless, the rules are not easy to master, and our phasing them in over the last few years and the regular publication of rule interpretations aim at making them more easily acceptable.

- UNIMARC. The Czech translation of this format is now also complete. It is the main machine-readable format used by Czech libraries, with the Czech Exchange Format becoming a secondary format. We have also translated the authority manual, although, unfortunately, our Aleph-based system does not accommodate many features of the UNIMARC-based authority control protocol.
- UDC. We have obtained some 60,000 classification numbers from UDC in The Hague, in a database version; they are now available on a CD-ROM (produced in collaboration with a Czech company, Albertina). However, the work is not finished as there are many addenda that we still have to work on.
- LCSH. We have discontinued the use of keywords to provide subject access. Although we will not translate the entire LCSH, the National Library in Prague recently decided to use LCSH in areas relevant to our collections. Our new subject-headings thesaurus—Subject Headings of the National Library of the Czech Republic (PHNK)—follows LCSH's philosophy and any newly formulated subjects are fully compatible with the spirit of LCSH.

While bibliographic description standards have by now been used by us for many years, the transformation of the subject-headings treatment is still unfinished. We still have to convince many of our colleagues about the wisdom and value of our approach. Just as in the case of bibliographic description, we believe that we will succeed in this task as well.

Despite our successes in many areas, others are still mired in shortcomings such as the lack of hardware and problems in software. The novelty of the implementation of standards does slow us down, especially when we encounter a truly new and difficult topic to deal with.

Future Goals

We still have work to do in perfecting the Czech interpretation of many AACR2 rules so as to adapt them to the UNIMARC-based Aleph (we cannot bend Aleph much further) and to prepare a "minimal level" cataloging standard applicable to all types of documents. We have a long way to go toward building and maintaining authority files. Last, but not least, since over the last few years we have spent great amounts of energy and attention to achieve standardization, we now have to resume and increase our productivity.

In addition to the available UDC, we need to complete the translation of UDC additions and prepare a modified version of "selected UDC symbols." We plan to analyze the relationship of UDC and PHNK and we need to reconcile LCSH and PHNK to provide sufficient examples. We would very much like to assign LCSH to all records for materials published in the Czech Republic that are now, monthly, being loaded into OCLC.

Summary

It should be clear that by now international standards are used in all aspects of cataloging in most Czech libraries, our records are available in the OCLC WorldCat database, and vice versa—we are able to use this database for cataloging our foreign acquisitions.

None of these results were easy to achieve. If the description of our results will encourage our colleagues from abroad to continue to introduce international cataloging standards, and if our identification of mistakes and errors can aid them in avoiding the same mistakes, we will be gratified, and proud to have helped them.

References

Anglo-americká katalogizační pravidla [American Library Association]; překlad Národní knihovna v Praze, Praha: Národní knihovna, 1994.

AACR2R/UNIMARC: České interpretace. Část I [AACR2/UNIMARC: Czech interpretations, Part 1] Pracovní skupina pro jmenné zpracování dokumentů při NK ČR, Prague: Národní knihovna České republiky, 1997.

AACR2R/UNIMARC: České interpretace. Část II [AACR2/UNIMARC: Czech interpretations, Part 2] Pracovní skupina pro jmenné zpracování dokumentů při NK ČR, Prague: Národní knihovna České republiky, 1997.

MDT: Mezinárodní desetinné třídění [UCD: universal decimal classification], UCD Consortium; překlad Národní knihovna České republiky, Prague: Albertina icome Praha, 1997, one CD-ROM.

UNIMARC/autority: univerzální formát pro autority [UNIMARC/Authorities: universal format for authorities], International Federation of Library Associations and Institutions; překlad Národní knihovna České republiky, Prague: Národní knihovna České republiky, 1995.

UNIMARC manuál: bibliografický formát [UNIMARC Manual: bibliographic format], International Federation of Library Associations and Institutions; překlad Národní knihovna České republiky, Prague: Národní knihovna České republiky, 1996.

Výměnný formát pro bibliografický, (dokumentační) a katalogizační záznam. [Exchange format for bibliographic and cataloging records], Prague: Státní knihovna, 1989.

Záznam pro souborný katalog : UNIMARC. Tištěné monografie [Minimum level record for the CASLIN Union Catalog: UNIMARC. Printed monographs]/ Pracovní skupina CASLIN pro standardizaci a jmenné zpracování . . . [et al.], Prague: Národní knihovna České republiky, 1996.

CHAPTER 19

Evolution of Authority File Work in Poland

ANNA PALUSZKIEWICZ

In 1989, intensive work was begun at the Warsaw University Library (WUL) to prepare for the implementation of an integrated library system. The library took advantage of a research grant from the State Office for Scientific and Technological Development (Urząd Postępu Naukowo-Technicznego i Wdrożeń) to develop a MARC bibliographic format for Polish scientific libraries—the resulting format was a FOKA (based on UNIMARC), for books and serials. There was one other important result: We realized how crucial authority files are for modern integrated library systems. Consequently, our library workers took the initiative and set up two working groups.

The first one was aimed at the creation of the rules for a name authority file. The second one was set up to design the rules for a subject authority file. From the very beginning it was clear that both groups were pioneering in these efforts on a national scale and as such they received support from the Ministry of National Education (Ministerstwo Edukacji Narodowej) and the State Committee for Scientific Research (Komitet Badań Naukowych). As work on authority files is a continuous process, in 1996 the Ministry of National Education established, at the WUL, a Center for Formats and Authority Files (Centrum Formatów i Kartotek Haseł Wzorcowych).

In this chapter I describe the importance of authority files in an integrated library system, and the history and organization of work on the union authority files created by Polish academic libraries. I also try to evaluate costs and benefits connected with such an undertaking.

Authority Files

The basic access points of the catalogue are the headings. To ensure consistency of data, and (as a consequence of this) effective searches in the catalogue, the headings must be uniform, according to strictly defined rules, and properly used in bibliographic records. As a source of uniform headings, authority files are created and maintained by the cataloging agencies. One of the methods of creating the database of correct uniform headings is to run a union authority file. Entering authority records into the union authority database and making them available to many libraries eliminates the unnecessary duplication of work and improves the efficiency with which bibliographic records can be exchanged. An authority file has the following main objectives:

- to specify the set of headings,
- to distinguish uniform headings from unestablished headings,
- to specify the scope of a heading,
- to establish relationships between headings.

Two types of headings are defined in the authority file: uniform (established) headings and unestablished headings. A uniform heading is a heading that is authorized for use in bibliographic records as a main entry or an added entry, a series-added entry, or as the lead element in a subject-added entry. An unestablished heading may be a variant of a uniform heading, a form of the heading used only for authority-file organizational purposes, or a subject subdivision that is authorized for use with a uniform heading in an extended subject heading. Headings may be names, name/title combinations, uniform titles (including series uniform titles), or topical terms; and there may be subdivisions, and extended subject headings. Further, a heading may be categorized as being suitable for either a name authority file or a subject authority file. Specifically, name, name/title, and uniform-title headings are suitable for a name authority file; name, name/title, uniform-title, topical-term, subdivision, and extended subject headings are suitable for a subject authority file.

General rules for authority files are defined in an IFLA document, *Guidelines for Authority and Reference Entries* (GARE).[1] This document deals with three types of entries: the authority entry, the reference entry, and the general explanatory entry. The authority entry is the key entry in any authority file—it not only contains the uniform heading, but may also contain the following: an information note that explains the relationship between that heading and related headings; tracings for the variant and related headings from which references have been made; or cataloger's notes documenting, for example, the source of the heading or the scope of the heading. The reference entry is essential not only in authority files, but also in catalogs, in order to direct the searcher from a variant heading to the uniform heading; or to direct him from one uniform heading to others that are related to it. The general explanatory entry is in fact a special type of reference entry—it directs the searcher from the form that is not accepted as a uniform heading (used only for authority-file organizational purposes) to a whole group of headings. Information contained in these three types of entries facilitates the proper use of headings and enables effective catalog searches.

Initial Work

Since the use of uniform headings requires the creation of authority files, it must be preceded by the development of:

- standards for the form and the structure of headings,
- rules for authority files,
- a format for authority data.

---

1. International Federation of Library Associations and Institutions (IFLA), *Guidelines for Authority and Reference Entries* (London: IFLA International Program for UBC, 1984).

None of these problems were solved in Poland before 1990. Only a draft of a Polish standard for the choice and the form of personal headings had been developed.

As the result of work initiated in May 1990, the guidelines for a personal-names and a corporate-names authority file were prepared. They were based on two IFLA publications—*Guidelines for Authority and Reference Entries*,[2] and *Form and Structure of Corporate Headings*[3]—and on the abovementioned draft of a standard for personal headings. In July 1991, a manual card file of personal and corporate headings was initiated.

In March 1991, the library received a grant from The Andrew W. Mellon Foundation. In 1992, the library purchased an integrated library system from VTLS Inc. In this, the Warsaw University Library was joined by the libraries of three other universities: Jagiellonian University, the University of Gdańsk, and the University of Mining and Metallurgy in Kraków (Akademia Górniczo-Hutnicza w Krakowie). To facilitate system implementation, the four libraries worked in close cooperation with each other. It was decided to use the USMARC format instead of the previously developed Polish format based on UNIMARC. So it was necessary to prepare Polish manuals for the US-MARC format for bibliographic data and for the USMARC format for authority data. It also became necessary to prepare guidelines for uniform titles. And so the rules for titles of anonymous classics, the Bible, other sacred scriptures, and liturgical works of the Catholic Church were established. Two IFLA documents—*Anonymous Classics*,[4] and *List of Uniform Titles for Liturgical Works of the Latin Rites of the Catholic Church*[5] —as well as *Anglo-American Cataloging Rules*,[6] turned out to be particularly helpful in this situation. The decision on establishing the form of a series uniform title was the most difficult one to make. Finally, we decided to establish a series uniform title following International Serials Data System (ISDS) rules for key titles.[7]

In December 1992, VTLS software was installed in the four Polish libraries cited above. The first half of 1993 was dedicated to library-staff training in USMARC formats, in authority files, and in VTLS software. At the same time, the other three libraries also initiated manual name authority files. In the second half of 1993, authority files of the four cooperating libraries were combined and the authority records were entered into the computer database. In the very beginning, the Warsaw University Library server was not connected to the Internet and data were transferred through the medium of magnetic tapes. In such a situation, it was impossible to avoid duplication and the overwriting of records. Fortunately, we worked under such con-

---

2. Ibid.

3. International Federation of Library Associations and Institutions, *Form and Structure of Corporate Headings* (London : IFLA International Office for UBC, 1980).

4. Rosemary C. Hewett, ed., *Anonymous Classics: a List of Uniform Headings for European Literatures* (London: IFLA International Office for UBC, 1978).

5. International Federation of Library Associations and Institutions, *List of Uniform Titles for Liturgical Works of the Latin Rites of the Catholic Church*, 2d ed. rev. (IFLA International Office for UBC, 1981).

6. *Anglo-American Cataloging Rules*, 2d ed., 1988 revision (Ottawa: Canadian Library Association; London: Library Association Publishing, Ltd.; Chicago: American Library Association).

7. *ISDS Manual* (Paris : ISDS International Center, 1983), 41–61.

ditions for only a few months. In March 1994, the authority file became available to the whole library community over the Internet.

Previously, in 1990, it had been decided to create a subject authority file, compatible with the French national authority file, RAMEAU (Répertoire d'Autorité Matière Encyclopédique et Alphabétique Unifié), and to give up the subject headings system that had been applied in the Warsaw University Library card catalog for over sixty years. For this purpose, *Guide d'indexation RAMEAU*[8] was translated into Polish and the first lists of free-floating subject subdivisions were developed.

In 1992, other Polish VTLS libraries decided to use this subject authority file, which was called KABA (Katalogi Automatyczne Bibliotek Akademickich [Automatic Catalogs of Academic Libraries]). From that moment on, the work has been continued in cooperation with several libraries (four in 1992; nine in 1997). Thanks to that cooperation, the pace of the work, its quality, and its efficiency have increased considerably. In March 1993, the building of the manual subject authority file, KABA, was commenced, and in January 1994 the first records were entered into the computer subject authority file.

KABA originated from the vocabulary of three subject headings systems: the American LCSHs (Library of Congress subject headings), the Canadian RVM (Répertoire de vedettes-matière), and the French RAMEAU, though the primary source is RAMEAU. It should be emphasized, however, that the KABA vocabulary is not simply a linguistic translation of the RAMEAU vocabulary; the libraries are developing the KABA vocabulary by way of the adaptation of authority headings that exist in RAMEAU, thus preserving the RAMEAU methodology but also taking into consideration the requirements of the Polish language.

The headings of our subject authority records are connected, by an equivalence relationship, to the respective French-language headings of the RAMEAU file and the English-language LCSHs, usually fixed on the basis of two-sided English and French indexes of the RVM authority file. For this purpose, 472 tags for authority records are used. In this way, French- and English-language headings can be searched in the VTLS database with a separate index (named the Z/search index). Hence, the KABA subject system gives the possibility of a trilingual access to the documents being searched.

The Center for Formats and Authority Files

Union authority files are maintained on the Warsaw University Library server. The creation of, and the changes in, authority files involve a continuous process. In 1996, after several years of mainly voluntary work, the Ministry of National Education decided to establish the Center for Formats and Authority Files at the Warsaw University Library. Its creation was the crowning event of a two-year effort of academic libraries that used VTLS software to establish just such a center. The center has its headquarters at the Warsaw University Library, which provides it with all the facilities it requires, while it is financed with special funds from the Ministry of National Education. The center is responsible for the following:

8. *Guide d'indexation RAMEAU 1992* (Paris: CNCIM, 1992).

- union authority files maintenance,
- coordination of library cooperation with respect to creation of authority files,
- work on the methodology of formats, authority files, and subject headings system,
- training in formats and authority control.

The staff of 16 people at the center is divided into two basic units: the Section for Formats and the Name Authority File (Ośrodek Formatów I Kartoteki Wzorcowych Haseł Formalnych); and the Section for Subject Headings Language and the Subject Authority File, KABA (Ośrodek Języka i Kartoteki Wzorcowej KABA).

The Management and Use of Authority Files

The following factors have a major influence on the organization of work in the union authority files:

- Authority files are created by librarians from several libraries.
- Authority records are used in many local databases.
- Authority records have to be modified and newly introduced changes may require subsequent changes to other authority records; modified records have to be passed on, without a delay, to local databases.
- Libraries using records from the union authority file use different software.

Seven members of the center's staff work as administrators of the name authority database. To ensure the coherence of data in the local catalogs of the cooperating libraries, the following procedure is used: Catalogers always check the union authority file to see if the authority record is already there, and they then copy it to the local database. If the record is not there, it is entered into the buffer of the union authority file database. Database administrators use printouts of records in the buffer to verify records and to eliminate duplications. After the verification, record control numbers are added and the records are transferred to the database and can be copied to the local catalogs. If the record has to be modified, it is modified only in the union authority file. Each modification is verified by a database administrator. In the process of verification it is checked as to whether a modification of the authority record requires changes to other authority records (for example, if a personal heading is changed, then the same modification has to be introduced into all name/title headings containing this personal heading). If it is required, all records that need a modification are changed. Every night, during buffer process, the file of modified records is created. Using FTP, this file is transferred to the servers of the cooperating libraries and used to modify data in the local catalogs.

The majority of libraries cooperating in the creation of the union authority file use the VTLS software and the ISO 6937/2 character set. At the moment, only one of the cooperating libraries uses the Horizon system and the ALA character set. Thus, data conversion is necessary. In the future, authority records are going to be used by other libraries that use the Horizon system. In order to facilitate such cooperation, a copy of the union authority file was installed at the server of the Nicholas Copernicus University Library in Toruń (Biblioteka Uniwersytetu Mikołaja Kopernika w Toruniu). This copy is continually kept up-to-date. Every night a file of new records is created.

This file, as in the case of the file of modified records, is transferred, by means of FTP, to the Nicholas Copernicus University server. After the necessary conversion, the copy of the union authority file is updated.

The organization of work on the subject authority file differs considerably from that on the name authority file. The proposals of authority records are prepared by the teams that are doing the subject cataloging in the cooperating libraries. To validate those records, the Interlibrary Validation Commission (Międzybiblioteczny Zespół Walidacyjny) was established. At its regularly convened sessions it collectively validates the records proposed by librarians. After the validation, the records are entered into the database by the staff at the Center for Formats and Authority Files.

Among the uniform headings, simple (nonextended) headings prevail. We introduce the extended headings in accordance with the principles defined in RAMEAU— namely, when they contain nonfloating subdivisions (also, chronologically arranged nonfloating subdivisions), when they are quoted in other records as examples, or when it is necessary in the fulfillment of semantic relationships in the language. The seemingly simple vocabulary of KABA is richer in practice, because many of its terms can be applied two ways—either in subject headings or in subdivisions.

Costs and Benefits

From the very beginning it was clear that the real advantage of library automation comes through cooperation. Setting up the union authority database was the first task completed by Polish libraries that use the VTLS software. Such a strategy was a policy choice suggested by the Warsaw University Library. It resulted from a conviction that, only by using headings that come from one source will we obtain consistent data in local databases; and thanks to this the avenue is now open for creating a union catalog in the future. So we decided to meet the costs of such cooperation, knowing that the benefits would be long-term ones and substantial (even if not immediate). The library's staff undertook additional tasks connected with the training of librarians from other libraries, with the preparation of manuals and additional unpublished rough guides, as well as with the maintenance of union authority files.

The inputting of bibliographic records was begun in January 1994. And the beginning phase of this task was very difficult: Although the union authority database contained about 15,000 records, it was necessary to create, on average, two or three name authority records for each bibliographic record. Experience that we have gathered since 1991 shows that, on average, the amount of time required for the creation of a particular type of authority record is as follows:

personal-heading record	0.5 h.
corporate-heading record	2.5 h.
uniform/series title record	2.5 h.
bibliographic record	15–20 min.

The great amount of work connected with the creation of authority records gave rise to delays in the cataloging of books. Such was the state of affairs for two years. The situation now is much better. For example, in 1996, while creating the catalog of the

Warsaw University Library, it was necessary to enter only one authority record for two bibliographic records. In 1996, for the first time, we managed to catalog, with no additional staff, a greater number of books than the number that entered the library that year.

The number of cooperating libraries continues to grow and, consequently, so does the number of authority records in the union database. By the end of 1997, fifteen libraries were participating in the making of the union name authority file. The four previously mentioned as cooperating from the very start were joined by the libraries of the following: the University of Wrocław (Uniwersytet Wrocławski); the Maria Curie-Skłodowska University in Lublin (Uniwersytet Marii Curie-Skłodowskiej w Lublinie); the Catholic University of Lublin (Katolicki Uniwersytet Lubelski); the University of Agriculture in Lublin (Akademia Rolnicza w Lublinie); the Technical University of Lublin (Politechnika Lubelska); the Krakow Academy of Economics (Akademia Ekonomiczna w Krakowie); the Agricultural University in Kraków (Akademia Rolnicza w Krakowie); the Kraków Pedagogical University (Wyższa Szkoła Pedagogiczna w Krakowie); the State Academy of Theater Art in Kraków (Państwowa Wyższa Szkoła Teatralna w Krakowie); and the Pontifical Academy of Theology (Papieska Akademia Teologiczna). All these university libraries use VTLS software. And in October 1996, one more university library joined us—namely, the one at the Nicholas Copernicus University in Toruń (Uniwersytet Mikołaja Kopernika w Toruniu), the first one that is using Horizon software. The dynamic growth of cataloging in the most advanced libraries and the increasing number of cooperating libraries led, at the beginning of 1996, to a daily inflow of data that was becoming impossible to manage, and cooperation in fact began to hamper cataloging. The establishment of the Center for Formats and Authority Files (on June 1, 1996) allowed for the entry and verification of 6,000 new authority records per month—we reached that number by June 1996, and since January 1997, the number has grown systematically. Indeed, the pace of the growth of the name authority file since 1994 can be seen in the following numbers:

January 1, 1994	(about) 15,000 records
June 1, 1996	66,365 records
August 1, 1997	145,743 records

By the end of 1997, more than 7,000 records were being added each month. And we expected the total number of records in the union name authority file to exceed 200,000 in January 1998.

On the average, a record entered into the name authority file was copied to three local catalogs. Of course, the libraries that started to cooperate more recently gain the greatest benefits, since the highest costs were shared by the libraries that initiated the creation of authority records—namely, the Warsaw University Library (the first in the group of all libraries that made the effort of maintaining a union authority file), the University of Mining and Metallurgy Library (the first and, for a long time, the only technological library involved), and the Main Library of the University of Agriculture in Lublin (the first of the agricultural libraries involved). Here is a better and more accurate rephrasing: These costs and benefits can be shown in the data below which give, as of June 1, 1997, the percentage of each library's authority records in the library online catalog that were created by that library (rather than imported from some other library):

University of Warsaw (1991)	72%
University of Mining and Metallurgy in Kraków (1993)	80%
Jagiellonian University (1993)	40%
University of Gdańsk (1993)	39%
University of Wrocław (1994)	50%
University of Agriculture in Lublin (1996)	55%
Maria Curie-Skłodowska University (1996)	16%
Technical University of Lublin (1996)	15%
Academy of Economics in Kraków (1996)	28%
Kraków Pedagogical University (1997)	10%
Agricultural University in Kraków (1997)	12%

The creation of subject authority records is very time-consuming. It takes an average of 4.5 hours to create just one record. However, each year's additions substantially increase the speed of file creation. The pace of growth of the subject authority file is illustrated by the following figures:

June 1, 1996	5,875 records
August 1, 1997	15,305 records

It should be stressed that the subject authority file, KABA, generally contains only the records of nonextended subject headings and the subject subdivision records that can be used in the cataloging process to create many other extended subject headings.

On August 1, 1997, the union authority files contained a total of 161,048 records; among them, there were:

116,238 personal-heading records
14,500 corporate-heading records
13,400 series-title records
821 uniform-title records
784 name/title records
15,305 subject records

The cost of the librarians' time needed to prepare these records exceeded by a factor of three the cost of the server and of the VTLS software bought by the Warsaw University Library. Yet, if we consider the fact that each of these records has already been used many times and will be used by many other libraries in the near future, the benefits of the maintenance of a union authority file cannot be underestimated.

Speaking about costs and the results of work done by the Warsaw University Library since 1989, we must not limit our praise to the benefits of using the union authority file. The great initial effort connected with preparing the manuals for formats and the rules for authority files, along with the creation of manual authority files, helped to extend the knowledge of library workers. As a result, library staffs could make competent and responsible decisions on the choice of an integrated library system. The staff of the Automation Department introduced the Cataloging Department to the work, so the Cataloging Department's staff had reasonable levels of expectations about what a library automation system could do and was not afraid of library automation. This was a great help in the successful implementation of the system. The effort put into the training of staffs from other libraries was so effective that gradually people from the most advanced libraries entered the training group. They are also the authors of some of the books and articles that resulted from the work. It should also be stressed that our experience gathered during the work on authority files greatly influenced the final contents of the Polish standards for personal headings, which are going to be published in the near future.

In analyzing the costs and benefits of the activities undertaken, we would like to stress the value of an activity that, for an outsider, may seem expensive and useless at the same time. This refers to the work on the FOKA format, started in 1989. This format was implemented only in a few libraries and only temporarily. The fundamental benefits of its creation are not connected with its implementation. The amount of knowledge on MARC formats and cataloging practices of other countries that was gathered during this work had a great influence on the choice and implementation of the library automation system. Without such experience we would probably have made many mistakes.

Training

Since 1992, librarians from other libraries were usually invited once a month to the Warsaw University Library for a one-day training session. Gradually those sessions turned into regular meetings of system librarians and other people responsible for the creation of union authority files. Such meetings became a normal aspect of our cooperation. Also, the workshops, organized in turn by various libraries, became an essential part of our cooperation. Subjects of subsequent workshops show various states of the work on system implementation. In September 1992, the Library of the University of Gdańsk organized a workshop on authority files and USMARC formats. Another workshop, which was also organized by the Gdańsk University Library, in August 1993, was devoted to the USMARC format for authority data and to the principles of entering data into the union authority file. In 1994, we were preparing for the implementation of a serials control subsystem. That is why the subject of the next workshop, organized by the University of Mining and Metallurgy Library, was on the USMARC bibliographic format for serials and on the USMARC format for holdings. To meet the growing interest in the subject authority file, the Warsaw University Library decided in 1995 to organize two workshops on the topic: The first one was set for in July, on the subject authority system and the subject authority file, KABA; and the second one, for October, on subject cataloging using the subject authority file, KABA. The year 1996 was rather difficult because of the substantial growth of the number of records entered into the union authority file, the organization of the Center for Formats and Authority Files, and the training of new employees of the center. That is why it was impossible to organize workshops for that year.

For 1997, we planned three types of workshops. During the workshop we conducted at the Warsaw University Library in August 1997, we presented and discussed two documents that were to be published: One was on updates and additions of rules for the name authority file; the other one was the Polish manual for the USMARC bibliographic format for computer files. Additionally, a project for a union catalog for academic libraries, prepared by a working group of VTLS libraries, was presented. The participants in other workshops were librarians from less advanced VTLS libraries and Horizon libraries. The subjects of the planned workshops were as follows: for the one in October, "The Rules for the Creation of a Name Authority File"; and for November, "Applications of the KABA Subject Authority File to Subject Cataloging." Staffs from the Warsaw University Library and other VTLS libraries, in many cases, also acted as consultants and lecturers at training sessions for various libraries that were preparing for the implementation of a library automation system.

Publications

From the very beginning, materials created at the Warsaw University Library were shared in unpublished form with other libraries that cooperated with the WUL. Since 1993, we have presented the results of our work to all interested libraries, with books being published by the Polish Interuniversity Consortium for Implementation of VTLS (Międzyuczelniany Zespół Koordynacyjny ds. Wdrożenia VTLS). And since 1997, our work has been published by the Polish Librarians' Association (Stowarzyszenie Bibliotekarzy Polskich). So far, 13 books have been published—these are listed in the appendix to this chapter.

We also present the results of our work in numerous articles published in scientific journals or in papers delivered at conferences. Special emphasis should be put here on two national conferences that dealt with the KABA subject authority file. The first one was held at the Jagiellonian Library on September 21–23 1993; the second, at the Gdańsk University Library on September 9–11 1997.

Plans for the Near Future

It would be a mistake to restrict the number of union authority file users to the 20 currently cooperating libraries. So, in the near future, our efforts are going to be concentrated on training staffs of new VTLS libraries and Horizon libraries. These libraries will be joining the system as so-called inactive users (who only copy authority records taken from the union authority file). Accepting new users to the so-called active-users group will be possible after the staff size at the Center for Formats and Authority Files is increased—a task already being undertaken.

So far, libraries enter catalog descriptions of books and serials. Entry into the database descriptions of other library materials has to be preceded by the development of the necessary Polish instruction manuals. A recently published manual for the format for printed music needs to be supplemented with the rules of the creation of uniform titles of musical works. This problem was handled by the revised and supplemental rules for creating the name authority file, which are being prepared for print. We are also going to publish instructions for the USMARC format for computer files and cartographic materials.

Changes entered into the USMARC format and other source materials used in our work require the gradual development of new editions of previously published instructions. That is why we plan to publish a new, revised edition of the format for serials, for bibliographic records, and for holdings records, as well as a new book on the KABA subject authority system.

References

Bagieńska, Ewa. Władysława Kostrzewa, and Anna Paluszkiewicz. *Zasady tworzenia kartotek wzorcowych haseł opisu bibliograficznego* (Guidelines for Name Authority File). Warsaw: Międzyuczelniany Zespół Koordynacyjny ds. Wdrażania VTLS, 1995.

Burchard, Maria. *Format USMARC rekordu bibliograficznego dla druku muzycznego* (USMARC Format for Bibliographic Data : Printed Music). Warsaw: Wydawnictwo SBP, 1997.

Chrzan, Ewa. *Format USMARC rekordu zasobu : instrukcja wypełniania rekordu w VTLS* (USMARC Format for Holding Record : Application in VTLS). Sopot: Międzyuczelniany Zespół Koordynacyjny ds. Wdrażania VTLS, 1994.

Głowacka, Teresa. *Kartoteka wzorcowa języka KABA : stosowanie w katalogowaniu przedmiotowym* (KABA Subject Authority File: Application to Subject Cataloguing). Warsaw: Wydawnictwo SBP, 1997.

Głowacka, Teresa, and Grażyna Jaśkowiak. *Listy określników swobodnych języka KABA* (The Lists of Free-floating Subdivisions of the KABA Language). Gdańsk: Międzyuczelniany Zespół Koordynacyjny ds. Wdrażania VTLS, 1995.

Lenartowicz, Maria et al., *Format USMARC opisu katalogowego książk: instrukcja wypełniania rekordu w VTLS* (USMARC Format for Books: Application in VTLS). Warsaw: Międzyuczelniany Zespół Koordynacyjny ds. Wdrażania VTLS, 1993.

Lenartowicz, Maria, and Anna Paluszkiewicz. *Format USMARC rekordu bibliograficznego dla książki* (USMARC Format for bibliographic Data : Books). Warsaw: Wydawnictwo SBP, 1997.

Lenartowicz, Maria, and Anna Paluszkiewicz, eds. *Katalogowanie książek i wydawnictw ciągłych w formacie USMARC : poradnik* (Cataloguing of Books and Serials Using USMARC Format: Guide). Warsaw: Wydawnictwo SBP, 1997.

Nałęcz, Barbara, Anna Paluszkiewicz, and Maria Lenartowicz. *Format USMARC rekordu bibliograficznego wydawnictwa ciągłego: instrukcja wypełniania rekordu w VTLS.* (USMARC Format for Serials Bibliographic Record: Application in VTLS). Warsaw: Międzyuczelniany Zespół Koordynacyjny ds. Wdrażania VTLS, 1994.

Paluszkiewicz, Anna. *Struktura danych bibliograficznych w zintegrowanych systemach bibliotecznych* (Bibliographic Data Structure in Integrated Library Systems). Warsaw: Wydwanictwo SBP, 1997.

Paluszkiewicz, Anna. et al., *Format USMARC rekordu kartoteki haseł wzorcowych: instrukcja wypełniania rekordu w VTLS* (USMARC Format for Authority Record: Application in VTLS). Warszawa: Międzyuczelniany Zespół Koordynacyjny ds. Wdrażania VTLS, 1994.

Paluszkiewicz, Anna et al., *Format USMARC rekordu kartoteki haseł wzorcowych: instrukcja wypełniania rekordu w VTLS* (USMARC Format for Authority Record: Application in VTLS), 2d ed., rev. Warsaw: Międzyuczelniany Zespół Koordynacyjny ds.Wdrażania VTLS, 1995.

Woźniak, Jadwiga, ed. *Kartoteka wzorcowa języka KABA* (Authority File of the KABA Language). Warsaw: Wydawnicwo SBP, 1994.

CHAPTER 20

The Union Catalog
Different Library Systems, Different Solutions

BŁAŻEJ FERET

My interest in union catalogs (or, rather, "union OPACs") began when nine academic libraries in Łódż Poland, started to implement a single, integrated library system. We were sure that after the successful implementation of the automation system at our libraries, we would provide users not only with nine separate OPACs but also with one access point that would serve all library catalogues. What is more, the question of how the union catalog would be created was one of the most important questions posed by our sponsor—The A. W. Mellon Foundation. What at first seemed to be an easy task became more complicated as time passed.

It is clear, from looking at access points to library consortium catalogs on the Internet, that there are many different solutions to the union catalog (OPAC) problem, ranging from the simplest—a web page with links to individual libraries and catalogs—to very advanced solutions, where a single consortial database provides all bibliographic and item details for all members of the consortium.

The idea of this chapter is to describe—on the basis of vendors' proposals—mechanisms that are used in different library systems to fit multiple library environments and to draw conclusions that may be useful for libraries or library consortia that are going to introduce an automated library system or set up a common catalog on the Internet. I tried to find out what the current status of the work is on consortial catalogs in Polish and other projects similar to the one run in Łódż. I also asked many union catalog managers about the solutions they use, and will also try to briefly describe the best-known of these, namely, OhioLink, ORBIS, and COPAC.

For the purposes of this chapter, I will use the term "union catalog" in the narrow sense of a union OPAC—the mechanism that allows one to search several consortium libraries (preferably with a single search) and that returns data on the location and availability of an item.

A Single Database versus the Distributed Search

Two general solutions for creating a single access point for a consortium of libraries are as follows:

1. The centralized solution (usually a single, large database), containing bibliographic records from all participating institutions—they are mostly high-quality managed

systems designed either as commercial services (as a source of bibliographic records), pure union catalogs (developed specifically as public access union catalogs), or shared union catalogs (a part of an integrated library system shared by several libraries).
2. The "virtual database," consisting of original distributed records with access via refined software (the distributed search)—this solution is characterized by heterogeneity and local autonomy in the design and management of individual databases.

The centralized solution may fall into one of three categories:

1. Only the bibliographic information is centralized; search results contain only the names of holding libraries; no item/status data are available.
2. Bibliographic information is centralized and has links to individual libraries for data on holdings. The user is switched to a local catalog where item information may be checked. The existence of item-status data depends on the implementation of the circulation module in the local library and on integration of this module with the on-line catalog.
3. The bibliographic and item data are centralized and then either all data are stored in only one (main) database and all libraries have direct access to this database for the modification of holdings, status, and other information (and then there may be problems regarding the full independence of libraries within the consortium—statistics, acquisitions, reports); or holding/status data are kept in local databases but mechanisms are implemented for "live" updating of the data in a central database; all transactions are immediately copied from the local database to the central database. In this case, all local information is duplicated in the central database and a user can also find full and current information on an item and its status in the central database. This model seems to be the best one but only a few library systems offer the necessary mechanisms for it.

In all cases of the centralized solution there are usually strong consolidation procedures implemented that allow the displaying of one—appropriate—bibliographic record and of attached holding/item/status data on copies. Additionally, the central databases are usually very homogeneous—which results in search and indexing consistency. It is also easier to perform resource-sharing tasks (for example, interlibrary loans) using the centralized approach. However, in every "centralized" case the process of adding a new library requires decisions on the top level since it is often equal to changing the parameters of the central database. The level of autonomy regarding the design and management of the databases of the participating libraries is not very high. This problem seems not to exist in the distributed-search approach. In practice, this approach is realized in most cases as an Internet web page with search options and the list of libraries that are to be searched. A query in the Z39.50 standard is sent to chosen libraries using the TCP/IP protocol. Z39.50 servers set up for local library catalogs process the query and send the answer back to the WWW server, which prepares, and sends to the client, the web page with the answer to the query. This approach requires a WWW server, Z39.50 servers at participating libraries, and software that allows the converting of WWW pages to Z39.50 (WWW-Z39.50 gateway).[1] Adding a new library requires only a slight modification of the central OPAC web

---

1. Distributed searches may also be done by a user directly (without the WWW-Z39.50 gateway) with Z39.50 clients such as Ameritech's WinPac, or BookWhere?, offered by the Sea Change Corporation. However, modifying the library list requires configuration changes in all users' workstations.

page. The whole setup may be quite easily done if Z39.50 servers are installed in libraries. Moreover, the libraries included in the distributed-search OPAC may use different library systems (a heterogeneous environment). However, here the positives end for now. Usually there are no consolidation procedures implemented for the displaying of search results. The same bibliographic record is repeated on the screen if it is found in different locations. The Z39.50 protocol currently does not support holding information (1). The installations where the item/status data are collected via the Z39.50 protocol use a more or less proprietary approach in retrieving this information. The search may be incomplete if some libraries are temporarily unavailable. It may also take a long time if the level of network traffic is high. In spite of this fact, the implementation of Z39.50 systems has dramatically increased in recent years and a number of cooperative projects have started (2–8). There are intensive features on the new, extended standard Z39.50 protocol that will not only request item-specific data but will also allow the introduction of consolidation procedures, which merge, sort and display results of search (in a manner similar to central database solutions). The extended standard will also provide access to the abstracting and indexing of databases and realize full interlibrary loan (ILL) requirements (9–17).

A Survey of Library Systems Vendors

To compare the solutions to the union OPAC problem that are proposed by different vendors, a set of questions was prepared by the group of Łódź libraries and sent to several library automation system companies. Library systems vendors were asked the following questions:

- Is the system they offer capable of functioning in a "consortium environment"—that is, does it have mechanisms to create and maintain the union catalog and OPAC of consortium libraries?
- Does the introduction of these mechanisms require additional hardware/software installations (for example, servers, disk space, server or client software), plus the main functions of a library automation system?
- Is there a requirement to create a separate large database with records from all consortium libraries or may the "union catalog" be created as a "virtual catalog" of original libraries' databases (for example, basing it on the Z39.50 protocol)?
- Does the system in question support both mechanisms (a physically separate, union database and a "virtual union catalog") and, if it does, which of these solutions is preferred by the vendor and by customers?
- Is the user able to find a specific book/journal in consortium libraries with a single search?
- What kind of information does the user obtain after a successful search of a union catalog (for example, location(s) of a book, bibliographic data, item data, book status in a specific library)?
- Is the option involving a search over all consortium libraries separated from the search over a specific library in a user interface—that is, how is a union catalog accessed compared to accessing a local library catalog)?
- What is the most preferred "front end" for an OPAC (a textual interface, or a WWW browser, some other specific solution)? If more than one OPAC type is available, do they have the same functionalities?

- Are any consolidation procedures implemented when the same bibliographic record is accepted from different libraries or when it is presented in the OPAC?

Vendors were also asked to provide examples of library clusters (consortia) that use the specific library system with an implemented union catalog and, if possible, to give the appropriate URL (address) for the Internet access point. The set of questions was sent to the following 13 vendors:

- Ameritech Library Services (ALS)—(Dynix Classic, Horizon)
- EOS International (T-Series, formerly TinLib)
- Ex Libris (Aleph)
- Innovative Interfaces, Inc. (III)—(Innopac)
- VTLS, Inc. (VTLS)
- GEAC Computer Corporation (Advance)
- Endeavor (Voyager)
- SIRSI (Unicorn)
- SLS (Libertas)
- Best-Seller (BestSeller, Portfolio)
- Elias (Dobis, Libis)
- Auto-Graphics (Impact/Online)
- Max Electronics (Prolib)

Answers were received from 7 companies: ALS, EOS, III, VTLS, Auto-Graphics, Max Electronics, and Best-Seller. Ex Libris replied that the company's staff was too busy to answer the questions. Fortunately, full support on Aleph was provided by Polish representatives of Ex Libris. The rest of the vendors did not answer at all.

Ameritech Library Services (http://www.amlibs.com/). Although, from the similar questions (listed above) that were sent to users of the library systems, it was clear that most of the union catalogs that are supported by ALS are run on the Dynix Classic system or on NOTIS, the official Dynix answer was related to Release 5.1 of Horizon. The proposed solution is based on three ALS products. The first of these is *WebPac (WWW OPAC)*. WebPac is the common user interface via WWW. It does the following:

- a search of Horizon union catalog;
- a search, via Z39.50, of all library catalogues of the union catalog project;
- a search of other Z39.50 catalogs, for example, citation databases;
- a display of holdings data and item status per location;
- an initiation of an ILL request from a patron;
- an initiation of document delivery requests from a patron;
- patron authentication.

The second ALS product is *Horizon (integrated library system)*. The cataloging module of Horizon will serve as a union catalog system including the following features:

- storage of bibliographic data of all libraries (if a separate huge database is created),
- loaders for MARC records,

- storage and maintenance of different authority records,
- 856 tag links to electronic documents or to home pages, in general,
- a replication feature from a local database to the union catalog and in the opposite direction,
- an initial load of bibliographic and authority data from local databases.

The third product is *RSS (resource sharing system)*. RSS will work in conjunction with WebPac, Horizon, OCLC, and other systems supporting the ISO standard for ILL and document delivery. Some of the features of RSS are as follows:

- patron-initiated management of intralibrary loans, interlibrary loans, and document delivery requests,
- verification of a patron's ability to place a request, by checking against patron privileges in the local ILS system using Z39.69 protocols or a copy of the local patron database on the RSS server,
- verification that a home library and a union catalog member do not own the material before requesting from a non-union catalog member,
- load leveling of requests to lending libraries,
- multiple formats for requests, including ISO 160/161, FTP, SMTP, and a fax,
- requests for materials located via WebPac searches,
- requests for materials as keyed into work forms, which potentially may provide capabilities for limiting access to pay-per-view databases.

Using these products, Dynix (ALS) is able to set up the system on the basis of either a single database or a distributed search, depending on customer needs. As a result of a successful search, all necessary data including the holding data, call number, location, and status will be displayed in the OPAC. The company proposes a WWW browser as a standard front end for the OPAC. For patrons without graphics, it will be possible to use a textual web browser (lynx). Some consolidation procedures will be implemented, but the company gave no details on these procedures.

This solution looks very promising and it will surely be one of the most advanced and complete solutions for the resource-sharing problem. However, what has been described is still in the planning stage; there is no real installation yet that runs this solution. Version 5.1 of Horizon was due to be released in 1998.

A lot of information on how ALS is going to solve consortium problems (including a common OPAC) in the near future may be found on the web pages of California State University, where a similar system is just being constructed (18).

From the answers of the users of existing library systems with union catalogs, it may be seen that Dynix Classic or Notis LMS is now more often used for the union catalogs than Horizon is. The examples of users include:

- Minnesota CLIC Consortium, using Dynix 161 (http://www.clic.edu),
- Flint Area Library Cooperating Online Network (MI), using Dynix 161 (http://www.falcon.edu),
- Northern Michigan University, using Notis 6.2 (http://www.nmu.edu/ais2/library.html),
- Louisiana Library Network, using Notis 6.3 (http://www.lsu.edu/OCS/louis).

These consortia are based on a single, centralized database. This solution permits a search of all consortium libraries in a single query, returns bibliographic, item, and status data (if the circulation module in the holding library is implemented), and is separated from the original library catalogs.

There were no replies on the centralized systems that are based on Horizon library system software. However, a further search discovered the following two consortia that have installed, or are going to install, a distributed-search system based on Horizon servers:

- State Library of Iowa Project (an experimental installation is already running) (http://www.silo.lib.ia.us),
- California State University UIAS Project, (in the preparation stage) (http://uias.calstate.edu).

VTLS Inc. (http://www.vtls.com). In addition to standard library automation software, a specialized union catalog module has been developed and implemented in multilibrary installations (19). The software is used to manage a hierarchy of catalogers; to provide distribution services for modified records, to update local databases of libraries that hold certain items; and to provide localized validation and quality control procedures. The software usually works on a separate, dedicated server. Although the VTLS software includes a Z39.50 server and the distributed search might be adopted, the company strongly recommends a solution via the single union database. The main reason for it is that such a solution allows (or even forces) uniform cataloging practices among the participating libraries. Such an approach "serves to standardize data among all participating libraries, to provide consistent and steadily improving and more complete data, and to provide a resource to reduce the expenses associated with local cataloging. This is particularly valuable where there is no commercial bibliographic utility available, such as in countries outside the United States where there are no repositories of records of, say, Finnish publications, or in specialized libraries with unique collections where OCLC and other utilities are of little help."[2] As we can see, the stress in the solution offered by VTLS is placed on the cataloging purity of bibliographic data rather than on item-specific information. The effect is that the union database contains only bibliographic data, with the libraries that hold items being identified. Although it is possible in this system to keep holding-specific information in the union database, none of the company's customers have implemented this. The searcher must then, after a successful search in the union catalog, check the local system of item-holding libraries to find out about the specific item and its current status. In the latest versions of the system this is automatically done and the user is presented with full on-screen information.

The basis of the described solution is the top-down approach to cataloging practices suggested by VTLS, which differs from the traditional approach of shared cataloging systems, where participating libraries contribute bibliographic records to the common database. Here, a defined set of catalogers is authorized to add the records to

---

2. Robert Goetz, VTLS Inc., private communication, July 31, 1997.

the common database. Local catalogers may request a bibliographic record for the new item from the union catalog if it is present there. Then they may update the holding information (if authorized) and send it back to the union catalog or (if not authorized) copy the original record onto the local database, adding the necessary holding data. If the record is not available in the union catalog, the library has to wait for it until the authorized cataloger enters it.

A new product of the company, Virtua, is fully compliant with Z39.50 and allows a dynamic connection to the union or local database as well as to several databases at once. The first versions of VTLS union catalogs were implemented with text interfaces only, while later ones were done so with Windows GUI. The trend to full access via web browsers is being currently realized by the implementing of most of the union-catalog specific functions in the current version of the VTLS-WWW gateway (Virtua Web Gateway).

The examples of VTLS installations in a multiple-library environment include:

- Swiss National Library (serials) (http://www.snl.ch/rpvz/english/);
- University Library Consortium in Catalonia (Spain) (http://consorci.upc.es/);
- West Virginia Library Commission (http://www.wvlc.wvnet.edu/);
- Finnish National Research Network (http://linnea.helsinki.fi/).

Innovative Interfaces Inc. (http://www.iii.com). At the heart of III's solution for consortia is INN-Reach software with a real-time union catalog (20). The idea is that the INN-Reach catalog contains all the necessary information that is continuously being taken from the databases of contributing libraries. Thus, the proposed solution falls into the category of IIIb. The participating libraries run local Innopac systems, which cooperate with the INN-Reach catalog. The Innopac INN-Reach catalog software contains specialized programs that do the following:

- receive records from multiple sites in real time;
- employ a master-record concept, with a holdings display of all libraries that hold an item;
- use sophisticated match software to merge individual libraries' holdings onto one master record;
- display detailed holdings information, including: circulation status, the call number, and the shelving location; a summary holdings statements of serial records; the on-order status for materials in the acquisitions process;
- provide extensive statistics.

What is interesting is that there is no need for any of the participating libraries to pass data to the central (INN-Reach) catalog. There is no direct keying or updating on the central database. The INN-Reach catalog is totally built and maintained by activity at the level of the local (Innopac) systems. In addition to the union OPAC function, the INN-Reach software permits advanced interlibrary circulation: The INN-Reach circulation subsystem allows patrons of a participating member library to borrow material from another.

The basic INN-Reach software and the union catalog database are installed on separate, dedicated servers. In addition, INN-Reach software must be installed on the local systems for contributing records and for transmitting circulation information.

It is also responsible for the easy transfer of a user's query to a local catalog and, further, to the union catalog, with only one keystroke.

Users can access the system (either a local or a union database) in both ways: via a text interface (telnet) or via a web browser.

Two of the best-known consortium-based OPACs using the INN-Reach software are the following:

- University of Oregon (ORBIS) (http://orbis.uoregon.edu);
- OhioLink Consortium (http://www.ohiolink.edu).

Further examples of consortia using the Innopac software (although without INN-Reach) include:

- University of Akron (Ohio) (http://www.uakron.edu/library);
- Dominican College of San Rafael (Calif.) (http://www.dominican.edu/Library);
- Five Colleges of Ohio (telnet://consort.library.denison.edu).

The Innopac software supports the Z39.50 standard and its catalogs may be searched via the distributed search.

Ex Libris (http://www.aleph.co.il). The latest version of the well-known library system of Ex Libris is the Aleph 500. The database of this system consists of units of three basic types:

- bibliographic data — BIB
- library data (holdings, borrowers, circulation, budgets) — HOL
- authority data — AUT

It is possible, in Aleph 500, to define any kind of relationship between the BIB, HOL, and AUT units. The relationship may be of a one-to-one type or a one-to-many type or a many-to-one or a many-to-many. Therefore, the system may be configured according to the structural needs of a library consortium. Units may be placed on one server or distributed over accessible servers, depending on the quality of the computer network. They all may be installed on a central server or every library may maintain its own server. There are two basic models. The first is the BIB1, with one bibliographic database (a central catalogue); and as many holdings and authority databases as there are libraries; i.e., HOL1, HOL2, ..., etc., in which every library maintains its holdings database, and AUT1, AUT2, ..., in which they maintain their authority databases. In this model, all bibliographic records are centralized and holding data are stored in each library. There is a mechanism (Expand) that allows for a virtual attachment of the item data to bibliographic records during a search.

The second model features a traditional approach. The central catalog is a separate database but every library maintains all units, including the BIB. AUT databases may be stored centrally and/or locally. Cataloging may occur either in the central database (and then a special "update" file for separate databases is automatically prepared and distributed) or in the local database (and then the "updated central catalog" file is prepared and imported to the central catalogue with the application of a "match and merge" mechanism).

After a search, all bibliographic and holding data, including status data, are displayed in both models. Catalogs may be accessed via the Windows OPAC client or via a web browser. Both have the same functionalities.

Examples of the Aleph (although not the Aleph 500) system in a consortium environment may be found at the following:

- National Library of the Czech Republic (http://www.nkp.cz/caslin);
- University of São Paulo Libraries (Brazil) (http://www.usp.br);
- Siena University (Italy) (http://www.unisi.it/ateneo/biblio/ccm.html).

EOS International (TinLib) (http:www.eosintl.com). Electronic Online Systems International currently sells the T-Series library software that for a long time was known as the TinLib Navigator. Because several installations of this system are implemented in Poland, it was interesting to check this company's solution of the union catalog problem.

The T-Series can provide support for multiple library environments using several different configurations. The most usual is to implement a union catalog located at one site that includes the holdings of each of the participating libraries. Each participating library will also have its own stand-alone copy of the T-Series to provide access only to the local catalog and to provide local support for circulation, acquisitions, and serials management. Each member of the consortium will therefore have its own system as well as access to the union catalog, showing holdings of all libraries in the consortium. Each library may have its own patrons, funds, policies, and circulation parameters. The union catalog will show the existence and location of all holdings but will not show the status of individual items. This must be determined by interrogating the local catalog database where the item is located. There are several ways in which the union catalog can be updated, depending on the rate at which the catalogs change at the branches and on the need for currency in the union catalog—for example, by extracting a file of new records once a day or once a week or once a month and sending it via FTP or mailing it to the union catalog site; and, whether the file is sent via FTP, regular mail, or e-mail, the resulting set of records is handled like an imported file for an addition to the union catalog database. Holding information can be included as well.

At the point of the submission of the bibliographic/item record to the union catalog, the software eliminates the duplication of titles and the item-holding information is merged under one bibliographic record, if possible. However, differences in cataloging practices from site to site may lead to instances in which the titles are not merged. Also, there may be problems with deleting holdings for lost copies, unless a newly supplied record is written over an earlier one. The catalog may be accessed via a text interface, Windows OPAC, or a web browser. The functionalities, however, are not the same. The text-based OPAC has the most sophisticated search features.

The vendor cited two contact points for library consortia using their software:

- Leuven Public Library (Belgium) (not on Internet);
- Northern Lights Library Consortium (http://nlln.org).

Best-Seller, Inc. (http://www.bestseller.com). Although this vendor is not very well known in Poland, it sells one of the more important library systems in the world—Best-Seller/PortFolio. The system is able to serve a multiple-library environment with the use of a common, shared database. Several libraries can share the same union catalog and yet operate as distinct, independent libraries with their own set of patrons, funds, and circulation policies. The only requirement is that the libraries must share the same server. In the OPAC, the user has a choice of displaying a summary or a full record. Both these displays are configurable by the library. Typically, the summary record displays, for a book, its title, author, subject headings, publisher, date of publication, and status. The full record display can contain all the fields of the record. The PortFolio BestOPAC supports multimedia and requires only a WWW browser. Best-Seller does support a textual interface accessible via telnet; however, multimedia are not supported. Bibliographic data are checked against existing records that are on import to the union database. Any overlay is flagged via a printed report. The system fully supports Z39.50 and distributed search. In fact, the Z39.50 client for distributed search is a built-in feature of the BestOPAC software. Best-Seller customers choose the centralized model over the distributed search, depending on their needs. The Z39.50 model is preferred for already existing independent libraries that support Z39.50. The separate-union-database model is preferred for consortia that share the same mandate (for example, the government's specialized libraries, neighboring municipal libraries).

Good examples of the union catalog that uses Best-Seller and PortFolio software include:

- City of Montreal Public Library (http://merlinweb.ville.montreal.qc.ca:1080/);
- National Library of Quebec (Montreal) (http://www.biblinat.gouv.qc.ca:6611/).

Auto-Graphics Inc. (http://www.auto-graphics.com). This company is also not well known in Poland, but has many customers in the United States. It offers a highly centralized solution in which all data are stored on the company's server and the participating libraries access the server over the Internet.

The family of products that together provide a consortium-based resource-sharing system is named Impact/ONLINE. The software is designed specifically for library consortia and enables libraries with divergent local systems to link together and share resources from anywhere in the consortium. It does not replace, but instead provides, a link between the local systems. Basic features include a public access catalog, interlibrary loans, cataloging, access to external databases (such as an index, abstract and full-text databases), and a Z39.50 information and Internet gateway. The software does not include the circulation component; thus participating libraries use it as an addition to their local systems. Updating of the central catalogue may be done in different ways. Library groups with circulation systems may send (via tape or FTP) daily, weekly, or monthly transaction updates, which are processed against the union database file. In addition, OCLC libraries arrange for a daily FTP of newly cataloged records from OCLC to Auto-Graphics for inclusion in the database. Other libraries use the Auto-Graphics database for their own cataloging purposes, and this automatically updates the union database, as well as providing a MARC record download for local systems. The union OPAC is accessed via graphic web browsers. For the text-based systems, it is possible to use textual web browsers (lynx) or set up a telnet server on which Lynx software may run. After a successful search, the information on bibliographic data, item locations (holding libraries), and call numbers is returned. However, an item's status is not given (after all, there is no link to circulation). Standard consolidating procedures (based on the company's experience with consolidation tasks) are used while new records are accepted in the union catalog. Additionally, every library may define "profiles"—that is, the manner in which the records are loaded, deduplicated, and items are created.

Since the Impact/ONLINE OPAC supports the Z39.50 search, the system can be configured to work with either a separate catalogue, or Z39.50 broadcast searching, or, most likely, a combination of the two. Until every consortium participant is current with Z39.50, Impact/ONLINE allows Z39.50 libraries to participate through Z39.50 and non-Z39.50 libraries to contribute to the separate union catalogue. The next versions of Impact/ONLINE will use the Z39.50 protocol to retrieve book status from a specific library.

The examples of union databases may be found directly on the company's WWW server:

- Kansas State University Library: (http://skyways.lib.ks.us/kansas/library.html);
- Texas Library Connection (http://www.esc13.tenet.edu/tlc/tlc.html);
- Oklahoma Department of Libraries (http://www.state.ok.us/~odl/).

Max Electronics (http://www.max.com.pl). Max Electronics is a Polish company that offers probably the most advanced library system of Polish origin, PROLIB. It has been implemented in a few libraries in Poland, although not in the consortium environment. Potentially it can be a much cheaper alternative for small academic or public libraries in Poland. The system is based on Progress RDBMS. All solutions for consortia are based on the general characteristics of RDBMS. Progress can search single or multiple databases, so the centralized location or the distributed locations of bibliographic data/holdings is possible. However, the Z39.50 protocol is not yet implemented. The access to OPAC is textual but work is being done to create a web interface.

Other library systems. Since replies to the questions were not received from several important library system vendors, the following list includes only the addresses of their web pages that contain information on their offered products:

- Geac Computer Corporation (http://www.library.geac.com);
- Endeavor Information Systems, Inc. (http://www.endinfosys.com);
- SIRSI Corporation (http://www.sirsi.com);
- SLS (Information Systems) (http://www.sls.se);
- Elias (http://www.elias.be).

A Survey of Consortia That Use the Vendors' Systems

A set of questions similar to those sent to library system vendors was also sent to individuals, via several library discussion lists posted on the Internet. The idea of this survey was to get the information on what has really been done and how the union

OPACs are being realized in practice, and to compare this with the statements and promises of the library systems vendors. A total of 38 people answered the questions, mainly from the United States. Library systems that were most often used were Innopac, Dynix (ALS), and Notis (ALS). There were also union catalogs based on Geac, consortia belonging to CARL network, and VTLS libraries. Almost all consortia reported the use of a centralized approach, but in many, Z39.50 mechanisms are implemented and it is possible to search Z39.50 libraries in the OPAC, while the local system is also Z39.50-accessible. In an appreciable number of installations the status information is accessible, although the text in the "status" line often says: "Check shelves." All systems have a text interface and many tend to use a web interface. It is, however, very often the case that existing web gateways do not present the same functionalities as the text interface does. Most of the consortia that replied to the queries and are on the Internet are mentioned previously. Below, there are short descriptions of two solutions that seem very interesting and successful.

OhioLink (http://www.ohiolink.edu) and the University of Oregon (ORBIS) (http://orbis.uoregon.edu) are two consortia that use the Innopac InnReach software. The user's web interface is very clear and there is a choice at the beginning of the central or the individual catalog. After a query is entered, a list of results is displayed on a screen split into 12 entry pages. Every entry is a link to further information, which depends on the type of search being done (author, keyword). Finally, at the level of a single bibliographic description, a user receives a page with basic bibliographic data, information on how many libraries of a consortium have the search title (with a link to full data), a link to ILL requests, and the option of a MARC format display. When the user follows the link to holding libraries, a page with a full report on where the title is located, and with details on the call number and the status of each copy, is provided. It is always possible to have the next/previous page or record displayed, return to browsing, start a new search, start from the beginning, or have e-mail results. It is also possible to limit or sort a search. Before starting a search, a user can follow the link to the extensive search tips and information about the catalog and its usage.

COPAC (http://copac.ac.uk/copac) is the national On-line Public Access Catalog, providing unified access to on-line catalogs of some of the largest university research libraries in the United Kingdom and Ireland. It's an independent project and not related to any of the integrated library systems. Records from participating libraries are loaded to the central database in the MARC format and, during this time, matching and consolidation routines are employed to avoid duplication. This results in the production of consolidated records, which provide merged bibliographic data and data on individual library holdings. COPAC may be searched via a web or text interface. The main menu offers author/title, periodical, or subject search options. After a form for a chosen search type is filled in, a page is displayed with a list of found records in a "brief display" format. Following the link at a certain title, the user is presented with a "full record" display, in which there are extended bibliographic data and information on holding libraries, with call numbers being included. The circulation status is not given. The catalog is Z39.50-compliant and it can also be searched in that way. More information on the initiative may be found on the project's web pages and in a journal article (21).

Union OPACs in Poland and Other CE/EE Countries

The Łódź project for implementing the integrated library system is one of many similar projects that were started in recent years in Poland and in other countries in Central/East Europe. Most of them, however, start from the introduction of a library automation system in their libraries, and the problem of the union catalog is put aside until the system is fully (or in a large part) implemented. Since the projects are relatively recent (1993–1997), and there is usually a lot of work with filling the databases with information (current cataloging and retroconversion) in order to make the catalogs suitable for public access, the idea of a union catalog (according to the definition used in this chapter) has not yet been realized.

Three main consortia in Poland are:

- VTLS Consortium—21 libraries, from 5 big cities, that have implemented the VTLS;
- Łódź Academic Libraries Automation Project—10 libraries in Łódź that have implemented Horizon;
- Poznań Library Consortium—11 libraries in Poznań that have implemented Horizon.

There are plans to construct a single access point for the catalogs of the libraries in the Łódź consortium. It had been planned that the union OPAC would be realized as a distributed-search access, similarly to that at the State Library of Iowa (http://www.silo.lib.ia.us). Plans for the union catalog of the Poznań consortium are not yet specified. However, there are several initiatives in Poland to create a virtual union catalog of chosen libraries, where the test installations are already running. Gateways to WAIS- or Z39.50-format libraries have been created for several technical universities (for example, http://library.p.lodz.pl/SFgate/; or http://www.ml.put.poznan.pl/SFgate/wais.html), and for the union catalog of the Lublin VTLS libraries (http://priam.umcs.lublin.pl/katalog). Both experimental installations work off-line (copies of real databases) but work on the access to "live" databases is in progress.

A similar situation exists in other countries. The Estonian ELNET (Consortium of Estonian Libraries Network) has introduced Innopac. A union catalog of the seven libraries in Tallinn and Tartu is being planned—work on it is in progress and a test installation was to be launched at the end of 1998. The Lithuanian Research Libraries Consortium has started to create the Lithuanian integrated library system LIBIS from the subsystem of the union catalog. The web pages of the project are on the Internet: http://vm.ktu.lt. The South African GAELIC consortium implements Innopac software. There are hopes that the consortium's union catalog will be available after the software installation and configuration are done.

Apparently, the only working implementation of a union OPAC is being currently tested in the CASLIN consortium of Czech and Slovak libraries. This system is based on Aleph software and is accessed via telnet or a web interface (http://www.nkp.cz/caslin). However, the data on item availability are not present in the catalog.

Conclusions

1. Most of the union catalog OPACs that currently exist are realized as centralized databases. Some of them allow one to see an item's status in the consortium OPAC

and some only allow one to find the location of a searched title. Among 38 respondents in the survey, only one described an existing distributed-data union catalog.
2. Although a distributed-search mechanism is easier to implement because many library systems work as Z39.50 servers, it is relatively rarely used since the current version of the Z39.50 standard does not permit the retrieval of holdings information from the server. This argument keeps many libraries and consortia from using the distributed search as the method of choice in the setting up of the union catalog. Any existing implementation of status retrieval in a Z39.50 client is a proprietary extension and thus cannot be used in other installations. Work on retrieving holdings data in the Z39.50 protocol is in progress. We may expect that in the future, use of the extended Z39.50 standard will be much more frequent than it is today.
3. Distributed search may work well in a multisystem (heterogeneous) environment. This property will in the future allow the creation of union OPACs for libraries using different library systems.
4. Distributed search is network-quality-dependent. Big systems may be unreliable since some servers may be down or inaccessible and response time may be very long. But on the other hand, there is only a small probability that all the servers of the libraries will be down, which would be a similar situation as a failure of the central database server.
5. The central-database solution permits the implementation of many resource-sharing functions that are not yet available in a distributed-search mechanism. Work on the extension of the Z39.50 standard to support ILLs are in progress.
6. Similarly, centralized solutions usually offer at least simple consolidation functions in the display of search results. The search in distributed databases results in a "messy" list of findings. An extended Z39.50 protocol should allow a comparison of records from different sources, and the sorting and merging of them.
7. Many OPACS are still available only via a textual interface. Even in the United States, where the technology is the most advanced, there is a large class of patrons using telnet access. Therefore, consortia and individual libraries putting their OPACs on the Internet should still plan to use old-fashioned textual-access methods along with modern web interfaces.
8. Due to the current limitations of Z39.50, library consortia that are going to introduce library automation systems and plan to set up consortial union catalogs should consider the implementation of a system permitting the centralized version of the union OPAC. Along with this, the system should also include Z39.50 servers that create the possibility of future developments toward a distributed-search system. Therefore, the two basic models for creating a union OPAC should be treated as complementary rather than competitive.
9. Currently existing consortia that use a common library system should discuss whether the centralized union catalog could be implemented and what functions it could provide. If there are too many limitations in the centralized solution for an existing library system, a distributed-search system should be considered.
10. Consortia that consist of libraries with different automation systems should consider a distributed-search union catalog.
11. It should be stressed that the union catalog (or OPAC) is only one of many aspects of the introduction of the library automation system and in many cases its existence and performance are not of much importance in the choosing of the system. On the contrary, consortia that declare as a main goal the existence of a union catalog also

have a choice of several solutions that do not necessarily contain full library automation functions (for example, there is no local circulation module).

References

1. "National Information Standards Organization [NISO] Home Page"; http://www.niso.org/; Internet; accessed 4 September 1997.
2. "Virtual Canadian Union Catalog Project"; National Library of Canada; http://www.nlc-bnc.ca/resource/vcuc/index.htm; Internet; accessed 4 September 1997.
3. Russell, Rosemary. "European Projects Involving Z39.50"; http://ukoln.bath.ac.uk/z3950/europroj.html; Internet; accessed 3 September 1997.
4. "Z39.50 Projects"; National Library of Canada; http://www.nlc-bnc.ca/resource/vcuc/z3950pr.htm; Internet; accessed 3 September 1997.
5. "Pennsylvania Academic Library Connection Initiative (PALCI)"; http://www.lehigh.edu/~inpalci/prospectus.html; Internet; accessed 3 September 1997.
6. "State Library of Iowa—Catalogs and Services Home Page"; http://www.silo.lib.ia.us/services.html; Internet; accessed 3 September 1997.
7. "North Bay Cooperative Library System—Super Search"; http://209.1.122.66/nbc/ss.html; Internet; accessed 3 September 1997.
8. Dempsey, Lorcan, et al. "Towards Distributed Library Systems: Z39.50 in a European Context." Program 30, no. 1 (January 1996) [journal on-line]; available from http://www.aslib.co.uk/program/1996/jan/02.html; Internet; accessed 3 September 1997.
9. "Union Catalogue Profile," National Library of Australia (August 1997); available from http://www.nla.gov.au/UCP/zupdmst2.html; Internet; accessed 3 September 1997.
10. Turner, Fay. "Report on Z39.50 and Holdings Meeting," National Library of Canada (18 June 1997); available from http://www.nlc-bnc.ca/iso/z3950/holds2.htm; Internet; accessed 3 September 1997.
11. "Technical Issues Associated with the Creation of the CIC VEL Public Catalog," Center for Library Initiatives (17 February 1997); available from http://cedar.cic.net/cic/cli/veltech.html; Internet; accessed 3 September 1997.
12. "Holding Retrieval Using GRS-1 and OPAC," DRA Information, Inc. (15 August 1997); available from http://www.nlc-bnc.ca/iso/z3950/holds3.pdf; Internet; accessed 3 September 1997.
13. Zeeman, J., et al., "Use of Z39.50 to Access Distributed Union Catalogues: Discussion Paper" (2 April 1997); available from http://www.nlc-bnc.ca/iso/z3950/holds.htm; Internet; accessed 3 September 1997.
14. Turner, Fay. "Z39.50 and Holdings Information," National Library of Canada (8 August 1997); available from http://www.nlc-bnc.ca/pubs/netnotes/notes50.htm; Internet; accessed 3 September 1997.
15. Lunau, Carrol, et al. "Issues Related to the Use of Z39.50 to Emulate a Centralized Union Catalog," National Library of Canada (April 1997); available from http://www.nlc-bnc.ca/resource/vcuc/ezarl2.htm; Internet; accessed 3 September 1997.
16. Payette, Sandra D., et al. "Z39.50. The User's Perspective," *D-Lib Magazine* (April 1997) [journal on-line]; available from http://www.dlib.org/dlib/april97/cornell/04payette.html; Internet; accessed 3 September 1997.
17. Lynch, Clifford A. "The Z39.50 Information Retrieval Standard. Part I," D-Lib Magazine (April 1997) [journal on-line]; available from http://www.dlib.org/dlib/april97/04lynch.html; Internet; accessed 3 September 1997.

18. "Unified Access Information System Home Page"; http://uias.calstate.edu/UIAS.html; Internet; accessed 4 September 1997.
19. Goetz, Robert. "Virtual Union Catalog Concepts," excerpts from "VTLS Proposals for Union Catalog Projects," VTLS, Inc. (1997). Private communication.
20. Innopac Inn-Reach Documentation, Innovative Interfaces Inc. (April 1997).
21. Cousins, Shirley. "COPAC: the New Nationally Accessible Union Catalogue," Ariadne. The Web Version, issue 8 (March 1997) (journal on-line); available from http://www.ariadne.ac.uk/issue8/copac/; Internet; accessed 25 May 1997.

CHAPTER 21

New Possibilities for Information Retrieval

GÉZA BAKONYI

The problem I deal with here is not a new one: Library patrons nowadays face so much information, both in terms of the amount of it and the varied content, that they either become helpless or, in their state of alarm, are satisfied with only a partial answer to the problem. It is even a problem for many that within the electronic environment of the modern library, they have evolved from being traditional readers to *users*, and thus they find it difficult to formulate their search terms (and in most cases they are not even aware that they are the ones who have to formulate queries).

Libraries, especially modern electronic academic libraries, which are established and operated in a modern electronic environment, have to cope with similar difficulties. The characteristics of the emerging academic library include locally loaded databases; graphics, imaging, and multimedia; networking; and graphical user interfaces (GUIs). Additional trends in academic libraries include a move toward client/server computing and the collaboration of libraries with other technology-based units on a campus. Only a few years ago, the local on-line catalog seemed to be a minor miracle to library users; now, hundreds of OPACs are available for worldwide access via the Internet. The explosion of networked information has contributed to an age of vast transformation in which librarianship as a profession is "caught in the swiftest and most encompassing changes—faster and more drastic than any other."[1]

At the same time that these transformations are taking place within libraries, the academic and nonacademic members/users of the libraries are also changing. During the microcomputer revolution of the 1980s, users in all disciplines became more computer literate. Many signs indicate that a considerable proportion of patrons are fond of making use of an on-line catalog on a frequent basis, and many patrons would like to be able to initiate library transactions from their homes or from their offices. These results suggest that faculty members find electronic library resources useful and would use such services if they were offered.

In spite of the fact that home, office, and faculty users today are better equipped to use information technology than their predecessors were, there are still many ob-

---

1. Patricia Fravel, Vander Meer, Howard Poole, and Van Valey: "Are Library Users Also Computer Users? A Survey of Faculty and Implications for Services," *The Public-Access Computer Systems Review* 8, no. 1 (1997): 6–31 (http://info.lib.uh.edu/pacsrev.html).

stacles to overcome in order to retrieve and manage the growing amount of on-line information that has become available. Moreover, the growth in electronic publishing creates a need for new user skills for searching full-text and, in some cases, multimedia- and hypermedia-based electronic resources. This trend also reinforces the need for traditional computer skills, such as word processing, text editing, searching databases, and using multiple search interfaces. End users trained in the use of computers, the Internet, and information finding can electronically retrieve, search, and manipulate information, and are better equipped to independently find information to suit their needs.

Because information technology is so closely related to computer technology, there is a growing interest in promoting cooperation between academic libraries and computer centers for the provision of services. Many campuses have developed an information technology infrastructure, which includes the following elements: a campus-wide communications network; an application architecture; and discipline-oriented databases. Ideally, such infrastructures are made available at the desktop of each member of the university community. Libraries and computer centers need each other to support such campus infrastructures and to more effectively use declining institutional resources. On the other hand, the development of the University Library of Szeged (Hungary) calls attention to another phenomenon in the shaping of information technology as well. Automated processing of bibliographic data began very early for the University Library. As a consequence, by the time that information technology had become widely known, the University Library had already collected considerable experience and knowledge in applying and spreading this technology. Therefore, at present the library has a well-developed local network; it possesses powerful, high-capacity servers, and software which makes effective use of these resources. Actually, the computer center does not deal with the library and in the dissemination of information, it fulfills tasks only in other fields.

In the area of user instruction, it is becoming increasingly difficult to stay abreast of rapidly changing technology in order to instruct others in how to retrieve electronic information, let alone how to manage the digital information once it is retrieved.

In general, we can state that the more specialized and technical work becomes, the more important it is that people collaborate and exchange knowledge. Otherwise, they may not be able to keep up with innovations or changes in techniques. However, this cooperation applies not only to the technical staff and to the use of information technology as a whole. It is at least as important that the library be able to cooperate with readers, with users of the traditional and electronic services of the library. The library has to face the problem that it is the library's job to convince users, who may be overwhelmed by the mass of information, that they should not be satisfied with large numbers of answers to their questions but, instead, only with high-quality information. What is more, the library has to convince users that it is the library that is able to provide that high-quality information.

This chapter will list those means and facilities that libraries generally have for the purpose of coping with this problem. At the end of the chapter I will show those types of solutions that we, using the new methods of information retrieval, tried to introduce in the University Library of Szeged.

Results Achieved so Far

I shall provide some examples of what solutions libraries were looking for in the past to cope with the problems of retrieval of data from the increased mass of information. However, before analyzing this, it is useful to summarize the expectations that an average user of a modern library has. The typical user would like to do and have the following:

- use the same interface to consult different catalogs (or CD-ROMs), without changing the style and functions of the application every time he/she wants to access a different catalog;
- execute the same search simultaneously on multiple catalogs;
- be assisted by the system in case of negative results (the message "no records found" does not help one understand if the subject of the search is not present in the catalog or if the query has been formulated in the wrong way);
- also receive assistance in the opposite situation, when the query has been formulated too generically and produces a result too broad to be used;
- use the results obtained as a starting point for successive searchs—similar to what can be done on the WWW in a hypertextual way;
- create complex queries without knowing the search operators (such as AND, OR, NOT, TRUNCATION, PROXIMITY);
- retrieve, print, and save bibliographic records without exactly knowing the structure of the bibliographic record (for example, ignoring the difference between the Title Proper and the Parallel Title);
- exploit the characteristics of a graphical interface, without being an expert on a specific operating system (for example, UNIX, Windows 95), but using only basic interactions, such as pointing the mouse and clicking on a button.

The European Union (EU) has initiated several library projects along these lines, which seek different solutions to the data-retrieval problem. More than one of these has come to the conclusion that one way toward the solution is the training of users. Indeed, today it is inevitable that users must be regularly informed about the new possibilities and methods. New technologies like hypertext, the WWW, and other tools (search engines, subject trees) available through the Internet provide significant help in this.

The EU Libraries Project

First, I would like to mention the EDUCATE project (EnD-User Courses in information Access through communication Technology) for end-user education in information access, retrieval, and handling.[2] EDUCATE has been designed as a set of multimedia programs that can be used in many ways; for self-instruction, as an instrument in formal courses and in distance learning, and as a tool for access to information sources. It is based on the WWW with hyperlinks. It seems important to note several of the program's objectives:

---

2. Documents in the program can be retrieved (URL = http://www2.echo.ju/libraries/respge.html).

- to be able to develop a systematic method of searching for information in connection with a person's studies;
- to become aware of the wide range of sources available for finding information and to select the sources which will best meet one's needs;
- to develop one's database-searching techniques for accessing both online and CD-ROM databases;
- to be able to use the international academic networks for getting information;
- to be able to compare and evaluate information obtained from various sources;
- to be able to construct a personal bibliographic system.

The WWW hypertext information system offers a very suitable tool for the development of global education programs. The WWW merges the techniques of networked information and a hypertext to provide a powerful global information system that is easy to use. The EDUCATE programs are based on an initial hierarchic structure on three levels, with many internal and external hyperlinks.

The HyperLib project provides a hypertext interface to a library information system. The library manuals and guides required for this have been in existence for quite a while and are being produced using a variety of word-processing and desktop-publishing software. These applications are not hypertext-editing tools per se, and the transport and reuse of information represented by such texts from one program or application to another remains difficult. The project needed a standard way of encoding the hypertext structures, thus enabling flexible transport.

The project therefore decided to use SGML, or Standard Generalized Markup Language. SGML is an international standard (ISO 8879) for coding the logical structure of documents. It does not describe a universal set of tags, nor does it define exactly what a tag means, in terms of how the items identified by tags are to be processed. SGML describes only the formal properties and interrelations of the components of a document. Regarding transmission over heterogeneous networks, the HTML (Hyper Text Markup Language) and the WWW provide a way to make the hypertext documents accessible through the net and have emerged as the most powerful content-oriented navigation and retrieval mechanisms on the Internet. The first Web clients were text-mode line browsers, but as richer data types (images, sound, video) were added to HTML documents, GUI (graphical user interface) browsers like Mosaic, Cello, and Netscape began to emerge. WWW browsers now cover all operating systems, thus guaranteeing client-server access to the HyperLib products.

This program calls our attention to an important problem of hypertext word processing—the problem of the segmentation of the processed text. A HyperLib manual or guide is an SGML instance that conforms to the HyperLib document type definition (DTD) and it is built from a sequence of topics. A topic is the smallest addressable unit in a hypertext network and it contains a structured text (headings, paragraphs, lists), embedded elements (foreground and background images), and hypertext references to other topics within the same manual, to other HyperLib manuals or guides, to other local documents or to remote HTML documents on the Web, or to Internet services in general (telnet, FTP, Gopher). All topics are organized in a hierarchical network of parents and siblings. As a result, all topics are defined with a unique location in the hypertext network. In fact, this structure resembles the structure of chapters and sections in a book (the URL for the HyperLib manuals and guides is: http://www.ua.ac.be/MAN/man.html).

The ILSES project aims to develop a service that enables individual users to access and retrieve documentary information and empirical data related to large-scale surveys such as the biannual Eurobarometer surveys. ILSES is designed to serve both end users and content-providers of socioeconomic information. ILSES will be designed as an open system that can be applied to different kinds of library and data holdings. In this particular project, however, a pilot application will be focused on socioeconomic information as collected by large-scale surveys, and on the associated literature.

ILSES is based on integrated relational databases of meta-information pertaining to both library and data-archive holdings, both of which are typically distributed over many different institutions. In order to productively connect such holdings with each other and with end users, ILSES provides a wide-area network interface utilizing the Internet and supporting browsing and retrieval tools such as the WWW. For end users ILSES facilitates the integrated access and retrieval of two different kinds of information: (1) documentary information as is commonly available from libraries, and (2) empirical data as archived by data archives.

ILSES allows end users to extend literature searches with a focused access to empirical data, which can, and have been, used in empirical research of the kind reported in the literature the users review. This allows them to extend classical literature searches with their own original empirical analyses of relevant data.

Of course, ILSES offers another route—namely, that of directing data analysts, who are searching for specific empirical data for use in secondary analysis, to literature in which results and outcomes of previous and similar analyses have been reported.

The following is another topic but one that still belongs to the EU library projects. The market for information technology for libraries, in general, and for information retrieval applications and tools, in particular, is evolving rapidly. Several categories of final users can be recognized, having different characteristics and needs. Consequently, a market for products that allows diversified access to information of a differing nature, according to the needs and expectations of heterogeneous categories of users, already exists today and will certainly grow in the future.

OLUIT intends to address the needs of the vast public of nonprofessional users of libraries, whose basic requirement can be expressed as follows: to interact with the library system through a simple and powerful interface that can be learned and used with a minimum of effort, without the users becoming experts on the library domain. During the project, an efficient and innovative Toolkit has been developed, which can be used to create a multiplatform graphical user interface for search and retrieval applications using the ANSI/NISO Z39.50 standard protocol.

The Toolkit has been designed and implemented with an object-oriented methodology and consists, in a library, of classes (of objects) related to specific types of information and management functions that are of crucial interest in search and retrieval applications. The Toolkit may significantly help the application developers to build their own user interface component using already existing or easily customizable software modules: By applying the object-oriented code inheritance and reusability mechanisms, it will be possible to save time and resources.

The style of the OLUIT interface, which is particularly suitable for the nonprofessional end users of libraries, is characterized by elements such as high-quality graphics, the use of metaphors representing objects that can be found in a library, and clear and simple screen layouts.

OLUIT functionality includes the main search and retrieval functions that can be performed on bibliographic databases using the ANSI/NISO Z39.50 standard protocol (version 3), and a full set of user-activated options (basket, sort, print, save) to exploit the retrieved records locally on the workstation. A context-sensitive help is available to support and guide the user in any place of work.

In the final report of the project there are some general conclusions. Specifically, it is important that a library can be regarded as a complex organization, the constituent elements of which are a set of variables—structures, documents, people, products—that interact with a series of given objectives. Its primary purpose is to create and spread information. Seen in this way, libraries are ideal for the object-oriented approach, in which applications are developed using software "building blocks" that mirror real-world entities. These software objects can be very quickly modified, or reused in different contexts, as requirements change.

The OLUIT objective was to demonstrate how an object-oriented approach can facilitate graphical-user-interface development to provide user-friendly information access and navigation that is effective, simple, and independent of language formalisms.

The approach OLUIT follows so as to study the characteristics of nonprofessional end users, and to implement a solution specifically tailored to their needs, is quite original with respect to the other EC projects. Nevertheless, OLUIT, by virtue of its design, dealing with the GUI module of a client/server-based solution, requires integration with other software components and access to real library databases and services in a Z39.50 environment.

During the life of the OLUIT project there have been, therefore, several occasions for contact with other EC projects—such as PARAGON, SOCKER, EUROPAGATE, ARCA, USEMARCON—to identify areas of possible cooperation, and in some cases a profitable exchange of ideas and experiences has occurred.

Search Types and Technical Solutions

So far I have been speaking about searching in general terms. I shall now examine the notion of searches and summarize what types of searches I mean:

1. Multidatabase search: At the beginning of the search session the user selects one or more databases (catalogs) on which the next searches operate. The DBs are clearly diversified by their physical location and by their content.
2. Single-criterion search: This search is carried out on the basis of the specifics of one of the following fields: author-name, title, subject, publisher.
3. Multicriteria search: This search is carried out by using a combination of multiple values specified by the user, for example, Title and Author.
4. Implicit use of Boolean operators, proximity, truncation: Even if the complex search operators are powerful tools, they are not very well known and are used very little by nonprofessional users. Therefore, it is necessary that the system use them automatically every time they are needed, without the user having to specify them.

5. Navigation: the possibility of continuing the search, using the already retrieved data without having to go back each time to the initial dialogue.
6. The display of the index content that matches the selected search field: The selected terms' initial part must correspond with the string entered up to that point by the user. The updating of the list is instantly made during the typing.

The main technical solutions adopted to meet end-user requirements are briefly described below:

- Automatic query expansion with implicit use of search operators: Only the basic entry points—for example, title, author, and topic (all fields)—are available to the user for the creation of simple queries, without the need for a search operator. The user's search is automatically expanded, by the application, into a complex query that utilizes, when necessary, the various search operators (such as AND, OR, TRUNCATION).
- Multidatabase search: The application makes available a list of catalogs (that can be configured by the system administrator); one or more can be selected by the user to make the queries. The mechanisms of simultaneous searches are "transparent" to the user, both in the search and the retrieval phases, with an indication being given of the origin catalog in the list of retrieved records. Therefore, from the user's viewpoint the search modalities on multiple catalogs are exactly the same as those on a single catalog.
- Navigation of catalogs: the possibility of selecting one or more words directly from the output of a previous search and using them for a new search, without having to type them in again. This is a very useful feature during an "explorative" search in which one does not have exact references. From the results obtained, the search context is expanded, as normally happens during the navigation of a hypertext or the WWW.
- System assistance in critical situations: In critical situations for the user, such as a "zero result" or a search with too many records, the application gives a series of alternatives that help to overcome the problem. For example, in the latter case some suggestions are given on how to reduce the number of retrieved records, introducing further selection criteria.
- Step-by-step implementation for complex tasks: Every task (including the search and the retrieval) is structured in a sequence of elementary steps. In this way users can focus their attention on one problem at a time and are guided by the application on the choices they can make. This kind of approach is good for users who are not experts but is "slow" for those who are more expert, for whom some "shortcuts" will be possible.
- Context-sensitive help: The "Help" command is always available and clearly visible in each window of the application. The content of the help displayed is connected to the operational context in which the application is located. In this way the information needed to perform the right task is immediately shown.
- The object-oriented graphical user interface: In this context an object-oriented approach has been followed to graphically reproduce objects of the real world in the user interface, such as the library reading room, the card files, the bibliographic cards. The objective is to put the user psychologically "at ease," reducing the distance between the abstract metaphors used in the standard GUIs and the real library world. A 256-colors graphic has been adopted, versus the 16 colors used in standard applications, to obtain a higher realism and a more attractive look and feel. Furthermore, all graphical objects and advanced interaction modalities that are present in a standard GUI (such as a "drop-down and pop-up menu," "scroll-bars," "drag and drop"), but that are not of immediate usage, have been purposely avoided.

Projects of the Past

If we browse in the library literature of the past years, we will notice that more and more authors emphasize that besides the new solutions, the first thing to do is to create a new approach as well.

After the creation of the alphanumeric interfaces, an obvious sign of the appearance of the new approach was the creation of the GUI OPAC. As Charles R. Hildreth wrote, very expressively, about this change of approach:

> Meet the GUI (graphical user interface) OPAC, what Crawford has described as "the user-friendly, bandwidth-intensive, hardware-dependent, slow for complex searches, GUI interface that is so much fun to use the first time around." It sparkles and fascinates. It draws you in. You ponder, "What's behind this cute little icon?" Just point and click to find out. Another click or two . . . ("Hmmm, this looks familiar") and a list of index terms to scan appears. Another click, . . . a list of book titles. Click on one of these, . . . a book catalog record to ponder. This book is not what you want? OK, move back over to the window with the list of terms (you may have to maximize it), or, maybe, click on the "New Search" button and try again. Some things change, some things remain the same.[3]

Naturally, the GUI is not all. Many users keep saying, "The enthusiastic application of graphical features has sometimes resulted in unnecessary complexity," complexity that may place unreasonable demands on the user.

The user interface in information systems constitutes a complex environment in which system features must appropriately match up with a bewildering variety of users' personal characteristics, cognitive abilities, and task requirements. In the best of cases, this environment, with its brew of tangibles and intangibles, affords the user a comfortable, supportive "space" to carry out information-seeking tasks. These tasks require not only appropriate information input and output, but also comprehensible decision-making support facilities.

Looking for documents or other publications in an on-line catalog is not just a mechanistic information-seeking activity. It is a dynamic, decision-making activity that requires that careful consideration be given not only to the information that is to be provided, but also to the manner in which that information is presented in displays and to the set of decision-making facilities available to assist the user in carrying out primary tasks and subtasks. Among these tasks are the following: identifying and locating documents; reviewing them; selecting some as suitable to the need or interest; and using retrieved, located data to modify or continue a search strategy. Thus, a major goal of information system design is to develop a user interface that will facilitate the semantically demanding cognitive tasks of user comprehension and decision making. This goal is only partially accomplished by presenting easy-to-use search input screens and legible displays of bibliographic information. Not all catalog users are the same, and a "one-size-fits-all" OPAC interface will be less usable for some users than for others. Bryce Allen, whose OPAC research has addressed the differen-

---

3. Charles R. Hildreth, "The HUI OPAC: Approach with Caution," *The Public-Access Computer Systems Review* 6, no. 5 (1995): 6–18 (URL = http://info.lib.uh.edu/pacsrev.html).

tial cognitive abilities of users, recommends that system designers "customize information systems for some users,"[4] and incorporate user-selectable options in the user interface. System designers, especially designers of user interfaces, must take into account the primary tasks that are to be performed with the system and the characteristics brought to the tasks by the users of the system. An understanding of these tasks and characteristics will inform the design of the appropriate information search, presentation, review, selection, and related decision-making facilities. Too often in on-line catalog interface design, only one or two of these facilities have been optimized. For example, search input may be simplified, but no dynamic review-and-feedback facility is provided to support a search continuation or enhancement on the basis of information that has already been found and displayed. In this age of distributed, client/server computing arrangements designed to support wide-scale information retrieval, it is all too tempting to believe that sufficient improvements in usability can be made at the client (user interface) level without regard to the server's search engine or to the database content and structure. However, search engines and databases impose fundamental limits on the search and interaction options that may be presented at the client level. For example, consider the OPAC whose database does not incorporate vocabulary control and has no hypertext linkages. GUI technologies cannot overcome limitations like these.

In his study, quoted above, Charles R. Hildreth describes two design principles that refer to the on-line catalog user interface as a complex environment for supporting the search, selection, review, and related decision-making activities; these led the present author to the articulation of principles and goals that should guide the design and development of the on-line catalog interface. The first principle is that the on-line catalog system should never permit a user's search attempt to fail to retrieve one or more bibliographic records for a review and action. Many searches in existing on-line catalogs fail to retrieve even a single record, and most on-line catalogs offer little or no assistance to the searcher when this occurs. The assumption behind this principle (always retrieve something for a display and review) is that something in a heterogeneous on-line catalog database might satisfy the request to some degree, or serve, even in its rejection by the user, to supply useful information that can be used to further the search. A second principle is that one should never assume that the display of a bibliographic record is the end of a search, that a record is merely to be selected or rejected, then "set aside." Bibliographic records are for use, not just as location devices, but as information-laden devices for furthering the search. This action role of bibliographic displays is often overlooked in system design. Bibliographic records can be generative; they may have a springboard effect in the search process, or serve as information "seeds" to fertilize subsequent searching. Several of these search problems are listed below:

1. initial system entry and orientation—Bates calls it the "docking" problem;
2. required use of unfamiliar commands or excessive keyboarding;

---

4. Bryce Allen, "Cognitive Abilities and Information System Usability," *Information Processing and Management*, 30, No. 2 (1994), 178. See also Bryce Allen, "Individual Differences, Values and Catalogs," *Technicalities*, 11, No. 7 (1991), 6–10.

3. entering or finding suitable search terms;
4. modifying a search strategy or a query to achieve better results;
5. having no way to provide feedback to retrieved information so that it can be exploited to yield enhanced search results;
6. interpreting and understanding information in bibliographic displays to support decisions regarding the suitability and usefulness of retrieved items;
7. knowing where one is in the search process or knowing what may be done next.

A common problem with flexible, hypertext retrieval systems that offer many alternative search paths is the feeling of disorientation that users experience after searching for a while. Faced with many choices and paths to pursue, users typically begin to wonder where they are and how they got there. Lacking sufficient markers and prompts, they often feel lost. This experience is exacerbated in nonlinear hypertext search systems that have been implemented in earlier screen technologies developed to support only linear modes of searching. A goal of interface designers should be to increase the quality of the interactions between users and information.[5]

An interesting article by Walt Crawford, from *The Public-Access Computer Systems Review*,[6] needs to be mentioned. The article discusses the alternative of the CCL as a secondary interface alongside the GUI. The point made in it is that not only is it surely better to give our users some information rather than no information. CCL, probably the most widely implemented but not-yet-adopted standard in the history of NISO and Z39, could become the universal secondary access technique, available to power-users and dial-up/network users as an alternative to the "user-friendly, bandwidth-intensive, hardware-dependent, and slow for complex searches, GUI interface that is so much fun to use the first time around."[7]

Probably not all of CCL, but most of the set-manipulation capabilities and macro-creation capabilities, are useful for professional on-line searchers but overkill for patrons. Instead, I would expect to see "secondary CCL" looking more like the partial CCL implementations that have been around (in some cases) for a decade or more: the West Coast Group—BALLOTS/RLIN (the original), Melvyl, Orion, Carlyle, and the like.

In the University Library of Szeged we developed a WWW OPAC interface (which will be discussed later); it is accessible with the help of a lynx browser as well, without a significant loss of data. Actually, this interface is based on the CCL interface of our OPAC and it domesticates the most important commands of that. Through that, even readers working in a less developed environment will be able to access the textual information the library provides.

Yes, you can implement the logic of CCL in a GUI with icons, buttons, and dialogue boxes for the inevitable search text, and it would make an interesting design; it

---

5. Marcia J. Bates, "Subject Access in Online Catalogs: A Design Model," *Journal of the American Society for Information Science*, 37, No. 6 (1986), 357–376.
6. Walt Crawford, "Future User Interfaces and the Common Command Language," *The Public-Access Computer Systems Review* 1, no. 3 (1990): 96–99 (URL = http://info.lib.uh.edu/pacsrev.html).
7. Crawford, quoted in Hildreth, op. cit., p. 97.

would be wonderful to try one out. But it makes sense to have plain old CCL available from the keyboard as well—why penalize library users who find text comfortable?

When we design the new search interfaces, it is worth asking, What are the most used services of the library? The statistics presented by Vander Meer, et al. in their article are very interesting.[8] Their data on what services are used, and by what percentages of faculty members, in university libraries, are shown in table 21.1.

In the area of libraries' electronic services, approximately 60 percent of the faculty members answering Vander Meer, et al.'s survey reported using the on-line catalog several times a month. Approximately the same percentage of faculty members reported the use of on-line electronic databases and other online catalogs, but they said used these services less often (less than once a month). On the other hand, only 45 percent of the respondents reported using CD-ROM databases at all, indicating an average use of less than once a month. It can be seen from these statistics that besides the on-line catalog, the usage of other databases and remote catalogs increases constantly and that the use of information transmitted by CD-ROMs also could grow if the library gave assistance in the usage of these tools. The basic demand is that all sources of information could be accessed from the same search interface.

The findings of this Vander Meer, et al., study have several important implications for university library services. The first relates to the scope and nature of the electronic services provided by libraries. At the time this study was conducted, the electronic resources made available by the Western Michigan University (WMU) libraries, like those in many other university libraries, necessitated the possession of basic computer skills (for example, the use of the keyboard, function keys, a mouse, and pull-down menus). In addition, these databases functioned using a variety of interfaces requiring very different search procedures and commands. These interfaces often required users to invoke help commands to obtain the information needed to perform all but the basic functions. As a result, library patrons, and in some cases even the library staff, were challenged by the need to master intricacies such as truncation, printing, downloading information, or field searching in more than one system.

This study indicates that a distinct "computer" bias does seem to exist among frequent faculty users of the libraries, one which focuses on experience and skill in the use of a variety of computer applications. Could it be that libraries, with their expanding electronic services, which often contain inconsistent interfaces and procedures, are not sufficiently user-friendly for faculty who tend not to use computers? Many people have noted that competitive market forces have led to the development of countless electronic products without uniform standards or conventions, which has created an unfamiliar environment for library users.

It seems possible that the rapidly growing number of electronic databases, coupled with the variety of electronic interfaces, may discourage use of the library among the segment of the faculty that are not frequent users of computers. If this concern is valid, what are some of the ways libraries might address this issue? Certainly, there is a great need for standardization among electronic interfaces in libraries. To address

8. Vander Meer et al., op. cit.

Table 21.1 Use of Services in University Libraries

Library Services	% Who Use Services	Average Usage Level*
Nonelectronic services		
Materials for borrowing	85.4%	3.03
Reference staff	82.5%	2.49
Work/study in library	79.6%	3.02
Electronic services		
Electronic databases	62.9%	2.56
WMU on-line catalog	61.2%	3.63
Other on-line catalogs	59.7%	2.48
CD-ROM databases	45.2%	1.97

* Scale of usage: 1 = not at all; 2 = less than once per month; 3 = once per month; 4 = a few times per month; 5 = weekly; and 6 = daily.

Source: Patricia Fravel Vander Meer, Howard Poole, and Van Valey, "Are Library Users Also Computer Users: A Survey of Faculty and Implications for Services," *The Public-Access Computer Systems Review* 8, no. 1 (1997): 6–31.

this need at our University Library of Szeged, a plan was recently implemented to minimize the number of different electronic interfaces that are necessary to use the library's resources.

During 1996, it was an emphatic intention of Hungarian libraries to install a Z39.50 server at as many places as possible and to assist remote users in searching. Libraries using similar systems prefer the solution that they make "relative" libraries accessible on their own OPAC interface. With the expansion of the Internet and the World Wide Web, there are even greater opportunities for libraries to become more user-friendly. The Web was designed to enable users to access different forms of media on computer networks in a consistent way, and addresses a variety of software and hardware standardization problems by offering access across different computer platforms. On many campuses the Web is already available at a variety of access points, including the library, and many of the computer labs, offices, and residence halls. Those who have access at home or through their offices can also use Web resources when needed, thereby accommodating their busy schedules.

Searches in Full-Text Databases

It is becoming commonplace that many such libraries are already accessible on the Internet in the virtual environment. We can state without exaggeration that these collections are well known and used by millions of people. However, it is less known that behind the collecting and processing of electronic texts in these institutions, there are considerable professional and scientific programs that deal with the digitization of texts, the computer-aided analysis and interpretation of digitized texts. These programs have great importance in the perfecting of the new methods of retrieval in many texts.

Therefore, it is useful to examine some significant foreign projects and their results. The first that should be mentioned is the CTI text analysis program, which is connected with the Oxford Text Archive, and which aims at the processing of the most important texts of English literature. On the one hand, the program deals with electronic text processing, and on the other, it focuses on research on the new tools of electronic text-aided instruction. Under new tools, the program means not simply the hypertext processing of the classical and modern texts but also research on, and elaboration of, the possible role of computers in instruction in the humanities. The program at Oxford University is in the lead, not only in creating software to assist instruction but also in the formation of the principles of the electronic classroom.

Similar important research is in process at several universities in the United States. One of the oldest is the Dante project at Dartmouth College. The main keywords of this program are (a) full-text processing of *La Divina Commedia* and the commentaries; (b) the retrieval possibility in the BRS/Search database; and (c) the downloading of the required keywords in context, or even sending them to one's home via e-mail. A similarly interesting project has been initiated in the United Kingdom at the University of Edinburgh: a digital text analysis program that deals with the computer-aided analysis of Machiavelli's *Il Principe*. Within the framework of the program, students, with the help of computers, can themselves investigate the principles of Machiavelli's new political terminology and can give their own opinions on this special linguistic-political text.

The projects launched in Italy in this field also deserve attention: For instance, the WWW pages on the beginnings of Italian literature or on the poetry of the duecento make possible the searching for rhyme pairs. The digital processing of Dante's *Commedia* and of the significant texts of modern Italian literature is also very important. The general aim of digital processing of texts is twofold: On the one hand, it means the processing of the text as an object (it implies the investigation of the so-called word and phrase patterns that comprise one of the fundamental principles of the publishing of dictionaries and of the renewal of the retrieval language of full-text databases); and on the other hand, it means the research into the text as the objectivized form of communication. The latter covers a wide range of research, from interactive text processing to text processing based on "intelligent algorithms" (like the preparation of translations or abstracts).

The background of these projects consists of such text processing standards, and plans related to them, as nowadays basically determine the digital text processing—just think about the most obvious one, the HTML technology of the WWW. Naturally, the hypertext versions include not only the preparation of Webpages; these became the bases of the modern text analyses, too. We will easily understand it if we think about the research of Genette, Connor, and others from the "culture of new orality," and about Roland Barthes's theoretical works that make a distinction between texts prepared for "reading" or for "writing" (and that practically became one of the fundaments of postmodern philosophy).

Furthermore, these theoretical research projects may be limited in their practical use. The text that escapes from the captivity of the physical existence of the printed book shows such new features as to make us rethink the legal aspects of the traditional copyright—and not necessarily for the sake of greater profits for the traditional publishers. The hypertext text variations strongly stress the intertextuality, which is an existing characteristic of the text itself. However, the importance of intertextuality cannot be exaggerated—it may lead to the overinterpretation of the text. Nevertheless, hypertext text processing may have great importance in the investigation of a well-defined mass of texts (like the whole of the texts of a given culture or cultural period) or in its appearance in instruction. Besides the abovementioned program initiated at Oxford, such a program is the Perseus, which works on the processing of the texts and context of texts of Greek culture, or the Intermedia, which focuses on texts written in English.

A dictionary program is available on the Internet, one which connects the principle of intertextuality with the increasingly popular SGML techniques, and, with the help of which, the usage of the dictionaries of several important languages can be connected through the network with the loading and translating of any text.

However, hypertext processing of texts is still far from that process that the text interpretation activity of readers consists of. Therefore, the results of research in the field of setting up text concordances, in text indexing (KWIC and visual indexes), or in the area of statistical-linguistic features of texts, are very valuable.

One of the text processing programs is the already mentioned program related to Machiavelli's *Il Principe*, within the frames of which such software was elaborated and serves the special aims of instruction and research. This program is TACT, a text processing and analyzing program. The essence of TACT is a KWIC (keyword-in-text) index and, with the help of this, the contextual relations of a certain keyword can be visualized on different levels (http://info.ox.ac.uk/ctitext/publish/comtxt/ct11/armstron.html). Naturally, several similar programs have been prepared, like the MTAS (Micro Text-Analysis System); the PAT (to process SGML documents); the OCP (Oxford Concordance Program); and the WordCruncher (which converts different indexes from ASCII texts). A very important experiment is the Multiconcord, which incorporates the results of previous research as well. The Multiconcord is a software for Windows (naturally, this principle is applicable for other interfaces, too) that is capable of comparing multilingual texts and, with the help of these, the linguistic and semiotic analysis of translations is also possible. With the use of SGML, this software can provide a solution to the central problem (the segmentation of texts) of text processing; it marks certain paragraphs, sentences, and compares their appearance in different languages. (At the same time, this is the weakness of the program, for if the segmentation of paragraphs and sentences is not the same, the declaration of the concordance becomes very problematic.)

Besides these experiments, we often meet programs created for statistical text analyses. These programs should not be underestimated since they provide valuable contributions to the background of text analyses. Those that aim at the renewal of the visual description of results are especially interesting, from among the statistics-based text analyses.

It seems that only the complex solutions can be successful—in itself, not one of the methods is satisfying. In the University Library of Szeged (http://www.bibl.u-szeged.hu), we started on several different ways and though we are still far from being able to speak about success or a final solution, it is worth summarizing our experiments.

One of our experiments is in relation to the mirroring of the belles-lettres material of the Hungarian Electronic Library (HEL). The full collection of the HEL is searchable in our Voyager database that was prepared by the library of Lajos Kossuth University, using the proper MARC fields. The selected texts can be downloaded immediately, but we have continued to experiment with this material. Our reason for that was that, in our opinion, the usage of the MARC (the extension of this standard to cataloging Internet sources is already widespread) suggests that the texts could be available only within the catalog, whereas we would not like to give such a central role to the catalog. We believe that it is quite significant that the texts and the mass of other types of information (biographic data, photos, scanned title pages and other pages) are not only accessible within the catalogue but also are in an equal position with it. Using the source code of a WWW browser, the further development of which was canceled, we prepared such a retrieval interface and, with the help of this, searches can be performed not only in the catalog but additional image and textual information related to the items will also be accessible. With this it is possible to visualize portraits of authors with biographic data, encyclopedia articles, and even full texts of works. This amounts to more than the solution offered by the USMARC, because texts can also be used that do not have any print counterparts. For example, if we search for the word 'Bible' in the title field, we will not only retrieve all the books in the title of which we find the word "Bible" but we will also be able to retrieve the HTML version of the text, too, even in cases of treatises on the Bible. No doubt, there are many arguable and subjective elements in this solution, but we believe that a search is not only a simple operational process in the library but also, paraphrasing of Benedetto Croce, it is the curiosity of mankind in a nutshell and like this it is originally subject-oriented.

Another program in progress is being handled jointly with the research conducted in the Department of Old Books of the Library and in the Department of Library Science. This program is a very significant contribution to the virtual catalog of old books. The program is aimed at processing inventories of old Hungarian libraries in such a way that it connects the texts to three BRS databases (the bibliographic database of the holdings of the library; the bibliographic database of the explanations of the original title items of the inventory; and the database of works referring to libraries). This software package (based on JAVA) is naturally available via the WWW as well). In this program the software makes possible the connection of the data of the databases with the textual data by means of a retrieval strategy.

For the future, we plan similar, digital processing of the material of two other important special collections of our library: On the one hand, we intend to establish a service for providing articles from dailies that were published between the two world wars and are available in the library. (The library receives many inquiries in connection with this historically very valuable material.) Our other plan is to realize the digital processing of the Oriental Collection and to prepare the publication of a certain part of the material on CD-ROM.

In conclusion, some thoughts concerning computerized text processing and text analysis: As for the interpretation of texts, the appearance of digital texts creates the possibility of providing new modalities for different levels of interpretation for various texts. The new methods enable us to search faster and more effectively in full-text copies of newspapers (available on CD-ROM and on the Internet), which makes the traditional research, and the preparation of background materials necessary for decision making, significantly easier. At present we are trying to develop such a method, which would help with the multilevel interpretation of literary texts (we make our experiments with texts of Italian and Hungarian literary works). This experiment is based on the proposition that the process of text interpretation can be derived from an interactive relationship between several models of interpretation and the text itself. On the other hand, the computerized analysis goes much faster through such processes required by the models, like the lexical interpretation of the text, and its comparison to basic-level grammatical and syntactical models and to certain logical text models (such a logical text model may be the parallel structure of proverbs, the verbal time structure of folktales).

Presently, this system is in an experimental stage and as the library information system grows, we will have a parallel plan to organize this interface on a higher and higher level.

CHAPTER 22

Why, and How to, Translate a Subject Heading System
Authority Control Provides a Solution

KLÁRA KOLTAY

The old card catalogs were difficult to handle; in fact, libraries had to keep several catalogs if they wanted to provide various types of access to their holdings. Copies of the same card had to be filed at their various access points in the author/title catalog, the subject catalog, the serial-title catalog, and the UDC catalog. With the emergence of machine-readable catalogs, catalog records indexed word by word promised much easier access to bibliographic data. However, librarians and their patrons soon discovered that while it might be easier to find a particular document in a catalog of this type, it would never give any information about the nature of a library's collection as a whole and about the hierarchy of disciplines it covers. A machine-readable catalog of a large number of records, with elaborate combinations of various indexes, lacks the coherence of a card catalog structured by its system of main entries, added entries, and subject headings with references interwoven in it. In this regard, the following has been said:

> Any individual item in a collection may itself serve little purpose; when included in a larger collection of like materials, its value is greatly increased. It is this fact that those who have invested great faith in a computer's ability to retrieve single, discrete records have ignored. Unless a machine readable database has a coherent underlying organization, sophisticated retrieval can only ensure access to individual items. If people do not have a precise idea of what they are seeking, computer access to a database (which does not exhibit a fundamental intellectual organization) will overlook many items that might be of use.[1]

Fighting incoherence, by providing an "underlying organization to the database and ensuring reliable subject access, is always among the most important tasks of library catalogs, which they try to fulfill in various ways.

---

1. S. Michael Malincomico, "Bibliographic Data in Base Organization and Authority File Control," in *Authority Control: the Key to Tomorrow's Catalog*, ed. Mary W. Ghikas (Phoenix, AZ: Oryx Press, 1982), p. 4.

Types of Subject Access

Databases without Subject Headings and Subject Classification

Theoretically, all databases can provide some kind of subject access, even without subject headings. Some of the MARC files of the British Library's Blaise-line system can be examples of another type of approach to subject retrieval. These files do not contain any type of subject classification system, either because they are based on old catalog records such as the British Library Catalog file consisting of main entry records converted from the printed British Library Catalog, or because they catalog antiquarian material such as the Eighteenth Century Short Title Catalog (ESTC) file or the Incunable Short Title Catalog (ISTC). On the other hand, the keyword searching facility is made as full as possible—it indexes all used fields, offers all the sophistication of logical operators, truncation, variable character symbols, string searching, date ranging, and provides access to all the computer indexes. The thoughtful combination of these possibilities can, to a certain extent, replace subject classification systems and offer some new possibilities.

The CD-ROM version of the British Library Catalogue offers even more search options than the number of MARC fields a record contains: Titles (ti/tk), authors (au/ak), publishers (pu/pk) can be searched as phrases or by keyword; or one can use the keyword (kw) option to search all the Author/Heading, Title, Series, and Content note fields and one can have access to the following indexes: Author/Heading, Author/Heading Keyword, Title Phrase, Title Keyword, Keyword Shelfmark, Accompanying Material, Place of Publication, Publisher, Publisher Keyword, Published Year, ISBN.

New types of questions, which, in the absence of enough indexed fields, cannot be answered, can be asked here—in a few steps one can collect all the British Library books published, for example, in Debrecen (Hungary) between 1500 and 1700 (see table 22.1).

Leafing quickly through the 425 items so as to select the one ones published between 1500 and 1700 (fortunately, the publication date is displayed first in brief citations), we find 18 documents that meet our original search criteria. Had the spelling variants of Debrecen not been found in "place of publication," only the last three titles with asterisks would have been found through browsing. Just as we could find the spelling variants used by the old printers, index files can be used for spotting cataloging mistakes: words spelled incorrectly, misused subfields (for example,

Table 22.1 Search Results for British Library Books Published in Debrecen

Search number	Search option	Search questions	Number of hits / relevant index lines	Relevant items	New items
1	keyword	pl=Debrecen and Debreczen	346		
2[a]	browse	place of publication—Debrecen	22 lines 425 items[b]		79

[a] The next logical step after search A would be to use the published-year search for the years 1500 and 1700, but it would take too much time for the computer. Instead, we can try to go into the browse option, find Debrecen in the place-of-publication index, and, with the help of the short citations, pick up the appropriate dates.

[b] Debrecen is spelled 22 different ways by old publishers and modern catalogers.

Table 22.2 Search Results for "Cambridge architecture"

Search number	Search option	Search questions	Number of hits/ relevant index lines	Relevant items	New items
1	keyword	kw=Cambridge architecture	30	3	
2	keyword	kw=church and Cambridge	449[a]		
3	keyword	cs[b]=2 and not kw=sermon	344		
4	keyword	cs=3 and tk=history	20	5	
5	keyword	cs=3 and tk=description	4	1	
6	keyword	kw=Cambridge and tk=college	939		
7	keyword	cs=6 and tk=description	8	2	
8	keyword	kw=Cambridge and tk=chapel	80		
9	keyword	cs=8 and not kw=sermon	55	14	
10	keyword	kw=Cambridge and tk=buildings	14	14	

[a] Too many items to look through, but if one has a look at the first few, one can see that some of them are sermons preached in the churches, and on the other hand, the ones that may be relevant contain the word "history" or "description" in their title.

[b] "cs" denotes a search that combines the results of the previous searches.

dates accidentally entered into the publishers' subfields would be collected on top of the file).

The topic "Cambridge architecture" is the type which would be much easier to search for in the presence of subject classifications. Instead, one has to be more careful in collecting the possible words that might occur in the title of a book like this (see table 22.2).

Our final results are that in 10 steps we retrieved 141 books, only 39 of which proved relevant; and one cannot help feeling that we have just given in at this point, and that better ideas for a keyword would result in more items.

Other Blaise-line files use more fields, which can provide more opportunities for circumventing the problem of subject searches—the ESTC file gives coded information concerning the author (whether his name is in initials, known or an unknown pseudonym)—and differentiating among five special genres (advertisements, almanacs, directories, prospectuses, songs) in the 008 field. The Blaise-line files also give bibliographical references in the 534 field and use general notes concerning the authorship, the language, the type, the subject or the content of the work, or give additional collation and publication details.

The field of bibliographical references can serve as a kind of subject heading if a clearly defined group of published bibliographies is used systematically throughout the cataloging process. The users of the ESTC files who are familiar with the bibliographies used here can, for example, choose D. F. Foxon's *English verse, 1701–1750: a catalogue of separately printed poems with notes on contemporary editions* so as "to extract verse without recourse to the many synonyms (epistle, poetry, poem, etc.) that would be otherwise necessary."[2]

2. M. J. Crump, *Searching ESTC on BLAISE-LINE: A Brief Guide, Factotum*, (Newsletter of the XVIIIth Century STC). Occasional Paper 6, January 1989, p. 22.

The lengthy, descriptive titles characteristic of eighteenth-century material, together with the subject and content notes, make a search like "sacheverell (tw) and not sacheverell h (au)," together with "sacheverell (ng)"—that is, a search for Sacheverell as a keyword in the title, but for works of which Henry Sacheverell is not the author, and for works the note field of which contains his name—retrieve a wide range of material from letters on him to a description of his trial.[3]

The search topic the Warsaw University Library has experimented with is typically one of the very broad topics that could be found much easier if a subject classification system were present. The library was looking for books of Polish authorship—and of specifically Polish interest—using the following search pattern:

- *Poland, Polish,* or *Pologne/Polen;*
- *Sski* or *Sky* or *Sskie,* typical endings of family names, like Poniatowski, Sobieski, Wielhorski, and their possible English spellings;
- names of major cities and provinces whose spelling was adjusted to those of *Encyclopaedia Britannica* (1773), with some French additions, like *Varsovie*;
- names of major figures of Polish life, like Bukaty and Kollataj, as well as other country-specific names like *Sejm*—parliament, plica polonica—a frequent disease.

Including the selection of the irrelevant items, the global result was 152 documents. Interestingly enough, the first and fourth patterns did not retrieve any relevant items.[4]

When having to find broad topics like the above, words with several spelling variants, the possibility of using single variable characters and truncation (which can be used at the end or in the middle of the words but not at the beginning) is valuable. The following example uses the ISTC file:[5] the name "William" can be used in Latin or Italian spelling, so if we want to find all variants within a search, we have to make use of the truncation: all gu:l:m: (aw) or all gu:l:m: (tw)

The 527 items retrieved contain one of the following 17 variants: Guglielma, Guglielmo, Gugliermus, Guilelmus, Guilhermus, Guilielmi, Guilielmo, Guilielmus, Guillaume, Guillelmi, Guillelmum, Guillelmus, Guillem, Guillermi, Guillemus, Gulielmi, Gulielmus.

A database like this can be of the greatest help if the search topic needs the combination of data contained in various fields; the sermons of the 1740s held by the Cambridge University Library can be listed in one search: sermon (tw) and c (lb) and all 174: (yr).

As we have seen above, the efficiency of keyword searches is basically determined by the fields indexed for them. If the catalog record does not contain any kind of subject headings and the fields and subfields that can be indexed are only those of the title, subtitle, series title, main and added entries, and content notes, the results of searches can be inadequate on the one hand and incomplete on the other. Inadequate

---

3. Ibid., p. 30.
4. Henryk Hollender, "Mapping the Image: English books on Poland in the 18th century," *Factotum,* no. 35 (August 1992): 20–21.
5. John Goldfinch, "Searching the ISTC on BLAISE-LINE," *Searching ISTC,*" in-house papers of the ISTC Project, September 1991.

items can appear because the wording of the titles is often figurative and they necessarily contain words that are far from the actual subjects of the books. Relevant items, however, can be left out of the list of located books if one of their important subject elements is not mentioned in the title or subtitle; they use variant spelling forms or they are simply not written in the language of the search terms. The latter problems can be overcome by indexing the field of subject headings, thus using the words appearing in them as the basis for subject searches.

Another disadvantage of keyword searches is that the more you increase the number of fields to retrieve the largest number of possible items present in the database, the longer are the lists of located items, with more and more irrelevant hits. Boolean searching, however, can be of great help for widening the basis of the search (for example, by giving search terms in variant spelling or languages with the help of an "or" operator) and can focus the result on a narrower topic more closely (for example, by using "and" or "not" operators, or pointing to a certain MARC field of the catalog record to be searched) at the same time.

Databases with Subject Headings

The efficiency and accuracy of subject searches can be greatly enhanced by adding subject headings to the records. The ways in which a retrieval system may use them are very different: They can simply be indexed together with title words in one large keyword index for subject retrieval purposes. In other cases, we encounter separate title words and subject keyword indexes or can browse the subject indexes. Other systems make use of subject authority records, with the result that they offer a system of references as well.

Several searches were performed by the author in the Libertas database of the University of London Consortium Libraries, which offer a combined title and subject keyword index, with the possibility of using truncation and Boolean operators. When more than one search term is used we are given "close matches" that contain all our terms and all other items that match at least one of our terms.

We can expect that the first search topic, "Jews in Hungary" (see table 22.3), will retrieve some items in the Hungarian collection of the Slavonic and East European Institute, but not too many to prevent us from following what is happening.

Besides the new title that search 5 gave us, we gained some additional ideas to widen our perspective toward the following possible related topics: the history of anti-Semitism; anti-Semitism in various countries and historical periods, anti-Semitism in art and literature. Similarly, the subject heading "Jews—Hungary" adds to our knowledge, structuring the nine books we have already found into the following pattern:

1. Jews—Hungary—Biography 1
2. Jews—Hungary—cultural assimilation 1
3. Jews—Hungary—fiction 1
4. Jews—Hungary—history 3
5. Jews—Hungary—history - twentieth century 1
6. Jews—Hungary—persecutions 1
7. Jews—Hungary—Szeged —history - twentieth century 1

Table 22.3 Search Results for "Jews in Hungary"

Search number	Search option	Search questions	Number of hits / relevant index lines	Relevant items	New items
1	Keyword	Jewish Hungary	927 (8 close matches)	8	8
2	Keyword	Jewish Hungarian	469 (1 close match)[a]	1	
3	Keyword (Boolean)	Jewish+Hungar?	8[b]	8	
4	Keyword (Boolean)	Jews+Hungar?	15	14	7[c]
5	Browse	Subject[d]—anti-Semitism–Hungary	2 lines/3 items	3	1

[a] If we want to avoid the several hundreds of "not closely matching" and, in fact, irrelevant items, we can try Boolean searching, making use of another advantage of it, the possibility of truncation. We cannot enter the truncation "Jew?," because it would result in too many search terms, but we can use "Hungar?".

[b] They are exactly the same as the first 8 "closely matching" items in search 1.

[c] We must be aware of the fact that 5 of the new 7 items—either as they are written in a foreign language or because their title does not contain the search terms—could be retrieved only because the catalog records contain subject headings, the elements of which are present in the keyword index of Libertas.

[d] As keyword searches of Libertas make use of the subject heading fields, as well, we cannot expect that the subject browse for "Jews" and "Jewish" can lead us to new items unless new terms have emerged. The first item in search 4, however, came up with another possible term, namely, "anti-Semitism."

Structuring the available material is especially important if we are dealing with a broader topic, for example, "Jews." The keyword search for "Jews" resulted in the discouraging number of 1,819. Subject browsing lays them out in roughly the following pattern: "Jews"; "Jews—History," further divided into periods; "Jews—rites and ceremonies"; "Jews—addresses, essays, lectures"; "Jews in various areas," often further divided into periods. Mingled with them, as alphabetical sorting requires, there appeared the subdivisions like civilization, colonization, commerce, cultural assimilation, dictionaries and encyclopedias, economic conditions, education, families, folklore, history, languages, legal status, mental health, migration, nobility, politics and government, psychology, restoration, statistics, and study and teaching.

Whether they add some kind of subject headings to their catalog records or not, most libraries use other subject classification systems as well. The Library of Congress, Dewey, or Universal Decimal Classification schemes determine the location of the books within the library and classmarks appear as "shelfmarks" in the records. Though they are not primarily intended as a means of subject retrieval, most systems offer a possibility of browsing the shelfmarks, which again can add to the results of our subject searches.

The different logic and structure behind the Library of Congress Subject Heading system and the Dewey and UDC classifications helped to get a more complete result for our search topic "history of biology," which suggests that in larger databases it is not superfluous to have more subject classification schemes (see table 22.4).

If we look at the subject headings of the additional 26 items we found with searches 2 and 3, we find that they are either classified under "naturalist," "genetics—history," "evolution," "biology—addresses," and "natural history," which would not

Table 22.4 Search Results for "History of Biology"

Search number	Search option	Search questions	Number of hits / relevant index lines	Relevant items	New items
1.*	Browse	Subject — Biolgy — History	2 lines/28 items	28	28
2	Browse	classmark: 011@574.09	5 lines/36 items	36	22
3	Browse	classmark: 012@574(09)	2 lines/11 items	11	4
4	Keyword	subject: history + biology	4,950 close matches		
5	Keyword (Boolean)	subject: history+biology	88	63	34

*The searches were performed in the union catalog of the King's College Library. The whole catalog has Library of Congress subject headings, while different locations use different classmarks: location "011" uses Dewey numbers while location "012" uses UDC. Thus the results of searches 2 and 3 together can be compared to search 1.

necessarily occur to the searcher, or have no topical subject headings at all. The hierarchical structure of classifications systems, however, group them as subtopics under the same main number, thus leading us to them.

After subject-browse and classmark searches, the third possible approach to the same topic lies in the two types of keyword searches offered by Libertas in search examples 4 and 5. The fact that they were able to add 34 new relevant items to our previous hit list teaches us that one search type alone is unlikely to find all relevant items, and the more options that are tried, the fuller the results will be.

A study by Adeline W. Wilkes and Antoinette Nelson proves that adding subject headings to the bibliographic records in itself is not enough by far.[6] A dramatic difference can exist between the performing of subject searches in a catalog, with and without authority control, and the references it provides. The number of unsuccessful subject searches in an "uncontrolled" catalog is relatively high and can reach 40.6 percent. If an authority-controlled classified subject vocabulary is introduced, 73.9 percent of the previously unsuccessful searches may retrieve at least one, and very often several records.

The subject heading systems, with their controlled vocabulary, their set patterns of subdivisions, their hierarchy of broader and narrower terms, provide a tool to reveal the structure and coherence of a collection, thereby guiding searchers toward relevant subject areas they have not thought of. User-entered search terms—regarded as set strings—are matched against the subject heading strings in the authority file and are shown in their alphabetical context. In the alphabetical neighborhood of his term the user may find thematically related strings or references to broader or narrower concepts, or to synonyms to be used, instead of the term originally entered by him. Thus, well-constructed subject authority files can strengthen the retrieving capabilities of an on-line catalog.

6. Adeline W. Wilkes and Antoinette Nelson, "Subject Searching in Two Online Catalogs: Authority Control vs. Non-Authority Control," *Cataloguing and Classification Quarterly* 20, no. 4 (1995).

Systems Offering Classmark-Based Searches

Many classification systems like UDC or Dewey reproduce the hierarchy of the broader and narrower concepts of a discipline, but they are not user-friendly and very often they are slow in following the new ideas emerging in scientific research. They were not designed for the purposes of on-line catalogues, which very often have difficulties in handling them. Most of the patrons consult UDC card catalogs with the help of the library staff and they simply avoid these indexes in the OPAC, which is mainly for self-service use.

There are systems, however, that try to make classmark searches more user-friendly by linking the classmarks to natural-language expressions in one way or another.

Another Libertas installation, in the Exeter University Library, offers the possibility of linking topical subject headings in the authority file to the appropriate classmarks. The subject heading–classmark connections appear on screen only when the subject-browsing option is used.

The search term "animal behavior," used in subject browsing, resulted in the following display:

1. animal behavior   4
2. animal behavior—congresses   1
3. animal behavior—history   1
4. animal behavior—measurement   1
5. animal behavior—classified at 591.5

At this point the searcher can either simply "expand" line 5 and find that there are 309 records for his search term, or, entering the classmark-browsing option, can find the same records there together with the neighboring classmarks and postings. The significant difference in the number of postings of "animal behavior" as subject heading and as classmark can give us the idea that the use of the "classified at" reference can make it possible to gradually introduce subject headings into a catalog as a new type of classification without any major disturbance.

The BLCMP system of the Birmingham University Library does not leave it to its users to judge the possible results of keyword and sequenced inquiries, and chooses the appropriate one. It offers fewer options at its initial screen, which, with the exception of searches by title and classmark, are keyword searches. When the results of the author/title, author, or keyword searches are displayed, however, the reader is invited to continue his search one step further by the option "other items at this classmark." Thus he can make use of the library's subject classification system and can easily switch between keyword searches and indexes without having to know much about their nature.

While in the previous examples the classmark browsing only complemented keyword and structured subject searches, since the 1960s there have been experiments with systems that are based on Dewey or UDC classification numbers as the main or only subject classification method used.[7]

---

7. Robert R. Freeman and Pauline Atherton, *Final Report of the Research Project for the Evaluation of the UDC as the Indexing Language for a Mechanized Reference Retrieval System* (New York: American Institute

Making use of the machine-readable version of the Dewey Decimal Classification used to produce the nineteenth edition of it, Karen Markey and Ahn A. Demeyer set up an experimental system to compare the efficiency of the widely used type of catalog similar to the Subject Online Catalog, offering keyword searches and "alphabetic inquiry" based on subject headings, and of the Dewey Online Catalog, which works with Dewey classmarks and terms of the Dewey Schedules and Relative Index. [8]

Though a detailed comparative experiment with the two catalogs showed that the Dewey Online Catalog is not significantly more efficient than the Subject On-line Catalog,[9] and calls for refinement at several points,[10] it can certainly add the advantages of a classified system to a catalog that, in the absence of classified subject headings, would have to rely on keyword subject searches alone.

It is not only experimental catalogs that base their subject retrieval on either the UDC or Dewey Classification schemes and try to translate the numbers into subject terms for the sake of their readers.[11]

The Library of the Swiss Federal Institute of Technology in Zurich developed a system call ETHICS, the subject register and the subject catalog of which are based on UDC.[12] The ETHICS standard register includes all the UDC numbers used in ETHICS, their descriptors in German, English, and French, and a chain of references and further codes. (The "auxiliary numbers" upgraded by ETHICS can be used as independent classification and search terms as well.) The standard register is the source of the following on-line subject registers.

The alphabetical register (either trilingual or separate, according to languages) contains as many synonyms as possible, and uses inversion, enumerations, and indentation. The personal and corporate names are also listed in the alphabetical subject register.

The systematic register is arranged by the UDC numbers:

    538.9   Physics of condensed matter
    538.91   Structure/condensed matter
    538.913 Structure/condensed matter. Dynamics and Statistics[13]

---

of Physics, Report AIP/UDC-9); a list and description of projects and systems using the UDC is given in Malcolm Rigby, *Automation and the UDC, 1948–1980*, FID Publication 565 (The Hague: Federation Internationale de Documentation, 1981).

  8. Karen Markey and A. Demeyer, *Dewey Decimal Classification Online Project: Evaluation of a Library Schedule and Index Integrated into the Subject Searching Capabilities of an Online Catalogue* (Final Report to the Council on Library Resources) Report number: OCLC/OPR/RR-86/1, OCLC Office of Research, Dublin, OH, 1985.

  9. Ibid., pp. 173–181.

  10. Ibid., pp. 220–224, 227.

  11. The ETH Library Information Control System (ETHICS) in the Library of the Swiss Federal Institute of Technology in Zurich, and the HELICON system, an economic database in the Helsinki School of Economics Library in Finland, an expert system for automatic UDC number assignment, are described in *The UDC: Essays for a New Decade*, ed. Alan Gilchrist and David Stachan (London: Aslib, 1990).

  12. Library of the Federal Institute of Technology, CH-8092, Zürich; and Klaus Loth and Herbert Funk, "Subject search on ETHICS on the basis of the UDC," in *UDC: Essays for a New Decade*, op. cit., pp. 35–46.

  13. Op. cit., p. 38.

The third register shows the concept environment of a chosen term with its generic-term cross-references and the subdivisions of the next lower hierarchy step.

The "real life experiments" with UDC-based on-line catalogues and cooperative databases have started to show the possible problems: The use of 350-450 comparatively general classes would result in thousands of references in certain UDC classes,[14] while the application of broader UDC versions would raise the question of differences in classification practices of libraries or even of individual classifiers.[15] (The problem is especially acute in the field of social sciences, where documents can be more diversely interpreted.) To help in the formulation of a more consistent and versatile classification policy, and in the design of more accurate tools for use UDC in retrieval, the Finnish Scientific Library Association started a comparative study of scientific libraries that use the KDOK/MINTTU databases.

Conclusions

What conclusions can be drawn? First, a database without reliable search techniques cannot really be of great help in finding the necessary information. The search results can only be trusted if the users are provided with the possibility of approaching their subject from various angles.

Keyword searches reaching as many fields as possible can be very useful if a specific topic requires a free combination of terms held in various fields. They are the easiest to start with, as they do not require the knowledge of subject strings or classification numbers. On the other hand, they may retrieve a lot of irrelevant items, especially if the OPAC is the type that "drops" one of the search terms; they may present the reader with hundreds of relevant but unstructured items in the case of broad topics, or they miss relevant items, especially if there is no subject-heading field, the words of which can complement the information in the title. They are very susceptible to spelling mistakes or to variant spellings.

Access to keyword indexes are very important as they can help both the cataloger and the reader to create and to find the correct forms of names. They can point out errors so that the cataloger can correct the record and the reader can find the record that would otherwise be hidden by the error.

The use of indexing languages that structure the database can give additional help in subject retrieval—the headings or numbers may contain subject information missing from the title; and even if the search results in a large number of documents, they are placed in the context of the given discipline. The authority files can, again, help in spotting mistakes, keeping the database tidy and allowing readers to find references, with broader or narrower terms.

The different inherent logic of classification systems can add to the capabilities of

---

14. Paivikki Karhula, "Use and usability of the UDC in classification practice and online retrieval," in *UDC: Essays for a New Decade*, op. cit., p. 48.

15. Ibid., note 5, p. 54.

on-line catalogs. The fact that these different approaches complement each other —and it is their combination that gives satisfactory results—justifies their parallel use in large bibliographic databases.

The Translation Project of the Lajos Kossuth University Library

We had all these considerations in mind when the Library of Lajos Kossuth University had a library system installed at the end of 1993 and started to build its machine readable catalog from scratch.

Subject cataloging had had a tradition of several decades in our library. We have been using "free," uncontrolled subject headings in addition to the general Hungarian practice of assigning one, or more often several, UDC strings to the documents. It was only a very small portion of the library's material that did not receive a UDC number. The UDC catalog built was considered to be the main tool of subject searches with scientific purposes and the subject specialists who assigned the numbers were always available to handle patrons' requests for specific subject searches. The subject catalog, on the other hand, was very selective, contained only a small part of our material, and originally was intended to be a tool of first orientation.

Realizing that starting the new machine-readable catalog is a never-recurring opportunity of rethinking subject-cataloging policy and putting it into practice at the same time, we had to decide what possibilities were ahead of us as soon as possible.

Not wanting to give up the longtime tradition of UDC altogether, the library decided to put more emphasis on subject terms, making them the main tool of subject retrieval. For that purpose, however, the "free," uncontrolled headings we had used were not suitable. On the other hand there is, at the moment, no general subject list available in Hungarian that we could adopt.

The solution was suggested by the fact that we started to use Library of Congress bibliographic records for both our retrospective and current cataloging, which contained Library of Congress Subject Headings.

Studying the nature of Library of Congress Subject Headings, we realized that the subject strings of a primary structure element, and the subdivisions it uses, resemble the structure of our old headings—which, from the point of view of our patrons, is a great advantage—and its striving for natural-language solutions is, again, not alien to our previous practices. As it has been a constantly growing vocabulary, aiming at incorporating new concepts as soon as they emerge in scientific literature with all the advantages of being up-to-date, there exist different layers of headings reflecting various phases in the hundred-year history of LCSHs. The coexistence of natural language ("minority lawyers, women lawyers") and of inverted headings ("lawyers, Jewish; lawyers, foreign") is an example of it. Despite the above and some similar stuctural incoherence, the LCSH system provides a vast number of headings, an elaborate reference structure, and a subdivision system with growing consistency. The present tendencies of creating "pattern headings," which systematize subject areas, of using indirect patterns for geographical subdivisions, of always placing the larger geographic area before the smaller, the gradual elimination of "rival headings" ("art,

American; art—United States"), the use of dual-concept headings and a progress from broad concepts to narrower ones—all these promise "a cooperative, comprehensive subject code" with a long future.[16]

The idea to adopt Library of Congress Subject Headings for a university library with a very broad scope of material—from sciences through law, to social sciences and various languages and literatures—as opposed to using a set of more specialized but not interrelated thesauri, seemed a very rational one. It was further supported by the general interest in LCSHs in the world's library community.

They are not only used throughout the United States and in many libraries in other English-speaking countries, but have also been translated into French by the National Library of Canada and are used in the French National Library. Among the present translation projects, the cooperative effort of several Polish libraries can be mentioned. The spread of LCSHs proves its value and enriches the original vocabulary with geographic and topical headings specific to the language areas that use the headings. It is especially true since the launching of the Subject Authority Cooperative Program (SACO) in the Library of Congress. The program provides a means for libraries to submit subject headings and classification numbers to the Library of Congress.

At this point we were strongly convinced that a Hungarian version of Library of Congress Subject Headings would meet all our requirements. The library turned to the Library of Congress in 1994, asking about the LC's attitude toward our using and translating LCSHs. They granted us their permission on the condition of being given a copy of the database created for review and reference purposes.

The Methodology of the Project. The methodology of translation, mainly determined by the library's immediate need for Hungarian terms for our everyday current and retrospective cataloging, followed the methodology of building the LCSH system itself. Instead of creating the complete Hungarian version, we translate a heading only when a need first appears for it in cataloging work.

It seems to be a dangerous approach at first, with the only advantage that it minimizes the preparatory period before Hungarian headings can actually be used. However, two factors—the reference system being attached to the subject headings, and the authority control module of our library software—ensure that the gradually created Hungarian vocabulary will become controlled and that the terms in it will keep their original position within the structure.

The elaborate reference system attached to the Library of Congress Subject Headings clearly defines a heading with the aid of a list of "use" and "used for" references, of narrower and broader terms. Translation in our case means creating a MARC authority record containing the Hungarian equivalent of all these (see table 22.5). Doing that, the subject specialist is always forced to consider synonyms and to be precise in picking the right word in the hierarchy. One of the most important guidelines we follow in our work is to stick to the original version as closely as possible. It is not always easy for people educated on "free" subject headings, but we always try our best. The

---

16. Willian E. Studwell, *Library of Congress Subject Headings : Philosophy, Practice and Prospects* (New York: Haworth Press, 1990), p. 110.

most flexibility we allow ourselves is in the case of "used-for" references. The language difference makes it unnecessary to translate all given English terms, while occasionally we have to add extra Hungarian words as suppressed synonyms of the term (see table 22.6).

Besides the references, the authority records will always contain the original English headings. It can be important in case we want to check if the term was translated correctly. As a recent practice, we add UDC numbers to enable us to gather up all the terms belonging to a topic.

Authority control, which we had learned to utilize for building an authority database of names and titles, became an important tool that maintains a very strict formal control on every subject-heading string we enter into our catalog records. When saving a new bibliographic record into the catalog, every subject string that proves to be unfamiliar to the system stops the saving process and catalogers have the opportunity to check the already existing database again. If the heading is really a new one, this is the time for creating the authority record containing the new translation; if it proves to be an unnecessary variant of an already-existing concept, it is deleted or, in case it is a term patrons are likely to use, it becomes a "see" reference to the existing form. Authority control keeps track of not only the accepted forms but also all the "see" and "see also" references. When browsing in the heading list, we see the accepted and unaccepted forms together, which calls the cataloger's attention to all precedents of a term. The third way authority control checks on consistency is by pointing out conflicts, like trying to use the same term as an accepted heading and a "see" reference at the same time. Another important rule of consistency is that of free-floating subdivisions. The subdivision "study and teaching" following the main heading "Hungary—History" and following another main heading "Geology, Stratigraphic" must look alike in both cases. Authority control cannot check it directly but the fact that not only the headings, but also the headings in all of their combinations with subdivisions, have to have separate authority records helps here.

Figuring out as much beforehand, being in possession of the Library of Congress's permission, of the Library of Congress Subject Heading List, a Library of Congress Subject Heading Manual, and the bibliographic CD of the Library of Congress, we started to work.

In the early phase, which lasted nearly a year, we translated only the headings that appeared in our catalog with imported Library of Congress records. Original cataloging and records from other sources were still given the old-type "free" subject headings.[17] We aimed at collecting the core concepts of all subject areas and as much deductive knowledge of LCSHs as possible. The imported records, keeping the English-language headings, were assigned to the translated ones as well. Before adding a Hungarian heading, we always check the database for precedents and let authority control

---

17. We put these subject expressions in an uncontrolled field (695), which is still in use when, in the retrospective-cataloging project, old free subject terms are keyed in automatically from catalog cards, and we may use it from time to time when a "proper" term cannot be found in LCSH. Allowing this practice was an important element in making subject catalogers accept LCSHs. As time goes on they use 695 less and less.

make the second check. If necessary, we create new authority records for a new term with its references and for every string containing new combinations of headings and subdivisions. When creating the references, we have to be careful with "see also" references, as often we have to retrieve the heading referred to and create the reference in the opposite direction, as well. The practice we follow here is not to translate narrower terms of a heading, since these might never be needed. (Table 22.5 contains a heading with only some of its narrower terms translated.) When it appears as a used-subject heading for the first time, we go back to its broader term and complete the record with it only then.

Trusting the effectiveness of authority control in the cleaning up of the database with global updates, we encouraged ourselves to proceed with the work even when feeling uncertain about one or the other solution. If the Hungarian term we have chosen is not the best stylistic variant, we keep using it till somebody comes up with a better idea. Then only a few authority records have to be changed to correct all the erroneous forms in the database.

When we started to feel more confident about what we were doing, the next important step was taken at the beginning of 1996: Using the accumulated Hungarian vocabulary and trying to assign new English LCSHs by ourselves, we widened the scope of our project to originally created records of Hungarian-published material. It was at this point that we started to use the LCSH file on-line to help us to find the appropriate headings.

The main source of the assigned headings is the already accumulated vocabulary of our catalog, and it turned out that the on-line authority database of the Library of Congress was much needed. This offers the most recent headings, as well as all references and scope notes. At this point, it became especially important to be aware of the rules that govern the creation of subject strings, which are provided by the Library of Congress's Subject Cataloging Manual 23. Its bibliographic database is, again, a valuable resource of current practice. In spite of all the help, on-line databases and manuals offer hope for organizing a subject catalog workshop with the participation of the Library of Congress staff.

Since earlier layers of our database contain records with only UDC numbers and/or free subject words, and since there are a considerable number of English headings that have not yet been translated, database maintenance has become a very important part of our work. Theoretically, whenever a new heading is translated, the earlier records that ought to contain it are retrieved by UDC numbers and/or free subject words, and they receive the new heading as well. In practice, how many old records can be revised always depends on the actual workload.

Much gratitude is owed to the subject catalogers who have undertaken the task of adopting a new system with all its thrills and tortures. While a great deal remains to be done toward a systematic catalog and a relatively full list of subject headings, the project continues now on a steady, routine basis. Besides widening the scope of the available headings as quickly as possible, our special plans for the future are to gain more theoretical knowledge of LCSH and to take a more active part in the Cooperative Cataloging Project of the Library of Congress. We are happy to work out the concept and the practice of cooperation with any libraries wishing to join this project.

Table 22.5 Illustrative MARC Authority Record

```
000    00189nz  2200085n 4504
001    autKLT00000051
005    19970905130744.0
008    940609nn acnnnbabn      un aaa   d
150 0  $aSemantics.
450 0  $aFormal semantics.
450 0  $aSemasiology.
450 0  $aSemiology (Semantics).
550 0  $wg$aComparative liguistics.
550 0  $wg$aInformation theory.
550 0  $wg$aLanguage and languages.
550 0  $wg$aLexicology.
550 0  $wg$aMeaning (Psychology)
550 0  $wg$aAmbiguity
550 0  $wh$aAntonyms
550 0  $wh$aCollocation (Linguistics)
550 0  $wh$aComponential analysis (Linguistics)
550 0  $wh$aComponential analysis in anthropology
550 0  $wh$aConnotation (Linguistics)
550 0  $wh$aDefinition (Logic)
550 0  $wh$aDiscourse analysis
550 0  $wh$aEmphasis (Linguistics)
550 0  $wh$aField theory (Linguistics)
550 0  $wh$aFormal languages$xSemantics
550 0  $wh$aGrammar, Comparative and general$xGrammaticalization
550 0  $wh$aHeteronyms
550 0  $wh$aHomonyms
550 0  $wh$aIdioms.
550 0  $wh$aLanguage and logic
550 0  $wh$aOnomasiology
550 0  $wh$aParaphrase
550 0  $wh$aPhraseology
550 0  $wh$aPlay on words
550 0  $wh$aPolysemy
550 0  $wh$aReference (Linguistics)
550 0  $wh$aSemantic differential technique
550 0  $wh$aSemiotics.
550 0  $wh$aSublanguage
550 0  $wh$aSynonyms
690    $aKK
999    $acatie


000    00229nz  2200133n 4504
001    autKLT00098407
005    19970905121243.0
008    951106nn acnnnbabn      un aaa   d
040    $aHuDeKLEK
080    $a801.54
150 4  $aSzemantika
450 4  $aFormális szemantika
450 4  $aSzemasziológia
```

Table 22.5 (*Continued*)

450	4	$aSzemiológia (szemantika)
550	4	wgaÖsszehasonlító nyelvészet
550	4	wgaInformációelmélet
550	4	wgaNyelv és nyelvek
550	4	wgaLexikológia
550	4	wgaJelentés (pszichológia)
550	4	whaKétértelműség
550	4	whaSzemiotika
550	4	whaSzövegtan
550	4	whaMezőelmélet
550	4	whaFormális nyelvek$xszemantika
550	4	whaNyelvtan, összehasonlító és általános$xgrammatikalizáció
550	4	whaNyelv és logika
550	4	whaSzójátékok
550	4	whaReferencia (nyelvészet)
750	0	$aSemantics
999		$acatie

Table 22.6 Illustrative MARC Authority Record

000		00229nz 2200133n 4504
001		autKLT00090980
005		19950907153924.0
008		950907nn acnnnbabn un aaa d
040		$aHuDeKLEK
150	0	$aGeology, Stratigraphic.
450	0	$aAge of rocks
450	0	$aRocks$xAge.
450	0	$aStratigraphic geology.
550	0	wgaPhysical geology
690		$aHM, KK
999		$acatie

000		00229nz 2200133n 4504
001		autKLT00090971
005		19960129161715.0
008		950907nn acnnnaabn un aaa d
040		$aHuDeKLEK
080		$a551.7
150	4	$aGeológia, rétegtani
450	4	$aRétegtan (geológia)
450	4	$aKőzetek kora
450	4	$aFöldtörténet
550	4	wgaFizikai geológia
690		$aHM, KK
750	0	$aGeology, Stratigraphic.
999	0	$acatie

000		00229nz 2200133n 4504
001		autKLT00110956

Table 22.6 (*Continued*)

005	19960329100655.0	
008	960215nn acnnnbabn un aaa d	
040	$aHuDeKLEK	
150	0	$aPoetry$xExplication.
690	$aBI	
999	$acatie	

000	00229nz 2200133n 4504	
001	autKLT00110957	
005	19960329100425.0	
008	960215nn acnnnbabn un aaa d	
040	$aHuDeKLEK	
150	4	$aKöltészet$xmagyarázat
450	4	$aVerselemzések
690	$aBI, KK	
750	0	$aPoetry$xExplication.
999	$acatie	

CHAPTER 23

Integrating Internet Resources into the Library Catalog

PÉTER GYÜRE

In the late 1980s, providing remote access to OPACs was the only way library systems used the Internet. Today, WWW services are considered by many to be equivalent to the Internet, and earlier solutions, like the telnet interface to databases, seem outdated. How could libraries, in competition with Internet content services, preserve the dominance that they had previously achieved with their on-line catalogs? One way is to catalog publicly available Internet services in the library catalog, and to provide library users with this information. When public Internet terminals become available in the library, users normally must discover the Internet on their own. This way of hunting for information is not as efficient and straightforward as using an OPAC. Though they are heavily used and popular, Internet search facilities are not as sophisticated as OPACs. Internet search engines often yield inappropriate results when one searches by keywords. Libraries, the mission of which is to provide easy access to well-structured information regardless of media type, cannot be content with such a situation. The solution for them is simple: Put the uniform resource locators (URLs) of Internet resources into library catalogs, and make these links "hot." If we store the URLs in addition to the usual metadata in bibliographic records, and enter subject headings as well, the Internet services provided by the library catalog can compete with those of popular Internet search services in terms of professional standards. Libraries, on the other hand, have to take the leadership in solving the problems caused by the ephemeral nature of URLs and should provide reliable, long-term access to information. Internet resources resemble conventional information sources in many respects; they all have the title, author or corporate author, issue date, place of publication, and publisher. The comparison is even more obvious in the case of electronic journals. Similarity allows librarians to catalog Internet resources and make them available through their OPAC. This chapter presents the technical possibilities of cataloging Internet resources, refers to appropriate standards and recommendations, and mentions the related problems through real applications: the ephemeral nature of URLs, acquisition policies concerning Internet documents, structuring resources, and handling multimedia capabilities. (5, 7)

Internet Search Engines versus OPACs

The first question is whether there is any reason for dealing with Internet resource cataloging and whether there is a place for OPAC-based Internet search. In a recent study, Taylor and Clemson try to answer a similar question and outline the advantages and drawbacks of Internet search engines (3)—we can add to their list of weaknesses:

- There is slow access for heavily used search engines.
- There are outdated—"blind"—links.
- Language specification can be wrong.
- There are no browsing capabilities by title, author, or subject (which is related to the point, discussed by Taylor and Clemson, that the vocabulary that search engines use is not "controlled."
- Subject and author entries have no structure and there are no links between them.
- They do not cover any subject area in its entirety.
- Document formats are totally different and many of them can be viewed by separate helper applications.

Most of these problems can be efficiently solved with proprietary or webbed OPAC interfaces. Searches are carried out locally within the campus, which ensures speedy access time. Links can and must be locally controlled, either by systematic checking or by using persistent URLs (PURLs) (6). In library catalogs, language specification and metadata are given more attention. Browsing capabilities are ensured in OPACs, more often together with "see" or "see also" references and sometimes with links to broader and narrower subject headings. The subject coverage of a catalog or a collection depends on the library's acquisition policy. Cataloging Internet resources ensures their seamless integration into the library's holdings as browsers can be configured to show all cataloged document types together.

Technology

The basic technology of using Internet resources in library catalogs is well defined. The two key issues are addressing technology and storage technology. Addressing technology is based on the URL, which is the de facto standard of the Internet document-addressing scheme. A URL consists of four parts: the protocol identifier, the Internet name or address of the servicing host, the optional port number, and the access path name. A URL is unambiguous, and always describes one, and only one, resource. Storing technology has its foundation in the USMARC standard. The USMARC bibliographic format allows us to record not only bibliographic descriptions of Internet documents, but also their location, access, and usage information. How and where to store individual URLs in MARC records is very well standardized. It uses tag 856, subfield "u," for the purpose of storing a URL related to the document. While other parts of the MARC record store other metadata, it was an obvious step to put URLs into the same structure. The name of the 856 tag is "Electronic Location and Access" and it can store other metadata besides URLs. A full description of field 856 can be found in Olson (1). A whole MARC record of an Internet resource is shown in table 23.1 as an example of the standard.

Table 23.1. Tagged MARC Record of the First Hungarian Internet Magazine

000		00424nas 2200289 4504
001		bibKLT00075411
005		19960404105033.0
008		c19959999hu w p 0uuu 0hun d
020		$a1219-4263
040		$aHuDeKLEK
245	00	$aInternetto$h[computer file]
260		$aBudapest :$bIDG Lapkiadó KFT,$c[1995-]
300		$bill.
310		$aweekly
362		$aVol. 1. No. 1. (July 1995)
500		$aTitle from screen
516		$aMultimedia electronic magazin
538		$aAccess: World Wide Web
710	2	$aIDG Magyarországi Lapkiadó Kft. (Budapest)
856	7	$2http$zMultimedia electronic magazin $uhttp://www.idg.hu/internetto/
949		$lIR

USMARC tags can have special content or can use additional subfields for describing Internet resources, such as the "h" subfield of tag 245, shown in the table. Another important advantage of using MARC records for describing and locating Internet resources is that the records can participate in the customary record exchange flow—they can be imported into any standard system and, thus, the documents once described can become a virtual part of any library collection. The records do not require any modification while they are moving across various systems, because the URL can be retrieved from any place in the world. The display format of exchanged records is locally configurable within the local system's framework.

The Internet documents described in standard USMARC records, with their related URLs, can be indexed and retrieved with the libraries' own user interface, its OPAC. Users can read the related URL on the screen, can write it down, and type it into a Web browser's navigating window. The connection between a retrieved MARC record and the Internet document can be created more efficiently and transparently if the URL stored in the records is "clickable," that is, it can be retrieved by pressing a button in the search window of the OPAC. Such an OPAC service is called a "hot link." Using hot links gives several advantages over manually copying URLs. It is faster, users have no chance to mistype the occasionally long and complex URLs, and it is more convenient. An OPAC interface must be window based to be able to use hot links. Without a windowing system, switching between the OPAC and browser would not be easy. Moreover, the windowing system must be graphical, because most of the electronic documents cannot be viewed in text format with browsers like Lynx. The ideal system for this purpose is based on a graphical user interface (GUI). Hot links have a natural domain in HTML pages. Indeed, hot links can be implemented in a very simple and natural way in webbed search interfaces, as the following case studies will show. The method described here gives a seamless integration of different media types into the library catalog and patrons can retrieve bibliographic information on books, articles, and electronic documents in the same way, regardless of media type.

Case Studies

Several projects for cataloging electronic or Internet documents are based on the MARC 856 tag (2). In the Internet Cataloging Project of OCLC, libraries have been asked to join and to contribute USMARC records of electronic resources. OCLC maintains the database of the records and provides a web search interface with hot links. The project was finished in March 1996. A more recent project, "WebDoc,"[2] runs under the leadership of PICA (Project for Integrated Catalogue Automation). The core of the WebDoc service is a centrally available catalog of electronically stored documents, called WebCAT, hosted at the central machine of the PICA in Louvain. The participating libraries contribute title descriptions and abstracts of journal articles and other material to the central catalog of electronic publications. Dutch and German libraries participate, and two publishers are involved as well, Academic Press and Kluwer Academic Publishers. The database is not open to the public, and charging and access control subsystems have been introduced.

Cataloging Internet Resources at the Lajos Kossuth University Library, Debrecen. The library staff is committed to using the Internet. Since the library system is based on USMARC records, it was plausible to experiment with cataloging electronic documents as well. A pilot project started in 1995–1996 because of general interest in the technology and the relative cheapness of Internet resources. The project resulted in the creation of several hundred reference-type electronic documents in the library collection.

The Electronic Version of Scientific Articles in Debrecen. The library has subscribed to Elsevier's electronic journals and, accordingly, receives several CDs per month along with articles and table of contents. Articles are in the ASCII, PDF, and TIFF formats and the tables of contents are in an SGML document. Elsevier has its own technology for making these documents available, but our library has decided to develop a new interface and integrate it into the OPAC. We are providing our users with two interfaces, of which one has the well-known hierarchical structure, while the other is the OPAC. In the hierarchical model, users can select a journal title from the sorted list and check the collected volumes and numbers. Issues of each number are highlighted, and can be clicked. Up to this point, we are using static HTML pages—one main page for the journal's list and one individual page for each journal. After one selects the required issue, the table of contents appears on the screen. Titles are highlighted as links to articles. After one selects the required article, a dynamic page displays in the browser's window with navigating and controlling buttons. On this page, users encounter pages generated by JavaScript. Users can see the standard information about the article (title,

1. http://www.oclc.org/oclc/catproj/overview.html
2. http://www.pica.nl/cgi-bin/wwwdoc.en

author, affiliation, abstract, language). Two different display formats can be chosen: ASCII or PDF. When ASCII is chosen, navigation is provided by forward and back buttons, and first page/last page buttons. The exact page number can also be chosen. When the PDF format is preferred, a helper application is started (Adobe Acrobat), and navigation is done through this program. Both Netscape and Acrobat provide printing facilities; hence printouts can be initiated from any workstations. The other search interface is the OPAC. USMARC records of the articles are automatically generated from the SGML document. The URL placed into the 856 tag of the USMARC record is the same as the URL of the article's JavaScript page mentioned above. These USMARC records are indexed into the database of electronic articles. If a user chooses this database from the OPAC, all the usual search facilities are available. Keyword and browse searches, the sorting of results, and the display of records are done through any OPAC interface (standard XWindow, Z39.50, ASCII, or webbed). When the user selects an article through the OPAC, the article is displayed by following the hot link. From this point, the navigation and display options are the same as described above. Access to the database is restricted to the campuses of the Debrecen Universitas. The document server checks the client's Internet address for validity.

The Audio CD Collection of the KLTE Library. As a special collection, the Audio CDs of the library have great importance. The Audio CDs are a part of our deposit collection that is supplied as legal deposit copies from the publishers. While searching and browsing in an audio collection, the detailed description of the individual music items and performers on a CD has special importance. USMARC allows a very detailed description of individual items, and the sophisticated search and indexing systems use a highly segmented data structure. For better use of the multimedia capabilities of the library system, the library decided to store and serve related multimedia objects for this collection. These include digitized audio segments and pictures related to the audio material (such as portraits of musicians, cover pages).[3]

As table 23.2 shows, all related multimedia objects are attached through a single URL. The CGI[4] program is called with only one parameter, the bar code of the item. The program retrieves the related objects, and creates an HTML page with additional information, such as the title, copyright, and links to the objects. Then this HTML page is displayed in the Web browser. Using this mechanism, catalogers are no longer responsible for filling in the 856 field. Instead, they provide a list of bar codes and documents. The list contains bar-code and document links, stating which part of the document must be digitized. Then digitizing staff digitizes the different media types on the basis of the instructions. They store the documents in the following way: Digitized documents are put into a directory, the name of which is equal to the first three characters of the bar code. Audio files get the extension ".au" while images are in the JPEG format with the ".jpg" extension. If more than one file with the same name is created, an additional distinctive number is put at the end as an extension to ensure

---

3. The cataloging and digitizing project is financially supported by the Library College Fund for Hungarian Culture.

4. Common gateway interface — the standard way of using search engines through HTML pages.

Table 23.2. Tagged MARC Record of an Audio CD from the Collection of the KLTE Library

000		01525njm 2200301 4504
001		bibKLT00021705
005		19970212140009.0
008		1992 xx nn 1 hun
020		$c1100.- Ft
028	0	$aQUI 903021$bQuintana - Harmonia Mundi
040		$aHuDeKLEK
041		$bhunengfreger
048	00	$aka
080		$a782.9.088:786.24$a786.24$a785.16.088:786.24
100	1	$aBartók Béla$d(1881-1945)
245	12	$aA csodálatos mandarin :$bNégykezes szerzői átiratok /$h[Hgf.] $cBartók
260		$a[Bp.] :$bQuintana - Harmonia Mundi,$c1992.
300		$a1 CD :$c12 cm +$emelléklet
306		$a(50 min 31 s)
505	00	$g1.$tA csodálatos mandarin (Pantomim egy felvonásban) = Le mandarin merveilleux = The miraculous mandarin : Négykezes szerzői átirat /$rBartók Béla +$g2.$tElső kamaraszimfónia Op.9 = Premiere symphonie de chambre = Erste Kammersinfonie (1906) : Négykezes szerzői átirat /$aArnold Schönberg
511	2	$aZoltán Kocsis (piano)$aAdrienne Hauser (piano)
500		$aA melléklet Wilhelm András ismertetőjét angol és német nyelven közli. A lemez a művek első hangfelvétele. (World premiere recording.)
695		$azongoraművek
695		$akamarazene - duó (zg.) - négykezes
700	1	$aSchönberg, Arnold$d(1874-1951)
700	1	$aKocsis Zoltán$d(1952-)$c(zongoraművész)
700	1	$aHauser Adrienne$c(zongoraművész)
856	7	$2http$zA CD borítója és zenei motívum$uhttp://www.lib.klte.hu/voyager/mc/mc.cgi?00132022
949		$aK.HCD 13160$lD1/Ztkhz00132022

uniqueness. When the staff has saved the related digital objects, the files are processed by a maintenance program. First, it creates thumbnails of images with an additional extension ".small." It then retrieves the records from the database, creates the corresponding 856 tags in the MARC records, and updates them. When the retrieving program (mc.cgi, where mc stands for music collection) is called with a bar code as an argument, it reads the image thumbnails and creates an HTML document that displays the thumbnails, and a violin clef for digitized media. Upon the clicking of the thumbnails or sound signs, the corresponding object loads or plays.

Implementation Issues

Launching viewers.   Webbed OPACs can follow hot links in the natural way, simply changing the context from the displayed bibliography to the document itself. When a nonwebbed OPAC uses hot links, a browser application must be launched every time the hot link is activated. Launching a new image of the viewer application for each document is not the way to conserve system resources, which is an important issue in multiuser UNIX environments. Therefore, we are using a well-configured Netscape browser as a general viewer and launching is done by controlling the already-running application. This means that if Netscape is already running on the user's screen, the running application is instructed to load the new URL, instead of starting a new one. A well-configured browser means that if a document type cannot be viewed through Netscape, a helper application is launched and used. Examples of such helper applications are a PDF viewer, an image viewer, or a Word document viewer. This setup conserves more system resources and keeps user screens as simple as possible.

More 856 Tags. Tag 856 is a repeatable field, which means that more than one instance of the tag can be in a MARC record. Multiple URLs can be used for a single document for several reasons. A document can have more than one related digital object. If there is only one related object (the document itself, for instance), it may have more than one access point through mirror sites. In these cases it may not be very clear how to deal with multiple URLs for a single document. Web interfaces can highlight all links but proprietary interfaces could not handle them in such a natural way. One solution is for one central HTML page to store all links, and only this page is linked into the record. This page should not necessarily be static or precompiled but may be dynamically created (see tables 23.1 and 23.2). This approach has the advantage that if, later, any extension or change is performed on those linked documents, the MARC records do not require a modification. This is very important if records participate in record exchange programs.

The "Moving Target" Problem. When we create search systems for Internet documents, we face the problem of a rapidly changing Internet world with ever newer services. Unfortunately, the URLs of services can change or services and locations can disappear. This phenomenon threatens the traditional reliability of libraries. Once they start cataloging Internet documents, catalogers have to take special care to keep their URLs up-to-date, if they want to live up to one of their most important responsibilities, that of providing access to their cataloged documents. For catalogers, checking and refreshing cataloged URLs would be extraordinary work. This problem does concern not only libraries; It does concern all Web indexing services as well, and thus there must be a more general solution. This could be either the new URN standard,[5] or the OCLC's PURL initiative (4). As of now, only PURL is available and should be used for the cataloged resource so long as it is available.[6] Fortunately, as every PURL is an URL, this requires no modification in networking technologies and applications. Where PURLs are not available, automatic consistency checkers could be implemented, with the task of regularly checking the availability of stored URLs, and of modifying (removing) records or, at least, notifying the staff in cases of unavailability.

Conclusions and Possible Enhancements

The most difficult process in Internet resource cataloging is record creation itself. Conventional documents can be more easily cataloged, because MARC records them-

---

5. Uniform resource name — a more stable and persistent version of URL.
6. See http://purl.oclc.org/OCLC/PURL/FAQ for PURL details.

selves are very available from several different sources and conventional access information is normally easier to read and type than URLs are. Sometimes, improvement techniques are also used when conventional documents are cataloged—the bar code, call number, and inventory number are the same and are read from preprinted tickets; shelf locations are simple abbreviations. These techniques cannot be used with electronic documents, because URLs must be typed and stored in their entirety. In cases of electronic documents, other parts of the record—for example, subject headings—are placed into the records the same way. There could be a closer integration between browsers and catalogers' screens, similar to the integration between browsers and OPACs. Today's library systems use hot links in the OPAC for facilitating the retrieval of documents. There should be a way of inserting URLs of retrieved resources into the MARC record, too. Graphical user interfaces provide an easy way of copying text through the cut-and-paste functions. Along with this, browsers could contain a function for generating prototypical USMARC records of HTML documents. Using favorite metatags, the titles, keywords, authors, dates, and much other information can be extracted as a skeleton. URL itself should be placed into tag 865, subfield "u." This kind of environment could greatly improve the creation of MARC records.

One may ask whether the cataloging of Internet resources needs the use of MARC records. Of course, MARC records are the handy solution for librarians, but users are not interested in storage or exchange record structures. The creation of MARC records is expensive and requires human intervention. Most of the Internet search engines choose another solution: They use automatic indexers (robots), they use very few metaelements, and process large volumes of documents with no selectivity and intervention.

Fortunately, there is an integrating element between the two methods. The OCLC/NCSA Metadata Workshop in March 1995 proposed a minimal set of metadata elements that is called "The Dublin Core."[7] This set consists of 13 elements, and uses no subfields. Those elements include the following: subject, title, author, publisher, other agents, date, object type, form, identifier, relation, source, language, and coverage. According to the proposal, a minimal MARC record and HTML (or any SGML) documents with the suitable metatags could be used. HTML has the advantage that the document and the metadata are inserted into one document and use the same structure; thus, there is no further need for separate surrogate records (6). This advantage cannot be exploited if the library decides to put both electronic and conventional documents into the same catalog, since separate metadata-only records are always required for nonelectronic documents. But SGML (HTML) documents corresponding to the Dublin Core can be automatically mapped to MARC records. With only a small chance of completely eliminating human intervention, this method should be implemented in the cataloging facilities of library systems so as to improve the cataloging process for electronic documents.

The main reason why cataloging electronic documents is justified, and can prove more useful than any automated process, is that the library can adapt its general ac-

---

7. http://www.oclc.org:5046/conferences/metadata/dublin_core_report.html for details.

quisitions policy to the selection of Internet resources. If libraries are selecting and cataloging Internet resources as responsibly as conventional documents, they can virtually extend their shelves for their patrons' satisfaction.

References

1. Olson, Nancy B. *Cataloging Internet Resources: A Manual and Practical Guide*. OCLC Inc., Dublin, OH, 1995.
2. "Cornell Guidelines for the Use of Field 856," http://www.library.cornell.edu/tsmanual/guide856/index.html.
3. Taylor, Arlene G. and Patrice Clemson. *Access to Networked Documents—Catalogues? Search Engines? Both?* Proceedings of the OCLC Internet Cataloging Colloquim, 1966, http://www.oclc.org/oclc/man/colloq/taylor.htm.
4. Morgan, Eric Lease. "Adding Internet resources to our OPACs." *Serials Review* 21, no. 4 (Winter 1995).
5. Gyüre, Peter. "Internet in the library system." Debrecen: NETWORKSHOP '96 Conference Proceedings, 1996.
6. Shafer, Keith, Stuart Weibel, Erik Jul, and Jon Fausey. *Introduction to Persistent Uniform Resource Locators*. OCLC, Inc., Dublin, OH 1996.
7. Husby, Ole. "Interfacing Libraries to the Net—Achievements and Standards", 15th NORDUnet Conference, Copenhagen, Nov. 14–16, 1995.

CHAPTER 24

Knowledge and Information Processing

TIBOR CSÍK AND KATALIN VARGA

> ΠΑΝΤΕΣ ΑΝΘΡΩΠΟΙ ΤΟΥ ΕΙΔΕΝΑΙ ΟΡΕΓΟΝΤΑΙ ΦΘΣΕΙ;
> ΣΗΜΕΙΟΝ Δ Η ΤΩΝ ΑΙΣΘΗΣΕΩΝ ΑΓΑΠΗΣΙΣ.
> —Aristotle, "Methaphysics"

We live in an information era. Information is a most popular commodity, and its circulation, processing, and dissemination are economically important businesses. Storing and processing information and gaining access to it are diminishing problems, thanks to the new technologies (cheap devices with great storage capacities, and increasingly common information skills). However, there is a growing problem of obtaining the relevant information.

The exponential growth of information, and new possibilities provided by computers, have changed not only knowledge representation but also information-seeking habits as well. Today's users need fast, precise, and specific information about publications available on a given topic. The places where they can find this are the on-line databases. Libraries are primarily required to collect and disseminate documents, but information about them comes from databases. The majority of these are very discipline oriented. If we look at the offerings of the main database vendors (DIALOG, DATASTAR, BRS, the European Space Agency), it is surprising to see the extent to which they are increasing in volume and their degree of specialization.

Knowledge-Representation Tools

The tools used today for knowledge representation were born in the nineteenth century. Two strands can be distinguished:

- Classification systems that are based on the division of the sciences:
  - Behind the separate branches of knowledge is the taxonomy of the sciences. Its basis can be for example, philosophy, "generally accepted" practice.

We would like to thank our teachers, Dr. Tibor Horváth and Mrs. Márta Környey, for their help and inspiration.

- The division of knowledge is based on logical principles: genus-species or whole-part relations. The significant aspect, which is the basis of the division (differentia essentialis), is relative. Classification criteria form a hierarchy.
- Codes are assigned to the criteria, showing their places in the hierarchy.

- Natural language indexing systems:

  - An unambiguous notation of the criteria is a key—ambiguities caused by the colorfulness of language must be eliminated (for example, homonyms, synonyms).
  - The principle of specificity—the uniqueness of the subject must be reflected.
  - To find similar subjects is secondary as compared to specificity—the use of cross-references is the solution. The suggested references are downward references (from generic to specific); upward references are allowed only in certain cases.

Classification and indexing coexist even today. This coexistence means some interdependence and they have to complement each other. The main role of classification is to generically place the subjects inside the disciplines (as is the practice in the United States), which endows a shelving system with character. Indexing serves the description of the individual subject criteria.

Library catalogs still use mainly one or two classifications and one indexing system (Library of Congress Subject Headings, Dewey Decimal Classification, Library of Congress Classification Codes). At the same time, the available subject access tools in discipline-oriented databases are numerous, and they form whole systems.

Knowledge Representation and Databases

The databases process well-distinguished knowledge areas. Special literature requires the representation of uniqueness. Databases apply subject-representation tools, which are able to cover a given discipline and/or group of documents. The representation of the information elements, which are outside the purview of the database, is also determined by the primary aspect. As we get further from the focus, the effectiveness and specificity of the representation are decreasing. Different databases use different information retrieval tools, but the concordance among them is an open issue. In a given field or discipline, subject representation is determined by the three factors shown in figure 24.1.

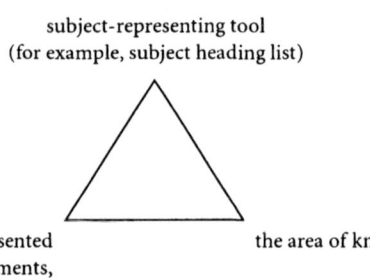

Figure 24.1 Three Factors That Determine Subject Representation

Knowledge and Information Processing 295

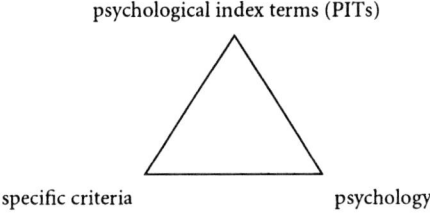

Figure 24.2 Database Criteria

The three factors have to be in harmony for effective subject representation; thus, in a reference database—for example, *Psychological Abstracts*—the natural language-representation tool has to refer to the criteria shown in figure 24.2.

Together, Terms of the thesaurus (PITs) and the relations among them have to fulfill the requirement in order that we can provide specific criteria in the field of psychology. Terms and their relations can be derived from the objective of the representation and the relevant knowledge. Though the list of PITs contains several terms related to education, these terms and their relations differ from an educational vocabulary. With them the representation of the education-related information would not be so effective.

Research Problem. In our survey, we examined, in a sample group of databases, all the fields and other tools used for representing any kind of subject element of the database. Our objective was to discover the existing solutions used for knowledge representation. We were especially interested in the question of how the biggest and most important on-line databases available use the existing tools for subject representation.

Every single criterion and category that represent the subject of the record in any way—beyond the identification of the object (author, title, publication data)—are taken into consideration. Thus, all fields that use any kind of classification or indexing system, all that have a preference for, or separate, one subject element (for example, the named person, human subject, document type), and all other elements that give additional information about the content (for example, weighting, qualifiers, subheadings) are examined. In the case in which a criterion is expressed in more than one way (with a code and natural language), we considered it to be two criteria, if one

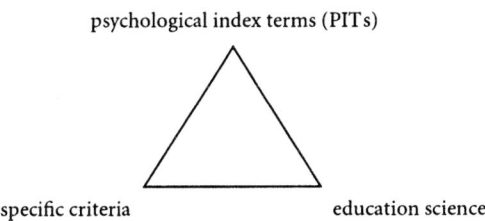

Figure 24.3 Database Criteria

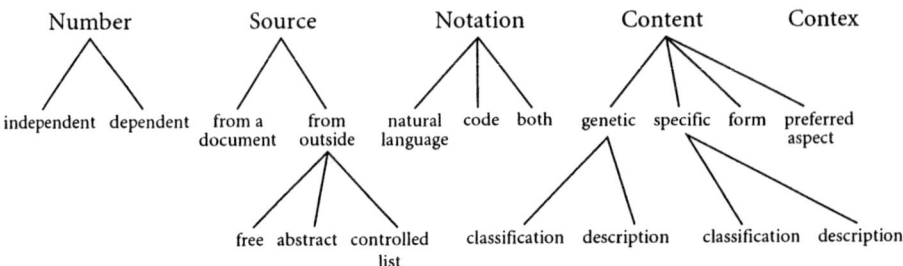

Figure 24.4 Survey Aspects

notation gives additional information. We examined the types of these subject-representing criteria, how they are expressed, their notation, where they are taken from (for example, free terms, controlled vocabularies), their characteristics (generic or specific), and how they represent the context of the document. Figure 24.4 shows the aspects we applied in the survey:

The Sample. Fifty databases were selected, with most of them available in DIALOG or DATASTAR. All significant subject areas and sciences are represented. We also tried to be international, selecting databases not only from the United States but also from different European countries and Japan. These databases provide answers for different information demands. The fifty databases can be divided into five broader groups. The objects and the knowledge area determine the applied subject-representation tools. The five groups are the following (for the complete list of the databases see appendix 24.1).

1. Directories, data banks
   - Objects to be represented: companies, enterprises, persons
   - Knowledge area: business facts
2. General bibliographies
   - Objects to be represented: general information incorporated into a definite document type
   - Knowledge area: general
3. Reference databases in the field of hard sciences
   - Objects to be represented: specific information in a given group of documents
   - Knowledge area: discipline oriented (hard sciences)
4. Reference databases in the field of soft sciences (social sciences and humanities)
   - Objects to be represented: specific information in a given group of documents
   - Knowledge area: discipline oriented (soft sciences)
5. Full-text databases—journals
   - Objects to be represented: the most specific information in one given document or in parts of it.
   - Knowledge area: selected published information (the selection was based on quantitative and qualitative criteria)—general

Research Methodology. The subject representing criteria can be examined from different perspectives (see Figure 24.4), and these give the main line of the research.

We counted how many criteria are found in one database which refer to the aspects. This kind of statistical analysis results in tables (these are available from the authors on request) that show the division of the different aspects among the databases. Further conclusions can be drawn from these numbers.

Summary of the Research

Number of Subject-Representing Criteria. Every element that gives information about content constitutes a separate criterion. The criteria may be independent ones, relating to the whole record, permitting separate searches (for example, descriptors, classification codes, section headings, preferred subject criteria, document types, treatment codes), or they may be dependent on other criteria—that is, modifying their meaning or giving additional information about the actual context (for example, weighting, qualifiers, subheadings). In the directories and data banks, subject-representation elements are a little different, and are often numeric (for example, products, geographical area, employees, sales).

Among subject-representing criteria, we counted the abstracts but not the full texts. If the database makes it possible to search some fields separately and also together (for example, DE(drug), DE(medical), DE(all)), we counted only the separate fields, not the common one (DE(drug), DE(medical)). In some cases, the same category is denoted by natural language and by codes or abbreviations. They count separately only if the notation indicates the system (for example, section headings and section heading codes are separate criteria, but document types and their abbreviations are not).

The tendency in current databases is toward a strong segmentation of the subject-representing criteria. The bigger a database is and the more current the information needs it observes, the more subject-representing criteria it uses. Ten or more criteria are not unusual. The average number of criteria in the different groups is instructive: group 1, 9.25; group 2, 5; group 3, 9.27; group 4, 5.92; group 5, 6.42. Subject representation is strongly discipline oriented.

Directories and data banks use relatively large numbers of criteria—which means a very detailed subject representation. These criteria are all independent ones—which emerges from the database characteristics. Only bibliographic databases have to deal with the problem of how to express that part of the information which is hidden in the context of the original document. The hard sciences use the most dependent criteria (mainly qualifiers and role indicators). It is here that the average number of criteria is the largest, and that the information needs are the most sophisticated General databases use the fewest number of criteria, and their subject representation is more generic.

Source of the Criteria (see table 24.2). Subject-representing criteria can be taken directly from a document (for example, lead paragraphs, a keyword in the title), or from outside the document. Criteria taken from outside can be controlled or free terms. For controlled terms, databases use different controlled vocabularies, thesauri, or authority lists. Abstracts are also among the outside criteria. The document as a source of the criteria is relevant only in the bibliographic databases. That is why in group 1, only the controlled-vocabulary column is filled. If a database uses codes and natural-language

Table 24.1 Number of criteria

Name	No. of criteria	independent	not independent
ABCE	7	7	
CZCO	7	7	
D & B	13	13	
Disclosure	20	20	
GDDB	5	5	
The McGraw-Hill Companies	5	5	
PLCO	7	7	
WWEB	10	10	
Current Contents Search	7	7	
Dissertation Abstracts Online	3	3	
WTI	5	5	
ABI/Inform	8	8	
Agricola	10	10	
BIOSIS	10	9	1
CAB	9 (5)	9 (5)	
Chemical Abstracts	10	7	3
Compendex Plus	9	7	2
Derwent Drug File	10	8	2
Econlit	5	5	
EMBASE	16	13	3
Enviro/Energyline Abstracts	11	10	1
FSTA	6	6	
INSPEC	8 (11)	8 (10)	(1)
INON	8	8	
JICST	10	10	
MMKA	8	8	
MEDLINE	12	10	2
NTIS	5	4	1
Pascal	9	9	
RILA	8	7	1
Artbibliographies Modern	4	4	
ASSI	2	2	
CELEX	6	6	
ERIC	9	7	2
Historical Abstracts	3	3	
ISA	5	5	
LLBA	8	8	
LISA	5	5	
Pais International	4	3	1
Philosopher's Index	4	4	
Psychological Abstracts	11	10	1
Religion Index	6	6	
Sociological Abstracts	8	8	
AGEN	2	2	
AP News	3	3	
FAZA	12	9	3
FTEE	7	6	1
HBRO	8	7	1
Le Monde	5	5	
Los Angeles Times	8	7	1

Table 24.2 Source of the criteria

Name	From document	Criteria taken from outside the document		
		Free term	controlled list	abstract
ABCE			2	
CZCO			2	
D & B			1	
Disclosure				
GDDB				
The McGraw-Hill Companies Publications			1	
PLCO			2	
WWEB				
Current Contents Search		2	4	1
Dissertation Abstracts Online			1	1
World Translations Index		3	1	
ABI/Inform	1	2	3	1
Agricola		3	5	1
BIOSIS		1	6	1
CAB		1	5	1
Chemical Abstracts		1	7	
Compendex Plus		1	4	1
Derwent Drug File			6	2
Econlit			3	1
EMBASE		2	8	1
Enviro/Energyline Abstracts	1	2	4	1
FSTA		1	3	1
INSPEC	1	1	7	1
INON	1	2	1	1
JICST		1	6	1
MMKA		3	3	1
MEDLINE	1	2	6	1
NTIS		1	2	1
Pascal		1	5	1
RILA		3	2	1
Artbibliographies Modern		1	2	1
ASSI		1		
CELEX		1	5	
ERIC		2	3	1
Historical Abstracts		1	1	1
ISA			3	1
LLBA		2	3	1
LISA		2	1	1
Pais International		1	1	1
Philosopher's Index		1	2	1
Psychological Abstracts	1	2	5	1
Religion Index		2	3	1
Sociological Abstracts		2	3	1
AGEN			1	1
AP News	2		1	
FAZA		1	4	
FTEE		3	5	
HBRO		5	2	1
Le Monde	2	2	1	
Los Angeles Times	3	3	1	

notations for one criterion, but both the codes and notations are taken from one list, it is counted as only one controlled list. There are relatively few criteria taken directly from the documents. But other fields, which serve as identifiers, also give subject information (for example, the title), and these fields can be searched in each database.

Our second table proves the significance of controlled vocabularies and authority lists in subject representation. Full-text and natural-language information retrieval would not make control unnecessary. The more specific a database, the more controlled lists it uses. The number of lists is the largest in the hard-science databases, where the most specific and precise information needs are served. In the soft sciences their number is smaller. Controlled lists may be applied even in full-text databases.

Notations. The next question in our survey was about how the different databases denote their subject-representation criteria. There are basically two kinds of notations available: natural-language notations or codes. Numerical data count as natural language. Quite often, the databases use two notations for the same element. Systematic codes make systematic searching possible. Behind the codes, there is the hierarchy, and a truncated search allows the searcher to step higher in this system. At the same time, natural-language expressions give direct information about the topic. In this case, although the two notations mean the same concept, the information transmitted by them is different (direct/indirect approach). If the code is simply another expression of the words, the codes are not counted in our tables. There are also elements that are not noted, for example, links, subheadings. But the notations of the weighting (for example, the asterisk) were counted by us as codes.

The role of natural language in subject representation is noticeably very strong. But at the same time that reference databases, especially in the hard sciences, are partial to codes, they often use two notations for the same criterion. In the soft sciences there are fewer codes.

The Content of the Subject-Representing Criteria. According to the concept system, covered by subject-representing criteria, they can be generic (covering broad subject categories) and specific (specifically denoting the topic). It is hard to decide where the limit is between the two, and only within the database can one decide which criteria are broader and which more specific. Both types can be classifications or descriptions of the subject. In the first case, the topic is assigned to one or more classes of a precoordinated classification system. In the second, the indexing tools are used to describe the topic mainly with natural-language expressions.

Besides classifications and subject descriptions, databases widely employ computer techniques to give preference to some elements and to label them with separate prefixes. These are separate aspects, criteria selected by their semantic meaning. The categories could be based on faceted analysis, but most often, practical considerations influence their selection. Examples of preferred subject criteria are named persons, geographic names, substance names, chemical names, and special features.

The same name can mean different content in various databases (for example, special features). The same category can be a classification system in one database and a preferred subject criterion in another, depending on a database's character. Directories of companies use the U.S. SIC codes for classifications, but in business journals the SIC codes function as preferred criteria used, only when relevant to the topic.

Table 24.3 Notations

Name	Nat. language or num. dates	Codes	Both
ABCE	6	1	
CZCO	2	3	2
D & B	9	4	4
Disclosure	12	8	
GDDB	5		
The McGraw-Hill Companies Publications	5		
PLCO	5	2	2
WWEB	10		
Current Contents Search	5	2	
Dissertation Abstracts Online	2	1	1
World Translations Index	4	1	
ABI/Inform	6	2	1
Agricola	8	2	1
BIOSIS	7	3	2
CAB	6	3	1
Chemical Abstracts	7	2	1
Compendex Plus	5	3	1
Derwent Drug File	6	4	1
Econlit	4	1	1
EMBASE	10	6	5
Enviro/Energyline Abstracts	9	3	1
FSTA	5	1	1
INSPEC	9	4	3
INON	5	2	2
JICST	7	2	
MMKA	7	1	1
MEDLINE	9	4	2
NTIS	3	2	
Pascal	5	3	
RILA	6	1	1
Artbibliographies Modern	4		
ASSI	2		
CELEX	4	1	
ERIC	6	3	1
Historical Abstracts	3		
ISA	4	1	1
LLBA	6	3	3
LISA	4	1	1
PAIS International	2	1	
Philosopher's Index	4		
Psychological Abstracts	8	3	1
Religion Index	6		
Sociological Abstracts	6	3	3
AGEN	2		
AP News	3		
FAZA	7	4	4
FTEE	5	1	
HBRO	8	1	
Le Monde	5		
Los Angeles Times	7		

The databases often separate the formal elements of documents: document types, article types, media types, target groups, and the intellectual level. These criteria specify the subject, so we counted them separately.

All databases lay emphasis on expressing the same topic with both generic and specific criteria. In generic subject categories, classifications and descriptions are equally used, but specific classifications are rarely applied. It is interesting that specific classifications are found only in some hard-science databases. These tools denote a specific topic, but at the same time they show it belonging to a class. For example, in Econlit the descriptors are expressed also by classification codes, but while codes show the systematic place of the topic, descriptors can be extended with more specific expressions:

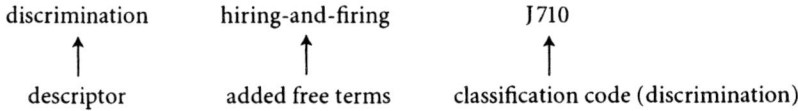

Directories and data banks favor preferred criteria and generic subject categories. In hard-science databases, specific descriptions and preferred criteria are the significant tools. Almost all apply both classification and description in generic subject categories. For the soft sciences, specific descriptions (descriptors, free terms, section headings) are the best tools for subject representation. Full-text databases do not apply classifications.

Connections between the Subject-Representing Criteria. Expression of the actual content of the document is the objective of every subject representation. This content has to be expressed not only by separate elements, but also by the connection between these elements, that is, by syntax. Terms in a context represent additional information, and the context itself is information. The last aspect of our survey focuses on how the original context of the terms can be reflected by the database tools.

The simplest way is to leave the natural-language context, the original context of the terms. This is used when abstracts or similar content-description tools are used. It is the most effective way for describing the real content, but natural-language problems make searching in the abstract a hard question. Another possibility is to emphasize the more important terms, those that represent the main subjects, by weighting them. This solution is quite widely used in bibliographic databases.tble 24.5

Some databases attach determinants to the terms. Determinants can be qualifiers or subheadings, which modify or specify the meaning of the term according to the actual context. There are generally usable determinants (for example, main headings, subheadings), where each term can be a determinant of another on the basis of the subject. Some qualifiers can be used only in special cases (for example, drug qualifiers, disease qualifiers), and thus they provide stronger specification. When using determinants, the databases mainly apply only two different criteria and deeper specification is not common. Determinants are applied in the sciences, but mainly in the hard sciences.

It is also possible to link those terms which relate to each other, and thus get closer to the natural-language-like expressions. It is interesting that full-text databases use this tool, though they also offer the full text.

Table 24.4 Content of the criteria

Name	Generic subject categories		Specific subject categories		Formal aspects	Preferred criteria
	Class.	Description	Class.	Description		
ABCE	1	1		1		4
CZCO	1	1				3
D & B	1	1		1		1
Disclosure	1			1		
GDDB		1			2	1
The McGraw-Hill Companies Publ.		1				4
PLCO	2	2				3
WWEB						10
Current Contents				2	3	
DISS		1				
WTI	1	1		1	1	
ABI/Inform	1	1		2	1	3
Agricola	1	1	1	2	2	1
BIOSIS	1	1		1	1	4
CAB	1	2		1	1	1
Chemical Abstracts	1	2		2	1	1
Compendex Plus	1	1		2	2	
Derwent Drug File	1	2		2		
Econlit			1	1	1	1
EMBASE	2	2	1	2	1	4
Enviro/Energyline	2	2		2	1	1
FSTA	1	2		1	1	
INSPEC	1	1		2	2	3
INON			1	1	1	2
JICST	1	1	1	2	3	1
MMKA	1	1		1	1	3
MEDLINE		1	1	2	1	3
NTIS	1			2		
Pascal	2	1		1	1	2
RILA	1	1		2	1	
Artbibliographies Modern				1	1	1
ASSI				1		
CELEX	1	1		1	1	2
ERIC				2	2	
Historical Abstracts				1	1	
ISA	1	1		1	1	
LLBA				2	1	
LISA	1	1		1		
Pais International				1	1	
Philosopher's Index				1	1	1
Psychol. Abstracts	1			3	1	2
Religion Index				1	1	3
Sociol. Abstracts	1	1		2	1	
AGEN				1		
AP News		1				1
FAZA		1				6
FTEE				1	1	4
HBRO				1	1	3
Le Monde		1		1	1	
Los Angeles Times		1		1	2	2

Table 24.5 Relation of the criteria

Name	Natural language context	Weighting	Determinants Generic	Determinants Specific	Role indicator	Link-syntax
Current Contents	1					
DISS	1					
WTI						
ABI/Inform	1					
Agricola	1					
BIOSIS	1	1				
CAB	1					
Chemical Abstracts			1	2		
Compendex Plus	1	1		1		
Derwent Drug File	2			2		1
Econlit	1			1		
EMBASE	1	1		2		
Enviro/Energyline	1	1				
FSTA	1					
INSPEC	1				1	
INON	1					
JICST	1					
MMKA	1					
MEDLINE	1	1		1		
NTIS	1	1				
Pascal	1					
RILA	1					1
Artbibl. Modern	1					
ASSI	1					
CELEX						
ERIC	1	2				
Historical Abstracts	1					
ISA	1					
LLBA	1					
LISA	1					
Pais International	1					1
Philosopher's Index	1					
Psychol. Abstracts	3	1				
Religion Index	1			1		
Sociol. Abstracts	1					
AGEN	1					
AP News	1					
FAZA						
FTEE						1
HBRO	1					
Le Monde	1					
Los Angeles Times	1			1		1

Search Engines. Computer-based databases offer further opportunities for subject-related information retrieval. These opportunities are available beyond the segmented data structure in the search engines. The segmentation of the data elements is possible only because during the search these segmented elements can be combined again. Contrary to what occurs with printed bibliographies, in databases several aspects can be handled at the same time. The existing search tools are the following:

- Computers can segment not only criteria but also phrases and words. It is possible to search for elements inside the criteria.
- Indexing methods also help in thematic searching. Content-bearing words and expressions are all indexed both by words and by phrases. Most of the databases also offer the opportunity to search for single words as terms and as parts of another expression. For example, DF (full descriptor), IF (full identifier), and FF (full term anywhere) are all single terms descriptors.
- The segmentation of data elements means that we can limit our search to criteria that are present in one given field or a group of fields. Basic indexes in all databases make subject retrieval easier.
- Traditional Boolean logic is still the most common form of combining the search elements. But in such segmented environments, simple Boolean searching is very noisy and it cannot give the desired relevant hits.
- Most database vendors offer a wide range of pseudo-Boolean operators, the so-called proximity operators. There are several levels of them, namely, elements (1) within one record—simple Boolean, (2) within one field, (3) within one sentence, (4) within one phrase, (5) adjacent to each other. The application of these search tools shows that information retrieval needs structures, not only segmented elements. With the help of them the original natural-language structure can be searched.
- With the help of truncation, full-text searching is much easier. It gives a solution for some language problems.

Answering the Challenges

Knowledge is changing, and information-representation tools have to follow these changes, answer the challenges. However, the databases, as organic systems, have some kind of inertia. New technology and the application of fast computers changes traditional indexing and classification. Some of their elements become stronger, some weaker.

Segmentation. The most evident impact of computerization on knowledge representation is found in the maximum segmentation of the data elements. Thanks to high-capacity computers, it is easy to separate information elements.

- First, disciplines are getting more segmented and there are more databases, covering smaller segments of the sciences. Expertise is needed to find the right databases.
- All the aspects of information and all types of data can be separated in a database. Effective usage of databases requires a perfect knowledge of their structure. From the point of view of subject representation, the database structures are strongly precoordinated. It is an additional problem that the database vendors provide databases in different formats and structures.

- Thanks to search engines (as noted previously), not only data types, but also words and expressions, can be segmented. Most databases allow one to search each element of a phrase, and some even permit one to find parts of words.

The question is where the limit of this segmentation is. How far can it go? What is the smallest part of the information-bearing element that can be separated, labeled, and made retrievable?[1] One thing is obvious: There is a limit to the segmentation.

Databases contain descriptions of documents. It seems that the basic unit of knowledge is the document. Subject-representing criteria also refer to the document. But in reality, in one document several knowledge units can be involved. The problem is how to define and how to represent these.

Control. Though the current trend is toward full-text databases and toward using the original text for information retrieval, our survey proves that there still exists a significant role for controlled lists and vocabularies. Users want fast and exhaustive information, but they want precise information as well. Without terminological control, this is not easy.

Beyond thesauri, databases use several lists in the different fields, such as those for document types, geographic names, and classification codes. The number of controlled lists is growing, but they no longer provide deep control. The majority of these lists are only for authority control and do not provide a systematic approach.

Classification. The hierarchy behind classification systems provides a kind of order. On the other hand, a hierarchy does not always mean subordination, but can also mean subsumption.

Equally, databases use descriptive indexing and systematic classifications. This shows that generic classification is still useful if it is combined with descriptive indexing; the representation of the topic is more sophisticated, and the two aspects can be combined in the search. It is also clear that traditional classification systems (for example, DDC, UDC, LC) are not applied in large databases, which use their own systems instead.

Databases with strong conventions have to carry their traditions within themselves. Most of them have a printed version, and the system of the printed version serves as a generic classification in the on-line one.

Context. Users are looking not for single words or expressions but for whole topics, where the words or concepts are in some relation to each other. Leading databases are aware of this requirement. Natural-language abstracts are not sufficient; we also need controlled vocabulary terms that form some kind of context. The most common tools are the weighting of the most significant terms, and the applying of determinants that qualify or modify the meaning of the term. The combination of two terms as a main heading and a subheading is also quite widely used. Role operators should have the same function, though they are very rarely applied.

Isolation and combination are the two basic processes that currently characterize

---

1. According to the present stage of linguistic research, morphemes are the smallest elements that convey information.

information retrieval. Subject-representation tools provide the regulation of the semantic space. Traditional classification systems and precoordinated subject-heading lists have reached their limits and the demand now is to regain the context of subject elements as it exists in the document. Some local solutions can be found for reflecting syntactic relations between isolated elements in discipline-oriented databases (links, subheadings, role indicators, qualifiers). Extending these possibilities, and finding general ways for regulating the syntactic space, could be the next steps toward enhanced knowledge representation.

The question is whether there are any general solutions for the representation of the actual context, the syntax. Powerful research is attempting to find such a general solution. But general syntax does not exist, only theories. According to Foskett, the two basic types of syntax reflection (1) provide the fact that a relationship exists, without specifying it, and (2) define the relationship.

The first happens whenever we use Boolean or proximity operators in a computer search, defining that two or more terms coexist in the same record. For defining the relationship, several theories have been developed (such as chain indexing, Austin).

Preferred Criteria. The result of segmentation appears in the form of numerous preferred subject criteria. Mainly data banks favor this tool, labeling all significant elements and separating them in different fields. In bibliographic databases, preferred criteria are those that have special significance in the given science. They are strongly connected to the disciplines, for example, geographic names, chemical names, and personal names. Retrieval of these elements can be important even if they are not the main topic of the document. Extensive use of preferred criteria obviously represents the impact of computers.

Natural Language. An unparalleled renaissance of natural language is occurring, because it is very user-friendly. However, the effectiveness of retrieval is limited because of variations in meaning, and control is always temporary. At the same time, there are some additional problems, too. Not only do the disciplines have their special expressions, but also, the language usage of the producers is also different.

Databases basically contain textual information, and figures and images are rare. Ongoing research in the field of expert systems also shows that natural-language knowledge representation and retrieval will not disappear in the near future. There is also a strong tendency toward using coding systems. The databases we examined give evidence that the two live side by side.

Conclusion

Looking at the available knowledge-representation tools and procedures, it is quite clear that the basic principle is the following: isolate and combine. Subject elements found in the documents are separated, and then some relationships among them are created. In the beginning, the collection was in the background, and later the disciplines took over the leading role. Since then, subject-representation tools could function only in limited domains.

The more elaborate a database, the more different aspects it applies. The aim is to show the difference and uniqueness of a field or discipline. This is the impact of the growing quantity of information. The result is that the users must have a solid knowledge about a database to be able to search it efficiently.

The known tools today handle only knowledge fragments. The knowledge quanta that are involved in the documents, and the whole message of the document, are represented only in an indirect way. The quantitative accumulation now should be followed by a qualitative change.

Appendix 24.1
List of Databases

1. Directories, data banks

ABCE — German Business and Industry Directory:
> The on-line version of the buyers' guide *ABC der Deutschen Wirtschaft*. It contains references to products manufactured and offered for sale by about 76,000 companies in Germany.

CZCO — Official Register of Czech and Slovak Organizations:
> The largest and most comprehensive collection of business-related information on the Czech Republic and Slovakia.

D&B — International Dun's Market Identifiers:
> Contains directory listings, sales volume, and marketing data for over 4.7 million establishments in more than 200 countries.

DSCL — Disclosure Database:
> One of the most comprehensive sources of financial and management information on public companies that trade their stock in the United States.

GDDB — Gale Directory of Databases:
> The most comprehensive source of detailed information on databases and database products, their producers, and on-line services and database vendors and distributors.

The McGraw-Hill Companies Publications Online:
> Provides the complete text for many major McGraw-Hill publications. The database covers not only general business but also specific industries.

PLCO — Directory of Polish Companies:
> A directory of companies and public organizations registered in Poland.

WWEB — Who's Who in European Business:
> An ideal source of information about Europe's top decision-makers.

2. General bibliographies

CBIB — Current Contents Search:
> Provides full bibliographic details of articles in every leading journal and book, in the sciences, social sciences, arts, and humanities, published in the world.

DISS — Dissertation Abstracts Online:
> The single most comprehensive source of dissertation information, with more than 1,000 participating institutions worldwide.

WTI — World Translations Index:
> The unique source for existing translations of literature relating to all fields of science and technology.

3. Reference databases in the field of sciences

ABI/Inform:
: The premier resource for information on the principles and practices of management.

Agricola:
: Provides selective worldwide coverage of primary information sources in agriculture and related fields.

BIOSIS Previews:
: The major English-language service providing comprehensive worldwide coverage of research in the biological and biomedical sciences.

CABI — CAB Abstracts:
: Provides coverage of the worldwide literature on agriculture in its broadest sense.

CA Search:
: The on-line version of *Chemical Abstracts*. Includes over 13 million quotes from the worldwide literature of chemistry and its applications.

Derwent Drug File:
: Presents information on all aspects of drug research and usage.

Econlit:
: A comprehensive bibliography of the worldwide literature on economics.

EI-Compendex:
: The machine-readable version of the *Engineering Index*, which provides abstracted information from the world's significant engineering and technological literature.

EMBASE (Excerpta Medica)
: A comprehensive index of the world's literature on human medicine and related disciplines.

Enviro/Energyline Abstracts:
: A unique source of information on all areas of the technical, scientific, socioeconomic, and policy aspects of a wide range of environmental subjects.

FSTA — Food Science and Technology Abstracts:
: Comprehensive coverage of research and new development literature in the areas related to food science and technology.

INSPEC:
: The database for physics, electronics, and computing.

INON — Insurance Information Online:
: The knowledge database for the insurance industry.

JICST-EPLUS — Japanese Science and Technology:
: A comprehensive bibliographic database covering literature published in Japan from all fields of science, technology, and medicine.

MMKA — Management and Marketing Abstracts:
: The specialist database produced by Pira International for information on all aspects of management and marketing practices, customer and industrial relations, in the European Market and worldwide.

MEDLINE:
: One of the major sources for biomedical literature.

NTIS—National Technical Information Service:
: Provides access to the results of both U. S. and foreign-government-sponsored R&D and engineering activities.

310 *Cataloging, Authority Control, Union Catalogs*

Pascal:
>One of the world's leading sources of life- and physical-sciences information.

4. Reference databases on the fields of social sciences and the humanities

RILA—Art Literature International:
>Abstracts and indexes current publications in the history of art.

Artbibliographies Modern:
>Provides comprehensive bibliographic coverage of the current literature on art and design.

ASSI—Applied Social Science Abstracts and Indexes:
>Presents a comprehensive reference service on modern society and its problems.

CELEX—European Union Law:
>Provides the full test and/or references for all European Union legislation.

ERIC:
>A bibliographic database that contains education-related documents and journal articles.

Historical Abstracts:
>A bibliographic database covering the world's scholarly literature in history.

ISA—Information Science Abstracts:
>Provides references and abstracts in the fields of information science and library science.

LLBA—Linguistics and Language Behavior Abstracts:
>Provides current selective access to the world's literature on linguistics and language behavior.

LISA—Library and Information Science Abstracts:
>Comprehensive coverage of international materials in the field of library and information science.

PAIS International:
>Database of the Public Affairs Information Services covers the full range of the social sciences, with emphasis on public policy.

Philosopher's Index:
>Provides indexing and abstracts from books and over 300 journals of philosophy and related interdisciplinary fields.

PSYCINFO — Psychological Abstracts:
>Provides access to the international literature in psychology and related behavioral and social sciences.

Religion Index:
>Comprehensive bibliographic database on religion and theology.

Sociological Abstracts:
>Covers the world's literature in sociology and related disciplines in the social and behavioral sciences.

5. Full-text databases—journals

AGEN —Agence France-Presse Newswires:
>The full text of Agence France Presse daily newspaper in French.

AP News:
>The full text of its coverage of the national, international, and business news, as well as sports and financial information.

FAZA—Frankfurter Allgemeine Zeitung:
: Germany's leading national daily newspaper.
FTEE—Financial Times Reports: Eastern Europe:
: Provides expert full-text comment on the business and political environment in Eastern Europe.
HBRO—Harvard Business Review Online:
: The on-line version of the prestigious journal.
Le Monde:
: The full text of Le Monde.
Los Angeles Times
: Full text of the journal.

References

Austin, Derek. *PRECIS: A Manual of Concept Analysis and Subject Indexing*. London: Council of the British National Bibliography, 1974.

Calderon, Federman. "Library of Congress Subject Headings: Vested Interest versus the Real Needs of the Information Society." *Cataloging and Classification Quarterly* 11, no. 2 (1990): 85–94.

Chan, L. M. *Library of Congress Subject Headings: Principles and Application*. Littleton, Colo.: Libraries Unlimited, 1978.

Chen, Z. "Role-limiting Methods for Automated Knowledge Acquisition: A Problem-solving Perspective." *Information Processing and Management* 32, no. 2 (1996): 239–245.

Chomsky, Noam. *Language and Mind*. New York: Harcourt, Brace and World, 1968.

Chomsky, Noam. *Syntactic Structures*. The Hague: Mouton, 1957.

Congrieve, Juliet. "Problems of Subject Access: Automatic Generation of Printed Indexes and Online Thesaural Control." *Program* 20, no. 2 (1986): 204–210.

Cousins, Shirley Anne. "Enhancing Subject Access to OPACs: Controlled Vocabulary vs Natural Language." *Journal of Documentation* 48, no. 3 (1992): 291–309.

Csík Tibor. "Ismeretek és könyvtári osztályozás." *Könyv Könyvtár Könyvtáros* (1996): 13–24.

Cutter, C. A. *Rules for a Dictionary Catalog*, 4th ed. rev. Washington, D. C.: Government Print. Office, 1904.

Dewey, M. *A Classification and Subject Index for cataloguing and Arranging the Books and Pamphlets of a Library*. Amherst, Mass.: Lake Placid Education Foundation, 1976.

Farradane, J. E. L. "A scientific theory of classification and indexing." *Journal of Documentation* 6 (1950): 83–99; 8 (1952): 73–92.

Foskett, A. C. *The Subject Approach to Information*. London: Clive Bingley, 1982.

Ingwersen, Peter. "Cognitive Perspectives of Information Retrieval Interaction: Elements of a Cognitive IR Theory." *Journal of Documentation* 52, no. 1 (1996): 3–50.

Lancaster, F. W., S. Herner et al. "Evaluation of Interactive Knowledge Based Systems: Overview and Design for Empirical Testing." *JASIS* 47, no. 1 (1996): 57–69.

Lin, J. "Integration of Weighted Knowledge Bases." *Artificial Intelligence* 83, no. 2 (1996): 363–378.

McMurdo, G. "How the Internet was Indexed." *Journal of Information Science* 21, no. 6 (1995): 479–489.

Morris, Anne (ed.). *The Application of Expert Systems in Libraries and Infromation Centres*. London: Bowker-Saur, 1992.

Notess, G. R. "Searching the Web with Alta Vista." *Database*, no. 3 (1996): 86–88.

Partridge, D., and K. M. Hussain. *Knowledge-Based Information Systems*. London, New York: McGraw-Hill, 1994.

Poynder, R. "Web Research Engines." *Information World Review*, no. (December 1996): 47–48.

Robertson, S. E., and M. Beaulieu. "Research and Evaluation in Information Retrieval." *Journal of Documentation* 53, no. 1 (1997): 51–57.

Shabas, Ann C. "Postcoordinate Retrieval: A Comparison of Two Indexing Languages." *JASIS*, no. 1 (1982): 32–37.

Vickery, Brian. *Classification and Indexing in Science*. 2d ed. London: 1959.

Vickery, Brian. "Conceptual Relations in Information Systems." *Journal of Documentation* 52, no. 2 (1996): 198–200.

Vickery, Brian and Alina Vickery. *Information Science in Theory and Practice*. London: Bowker-Saur, 1987.

Vickery, Brian. "Knowledge Representation: A Brief Review." *Journal of Documentation* 42, no. 3 (1986): 145–159.

Vickery, Brian. "Knowledge Discovery from Databases: An introductory Review." *Journal of Documentation* 53, no. 2 (1997): 107–122.

Weinberg, Bella Hass. "Complexity in Indexing Systems—Abandonment and Failure: Implications for Organizing the Internet." *ASIS 1996 Annual Conference Proceedings* (19 October 1996).

CHAPTER 25

The Dissemination and Archival Storage of Old Materials as Electronic Documents

ADOLF KNOLL

The world is rich in culture and in various types of knowledge, substantial parts of which have been recorded. However, with the passage of time, some recorded knowledge becomes endangered, because it may no longer be possible to decode it. This pertains not only to modern electronic communications or to the preservation of the printed, mostly paper-based, heritage.

This has always been the case. Just note the Etruscan inscriptions; we are lucky to have them; we can even distinguish the characters, but we are unable to understand them. Even if frequent use has contributed to the preserving of the unrecorded oral heritage, in some countries its recording is the first step toward its safeguarding. We are becoming increasingly aware that our existence is closely bound to the richness of our ideas. It is thanks to this added value that mankind is creating civilization, the core of which is culture.

It is also true that civilization grows by building on previously created cultural values; hence it is very important to preserve the immense diversity of cultural representations of the world we have inherited. We would like not only to have cultural objects themselves; we would like also to understand them properly in the future. We are uncertain about the proper functions and meaning of many earlier cultural objects. This occurs frequently in the case of ancient civilizations, in spite of the fact that they have left us many artifacts. However, in many cases, we feel that a substantial part of the memory of them has been lost. This can happen also with our own civilization if we are not clever enough to record our knowledge in a way that will permit not only its safeguarding, but also, and especially, its proper understanding.

We are unable to understand Etruscan texts, because we lost their context, because there is no metainformation added to them to help us with their decoding. The same works also in the realm of electronic communications.

With this in mind, UNESCO, in 1992, launched the Memory of the World program, with the aim of safeguarding the world's documentary (and also oral) heritage.[1]

---

1. See Abdelaziz Abid, "Memory of the World: Preserving our Documentary Heritage" (http://www.unesco.org/webworld/memory/Abid.htm).

The program has grown since that time and has covered many aspects of preservation, both classical and electronic.

Recorded Information

Two things need to be in place in order to record information: first, something that helps encode information, and second, a supporting matrix on which it can be written. It is clear that the latter is always material that can change in time as technology develops. It was stone or terracotta in the distant past; it was parchment, palm leaves or silk, and, especially, paper in later times. Many kinds of plastic materials have been introduced in this century, especially to support the development of sound and motion picture recording, and lately for electronic publications. The main revolution in recording information has occurred in encoding systems, because a new immaterial system needs to be added to the material supports (inks, colors, and various chemicals).

In the case of the digital encoding of information, it does not react with the carrier of information. Even if it can migrate from medium to medium, the encoded information remains the same. Thus, it has been frozen in the form that was shaped by its production.

The classical encoding of information, however, is materially and chemically conditioned; the information changes over time, and also reacts with its carrier. It can never be conserved or frozen in one of its states and its deterioration can never be stopped.

The classical preservation discipline was mostly chemistry based, and many preservation debates are about the stability of materials (the most common being about the problem of acid paper). The arguments become more complex when we deal with older materials (parchment manuscripts) or special documents (photographs, films, and analog sound or video recordings), because they are about an interface of the two material media.[2] Chemistry-based research is object oriented and is aimed at the preservation of documents as physical objects, even the reformatting of them on a new medium (newspapers, for example, were recorded on microfilm). In this area, preservation discussions are about the stability of materials. The Etruscan inscriptions in stone may be considered an ideal example of material stability, which can hardly be achieved for more recent documents. Etruscan inscriptions are often relatively well preserved, but in spite of this, the basic message contains no information for us. In fact, there is information, but we are unable to understand it. How typical for our modern computerized world!

The Need for Additional Information

It is now clear that, in principle, the problem of the preservation of new electronic documents is not new. The concern is that the computer-created documents, even if preserved on some media, are in danger, because they might not be decodable in the future.

---

2. These discussions arise because very rare materials need to be preserved (special research concerns historical bindings, inks, colors, parchment), or else whole groups of documents are endangered (newspapers, recordings on tape).

It is also important to keep in mind what aspect of the document we actually want to preserve—it is neither the carrier nor the representation of the message on the carrier; it is the information that is encoded with the help of both of these, and it is information that we must take care of much more than we did before.

It is very interesting to review classical-library and archival activities. Libraries sometimes insist very much on the preservation of objects, claiming that it is their role (especially in the case of national libraries), imposed on them by law or regulations. They often spend lavishly on the safeguarding of objects that contain information that, for the most part, is not in fact endangered. For example, it is highly probable that Shakespeare's, Goethe's, or Dante's texts are not endangered and that the ideas contained in them have a good chance of surviving, simply because copies of these texts exist in large quantities in the original language as well as in translations. Such is also the case with many sound recordings or even films. This can be explained by the high demand for, and frequent use of, the information contained in them.

A serious problem that must be faced, even in the area of preservation, is the problem of selection. More precisely, we need to weigh the trade-off of preserving all documents as objects against preserving all information. It can create a serious management problem if funds are to be allocated to both objectives. While some national librarians might object, a third edition of Goethe's *Faust* in Czech is not important, in light of the many unique documents whose content has not been duplicated as often. To take another example, one should be willing to consider that the work of Dickens is in no danger of disappearing, since the text is much more important than the various individual documents in which it is published. Among these documents, there is only a small number that represent important editorial practices of various publishing houses or editorial approaches of graphic or bookbinding schools. These practices are not represented by the texts themselves, because they are artifacts produced in the process of making the text available.

On the other hand, there can be outstanding editions of a concrete work. In this case, the value added to the text by the manufacturer of the book is so high that these editions should be preserved to demonstrate the evolution of the interpretation of a text or a writer in a society.

In effect, museums are needed for collecting these artifacts, and the national libraries of today, dedicated to the acquisition and storage of the entire documentary heritage of a nation, are such museums. They can possess many artifacts containing the same text and not be concerned, because they are used to focusing on physical objects. As a result, in the case of electronic documents, they may have problems in adopting new ideas that are based on the concern with information as such, rather than on its containers. If they continue to follow their old collection development policy, they can become new media museums and end up preserving artifacts as mere containers, without understandable content. The question for the future behavior is twofold: Should they apply the same policy toward new media (videotapes, CDs,) and should they not rethink their archival policy for both classical and new documents?

Perhaps it is more accurate to talk about the preservation of texts, graphics, sound, and motion pictures than about the preservation of documents such as books, CDs, films, photographs, postcards. Perhaps we should distinguish between common and unusual document objects in order to cope with preservation tasks. This will certainly have an impact on our financial management as well.

Libraries and archives are concerned with the condition of rare documents as objects,[3] and they apply to them the same, old technique, namely, the duplication of information. But the responsibility for such duplication is really driven by different concerns. If there is a good market, the duplication is generated by the need to use such information; if the market is poor, the duplication must lie with the documents' owners. In this sense, then, two points should be made:

1. Libraries are not key players in safeguarding information which is in high demand since this is taken care of by publishers (Shakespeare's texts have been preserved, thanks to publishers).
2. Libraries should do their utmost to safeguard rare information that is not used very often because of limited access to it (old newspapers, graphically important collections, and rare documents, old and new).

As recipients of the legal deposit, national libraries should monitor the book or document market to help ensure their own compliance with point number 1. Only as book or document "museums" are libraries "information institutions," and they should not be in the business of reproducing information that should be generated by publishers.

Where information is endangered independently of its character,[4] it is incumbent upon libraries to start behaving in a way that preserves it, either in its original format or in another one. And they have the responsibility not to create new Etruscan inscriptions in cases where reformatting takes place.

Understandable information about the encoding of Etruscan information is what we are lacking. A parallel Latin translation, an Etruscan grammar in Latin, or a small Etruscan-Latin dictionary would suffice. It is the metainformation that is missing and this should be a warning when we apply digital reformatting technology. We need to add to reformatted documents information about what we have done and how we did it. If not, we contribute to the disappearance of our culture.

The Digital World

We are living in a digital world, because digital technology enables easy communication and sharing of information. We have electronic texts and databases; we have and use digital sound recordings; and we use computer graphics not only for speeding up printing, but also for sharing graphic information from classical and rare documents. The digital television and digital video are on the verge of entering into everyday life.

In view of this, it is natural that UNESCO emphasized digital technology in the Memory of the World program. After the initial enthusiasm about the fact that this technology would be able to solve preservation problems, some pessimism also emerged because of a lack of appropriate analysis of what preservation tasks were aiming at.

---

3. These include manuscripts, incunables, rare prints, rare graphics, and important archival documents.
4. This means the analog or digital nature of the information, or the textual, graphical, or sound aspect of it.

It is clear that digitization solves the problem of the preservation of documents published in digital form, because the copying of files enables the exact reproduction of the original record, provided it has not been critically damaged. We then decide whether the accompanying material is important enough to be reproduced, for example, as a CD publication or booklet. The most important and interesting sound recordings are digitally rewritten and republished in this way. Furthermore, the analog sound recordings are digitally remastered. Specialists may say—and they sometimes do—that the digitally remastered sound recording is different from the analog one and that, perhaps, the analog recording is better. Other specialists argue that it is not the case. In any event, the point is that in the digital world, the fundamentals of reformatting—namely, the format, resolution, and compression—can be exactly measured and controlled, and, with them, the quality of the recording itself.

The same holds for the reformatting of materials, such as hand-written and printed (especially old) documents, where we are interested in more than the text itself. While graphic documents or newspapers are good sources for digital reformatting, there is no doubt that the results of this conversion are new documents, which are different from the originals.

Originals, and especially the rare ones, should be preserved as long as possible. Their digital copies can help share the information they contain, and they can also eliminate the direct use of originals and thus contribute to their preservation, because one of the most dangerous agents of deterioration is handling and frequent use.

Originals and their Digital Copies

Many approaches to digital documents produced from the reformatting of analog originals follow only the logical properties of originals. This can lead to an interdependency between copy and original such that copies, if originals are not taken into consideration or external information about them is disabled, can become the future equivalents of Etruscan inscriptions.

In many programs, the digital copy is a sum of computer graphic files, which are usually copies of pages of the original document. In such cases it is recommended that file names express the order of the original parts of the document. When stored, a mapping between these data and a catalog record of the original can be set up, emphasizing that the discussion is about today's, and especially tomorrow's, access to digital copies.

Access then depends on the readability of the data obtained during the process of digitization (for example, image files) and on the readability of the data that enable access to it (added information). Discussions of image digitization have mostly focused on the first category. Recommendations have concerned data formats and their properties, such as those of compression or resolution,[5] and stress has been on the quality of digital files. Many people were and still are reluctant to accept data com-

---

5. See, for example, "Technical Aspects of Preservation—Recommendations of the Sub-Committee on Technology," in *Memory of the World. General Guidelines to Safeguard Documentary Heritage*, prepared for UNESCO on behalf of the IFLA by Stephen Foster, Jay Lyall, Duncan Marshall, and Roslyn Russell (Paris:

pression. They say that the image files must be as large as possible and that they should be stored mostly in the Tagged Image File Format (TIFF). They forget that *any* image of reality is a compression and that the files far exceed the resolution of human perception and the intentions of the creator of the digitized original.

Nevertheless, some preferred standards exist. Internet communication, for example, requires for images the Graphic Interchange Format (GIF) or the Joint Photographic Expert Group (JPEG) format. Recently, the Portable Network Graphic (PNG) format has been recommended. The TIFF is also frequently used. Of course, there are more varieties of the GIF, TIFF and JPEG, different compression algorithms, and the images can vary in the number of colors and the degree of resolution. The most important criterion, however, is the purpose for which the digital image has been created.

This is quite understandable with respect to so-called user quality images since a small-preview GIF image can give enough basic information using 256 colors and occupying 50 KB. The same image is not satisfactory for a detailed study of the original, and the question becomes, How large and detailed should the image be to meet specialists' needs? In other words, the object studied is what is at issue. It is simply not the case that the digital copy somehow remakes the original; it only creates its illusion. We study the original through its illusion and the concern is the latter's veracity. Different specialists agree on various degrees to which the illusion satisfies their particular access need, while a few specialists need access to the original because we are unable to provide them with a sufficiently true illusion of the studied reality.

Old documents were prepared for generally accepted technological levels of communication. But some information may have been unintentionally created at other levels, and the question is, To what extent this should be electronically supported? The material features of the document that are beyond the perception of the creator and the user can have a certain relevance for study, but in general they are not part of the original message.

We think that extreme digitization does not make sense and that a certain degree of compression should be allowed — digital files that represent classical documents should reflect user and archival needs (and these, too, have their limits.)

The above considerations have convinced us about the appropriateness of using JPEG compression even for archival materials. We arrived at this conclusion after a series of careful testing procedures,[6] in which we obtained the following products from each original TIFF image:

- excellent-quality image for archives (JPEG);
- high-quality image for CD-ROM usage (JPEG);
- low-quality image for the Internet (JPEG);
- preview image (GIF) (see figure 25.1);
- gallery preview image (GIF).

UNESCO, 1995), vii, 77pp., Annex D (see also URL—http://www.unesco.org/webworld/mdm/administ/en/MOW_findD.html).

6. Psohlavec, Stanislav "Digitization of Old Manuscripts: A Technical point of View" in: *Digitization of Old Manuscripts*, Knoll, Adolf and Psohlavec, Stanislav (eds.), Prague: National Library of Czech Republic, 1995.

The Generation of Digital Data

The Digital Processing of Originals. As shown below, the original pieces of information are digitally converted into computer files. In this way, pages can become images, or only texts, if we do not insist on having images of the original medium; motion pictures can be converted into digital video files, while the analog sound recording can be converted into the digital sound files.

Thus the immediate result of the digital reformatting can be one of the following:

- image files
- text files
- sound files
- video files

These files can be in various formats, and dozens of graphic formats are used for different purposes.[7] In the WWW domain, it is GIF and JPEG that are recognized as well as PNG, which may also be admissible. In addition, there are the compression algorithms, the most common being LZW (for GIF), JPEG, and PNG. It is interesting to note that the TIFF format can be uncompressed or compressed by any of the three other methods.

When an image is digitized, it is represented as an image file, mostly as an uncompressed TIFF. Before storing it, one has to cut out the unnecessary parts of the computer image. Then the image can be stored in any other format or it can be used for the production of derived images.[8]

This work results in data files, that is, copies of original parts of the document. It is at this juncture that another problem arises: What should be added to these files so that they can be easily understood and shared?

1. As the data are placed on a carrier, say an optical disk, it is important to add information about the relationship of this carrier and the document, mindful that a document may be large enough to require more than one disk or that several smaller documents may be placed on one disk.
2. Since the data and other added material are arranged in a structure and may be in different linguistic versions, appropriate information about this is needed, especially for processing by special access software.
3. Since the digital document is created on the basis of an original, information about this is also needed. A short catalogue description with specific data for each type of document may be sufficient. This may be used for an information system about the digital archives in which the digital copies are stored.
4. Since specialists may be interested in detail descriptions of document features, a system for structuring such data is needed.

---

7. The graphic formats can also be the following ones: CompuServe (GIF); Deluxe Paint (IFF/LBM); Ventura (EM/IMG); Halo (CUT); MacPaint; Microsoft Paint (MSP); PC Paint Pictor (PIC), PC Paintbrush (PCX); TIFF; Truevision Targa; Windows 3 (BMP / DIB); Windows 3 (RLE); WordPerfect Graphics (WPG); JPEG; Kodak Photo-CD (PCD); Sun raster (RAS); Windows Metafiles (WMF); Corel Draw Preview (CDR); Corel PhotoPAINT (CPT); Portable Network Graphics (PNG); Photoshop (PSD), etc.

8. Much work has to be done, because each category of material needs a special tuning of the camera computer control with respect to color, resolution, and the adjustment of the original on the vacuum

This is a preview image of a manuscript at the National Library of the Czech Republic—VIII H 73, digitized in 1996. On the CD, it is in the GIF87a format; packed size, 69,554 bytes; unpacked size, 76,328 bytes; GIF LZW compression, 9 percent. In the same manuscript, more simple images with fewer ornaments have the compression of 40-50 percent in the same format. A smaller gallery preview image in the same format has 9,464 bytes, while the low-Internet-quality JPEG has 147,055 bytes, to which the corresponding unpacked size is 611,392 bytes, and the JPEG compression, 76 percent. The high-quality image in JPEG has 1,040,230 bytes, to which the corresponding unpacked size is 1,753,624 bytes, and the compression 41 percent. The excellent quality of the JPEG image is even larger. It has 2,139,567 bytes, which corresponds to the unpacked image of 4,843,608 bytes; compression, 56 percent.

Figure 25.1 A Preview Image

These four categories of added data can be called metadata. It is important to have a processing capacity to create such metadata for each digitized document. But some basic standards need to be agreed on—for example, on what to base the catalog description (the National Library chose the minimal set of AACR2), or on what to base the description of other features of the document. We need also to decide which substandards to apply for character encoding, dates, numbers, and an indication of the linguistic version of the document. Figure 25.2 shows the main categories of data that are necessary for the production of a digital copy of a classical original document.

The Metadata. During the production of the digital document, in which graphic files carry the relevant information, a very important role is played by the metadata that provide the context and additional information for these data files.

It may seem strange that the metadata may become a relatively more important part of the digital document than the data themselves. However, the metadata are a gateway through which we can get access to data. If the metadata are well organized and contain much useful information, our access to data becomes easier.

---

holder of pages. Many prior problems have to be solved, such as vibrations of the floor, lights, the automation of all routine work, including the writing of supporting software. Stanislav Psohlavec, a specialist from Albertina Icome Praha, Ltd., will describe this process in a later work.

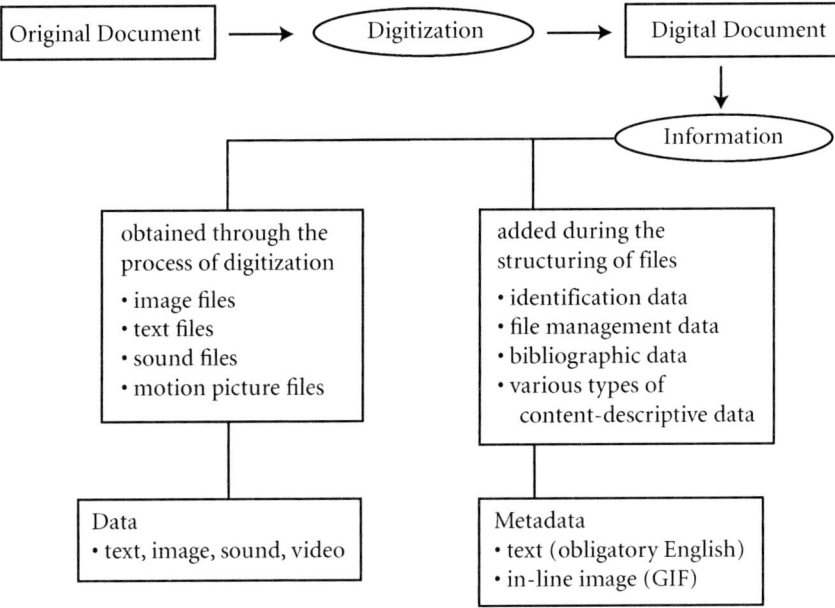

Figure 25.2 Main Data Necessary for the Production of a Digital Copy of a Classical Document

A researcher is mostly interested in data—in our case, in image copies of manuscript pages. However, he can also be interested in producing descriptive metadata; after all, this is the primary work of many specialists in old documents—their work is indeed metadata production. Such a scholar may also be interested in making his findings available in the digital environment. And, if he is not interested in the metadata of others, he may still be interested in the storage of his own metadata and in digital publishing.

For the storage of metadata, we recommend an SGML-based format. However, these metadata must be produced and structured and, therefore, we need some basic tools for specialists to write and structure the necessary data. There must be an editor for the defining of the metadata categories to be applied and for the merging of the metadata with the image data.

In our program we use an HTML Generation Kit that was especially developed for this purpose. It allows the definition of a specific template, the entry of metadata into this template, and the generation of the HTML structure, which enables access to image data that are external to metadata.[9] HTML has been chosen as the language in which the metadata skeleton will be constructed.

---

9. With the exception of very small in-line images, which can also have a metadata function from the user's point of view.

The Structuring of Digital Copies

Today we understand and accept much more than we did in 1995, when we maintained that it would not be possible to have a databaselike organization for a digitally reformatted manuscript.[10] In fact, the master file of such a database consisted of records containing information—in each case, about a page—from the original manuscript. Image files were associated with those records.

In principle, there is nothing wrong with such an approach, since the image data have their explanatory (meta)data in the digital document within the master file records. In effect, there was some added explanatory metainformation within the document. The problem was that our approach was tied to the use of a specific database machine (WiniFRET), whereas other publishers used different database machines, which required that the data be organized in separate file sets.

It was naive to think that the struggle was about building the best database machine. We spent a lot of time in shaping the access software, but we were also getting concerned about the fact that this approach was leading us toward data incompatibility. In the spring of 1996, we articulated the need to use a structuring language that would enable open access and would be user-friendly for both producers and users. UNESCO supported HTML as the basic access platform for the data produced under the Memory of the World digitization subprogram.

We wrote two sets of rules for embedding metadata into HTML. Our first proposal concerned only manuscripts and old printed books,[11] and we decided to use HTML comment tags for structuring the metadata added to images. In 1997, on the basis of one year of practical work with this structure, the generalized version 2.00 of these rules was written. This version contains a very detailed analysis of the categories of metadata necessary for structuring digitized documents,[12] and we obtained results that are satisfactory both from the structural and descriptive points of view. The new tags are not too numerous, they do not disturb the basic viewing of the digital document in Internet browsers, and they contain such data that can be used with better indexing and viewing tools that are yet to be created.

The only problem involved the use of comment tags and our reluctance to accept a pure SGML (Standard Generalized Markup Language) syntax for the structuring of data, be it our own application or an application of the Text Encoding Initiative (TEI). Our most powerful and simple argument is that we do not want to complicate the accessibility of structured data by limiting the user to access via an SGML browser.

It is well known that SGML browsers and editors are expensive, while the WWW

---

10. See our publication of the manuscript "Antiphonarium Sedlecense" (Prague: National Library of the Czech Republic and Albertina Icome Praha, 1995), 1 CD-ROM, and of the manuscript "Chronicon Concilii Constantiniensis" (Prague: National Library of the Czech Republic and Albertina Icome Praha, 1995), 1 CD-ROM.

11. "Proposal of the Structure of Digitized Old Books and Manuscripts, Version 1.11 of 31 July 1996," Tomáš Mayer and Adolf Knoll (http://digit.nkp.cz/Structure_Proposal/navrh111.htm).

12. "Digitization of Documents. General Structuring Rules for Storage of Metadata," Jan Vomlel and Tomáš Mayer, with the participation of Adolf Knoll (http://digit.nkp.cz/Structure_Proposal/Version_200/Version200.html).

browsers and some WWW editors are free, at least for the academic community. In the WWW environment, the access problem is usually solved by an SGML-to-HTML conversion when the server sends the requested data to the user's PC. However, we expect that data will often be used locally from CDs.

It is also true that HTML is a part of SGML, having been defined by a special Document Type Definition (DTD),[13] so that a basic compatibility does indeed exist. It is, however, also true that HTML is much simpler than SGML. This can be a positive as well as a negative feature, especially when talking about the archival storage of textual information.[14]

We have defined all pieces of metainformation necessary for constituting the minimal basic set that is to be added to the digital images produced from original documents. We know that in such cases the specialists need more space for descriptive information than for structuring information; therefore, we think that in cases in which the message is preponderantly supported by data other than the textual kind, an enlarged HTML framework would be enough. If necessary, this framework can introduce an SGML-structured text or any other special data format.

Accordingly, we decided to write a DTD for an enlarged HTML, an HTML with our own specific tags. If successful, such structured documents will be understood by SGML viewers as well as by HTML ones, especially Netscape and Microsoft Internet Explorer. As to HTML, we are not using complicated tags (only up to the version 2.0), and for added tags, we distinguish between bibliographic and various types of content-description data. A separate text file contains identification and file management data.

Another important feature is that we can tag added (meta)data such as a main title, an annotation, or any object-description category, as well as data that are represented by any external files to which the metadata skeleton of the document may point.

In an American publication about the use of SGML for digital access and preservation, a very special category is used for the types of documents that we are interested in.[14] They are called *compound documents*. Most people feel that a hypertext-based organization of data could be very suitable for these. There is perhaps a general agreement that this holds for access, because the HTML protocol is an Internet access standard. However, the problem is how to encode the content to allow for multiple outputs. In this case, there is a general agreement that an SGML platform should be used.

Many have the same problem that we had in 1996 concerning the application of HTML to the structuring of compound documents. We felt that we had to add something to this language. In fact, since HTML is mostly a formatting language, rather than a content-description language, we had to add various tags for the description of contents on different levels of the document. In this sense, we can agree with the authors of the publication cited above. We can even imagine the use of a special DTD SGML or a TEI SGML for this work.

---

13. "HTML as an Application of SGML" (http://www.w3.org/pub/WWW/MarkUp/html-spec/html-spec_3.html).

14. See James Coleman and Don Willis, "HTML-HyperText Markup Language," in *SGML as a Framework for Digital Preservation and Access* (Washington, D.C.: Commission on Preservation and Access, 1997).

However, at the beginning, a digital copy of a book was based on almost the same philosophy as a microfilm copy is based on. They both involve a set of reformatted images, and everything else only helps the user to become better oriented in a collection of such products or within the microfilm or digital copy itself. There is a reluctance to introduce too much metadata into overly complicated structures. And, at times, it's not even desirable. For example, if we listen to a sound recording, we are interested primarily in the sound and need only few supporting metadata, usually supplied by the CD insert. On the other hand, we could publish music on CD-ROM and use a supporting metadata framework from which parts of the music (digital sound files) could be referenced. This becomes an important publishing tool for embedding our findings and comments. In this way, digitization involving large amounts of metadata can be a very attractive research and publishing tool.

We have now digitized thousands of pages of historical manuscripts. Practically speaking, while the digitization process is difficult in the beginning, when many devices must be fine-tuned, this process becomes, over time, mostly routine work. It is the preparation of basic metadata for the structuring of a new digital document that is the most critical stage in the production process.

The minimal set of metadata usually contains a very short bibliographic record and a list of folios and/or pages as they exist in the original document. We use special software tools to help the specialists prepare these data and we have other tools for generating the HTML structure. When everything is ready, data for the CD sets are written.

If we want to speed up the work, we must accelerate the work of specialists who prepare the descriptive data. This can hardly be just a routine. It is clear that a basic digitization program should work only with basic sets of data; otherwise our expensive digital equipment is not well used. Only in special cases can we afford more elaborate descriptions. A digital publication is then a matter of additional funding as well as of much additional work. A basic program to provide access to as large a number of rare documents as possible does not usually cover these hidden yet large expenditures.

The History and Future of our Digitization Program

The milestones of our digitization program are as follows:

1992–1993   The preparation and publication of the first CD-ROM with a database of rare old documents and sample images (UNESCO pilot project for the Memory of the World program).

1994–1995   The testing of digital cameras, and the development of a professional viewer.

1995   The publication of two complete medieval manuscripts on CD-ROM.

1996   Membership in the Memory of the World Subcommittee on Technology; the formulation of initial proposals for standardized access; the building of a complex digital production center in the National Library; the mass production of digital copies of old manuscripts.

1997   The reformulation of the structuring rules for the storage of metadata; decision reached on the use of the appropriate format (special SGML DTD for an enlarged HTML).

1998 A state grant was awarded for the digitization of rare old documents, including sound recordings, and for starting the digital archives for our own data production.

A good deal of further information, mostly in English, can be found at our Web site at the URL (http://digit.nkp.cz). There are articles and information about the different stages in the development of our program, a search database of digitized documents, samples, and key materials.

Until now, the digitized manuscripts have been structured according to version 1.11 of our structuring recommendations. The HTML Generation Kit and the first version of the new specialized viewer and the indexing machine work on this structure. The new data containing the SGML-based system have been prepared and implemented.

The first version of the database of the digital archives has been created and it is now being tested. Within the program called "Memoriae Mundi Series Bohemica," each digital copy has, as its basic output, a set of two excellent-quality copies and a set of two high-quality user copies. One user copy is delivered to the Manuscript and Old Printed Books Department, the other three copies are stored in the digital archives. From these copies, other additional copies will be manufactured and offered at affordable prices. These copies can be viewed in a WWW browser. In the archives, a special program automatically extracts from the CD the necessary data for building the database. This database is searchable and it is accessible on the Web (see the URL above).

A special ManuFret viewer is able to read the metadata from the disk and to index it, thereby enabling document searches. We anticipate having a freeware edition and a professional one with added features, such as the ability to correct for brightness or edges.

A special part of the program is the digitization of endangered sound recordings. They will, presumably, also be structured according to the agreed-on structuring rules.

The work of the UNESCO Memory of the World Subcommittee on Technology is continuing, and we look forward to introducing it to our new solutions, which will require the assistance of specialists in the area. It is expected that the development of ideas, know-how, and software tools, as well as the data production, will move quickly ahead. Our WWW home page is continuously updated with the latest information on our progress.

A New Solution for a Data Container System

Data and metadata form a compound digital document, for the storage of which an SGML-based data container system has been defined. The compound document can consist of a large number of computer files, be they the text-based SGML metadata files or graphic, sound, or video files. One of the SGML metadata files is a root file from which the document starts.

The SGML file of this document is defined by the special DTD. We call it the DOBM DTD. It represents an enlargement of the HTML, permitting any descriptive system related to documents to be encoded. This descriptive system can include any cataloging rules or any special descriptive rules concerning the objects definable in the document. Further, this descriptive system or these descriptive rules can be another standard (for example, AACR2), recommendations used as a de facto standard, or so-called good practices.

Seen from this point of view, the data container system offers a software-independent platform for any already-existing standards that are recommended for use with a compound document. This way the basic compatibility with existing partial systems can be achieved. If a library applies a certain system for the description of artistic objects in manuscripts, the categories of this system can be used in the data container. If it uses certain cataloging rules, the objects defined by them can be defined in this data container system. The application of such standards or good practices is recommended wherever possible.

The DOBM DTD opens the way for a content-oriented description and it indicates whether this description concerns the DOBM file as a whole (taken as an object), or a metadata object in a DOBM file, or a data object represented by a referenced file.

The parameters of these objects mirror the standards applied to the encoded descriptive subsystems. These parameters are given in a special SGML file called the DOBMENT, which maps the concrete describable objects in the document. Of course, the general structure of the DOBMENT has also been defined as a DTD (DOBMENT DTD). Thus, each concrete application of the data container system is mapped by its DOBMENT.SGM and the concrete application for manuscripts and old printed books has been finalized. It follows that our SGML-based data container is a very complex solution in which three levels can be distinguished:

1. The general level permits the description of contents in an extended HTML application of SGML called the DOBM and it enables the mapping of describable objects in a DOBMENT SGM. On this level, these features are enabled by special SGML DTDs called the DOBM.DTD and the DOBMENT.DTD. Also, some other general rules are given concerning the application of character sets or other related ISO standards. A special carrier-definition text file is also defined.
2. The concrete-application definition level establishes the definition and mapping of concrete objects, which is carried out in the DOBMENT.SGM. Here it is decided which standards, quasi-standards, or good practices are applied for the description of the document as an object (cataloging rules) as well as for the description of its metadata objects or data objects on lower levels (for example, within pages).
3. The data-entering level provides the detailed rules for solving the concrete-application problems that can occur—for example, how to interpret the difficulties of marking the foliation of manuscripts where pages are missing, and how to interpret the occurrence of errors, made even by scribes, that interfere with logical numbering.

All these levels are described on our CD-ROM "Digitization of Rare Library Materials. Storage of and Access to Data: The Solution for the Compound Document. Manuscripts and Old Printed Books." The disk is now being published and it also contains rich examples of, and supporting software tools for, generating and accessing data.

CHAPTER 26

The Automation of Special Collections
General Issues

JOANNA PASZTALENIEC-JARZYŃSKA

In the 1990s, we have observed an unusual development in computer technologies: Relatively small processors used by libraries have been superseded by multimedia workstations with Pentium processors, offering previously unobtainable storage capacities and information-processing rates. Multimedia systems have developed rapidly since the mid-1980s. And a new type of document appeared on the book market, which has become generally accepted by readers, publishers, and libraries, and which combines text, graphics, sound, animation, and video; offers interactive access to information; and provides a totally new quality in teaching, education, research, and in ordinary communication and entertainment. The quality of the image, sound, color, speed, and the methods of access to the content of the multimedia electronic documents, generate confidence even in users who have been most skeptical about the technological novelties. The pace at which these changes occur was realized during a 1992 visit of a group of seven librarians from the Polish National Library to the United States, the purpose of which was to get acquainted with automation in American libraries. At the Library of Congress, the Polish librarians saw a presentation of the project "American Memory," which was designed to digitize—most often to a multimedia format—the most precious items of the American heritage.

The effects of this impressive, pioneering project seemed to indicate at the time that in the future the quality of the image and sound unobtainable through digitization would give way to mechanical or optical methods—photographic techniques (microforms) or analog sound recording. Thus, multimedia documents appeared to be mainly useful for entertainment, games, and to support the educational process. The current technology and software packages allow for the creation of ever more perfect copies of documents for the purpose of archiving and preserving of original documents, which helps to restore the former quality of even barely legible documents. By clearing the sound layers of the recordings of the oldest phonographic media (for example, Pianola rollers or vinyl records) or by reproducing, through the use of infrared rays, the normally invisible, destroyed fragments of manuscripts or etched plates in an original document, the electronic duplicates of the old documents become clearer and open up new possibilities for scholarly research.

The special collections of the big research and national libraries, archives, and museums have developed an increased interest in library automation and digitization, because of the numerous benefits of modern electronic technologies, such as the preservation of original documents, the creation of effective ways to spread knowledge of the national and world heritage, and the possibility of providing scholars with modern research instruments in the humanities and in the history of art. In Eastern and Central Europe, this interest has been particularly fostered by the UNESCO program "Memory of the World," by the activity of the Commission on Preservation and Access in the United States and in Europe, and of its European counterpart, the European Commission on Preservation and Access; by the projects carried out in the 1990s by European national libraries—the British Library, the Bibliothèque Nationale, the Deutsche Bibliothek; and also supported by the European Commission's Directorale General XIII, whose objective is to create virtual libraries, including electronic copies of items of European heritage. The goal of these projects is to modernize library services through the use of modern technologies and modern methods of work.

The present situation of the National Library in Warsaw and of Polish university libraries is a typical Central and East European example of automation of special collections, where individual initiatives to create electronic copies of precious items encounter new down-to-earth problems, such as an absence of universally used standards of bibliographic description of special documents.

Since the early 1990s, PCs and the National Library's own software, MAK, have assisted the special collections of the National Library in the use of computer technology to create catalogs of fragments of manuscripts, music, microform, or rare print collections, in which the in-house MARC BN format was used—the format developed at the National Library in the 1980s for the registration of the current national bibliography. Most of these initiatives arose from immediate information needs, from publishing needs, or from research projects carried out by various divisions, but they were not a part of a uniform and consistent program of automation of catalogs and of digitization of special collections. International cooperation is also an important element of educating people in the use of computer technologies for the needs of special collections, because for many years the National Library has regularly supplied data to international and European computerized information systems, such as the Eighteenth Century Short Title Catalog (ECSTC), the Répertoire International des Sources Musicales (RISM), the Répertoire International de Literature Musicale (RILM), and, from 1997, the European Register of Microform Masters (EROMM).

The current state of preparations for the automation of the special collections at the National Library was influenced mainly by two facts. The first was the decision made in 1994 to eventually switch all computer services of the National Library to the USMARC format and to stop work on the development of its own MARC BN format. The second was the purchase of the INNOPAC integrated library system and the fact that special-collections librarians have also been engaged in testing and implementing INNOPAC.

Both these facts speeded up activities at the National Library that were indispensable for the implementation of an integrated system and the creation of good conditions for cooperation, among libraries on the national level, in the standardization of the description of special collections. The years 1995–1996 were marked by intensive work and discussions about Polish rules concerning the standardization of the bibliographic description of special collections and the preparation of a manual for USMARC formats for all types of documents.

The question of bibliographic standardization in Poland still falls short of expectations. In 1994, a long-awaited standard of bibliographic description of rare books was accepted, covering books published from 1501 to 1800 (PN-N-01152-8). The standard for describing post-1800 music prints (PN-83/N-01152.06) has been in use since 1983, and the standard for the bibliographic description of published music and of nonmusic sound recordings (PN-85/N-01151/07) has been in use since 1985. There are still no standards for the bibliographic description of manuscripts,[1] cartographic collections, collections of pictures, audiovisual material,[2] gray literature (leaflets, posters, brochures), and electronic documents. The absence of such standards means that there is a great deal of freedom in cataloging these types of collections.

During the installation of INNOPAC and the preparation of the Polish version of USMARC, automation activities in special collections concentrated on several issues, such as the following:

1. Does the USMARC format in its final version allow for the appropriate identification of the data elements of all types of documents, in line with the expectations of Polish users of special collections who are accustomed to catalogs containing detailed bibliographic and catalog data?
2. What problems may appear in the maintenance of a single bibliographic database for monographs, serials, and special collections?
3. Will such common authority catalogs prove to be satisfactory for both students who borrow new books and serials and scholars who use rare books?
4. Will the indexes, which are the same for all types of collections and are supposed to help in searching the automated catalog, be sufficient for the needs of special collections (for example, doing searches according to the publisher, the printer, or the year of publication)?
5. Should subject cataloging be introduced into special collections (so far most of them have no subject catalogs), and if so, could one set of subject headings be used if appropriately extended by subject headings specific for special collections?

The search for replies to these questions involved intensive work to prepare complicated examples of descriptions of all types of special collections in the USMARC format, which were later tested in INNOPAC and in the preparation of cataloging instructions for USMARC.

Compared to other problems of implementation of the integrated system, which deal mainly with newer collections, we have spent much less time on how special-collections records will function in a single database with other collections. Cataloging problems are particularly evident for manuscript and pictorial collections, especially because of the anticipated cooperation with archives and museums. Dur-

---

1. But note the Mellon Foundation grant to the Hill Monastic Library at St. John's University in Minnesota, for developing a MARC format for medieval manuscripts.
2. Standard descriptions of film are of some help in this.

ing the preparations for INNOPAC, most of the staff members in special collections were engaged in an accelerated education process covering the use of computers in special-collections cataloging and circulation.

At the same time, thanks to the Internet and to our foreign library visits, we have had a chance to see the operation and usefulness of automated catalogs in special collections where they already serve as the basic instrument of bibliographic searches. In the initial period of automation, libraries do not always realize the role of special collections and of their catalogs as sources for scholarly research. Thus, awareness of certain distinctive features of this part of the collection should be widespread among the managerial staff of a research library. In the cataloging process, one should not overlook the specific bibliographic features of a document and the individual description of each copy. Poorly constructed records and wrong search elements result in limited access to these sources. For example, the description of a rare document cannot be limited to a basic set of bibliographic and catalog data, since it must also contain additional information about the special features of a specific copy, as well as provenance data,[3] various manuscript notes,[4] data on the typographic material,[5] and data on the type of document.[6] It would also be desirable to include in the database information about the state of the preservation of the document and the conservation treatment performed in the past. Only a description containing at least a part of this information, indispensable for historians of the book and of a document's heritage, may meet users' expectations. Special-collections data should be entered so as to ensure access to information about the specific features of each type of library material and each copy of it.

Users of the automated catalog of special collections should be convinced that the system offers them more possibilities and a quicker retrieval of the necessary information than the traditional card indexes and catalogs. The analysis of the content of a number of catalogs of special collections and of retrieval systems used in them reveals the causes of certain reservations expressed by scholars and researchers about the usefulness of electronic catalogs. Usually, the descriptions contain only basic bibliographic data that are sufficient to identify the documents, but do not enable us to search by specific features of a given item in the catalog. In addition, subject cataloging does not exist, the headings used in authority files are imprecise, and one cannot search by provenance, names of printers, typographical material, or binding. This type of a catalog enables the researcher to identify the item, but does not satisfy his information needs.

During the implementation of INNOPAC, we have tried to answer the questions about the limits of the catalog description and about the minimum and maximum

---

3. That is, the last owners and previous owners of the document, the type of proprietary marks (superbookplate, bookplate, a note supplied in the manuscript).

4. Such as glosses, marginalia, a censor's deletions, dedications, the description of a binding type, the description of the printing and publishing process (e.g., a false place of printing, a printer's device).

5. Types used; vignettes, headings, and ornaments used.

6. For example, correspondence, sermons, constitutions, essays, poems, bibliographies, Psalters, speeches, commemorative literature.

number and content of search indexes. The preparation of standard rules for descriptions created a rapprochement among the librarians responsible for newer collections and those for special collections. We are convinced that it is possible to use, in a single database, all types of library collections, provided that there is no limit to the number of fields, subfields, and the information content of records in any type of collection, so that their specific features are taken into account, and also provided that there is easy access to particular data groups. Thus, the replies to the questions posed earlier will be in the affirmative, although effecting a common database makes large demands on both software and database content, and will also require adequate hardware.

However, the true revolution in the use of electronic databases for special collections consists of multimedia technologies, which additionally enable us to identify items in the database through linked images of the text (the entire document, the title page or the contents page, the colophon) or, in the case of music documents, through linkages to digitized sound recordings. The possibility of easily using such databases on-line on the Internet or in a local area network (LAN) a challenge for all national and academic libraries.

Though the National Library of Poland is in an early stage of creating electronic databases for special collections, the endeavors of libraries in other countries, and the technical possibilities offered by hardware companies and software vendors, create incentives for facing the new challenge. Libraries are expected to not only provide access to catalogs, but also to offer related collection-based services. The possibility of identifying the work not only through the text of the bibliographic description, but also through the image, sound, and animation, opens up new prospects for the development of information and retrieval systems and of different types of indexes. This also encourages one to reflect on the future of the profession of librarians, and on the possible modification of cataloging rules and of collection indexing. In the case of documents in the electronic format, a new task is to standardize both the encoding of bibliographic information that describes the document and the ways of access to it.

To sum up the dilemmas that are involved in the introduction of electronic technologies in special collections, we need to stress that the National Library is going through a special period: Though it is only beginning to create electronic catalogs of special collections according to international standards, staffers are already preparing to broaden and diversify library services—which has become possible thanks to today's computer technology.

PART IV

Management Issues

CHAPTER 27

The Sequencing of Automation in Central and East European Research Libraries

HENRYK HOLLENDER

When trying to evaluate the automation efforts of Central and East European libraries, we have to pose the question of how particular projects were scheduled and managed. It is obvious that implementation of an automated system involves an arduous, multiphase, and multilayer process. Looking at the social, institutional, and economic contexts in which libraries operate in this region, we would not be surprised if these phases and layers were indeed numerous and distinctively interrelated.

What is, after all, a model of library automation? It is a model of the execution of certain library routines, in such a way that these routines can be explained as work flows, and that particular work flows are encompassed by subsequent modules of an automated system. It is then the job of a manager to select a system that will affect the work flows in the manner in which they need to be affected, and then to choose which modules are to be implemented first. The whole undertaking is thus ordered or arranged; it uses system modules as equivalents of subsequent phases of the project. This is what may be called "sequencing."

If systems selected for libraries could automate all those routines (and those only) that are performed in a library, there would not be a better way to study library policy than to study the scheduling of an automation project.

This general model will be used here to study a very complex setting. We are dealing with libraries from a region which, in recent decades, happened not to play a leading role in the development of librarianship. The progress of automation before 1990 was severly hampered by several factors, which need not be listed here; technical and organizational innovations elsewhere were watched and did percolate, but with delays and limitations. It has always been referred to as just a case of retardation; but what was actually more retarded—the machines and the programs that run on them, or our perception of a library's tasks and processes? It has to be kept in mind that we are not speaking about newly created libraries, endowed with some narrow function, which require just a one-step action. Instead, we are speaking about traditional, if not historic, institutions, identified generally by their ability to keep their continuity, rather than by their ability to set goals and achieve them. Béla Mader has given a clear account of the situation.[1] We are yet to describe in depth the behavior of library managers, including, for example, their relations with computer specialists. I will try not to elaborate on this seductive theme, but let me just observe that the discourse of library automation in Eastern Europe has been dominated by the concept of human adjustment to computers, and not by that of the computer's adjustment to needs specified by a human.

The integrated, expensive automation packages that appeared in some former Council of Mutual Economic Assistance (COMECON) countries in the 1990s were not simply considered "advanced" when set against the current practices in librarianship and information management. They were tools for automation of a different type of library. It is not only—and not really—a matter of a stage of organizational and technological development, but of a historically and culturally defined profile of a library institution. Most new systems were designed in an Anglo-American environment, to serve an Anglo-American library with features not necessarily in operation (or even known) in countries like Poland. Consideration of these inadequacies is another temptation that I will now resist, yet we have to keep the whole issue in mind: Has it not been the case that some activities now recognized as priorities were simply avoided because they belonged to new, unexplored areas of library work? With a sense that a comparative study of library automation has merely started, but indeed started with a journal article that will long remain unsurpassed, rich in insights and explanations,[2] I will later point to some of these areas.

Any essay on sequencing the implementation of automated systems should consider not only global differences between library cultures, but also the actual differentiation in, for example, missions, tasks, functions, and sizes of libraries within a country. Libraries we have dealt with were of different types: national, university, and special. In Europe, a chief duty of a national library is the production of a national bibliography, while for a special library, the absolute priority may be on-line access to remote databases. In the future, a study focusing on a particular type of library could be useful, but for the time being, we have not classified libraries at all. Moreover, in our search for sequencing patterns, we have identified phases not only on the basis of existing modules of automated systems, but also on the basis of some selected aspects of library work, whether they are actually served by a separate subsystem or not. In other words, we decided to describe library policies and automation's impact on library work rather than just the subsequent technical steps involved. We thought that this approach would provide more information about what libraries can achieve. We were aware that we will simultaneously blur the perception of the librarian and the perception of the systems analyst; that we will confuse strategies, plans, and timetables with actual case histories; and that we will invite some wishful thinking. We could not think, however, of a methodology which would accommodate a strict observance of all these distinctions.

---

1. Béla Mader, "Library Automation Systems in Academic Libraries in Hungary," *Program* 29 (July 1995): 285–293.

2. Christine L. Borgman, "Automation Is the Answer, But What Is the Question? Progress and Prospects for Central and Eastern European Libraries," *Journal of Documentation* 52 (September 1996): 252–295.

It was necessary to write about libraries supported by The Andrew W. Mellon Foundation, that is, about those in the following countries: the Czech Republic, Hungary, Poland, and Slovakia. I was naturally exposed to writings in Polish, and knew the Polish library scene as a member of the group of library directors responsible for the implementation of software supplied by VTLS, Inc. Hence it was reasonable that the main source of information on the Polish scene would consist of publications and personal contacts. However, information from libraries in other countries needed to be collected by means of a survey, and it was also reasonable to use English as the language of the survey instrument. The choice of English reinforced my decision not to send the questionnaire to Polish libraries—it would have been artificial to have used a foreign language to contact colleagues with whom a conversation is maintained in the native language, and any additional exchange of opinions in Polish would have brought about a substantial amount of Polish bias in this chapter. However, in retrospect one cannot be fully satisfied with the solution, mostly because information derived from questionnaire responses is difficult to compare with information acquired in other ways.

It was not my intention to evaluate software packages or even to name them. Nevertheless, I was aware that, in so far as Poland is concerned, some systems would have to be mentioned. Since the first group of Mellon libraries selected VTLS, the second group opted for Horizon, and the National Library is currently implementing INNOPAC, the situation can be more easily described on a consortial level rather than on an individual-institutional one. VTLS libraries—not a consortium in the legal sense—cooperated intensely from the beginning and set new standards of library work. Their original decisions, adopted somewhat tacitly, deeply affected the sequencing of automation.

Our perception of the situation in Poland is thus dominated by the VTLS library group. It is then relevant for another large group of Polish academic libraries, which, having never applied for a Mellon grant, also did quite well in automation efforts. Using CDS/ISIS, and then the National Library's product, MAK, or other packages designed and marketed in Poland, they usually focused on cataloging and circulation. They wanted quick results, they achieved them, and their current or future efforts to regain ground they might have lost by their carefree ignoring of standards are beyond the scope of this chapter.

For VTLS libraries, we have several descriptions of planning and of steps of implementation, such as an article by my colleagues from the University of Gdańsk. Having dealt with the prehistory of a system and the story of all the preparations, they admitted (in December 1993): "Currently we work intensively to have the OPAC operational, which will prove to the users that the library is really getting automated. Up to now, only the personnel in some departments have experienced any automation."[3] The authors thus declare that the end-users' access to library collections—

---

3. Ewa Chrzan and Jadwiga Łuszczyńska, "Komputeryzacja w Bibliotece Głównei Uniwersytetu Gdańskiego" [Automation in the Central Library of Gdańsk University], *Przegląd Biblioteczny* 62, nos. 1/2 (1994): 24.

no matter how small they are in numbers—is their urgent goal; full mastering of monograph-processing routines is only to follow. Yet later, core records would be created in the acquisitions department, without even implementing the respective module (which has not been purchased). Connectivity to other VTLS libraries is also marked as a priority, but without any explanation, we can only guess that at that time it meant input/output operations on the union authority file, mounted on the Warsaw University Library server,[4] rather than full-fledged shared cataloging. Next, the closing of card files and automation of lending are listed, and the authors inform us that to print order slips in a closed-stacks store, it is necessary to purchase a *document delivery* subsystem.

At VTLS libraries, authority records were created first, before the actual cataloging started. Even earlier, extensive work had been undertaken on formats. At the same time, the new system of subject headings was designed, based on the French RAMEAU and thus akin to U.S. Library of Congress subject headings (LCSHs). Then rules of cooperation were agreed upon, and the actual work flows designed. What we created is indeed a unique way to sequence a library automation project. Its basic features are:

- a stress on authority control and a clean file syndrome as the foundation of shared cataloging;
- strict on-line cooperation between the libraries;
- the bottom-up nature of all this work, conducted with some government support but no government leadership.

It is easy to guess that the growth of the files in VTLS libraries in Poland was not too quick at the beginning. The extensive authority file, however, is now giving more support for current cataloging and retrospective conversion projects. Another central file—that of serial records—is fully operational, and the designing of yet another one—for bibliographic descriptions of books—was advanced at the time of the Warsaw Library Automation Conference in October 1997. In the meantime, circulation had been automated in most of the libraries.

But if we skip the phase of getting ready for authority work, of necessary bibliographic standardization, and of training, we arrive at a generic pattern of automation sequencing. Let us look at a library in Poland, which is neither a VTLS library nor a beginner in the automation field. Its sequencing, as reported by one of the managers, looks more or less like this:

- monographic cataloging
- serials control
- acquisitions
- the circulating of open-stacks items

The manager there has reported that the only alternative was to begin with acquisitions (but this was turned down, because the module supported several features not

---

4. Maria Burchard, "Problemy komputeryzacji bibliotek na podstawie doświadczeń Biblioteki Uniwersyteckiej w Warszawie" [Library automation issues: experience of the Warsaw University Library], *Przegląd Biblioteczny* 62, nos. 1/2 (1994): 31.

considered essential for the library, and failed to support some useful others, like the extensive book exchange found widely in Poland). She also admits that the closed-stacks circulation subsystem needs some refinement by the system vendor.

Similarly, a Hungarian colleague wrote to me about the building of a bibliographic database as the first priority. The urge to collect as many bibliographic records as possible was so strong that this colleague's library considered starting with a retrospective conversion, but having discovered that "the most efficient way of retrospective conversion with lots of Hungarian materials [at the library] is to do the cataloging work in-house," the library installed ISIS before the target system could be used. The records accumulated in the ISIS file were later converted to the target system. Also, bibliographic databases on CD-ROM were purchased for use in copy cataloging. Then the actual cataloging started, and the card files were closed. Authority control was maintained despite the temptation to get rid of a routine that added a "serious additional workload," and some problems with copy cataloging were successfully addressed. Then some acquisitions features were automated with the cataloging module.

The second priority was circulation, and there are plans to automate the interlibrary loans. The third priority is acquisitions, and yet the next is automation of "accession registers," which are referred to as "unique in Hungarian libraries," although Polish libraries have them as well. This novelty, apparently minor, my Hungarian colleague said, "will probably cause the greatest change in the work flow since we started automation: We are planning to introduce a phase of a database check for all the arriving books, which will pick out all the documents the processing of which do not require a professional cataloger. They will be dealt with when entered into the computerized version of the accession registers and they will find their way into the stacks at once." What we are getting here seems a genuine simplification; Polish libraries know about the issue of inventories (*inwentarz*), but have resolved it mostly to get printouts that could be bound as required by the rules, and not to save some of the books from being sent from the Acquisitions Department to Descriptive and Subject Cataloging.

It was clear that I would not be able to obtain a detailed report from my Hungarian colleagues that would serve to compare a larger number of libraries. Instead, I wanted a statement on priorities and strategies, and a comprehensive, standard list of steps that were, or might have been, taken in each of the libraries I contacted. The former was to be achieved by several open-ended questions contained in a letter I sent to all the Mellon libraries I located south of Poland; the latter was left for a questionnaire that I hoped to design after the answers to the first letter arrived.

The letter requested help in finding out how objectives were prioritized and what sequence of tasks was adopted. I asked the addressee (always a library director, but she or he could, I added, "delegate the task to someone at the library whose views and work he or she accepted") to list the major steps in library automation and to describe how they affected the functioning of the organization. I counted on very personal and local approaches, which never seem present when it comes to collecting data from a questionnaire. The letter could then have served as a good pilot study for determining the content of the questionnaire, and for making the questionnaire solicit information on the social aspect of each project. But it did not: I received only two answers, and only one library referred to my questions. (I quoted it extensively above, citing the respondent as a "Hungarian colleague."

I then designed a questionnaire of modest length—and sent it to 22 institutions, which I believed to be either "full" Mellon libraries, or libraries with partial Mellon grants.* I received good answers from 10 of the 22, and, I am now going to discuss them. Although this number is too low to provide statistically valid data, I think that it provides some insights, and makes a point of departure for further study.

The first question was merely a starter. I wanted to know whether, before the current automated project at a particular library, any automated system had worked at that library. Three libraries declared that they had nothing before, and most had in-house-built or ISIS-based systems, partial and nonintegrated ones, yet usually permitting a substantial accumulation of bibliographic records.

The second question was on features of the system that attracted the attention of the selecting team and helped it to make the final decision. Most answers were very general (for example, "shared cataloging features"; "UNIMARC data structure capability"; "integrated environment"). Few went into details by revealing some particular intention of the selector ("an open system"; "graphical user interface"; "*capability of handling music, sound*" [italics mine]). I do not think that the answers were directly linked to the strategies of the selectors; what they seem to communicate is just the intention to use an advanced system to its fullest potential.

The third question was on standards. I wanted to know what data transmission protocol, format, authority control, bibliographic description, and subject headings and classification were in use at the beginning of the project. Answers were incomplete, possibly because I might have ambiguously phrased the question, which must have confused the respondents. What I had in mind was how widely the standards were accepted and used and in what types of libraries, but the question might not have been all that clear. Nevertheless, the answers seem to have shown a familiar scene: Professional systems were purchased at a time when many normal features of library work (such as authority-controlled subject headings) or information technology (such as TCP/IP) were not available. As was the case in Poland, the implementation of an integrated system might have been preceded by a "nonimplementation" period, in which all the necessary foundations were being put in place.

The fourth question was stated as follows: "Evaluate the stress which you put on the following aspects of your automation policy. Please use grades: 0 (no stress), 1 (very weak stress), 2 (weak), 3 (secondary), 4 (strong), 5 (very strong)." Then I listed the "aspects," which were actually parts of library work or of modules that systems normally consist of. The list was not designed to suggest any priority, although it did start with the "production of bibliographic records." The following list shows the sums of the grades that the 10 respondents gave to each aspect of their work, beginning with the total grade of 45 points that was given to the "handling of national diacritics," and then proceeding in descending order of stress attached to the various aspects:

---

*I did so on advice from Miklós Fogarassy, to whom I am deeply indebted for his assistance.

45: handling of national diacritics
41: circulation
39: retrospective conversion;
    subject access
    WWW availability of your file(s)
38: authority control
37: database access
34: electronic mail and other Internet applications
    OPAC
32: other libraries' OPACs are accessible for a library's users
31: serials control
30: availability of a library's bibliographic records so that other libraries can import them into their files
29: acquisitions
    closing of card files
    printing of catalog cards
28: cataloging of special collections
26: classification
24: interlibrary loans
22: journals indexing
    union catalog
20: production of bibliographic records
18: automation of clerical routines
17: document delivery
16: cataloging of electronic and Internet resources
14: funds accounting

While the overall result here seems very consistent with trends elsewhere, the low position of "production of bibliographic records" can be explained only by a methodological error. Indeed, that is what happened. I broke down this category into three subdivisions, namely, "original cataloging," "copy cataloging," "conversion of the existing database"; and some respondents neglected to grade the main category, while the others concentrated on it and ignored the subdivisions. Eventually, original cataloging received 38 points; copy cataloging—28; and conversion of the existing database, 40. Therefore, if not for mutual competition between the main category and its components, the general position of this basic, indispensable feature of library work would be much higher. Still, the grading we received showed that librarians valued retrospective conversion much more than copy cataloging, which indirectly confirms that the scope of retrospective conversion projects was for the time being a very limited one; what was actually converted was the set of files already owned by libraries, accessible via their previous systems.

Other catagories which might otherwise have reached higher positions are classification, subject access, and the union catalog.

"Classification" was subdivided into the "adoption of some well-established schedules" (which received a total of 26 points); "designing new schedules" (15); and "classification symbol for any bibliographic record" (20). It is obvious that libraries chose to use existing classifications, like Universal Decimal Classification, and it remains for further research to reveal whether any new schemes were actually designed. I know of such a case in Poland, but in fact it is supplementing a classified catalog with notations permitting shelf arrangement (call numbers), rather than introducing a completely new endeavor. In addition, the third option is just an unclear phrase; it should probably have read, "Assigning each bibliographic record a classification symbol."

As for "subject access," it was subdivided into "adoption of some well-established subject headings" (33); "designing new subject headings" (30); and "subject access for any bibliographic record" (30).

A proximity of the scores received by "adoption" and "designing" is a little suspicious —it suggests that both might be practiced within one system: "Adoption" would mean assigning a subject which already existed, and "designing" would stand for the adding of a new subject. What I had in mind was using a system like LCSH, or the Polish Biblioteka Narodowa's JHP, as opposed to starting a new system (like the KABA of the VTLS libraries in Poland). It is worth remarking, however, that altogether, "subject headings" passed "classification," which seemed to have had more roots in this part of the world. It is probably the automated systems which facilitated this essential step from classification to the use of subject headings as the best way to access contents of library materials.

The "union catalog" was subdivided into "national" (26); "regional" (9); "consortium" (22). While the result is very good for national union catalogs (or rather for the intention to contribute toward them), it is also good for consortium ones. Probably both subcategories stole some points from the "regional union catalog" entry, which would have been rated much higher had it lacked qualifiers. Apparently, regional cooperation is nearly nonexistent, and the German pattern in this respect will probably not be followed.

It is a characteristic of questionnaires that they always leave a feeling of unfulfillment and inadequacy; they seem to be composed for some institution other than ours. We expected that our respondents might show the same disbelief toward this questionnaire, and we wanted them to express it. We asked them (in question 5) to "evaluate the applicability of the above list to [their] actual strategy," by also using a 0–5 scale. The mean here was 3.72, which may be verbalized as "fair applicability but far from good." However, the questionnaire also contained at this point some encouragement for respondents to suggest other work features and aspects, yet no respondent acted on this.

To check the consistency of answers to question 4 and to acquire additional information, question 6 was included. In this, we asked the respondents to outline the actual order of their automation phases by using the elements listed under question 4. Here are the "emphasis leaders," or the areas receiving the most stress, with numbers specifying the positions each phase occupied in the order of phases reported by respondents who cited it.

- production of bibliographic records (1, 1, 1, 1, 2, 2, 3)
- OPAC (1, 1, 2, 2, 2, 2, 3, 4)
- Authority control (1, 1, 3, 3, 7)

- WWW availability (1, 4)
- Circulation (1, 3, 4, 6, 6, 7)

The handling of national diacritics, receiving so much emphasis in the previous question, was never marked in this one, certainly because it is never a phase of an automation project, but it does make the production of bibliographic records possible.

So we see that bibliographic ability is the core of any library database, that it is tightly clustered with OPAC and circulation (at least in a sense that automation of circulation is not available without the production of bibliographic records), and that it is reinforced with authority control.

The next areas on the list—the secondary emphasis leaders—are:

- serials control (4, 5, 5, 7, 7, 8)
- subject access (2, 2, 3, 4, 5, 7)
- classification (4, 6, 6, 7)
- retrospective conversion (3, 4, 5, 5, 5, 6)
- electronic mail and other Internet applications (4, 4, 5, 5, 7)

The next question made the respondents approach the same issue in yet another way: We asked them to outline the actual order of their current automation phases by using their own grouping and naming of the phases. Some respondents referred here to the sequences outlined under question 6, which means they approved of names we put forward. Others did not necessarily conform. One respondent mentioned "hardware" as the first item, and she (or he) was the only one that followed with "circulation, serials, authority control, and retrospective conversion." Two directors opted to first provide Web access, which is logical when you have all the necessary equipment and Internet-oriented software, but in those cases the actual library program has not yet been implemented. The others provided here various versions of the following story:

- conversion of existing database, and then OPAC
- cataloging, the results of which also went to OPAC
- authority control and subject headings
- circulation
- serials

One may ponder, however, how it is possible to introduce authority control when it has not been prepared in terms of, for example, software, standards, and model routines. In the case of VTLS libraries, we practiced and preached it in a very orthodox manner, taking for granted that if we did not start with it, we would end up endlessly cleaning our dirty file. We know, however, that approaches here may differ from community to community and from organization to organization. Some say that a "quick file" (rapid growth of the database) is a feature the user needs more than a clean one. The others assert that, with big files, what seemed to be harmless impurities at the beginning will soon lead to chaos, which will affect the search capabilities and reduce users' satisfaction. This issue requires more study and a broader context. It is true that VTLS libraries could not rely on any utility to organize authority work, and some libraries label "authority control" as merely any technique of cross-referencing.

Generally, the study shows that library automation in Central and Eastern Europe tends to reflect a traditional model of a library, concentrating on catalogs and circulation as its basic features. It contradicts my expectation that circulation would easily be left behind as not dealing with conceptual representations of holdings. On the other hand, automated catalogs are main catalogs, and this may leave other search tools unaffected, and the lack of stress on cataloging of special collections is of much concern here, if we take seriously the respect for the historical heritage declared in public by knowledge brokers in this part of the world.

Another missing piece is the vast domain of library cooperation. Although access to other libraries' catalogs ranks quite high on the list of priorities, and availability of a library's bibliographic records for downloading to other libraries' files follows closely, it does not seem to be integrated into cataloging routines as a basic feature; instead, it seems an important element that has yet to be given some consideration. Natural fruits of library automation, like interlibrary loans, document delivery, and an orientation toward digital libraries, are given little emphasis. In this context, the "database access," as listed in question 4, may mean just access to the main file, and not remote access to on-line services or databases published on CD-ROM. And, last but not least, statistics provided by professional software, so essential to systems management, were not mentioned by any of the respondents.

Have the libraries, then, been able to learn from the packages which were designed to handle much more diversified sets of operations than they were initially assigned in Central Europe? The experience with subject access would permit a positive answer. The lack of interest in such useful features as reserve modules (students' course readings as selected by professors, arranged physically for short-term loans and retrievable in the OPAC by the course title and the professor's name) provides a negative one. The general impression is thus mixed.

This is not to minimize the amount of work done in libraries which set upon automation in an unstable economic and political context, and for which purchasing an integrated system was often the first major opportunity to modernize. It is still very likely that systems implemented in the nineties will gradually grow to encompass all the aspects of library work. It is also obvious that the chance for progress came abruptly and without sufficient background preparation, and thus the development, while rapid, could not be harmonious. Persisting patterns of sequencing constitute common sense and could not be greatly altered.

There is, however, a danger, that with prolonged economic difficulties and a lack of awareness in academic communities, the gap between the most advanced libraries of the world and the automating libraries of this part of Europe will fail to diminish. The basic repertoire of automated services may then, paradoxically, remain frozen, with a positive feedback from library users, happy with what they received, and with the undoubted, yet restricted efficiency of well-known library routines, slightly improved by automation.

CHAPTER 28

Managing Delays
The Micropolitics of Time in the Czech and Slovak Automation Projects

ANDREW LASS

> One of the highest leverage points for improving system performance is the minimization of system delays."
> —President of a U.S. computer company

> And why would you want to save time, Mr. Lass?
> —A bureaucrat in Prague, circa 1949

In a book that has quickly become a best-seller in modern management theory, Peter Senge points to the importance of incorporating the phenomenon of delays into the analysis of organizational behavior: Delays—"when the effect of one variable on another takes time"[1]—are, together with reinforcing and balancing feedbacks and limiting conditions, the basic components of the systems analysis advocated by Senge. Any organization or, for simplicity's sake, any task that involves goal-oriented action, can be described as a series of mutually interdependent activities or, more exactly, feedback loops.

Senge uses an everyday example, from the world of plumbing, to focus our attention on the importance of understanding the play of interlocking processes and of delays in the behavior of complex systems. Thus, adjusting a shower faucet can be described as a sort of balancing act in which, as we turn the knob in response to our skin's reaction to the water temperature, we look for the ideal point of mixture for the cold and hot water. But this relatively simple task can become frustrating when our adjustments are affected by the distance between the faucets and the shower head, or by decreased skin sensitivity or the simultaneous use of other water outlets (showers, sinks, or toilets) in neighboring bathrooms attached to the same water main. Add to this a hot water boiler with limited capacity and its own (delayed) recovery time, and you have the makings of a type of organizational behavior characterized by the presence of multiple agents vying for access to limited goods and by what appears to be an

---

1. Peter M. Senge, *The Fifth Discipline: The Art & Practice of The Learning Organization* (New York: Doubleday, 1990), p. 89.

endless series of delays. Our response to the actual water temperature—as we compare it to our ideal and turn the knob—is not really an adjustment to our previous input. Instead, we are affecting our own results through the impact that our behavior has on that of others.

In the business world, where there is a clear bottom line by which to judge a company's health, time is of the essence. In the words of a vice president of a Boston consulting firm, "The way leading companies manage time—in production, in new product development, in sales and distribution—represents the most powerful new source of competitive disadvantage."[2] And, in the past few years, the same philosophy is increasingly being applied to our state-run bureaucracies and not-for-profit organizations devoted to the delivery of services (such as health providers, educational institutions, and, in our case, libraries). Has it always been this way and, more important, is the culture of "time management" the same in different places? What about the bureaucrat from Prague, quoted at the beginning of this chapter? What exactly could he have meant? By paying attention to the interplay of agents acting at varying degrees of organizational and temporal distance, we can begin to approximate a model of dynamic complexity that does justice to the specificities of state-run organizations that have operated under the political economy of socialism for close to half a century and that are now undergoing a whole sequence of stress tests as they grapple with innovative change.

The purpose of this chapter is to give an initial feel for the play of delays that have been so characteristic of the library automation projects in Eastern Europe. My aim is to identify the parameters, draw attention to the micropolitical underpinnings of these delays, and make the simple point that, objective conditions notwithstanding, the phenomenon constitutes a case of a deeply embedded social practice with ramifications that go beyond the institutional setting of a library. Practically speaking, delays are not only a hiatus in a projected flow of time. Their "silence"—for that is one of delay's distinctive qualities—is deceptive, so that any attempt to manage delays in such a setting would do well by first learning about what it has to say.

The CASLIN Project

In 1993 a library automation and consortium project funded by the Andrew W. Mellon Foundation and the Pew Charitable Trusts commenced in the Czech and Slovak republics. It involved four major libraries, two in each of the countries, and was scheduled to run for three years. During that time three other projects were launched and all of them involved different kinds of library consortia that were meant to become, together with the original CASLIN project, equal partners in a single network of cooperating institutions.[3] These too were scheduled to take about three years each. At present, as far as the U.S. side is concerned, the initial project has ended. In other words, the grant money has been spent, the account is closed, and the final report has

2. Ibid.
3. Other chapters in this volume discuss these projects in greater detail.

been submitted to the Foundation. The subsequent projects are at various stages of completion but in all cases, I think it is fair to say, we will be able to close the accounts within about a year after the originally planned three-year schedule. It is worth recalling that during the initial discussions the librarians, specifically the computer automation experts, placed their estimates of how long "it would take" at about two years. We could simply conclude from this that, insofar as both estimates were (in hindsight) naive, the whole project took between a year and two years longer than planned. After all, in the grander scheme of things, assisting large libraries out of the doldrums of a half a century of neglect and into the electronic age and the world of international library standards was no simple task. Considering the enormity of the undertaking, a delay of this magnitude is insignificant if not irrelevant. And, in fact, so much has been accomplished in the three to four years of the initial CASLIN project that it is easy to forget where things stood in the early 1990s.

But it would be misleading to leave the question of a project's duration at that. As I indicated above, it is from the granting agency's point of view that we can speak of a completion—as the funds are expended, my task as project manager comes to a close. Only if one takes a closer look, and from the perspective of the implementation process itself, does the question of the project's duration take on an opposite significance. How much of what had been planned, as outlined in the proposal, was actually accomplished? There is no such consensus on the grantees' side, partly because we are speaking of multiple site installations with not one goal but several, partly because there are many voices that are to be heard from on this side of the equation: librarians, users, vendors, and government ministries, as well as other libraries not participating in this project (to name the key players). But there is much more to it than that. The sense of accomplishment assumes a benchmark, some way of knowing that a goal has been reached. And there lies the problem. The many benchmarks thought to be in place seem rather susceptible to the micropolitics of time.

One of the more striking features of the project, and of the phenomenon of delays, is the number of initiatives that appear to dissolve into a kind of infinite regress rather than an ending, marked by an act of closure. There have been, to date, only a few instances of public recognition of a completed project or phase. The official opening of the Czech National Library's new book depository in Hostivar (January 1996) is one notable example,[4] the launching of the Aleph library system—symbolized by the introduction of the lending module—at the Slovak National Library (1996) is the other. In neither case could it be said that the task was finished "to perfection." The point is, that the celebrations marked the recognition that a stage was reached that allowed and demanded moving the project from "construction" to "use." In the former case it was a building—it would take another year before the books and departments would move and the whole setup became fully operational; in the latter case it was a complete on-line library system, even though several components in the processing line (for example, acquisitions and lending) involved some improvising.

4. The building of the Hostivar book depository was not a Mellon-funded project, though, historically speaking, it came out of a U.S. initiative to evaluate the condition of the NL in Prague in 1990. More important, it is part of the library system and therefore an integral part of the automation project.

For the most part, however, there is a sense that a significant number of project phases remain incomplete or, more exactly, forever on the verge of "being there" but never close enough, or good enough, for completion. And among those that are completed, it seems as if their significance is lost because their timeliness is (perhaps they are just lost in the buzz of activity that characterizes any large institution.) One learns about them because, as is often the case, "one day things are done differently" and then it is the imperfections that are noticed first—whether it is that way for the librarians or, more important, noticed by the users. In my case, it was my semiannual visits to the individual library sites that made me aware of some dramatic changes that, as far as I can tell, had gone publicly unannounced. Most notable among these were the visits to the Moravian Regional Library in Brno, where the project's implementation appeared to progress in definable (visible, *hmatatelný*) stages, so that, during my January 1997 visit, I had the sense that they had, in that basic sense mentioned above, reached an acceptable point of completion, similar to what took place at the Slovak National Library a few months earlier. Best of all was the time I "happened" to pass the circulation room of the National Library in Prague, and noticed that there were students sitting in front of OPAC terminals.[5]

For many there is, no doubt, a sense of genuine accomplishment. But equally there is also a feeling—so familiar in this part of the world—that it "just drags on forever" (*trvá to věčnost, táhne se to do nekonečna*) and "doesn't really work" (*nefunguje to*). I would argue that the truth of both of these positions lies as much in the fact that these are expressions of attitude, of how people actually experience what is going on and, therefore, that inform their actions, as it does in any correspondence to an actual state of affairs. Negative evaluations, especially in the form of gossip, play their part in the micropolitics of organizational behavior and are key components of the implementation process. Take, for example, an attitude shared by some of the librarians: that "this automation project can never work." Not only did it play into others' less-than-enthusiastic work morale; but also, persistent problems with the local area network (LAN) installation and the resulting delay confirmed the prophecy and, as angered and disappointed employees quit their jobs, the prophecy became—at the institutional level—self-fulfilling.

The fact of the matter is that throughout the project just about every step was accompanied by two features: It was complicated and it was late. And I can't think of anybody who would disagree that most activities involved an inordinate amount of waiting, complaints about delays, and attempts to speed things along. We can easily imagine, for that to be the case, a whole set of players locked in a relationship of codependency in which the transfer of goods, services (information), or payments is somehow awash in a sea of delays! Needless to say, such an interlocking system of delays will add a particular spin to an organization's behavior—in this case, to a whole network of players implicated in the CASLIN project. With reference to the model mentioned earlier, there is no doubt in anyone's mind that the situation poses a limit

---

5. Though, to be fair, in the case of the National Library the monthly in-house newsletter has become a good source of information and of progress reports.

to growth and is therefore a case of diminishing returns. But it is not enough to speak of the balancing feedback alone, though that is still one of the overall effects. This dense temporal structure of delays is itself dynamic in character, quite the reverse of its dampening effect—we are here faced with a case of reinforcing feedback. Simply put, delays engender more delays as people spend their time trying to bring their instance of waiting to an end.

The Play of Delays

But how is such a situation possible? What exactly lies behind these delays and how do they work? Since we have, in the case of the original CASLIN libraries, four institutions presumably cooperating in the implementation of a single system, it would seem reasonable to expect a more or less simultaneous progression through a series of stages toward a definable end. That was certainly the original intent. But with each new stage in the implementation, the differences between the sites became more apparent and the levels of completion more disparate. It has also become obvious that the tender link of cooperation between the four libraries—tender because it was de facto shouldered by those directly responsible for the system's implementation, the technical and library experts, rather than by the library directors—became, over time, the only real and progressively weaker link.

To begin with, the participating libraries were different in their organization, ways of doing things, special needs, and, perhaps most important, ties to other institutions. The introduction of a new system with an overarching library standard inevitably necessitated adjustments. Furthermore, as libraries depended on the other partner libraries for the completion of certain tasks (for example, solving the problem of Aleph data output necessary for doing acquisitions or printing paper catalog cards), they also found themselves waiting. With each stage in the implementation, the actual functioning of a library became increasingly more involved and so, not surprisingly, the response was not to wait but, instead, to look for its own solutions. As a result, local solutions were found for some of the functions (though, as far as I know, not at the cost of maintaining interlibrary standards.) This explains some of the disparity in the results and also in their timing. More to the point, if the four libraries started off on a different footing, the "delay response" not only reinforced it, but it also played into the underlying tensions already in place. In one memorable case, the anticipated delay in the development and launching of the CASLIN union catalog was used by the director of another "waiting" library to take the initiative and try to organize a union catalog of an altogether different association of libraries, of which his library was a leading member. Fortunately, this attempt was stopped. On the other hand, upon learning that this very same library had figured out a way around a long-standing technical problem with the system software, I was told, by a member of the partner library, that "the solution was suspect; it was not a real solution and, in any case, couldn't be used given their particular needs." Be that as it may, the fact is that in both cases the delays and responses to them were viewed with suspicion and it takes very little for this to develop into a reinforcing cycle of growing disparity as delays become visibly more politicized and cooperation more unstable. Not surprisingly, among the

350   *Management Issues*

various goals that failed to materialize as they receded beyond the horizon, the consortium itself looms high.

The Parameters

In order to come to grips with the multifaceted aspect of delays in the CASLIN project, it is useful to make the following distinctions.

First, we need to mention those limiting factors that are perceived as the constraints under which the libraries operate and that are arguably behind much of the behavior, including the delays. Three such limiting factors stand out: funding, regulations, and the labor force.[6] All three tie the libraries as state-funded organizations to the political economy of the city and country that they are operating in. Simply put, state funding of institutions such as libraries has been decreasing (while the operational costs have been increasing), the administrative rules continue to be confining and leave little room to maneuver; and, finally, with salaries that cannot compete with those offered to individuals by the private sector, it is very difficult to maintain a qualified labor force. It is not just the restricted funds, however, that frustrate the management's ability to fulfill the library's mandate, let alone pick up where the Mellon funds left off. There is also the fiscal schedule itself: Budgets are announced in January for the given year but the funds may not be available until months later. Expenditures must be made within that year and accounted for by its end and any surplus as well as income (!) are to be returned to the state (budget). This, as it now turns out, holds for grants given by the Ministry of Culture in 1997 as well. The existence of grants was announced in January, with applications deadlines being posted for March. Awards were announced in May but funds were not made available until late August. This means that in the four months that remain before the year is out, the full cycle of ordering, invoicing, delivery, and payment must be taken care of. These fiscal schedules result in a series of uncertainties (about funds) and pressure points (of deadlines) that alternate in a cycle that is best described as organizational arrhythmia. It means that "production" goes into "high gear," people work overtime and are chronically overextended. It does not mean that productivity goes up but, rather, that the use of shortcuts does and with it, ironically, the bottlenecks of delays.[7] I found, throughout the

---

6. Actually *time* and *space* are two other limiting factors that need to be considered. I have deliberately chosen to ignore them in the present discussion. They are complex enough to warrant a separate analysis. See an earlier study for a more in-depth analysis of the external ties, their transformation from the socialist to the post-1990 era, and their influence on library politics especially their interest in consortial activities: Andrew Lass, "The Cross-Currents of Technology Transfer: The Czech and Slovak Library Information Network," in *Technology and Scholarly Communication*, Richard Ekman and Richard E. Quandt (eds.) (Berkeley: University of California Press, 1998)—an electronic version of this collection has been published on the Web at: (http://arl.cni.org/scomm/scat/index.html). The project also exemplifies some more general issues in technology transfer to post-socialist Eastern Europe. See, Andrew Lass, "Portable Worlds: On the Limits of Replication in the Czech and Slovak Republics," in *Uncertain Transition*, edited by Michael Burawoy and Katherine Verdery). Lanham: Rowan & Littlefield, 1999.

7. Katherine Verdery (in her "The 'Etatization' of Time in Ceausescu's Romania," in *What Was Socialism and What Comes Next* [Princeton, N.J.: Princeton University Press, 1996]) uses the term "arrhythmia"

project, that as December approached it became close to impossible to move on those matters related to CASLIN that were not tied up in domestic budgets. Needless to say, the administration of the library is increasingly one engaged in crisis management, which, in turn, makes it very difficult to keep an eye on long-term trajectories.

Second, while it is possible to point to the objective condition of any delay (one can think of a narrow bandwidth or a slow processor speed as ideal examples), in practice, as the terms "delay" and "waiting" imply, we are dealing with a value judgment and in that case it is hard to imagine a delay as anything other than socially mediated. What seems clear enough is that it is inevitably the subject of a micropolitical action. An actor (individual or organization) may (or may not) respond, to a delay, regardless of its justification, although the fact that the reason for the delay is (or is not) ignored, and how the actor justifies his or her own response, are themselves important factors to keep in mind since they form an essential part of the discursive practice of delay. We should be careful to assign the same truth value to statements made about one's own reason for not waiting, and for the actions taken, that we do to the explanation (that can take the form of reproaches and outright accusations) for what is taking others "so long." In other words, the distinction between the objective circumstance (of a delay) and statements about it becomes clouded once we consider the possibility that, in pragmatic terms, it is statements (explanations) that emerge and circulate in both cases and that the actions that they inform amount to statements as well, and politicized ones at that. I can, for example, think of several cases in which the presumed responsibility for a delay was a primary reason for dismissing a library division head. This is not to argue that there was no real case to be made (the evidence seemed clear enough to all) but, rather, that the actual existence of the delay was only part of the picture. The statements that accompanied it, and the actions that followed, were the other parts.

The third distinction, alluded to above, regards the quality of otherness that is characteristic of a delay. After all, waiting implies waiting for something and, in organizational behavior, the "other" is inevitably someone else or, more exactly, some organizational level of otherness personified. More often than not, it is a concrete individual who represents for us our experience with an organization. Figure 28.1 represents some of the key players in the CASLIN project, with some indication of the ties that extend beyond the organizational horizon of the libraries themselves (but in which they are nevertheless implicated.) Since all of the ties involve some type of transfer, they also involve possible delays—like before, the different points of exchange correspond to existing institutional settings with their particular official rules and unofficial micropolitical games, all of which are implicated in the delay. It is important to keep in mind that all organizations have more than one thing they are involved in at any point in time (indicated as "oc" on the flow chart), and that they all have their internal politics (indicated as "idr"), for that is what makes for the complexity of scheduling and the potential for bottlenecks. But, in some situations, the

---

to describe the consequences of socialist planning (and the economies of shortage) that required that "all stops be pulled" to fulfill the plan.

352 *Management Issues*

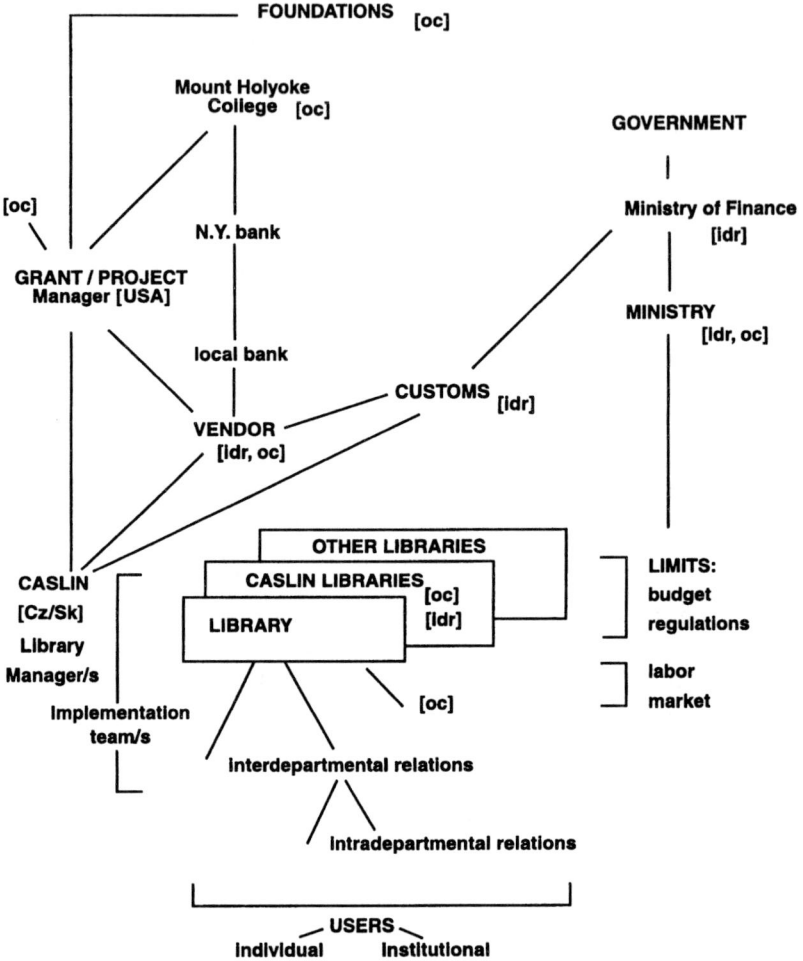

[oc] = other commitments

[idr] = inter/intra dept. relations

Figure 28.1 CASLIN Project Implementation Network (partial view)

setting of priorities and crisis management can become synonymous. This is particularly the legacy of organizations that had previously adjusted their functioning to the command economies of socialism, where the separation between the organization's distinct levels, as much as its rules of conduct, were somehow negotiable. Often, the very practice of delay worked to both alter and reinforce these rules while the process of negotiation (whether official or unofficial) between the parties involved was aimed at reversing the situation. The result was a reinforcing cycle of favoritism: The over-personalized character of professional relations was both one of the causes of delay and one of the indispensable tools for resolving it.[8]

The delays experienced in any one of the CASLIN libraries as part of the implementation process occurred, for the most part, at the same junctions that already existed within the given organizational setup. By this I mean both the organizational divisions inside the library and those that existed between the library and other institutions. The former would correspond to intradepartmental relations and interdepartmental relations, and the latter, to the existing relations between the library and, let us say, the Ministry of Culture. The existing ties, such as the very tense one between the ministry and the library, and between departments or individuals within the library, were micropolitically rich before the project began and so, not surprisingly, it was not going to be clear sailing with these preexisting conditions having a direct and inhibiting effect.[9] Initially, however, the project involved (in addition to the library director) a small group of specialists who were perceived as tangential to the mainstream concerns of the library. Insofar as we experienced sluggishness in the response time (such as in choosing the primary vendor), it could be easily attributed to the lack of previous experience and to what could be seen by outsiders as an exaggerated need for caution. But it had also to do with another factor: There was no precedent for direct dealings with a private company (the vendor), let alone a foreign one. Moreover, this was the first instance of practical cooperation between the four participating libraries. Until that point, CASLIN was a promise and a commitment (on paper) that was to be realized (or not) through the very implementation process.

The Project's Implementation Network. And so, as the project unfolded it put in place new relationships next to the old ones. In particular, the vendor(s), the grant administrator and project manager (myself), the customs office, and the CASLIN library managers evolved into a series of interdependent liaisons that were required to get the job done but that were inevitably fraught with difficulties that either resulted in delays or were caused by them. The following is a somewhat detailed account of the series of steps required to purchase a piece of hardware and get it delivered and installed.

Placing an Order. The initial order of HWs (the Digital Alpha servers) was included in the contract with the library software vendor (Ex Libris) as a subcontract. This was meant to help minimize conflicts as possible incompatibilities or problems in coordination occurred between them (as indeed they did). All subsequent orders—and there would be many—were made either by individual libraries or by one library

---

8. The argument could be made, in anthropological parlance, that the experience of delay is in some sense constituted through the existence of different levels of organizational "otherness," as it is itself constitutive of those differences. The anthropological study of segmentation in both complex organizational settings and traditional kinship systems provides a useful model for looking at the shifts in alliances that occur between different segments in the whole network as one of the functions of delay (cf. Michael Herzfeld, *The Socialist Production of Indifference* [Chicago: University of Chicago Press, 1996]).

9. The real challenge lay in the (faint) possibility that the project would become a vehicle for a new vision that would unify the employees behind a single cause. The opposite—that it would be eaten alive—was, of course, equally likely. To date, neither has happened (though we have touched base with both possibilities).

(usually the National Library) on behalf of the CASLIN group.[10] These orders—for products ranging from fax machines and disk upgrades to microfilm cameras and lab equipment—required the libraries to look into possible options, negotiate with local or foreign vendors, and work out a contract agreement that, depending on the size and complexity of the order, involved the grants administrator and project manager as well. But orders initiated separately by the CASLIN managers, or those that originated within individual divisions in a library organization, were often caught in the crossfire of confusion over procedural matters. The question of authorization would inevitably come up: Who was entitled to take such an initiative and on behalf of whom? Through whom were these requests supposed to move? Finally, the actual paperwork often required the services of the library's business office, which was unequipped to handle nonstandard (that is, foreign) forms and requests. Matters were not helped by the fact that some of the initiatives come from the grants administrator and project manager, essentially from the "outside." Not surprisingly, this confusion was not only a cause of interpersonal tensions, but it was also, in effect, an expression of them.

Initial Payment. Once an agreement on the purchase was reached (and signed), a copy of the invoice—signed by the vendor, the library director, and the local CASLIN manager (or the library division head)—was faxed to the grants administrator and project manager in the United States (the grant money was deposited with a U.S. institution of higher education). Once received, this invoice, which I countersigned, was passed on through a secretary (who kept an account of all transactions), with instructions to transfer the payment to the vendor's account. From there the invoice was passed on to the comptroller's office, where the actual instructions were given to a New York bank that in turn initiated an international electronic money transfer. Again, mishaps could and indeed did happen along this part of the route as well. If funds did not reach their destination in a reasonable amount of time, a search would be initiated from the U.S. side. It is worth noting that this particular sequence was set up to be as simple as possible—that is, there were no forms to be filled out and payment was initiated on the basis of a faxed invoice. Invariably, simple misunderstandings (such as the vendor's mailing of an invoice directly to the grants administrator and project manager in the United States, instead of to the Czech or Slovak library for signatures) would translate into extensive delays.

Delivery. It has been my policy not to allow grant funds to be used for the payment of a VAT or any other fees associated with customs. The reason, of course, was both a matter of expediency and a matter of principle. It seemed clear that paying a VAT would cut into the budget, and it seemed just as clear that since the funds follow a not-for-profit route all the way, there should be no reason for levying a VAT in the first place. Consequently, the project found itself involved with trying to change leg-

---

10. Here it is important to remind the reader that one of the unique (and complicating) features of the CASLIN project is the fact that it involves an attempt at introducing a single system (and network of cooperation) in two countries that were, from the project's outset in 1993, continuing to grow apart. This meant, and continues to mean, that the purchase and delivery of products intended for one system had to take different bureaucratic routes.

islation (and therefore dealing with the Ministry of Finance) but, at last, no VAT has been paid on any CASLIN-related Mellon purchases. In principle, the agreed-upon "VAT exemption" procedure was simple enough—it required that a letter written by the grants administrator, certifying that a particular delivery was indeed purchased by the Foundation's money, and was intended as a gift to the CASLIN library, had to accompany the actual goods through customs. But that turned out to be no easy task, not only because this letter required knowing the invoice number of the actual shipment, but also because the procedure was never the same and therefore could not be replicated in the future. Depending on the vendor's policy (and attitude), where the equipment was being shipped from and through what point of entry, the mood of the customs officer, and the particular stage in the ever-changing tax law (not to mention the particular abilities of the librarian in charge), the actual movement of goods through customs could go with ease or not at all. The point is, the procedure was never the same.[11] At times it seemed like endless exchanges were required between myself, library project managers, customs officials, and vendors, before things were straightened out and the HW released for delivery. This stage was not only a major source of irritation. It was also very time-consuming and a significant source of delay.

Installation and Final Payment. The final and, usually, second payment followed the same mechanism as outlined above but was contingent on the satisfactory delivery or, in some cases, satisfactory installation of the hardware. In the latter case, some type of test would be required but once it was passed, a request for payment would be initiated.[12]

Some of us take these steps for granted while others have never given them much thought (someone else "takes care of it") But, in a situation where both the practice itself and the particular chain of command are new, not one of the steps could be taken for granted. If anything, each step provided an opening for miscommunication and the prevailing expectation that "once I move 'it' (a message or a piece of paper) along, the next one in the line will take care of it" often proved fatal. As a result, while the various transactions were established (since most of them were new) as direct and certainly official, they nevertheless demanded extra indirect and unofficial attention—ranging from actual time spent "taking care" of them to using personal contacts to resolve a bottleneck—to help see things through. It is precisely in this move that involves the existing habit of supplementing official lines of exchange (which are always already suspect) that the new—in this case the CASLIN project—eventually succeeds and at the same time gets domesticated by the old.

---

11. In one case the local dealer for a large international computer company, after dealing with an intransigent customs officer, put the sealed merchandise back on his truck, drove it out of the country into Slovakia, where he turned around and brought it back into the Czech Republic but to a different customs office in Prague, known for being more congenial. There it was promptly released, exempt from a VAT.

12. The above description, as detailed as it may seem, is based on a typical transaction involving hardware (such as PCs). The situation becomes significantly more complex in the case of the delivery and implementation of the library software. The issue of a timely delivery of library software is intricately tied to the topic of installation and acceptance protocols. While I make reference to the Aleph system and, in particular, the launching of the cataloging process, I have chosen not to focus in detail on this critical part of the project in this chapter. I hope to do justice to this complicated and controversial topic in a separate study.

When you have a volatile baseline, dramatic changes—such as the library automation project—make it very difficult to follow through. Instead, the problems and difficulties that change brings anywhere have the wonderful ability to reinforce negative feedback mechanisms already in place. Complex organizations, such as the libraries, have a deeply entrenched way of going about doing their business, not only in terms of their mandate and in terms of their informal organizational structure, but also in terms of the informal ties that bind individuals in a dense, overdetermined network. Some speak of a corporate or institutional culture, but I have chosen to use the term "micropolitics" in order to emphasize the dynamic that informs decision-making with the subtle or not so subtle moves that individuals engage in as they position themselves in relation to what appears as the moving targets of power. It is all the more important to keep this in mind as one evaluates projects initiated in former socialist countries. The libraries of the former Czechoslovakia operated under particular constraints and developed, like other organizations, certain micropolitical climates. In the years since 1989 some constraints have remained in place while new ones have formed. Likewise, as the web of social networks worked its way through the "post-Communist" transformations, people discovered, once again, that it is the continuities that informed the discontinuities rather than the other way around.

As the project continued to unfold it also moved from the sidelines to center stage and began to directly affect the functioning of the library, as it was, indeed, meant to. Intralibrary problems and needs, as well as the history of the relationship between libraries or with the Ministry of Culture, affected the ability of the CASLIN managers to concentrate on the newly formed relationships.

The parameters of delay, discussed earlier, should help explain how the external constraints affect patterns of stress in the work flow (arrhythmia), which, in turn, feed off the preexisting micropolitical climate without which, under such circumstances, it would not be possible to get things accomplished. In other words, as the work flow becomes hectic it also becomes more unsettled and chaotic; in order to get anything done, one must interrupt what one is doing in order to help "move something else along the way." In using the unofficial social relations of production, one simultaneously reinforces them but that means that in order to interrupt someone, one must also be interrupted, thereby adding to the cumulative quality of delay. Everyone is terribly busy, nay, exhausted, though in the end, somehow, things get done (*ono se to nakonec nějak udělá*). But not always, and most important, not with the desired effect. Continuing problems in implementation (increased delays) may give the impression—to those who are waiting (other librarians, users)—that there is much to do about nothing. I have, on repeated occasions, observed the following two scenarios play themselves out: In the first case, individuals who have joined the library to help with the automation process find themselves engaged in a multiplicity of tasks that are short-term ones, usually the result of a crisis (arrhythmia) and that have little or nothing to do with automation. They are in effect "waiting for the real thing to finally take off" and are meanwhile "running around" helping with other people's tasks. In a significant amount of cases these employees leave to pursue other careers, usually not in library settings. In a few cases their departure was motivated also, but not entirely, by financial needs; in all cases discouragement was a key factor in their decision to leave. For the most part, these were not trained librarians but skilled, usually young, individuals drawn by the prospects of working with IT. In the second case, which, in contrast to the first, involves professional librarians, continuous problems in the installation of the LAN (and subsequent problems with the library system software) often meant that their retraining—an already steep learning curve—became wasteful. With no way to reinforce new habits through practice, the time between training sessions was basically lost and, worse, the initial momentum—during which it would have been easier to get people on board and capture their enthusiasm—was lost as well. By the time the processing line was running, the doldrums had set back in and the librarians, who now find the system much too complicated and the working conditions (including the payroll, frequent down time) unsatisfactory, "refuse to cooperate." The final result of this series of diminishing returns is an underutilized library automation system and a growing backlog of uncataloged books. In the first case it was disappointment that drove people away; in the second it was the cynicism that kept them uninvolved.[13]

If, as has happened on more than one occasion in the CASLIN project, the basic attitude among a large percentage of employees is that of suspicion ("you just wait, this can never work"), then we must understand that this script finds its support in the fact that socialism was notorious for grand plans that amounted to, at best, faked results and that, therefore, prolonged delays in the implementation of the library automation project only confirm this historical experience in the present. In a world where "things take forever" there is very little patience for "things that take time." Under these circumstances it is almost impossible to change lethargy or cynicism into their opposite or make the point that the institution is locked in a cycle of self-fulfilling prophecies regardless of the regime.

Conclusion

There would be plenty to reflect on in a careful study of delay (the present essay is but a hint). There is the contribution that this sort of material and analysis can provide, more generally, for an increased understanding of complex organizations and, particularly, of the different ways in which processing time and social time interact. Since we are speaking about a case of organizational change in Eastern Europe, we need to also consider to what extent our models, such as the Senge model with which this chapter began, need further development. One thing is certain: There are very few (I sometimes wonder whether there are any) incidents that occurred in the CASLIN project, or were related to it, that could not literally happen in other "Western" democracies—with so-called capitalist rather than once-socialist economies—or at

---

13. A note of caution: There are perhaps few topics in the scholarly literature that have received more attention than the relationship between new technologies of production, retraining, productivity, and labor unrest. The case could and should be told again for libraries, particularly those in Eastern Europe. My present discussion cannot possibly do justice to this important topic, nor does it make any claims on fully explaining the reasons why some (not all!) of the libraries have experienced serious delays in technical services or public services.

least for which one could not find an analogy. Rather, the challenge of description and, finally, of explanation would lie in trying to come to grips with the intensity and chronic pervasiveness of the phenomena and in figuring out what it is that sets this collective syndrome apart from others.[14] But there is also the practical side to what I have said up to this point. What is it that we can learn from all of this? It is to this question that I turn in my concluding remarks.

The preceding description of the trajectory that is traveled by goods and by information about goods (for example, invoices) makes it clear how easy it is, with so many points along the way, for delays to occur. I think it is important to underscore those junctions that have turned out, in my experience, to be critical in bringing about delays that had a serious impact on the project: First, the opening move required the ability to actually place an order and this, as we have seen, was not a straightforward process; instead, it was laden with micropolitical agendas. Second, delivery delays, especially where defective products arrived or products were missing, caused cumulative complications due to their interference with an implementation schedule. Third, the closing move was, of course, the most critical if by "installation" we also mean "implementation," or putting into operation what has been delivered. As illustrated above, of all the delays, it is this one that was most transparent to others: If, once things have "finally appeared," they "still don't work," and yet their employment is of direct and immediate consequence to the transfer of existing operational procedures to the new system, then the consequences can be disastrous.

Two singular features stand out in the way the CASLIN project was handled by the libraries and their supervisory organizations (for example, the Ministry of Culture), and these account for much of the delay and therefore for many of its consequences. First, there was a fundamental misjudgment of the expertise needed and of the demands made on the library in the implementation process and, therefore, an insufficient investment or, in one case, no upfront investment, was made in funds, human resources, and publicity.[15] Indeed, all needs were taken care of, but minimally and, in some cases, in the same improvisational manner as other library activities were handled. Second, the challenges that the project posed to the existing organizational setup were not taken up in a serious, systematic way. It is not that the organizations did not respond to the pressures. On the contrary! But, once again, these were mostly reactive rather than proactive responses—it's no wonder, then, that not all of them were forthcoming. After all, the project offered the library an opportunity to not only improve its functions but to also act as an independent subject. This means that the organization would be affected directly in two ways: (a) how it went about doing what it was used to doing (the electronic challenge to librarianship); and (b) how it arranged the organizational structure to facilitate management (delegating authority,

---

14. For the sake of simplicity, I have not discussed any of the many studies devoted to former socialist economies. An excellent review of the extant literature, as well as a serious contribution to the debates, can be found in Verdery, op. cit.

15. Actually "matching funds" were promised by the Ministry of Culture of the Czech Republic at the very onset of the project in 1993. Two years and three ministers later, those funds were appropriated.

improving work flows, and learning better time management). That the two are related is indisputable but they can and need to be kept apart: if, for example, there is good reason to debate the impact that automation and networking may have on the library's traditional cataloging needs (though I wouldn't drag this one out forever, either), then, to use another example, there is no excuse for not having a well-informed purchasing office that works to assist different departments with their varying needs in a timely and courteous manner.

If it is the case that interlibrary cooperation does make sense to the libraries that have participated in a joint automation project, then it is not enough to implement the system and assume that the rest of the cooperation will emerge as a consequence of piecemeal exchanges. It demands a coordinating body and that means that libraries need to have their representatives or consortium managers. They need to be compatible with the position of someone whose primary role is reaching out and working with other libraries, vendors, granting agencies, and other (international) library associations as part of the libraries' own internal structure. That is, of course, if the libraries are genuinely interested in reaching out. If they do, they may find that many of their internal concerns have external solutions. But a commitment must be expressed in more than just words or initial gestures. It must involve a continuum of well-publicized structural adjustments. It is essential that employees are kept informed and are listened to, and that most of them are kept on board most of the time.

An examination of what I have said indicates to me that perhaps the problem is not in delays themselves but, rather, in our chasing after them. Why indeed should we save time? Shouldn't one just accept, as the saying goes that "things take their time" and leave it at that? My answer to these philosophical questions is to suggest that while it is indeed the case that "things take their time," it is also the case that this "taking of time" is akin to a timepiece in which the mechanism is social (and not "natural") and the spring is micropolitical (and definitely not digital). The consequences are not neutral, either: The feeling that "things go on forever" (even when they don't!) and that "things don't really work as promised" (when the point is that they do work!)—this indefinite state of affairs can have quite unsettling results, as we saw. After all, how long are you willing to wait for Godot?

The faces of delay, in the CASLIN project, are numerous. It would be impossible to identify them all, let alone describe them in full. To try to do so would be to miss the point. It should be clear that—mimicking delay itself—the story of delay is a never-ending one. What I hoped to do here was to point to the importance of studying delay as a principally social and micropolitical process. This phenomenon is pervasive and lies at the core of all organizational behavior if only because, as the quote at the opening of this essay indicates, the basis of modern production, and one of its key measures of success, is speed. As systems get faster and more complex, opportunities for delay become more numerous and, potentially, more disruptive. It seems as if all we know how to do is to repeat ourselves as we look for ways to smooth out the kinks and develop more sophisticated and faster ways and then learn to live with the newfound delays.

CHAPTER 29

The Kraków Project
Problems of Management

EWA DOBRZYŃSKA-LANKOSZ

The Mellon Foundation began its Polish program at the beginning of 1990. Its first library grants were made to individual libraries (for example, the Jagiellonian Library in Kraków). Many other libraries felt that they had a good chance of receiving support from the foundation. Thus, many grant applications, often several from one university center, were submitted by Polish institutions. Subsequently, the foundation decided that it was more effective to consider joint applications from groups of libraries. This insistence by the Mellon Foundation that libraries apply for grants in a consortial setting stimulated the great academic centers not only to pool their efforts in preparing applications, but also to design joint implementations of the projects.

Appropriate management is one of the important factors in the achieving of a successful project performance, and this is particularly the case for joint projects. Hence, several chapters in this volume deal with issues of project management.[1] It should be noted that most Polish librarians were familiar with management issues only from the literature, and not from experience. The 1990s witnessed a rapid development of the management faculties at Polish universities. But in these faculties, the academic staff is mainly involved with the problems of managing industrial and commercial enterprises. The management of library projects was a novel concept. But since the opportunities provided by foundation grants represented a significant challenge for libraries, they mobilized themselves to develop the necessary management structures.

The projects in Kraków, Lublin, Poznań, and Łódź can be counted among the biggest joint library projects in Poland. In addition to these joint projects, individual libraries across the country started to coordinate their actions and a broad-based program of cooperation among all libraries with the VTLS system came into being. The objectives of this chapter are (1) to discuss the problems that arose in managing the Kraków project, and (2) to compare it with other, similar projects. It should be noted that some problems arose from the lack of a clearly defined management structure for countrywide cooperation. At present we are working on refining and perfecting the principles of cooperation. Brief comments about this will be provided at the end of this chapter.

I am indebted, for important information, to various individuals engaged in implementing the projects discussed in this chapter.
   1. See, for example, the chapters by A. Lass and by M. Fogarassy.

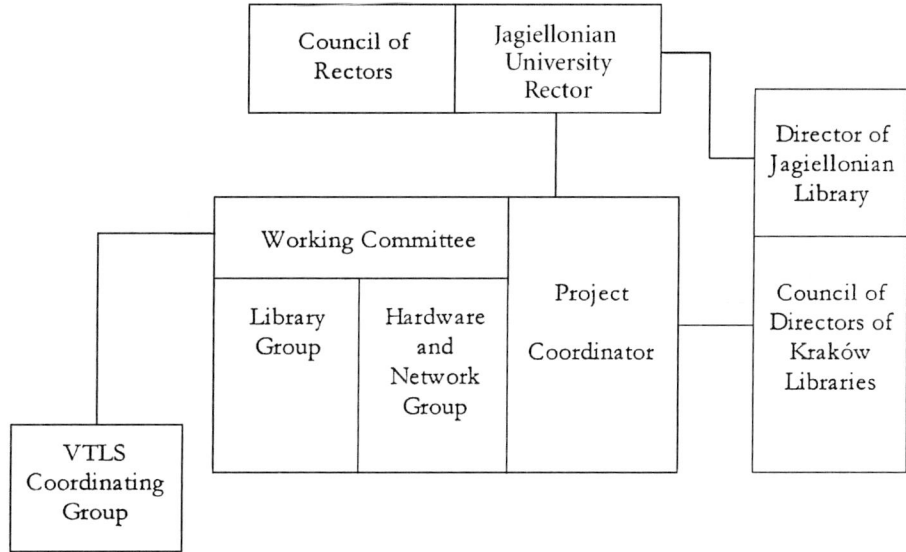

Figure 29.1 Stage 1 of Project Management

Managing the Kraków Project

Initially, three stages of project management were developed: stage 1, involving the preparation of an application for grants from the Mellon Foundation and from the State Committee of Scientific Research; stage 2—the implementation of the Kraków project of library automation, and stage 3—the use of library system.

The management scheme for stage 1 is presented in figure 29.1. Stage 1, apart from the preparation of applications for grants, was also devoted to the development of the metropolitan area network (MAN), administered by the Academic Computer Center, and of the local academic networks of Jagiellonian University, and the University of Mining and Metallurgy (UMM), and the University of Technology, as well as to the implementation of the VTLS system at the Jagiellonian Library and at the UMM Main Library.

From the beginning, there was no doubt that the library automation project should be firmly anchored within the existing metropolitan network project. Therefore, a representative of the Academic Computer Center participated in the preliminary work on the library project and checked for possible inconsistencies between the two projects.

It was decided to establish, for stage 2, various implementation and working groups for the different tasks that had to be carried out (see figure 29.2). After the Mellon Foundation approved a grant for the project, we immediately proceeded with this stage. Soon thereafter, the importance of organizing the project and managing people and tasks became obvious. A competitive search for a project manager was announced, and one was duly appointed. Then, in order to build a proper foundation

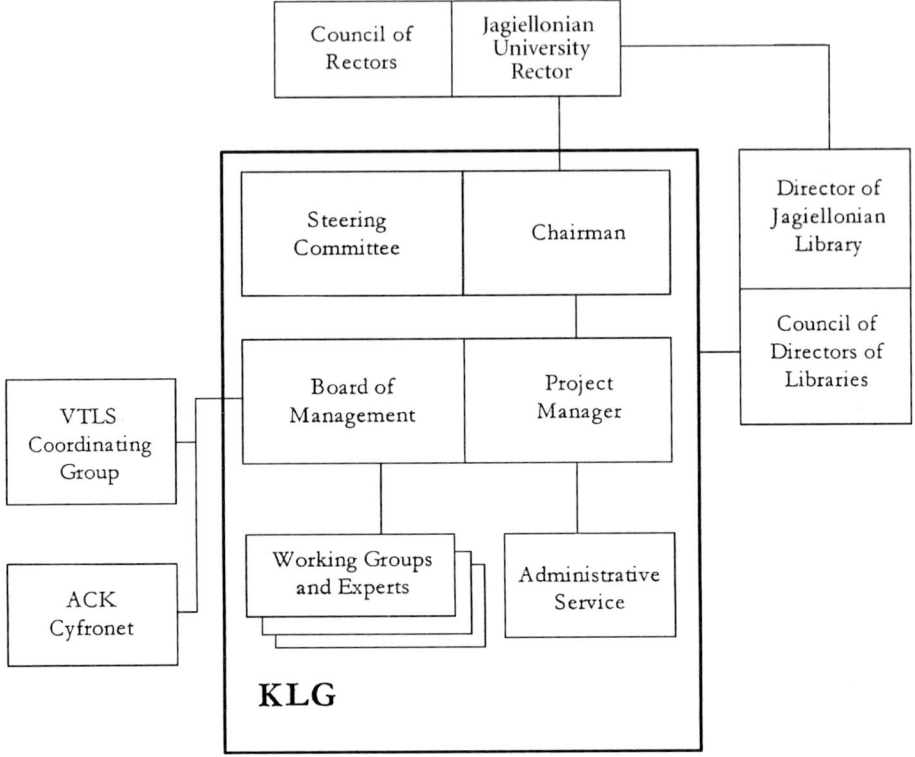

Figure 29.2 Stage 2 of Project Management

for further activities, the scope of the duties and responsibilities of various groups and persons working on the project was defined, and formally adopted in an agreement, which established the Kraków Library Group (KLG) for the carrying out of the library automation project. This agreement defined the organizational scheme of the KLG. It specified that the Steering Committee, appointed and recalled by the Council of Rectors, is the highest authority within the KLG. The committee includes representatives (on the level of vice rectors) of the four largest Kraków universities or academies, the director of the Academic Computer Center, and the director of the Jagiellonian Library.

The executive body of the KLG is the Board of Management, which includes the project manager and managers of the technical, training, and library-system implementation working teams. In response to current needs arising from time to time, additional teams or consultants were temporarily appointed for particular tasks.

While the agreement defines the general duties and responsibilities of the Steering Committee and of the project manager, its primary function is to empower the Steering Committee to chart general KLG strategy, to coordinate the activities related to the performance of the project, and to make financial decisions (excluding an operating fund that is at the project manager's disposal).

The competencies and duties of the project manager were set as follows: (1) to be responsible for project implementation; (2) to prepare performance schedules for given tasks; and (3) to report on the activities of the Board of Management to the Steering Committee. In practice, the project manager's principal tasks are the organization of the work of the Board of Management; the supervision of implementation of the library system; the supervision of the organization and training activities; as well as the maintenance of contacts with the Polish VTLS Consortium, so as to be able to proceed in accordance with the provisions laid out by the consortium for developing common solutions and preparing common undertakings. The agreement also includes basic financial regulations, and covers such items as sources of the project's financing, the allocation of the foreign and Polish funds, and the so-called operating fund.

The operating fund was established to cover expenses connected with project management. In the initial phase it was necessary to work out the ground rules for drawing from the operating fund and the principles of account settlement. It was also necessary to work out rules of compensation for key individuals within the KLG. The detailed solutions were in conformity with the original stipulations of KLG, although some details had to be modified in accordance with the lessons learned from experience.

Training was considered to be extremely important in the Kraków project and the decision was made that this was a principal element of project management. Parallel with the purchase of hardware and software, the Board of Management organized training for librarians that covered in (1) MARC formats for different type of documents; (2) bibliographic descriptions; (3) rules for authority files; and (4) the organization of work within the system, including data entry into the union database as well as into other data structures in the integrated library systems.

Due to the various educational levels of librarians and to the fact that training was needed in various subject areas, it was necessary to appoint a coordinator for the education of librarians. The coordinator is responsible both for the preparation of training programs, and instructional and other materials, and for keeping to time schedules, making physical arrangements for lectures, and appointing lecturers.

The technical team supervises, and ensures the compatibility of, the library project and the Metropolitan Area Network project.

The team for the implementation of the library system is responsible for the design and proper operation of the library system, its everyday maintenance, database backups, and archiving. The experience gained from the UNIX version of the VTLS system indicated that if several databases are installed on the same server, it is necessary to provide a single management team for the daily operations of both the databases and the system, contrary to what occurs with the MPE versions, where the administration of individual databases can be clearly separated.

The generation of the reports is an essential aspect of project management. The following three types of reports are prepared:

- reports on the activities of the Board of Management—submitted to the Steering Committee
- reports on the activities of the KLG—submitted to the Council of Rectors
- reports on the performance of project—periodic or final—which are required by all project sponsors, both Polish and foreign.

During stage 3, a management organization similar to that of stage 2 was foreseen. It is anticipated that the Steering Committee will be dissolved, but that the team working under the project manager will remain. This team is to be responsible for the supervision of the proper use of the system, for the day-to-day handling of the databases, for cooperation with the Polish VTLS Consortium, and for the further development of library automation in the Kraków academic environment. If this concept is accepted, further work will need to be done to work out detailed solutions and to coordinate future activities.

Management of Other Library Projects

The forms of management structures in other large Polish library projects differ from one another, although there are numerous family resemblances.

The Lublin Project. This project was started by an agreement between the rectors of four Lublin universities. A team consisting of the following people was appointed by the rector's office of the UMCS:

- a technical specialist (in computer network, too);
- a library specialist;
- a financial specialist;
- a team secretary.

The chairman was appointed to supervise the Lublin Consortium. Financial decisions of significant size were taken by the rector of the University of Marie Curie–Skłodowska, or, for lesser amounts, decisions were made by the team. The project did not anticipate covering project management costs on a permanent basis, except in the initial period, when the labor costs were covered out of the grants obtained by the consortium.

At present, the retroconversion program is performed as a common enterprise. The chairman of the consortium coordinates the program; administrative activities are carried out by the secretary.

The lack of a clear structure and of strictly defined competencies for the persons engaged in various tasks leads one to the conclusion that in the case of the Lublin Consortium it very difficult to say anything about the management of the consortium. Neither experts, nor teams to solve new problems, have been appointed. However, this does not mean that coordination is nonexistent. Coordination is performed to a great extent due to the close cooperation of the Lublin libraries with the Center for Formats and Authority Files, and is thus due to their participation in the work carried out on the national level or at least the interregional level. The system implementation policy depends to a large extent also on decisions of the library directors.

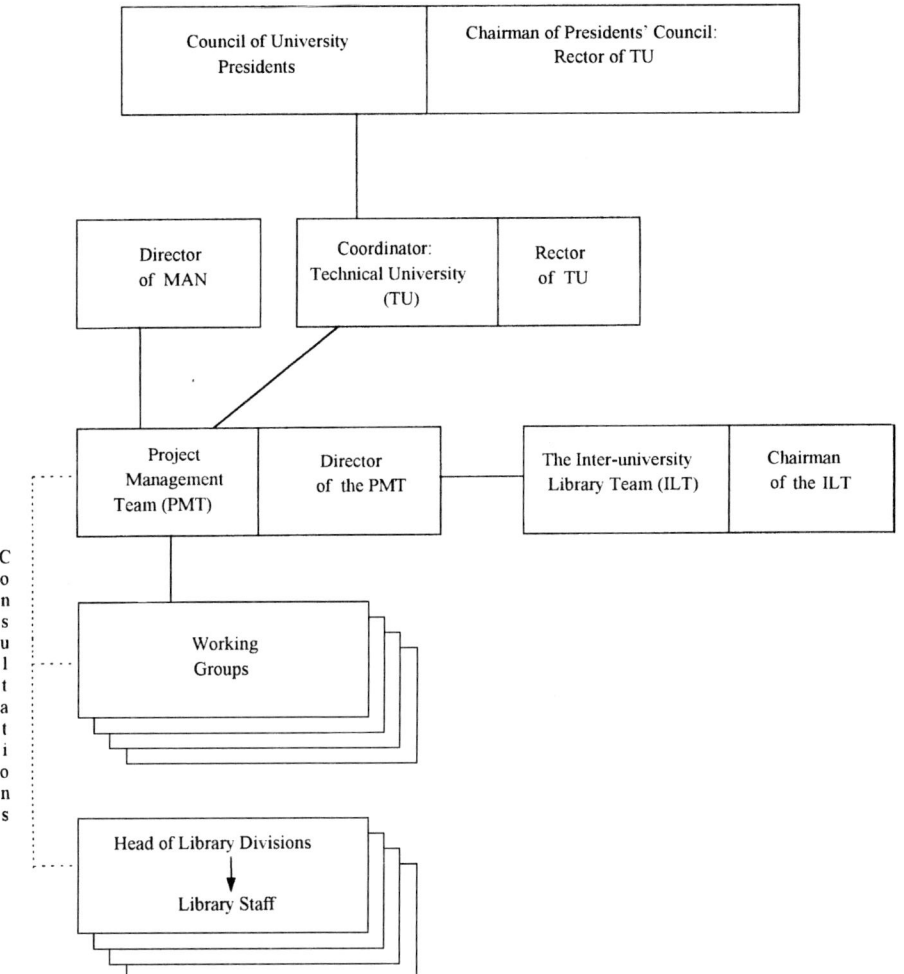

Figure 29.3 The Łódź Project's Management Structure

The Łódź Project. The project at Łódź, like the projects at Kraków and Lublin, was also begun under an agreement between rectors (1995). The project management structure (see figure 29.3) was developed at the time that an application to the Mellon Foundation was in the stage of preparation. According to the adopted stipulations, the project implementation is supervised by the Conference of Rectors, with the assistance of the following:

- the coordinator and financial manager—the rector of the Technical University of Łódź,
- the Interuniversity Library Team (with a chairman),
- the Project Management Team (with a director).

The Interuniversity Library Team was appointed by the chairman of the Conference of Rectors. The team includes the directors of the libraries in Łódź that are participating in the project. The main tasks of the team are:

- the supervision of the project's implementation—in particular, obtaining information from the Project Management Team about the progress of the project's implementation and evaluating the quality of grant implementation by the Management Team;
- the coordination of the execution of the project.

The rector of the Technical University, in agreement with the chairman of the Interuniversity Library Team, appointed the Project Management Team to operate the project. The Project Management Team has at its disposal two working groups: a library working group (system-librarians from individual libraries) and a technical working group. The tasks of the library group include:

- the preparation of preinstallation sheets required by Horizon;
- the coordination of work related to testing the database configuration;
- the organization of training for librarians.

Training is among the principal tasks of the project. In addition to training provided by the software vendor, additional training was also organized, such as lectures on library automation (with lecturers invited from all over the country); training in book cataloging (such as in the operation of the cataloging module, or in the creation of bibliographic records or authority records, training in data export and import, and in the OPAC); training for the system and database administrators; and consultations for the system and database administrators, catalogers, and system-librarians. The training pertaining to the acquisition, circulation, and serials-control modules is planned for a later date.

Apart from training organized by the library group, the libraries conduct an internal training for its own staff—like, for example, the Kraków Consortium conducts.

The training and work in systems are also based on instructions and methodical material developed by a group of the VTLS libraries, although work on the preparation of the project's own, new instruction materials is conducted.

The technical group is responsible for the configuration of librarian workstations, the configuration of local networks, and its connection to the MAN backbone.

In addition, the library server-managing team was appointed (three administrators, one for each server). They are responsible for proper server operations. They are engaged in system work and prepare the system and database backup. It is planned to extend the team as its tasks become widened.

Costs connected with project management are shared among all institutions participating in the project.

The Poznań Project. The Poznań Foundation of Scientific Libraries was established in 1996. The structure, competence of individual teams, tasks, and decision-making process were clearly stated in the foundation's statute.

According to this statute the foundation includes the following organs:

- the Assembly of Founders;
- the Council of the Foundation;
- the Board of the Foundation (see figure 29.4).

The assembly of Founders is composed of representatives of founders (rectors or heads of other institutions) who determine the foundation's policy. Their tasks also include the assignment and recall of the board's members and its chairman, the approval of an annual blueprint and an annual budget, the acceptance of reports prepared by the Board of the Foundation and the Council of the Foundation.

The council consists of six representatives of the founders. The board performs such tasks as deciding on the annual blueprint, supervising the board's activity, and providing opinions on the annual budget.

The foundation is directed and represented outside by the board, which consists of three persons. The chairman, chosen after a competition, is the head of the board. The board is responsible for the implementation of the library system. Its tasks include the preparation of annual plans of activity and of annual reports, and supervision of the activity of experts and working teams.

There are permanent teams such as library teams, and temporary teams appointed

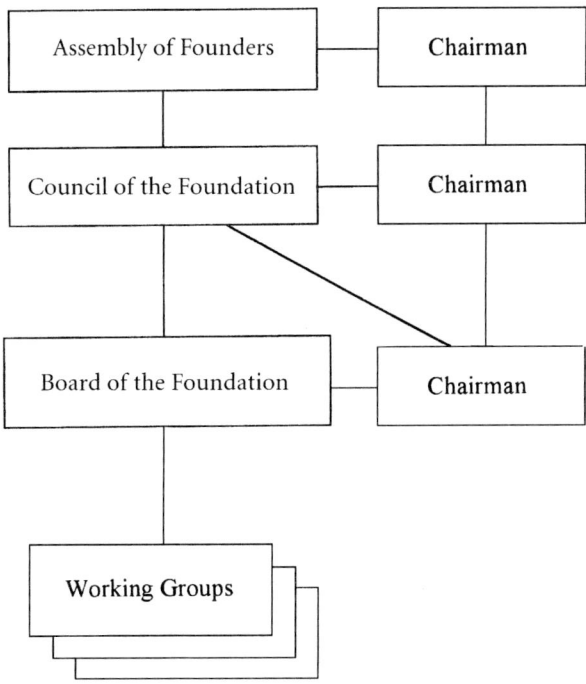

Figure 29.4 The Poznań Project's Management Structure

to perform specific tasks. The library team includes system-librarians and its operation is directed by the deputy of the chairman of the foundation. The task of the team is to coordinate the work of libraries participating in the project, to assist in the preparation of development plans for individual libraries, to supervise the implementation of the system, and to organize training.

In addition, the system administrator and system-librarian are employed on each of three servers. These teams are responsible for the operation of the system. Costs related to the project's management are borne by the foundation. The foundation's revenues originate from subsidies, legacies, donations, and from membership fees paid by institutional members of the foundation

The All-Polish Project of the VTLS Libraries. Before common local projects were established, the leaders of four Polish libraries, which had decided to purchase the same library system, entered into a program of cooperation. Due to the exceptional imagination of some of the individuals involved, four libraries—the University Library in Warsaw, the Main Library of Gdańsk University, the Jagiellonian Library (Kraków), and the Main Library of the University of Mining and Metallurgy (UMM-Kraków)—coordinated the work connected with the implementation of the integrated library system.

In 1993, the rectors of the universities mentioned above signed an agreement on cooperation. Under this agreement the Interuniversity VTLS Coordinating Group was appointed. The agreement was of a very general nature. It was assumed that shortly after the signing of the agreement, detailed rules for group operations would be specified in a formal document. Unfortunately, such a document has never been prepared. Since neither the management structure for such an all-Polish enterprise, nor its responsibilities and competencies, have been clearly defined, the group practically terminated its operation, although cooperation between libraries has not been suspended. An initiative related to the most urgent common tasks was taken over by the working teams: the system-librarian team, the validation team, the journals' union catalog team, and the most recent one, the team for developing specifications for a consortial union catalog. The system-librarian and validation teams were created because of the need to maintain permanent work contacts between persons responsible for individual catalogs and the staff engaged in subject preparation. The task of this team is to set up detailed principles of cooperation within the scope of the establishing of the Union Authority Files. The work of both teams is coordinated by the Center for Formats and Authority Files. The Journals' Union Catalog team coordinates work connected with the creation of the periodicals database.

In such a situation it is difficult to conduct common enterprises, and thus at the end of 1996, the problem related to the management of the all-Polish project was resumed and work on implementing considerable changes was begun. At the time when this chapter was being prepared, the work on a new document was completed, in principle. According to the document under preparation, the new structure of the VTLS Library Consortium includes:

- the Council of Directors;
- the Presidium of the Council of Directors;
- the Coordinating Group (see figure 29.5).

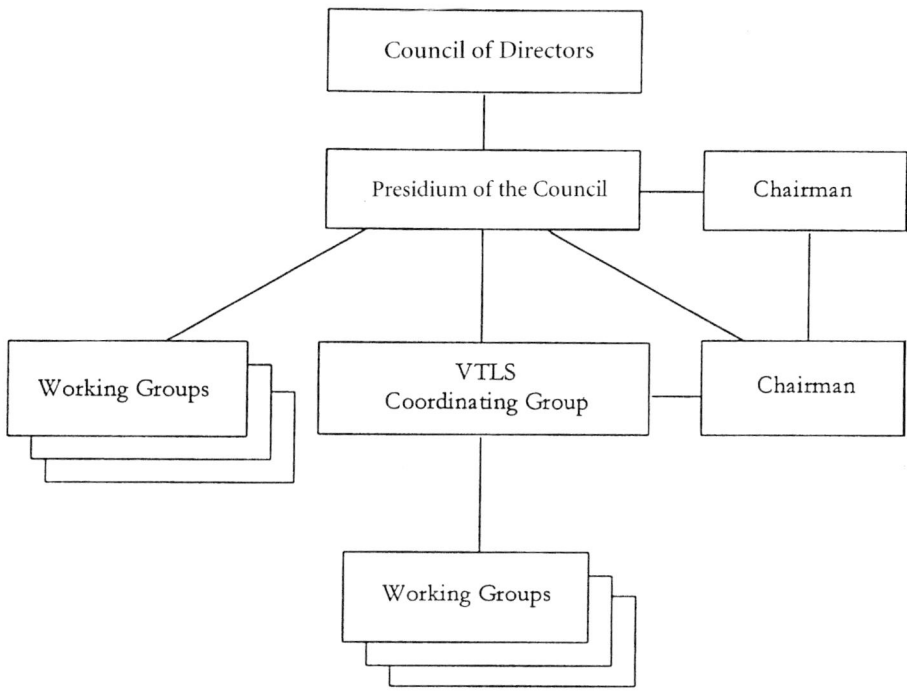

Figure 29.5 The Polish VTLS Consortium Project Management Diagram

The Council is composed of directors of the libraries in which VTLS is used. The Council elects the Presidium, consisting of seven persons, from among its members. The chairman is the head of the Presidium. The Coordinating Group is also appointed by the Council. The group's members elect, from among themselves, a chairman and a science secretary.

The proposed solution permits a straightforward extension of the consortium to new VTLS libraries (each director is, ex officio, incorporated into the Council of Directors) and at the same time it defines the procedure for the election of the representatives to the Coordinating Group. The tasks and competencies of individual units are also set in the agreement.

It was also assumed that the permanent operating fund, designed for covering costs connected with the all-Polish project management, would be created.

Conclusions

The solutions for designing project management structures that are presented above differ among themselves to a greater or lesser extent. In some cases, the responsibilities and competencies of particular units have been clearly specified (Kraków, Poznań), while this is not the case in others (Lublin) (see appendix 29.1). Typically, each structure contains several tiers, and there are executive units as well as supervising ones. In the majority of cases, the projects are executed on the basis of a work schedule. The reports on the execution of tasks constitute a control tool. All consortia that work on the basis of clearly specified principles are able to operate efficiently. When competencies and responsibilities for particular teams or persons are clearly indicated, it is possible to control and coordinate their work (provided that a supervisory unit is competent and is able to assess tasks properly and account for them consistently). The failure to perform tasks then leads to the recall and replacement of the team in question. In the draft of the VTLS libraries' agreement, it was anticipated that the terms of office for the officials would be three years, but in the event of nonperformance, team members can be relieved of their duties.

The project managers take on a great deal of responsibility. These persons must have special skills, not limited to ordinary managerial abilities, but must also include such skills as the ability to anticipate and they must be able to solve difficult problems, and must be stable and even-tempered. Needless to say, it is not easy to find such persons.

The solution applied in Poznań differs considerably from the majority of solutions discussed in this chapter. The Poznań Foundation seems to represent the clearest and most stable solution, while the management system seems to offer the most professional solution. Due to having its own foundation, the Poznań solution is able to avoid many financial difficulties or property squabbles, as well as problems related to employment issues, which were experienced by the KLG, especially at the beginning. However this does not mean that such a solution is an ideal one. For example, the Poznań Scientific Library Foundation encountered a problem, resulting from Polish customs regulations, that could not have been predicted.

The above assessment is based only on theoretical considerations. So far, the projects of the VTLS libraries have shown the most distinctive progress. This is probably because, despite some organizational problems, the group of the Polish VTLS libraries is the only group that has entered into close collaboration on an all-Polish level, so far, under a formal agreement of collaboration. Although the statute of the Poznań Scientific Library Foundation anticipates its cooperation with other domestic library networks, this has not yet begun. Consultations conducted between representatives of particular local projects, (Łódź, Poznań, Toruń) allow us to expect that the Polish libraries that use the Horizon system will enter into closer cooperation very soon.

There are also plans for cooperation among libraries that use different systems. It is possible that formal agreements will be signed in the future. As yet, there are no such agreements, but this does not mean that particular groups operate independently and separately. For example, the University Library in Toruń, using the Horizon library system, cooperates with the VTLS Library Consortium in order to develop the union authority files. It should also be added that many libraries outside the VTLS group obtain benefits from the publications of the VTLS Consortium, and participate in training, workshops, and system-librarian meetings that are organized by the VTLS group.

Conclusions resulting from the work performed by the team for the preparation of a union catalog (WuKa) are also unique: It is necessary to achieve agreements between libraries using either the same or different systems. Similar conclusions have been drawn by other teams and persons representing various environments (for example, from Łódź or Toruń). It should be noted that many tasks are often duplicated (for example, translations of the MARC format). This is caused by a lack of coordination on the system level. Because many activities are undertaken individually, the same work is repeated many times, which leads to discrepancies and inconsistent solutions.

It is quite likely that agreements will be concluded in Poland in order to minimize the duplication of work, and to ensure that everybody uses the same sources, such as authority files and union catalogs.

Appendix 29.1

Kraków Library Group's members:

1. Jagiellonian University—Uniwersytet Jagielloński
2. University of Mining and Metallurgy—Akademia Górniczo-Hutnicza
3. Academy of Economics of Kraków—Akademia Ekonomiczna
4. Agricultural University of Kraków—Akademia Rolnicza
5. University of Technology—Politechnika Krakowska
6. Pedagogical University—Wyższa Szkoła Pedagogiczna
7. Academy of Music Art—Akademia Muzyczna
8. Academy of Fines Arts—Akademia Sztuk Pięknych, Kraków
9. State Academy of Theatre Art—Państwowa Wyższa Szkoła Teatralna
10. Pontifical Academy of Theology—Papieska Akademia Teologiczna
11. Medical College of Jagiellonian University—Collegium Medicum Uniwersytetu Jagiellońskiego
12. Polish Academy of Science—Polska Akademia Nauk
13. Institute of Nuclear Physics—Instytut Fizyki Jądrowej

Łódź Project's members:

1. University of Łódź—Uniwersytet Łódzki
2. Technical University of Łódź—Politechnika Łódzka
3. Medical University of Łódź—Akademia Medyczna
4. Military Medical Academy—Wojskowa Akademia Medyczna
5. Academy of Music—Akademia Muzyczna
6. Strzeminski Academy of Fine Arts—Akademia Sztuk Pięknych im. W. Strzeminskiego
7. Catholic Theology Seminary —Wyższe Seminarium Duchowne
8. National Higher School of Film, Television, and Theater—Państwowa Wyższa Szkoła Filmowa, Telewizyjna i Teatralna w Łodzi
9. Center of Molecular and Macromolecular Studies of the Polish Academy of Sciences—Centrum Badań Molekularnych i Makromolekularnych PAN

10. Jozef Pilsudski Scientific Public Regional Library of Łódź—Wojewódzka i Miejska Biblioteka Publiczna im. Marszałka Józefa Piłsudskiego w Łodzi

Lublin Project's members:

1. Marie Curie-Skłodowska University—Uniwersytet Marii Curie-Skłodowskiej
2. University of Agriculture of Lublin—Akademia Rolnicza, Lublin
3. Technical University of Lublin—Politechnika Lubelska
4. Catholic University of Lublin—Katolicki Uniwersytet Lubelski
5. Hieronim Łopaciński Voivodship Public Library of Lublin—Wojewódzka Biblioteka Publiczna im. Hieronima Łopacińskiego w Lublinie

Poznań Project's members:

1. Adam Mickiewicz University in Poznań—Uniwersytet im. Adama Mickiewicza w Poznaniu
2. Poznań University of Technology—Politechnika Poznańska
3. Agriculture University in Poznań—Akademia Rolnicza w Poznaniu
4. Poznań University of Economics—Akademia Ekonomiczna w Poznaniu
5. Karol Marcinkowski Academy of Medical Sciences—Akademia Medyczna im. Karola Marcinkowskiego w Poznaniu
6. Eugeniusz Piasecki University School of Physical Education in Poznań—Akademia Wychowania Fizycznego im. Eugeniusza Piaseckiego w Poznaniu
7. Ignacy Jan Paderewski Academy of Music in Poznań—Akademia Muzyczna im. Ignacego Paderewskiego w Poznaniu
8. Academy of Fine Arts in Poznań—Akademia Plastyczna w Poznaniu
9. Pontifical Faculty of Theology in Poznań—Papieski Wydzial Teologiczny
10. Polish Academy of Sciences—Polska Akademia Nauk, Oddzial w Poznaniu
11. Poznań Society of Friends of Arts and Sciences—Poznańskie Towarzystwo Przyjaciół Nauk
12. Edward Raczyński City Public Library of Poznań—Biblioteka Raczyńskich

VTLS Consortium (libraries from Gdańsk, Kraków, Lublin, Warsaw, Wrocław):
1. Warsaw University—Uniwersytet Warszawski
2. Jagiellonian University—Uniwersytet Jagielloński
3. University of Gdańsk—Uniwersytet Gdański
4. University of Wrocław—Uniwersytet Wrocławski
5. Marie Curie-Skłodowska University—Uniwersytet Marii Curie-Skłodowskiej
6. Catholic University of Lublin—Katolicki Uniwersytet Lubelski
7. University of Mining and Metallugry—Akademia Górniczo-Hutnicza
8. University of Technology in Kraków—Politechnika Krakowska
9. Technical University of Lublin—Politechnika Lubelska
10. Pontifical Academy of Technology in Kraków—Papieska Akademia Teologiczna
11. Medical College of Jagiellonian University—Collegium Medicum Uniwersytetu Jagiellońskiego

12. Agricultural University of Kraków—Akademia Rolnicza, Kraków
13. University of Agriculture of Lublin—Akademia Rolnicza, Lublin
14. Pedagogical University—Wyższa Szkoła Pedagogiczna, Kraków
15. Academy of Fine Arts—Akademia Sztuk Pięknych, Kraków
16. State Academy of Theater Art—Państwowa Wyższa Szkoła Teatralna, Kraków
17. Academy of Economics of Kraków—Akademia Ekonomiczna, Kraków
18. Institute of Nuclear Physics—Instytut Fizyki Jądrowej, Kraków
19. Polish Academy of Science—Polska Akademia Nauk (several libraries from Gdańsk and Kraków)
20. National Ossoliński Institute—Zakład Narodowy im. Ossolińskich
21. Hieronim Łopaciński Voivodship Public Library of Lublin—Wojewódzka Biblioteka Publiczna im. Hieronima Łopacińskiego w Lublinie

CHAPTER 30

Staffing Patterns for Academic Libraries of Central and Eastern Europe, Russia, and the CIS Countries

ROBERT M. HAYES

This chapter presents the background, methodology, and results of a research project that obtained data concerning staffing patterns for major academic libraries in Central and Eastern Europe, Russia, and the countries that belong to the Commonwealth of Independent States (CIS). The project analyzed those data for the purpose of establishing a set of benchmarks as a basis for assessing the effects of future changes, especially those resulting from library automation.

The objectives of the investigation were threefold:

1. to establish objective means for relating the staffing of selected libraries to the workloads in services to clients (populations being served) and processing of materials;
2. to do so in a manner that will permit library managers to easily assess the effects of changes in both the workloads and the means for the management of them (especially the latter as represented by the introduction of automated systems);
3. to establish, to the greatest extent possible, broadly applicable values for underlying parameters that determine or, at the least, affect the relationships between workloads and staffing.

The following issues provide the rationale for these objectives: First, Funding agencies, such as the Mellon and Soros foundations, need to assess the effects of their support of libraries upon the services, operations, staffing, and management of the libraries for which each has provided support. To do so, consistent benchmarks should be established for the objective assessment of current patterns within a framework that, to the maximum extent possible, is externally confirmed and uniformly applicable. Second, effective management of change within the libraries themselves requires that they have externally justifiable, objective criteria against which to assess needs and effects of changes.

Third, support by institutions of their libraries requires that there be a rational, objective basis on which to assess the needs for the staffing of those libraries.

Methodology

The hypotheses and conjectures that served as the frame of reference for analyzing these issues are presented in the next section, together with a discussion of the extent to which each was confirmed or denied by the results of the analyses. The question that underlay them is whether the patterns experienced in Central and Eastern European countries are at all similar to those in Western countries. To answer that question, an existing, well-tested model, the Library Staffing Model (LSM), was used. It relates staffing requirements to workloads in the providing of services to various populations of users and in the processing of materials acquired. It is based primarily on experiences of libraries in the United States, although it has been successfully applied to libraries in a number of other countries (in particular, Canada, Australia, Japan, and Brazil). An overview of the nature and use of the LSM is presented later in this chapter.

The LSM was the structure into which data acquired from participating libraries were recorded in a uniform, consistent fashion. Worksheets provided means for obtaining those data. They were distributed by e-mail to participating libraries, who recorded data in a standardized format about populations they serve, materials they acquire, and current patterns of use and of staffing. Applications of the model were made to those data, independently for each library and then to a "Study Composite Library" (generated as the average for each field of relevant data over all of the participating libraries). In this chapter, only the application to the Study Composite Library will be discussed, in order to avoid any possible breach of confidentiality. However, the Study Composite Library is in fact representative not only of the group as a whole but also of individual libraries themselves, since they were remarkably similar in most significant aspects, even though they were of a wide range of sizes and coming from different countries.

A further application of the model was made to a real U.S. academic library, called the "U.S. Comparison Library," which was selected as being sufficiently similar to the Study Composite Library to serve as a basis for the comparison of results and the interpretation of them.

Later in this chapter, details of the process of data acquisition and analysis will be provided. In this process, 12 academic libraries served as the context for the analysis. For each library and for the Study Composite Library, the data acquired served as the input to the LSM.

Summary of the Results

A later section of this chapter presents the detailed results of the analysis, based on the application of the LSM to the data from the participating libraries. The results are presented in terms of three patterns: (1) patterns of use, (2) patterns in the acquisition and processing of materials, and (3) patterns of staffing.

With respect to patterns of use, the decision was made to make the overall patterns for the Composite Library identical to those for the Comparison Library, since those are the default values for the LSM. Differences were therefore only with respect to the size of each type of population included and to the then resulting distributions of the uses of services and materials. The distributions were determined from the reported data concerning actual levels of use of each type of service or material (as discussed in a later section, which describes the procedure for data entry and analysis). The results for the frequency of use at the Study Composite Library are approximately half of those in the Comparison Library with respect to the uses of both services and materials.

With respect to patterns in the acquisition of materials, the amount of acquisitions for the Study Composite Library is about half that for the Comparison Library (although that ratio must be treated with caution, since the two are not completely comparable). The most meaningful differences are shown with respect to the distributions of processing of materials.

With respect to patterns in staffing, for both the Comparison Library and the Study Composite Library, the estimates for total staffing and for staff distributions by functional area provided by the LSM are very close to the actual figures. The distributions among levels of staff are substantially different for the Study Composite Library. Specifically, in the Comparison Library, as in the United States generally, 25 percent of staff are students, but in the Study Composite Library virtually none are students. And the ratio of professional-to-support-staff members in the Comparison Library, as in the United States generally, is about 1 to 2, but in the Study Composite Library it is nearly 4 to 1.

Implications of the results of the analysis are presented, in three major categories: (1) those with respect to hypotheses, (2) those with respect to library automation, and (3) those with respect to management policies.

Hypotheses and Conjectures

The following are the specific hypotheses that guided the investigation and, for each, the conjectures formed at the initiation of it and the extent to which the hypotheses and conjectures were confirmed or denied:

1. Workloads for the use of libraries by populations served in Central and Eastern Europe, Russia, and the CIS countries are, at the moment, different from those in the United States and other Western countries. It was conjectured that hypothesis 1 would be confirmed. Specifically, it was conjectured that the identifiable bases for differences would include policies with respect to the access to materials (for example, closed stacks versus open stacks and restrictions on lending); user orientation (for example, lack of experience in the use of electronic services); and the effects of library automation. This hypothesis was clearly confirmed. The workloads for uses and services are substantially different, both in overall totals and in specific distributions. Those differences are identifiably related to policies, the nature of uses, and the effects of library automation.
2. Workloads for the acquisition and processing of materials by libraries in Central and Eastern Europe, Russia, and the CIS countries are, at the moment, different from those in the United States and other Western countries. It was conjectured that hypothesis 2 would be qualitatively confirmed. Specifically, it was conjectured that the

identifiable bases for differences would include economic conditions (for example, lack of financial resources and lack of centralized bibliographic utilities), and the effects of library automation. This hypothesis was clearly confirmed. The workloads for the acquisition and processing of materials are substantially different, both in overall totals and in the specific distributions. Those differences are identifiably related to economics and to the effects of library automation.
3. Overall patterns for the staffing of libraries in Central and Eastern Europe, Russia, and the CIS countries are essentially similar to those for the United States and other Western countries in relationships between the workloads and the staffing required to handle the workloads. This hypothesis was clearly confirmed. In fact, the only change in workload factors (which are the underlying core of the LSM) needed to reflect the staffing in the participating libraries was in stack paging and maintenance (because of the need for paging from closed stacks), and that change was derived from the U.S. experience in such closed-stack-contexts.
4. Distributions of staffs in libraries of Central and Eastern Europe, Russia, and the CIS countries are similar to each other. It was conjectured that there would be similarities among the libraries in Central and Eastern Europe, Russia, and the CIS countries with respect both to the staff distributions by functions that are similar to the United States in staffing patterns and to those that are not similar to the United States (that is, even where there may be differences between these libraries and the United States, there will be similarities among them). This hypothesis was clearly confirmed. The several participating libraries, across the six countries included among them, were remarkably similar in both staffing patterns and workload patterns.
5. Distributions of staffs in libraries of Central and Eastern Europe, Russia, and the CIS countries are similar to those in the United States with respect to their relative numbers of professionals and nonprofessionals. It was conjectured that this hypothesis would be denied, given the egalitarian wage scales in Central and Eastern Europe, Russia, and the CIS countries. This hypothesis was completely denied (as it was conjectured that it would be). In fact, while the total numbers of staff in the participating libraries are consistent with the workload requirements, there is essentially no use of a student staff and the ratio of professional-to-support staff members is 4 to 1. This is in sharp contrast to the U.S. experience, in which 25 percent of staff members in academic libraries are students, and in which the ratio of professional-to-support staff members is about 1 to 2.

It is important to note that given the size of the sample (12 libraries that were highly self-selected), there is at best a minimal basis on which to make any statement about the extent to which the confirmation of the hypotheses can be generalized to a larger population. These results are therefore presented solely as they apply to this specific context. Having said that, one must also say that the results are remarkably consistent across the entire set of libraries, as will be demonstrated later.

LSM—The Analytical Tool Used in the Project

The methodology in this study (as noted previously) is based on the use of an existing model, the Library Staffing Model, which provides the means for representing the workloads generated by various populations of users and by types of acquired materials and for estimating the staff required to meet those workloads. The representation of users and materials is based on six matrices: three matrices of clients (or populations served) and services for them, and three of materials and technical processes for them. In each case, the first matrix contains data for determining workloads involved; the second contains data for the extent to which workloads use specific services or processes; and the third contains workload factors as means for estimating the required staff.

Workload Matrices

In the model, the workloads are considered in two major categories: those related to services to the populations served, and those related to the internal (technical) processing of the materials acquired. In each case, the model separates the measurement of the workload into two matrices, the first measuring the size of the populations involved and the frequency of their use, and the second measuring the distribution of uses across the set of services provided.

The value of this approach in developing the model is that it separates the tasks of measuring the populations from that of measuring the uses of services. In that way, each can be investigated without worrying about the other.

The value of this approach in applying the model is that, given the matrices measuring using populations and their use of services, the workload for each of the services can be calculated by simply multiplying the two matrices. In the same vein, given the matrices measuring materials acquired and their use of processes, the workload for each of the processes can be calculated by simply multiplying those two matrices.

Workload Factors in Estimating Numbers of Staff and Costs

The third pair of matrices (one each for populations served and materials acquired) provides workload factors as the means for estimating staff sizes and costs. For each item included in a set of library services and processes, units of work have been defined. The workload factors then are expressed as percentages of yearly FTE (full-time equivalent) staff required for the performance of 1,000 units of work for each library function and subsidiary process.

The model incorporates default values for the workload factors but they can easily be modified to reflect experiences and detailed data at each library. The default workload factors in the model are consciously and deliberately used with minimal precision—typically on the order of 10 percent. This reflects the fact that there is great variability among institutions and, even within a single one, there are differences in the qualitative character of the workload. It would be spurious to imply high levels of precision simply not warranted. As a result, there is no reason to anticipate that the use of these default values in a given library will match actual data any closer than the precision implies—that is, within, say, 10 percent. It is for that reason that the model provides the means to change the defaults if there is sufficient confidence in the data to warrant the use of workload factors of higher precision than is represented in these default values.

Despite the low precision, though, the default values very closely fit the actual data for many libraries. Therefore, they should be used as the starting point in applying the LSM to any particular library; changes in them should be very carefully made, especially if there is to be comparability among institutions. The default values for the workload factors were developed by an iterative process that involved hundreds of libraries, of all kinds and sizes, over a period of decades. Beyond the use of actual data from visited libraries, other means were used to determine default values: time and motion studies; analyses of the rich array of relevant published data to reduce them to a consistent accounting structure; and analogies with various kinds of operations, both within libraries and between them and industrial and commercial counterparts.

Overhead

A major component of the model is "overhead," which includes those costs that cannot be directly attributed to "productive work." That in no way means that such costs are not necessary or significant; it simply means that it would be difficult or irrational to attempt to associate them directly with productive work. Supervision, for example, is clearly necessary, but in no way does it, in itself, produce catalog entries, bind volumes, provide reference services, or do the actual work, whatever it may be. A typical rule for allocating these costs is to make them "proportional to direct labor costs," and that is the rule used in the model.

Data Acquisition and Analysis

The process of data acquisition and analysis involved the following steps:

1. identify librarians and libraries as potential participants;
2. obtain e-mail addresses for them, to the extent possible;
3. obtain their approval regarding their participation;
4. acquire standard data from them, using e-mail for sending the worksheets and for receiving the responses;
5. analyze the data by the use of the standard LSM model, and determine what changes, if any, are needed to represent the data for each library and for the group of libraries as a whole;
6. communicate with participating libraries, as needed, to assure mutual understanding and agreement regarding the data and the results of the analyses.

The project took nine months. It started in October 1996; the final set of data from the last participating library involved was received in June 1997; and the analysis and the writing of this essay were completed by the end of July 1997. The nine-month period for this effort was completely adequate, because e-mail communication of data, results, and resolution of differences could be easily carried forward, given the commitments on the part of the participants. The time schedule in the conducting of the data-gathering process has been completely consistent with prior experience. The following table indicates, by country, the number of persons and/or libraries actually involved in the succession of steps:

Country	Step 1 Individuals	Step 2 Individuals	Step 3 Libraries	Steps 4, 5, 6 Libraries
Bulgaria	2	1	1	
Croatia	2	1		
Czech Republic	14	14	2	
Georgian Republic	4	4	2	1
Hungary	12	11	5	3
Latvia	3	2	1	1
Poland	26	23	9	5
Romania	1	1		
Russia	25	6	3	
Slovakia	19	19	1	1
Ukraine	5	3	2	1
Total	113	85	26	12

The Selection of Participant Libraries

The first of those steps involved obtaining lists of libraries and individuals from a variety of sources. During Crimea '96, the conference held in June 1996 (at Foros in the autonomous republic of the Crimea, in the Ukraine), the research program presented herein was discussed with staff members of about a dozen Central and Eastern European, Russian, and CIS libraries; in each case there was enthusiasm about the project, and they clearly expressed interest in participating. Furthermore, in several cases, they were willing to identify other libraries as potential participants. Those libraries and further referrals from them became potential participants. Besides them, there were libraries and institutions of specific interest to the various funding agencies (such as the Mellon and Soros foundations).

In the second step, to the extent possible, e-mail addresses were obtained. That reduced the list to 85 individuals. (It is difficult to assess the number of libraries involved in step 2, since the affiliations of the individuals were not in every case well identified or the e-mail addresses may not have reflected them.) E-mail messages were sent to them, identifying the objectives and asking them to participate. The key point is that, given the use of e-mail as the means for communication and data acquisition, there was no real limit on the number of libraries that could participate.

Responses were received from 45 persons, who represented 26 libraries in 8 countries, and in every case there was an enthusiastic commitment to participate. That level of acceptance was within the range of 20 to 30 that had been hoped for. To those positive respondents, e-mail messages were sent that provided a detailed description of the methodology, copies of the worksheets to be used for recording the relevant data, and promises that all data would be treated with strict confidence.

It had been expected that in the fourth of the steps—receiving data—some of the libraries would not actually respond, despite having agreed to do so. Indeed, that was the case, with only half of them providing data (12 academic libraries from 6 countries). The reasons for not participating are not known, since no further contact was made with nonrespondents after sending out the worksheets. However, it is reasonable to conjecture that at least three reasons were operative: (1) filling in the worksheets required an extensive effort on the part of the respondents, and some libraries concluded that it was too burdensome; (2) it is likely that some libraries felt that they did not have available sufficiently accurate data on which to base responses to the worksheets; (3) it is likely that, despite the assurance of confidentiality, some libraries were reluctant to provide data, even if it was available.

After receiving the data, and entering them into the LSM for analysis, further contact was made with some of the participating libraries to confirm the data and to test the implications of the results as revealed by the model.

The Use of Worksheets and E-mail for Data Acquisition

Worksheets were sent by e-mail to each participating library, with the request that they fill in the data to the greatest extent possible. In prior studies of this kind, using e-mail as the means for data acquisition, the process of data acquisition has involved a repetitive cycle of submitting worksheets to the participants, responding to questions about specifics, receiving the resulting data, and responding to those data. To arrive at a final set of data usually takes on the order of three to four months. The time required is not really determined by the number of participants, since they all interact in a parallel manner, but rather by the process of arriving at a mutual understanding of the data. In this study, however, the data received were sufficient for the purposes and minimal interaction was necessary. The time required in fact was determined not by either the process or the number of participants but by the responsiveness of participants in sending data.

Analysis of the Data

This step proceeded in parallel with data acquisition and is an integral part of the process of communication and reconciliation. It involved the entry of the data into the LSM and then the output of the comparisons of the results from the model with the data on actual distributions of staff.

The following were the specific steps in the entry of data and the analysis:

1. The values in worksheet 1 ("Populations Served") from the first column ("Total Population") were entered into the corresponding fields of the first user matrix of the LSM (except for "Institutions," for which the value from the "Total Use" column was entered, to represent the total for ILLs). The value for "Students" was entered for undergraduates, since there was no basis for dividing it between graduates and undergraduates.
2. The values in the columns for percentages of use and of frequency of use in the first matrix for users were taken at the default values, and the total-frequency-of-use column was then automatically calculated by the LSM from the input data for total populations, multiplied by the other two columns of default values.

3. The values from worksheet 2 ("Collections of Materials") were entered into the corresponding fields of the first materials matrix of the LSM, for both "Total Holdings" and "Yearly Additions." Parenthetically, it should be noted that at present the LSM does not use "Total Holdings" in estimating workloads, so only the "Yearly Additions" actually affect the results. However, the Total Holdings data were very useful as part of the basis for identifying an appropriate U.S. Comparison Library.
4. The values from worksheet 3 ("Actual Staff Distributions") were then used to determine the values in the two matrices "Distribution of Use of Services" and "Distribution of Use of Processes." Those values were calculated to provide estimates from the LSM for the number of staff members in each category that would be as close as possible to the values reported in worksheet 3. The intent in doing so was not to provide matches for any individual library but, rather, to establish generic values that would apply to all of them and to the Study Composite Library. Given the deliberate limits on precision, exact matches were unlikely, but the matches could be made close enough for the purposes of this study.
5. The values from worksheet 3 ("Actual Staff Distributions") were then entered into the display in the LSM that provides a comparison of the actual distributions of staff members by function with the estimates from the LSM. Given the fact that the values for distributions of use of services and for use of processes materials were chosen to make the generic LSM estimates close to the actuals (in step 4, above), it would not be surprising if they turned out to be so, although it must be recognized that the use of generic values does not mean that each library, individually, will necessarily match well.
6. The values from worksheet 4 ("Actual Workloads on Services") were then used to determine the values in the "Distribution of Uses of Materials" matrix. Those values were calculated to provide estimates from the LSM for the use of each type of use of materials that would be as close as possible to the values reported in worksheet 4. Again, the intent in doing so was not to provide matches for any individual library but, rather, to establish generic values that would apply to all of them and to the Study Composite Library. The results from the LSM were then compared with actual circulation-staff data from worksheet 3 ("Actual Staff Distributions") to provide a further calibration. Given the generic values and the deliberate limits on their precision, exact matches with any of the values were unlikely, but the matches were close enough for the purposes of this study.
7. Further processing in this step depended upon the nature of the comparisons. If there was substantial agreement (generally taken to mean within 10 percent, more or less) of the model with reality, the model and its results could be accepted; in our prior experience, that has turned out to be the case in about 75 percent of the libraries. For participants in which the results from the model are substantially different from the actual data, there needs to be an exploration of the data and of the operations of the library. That may lead to the identification of portions of the operation that need to be separately treated; an example might be a major publishing activity or responsibilities that range beyond the institution. In such cases, an effort will be made to accommodate such activities within the model or, if that cannot be done, simply to deal with them separately. In this study, the results were sufficiently consistent with the model for analysis to proceed, but the effects of publishing needed to be recognized, as had been anticipated.
8. Steps 1 through 7 were repeated for each participating library, for the Study Composite Library, and for the U.S. Comparison Library. As each participating library

was considered, the values for the two distribution matrices were reassessed for their generic applicability, but rapidly converged to their final generic values (as shown later in this chapter).

9. Upon the completion of step 8, the generic values for the two distribution matrices were applied to each of the participating libraries, and the estimates from the LSM were compared with the actual staffing for each functional area.
10. Upon the completion of step 9, the values for the reported uses of materials (that is, circulation and in-house uses) were used to replace the corresponding generic values in the distribution-of-uses matrix, and again the estimates from the LSM were compared with the actual staffing for each functional area.
11. Upon the completion of step 10, data reported for publishing activities were used to determine an estimated FTE staff requirement for the resulting workload. This function is not part of the LSM as generally applied, but workload factors have been developed for it; they total 1.2 FTE persons per 1,000 pages published, primarily professional-level people. Those FTE people were divided equally between the reader-services staff and the materials-processing staff, and again the estimates from the LSM were compared with the actual staffing for each functional area.
12. The entire set of data for each library—(1) reported actual staff; (2) LSM estimates using only the generic values for the distribution matrices; (3) LSM estimates using the reported data for circulation use and in-house use; and (4) LSM estimates including allocations for publishing-related FTE people—was placed into a spreadsheet, sequenced in order of total reported number of staff members, together with calculated averages over all libraries for each value. (The results are presented later in this chapter.)
13. The analysis then examined the values in the two generic distribution matrices for the Study Composite Library, and compared them with those for the U.S. Comparison Library. (The results are presented later.)
14. The analysis then examined the estimates from the LSM for the distribution of staff by levels of appointment (professional, support, and hourly) and by functions, and compared those estimates with the reported actual distributions.

There are several aspects of this process that are worthy of emphasis. First, note that values for all but one workload factor were the default values. The one workload factor that was changed was the one needed to recognize staffing requirements for paging from closed stacks. The need for that change was almost immediately evident when the relatively low values for circulation and the high proportions of in-house use were combined with the reported values for circulation staff that were inconsistent with the LSM estimates. Queries to the participating libraries confirmed the conjecture that they had closed stack operations, so the workload factor was then modified to reflect the known U.S. experience in such environments.

Second, note that the values for distributions for uses of services and of processes are determined so that the LSM estimates for reference-services staff and technical-processing staff will equal the reported actuals. This is in sharp contrast to the means for the determination of distributions for uses of materials, which are based on using the reported actual workloads on uses of materials, and the LSM estimates for circulation staff are then derived from those distributions, rather than vice versa. The underlying reason for treating circulation staff differently than other staff is the fact that reported data for use of services are notoriously inaccurate; in contrast, reported data for the use of materials are usually very good, since they are directly measurable from statistics of circulation or reshelving.

Third, note that in step 11 recognition is given to the effect of publishing upon library staffing. Worksheet 4 ("Actual Workloads on Services") explicitly makes provision for the reporting of such activities (as well as other activities, such as retrospective conversion, for which there is adequate provision within the LSM). This was precisely because our prior experience with libraries of the kind involved in this study has been that publishing can be a major responsibility, but one whose impact on staffing is frequently unrecognized. The workload factor for publishing, as a supplement to the LSM, is taken at 1.2 FTE persons per 1,000 pages (primarily those of the professional-level staff).

Communication

As indicated above, throughout there was some repetitive communication with the participants during the receiving of data and the sending of the results of the analysis. The purpose in doing so was for feedback, a resolution of problems in definitions and in inconsistencies with respect to the data. The end result could have been a modification, as necessary, of the model and parameters, but the actual result was a confirmation of the conjectures concerning the likely basis for results (such as that regarding the workload factor for circulation paging).

Details of the Results

The results include the data and the tables that present the analysis of them. They also include copies of the model as it may have been modified during the project to reflect the reality of patterns in the participating libraries. Copies of the model, with their data included in it, will be sent to each participating library, with complete documentation for the model, including description of the means for using it.

This will serve to provide the confirmation of validity of both the data and the analysis. Such confirmation is necessary because each participating library was guaranteed confidentiality, so only statistical summaries are presented in this chapter (with the single exception of the table that compares various LSM estimates with actual staff distributions by function for each library, but without identifying the libraries themselves). That means that there is no means by which the reader can be sure that the data and results are valid, beyond the fact that LSM is readily available and can be independently tested.

Patterns of Use

The worksheets provide means by which the patterns of use can be identified both in detail by type of user and in aggregated statistics. The latter are the easiest to measure and are the ultimate input to the staffing model, but the former allow the library manager to relate patterns to the nature of each type of user.

The most evident fact, almost universal across all of the participating libraries, is the high ratio of in-house use to circulation use. On average, for the participating libraries, it was nearly 4 to 1, and in some cases, as much as 20 to 1. This is in sharp contrast to patterns in the United States, in which the ratio is 2 to 1.

When this ratio was explored with the respondents, the reason for the high ratio became clear. It is a result of library policies that force the users to use the materials within the library and, furthermore, a result of policies that close the stacks to users. Of course, this was expected, given the differences in library traditions between the relatively open policies of libraries in the United States and the policies in Europe, which tend to adopt the view that libraries should primarily emphasize preservation of the materials rather than use of them.

Population Distributions. For an application of the LSM to the Composite Library and to each of the individual libraries, the data reported by the participants were used for the total size of each population, but the values for the percentage of users and the number of annual uses per user were taken as the default values for the United States. The LSM has also been applied to a U.S. Comparison Library, which serves as the means for comparison in all of the elements of analysis. The following compares the resulting population matrix for the U.S. Comparison Library with that for the Study Composite Library:

	U.S. Comparison Library			Study Composite Library		
	Total Population	User %	Uses/User	Total Population	User %	Uses/User
Service points	10	100%	250	10	100%	250
Institution staff	600	25%	50	1,939	25%	50
Faculty	974	100%	90	2,182	100%	90
Graduate students	2,586	100%	60		100%	60
Undergraduates	19,289	100%	45	16,300	100%	45
ILL-lending	5,920	100%	1	2,659	100%	1
Other researchers	100	100%	25	1,108	100%	25
Informed public	100	100%	25		100%	25
General public	100,000	1%	9	36,202	1%	9

The U.S. Comparison Library is a real library and the data for it are actual data. While there are evident differences between it and the Composite Library, the populations are, overall, similar.

Distributions of Services. For the application of the LSM to the Composite Library and to each of the individual libraries as well as to the Comparison Library, values for the distributions of workloads among services to users were chosen so as to bring the results from the model into matches with the reported totals for the number of staff members in reference services.

The final generic values for the Study Composite Library, with three minor exceptions, are exactly half the default values used for the U.S. Comparison Library. The first exception is the trivial one related to reference service points, for which the values, by definition, are identical. The second exception is equally trivial, since it reflects the necessary fact that ILL services require reference work in the checking of bibliographic data. The significant exception is the estimate of the use of ILL-Borrowing, for which the reported actual level of use was used to determine the distribution of use. The relative difference for that value between the Comparison Library and the Composite Library is worthy of comment: In the U.S. experience, the combination of borrowing and/or photocopying of documents for delivery has become a very significant service. Ten or so years ago, it was at the level of about 1 percent of uses (as exhibited in the Composite Library, in fact), but today in the United States it is running at about 3 percent of the uses of materials.

Comparisons of the resulting generic values with the default values, as used for the U.S. Comparison Library, are presented in the following tables.

The values shown in each table are intended to represent the percentages of total use of the library by each type of population that involve the given service. The services, represented by the columns, are: Regular Reference (frequently called "Ready Reference"), Extended Reference (reference work requiring extended periods of time, taken as more than 15 minutes), Database Access (the use of online database services and/or CD-ROM databases within the library), ILL Borrow (the request for materials from other institution, either by borrowing the document or by receiving a photocopy, also called "document delivery"), and Consult/Instruct (services of reference staff in consultation and instruction in use of the library and of information resources).

U.S. Comparison Library

Services	Reference		Database Access	ILL Borrow	Consult/Instruct
	Regular	Extended			
Service points	100%				
Institution staff	5%	1%			.2%
Faculty	5%	1%	.2%	5.0%	.2%
Graduate students	5%	1%	.1%	2.5%	.2%
Undergraduates	5%	1%	.1%		.2%
ILL-lending	100%				
Other researchers	2%				
Informed public	2%				
General public	2%				

Study Composite Library

Services	Reference		Database Access	ILL Borrow	Consult/Instruct
	Regular	Extended			
Service points	100%				
Institution staff	2.5%	.50%			.1%
Faculty	2.5%	.50%	.10%	1%	.1%
Graduate students)	2.5%	.50%	.05%	1%	.1%
Undergraduates	2.5%	.50%	.05%		.1%
ILL-lending	100.0%				
Other researchers	1.0%				
Informed public	1.0%				
General public	1.0%				

The choice of those values as uniformly 50 percent of the defaults (except for the three minor exceptions) is consistent with the general approach used in the LSM, which is to minimize the variations among values to the maximum possible extent.

Distributions of Workloads among the Uses of Materials. For the application of the LSM to the Composite Library and to each of the individual libraries, values for distributions of workloads among uses of materials were chosen so as to bring the results from the model into matches with the reported totals for such uses.

There are several relevant points here worthy of emphasis. First, the general level of use of materials in the Composite Library is substantially less than that in the Comparison Library; presumably that reflects either the effects of policies on access to materials or reduced expectations on the part of the users or, most likely, a combination of the two. Second, note the relative ratios of in-house use to circulation use; in the United States that ratio is generally 2:1 but in the Composite Library it is about 3.5:1. Almost certainly, this reflects the effect of closed stacks and restrictive policies on circulation. Third, note the relative magnitude of photocopying by library staff; the reduced value in the U.S. Comparison Library reflects the fact that most copying is done by users themselves, with the bulk of staff copying representing ILL document delivery; in the composite library, only one-third of photocopying is done by the users.

Comparisons of those values with the U.S. Comparison Library, as represented by the default values used for it, are as follows:

The values shown in each table are intended to represent the percentages of total use of the library by each type of population that involve the given use of materials. The uses of materials, represented by the columns, are: Circulation (the traditional charge-out of materials for use outside the library), Inhouse Use (includes uses of materials for reading within the library, for browsing on the shelf, for checking references and obtaining data from materials, and for photocopying of selected pages), Reserve Use (uses of library materials specified for controlled access, usually limited to in-house use for brief periods of time, typically, to assure that readings assigned to a class are readily available during the day for all students in that class), Photocopy (to be done by library staff, not by users themselves), AV- Multi-Media (intended to cover the entire range of uses of library materials that require equipment, including use of audio-visual materials, microforms, and computers).

	U.S. Comparison Library				
Service points	Circulate	Inhouse Use	Reserve Use	Photocopy	AV,Multi Media
Institution staff	33%	67%		.1%	.1%
Faculty	33%	67%		.1%	.1%
Graduate students	33%	67%			.5%
Undergraduates	16%	33%	7%		1.5%
ILL-lending	50%			50.0%	
Other researchers		100%			
Informed public		100%			
General public		100%			

388 *Management Issues*

Study Composite Library

Service points	Circulate	Inhouse Use	Reserve Use	Photocopy	AV,Multi Media
Institution staff	16%	55%		.2%	
Faculty	16%	55%		.2%	
Graduate students	16%	55%		.2%	
Undergraduates	16%	55%	.6%	.2%	.2%
ILL-lending	50%			50.0%	
Other researchers		10%			
Informed public		10%			
General public		10%			

Patterns in Acquisition of Materials

Workloads in the Processing of Materials. For the application of the LSM to the Composite Library and to each of the individual libraries as well as to the Comparison Library, values for the magnitude of workloads among categories of materials were taken as reported. Comparisons of those values with the U.S. Comparison Library, as represented by the actual data for it, are shown in the following table. In the LSM, values for microforms, special collections, and documents are taken in linear feet (using a nominal value of 100 items per linear foot), so the values shown in each column for those types of materials are also in linear feet:

	U.S. Comparison Library		Study Composite Library	
Materials	Total Holdings	Annual Additions	Total Holdings	Annual Additions
Monographs	642,822	19,338	789,234	12,298
Mono series		6,000	37,736	855
Periodicals	138,912	7,498	299,695	4,650
Microforms	15,275	1,384	240	7
Special coll.	515	19	2,569	21
Documents	3,377	154	479	4
Media	55,988	4,588	11,406	169

The Comparison Library and the Composite Library differ somewhat in size, both in overall number of volumes and in the relative number of bound periodicals. They also differ, more substantially, in the current rates of annual additions, the Comparison Library having overall acquisitions about twice those of the Study Composite Library. For the participants in this study, this surely reflects the effects of economic conditions in their countries. Clearly, those differences are important and raise the issue of whether the chosen U.S. library is appropriate for a comparison; however, any real library to be used for the comparison would differ at least to the extent shown here. For the purposes of this study, the Comparison Library and the Composite Library are regarded as sufficiently similar.

Distributions of Workloads among the Use of Processes. For the application of the LSM to the Composite Library and to each of the individual libraries, values for distributions of workloads among types of processes were chosen so as to bring the results from the model into matches with the reported totals for collection development staffing. Comparisons of the values for processing involved in collection development with the U.S. Comparison Library, as represented by the values used for it, are as follows:

In the following table, the values shown are intended to represent the percentages of acquired materials of each type that involve alternative means for selection, two of which are identified: Firm Order (in which the entire decision process is conducted by staff of the library, typically by a commercial service, and library staff then selects from those presented "on approval"). In all cases, the materials must be ordered and paid for, and that is represented by the column Acquire. In each case, the values shown are intended to represent the percentage of acquisitions of a given type of material by the library that involve the given process. For two rows, Monograph Serials and Periodical, the value are blank; for monograph serials that is because none of the participants could provide these data and for periodicals it is because selection arises only when new titles are involved, and the percentage of that is small.

	U.S. Comparison Library			Study Composite Library		
	Collection Develop			Collection Develop		
Materials	Firm Order	Approval	Acquire	Firm Order	Approval	Acquire
Monographs	50%	50%	100%	25%	75%	100%
Mono series						
Periodicals						
Microforms	10%	90%	100%	25%	75%	100%
Special coll.	100%		100%	100%		100%
Documents						
Media	50%	50%	100%	100%		100%

For the specific real library that is serving as the U.S. comparison library, the values used differ substantially from the default values (which are 25 percent firm order and 75 percent approval plan); that reflects a policy at that library for the past several years in which there has been a significant effort at retrospectively building the collection. With respect to the study composite library, the values shown differ from those used in the first draft of this chapter, which was the basis for the presentation at the Mellon Conference on Library Automation; the change to the values shown here was a direct result of evidence, revealed during that conference, that a major portion of acquisitions at these libraries is accounted for by "deposit" which operationally is equivalent to the use of approval plans.

The comparison of the values for the receiving and handling of materials, both monographs and serials, at the U.S. Comparison Library, as represented by the default values, with the values at the Composite Library, are as follows:

In the following table, the values shown are intended to represent the percentage of acquisitions of each type of material that involve handling. Two processes in handling are identified: Receive & Handle (which involves the physical processes in receiving materials when they arrive at the library) and Serials (which covers the work involve in maintaining serials records).

	U.S. Comparison Library		Study Composite Library	
Materials	Receive and Handle	Serials	Receive and Handle	Serials
Monographs	100%		100%	
Mono series	100%	100%	100%	100%
Periodicals	100%	100%	100%	100%
Microforms	100%		100%	
Special Coll.	100%		100%	
Documents	100%	100%	100%	100%
Media	100%		100%	

There is no reason to expect there to be any significant differences in such a set of procedural and manual activities.

The comparison of the values for the cataloging of materials at the U.S. Comparison Library, as represented by the values used there, with the values at the Composite Library, are as follows:

The values shown in the following table are intended to represent the percentages of acquisitions of each type of material that involve two alternative means for cataloguing: Original Cataloging (intended to represent cases in which staff of the library create the relevant data, whether descriptive or subject/classification, directly from the "book in hand" rather than using other sources for the data) and Copy Cataloging (which draws upon existing data, usually from one of the bibliographic utilities, such as OCLC or RLIN). Beyond cataloging as such, Authority files for both names and subjects, are needed for effective cataloging but they are absolutely essential in the use of automated cataloging systems.

	U.S. Comparison Library			Study Composite Library		
	Cataloging		Authority	Cataloging		Authority
Materials	Original	Copy	Files	Original	Copy	Files
Monographs	7%	93%	5%	75%	25%	5%
Mono Series		100%	5%	75%	25%	5%
Periodicals			5%			5%
Microforms			5%	75%	25%	5%
Special Coll	100%		5%	100%		5%
Documents		100%	5%	75%	25%	5%
Media	15%	85%	5%	75%	25%	5%

Note that the values for the U.S. Comparison Library are those actually experienced there; the default values are 10 percent original and 90 percent copy. With respect to the Study Composite Library, the values shown here differ from those used in the first draft of this chapter (which was the basis for the presentation at the Mellon Conference on Library Automation); the change to the values shown here was a direct result of evidence, revealed during that conference, that the use of original cataloging was substantially greater than the values used in the draft. The important point, of course, is the much greater dependence at the Composite Library on original cataloging, which is far more labor intensive than copy cataloging.

Patterns of Staffing

Workload Factors. For the application of the LSM to the Composite Library and to each of the individual libraries, a change was made in only one workload factor (the hourly staff in stack maintenance in circulation and in-house use, which was increased by 50 percent from the U.S. experience to reflect the need for the paging of materials from closed stacks). All other workload factors—services to users, processing of materials, and overhead—are identical with those used as the default values, based on the U.S. experience. This is the ultimate test of the hypothesis that patterns of staffing, as far as basic productivity is concerned, are similar to the U.S. patterns, for the libraries that participated. Let us now see what the effects are of the values used in the several matrices.

Comparison of Estimates with Actual Staff Distributions. On the basis of the values for the six matrices as presented above (the basic workload matrices, for the population served and the materials processed; the distribution matrices, for services provided and for processes; the workload-factor matrices), the model provides estimates of the required staffing levels.

The following table shows four sets of data for each library—(1) reported actual staff; (2) LSM estimates using only the generic values for the distribution matrices; (3) LSM estimates using the reported data for circulation use and in-house use; and (4) LSM estimates including allocations for publishing-related FTE people—sequenced in order of the total reported number of staff members, together with calculated averages over all libraries for each value.

In the following table, the figures represent numbers of FTE people in three categories of responsibility: services to reader (including circulation and reference work), processing of materials (including selection and acquisition, cataloging, conservation, and handling), and supervision and management.

Library	Basis For Estimate	Reader Service	Materials Processing	Manage/ Supervise	Total
Library 1	Actual	9	6	2	17
	Use Average Data	4	11	3	18
	Use Actual Circulation	4	11	3	18
	Add Publishing	4	11	3	18
Library 2	Actual	12	20	5	37
	Use Average Data	12	21	5	38
	Use Actual Circulation	12	21	5	38
	Add Publishing	12	21	5	38
Library 3	Actual	29	27	10	66
	Use Average Data	25	30	11	66
	Use Actual Circulation	25	30	11	66
	Add Publishing	25	30	11	66

Library	Basis For Estimate	Reader Service	Materials Processing	Manage/ Supervise	Total
Library 4	Actual	35	35	8	78
	Use Average Data	18	30	9	57
	Use Actual Circulation	25	30	10	65
	Add Publishing	27	32	11	70
Library 5	Actual	26	50	8	84
	Use Average Data	23	41	12	76
	Use Actual Circulation	23	41	12	76
	Add Publishing	25	43	12	80
Library 6	Actual	40	29	17	86
	Use Average Data	70	12	16	98
	Use Actual Circulation	40	12	10	62
	Add Publishing	40	12	10	62
Library 7	Actual	60	40	10	110
	Use Average Data	19	28	9	56
	Use Actual Circulation	54	28	9	91
	Add Publishing	55	29	9	93
Library 8	Actual	61	49	10	120
	Use Average Data	121	34	29	184
	Use Actual Circulation	60	34	18	112
	Add Publishing	60	34	18	112
Library 9	Actual	52	49	26	127
	Use Average Data	46	42	17	105
	Use Actual Circulation	46	42	17	105
	Add Publishing	52	48	19	119
Library 10	Actual	71	49	22	142
	Use Average Data	45	27	14	86
	Use Actual Circulation	45	27	14	86
	Add Publishing	69	51	20	140
Library 11	Actual	84	47	25	156
	Use Average Data	30	28	11	69
	Use Actual Circulation	71	28	19	118
	Add Publishing	71	28	19	118
Library 12	Actual	109	48	27	184
	Use Average Data	110	44	29	183
	Use Actual Circulation	110	44	29	183
	Add Publishing	110	44	29	183
Averages	Actual	44	36	14	94
	Use Average Data	47	29	15	91
	Use Actual Circulation	39	29	13	81
	Add Publishing	44	33	14	91

Note that for five of the libraries (1, 2, 3, 4, and 12), the use of the generic distribution matrices provides LSM estimates within 10 percent of the actual totals; two others (6 and 9) are within 20 percent; the remaining five libraries differ by ratios between 27 percent and 56 percent. When actual data are used to replace the generic values for the use of materials in circulation and of materials in-house, six are within 10 percent, three within 20 percent, and the remainder between 24 percent and 39 percent. And when the workload represented by publishing is recognized, nine are within 10 percent, and the remaining three are from 15 percent to 28 percent.

Comparison of Estimates with Actual Staff Distributions by Level.   As shown above, the results from the model quite closely match the total actual staffing and the functional distributions. However, the distributions among levels of staff are different and that will be illustrated by the Composite Library and will be contrasted with the Comparison Library. The differences between the LSM estimates and the actuals for the Comparison Library reflect specifics there with respect to staffing policies, especially during the past five years of reduced financial resources.

In the following table, the data are FTE people in each category of staff: Professional, Support (or clerical), and Hourly.

	U.S. Comparison Library				Study Composite Library			
	Prof	Support	Hourly	Total	Prof	Support	Hourly	Total
Actual	31	53	30	114	72	22	0	94
Model	40	53	23	116	34	29	24	87
Model + Publish					36	32	24	92

Note that the effect of publishing needs to be recognized, so, to do so, this table includes an added row.

It is worth commenting on the basis for the distribution of levels of staff made in the LSM. Leaving aside whatever may be the implications of the terms "professional," "nonprofessional" (or "support"), and "hourly" (or "student"), there are fundamental differences in the extent to which a given service or process involves "intellectual," "procedural," or "physical" actions. It is that distinction that the structure of LSM makes in its assignment of functions to the three levels of staff.

The differences for the Composite Library are apparently due more to economics than to such theoretical issues, and probably reflect the effect of egalitarian salary structures, in which there are relatively small differences in average salaries for professional, support, and hourly employees. In the United States, those salaries are in the ratio of 5:3:1, whereas in the countries covered by this study, they are probably more in the range of 3:2:1.

Comparison of Estimates with Actual Staff Distributions by Function.   The following tables show the actual distributions of staff by function, for both the Comparison Library and the Study Composite Library. At the end of each table the distributions as estimated by the LSM are shown. For the Study Composite Library, two such LSM estimates are shown, the second with the inclusion of the staff estimated as required for publishing (a total of 5 FTE people—2 in reader services and 3 in technical services—based on a requirement of 1.2 FTE people per 1,000 pages for the total of 4,221 pages).

In the following tables, the data are FTE people in each area of responsibility: services to reader (including circulation and reference work), processing of materials (including selection and acquisition, cataloging, conservation, and handling), and supervision and management.

U.S. Comparison Library

	Reader Service	Material Process	Supervision & Management	Total
Reference	19		2	19
Circulation	33		3	36
Collection development		26	2	28
Catalog		18		18
Supervise			12	12
Total	52	44	19	114
Model	54	44		18	116

Study Composite Library

	Reader Service	Material Process	Supervision & Management	Total
Reference	13			13
Circulation	33			33
Collection development		18		18
Catalog		17		17
Supervise			13	13
Total	46	35	13	94
Model	38	35	14	87
Model + Publishing	40	38	14	92

Given the simplicity and uniformity of the values in the workload-distribution matrices and the overall precision of the values used for workload distributions and for workload factors, the match is in each case remarkably close, and this is the evidence on which the validity of hypothesis 3 (cited earlier), the most central of the hypotheses, is regarded as confirmed.

Implications

There are several implications that can be drawn from the results presented in section. They will be discussed in three major categories: (1) the implications with respect to the hypotheses that guided the conducting of the study; (2) the implications with respect to library automation; and (3) the implications with respect to management policies.

Implications with Respect to Hypotheses

With respect to hypothesis 1 (that there would be differences between the study libraries and U.S. libraries in the workloads in the use of services and materials), the extent to which the calculated distributions of the use of services and materials differs from those of the U.S. Comparison Library provides the basis for the assessment that hypotheses 1 has been confirmed. Overall, the use of the libraries that were studied appears to be about half that of a comparable U.S. library.

With respect to hypothesis 2 (that there would be differences between the study libraries and U.S. libraries in the workloads in the processing of materials), the extent to which the calculated distribution of the use of processes differs from that of the U.S. Comparison Library provides the basis for the assessment that hypothesis 2 has been confirmed. Overall, the level of the acquisition of materials appears to be half that of a comparable U.S. institution, and the economic reasons for that are virtually self-evident. Beyond that, the distribution among processes is substantially different, and the reasons almost surely reflect the effect of automation (as will be discussed below).

With respect to hypothesis 3 (that there would be similarities in staffing patterns between the study libraries and U.S. libraries), use of the LSM required a change in only one workload factor (that for the paging of materials from closed stacks), and the value used there was derived from the U.S. experience. This substantiates the view that those workload values can effectively be used for the analysis of data from the participating libraries and is regarded as evidence in support of hypothesis 3. It must be said that it is difficult to separate the effects of the distribution matrices from those of the workload matrices, and it is possible that the value for a workload factor might really be less but be counterbalanced by an increased value for a related distribution. However, the fact is that the distribution matrices turned out to be generic in an exceptionally simple and uniform manner, and any significant effort to counterbalance them with the workload matrices would require a substantial departure from that.

With respect to hypothesis 4 (that there would be similarities among the staffing patterns in the study libraries), the distribution matrices for each of the participating libraries turned out to be nearly uniform and well represented by the one used for the Study Composite Library in this chapter.

With respect to hypothesis 5 (that there would be similarities in the use of levels of staff between the study libraries and U.S. libraries), the evidence is clear that this hypothesis is denied. In fact, the staffing in these libraries is done largely with professionals, whereas in U.S. academic libraries there is a heavy use of support staff and hourly staff.

Implications with Respect to Library Automation

With respect to library automation, there are five implications. The first, and most evident, effect of library automation, including, in particular, the use of bibliographic utilities for access to standard catalog data, is a dramatic reduction in the need for professional cataloging staff, with the likelihood of both a reduction in overall staff time and a shift of workloads to nonprofessional, support staff. This has been the experience in U.S. academic libraries during the past two decades, especially since the bibliographic utilities (such as OCLC and RLIN) were established. While there had been prior use of the Library of Congress card services and commercial counterparts, they were inadequate for most academic libraries, especially the major ones. Once the on-line bibliographic utilities were established, and especially after the local integrated library systems were installed, the use of copy cataloging became the rule. Only the very largest of the research libraries (the major members of the Association of Research Libraries) depend to a significant extent on original cataloging. The default values in the LSM for the relative mix of cataloging are 10 percent original cataloging and 90 percent copy cataloging. For the Composite Library, that mix would reduce the cataloging staff from a current total of 32 FTE people (21 of which are professional staff and 11 are support staff) to a total of 15 FTE people (2 professional and 13 support)—a decrease of 17 FTE people. That clearly is a dramatic change and would require very careful management. Fortunately, such a transition will take several years to occur, but the sooner planning for it is initiated, the better.

A second evident effect of library automation, one which in the long run is likely to be even more significant, is a dramatic increase in the need for professional staff who directly support users—in consultation and in bibliographic instruction. Again, this has been the experience in U.S. academic libraries during the past two decades, and it is now accelerating, as the overall information economy is doing. In the default values for services in the LSM, this is exhibited by the high values for distributions of the use of all reference services, but especially in the roles of consultation and instruction. For the Composite Library, use of those default values would imply an increase in reader-services staff from the current 31 to 47—an increase of 16 FTE people, all professionals. It is worth noting that this increase in reader-services staff is essentially equal to the decrease in cataloging staff, as identified in the first implication. Clearly, a shift of professional staff provides a tactical answer to the strategic objective, assuming that the staff can be reoriented in this way.

A third effect, not so evident perhaps but still very real, is the necessity for increases in both management staff and professional staff with substantial technical qualifications for handling automated systems. This appears most directly in the need for systems staff within the office of the library director, but it also appears within both reader services and technical services. In the LSM, the functional category "management/supervision" includes a number of functions, such as the director of the library and such management staff as accountants and personnel officers. Of increasing importance among them over the past two decades have been systems managers for computers, which have their related devices such as terminals, and for telecommunication networks. At the U.S. Comparison Library, they now represent half of the library's central management office. In general, these staff constitute additions rather than shifts, because of the technical qualifications. Beyond those general staff additions, there is an increasing need for technical expertise within reader services and materials processing; however, that can be accomplished by a shift of staff who develop the technical expertise.

A fourth effect is due to a combination of the implications related to technology and those related to management policies—it is the increasing role of interlibrary cooperation, exhibited in part in the sharing of materials among libraries but also in the cooperative management of automation development. The default values for the frequency of the use of interlibrary borrowing (including "document delivery") are three to four times those for the Composite Library. Experience in the United States during the past two decades has been that the level of use of these services has been dramatically increasing, and the reasons are largely that library automation has both increased the frequency of need (because of the improved reference databases that identify materials needed) and increased the ability to meet the need (through the electronic ILL referral systems, such as that operated by OCLC). Of course, for such expanded use of ILL to be effective, there must be policies favoring cooperation among libraries and a willingness to share resources. The economic benefits are clear, given the more efficient use of expenditures for acquisitions, but the changes in policy may be difficult to implement. Beyond these operational effects, it is also a fact that interlibrary cooperation is especially consuming of the time and energy of the highest levels of library management. Participation in the development of OCLC and the Research Library Group was by no means a trivial commitment on the part of the libraries and librarians involved.

A fifth effect arises from the increasing role of electronic resources in library services, with a resulting impact on collection development decisions, whether in the acquisition of electronic media or in the replacement of acquisitions by electronic document delivery. The impact of library automation on collection development decisions has been a matter of increasing concern, but the real impacts are still to come. The role of electronic document delivery has already become a big one, and the transition of publishing (especially of scholarly journals) to electronic formats is accelerating. The role of the network, as represented by the World Wide Web, is still unclear but, if its rate of growth is any measure, the impact will be great. The resulting effects on collection development staff are difficult to foresee, but it is likely that there will be a shifting of them into greater reader services, where they will work more directly with faculty in decisions, not so much about acquisitions but about overall information resource access.

Implications with Respect to Library Management Policies

With respect to management policies, there are two implications. There is much to be gained by instituting policies that encourage increased access to, and use of, collections. This relates both to services to each library's primary clientele and to the gains from the increased sharing of library materials among libraries. The role of information resources in general is clearly increasing as the industrialized countries move into information-based economies. There is economic value in facilitating that access for the institution that the library serves, and the library itself needs to maintain its position in the institution as the primary provider of that access. There is therefore a dual reason for establishing policies that encourage increased access to, and use of, the library's collections and of information resources generally by library services. In the application of the LSM, the difference between the U.S. Comparison Library and the Composite Library in this respect is exhibited by the increased level of use in the former—by a factor of 2. At least that level of increase should be planned for.

There is much to be gained from increasing the relative role of nonprofessional support staff and students in library operations and services. One of the likely effects of the transition into market-based economies is increasing salary and wage differentials. In the United States, that differential results in economic benefits to the library in the form of the employment of relatively low-cost hourly staff (such as students), instead of their having to employ the higher-cost professional and support staff, and in the shifting of workloads, especially those in procedural tasks, from professionals to support staff. The default values in the LSM recognize this in the assignment to the hourly staff (usually students) of tasks that are largely physical (such as the reshelving of books, the handling of materials being received and physically processed). For the Composite Library that would imply an increase in student staff from 3 to 20, with a corresponding shift of support staff to procedural work and of professional staff to intellectual work and, especially, to reader services. Again, this provides a means for dealing with the likely impacts of library automation—a value beyond simply the economic benefits.

CHAPTER 31

Staff Preparation for Automation

MARIA ŚLIWIŃSKA

The library staff's preparation for automation is an important and complicated issue. Although I could simply have asserted that the library staff was not prepared for automation, I decided to investigate this issue, with the aid of a questionnaire I sent to all Polish libraries that were introducing integrated library software (VTLS, Horizon, Aleph, Tinlib),[1] and another questionnaire that went to librarians who had been educated at library schools. In response, I received 39 completed questionnaires from libraries, and 227 from librarians. Before discussing the responses, I will provide some background data.

Poland is a country with a population of about 40 million people. The public is served by public, research, and special libraries operating under the Library Act of 1997. There are also information centers whose activities are conducted in accordance with the 1974 Information Act.

Library Network

In Poland there is a network of scientific (research) libraries, including academic libraries, libraries of research institutes, selected county libraries, and the National Library; the latter also belongs to the system of public libraries.

In 1980 there were 1,329 registered scientific libraries. In 1991, the number decreased to 1,235, but in 1993 it increased again to reach 1,285. In 1996 (the last year officially on record), we had 1,274 registered scientific libraries (11 fewer, although since 1991 about 130 private high schools (not in the American sense of the term—they are more comparable to British polytechnics) came into existence.

There are also public libraries, and the National Library is responsible for their coordination, training, scholarly activities, and standardization. The system of public libraries includes county and city libraries as well as very small-scale, village-level book distribution points ("library points"). Public libraries suffered the hardest blow from the introduction of the market economy—many of them were closed or are surviv-

---

I am indebted to Dominika Czyżak for assistance with this chapter.
 1. At the time the questionnaires were distributed, there were not enough INNOPAC users to include them.

ing on minimal resources. The more ambitious ones try to improve their situation by introducing paid services—for example, renting videos, leasing conference halls, or organizing book sales. Despite the fact that the public libraries underwent a serious crisis in the 1980s, their number still grew (from 9,315 in 1980 to 10,269 in 1990). Later, their number fell steadily (to 9,770 in 1992; 9,605 in 1993; and 9,505 in 1995).

School and pedagogical libraries did not really suffer from the changed environment. Only seven of the pedagogical libraries were closed between 1980 and 1990. The school library system has even grown (from 19,868 libraries in 1985 to 20,879 in the school year 1991–1992).

The majority of special libraries (in enterprises, hospitals, and prisons) were liquidated in the 1980s and the decline continues. Among libraries belonging to enterprises, we distinguish libraries holding professional literature (3,751 such libraries in 1980; 1,925 in 1991; 1,591 in 1993; 1,426 in 1995) and leisure-reading materials (3,736 in 1979; 864 in 1991; 667 in 1993; and only 546 in 1995). Some of them merged, and in the 1991 census, a new category of professional/leisure libraries appeared (170 in 1991; 113 in 1993; and 84 in 1995). Information about prison libraries was published for the first time in 1981 (earlier, the data had been considered classified.). In 1979 there were 146 registered prison libraries. Their number increased until 1989 (157 libraries), fell slightly in 1990 (150), and rose again in 1991 to stay unchanged until today (154).

Library activities are complemented by the activities of scientific, technical, and economic information centers. There were 1,723 of these in 1980; 522 in1991; 412 in 1993; and only 312 in 1995. It does not seem to help to enter into the Information Age.

It was alleged at a conference in Zakopane,[2] held in September 1997, that some of the information centers having financial difficulties, because of the problems of their parent organizations, decided to privatize. Their staffs were subjected to risky decisions, to which people in Poland are still unaccustomed, since they do not yet have a tradition of private provision of such services.

Library Staff

It is difficult to estimate the number of librarians in Poland. Some of them are not in fact employed as librarians but as teachers or clerks. In all library systems there were reductions in employment. The librarian profession does not enjoy high prestige and is poorly paid. (The majority of librarians were happy with their work at the library, but complained, in the questionnaire, about salaries). One of the indicators of this is the fact that it is difficult to find candidates for the position of chief librarian in scientific libraries. But there is a sign of change in this matter as well, as reported by the academic staff at library schools, because there are more candidates interested in library schools, and gradually, more males are applying. The reason for this visible change is the growth of library computerization and of attractive computer classes at library schools.

---

2. The Fourth Forum of Polskie Towarzystwo Informacji Naukowej (Polish Society of Scientific Information).

Preparation for Automation

General Information about the 1980s

Immediately following the great political changes, the librarians were not prepared at all to deal with automation. The only computerized library sponsored by the government before 1989 was the Technical University Library in Wrocław, where the CDS/ISIS system was used for bibliography preparation and for new-acquisitions cataloging.

At the National Library, the quite primitive ARCA system was used for central catalogs. Other libraries started using computers when cheaper PCs were imported to Poland in the 1980s. They were initially used in rather primitive ways. Standards and formats were unknown, and as a result, everybody created his own internal format, using mostly the CDS/ISIS, a free product obtainable from UNESCO. But it needs to be underlined that "everybody" does not mean too many people, since the computer experts did not understand the library operations, while librarians did not understand the technical problems connected with computers. This situation changed during the 1990s.

To improve the situation, the Institute of Information organized courses devoted to learning the ISIS system. Subsequent courses, sponsored by the Ministry of Education and devoted to basic automation problems, were organized by the Technical University Library in Wrocław.

Library Schools Were Unprepared for Computerization. Library schools did not possess computers at all. Students could hear about them, and could see what a computer looked like only if an educated teacher could draw a picture of a computer on a blackboard. Thus, library schools were mostly interested in historical problems and did not prepare students for automation. This situation is changing gradually, but still only slowly, since at a 1996 conference in Kraków,[3] which I attended, the programs presented contained no information concerning RFI, RFP preparation, bid evaluation, or license-agreement preparation and signing.[4]

Preparation for Computerization in Libraries in the 1990s

This section is based mainly on the author's personal experience. When, in 1989, I (knowing nothing about computerization, but with expertise in using OPACs at American libraries), accepted a position in the automation division of the Nicholas Kopernicus Library I could attend CDS/ISIS system courses, but could not find the proper format for bibliographies anywhere. In that time the so-called BN-MARC format was used for the preparation of the national bibliography, which we eventually

---

3. See *Rynek pracy a studia bibliotekoznawstwa i informacji naukowej w Polsce. II Ogólnopolska Konferencja Naukowa, Kraków, 4–5 czerwca 1996* [Relation of library and information studies to the job market in Poland. 2d National Conference, Kraków, 4–5 June 1996], edited by Maria Kokojowa (Kraków: Jagiellonian University Press, 1997).

4. A brief listing is contained in appendix 31.1.

accepted for importing bibliographies into our catalogs. Reading all possible materials, I came across information about a format for articles and book paragraphs that was under preparation by a group headed by the Polish Academy of Science. Unfortunately, it was not permitted to lend this format or to copy it. Reading it for a few hours was not enough to learn all the MARC fields and subfields and use it for the preparation of a bibliography. Even today, no analytical format has yet been accepted, but at that time we agreed with the Center for Formats and Authority Files (established in 1996 at Warsaw University), on the possibility of preparing it at my library, drawing from the USMARC Format and the USMARC discussion list, where this issue is discussed.

Starting in 1991, I went to Warsaw to look for help at the University Library, where a group was developing the UNIKAT system. I learned a lot there, but did not expect at that time that it would become the most important center for developing the necessary tools for library automation, which did not yet exist in Poland. Automation started later, when three libraries made the first decision to purchase the same automated system with Mellon Foundation grants. At the meeting organized at the National Library in 1992, the Jagiellonian University Library and the University Libraries of Gdańsk and of Warsaw (the only libraries with grants at that time) decided to select the VTLS system. Others present at this meeting declared that they would make the same selection in the future. The Nicholas Kopernicus University Library was the only one that was looking for another, more modern system based on the newer technology of the ORACLE library database management system. But we were interested in all library work that had to be done before computerization, such as the preparation formats, cataloging standards, and authority files.

At that time, Anna Paluszkiewicz was an emerging star at the University Library in Warsaw.[5] Supported by Maria Lenartowicz, a very knowledgeable librarian in cataloging rules, and by many others who were perhaps less advanced but with a strong determination to prepare the necessary tools, she started working with the so-called FOKA format, based on UNIMARC. It was a good format and it was the only one available at that time. But after some time, the Warsaw group changed its decision and started to use the USMARC format—which I dislike because it requires the use of separators to end each field and subfield. Another problem was the dissonance between European cataloging rules and the American format. The decision was made for other reasons as well. Most notably, because of the functionality and features the system already had and the functions which were under development and planned for future releases. And so the Kopernicus Library followed the lead even though, in the end, it decided to buy another system. We were not the only ones with strange combinations, since other European libraries selected UNIMARC and Anglo-American cataloging rules.

Another difficulty at that time was the problem of subject headings. The VTLS group had decided to customize the Library of Congress Subject Headings. I had no

---

5. See Anna Paluszkiewicz's chapter in this volume.

doubt that the most common language for the library world should also be accepted by our libraries. But there was a great controversy in Poland about it, since the majority thought that we Poles were smart enough to create our own subject headings. Just such a set of subject headings was developed by the National Library. It was a long, difficult historical battle, which was finally won by the minority—for the benefit of all our libraries. The risky decision of Teresa Głowacka—the head of the unit responsible for subject headings—was most admirable. Not knowing English, she started with the Library of Congress Subject Headings with reference to the French RAMEAU and the Canadian LAVAL. Thanks to her, to Jagoda Woźniak of the Warsaw library school, and to a group of dedicated librarians, we have two other European languages—English and French—in preparation for joining the European Community. There are still some doubts and there are people who do not appreciate this decision and this tool, because they are impatient and would like to see all the subject headings that *they* need. But "it's a long way to Tipperary." Nobody can prepare tools overnight, if they did not exist before the introduction of automation. Perhaps the situation is not ideal yet, but the retrieval language is growing significantly each month. Thus, the principal problems that needed to be solved were attacked by some individuals, supported by those who first needed these tools for computerization.

Other library staff members were not prepared for automation at all. The reason that some libraries selected a system at all was only because some help was obtained by them from some knowledgeable source. No Polish library selected its system using the Western selection style, which relies on RFP preparation or on evaluation of tenders. The Kopernicus Library was the first to use such a Western approach, and was followed after two years by the National Library and the Parliamentary Library. How experienced were libraries that were introducing integrated systems? To provide some statistical evidence, I distributed questionnaires to all libraries that had introduced the following integrated library systems: VTLS, Horizon, Aleph, and Tinlib. In response, I received 15 answers from VTLS libraries; 14 from libraries using the Horizon system; 4 libraries with Aleph; and 6 with Tinlib. At 9 libraries (2 with Horizon, 5 with VTLS, 1 with Aleph, and 1 with Tinlib), there had been no prior, even temporary, system. At other libraries there were predecessor systems: ISIS (12); SOWA (4); SOB (3); MAK (2); Lech (2); Unikat (2); Schola (1); and unspecified (3). Only two (small) libraries considered temporary systems good ones and the staff at these was unhappy that the leadership had made an alternative decision. Others realized that the hitherto existing system was effective only temporarily, and this helped overcome their fear of the computer.

In answering the question of whether library staff had been trained for automation, 7 out of 39 libraries replied that their staff had been trained for automation at schools of library science or in other postgraduate studies. A fair interpretation of the replies would seem to be that the respondents did not understand the situation, since students had not been receiving training in computerization at library schools at that time. All other libraries organized training themselves, carried out by software vendors and at cooperating libraries. Most important were courses organized by the Center for Formats and Authority Files. Also very important were visits to Western libraries, organized under the TEMPUS program.

One question inquired about problems encountered. The majority of the replies commented on the limitations on staff size and on poor salaries. There were also suggestions that Poland lacked new staff trained according to Western standards; and a suggestion to organize modern postgraduate training for librarians.

The majority underlined the need for intensive foreign-language courses and many stressed the need for training in computers. The following are some of the problems that libraries and librarians considered the most important—in the replies to the question about the most important problems to be resolved at libraries in Poland, those most often cited were priorities:

- to prepare a new library hierarchy of positions;
- solve the problem of low salaries;
- to create strong representation for the interests of libraries and librarians;
- to improve coordination;
- to organize a center for postgraduate training;
- to change the system of education for librarians.

We are working on the first problem cited and we hope that it will be resolved within a year. The salary problem is a difficult one to solve, but this unfortunately creates a serious brain drain in that the best-trained library staff members tend leave the libraries for better-paid jobs. There is some hope that we are approaching a solution for the lack of coordination in and among libraries, since we were able to form consortia of VTLS libraries and of Dynix/Horizon libraries that are willing to cooperate with the Center for Formats and Authority Files. The last two problems cited can be solved somehow by the newly opened International Center for Information Management, Systems, and Services (ICIMSS).

Librarians responding to questions about their library-school preparation for work amazingly found it to be good (older respondents) and not good enough (younger respondents). The older respondents appreciated the general knowledge and the theory taught at library schools. The younger ones indicated that there is not enough practical training, language training, and computer training in library schools.

Answers concerning the desire to develop new job competencies and about work satisfaction did not appear to be age-related. Also amazingly, even the oldest respondents, just before retirement, were frequently very proud that they could deal with automation and found lifelong education in whatever form as an absolutely necessity. Of course, there were also many not interested at all in education—they felt themselves to be educated enough. Unfortunately, the majority of librarians do not read professional journals, or read them only from time to time. The majority read the lower-level journals; only a few people read foreign journals. It appears to be the case that those librarians who are less interested in continuing their education are also the ones who are less satisfied with their jobs. Some librarians were unhappy with their supervisors and library directors, but they characteristically did not reply to the question "What journals do you read?" and the question concerning the development of their professional activities. Probably, many librarians did not fill out the questionnaire *at all*—including some at Nicholas Kopernicus library, which is my own library. Responding to questionnaires is perceived by many as an unpleasant chore, and caused some librarians to respond with caustic remarks—for example, answering the question "What occupation do you find more attractive"? with "Top model, businessman's wife, housewife." But at the same time, others responded to the question "What would you change at your library"? with the answer "Some people." I must admit, though, that this item was left blank in the majority of questionnaires, as was the item "What would you change in the Polish library system"? All this gives us a picture of the general state of Polish librarianship.

I am forced to conclude that nobody had been properly prepared for library automation—neither library schools nor libraries. Also unprepared were the university and the leadership at other schools, let alone the users. How did we achieve so much? One answer is that Polish librarians felt that they owed a responsibility to grant-giving organizations and that they had to live up to the challenge posed by these. We had a serious responsibility not to waste the opportunity given to us by these grants; and in spite of our national character, we carried out this work with the collaboration of those who were more talented and advanced. But we are also aware that it is the beginning of our work—hopefully, it will continue without so many other dramatic choices to make.

Appendix 31.1

Summary of Polish Library School Programs in the Area of Computerization

Bydgoszcz: introduction to information science and computers, information technology
Gdańsk: no single computer used in teaching
Katowice: introduction to information science, retrieval languages, automated systems, automation of information processes, library automation
Kielce: introduction to information science
Kraków: information sources, introduction to informatics, databases, programming languages, library and computer networks, on-line searching, CD-ROMs, multimedia, and expert systems,
Kraków II: introduction to information science
Lublin: information science
Łódź: introduction to information science, computer laboratory
Olsztyn: introduction to information science
Poznań: basic introduction to using computers, computer at a library, computer desktop publishing
Toruń: information science, information processes automation, cataloging
Warsaw: information science, information tools, analysis and projection of searching systems, retrieval languages, databases, library automation, electronic publishing
Wrocław: library automation

References

Edukacja z zakresu bibliotekoznawstwa i informacji naukowej na poziomie wyższym w Polsce. Status i przyszłość. Ogólnopolska Konferencja w Krakowie, 26 kwietnia 1996 roku. Red. Maria Kocojowa. [Education in library and information science in Poland. Present status and future. National conference, Kraków, April 26, 1996. Edited by Maria Kocojowa]. Kraków: Polskie Towarzystwo Bibliologiczne, 1995.

Rocznik statystyczny [Census data] 1996. Warsaw: Central Bureau of Statistics, 1997.

Rynek pracy a studia bibliotekoznawstwa i informacji naukowej w Polsce. II Ogólnopolska Konferencja Naukowa, Kraków, 4–5 czerwca 1996. Red. Maria Kocojowa [Relation of Library and information Studies to the Job Market in Poland. Second National Conference, Kraków, June 4–5, 1996. Edited by Maria Kocojowa]. Kraków: Jagiellonian University Press, 1997.

CHAPTER 32

Interactions between Library Automation and Staff and Patron Training

EWA KRYSIAK

> Teach people to *surf* the Internet and they can *tour* the world. Teach people to *serve* on the Internet and they can *touch* the world.[1] (Emphasis added)

With Internet access and information technology at hand, librarians and information providers have gained unpredicted vast possibilities for enriching and upgrading our services. Those who have spent hundreds of hours navigating the information superhighway are aware of how difficult it is to find exactly what is needed. But the deluge of data can be both a blessing and a curse.

Librarians can and should be aware of the tools available, in order to improve the performance of their duties—that is, to provide patrons of their libraries with the best possible service. The tool is out there, but skills have to be gained in the most economical and humane way. One cannot just sit at the computer and start surfing the information superhighway without proper awareness, knowledge, practice, and—the most important asset—*motivation*. This issue has to be understood, organized, and led by those responsible for library management. With their support and blessing, as well as their thoughtful guidance, the goal, by which most people have a better understanding of library services and of a library performance, can be achieved. The basic questions are the following:

1. What is our goal?
2. Why should we aim at achieving this goal?
3. How are we to achieve this goal?
4. Who is going to do it?
5. Who is going to manage this?

Our goal is to raise the awareness of librarians in regard to new and powerful tools, such as Internet resources and surfing the Net, in order to locate the most relevant data needed by the user. At the beginning, librarians have to switch themselves from

---

1. Harry M. Kriz, "Teaching and publishing in the World Wide Web," 1994 (URL: http://learning.lib.vt.edu/webserv/webserv.html).

information description, arrangement, and preservation to information provision. With the passage of time, one can witness interactions between librarians (information providers) and users (information seekers). The heightened awareness, the changes in functions, and the new interactions can easily upgrade the services and traditional functions of the library.

We should aim at achieving this goal in order not to be left behind on the information superhighway. Although users learn quickly and easily, there is always a need for guidance.

The goal can be achieved in many ways, starting with special Internet training of staff members, providing them with relevant facilities, like on-site Internet classes; distance learning on the Net; bulletin boards on the Intranet; on-site Internet workshops; printed flyers; handouts, distributed among library employees and users; library-focused on-line training; and numerous other techniques.

One has to find the people who can handle the introduction of new technologies in libraries. Some librarians have special computer-literacy skills and it is the role of library managers to find them and support them, so that they can then transfer their knowledge to their coworkers (training the trainer).

Managers need to create task groups with precisely defined goals. Their duty will be to organize and carry out training programs, carefully monitored and occasionally redefined to fit the needs of the individual library and its users. These are the most important questions to be answered and each library has to answers them in its own individual way, which takes into account the library's own characteristics and context.

When a library applies for a grant to automate its operations, it is often the case that it has not previously encountered costs involved in staff and patron preparations for new technologies; some libraries have underestimated these costs and have not even been aware of their importance. However, over time—especially since the successful implementation of the new system—this issue has become much more important.

The implementation of a new library system must be approached as a complex process, involving, in the first place, a change in the management of the library, and changes in everyday library procedures, both in processing new materials and in user services, but, above all, in librarians' mind-set.

Librarians are rather conservative when it comes to innovative operations. That is why this problem has to be explored, and then carried out with extraordinary precautions, tact, and reliance on incremental steps. The librarians' role is also changing, from having been information guardians to being information and data providers, which requires ongoing and organized training and self-training. Hence, it is essential that librarians be provided with the relevant opportunities. The whole repertoire of everyday procedures has to be turned, if not aside, then upside down, in order to meet requirements. "Technological change is always a Faustian bargain: Technology giveth and technology taketh away, and not always is equal in measure. A new technology sometimes creates more than it destroys. Sometimes, it destroys more than it creates. But it is never one-sided."[2]

---

2. Neil Postman, "Informing ourselves to death," 1990 (URL: http://www.eff.org/pub/Net_culture/Cr...ms/informing_ourselves_to_death.paper).

Review of the Literature

A search of on-line databases and electronic resources on the Internet reveals much interesting literature on the interactions between library automation staff and patrons who receive training. The most interesting of these that deal with the impact of IT on people are listed at the end of this chapter.

A useful starting point is Neil Postman's "Informing ourselves to Death,"[3] which describes his ideas about the advantages computer technology offers in dealing with masses of people—treated by machines like numbers—who become easy targets for advertising and for political, commercial, and religious organizations. In considering who might be the winner and who the loser in this competition between man and computer, Postman says, "Technology always has unforeseen consequences, and it is not always clear, at the beginning, who or what will win, and who or what will lose." He also warns about what makes computers dangerous and why. People are drowning in information, have no control over it, and do not know what to do with it, for two main reasons. First, we no longer have a coherent conception of ourselves and of the universe; we no longer know where we come from and where we are heading or why. Thus, it is hard for us to know exactly what data are, and what are not, relevant for our lives. The second reason is that we have directed so much of our intelligence and energy into inventing "new toys" that do nothing else but increase the supply of information. The information overflow weakens our immune system and there is no way to reduce or filter data, which leads directly to an illness that Postman calls "a cultural AIDS."

Several interesting articles are devoted to technostress. Ann Zimmerman warns that computerized information networks are a mixed blessing, not only giving us better opportunities, but also placing us in a psychological condition knows as *technostress*.[4] Her work is a review of the literature on this topic. She quotes Craig Brod's definition of technostress,[5] which calls it a modern disease of adaptation resulting from an inability to cope with the new technologies in a healthy manner. Brod depicts the stress of technology, how people in a postindustrial, computer-based society are attempting to control their lives and environment. Our flirtation with computer-mediated communication gradually replaces public spaces and human interaction, and we start to suffer from another malady—namely, "analysis paralysis," or the inability to make decisions—while being overloaded and overobsessed with information. What we need now more than ever is "intelligence technology," a way to make sense of the information we are faced with. Zimmerman summarizes several negative aspects of IT's impact on individuals and society, and suggests a framework for reducing this impact. We should become aware of the limits of technology and we should recognize the advantages of human intelligence and interaction. She concludes her essay with an appeal to the federal government to provide its citizens with education, regulation, and research that could lead to an outlining of the proper role of computer technology in solving everyday problems.

---

3. See number 19 in the "Recommended Further Reading" section of this chapter.
4. See number 25.
5. See number 7.

Computer-related stress, a common problem for reference librarians—consisting of a combination of performance anxiety, information overload, role conflicts, and organizational difficulties—is also analyzed by John Kupersmith,[6] who describes the same illness as a "modern disease" of information professionals. He identifies the components of technostress as well as its remedies (relaxation, staying healthy, cultivating a positive attitude, managing time, setting realistic goals). He also gives some hints concerning managing technostress within the organization (by believing in the individual; fostering cooperation and the exchange of experiences; organizing and filtering the barrage of information; providing opportunities for hands-on practice; disttributing expertise; simplifying technicalities; lowering anxiety; and setting clear priorities). He concludes his essay with the observation that there is no "magic bullet" that can banish technostress from libraries. We shall deal with continual change for the rest of our working lives. Positive attitudes and sensible management strategies will ease this process and benefit both librarians and users—which will, in turn, enable us to concentrate on the excitement of being at the heart of a true revolution.

Several works cover the change in the educational environment of libraries and information science. Nancy A. Van House and Stuart A. Sutton broadly explore the fundamental changes that are shaping the future environment of library and information-science educational programs in the context of two overlapping ecosystems—namely, the rapidly changing information universe and the university settings in which these programs are housed.[7] The authors warn that the survival of library and information-science programs does not necessarily mean the survival of current programs, and certainly not in their current form and with their current curricula. The increasing value of information lies in bringing other professions into the information field and changing the boundaries and the rules of competition.

Christine Barry discusses the problem of the changing environment of academic research from the standpoint of "information behavior" in research.[8] She concentrates on the formulation of information skills, involving the following: formulating and analyzing information needs; identifying likely sources; locating particular resources; examining, selecting, interrogating, and rejecting sources; recording and storing information; interpreting, analyzing, synthesizing, and evaluating information; presenting and communicating the resulting work; and evaluating what has been achieved.

All these authors as well as others, have provided considerable insights into the evolution and impact of technostress and often point to ways in which its worst effects may be alleviated.

A Questionnaire

I have prepared a special questionnaire designed to find evidence that would shed light on the hypothesis that as a library approaches full automation, human factors

---

6. See number 18.
7. See number 24.
8. See number 4.

are underestimated and sometimes even neglected (see appendix 32.1). If true, that is why the whole process of the new system's implementation becomes a nightmare. One has to fight with system vendors, with understanding the system in a practical way and on-site in its everyday performance; then with staff members, because of a lack of support and awareness; and, at the end, with patrons who are impatient, and wait endlessly for the promised better service.

The best way of achieving the goal is to find the right people among the staff, who should be enthusiastic and willing to undertake new, difficult, and challenging procedures. These people are at the outpost of the new environment, and should be given credit for their achievements and support for their work. They should also be given time to do the research and then to practice new, technologically advanced procedures. They need to organize and carry out automation classes for the staff and patrons. They need to handle the preparation of written and on-line instructions in their native language (most library systems available on the Polish market are foreign language systems), and they must be provided with special computer rooms to carry out training. These employees, the trainers, should in time enlarge the cadre of trainers and then the process of training the trainer can continue indefinitely. But the problem is to give the trainers adequate support and relevant means.[9] With a constructive response and approach, one can achieve the goal. The more instructions that are given to the staff, the more effectiveness can be achieved in everyday procedures.

It is obvious that staff members' response to this activity can be both positive and negative. However, existing stereotypes can be changed as soon as performance is upgraded and our patrons are better served.

While the transition to an integrated automated system may involve an intense and temporary initial period, the development itself is not temporary. Once a library has embarked on a path of complex library automation, it has to be aware of its ongoing, long-run character. The technology is developing rapidly, information sources are growing in number and quality, and in order not to be lost along the way, everybody must keep the pace and not give up. The librarians' duty is to serve better, to provide better quality and relevant data more quickly, and nothing can change this fact.

The answers to my questionnaire have confirmed the hypothesis that the human aspects of library automation are not given the right attention. Most libraries have instead focused on first acquiring the right tool and, only then perhaps, on exploring it with staff members. If there have been any delays in the implementation of the new system, they must have resulted from the fact of not taking into account human factors involving both employees and patrons of libraries.

One has to bear in mind that a decent part of any grant for automation purposes must be devoted to staff training. This is also the case for working hours. A reason-

---

9. Every director of a library that has received a Mellon Foundation grant (and in the case of academic libraries, every university rector) has been alerted to the necessity of releasing library staff involved in the transition to an automated system from at least some of their customary duties, because no person can work full–time in a traditional job and, at the same time, learn a new system and teach others its use. In only the rarest instances has this recommendation been adopted.

able, wisely controlled time has to be "lost," that is, given away, for learning the new environment of the librarian. It is absolutely not enough to just install the new system, to give the staff nice and powerful PCs with the new software, neatly installed and configured, and to start working with the new system. We have all experienced the fear of touching the keyboard, switching the PC on or off, or trying to understand what is going on "inside" this new toy.

The National Library in Warsaw has undergone the process of staff and patron education in the field of automation in a very complex, evolutionary way. The narrow circle of those who were, early on, introduced to computers by the use of mainframe computers for creating bibliographic records, and of the computer specialists who maintained databases in early 1970s, grew in the 1990s into a much larger group of PC users who could use their bibliographic workstations to create records in a much more modern manner.

Staff members, reluctant to adopt changes, have been provided with new possibilities in a practical and systematic way. In 1992, we founded at the National Library a special unit entirely devoted to exploring new technologies to be introduced into the everyday library procedures. The Internet boom (a buzzword that has ruled the information world ever since) has helped to convince people that the exploration of new technologies is important—indeed, unavoidable. We organized a computer room for staff members, in which each employee could explore the use of PCs, the Internet, and the local area network system. Many training courses have been carried out, including lectures on new technologies, demonstrations of the use of on-line and off-line databases, and the use of CD-ROM's. We have joined the special Classroom Instruction Program of the DIALOG firm (now Knight Ridder), in order to give our staff members, librarians from other libraries, and library and information science students the opportunity to get to know the state-of-the-art system of accessing the world of information. Staff members were attending those classes with great reservations at the beginning, but after a while, with increasing interest, understanding, and willingness. It was a difficult time for managers, who saw their employees as being trained in some not-fully-justified procedures; and for the personnel, who were dragged from their desks to do something perceived as not very necessary at the time, and for trainers who were trying to explain the new approach to information provision. In addition, we also encountered shortages of important hardware, software, and expertise.

The Impact of Library Automation on People

Traditional ways of training, like classes, demos, or lectures, have to be enhanced in order to cover new topics. New technology brings new opportunities, and interacts with those who are being trained. On-line classes, electronic discussions, electronic help desks, WWW technology home pages are available for use by the staff and patrons. However, someone has to prepare such tools, configure the easiest interface, and convince people to use those tools.

Should we hire more computer specialists, or train the future trainers? Should we rely entirely on our own resources, or use some external experts? Should we invest in people or in technology? Should we ever make such choices?

These are, again, questions for us to answer individually, bearing in mind that the goal is to keep up the pace, to develop, to enhance, and to upgrade our performance level—while maintaining the standards—and to be treated as partners, not "beggars," on the information market. Information is money, and libraries are full of information to be transferred to those that need it, which means that libraries hold treasures that should be treated as valuable resources. "All roads lead to Rome," as long as one does not forget the goal, and does one's best to keep the pace. As Zimmerman notes: "Computerized information networks are a mixed blessing. On the one hand, they enable people to communicate, share, and deliver information with speed and efficiency. On the other hand, they can result in a psychological condition known as *technostress*."[10]

Technostress is something that we deal with in our libraries on everyday basis. The only way to overcome it is to gain awareness, to gain expertise through practice, and to continue interacting with what technology brings.

Conclusion

We must deal with the automation challenges of the 1990s with care, managerial support, and respect. If we pretend that there is no problem, we are fooling ourselves and the whole process of staff and patron adoption of new technologies could be seriously set back. Any method of getting staff members and patrons acquainted with new technologies, carefully explored and proved useful, should be introduced, even if it is not very popular.

Not all problems have been solved so far. There are still issues to be coped with, but I think that the hardest part is over. In the present, as well as in the future, libraries must never forget the human factor, which is crucial for coping with technological changes.

Appendix 32.1

Questionnaire

1. When applying for the library automation grant, did you encounter any costs involved in the staff and patron training?
   a. yes____   b. no____   (if no, go straight to question 5).

2. If yes, what sum (in percent) of the whole grant amount has been estimated for this purpose?
   a. ____%

3. Was your estimation correct?
   a. ____ (go straight to no. 5)   b. ____

---

10. Ann Zimmerman, "Seeing through the promise of technology," 1996 (URL: http://www.s:umich.edu/spp/courses/744/writings/Zimmerman–memo1–2.html).

4. If no, did you split the grant, adding more to staff and patron training?
   a. yes _____%   b no_____

5. What kind of staff and patron training has your institution introduced? (please tick off all relevant items)
   a. automation classes for the staff
   b. automation classes for patrons
   c. written/printed instructions in native language
   d. on-line instructions in native language
   e. new system computer room for the staff
   f. new system computer room for patrons
   g. hiring instructor from the integrated library system (ILS) vendor to train the staff
   h. hiring instructor from the ILS vendor to train patrons
   i. translation of the documentation provided by the ILS vendor
   j. training the local trainer(s) from the staff at the ILS vendor's headquarters —or at the regional office, or on-site
   k. obligatory subscription to new ILS electronic discussion lists for the staff
   l. translation and circulation of printed or electronic newsletters supplied by the ILS vendor among staff members
   m. preparation of special leaflets (in a printed or an electronic format) for the staff—and for patrons
   n. regular general training sessions (e.g. once a week, the same place, the same hour, the same trainer) for the staff—open to patrons
   o. regular training sessions on a particular module (e.g. OPAC, circulation) for the staff—open to patrons
   p. establishing special training unit within the library organizational structure, especially devoted to the introduction of new automation technologies (if yes, please describe this unit in a few sentences)
   q. incorporating information on special training for the staff—and for patrons— as well as on-line training, within the OPAC
   r. other (please describe briefly)

6. What was the general response of the staff to the automation training offered?
   a. positive _____%
   b. negative _____%
   c. ambivalent/indifferent _____%

7. What was the general response of patrons to the automation training offered?
   a. positive _____%
   b. negative _____%
   c. ambivalent/indifferent _____%

8. Have you done any polls among the staff—and patrons—in this respect?
   a. yes_____   b. no_____

9. If no, do you plan to do so?
   patrons   a. yes _____   b. no _____
   staff   a. yes _____   b. no _____

10. Do you have at your institution a special room or place with computers "to play with," as a method of self–training?
    a. yes____   b. no____

11. If no, please describe in a few sentences the reasons:

12. Is your institution maintaining special training for the staff—on the use of the Internet resources and facilities in everyday work?
    a. yes____   b. no____

13. If no, please describe, in a few sentences, the reasons:

14. Have you experienced at your institution any staff stress reactions to the automation?
    a. yes____   b. no____

15. If yes, please describe briefly their nature (e.g. the fear to use the PC):

16. Have you experienced at your institution any patron stress reactions to the automation? NA. (too early to answer)
    a. yes____   b. no____

17. If yes, please describe briefly their nature (e.g. persistent use of the card catalog instead of the OPAC)?

18. In your opinion, training for library automation is a temporary—or a permanent—task?

19. How are you planning to meet the staff's, and patrons,' needs with respect to the library automation (please describe briefly).
    a. budget (increase in budget allocations)
    b. training (permanent training)
    c. trainers
    d. facilities

20. Who, personally, is responsible in your institution for the staff and patron training for library automation:
    a. the staff: _____
    b. patrons: _____

21. Who is responsible for library automation developments in your institutions? (describe)

Thank you very much for returning the filled–in questionnaire by the end of September 1997 to my e-mail address: ekrysiak@bn.org.pl (a cc copy to quandt@pucc.princeton.edu)
Respectfully,
Ewa Krysiak
The National Library, Poland

The Answers

1. a. 7
   b. 8
2. a. 15.5%, 28%, 4%, 7%, 1.5%, 0.5%
3. a. 5
   b. 2
4. a. 3 (10%)
5. a. 12
   b. 3
   c. 13
   d. 9
   e. 5
   f. 2
   g. 10
   h. 1
   i. 6
   j. 11   (mostly on-site for both staff and patrons)
   k. 4
   l. 3
   m. 9
   n. 3
   o. 9   (mostly on demand for both staff and patrons)
   p. 4   (special task groups)
   q. 3   (usually upon request)
   r. 3
6. a. 5   (25%, 90%, 10%, 10%, 75%, 65%, 100%)
   b. 2   (30%, 5%, 60%, 0%, 0%, 0%, 0%)
   c. 2   (45%, 5%, 30%, 60%, 25%, 35%, 0%)
   d. 2   (difficult to estimate)
7. a. 3   (15%, 80%)
   b. 1   (15%, 0%)
   c. 1   (70%, 29%)
   d. 2   (difficult to estimate)
8. a. 2
   b. 10
9. a. 8
   d. 4
10. a. 6
    b. 8
11. –lack of space and no IT
    –all machinery should work and there is no need for that
    –no space and no additional PCs
    –cannot afford additional terminals but plan to set up a training room
    –not enough PCs
    –no room and no PCs
    –shortage of equipment and staff
    –staff well equipped with PCs at their desks

12. a. 13
    b. 1
13. No appropriate Internet connection (only X.25)
14. a. 12
    b. 3
15. –unrealistic expectation that the system would work completely from the beginning
    –need to change existing stereotypes
    –fear associated with the introduction of new standards and new software
    –fear of PCs in general and of radiation
    –fear by older personnel of revealing less experience with new technologies
    –unwillingness to change traditional methods of everyday work
    –unwillingness to put in additional effort
    –fear of using the system to its full potential
    –fear by elderly personnel of having to learn the system by heart
    –fear of changes in the work flow
    –fear of losing data if stored only in the electronic form
    –general fear and resistance to change
    –fear of new technology
    –fear of changing the work environment, of additional tasks, of becoming redundant
16. a. 3
    b. 9
17. –not using PCs earlier
    –avoiding the formal training that is being offered
    –resistance to using PCs at all
18. temporary 0
    permanent 14
19. a. budget increase, grants, external sources, vendor training
    b. vendor training of the trainer, permanent training, 5% of salaries allocated for training
    c. training sessions for "superusers," staff members, ILS vendors
    d. sufficient reallocation of space, more terminals needed, PC classrooms
20. the staff:
    systems librarian, library information center, the staff, special training unit with a designated staff academic secretary, automation department, heads of subject-specialist and automation departments, head of library, head of training and information system department, deputy director for automation
    the patrons:
    head of reader services, individual central libraries, patrons themselves, special training unit, reference department, head of reader services, head of information and customer services, systems librarian, head of library services
21. directors of library divisions are assisted by deputy director and systems librarian, library information center, systems department, automation department, library departments, systems librarian and others involved in automation, head of automation department, head of authority files, library director, automation department and deputy director, director together with head of computer depart-

ment and head of library department, head of information services and head of information system department, deputy director of automation together with systems librarian, and head of automation department together with library management team

Recommended Further Reading

1. Allan, Ferne C., and Joyce M. Shields. "Automation challenges of the 80's: what to do until your integrated library system arrives." *Special Libraries* 77, 1 (Winter 1986): 15–19.
2. Nuckolls, Karen A. "Humanism and automation: working with people in the library automation process." *The Reference Librarian* 38 (1992): 109–114.
3. Barry, Christine A. "Critical issues in evaluating the impact of IT on information activity In academic research: developing a qualitative research solution." *Library and Information Science Research* 17, 2 (1995): 107–134.
4. Barry, Christine A. "Training the next generation of academic researchers to operate in an electronic world." URL: http://www.kcl.ac.uk/kis/schools/education/cbaera.html (1996).
5. Bartlett, Virginia. "Technostress and librarians," *Library Administration and Management* 9 (1995): 226–230.
6. Bichteler, Julie. "Technostress in libraries: causes, effects, and solutions," *The Electronic Library* 20, 5 (1987): 282–287.
7. Brod, Craig. *Technostress: The Human Cost of the Computer Revolution.* Reading, Mass.: Addison-Wesley, 1984.
8. Callahan, Diane R. "The librarian as change agent in the diffusion of technological innovation." *The Electronic Library* 9, 2 (1991): 13–15.
9. Caputo, Janette S. *Stress and Burnout in Library Service,* Phoenix: Oryx Press, 1991.
10. Commings, Karen. "Ongoing training for integrated library automation systems." *Computers in Libraries* 11, 10 (1991): 42.
11. Dobb, Linda S. Technostress: surviving a database crash." *Reference Services Review* 18 (1990): 65–68.
12. Engle, Michael O. "Instruction and the Web: the development of a library research tutorial." In *The Library Web,* edited by Julie Still. Medford, N.J.: Information Today, 1997, pp. 167–177.
13. Engle, Michael O. "Remythologizing work: the role of archetypal images in the humanization of librarianship." URL: http://fox.cs.vt.edu:80/talks/UNC96/lphilo.html, 1996.
14. Engle, Michael O. "Using World Wide Web software for reference and instruction." URL: http://urislib.library.cornell.edu/wwwpaper.html (1996).
15. Fox, Edward A. "Rethinking libraries in the information age: lessons learned with five Digital Library Projects." URL: http://fox.cs.vt.edu:80/talks/UNC96/1philo.html, 1996.
16. Hallmark, J., and C.R. Garcia. "Training for automated systems in libraries." *Information Technology in Libraries* 15, 3 (September 1996): 157–163, 166–167.
17. Kalin, Sally, and Katie Clark. "Technostressed out? How to cope in the Digital Age" *Library Journal* 121 (August 1996): 30–32.
18. Kupersmith, John, Technostress and the Reference Librarian." URL: http://www.greatbasin.net/~jkup/tstr_ref.html, (1992).
19. Postman, Neil, "Informing ourselves to death." URL: http://www.eff.org/pub/Net_culture/Crms/informing_ourselves_to_death.paper (1990).
20. *Staff Training for Automation in ARL Libraries.* Washington, D.C.: Association of Research Libraries, 1984.

21. *Teaching Information Skills: A Review of the Research and Its Impact on Education.* Edited by Rick Rogers. London: Bowker-Saur, 1993.
22. "Teaching Research Skills: Innovative Strategies for Library use Instruction." URL: http://iti.acns.nwu.edu/slatran/teach.html, (1996).
23. *Training of Technical Services Staff in the Automated Environment.* Washington, D.C.: Association of Research Libraries, 1991.
24. Van House, Nancy A., and Stuart A. Sutton. "The Panda Syndrome: an Ecology of LIS Education." URL: http://sims.berkeley.edu/~vanhouse/panda.html, (1996).
25. Zimmerman, Ann, "Seeing through the Promise of Technology,"). URL: http://www.s:umich.edu/spp/courses/744/writings/zimmerman–memo1–2.html, (1996).

CHAPTER 33

Special Role of the Hungarian National Library in the Formation and Management of Consortia

MIKLÓS FOGARASSY

The present chapter is a Hungarian case study and deals with the special, practical, and historical role of the Hungarian National Library. I first outline the working environment in which we have been operating for some years. The activities of the National Széchényi Library have been managerial in nature and concern a major segment of the national library system, the libraries of key importance.

The National Széchényi Library provides classical central services. For some decades, it has had a special, central section—a library institute called the Center for Library and Information Science (previously called the Center for Library Science and Methodology). This center has had a major influence, beginning in the late 1950s, upon the whole Hungarian library system. It undertook the roles of service provider, manager, and organizer. One might conclude from its history that it was better able to fulfill its role under the conditions of a Communist society than in the years following the 1980s.

There are several reasons for this, but an analysis of them would be a digression. However, its staff was in fact an excellent intellectual collective that strove to participate in the realization of modern library and information policy. The institute not only made efforts, but succeeded in transmitting and adopting the organizational and service patterns of more developed and richer democratic countries, in the fields of library research and in the development of certain central services—with a considerable delay, of course. Since it was largely free from political influence, it successfully maintained open and effective access to information. The center's activities have been concentrated first on the needs of public libraries, but its initiatives have actively involved research and academic libraries as well. However, following the political changes in the late 1980s, there was a slowdown in the extent to which it initiated changes.

The Széchényi library itself was probably the first Hungarian library that started to introduce library automation (at first, in the field of national bibliographic services). Its library institute—the former protagonist of modernization, the initiator of library developments—was, however, not able to take a leading role in the revolutionary new field of library technology at the time of its appearance in Hungary. Beginning in the 1980s, the challenges of library technology pointed toward new directions for university, research, and large public libraries. The National Library's Center for Library and Information Science was not able to fulfill its previous role—to be an effective agency of library policy concerning the planning and organizing of the Hungarian automation on a unified basis. Library automation had started in university libraries 15 years earlier, in a rather individualistic manner, but was ready to spread significantly. Automation not only lacked financial resources, but also comprehensive national plans for a unified computer network. However, some temporary and limited improvements in this situation could be brought about by the Coordination Department of the National Library's center, which acted as a clearing house for foundation initiatives. Cases in point were the consortial applications for grants, and the cooperative development projects of The Andrew W. Mellon Foundation and the Soros Foundation. These projects dealt mainly with library automation and involved organizational and managerial tasks. I shall draw up a balance sheet for this six-year activity and indicate its limitations, in the hope that useful lessons can be learned.

The First Two Consortia—Or, Who Submitted Proposals for Funding?

In the years 1985–1989, a team was formed that later became the manager of foundation initiatives—first of all, by American foundations. These initiatives were directed toward the development of library holdings via enormous gifts of books. The team soon started to operate an efficient information and distribution system tailored to needs—one of the first in Central Europe. As a result, several hundreds of thousands of valuable books and journals were received by Hungarian libraries that ranged from the academic level to small village and school libraries. The success of these ventures resulted in the establishment of a team, which was to be responsible for organizing and managing cooperative proposals for the development of automation programs by research and university libraries.

Being conscious of its responsibilities and the limitations thereof, the team could achieve this aim only in some careful steps. At the end of the 1980s—stimulated by the urgent needs of users—the leading 30-40 large Hungarian libraries (including almost all university libraries) began almost independently, and under difficult financial conditions, to use local area networks for operating their technical processing, catalogs, and services. These libraries had been competing for state funds, and the need for grants for automation had increased tremendously. The difficulties arose for two reasons: first, because of the earlier limitations on the export and import of information technology, and second, because of the need to reunify artificially separated libraries into a campuswide system. Although the National Library was itself short of funds and was among those submitting applications, its success depended on the according of priority to, and representing, the mutual requirements of several institutions within national consortia.

The two consortia set up in 1990 and 1992 for library development, encouraged by the Mellon Foundation, can be called "consortia" only in a limited sense—they were basically only joint proposals for funding their separate objectives. They were connected only because the National Library undertook responsibility for the projects and for their common financial administration.

One may ask why the Hungarian libraries did not attempt to organize a more extensive automation system, and whether it would have been too late to start a Hungarian CASLIN?[1] The basic reason has to be seen in the nonexistence of the preconditions, either in the library community or in the staff of the institute, for undertaking a more encompassing project. The nine proposals for funding, which were submitted by leading Hungarian research academic and research libraries in 1990, and whose transmission to the Mellon Foundation was undertaken by the National Széchényi Library, provide some insight into the state of the art of Hungarian librarianship in the years of the system change. It is important to note that the participants (1) were libraries taking leading positions in the national provision of special literature, and (2) used the grants received as part of a consortium for the most urgent developments in the automation efforts that they had already started.

They requested support for enlarging local networks, for access points, disk capacities, and network-based services at the university campuses. Six of the eight proposals, supported by a total grant of $275,000, formulated such objectives and related ones for the acquisition of CD-ROMs and other library materials.

The participants in the first proposal (1991) were large research libraries, partly in the humanities and the social sciences and in medicine. In particular, the needs of the latter forced the library systems of medical universities to provide up-to-date information on electronic media.

The participants in the second consortium (1992), and the contents of the proposal differed somewhat from those of the previous project: The 12 participants were mostly libraries of technical and agricultural universities, and particularly academic and special libraries that had already been able to formulate ambitious local development plans. By this time, the National Information Infrastructure Development Program had already started and had begun to build an X.25 network that served as a solid basis for accessing the local databases—that is, for making use of library information throughout the country. As a consequence, institutions were in need of bigger storage capacities, IBM-compatible PCs, OPAC modules, and other software.

These two projects represent an organizational framework in which the objective was to submit joint proposals for building local networks within institutions. The National Library's role in implementing and managing this was to verify the feasibility of the proposals, summarize and report on the results of the projects, and undertake a program of financial administration.

---

1. Czech and Slovak Library Information Network, consisting of the Czech and the Slovak National Libraries, the Bratislava University Library, and the Brno State Library.

The HUSLONET Consortium

I am convinced that the third phase, which involved a venture undertaken in the period 1993–1996, is a more realistic and a more effective example of the organizing of consortia. Its aim was to acquire and provide on-line access to databases by the university libraries of two Hungarian cities (Debrecen and Miskolc) and one Slovak city (Košice), by building a wide-area network. The idea was raised and outlined by the staff members of the National Library. The two university centers in northeastern Hungary and Šafárik University in Košice are in geographical proximity, in disadvantaged regions of their respective countries, and were at a comparable level of development in the area of library automation. These libraries had all previously received Mellon grants, and so their former success seemed to constitute a good basis for further grants. It was assumed that if their needs and development led to cooperation among them, this would have beneficial effects on the cooperation between the universities of the two countries on a broader scale as well. It is debatable as to the extent to which these presumptions have been proved, and whether an international consortium is too bold an experiment. I shall describe the difficulties we have encountered.

I mentioned three university sites, but on the Hungarian side it meant actually four institutions. In Debrecen, in addition to the prestigious Lajos Kossuth University, which has numerous faculties in the arts and sciences, the libraries of the medical and agricultural universities appeared as independent units. But in parallel with the preparation of the proposal, the librarians in Debrecen started to implement a unified local network for connecting the three organizations; these steps may be viewed as the first ones toward creating a unified system of higher education in the city, called a "universitas." This aspect was an important factor in the planning of the Hungarian-Slovak Network (HUSLONET).

The concept seemed promising to the Mellon Foundation. The preparation for the proposal consisted of several phases. The National Library contacted the managers of the libraries concerned, and later organized several working sessions where the framework for the joint project was formulated and individual roles for the various participating institutions were specified. The working sessions were held at different locations and involved computer specialists. The aim was to reach a consensus. The staff of the National Library participated as moderators, initiators, responsible managers, and representatives of the plan. This role, being involved as the manager but not as a beneficiary of the project, was undoubtedly an ambivalent one. After the first brainstorming discussions, the institutions prepared their own proposals, and presented the final versions to the National Library, for submission to the Mellon Foundation.

The proposal of each institution consisted of two parts: a minimal version, which calculated the costs of network infrastructure, and a longer-range, maximal version that cited the CD-ROM databases accessible to the users of the three universities. The latter also considered the costs of database construction, cases of a retroconversion, in some instances, and the joint acquisition of multimedia capabilities. The preliminary cost calculations indicated, however, that we had to separately treat the remote CD-

ROM network (WAN), operated by three Logicraft gateways, and the complementary developments. Later, it turned out that the realization of even the minimum exceeded the preliminary calculations.

The ideas emerging from the universities in Košice and Debrecen (the latter meaning the universitas connected onto a joint network) basically determined the plan, and their needs were approximately the same. The backbone of the consortium was formed out of compromises, but the final decisions were always made by the National Library.

The management role of the National Library was very special: It coordinated, it harmonized, and it represented the plan, whose implementation opportunities had to be calibrated to, and developed by, the participating organizations. Nevertheless, the National Library itself was not a beneficiary of the project. One may wonder whether this was the best possible solution, and whether this limited function did not contribute to preserving the centralist, paternalistic memories of a former library management structure. This question is particularly relevant, because not only HUSLONET, but also the other recent consortia of Hungarian libraries (in some cases, with the National Library's participation), aimed at the elimination of a central organization, through a consortium organized on an equal basis. Three years later, 15 large Hungarian libraries submitted proposals, to the Open Society Institute and to the Hungarian Soros Foundation, for the establishing of the national shared cataloging system, in the spirit of the inherent natural democracy of the Web.

The use of the grant of $425,000 obtained from Mellon Foundation in June 1993 for the HUSLONET proposal, and the technical details of the plan's realization, are only highlighted here:

1. It was already clear, in the proposal-preparation stage, that the geographic proximity of the three cities did not correspond to an optimal proximity from the standpoint of communication. The costs of laying a direct Miskolc-Košice cable far exceeded the budget of the maximum version ($800,000). We had to be satisfied with a Hungarian-Slovak network connection using Hungarian X.25 and Internet lines. The latter involves a very roundabout path through Austria and the Czech Republic, with numerous intermediate servers, and is therefore very slow, on the average. The resulting disadvantages could not be foreseen and the consortium had to later make significant compromises.
2. The decisions of the consortium concerning tenders for the hardware and software, and concerning technical implementation, were the result of a difficult but conscientiously undertaken process. However, the points of view of the Hungarian and the Slovak parties differed considerably with respect to the evaluation of bids and priorities. The firm Dataware that was awarded a contract had submitted a more favorable price quotation than the others. At the same time, while the firm had had successful applications in Hungarian libraries, and was known in Slovakia, it had no capability for providing adequate service there. Its system was better adapted to the existing Hungarian systems than to those systems in Slovakia. The parties had to reach an agreement and make a joint decision. This raises the question we had considered before: Should the management exercise strong leadership in cases of international library consortia, and should the management perhaps be provided by an outside organization, rather than by the national library of one of the countries concerned?

The installation and the training of system managers and users have been successfully carried out in Košice, as in Hungary, although the Košice University Library has had many more difficulties with customs clearance and the importation of products, and with further relations with the vendor. These difficulties could not be avoided by the National Széchényi Library, in spite of the very thorough preparations given to the draft contract with Dataware.

3. Another question, which emerged around the time of the Mellon Foundation's favorable decision, was whether additional funds could be obtained for the project from the Open Society Institute. The National Library was of the view that this second proposal—in fact, a matching-grant proposal—was to be prepared by the consortium after its infrastructure was already in place, and after it could exhibit a track record that would justify another project. This view may have been excessively conservative and, in fact, the proposal was submitted only in 1997, the year in which HUSLONET became independent of the Széchényi Library.

4. In the next phase of decision-making, another delicate question concerning the entire consortium has to be faced. When the consortium was ordering bibliographic databases on CD-ROM, jointly chosen as the most important for use via the network, the copyright (licensing) problems of WAN use, and the question of the correct number of simultaneous users, had to be faced. It turned out that the consortium obtained more favorable terms if it placed orders in duplicate copies for the WAN. It became clear that the original conception had to be modified, since originally the consortium meant to buy databases in a single copy for mutual access by the several participants. But the arguments for saving on costs were very convincing. In any event, one might argue that this should have been foreseen in the preliminary phase of the project and may be a good lesson for the future.

The system, whose finances were being administered by the National Library, was ready to operate by the end of 1995, but the first experience showed that the data exchanges among the three universities needed continuous attention and substantial e-mail traffic. At this time, an inauguration ceremony for HUSLONET was organized, with the participation of the rectors and leading staff members of the universities, at two locations, namely, Miskolc and Košice.

The National Széchényi Library was initiator and organizer of the consortium. This function has ceased with the issuing of final report to the Mellon Foundation. In the meantime, the members of HUSLONET entered into a legally binding agreement, which stipulates the rights of HUSLONET as a consortium cooperative and the obligations and responsibilities of its members. The organizational phase of HUSLONET ended with the negotiation, and the acceptance by a consensus, of this agreement. The members of the consortium agreed on property rights pertaining to jointly acquired equipment, on the framework for mutual services, and on the establishing of a board of directors. It was this board and its executive officer (elected annually), the director of one of the participating libraries, who took over the National Library's role.

Conclusions

- The former leadership and development structure of Hungarian libraries, as well as the features of the National Library and the role of its Central Library Institute, have become considerably modified through the organizing of consortia for the purpose of

submitting proposals and fostering cooperation. Some of their roles have now been taken over by special-purpose organizations that have been created in the process of establishing consortia.
- Between 1990 and 1996, the emphasis has been increasingly on actual network construction and effective cooperation. It is in part thanks to the Mellon Foundation that Hungarian library automation has experienced substantial development. We can now count on cooperation among many libraries in a smoothly functioning system. While it is true that the present situation is quite different from what was expected in the early part of the decade, important morals have been learned from the experience of the Hungarian consortia, be they positive or negative.

CHAPTER 34

The Human Aspects of Library Automation

MÁRTA VIRÁGOS

> We live in "the rapids of change." The white waters carry us quickly on;
> we cannot slow down the changes coming to our culture, our society,
> our families, ourselves. But we do have a choice: we can learn
> to enjoy turbulence rather than being overwhelmed by it.
> —Theobald, 1987

With the new Act of Higher Education (1993), the Hungarian university system is facing a radical restructuring, which will result in a doubled intake within five years and lead to substantially new methods of teaching and learning. The reform of higher education involves both the actual contents of curriculum development and the structural organization of university education, with a substantial increase in student enrollment, which, in turn makes the updating of the institutional infrastructure—including the operation and the services of university libraries—an issue of top priority.

In the complex development of Hungarian education and research, the Higher Education Act assigns an important role to the following:

- the abolition of scattered institutions;
- the integration of education and research;
- integrated, wide-range specialty education;
- a flexible educational system (openness of universities, exchangeable education models);
- postgraduate training; and
- retraining.

Libraries, which provide essential access to reading material and information, are crucial components of higher education and their efficient and cost-effective development will produce benefits for the whole university community. University administrations lay special emphasis on the automation and development of library networks. The main goal is for libraries to be completely accessible to all, in offices, laboratories, classrooms, and public clusters throughout the university network system.

The period that witnessed the emergence of various ideas concerning the development of libraries of higher education institutions from domestic resources and from World Bank loans offered new perspectives and resulted in new developments. The first concept, which gave a priority to the expansion of library holdings, was gradually replaced by ideas calling for a fundamental overhauling of the entire library system.[1]

The Cooperation of University Libraries

Although the idea of sharing resources is not new, there is about it a sense of urgency not seen in the past. The world of scholarship has been expanding and the spread of interdisciplinarity into the recesses of nearly every discipline has become the rule, not the exception. The locus of concern, then, is how to create an infrastructure so as to share resources efficiently, rather than what resources will be available to share (Dowler, 1995: 5).

"Resource sharing" may appear to be nothing more than a new term for the familiar concept of library cooperation, but, as stated by Dowler, "resource sharing" may be seen as a term for working out interinstitutional relationships for the benefit of users.

Budgetary constraints and the so-called information explosion compelled the university libraries in Debrecen, as early as the 1980s, to establish a joint acquisitions policy. This was the first step in the drawing up of a resource map of the Debrecen Universitas libraries, which helped to focus on areas of collection overlap for journals, complementarity, weaknesses, and strengths. Consequently, the emphasis has shifted from a collection-centered approach to a client-oriented one.

In other words, informal cooperation was replaced by a more deliberately planned relationship and services moved from a "holdings" strategy to an "access" strategy. Owing to a World Bank grant, the participating libraries of the Debrecen Universitas have been able to purchase and install a state-of-the-art local area network and requisite software that enable them to computerize their operations and make available an on-line public access catalog for efficient access and resource sharing.[2]

The Management of Automation Procedure

Sanchez states:

[T]he initial installation of an integrated library system to automate library functions and services is becoming a distant memory for many libraries. Each library automation project is different from that of the other as each library has its own history, resources, personnel, goals, and organizational structure. These unique attributes cause each library to need different types and levels of decision-making groups, project staff, and automation project implementation plans. (1996: 97)

---

1. A Library Subproject Team was established within the Ministry of Culture and Education in order to further define all those aspects which required more detailed study, as well as related actions and research in 1994–1995. The team rapidly decided to approach the issues involved by defining four key areas of concern: collection augmentation, automation, structure, and training.

2. The Universitas of Debrecen was formally reestablished, initially as a loose association that consists of the University of Agriculture, the University of Medicine, the Academy of Theology of the Reformed Church, the Lajos Kossuth University of Arts and Sciences, and the Institute of Nuclear Research of the Hungarian Academy.

The magnitude and complexity of the task required of an institution that is planning to introduce an automated system have to be fully understood by all before they attempt the process, but this is hardly feasible. In my view, there are two very critical phases in automation: the planning process, and the phase that runs from contract to acceptance. Even though the individual projects are different, several common management considerations exist that make library automation project planning and implementation more effective and successful. Rosenau (1992) states that library automation is a project with the same characteristics of any project and not of an ongoing working environment. The most important characteristics are the following:

1. Projects are temporary events with set objectives that are accomplished by the organized use of the correct resources;
2. Projects require the simultaneous achievement of the performance specifications, the time schedule in which to complete the project, and the cost-budget estimate.

Planning

Strategic planning is an important element in the achieving of a vision of transformation. Planning for the application of information technologies and information management cannot be done in isolation—technology planning must be part of an institution's overall strategic-planning process.

In the case of the libraries of the Debrecen Universitas, their vision statement can be summarized as follows: Improve scientific research work by (1) building a joint information network, laying the foundation for computerized bibliographies and library documentation and databases; and (2) encouraging joint research projects.

The aim of the application of the integrated library system are the following:

- to process and make available all materials possible that can serve as the bases of instruction and research at the university;
- to offer possibilities for the unified handling of the databases of cooperating libraries, and the accessibility of one another's databases with proper authorization;
- to be capable of providing and receiving information for and from domestic and foreign networks, respectively.

Woodworth and Maylone state, "[It] is commonly accepted that the rapid infusion of information technology into universities is bringing computing centers, libraries, and telecommunications operations closer together" (1992: 66).

There are many campuses where this integration has led to the administrative merging of libraries with a computing center and other "information partners." In the case of Debrecen, the concept of "reengineering" was critical, and the traditional organizational structure was redesigned and a Task Force Group was created, of which both the managing directories of the libraries and the computer centers were members.

The management team conceived of the library automation project as a number of smaller projects that must be accomplished in order to achieve the larger project goal of a fully integrated on-line library system. Since the integrated library system initially operates in the automation of cataloging, circulation, acquisitions, and other library

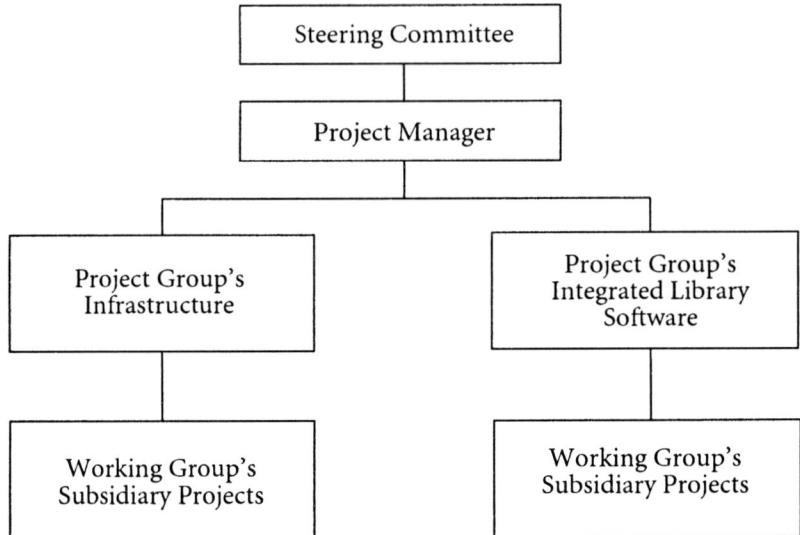

Figure 34.1 Project Management Structure

areas, it seemed reasonable to assume that project leaders for these areas would be well acquainted with the history, staff, and work processes for their area of the project.

The project was supervised by a steering committee, of which both the managing directors of the libraries and the computer centers were members (see figure 34.1). The general project manager was assisted by two coordinators (one is a librarian; the other, the head of the library computer department), who were responsible for the logistics and the flow of information to the distinct project groups.

Systems Analysis

Systems analysis is frequently taken to be a concept entirely related to computing, but it is in fact a technique designed to help one look at the world in a more structured way and identify the system that exists within it, the inputs and outputs, and how things flow through them. Systems analysis will progress from a general analysis to a more detailed one, listing all the inputs, outputs, and relationships of each part of each process. For systems analysis, we had to set out the management methods and project goals that can best work with the local resources and are acceptable to the administration.

To achieve an accurate analysis, we had to carry out two studies. First, we had to draw up a series of flowcharts showing how our current system worked. All the libraries of the Universitas were conveniently organized by a combination of functions (acquisition, circulation, reference), activities (orders, repairs, extensions) and forms of material. The second study had to be carried out to identify what the library users' expectations from the new system were, and how these expectations overlap with our objectives.

This part of the process is critical to the ultimate success of the project. Producing a system based on false assumptions about what is actually going on is a recipe for, at best, a disappointing performance from the new system, and, at worst, a disaster. Our system analysis was in reality a feasibility study, even though we did not identify it as such at the time.

The main purposes of the study were

1. to define the goals of the automated system, based on the libraries' objectives;
2. to describe a new system to achieve the objectives;
3. to establish hardware and software requirements and request proposals;
4. to determine the costs, staff, and accuracy and quality of information of the system.

To illustrate the method we used, there are two flowcharts for the cataloging process. The first one is for our manual operations and the second is for the automated system (see figure 34.2). In this state of the study we tried to define those areas where the greatest problems lay—analyze each individual difficulty to confirm the problem (a different system or method for subject cataloging, indexing, serials cataloging).

What we can see in these charts is that the number of steps in the process can be reduced by roughly half. It is assumed that the new system will require data to be entered only once to create both an order and a catalog record. The other important element is to draw a flowchart for human tasks and match it to the data work flow. The flow of work and the movement of items through technical services had been affected by automation and the tasks that the staff performed had changed. "The optimum way to redesign work flow in an automated system is to use the management concept of reengineering—a complete restructuring of technical services operations. To re-engineer means that library administration and staff need to be willing to look at what they do with a fresh eye rather than continuing 'business as usual.'" (Joseph and Fricke, 1996: 112). Reengineering is critical if the library is going to be effective in improving its productivity and utilizing the increasingly scarce resources that are available to it.

The Request for Procurement (RFP)

The RFP actually translates into the developing of timetables, charts, and graphs that are logical and realistic, and that would best explain to all the enormity of the venture that was being undertaken. Plans for a procurement cycle for an automated system should be synchronized with technological advances (see figure 34.3). By planning each step in advance, the library can avoid potentially damaging and wasteful errors caused by the omitting of some vital step that must be completed before a later task can be started.

There are several ways of presenting the time frame required to procure a new system:

1. by listing the major tasks involved and indicating an approximate length of time needed;
2. by listing the anticipated schedule of events, indicating specific calendar dates where milestones will be met; it is known also as "key-events planning";
3. by showing individual activities as bars against a time scale (bar-chart planning), as shown in figure 34.4, which is also known as "Gantt-chart planning."

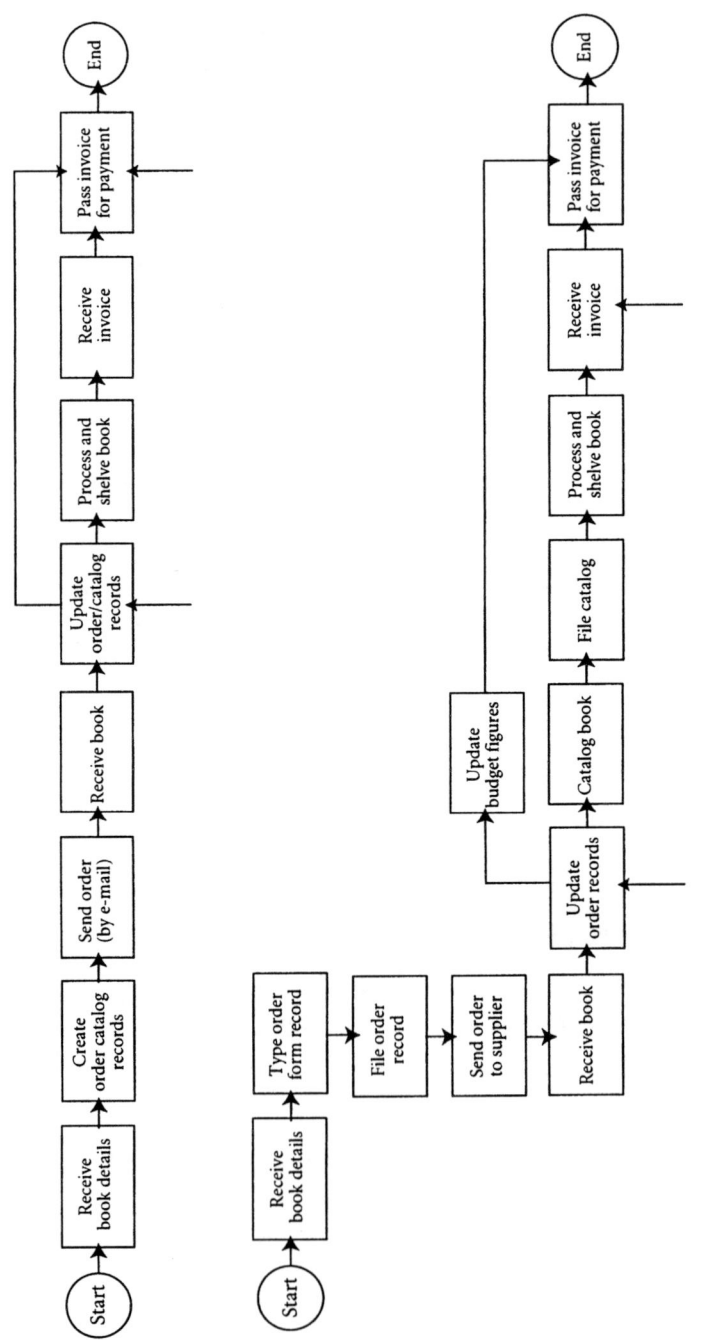

Figure 34.2 Flowcharts for Cataloging

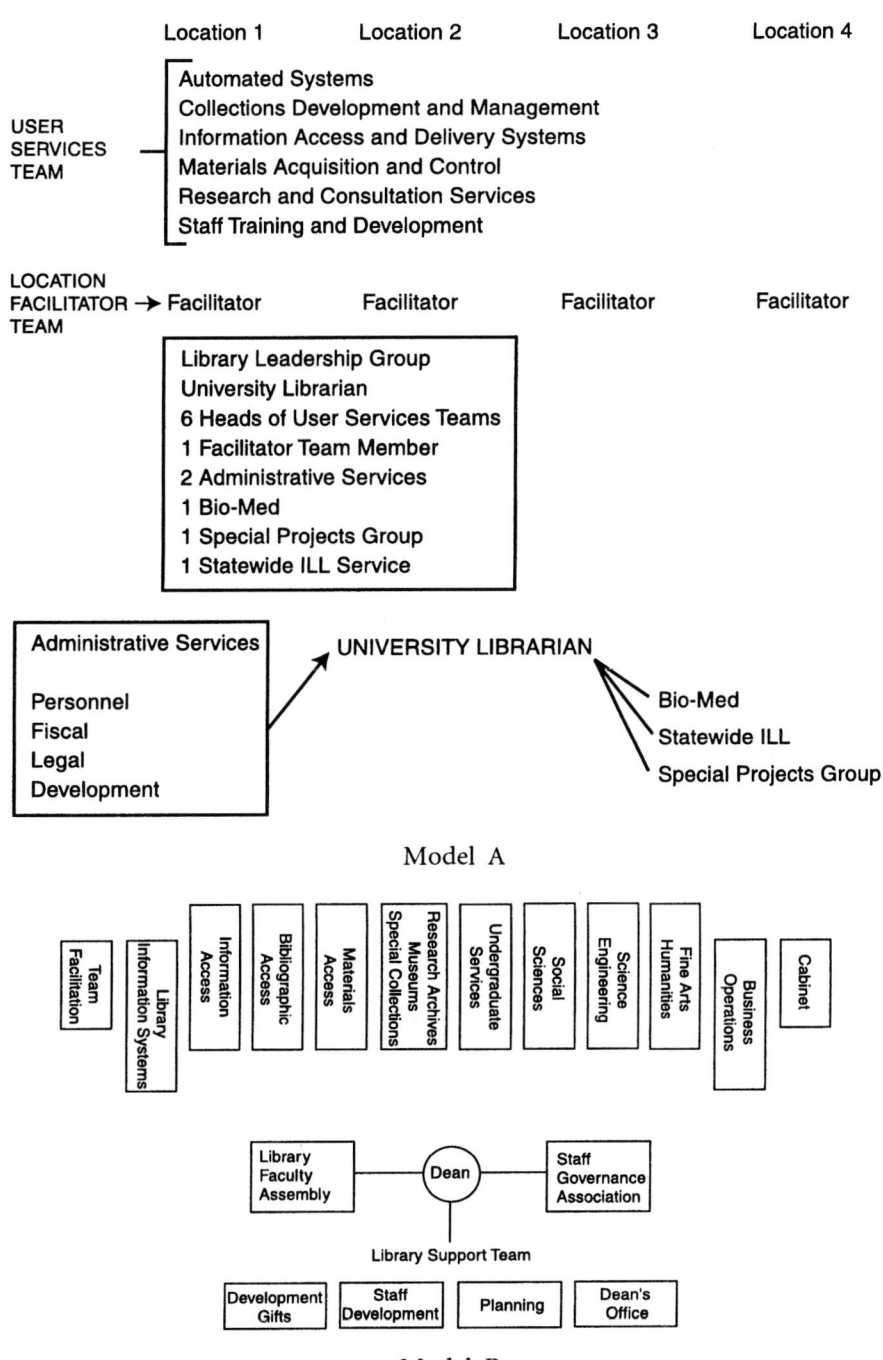

Figure 34.5 Analysis of Teams

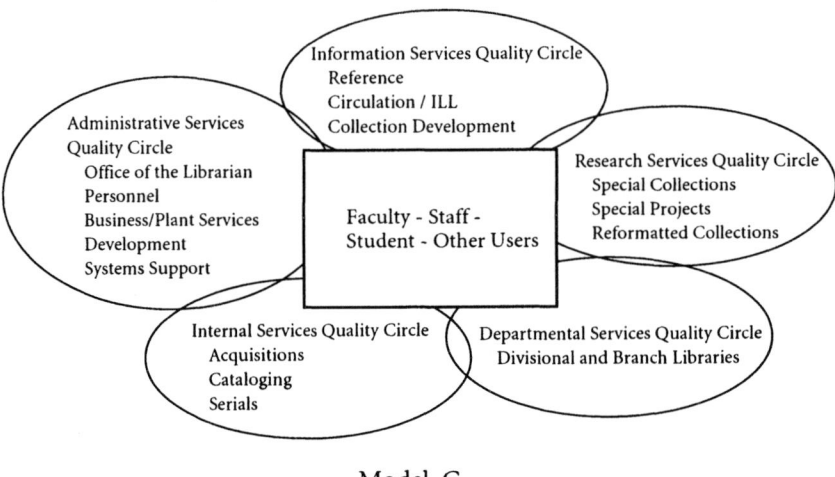

Model C

Figure 34.5 (continued)

One of the most important functions of the management in the process of change is to minimize the negative impact on the staff. Craig Brod defines a malady, called technostress, as "a modern disease of adaptation caused by an inability to cope with the new computer technology in a healthy manner" (1984: 16). A number of systems could be identified among librarians, such as anxiety, denial, resistance, panic, intolerance, and physical discomfort. Resisting force can be articulated in milder and more spectacular manifestations. The "Why do we have to do all these silly things?" or "I am uneasy about computers" attitudes can finalize in an early retirement or in sick leave.

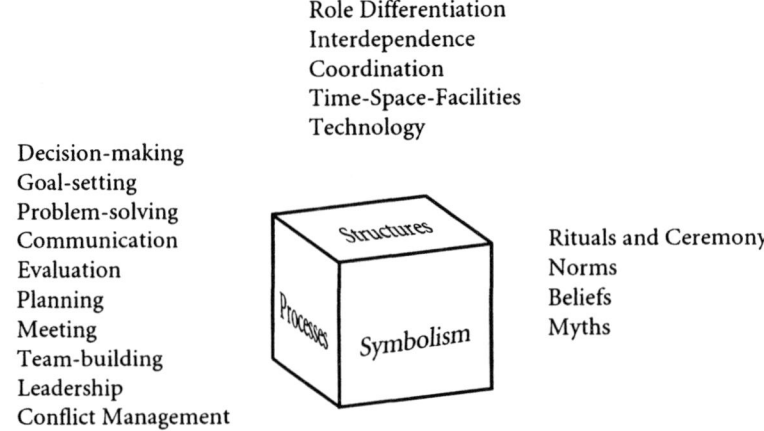

Figure 34.6 Three-dimensional Theory of Change

New Managerial Methods

Both the organizational change involved and the automation process needed a new managerial form with participatory decision-making. Issues relating to participatory management have been debated in the professional literature for more than twenty years.

John Millet, one of the advocates of collegiality, assumes that the collegial model can work better in the place of the bureaucratic model.

> I would argue that that there is another concept of organization just as valuable as a tool of analysis and even more useful as a tool of analysis and even more useful as a tool of generalized observation of group and interpersonal behavior. This is the concept of community. The concept of community presupposes an organization in which functions are differentiated and which specialization must be brought together, or coordination, if you will, is achieved not through structure of superordination and subordination of persons and groups, but through a dynamic consensus. (1962: 234–235)

Management should utilize the strengths of the collegial model, which are the following:

1. Staff members can express themselves and practice a higher degree of autonomy.
2. Group-decision making exists, which means that majority rule of a consensus prevails.
3. It is expected that decisions made by a group tend to be more accurate.
4. It provides better communications of ideas across all levels of library staff.

The internal communication level is one of the critical success factors in human resource management. Managers need to be very careful in involving their staff in decision-making; honesty in group dynamics is of the utmost importance. The staff needs to be involved to the greatest possible extent. Communication permeates all management functions and affects both how the system change is structured and how the staff and patrons accept it. The forum and the way for informing the staff depend a great deal on the library's organization. In our case, this was accomplished mostly in face-to-face meetings. A free expression of ideas and viewpoints is the essence of the collegial concept. Librarians may feel that their ideas and opinions are being ignored in the bureaucratic settings of their libraries, and therefore, they think of collegiality as a way to express themselves and practice a higher degree of autonomy.

One of the most important managerial tasks during the changing process is the managing of conflict. For most people the term carries a negative connotation—but there is another view of "conflict." This one argues that conflict improves an organization's effectiveness by stimulating change and improving the decision-making process. There are several techniques for reducing the intensity of conflict. Mutual problem-solving has been described as the soundest method for resolving intergroup conflicts. This technique requires that the conflicting parties come face-to-face with the underlying causes of their conflict and share the responsibility for seeing to it that the solution works. Mutual problem-solving requires that the conflicting units have the potential to achieve a better solution through collaboration.

We can conclude that the program manager must be a good communicator in order to convey to the staff and users, at various levels of understanding and interest, what outcome is desired from the implementation of an integrated system and what work flows are necessary. Excellent analytical skills are required to communicate well. Leaders must focus on honing skills in group dynamics. There is no question that the implementation of automated systems in libraries offers opportunities to move decision-making down the managerial chain. As a matter of fact, to function well, our sophisticated systems require substantive independent thinking for even the most elementary tasks.

Warren Bennis (1990) identified the following four areas of competence for leadership: (1) management of attention: the ability to communicate clear objectives and directions to others; (2) management of meaning: the ability to create and clearly communicate meaning, thereby achieving understanding and awareness; (3) management of trust: the ability to be consistent in circumstances that are often complex and are fraught with dilemmas, so that people can depend on them; (4) management of self: the ability to know oneself and to work with strengths and weaknesses.

Assessing Staffing Needs

The library staff is the most important resources the library has in anticipating new and evolving uses of the network. Staff members work with a variety of users, communicate with faculty about research needs, and guide students to information resources. They can serve as constant environmental scanners who look for indications of changes in users' information behavior and expectations. It is very important that each person's job be explained to him or her, and that employees should be quite clear about what they are to do, when they are to start, and how long they are expected to take with each task they are given. Automation profoundly affects library organization, and the management must find ways to minimize negative elements and emphasize the positive.

In the case of our library, one of the first issues dealt with was in regard to what functions would be necessary for efficient operation, and who should perform these functions. The second step was to create a chart with the new processes and combine these with the previous ones to help the librarians visualize work flows after automation. Over the years, some tasks have been allocated to personnel on the basis of individual interest and ability.

The library management used Grover's model, in which he shows an entirely new approach to organizing the staff and developing job descriptions. He gives criteria that distinguish between professional and nonprofessional levels of work. The approach to the analysis is by means of a set of standards applied to every service or activity requiring staff action. These standards are the following: the degree of complexity, specific procedures and modes, degree of responsibility, level of involvement between the staff and client, time frame of the service, value of the activity, degree of supervision, and level of formal education (see table 34.1).

Table 34.1. Library Staff Activities and Associated Attributes

	Attributes		
Set of Standards	Technician	Librarian	Information Manager
complexity	transactional	reactive	diagnostic
process/mode	procedures	recipes	theory
responsibility	organization	client needs	professional
level of involvement	impersonal	interpersonal	personal
time frame	immediate	short	extended
value	task	information	person
independence	supervised	supervised	independent
education	high school	college	M.L.S.
objective	efficiency	relevance	customization

We defined three categories of activities and associated them with three distinct classifications of staff: information manager, librarian, and technician. The analysis of the required skills for the three groups was made according to their respective tasks in the automation process. For the information manager, the skills involved in network integration, navigation, database design for local documents, and client/server architecture are basic. For librarians, a second level is required with skills of repackaging and synthesizing information, document management, and electronic document delivery. For technicians, topics at the basic introductory level could be of relevance. We can also state that the team leaders take the role of middle managers and they function as "coaches." This is a job in which the manger is both a delegater and a doer, a strategist and an operator, and a long-range planner as well as an immediate implementer. Kantor (1986) has done a considerable amount of research and writing about the changing role of the middle manager in organizations in the United States. A particular theme in her work has been the shift from the traditional role of an "approver or message carrier": to one as an innovator or "idea entrepreneur."

Successful planning and management of human resources is critical for overall organizational effectiveness. Every library has to be concerned with human resource management, especially when a new task arises and the library is therefore forced to plan for the more effective and efficient use of its staff.

The micro approach to human resource planning reflects the interface between individuals and their jobs. The micro approach is systematic, beginning with a job analysis (see figure 34.7) and ending with the exit interview. Depending upon the intended purpose, project management can use the whole, or some parts, of the model very efficiently in finding the right person for the specific task.

Training

The content of the training program must be revised as the library progresses and new features are added to the system. The training sessions we organized at Debrecen

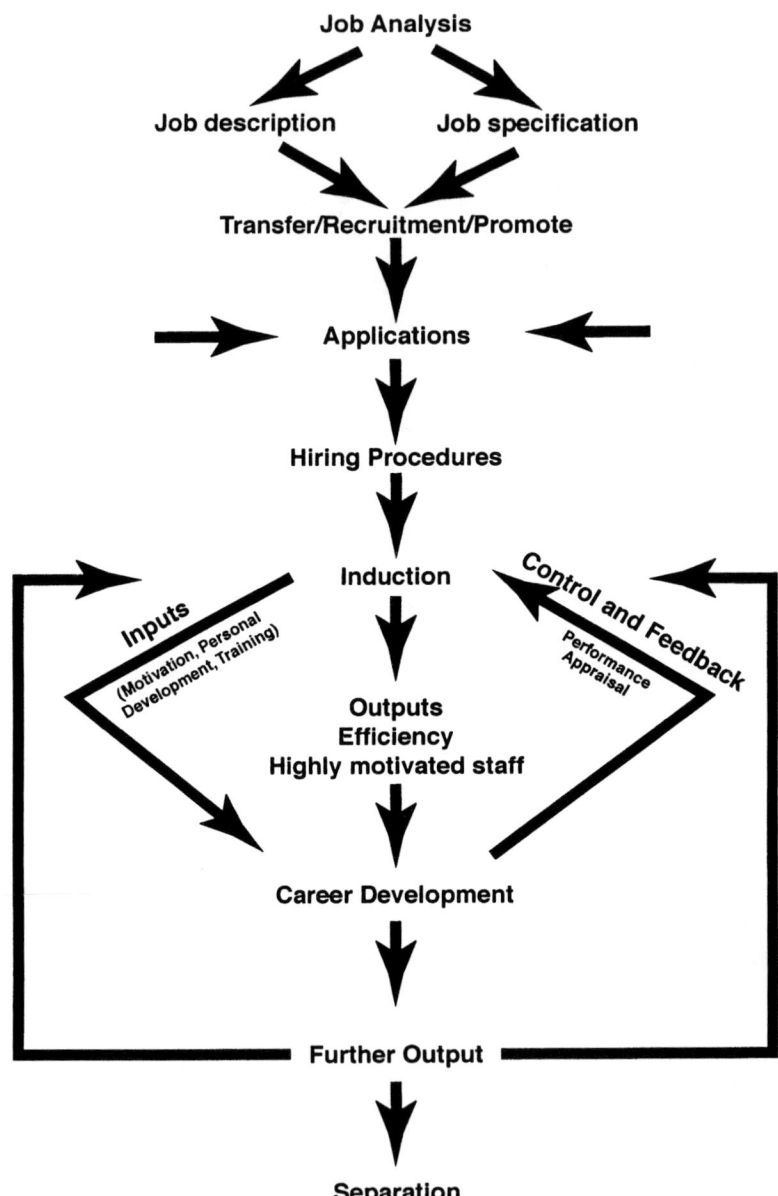

Figure 34.7 Job Analysis

were a combination of training sessions by the system manager and vendor training. For the OPAC model we got a beta version to organize in-house training sessions. Each session cover the basic structure of the system, how each function is tied together, data contents, and screen displays.

As part of the whole training and development process, we made the staff aware of expected standards of performance. Accuracy is a critical factor in the use of integrated library systems, and hence a method for checking error rates and monitoring trends was established to ensure standards.

Training could be a waste of time and money when the staff members are not eager to learn because they were never part of the planning process and did not have enough basic knowledge about the system. Also, the success of the team approach requires a commitment by all members to the goals of the team rather than to individual goals. The team members must also have the willingness to share authority and responsibility.

For the overall success of the new system, there are two human elements are fundamental: staff motivation and job satisfaction. I wish to conclude by quoting from a study by Bradford and Cohen:

> In a well-functioning organization, staff working at or near their full potential are likely to be characterized by a sense of commitment. There are collaborative team-efforts, concern about the whole of the organization, active problem solving, acceptance of unit and library-wide goals, and focus on quality services and performance. Staff who are satisfied with their job tend not to wait for the department head to notice a problem with service, methods of operation, coordination, or other functions. They assume responsibility themselves for the unit's success and take the initiative to deal with problems and meet objectives, thus avoiding the passive acceptance of things gone wrong because "it's not my job." (Bradford and Cohen, 1984: 7)

References

Boisse, Joseph A., and Stella Bentley. "Reorganizing Libraries." In *Advances in Librarianship*, vol. 20, 1992, pp. 27–45.
Bradford, D. L., and Cohen, A. R. 1984. *Managing for Excellence*. New York: John Wiley and Sons.
Brod, Craig. *Technostress: The Human Cost of the Computer Revolution*. Reading: Addison Wesley, 1984.
Derr, C. B., and Deal, T. E. 1979. *Towards contingency Theory of Change in Education: Organizational Structure, Process and Symbolism*. In E. J. King (ed.), *Education for Uncertainty*. London: Sage.
Dowler, Lawrence. 1995. "The Research University Dilemma: Resource Sharing and Research in a Transinstitutional Environment." *Journal of Library Administration* 21 (1/2): 5–26.
Grover, Robert. "A Proposed Model for Diagnosing Information Needs." In *School Library Media Quarterly*, vol. 21, no. 2, 1993, pp. 147–152.
Johnson, Peggy. 1991. *Automation and Organizational Change in Libraries*. Boston: G. K. Hall and Co.
Joseph, Myrtle, and Fricke, C. Nancy. 1996. *Issues in Managing Automated Cataloging*. In J. W. Head (ed.), *Introducing and Managing Academic Library Automation Projects*. Westport, Conn., and London: Greenwood.

Kantor, R. M. 1986. *The Reshaping of Middle Management*. Management Review (January): 19–20.

Millet, John. *The Academic Community*. New York: McGraw-Hill, 1962.

Roseanau, Milton, D., Jr., *Successful Project Management: A Strategy by Step Approach with Practical Examples*. New York: Van Nostrand Reinhold, 1992.

Sanchez, Elaine. 1996. Project Management and Organizational Change from the Advent to the Aftermath of Automation: Library and Cataloging Department Perspectives." In J. W. Head (ed.), *Introducing and Managing Academic Library Automation Projects*. Westport: Greenwood.

Saunders, Laverna M., "The Management of Change: Minimizing the Negative Impact on Staff and Patrons." In *Library Systems Migration*, edited by Pitkin, Gary M. Westport: Meckler, 1991.

Theobald, Robert. 1987. "The Rapids of Change: Social Entrepreneurship." In *Turbulent Times*, Indianapolis: Knowledge Systems, 1987.

Warren, Bennis. "Managing the Dream: Leadership in the 21st Century." In *Training* 27, May 1990, pp. 44–49.

Woodworth, Anne, and Maylone, Theresa. 1992. "Chief Information Officers, Academic Libraries, and Information Job Family." In Gary M. Pitkin (ed.), *Information Management and Organizational Change in Higher Education*, Westport: Meckler.

CHAPTER 35

The Contribution of Integrated Library Services to the Ensuring of Quality Services

JUDIT SKALICZKI
ÉVA ZALAI-KOVÁCS

Even in the 1970s, Hungarian libraries had already been considering the questions and possibilities of automation. In the beginning, the libraries used mostly the Microisis-based software that had been developed by their own computer specialists to automate different work processes. From the mid-1980s on, librarians at mainly the academic and specialized libraries drew encouragement—from articles in library journals and from personal experience gained abroad—for efforts to formulate their own plans and ideas regarding automation. The introduction of integrated library systems received a strong boost at the beginning of the 1990s. At that time, no Hungarian integrated software had been developed, yet the libraries purchased foreign software, primarily software that had already been translated into Hungarian. Foreign companies were quick to recognize the good market potential in Hungary and products of more and more of these companies appeared on the market. The libraries' choices were strongly influenced by their financial status, and the methods of acquisition were influenced by the changing economic regulations and by the conditions stipulated by the tenderers in the event that the libraries obtained their systems through tendering.

Modern management methods began to appear in Hungarian librarianship in the 1980s. The political, social, and economic changes of the 1990s made it even more important that librarians become familiar with, and apply the methods of, the managing of change. The need for increased efficiency, flexibility, and continual quality assurance made it necessary to introduce total quality management (TQM) methods as well.

The selection and the introduction of an integrated library system bring about great improvements in the quality of life of a library, regarding both its environment and its services.

The Aim of Hungarian Library and Information Policy

The objective of Hungarian policy is to make our libraries become the foundational institutions of the emerging information society. This aim can be achieved primarily by the development of the information technology of not just one or two libraries but of the entire library system. As a first step in this direction, information science infrastructure must be developed nationwide in a way that information available in the libraries becomes freely accessible, creating a virtual single library in Hungary. And the development of infrastructure must be followed by the development of computer technology in libraries, taking into account the library's technical possibilities and aiming toward the use of integrated library systems.

At present, the ministry has two options for financing this development:

- central financial aid from the ministry for the purpose of infrastructure development of libraries, as stated in the draft of the new library bill (which was enacted as a law in 1997; and
- funds appropriated by the government for information technology development.

These options provide a guarantee—to all academic libraries, major special-purpose libraries, and county and city libraries—regarding the acquisition of integrated library systems.

How Does Automation Change Libraries?

We propose to answer the question of what changes in a library due to automation and how this change takes place. It is in fact a threefold question: what the introduction of an integrated system changes in the everyday operations of the library; how it changes staff attitudes toward their work; and most important, how it changes librarians' efforts to more effectively meet the needs of the library's customers, and in a more user-oriented way. The question underlying all this is how the operation of an integrated library system raises quality.

It is a cliché in library circles that the library is doing its job only if customers' needs are being met. The use of an integrated library system is only a tool in the realization of this goal. We believe that one of the tools of TQM today is the use of appropriate software.

This notion was our working hypothesis and we prepared a questionnaire to find out whether we were right or not. This questionnaire (appendix 35.1) was sent to eight different libraries (their addresses and statistical data are given, respectively, in appendixes 35.2 and 35.3).

Integrated Library Systems

We chose four different computer integrated library software systems used in Hungary: TinLib, OLIB, Aleph, and Voyager. These were chosen because they are the most frequently used systems in Hungary today. In the case of each of these systems, we asked two libraries to participate in the survey and attempted to pick ones that represented different library types. Thus, among the participants, we find academic, public, and specialized libraries.

Reasons for Choices. First, we wanted to find out their reasons for choosing their particular system. Among the respondents, the academic library that chose the OLIB system was replacing an already existing Microisis-based system; professional and economic factors, as well as the development of further services and the terms of the guarantee offered, were decisive in the making of this choice. The system was chosen by a two-step procedure in which the library invited several system vendors, tested each system for a month, and held a one-week demonstration for every system invited. The systems were judged on the basis of a point system devised by the library and the final decision was made by means of a professional evaluation.

The county library that chose OLIB based its decision on three factors: the system's most up-to-date relational database management, the distributor's professional and business expertise, and the favorable long-term cooperative agreement made with it.

The decision of the academic library that chose the TinLib system was influenced by the fact that at the time of the decision, this was the only system with a Hungarian menu and user's guide and that it worked on the hardware and network available to the library. At the same time, the system was not too simple or overly complex; the library was able to convert the data already in existence; the favorable prices made it possible to obtain the complete system and to increase the number of user and staff workstations. The library's decision was also influenced by the fact that a major library with a specialization similar to its own was already using this system.

The city library's decision to choose TinLib was influenced by a need for full-scale automation, the up-to-date development possibilities, the system's easily masterable operation, and the possibility of operating the system from PCs.

Among other professional aspects, the ability to process images was a major factor in choosing the Voyager system for the library of an academy of arts. Its decision was also influenced by the fact that Voyager has a representative in Hungary, and by the fact that the company's offer took into consideration the library's professional needs and was financially favorable.

Another academic library surveyed chose this system through a call for tenders. Its major considerations were the need for up-to-date software and hardware, the openness and the level of integration of the system, user-friendly interfaces, and the authority control option.

The academic library that chose Aleph made its decision on the basis of the flexibility of the system and the possibility of adapting the modules to current local needs. It was decisive that the system met the requirements of the library's technical and financial conditions.

The specialized library that chose this system learned about it when it made the decision to change directions in the area of automation, due to its unfavorable experiences with the system it was using at that time. Its decision was motivated by the good experiences it had had with the operation and the distributor of the system. It is worth noting, though, that at the time it made its decision, no other integrated system was present in Hungary; hence the decision was naturally directed toward the Aleph system.

How Libraries Learned about Systems. In the next question, we asked the libraries where and how they found out about the systems. Most of them first saw their system at a trade show or read about it in the professional press. It is worth noting that visiting a library already using a particular system also helped the others to make a decision.

Most of the respondents gave the possibility of both fast and up-to-date availability of information as their professional reasons for automation. Most of the libraries had already been using automated processing in certain areas and the need for using an integrated system inevitably surfaced. This need was natural in the case of a newly built county library—especially so because its network was developed as part of the building project. Other professional reasons included the increase in the workload, the lack of adequate staff, the growing amount of information appearing in the electronic form, and the need to raise the quality of services.

Almost all the respondents answered the question regarding user needs from the point of view of both customers and staff. The librarians saw the systems as providing a possibility for faster and more accurate work in processing; from the point of view of fulfilling customers' needs, the aim was to make multifaceted searching faster and more efficient through the use of these systems.

The Context for Automation. The next questions dealt with the circumstances that surrounded the introduction of automation. In libraries where processing was already automated, either partly or fully, the introduction of the system began with the creation of a new hardware environment and the conversion of the data already in existence. Libraries, which had previously worked with traditional methods, prepared for the introduction of the new system by reviewing their work processes, by putting their records in good order, and by taking an inventory. In several libraries, the staff was trained in computer technology.

Usually, the first step in the automation process was the introduction of the cataloging module and the OPAC module, and the next step was the introduction of the circulation module. In libraries where an integrated system was already being used, the transition happened simultaneously in all areas, but of course, not all functions were used right away.

In every library, the training and preparation of staff members first took place through courses offered by the distributors of the various systems. Following these courses, most libraries held further internal courses taught by staff members in charge of individual modules and prepared internal guides and regulations.

With regard to systems managers and local computer specialists, the picture is quite varied. In most libraries, there is a systems operator and a computer specialist but, especially for provincial libraries, the entrepreneurial sphere, offering much higher salaries, has proved a fierce competitor and succeeded in luring away experienced professionals.

It was interesting that staff members in every library had feelings of anxiety and even some fear in the beginning. This is understandable, because many of them not only had to master the given system, but they also had to learn to use a computer for the first time. Later on, most librarians got to like their systems and they now see their tasks as providing a new and good job opportunity.

The most varied answers received were the responses to the question about the nature of the guarantees for the continuing conditions of operation. The difficulties surfaced in the forms of capacity and appreciation problems, especially in the case of libraries that began automation four or five years ago. It can generally be said that this is what poses the greatest problem for libraries because the originally determined and continually decreasing operating budgets are no longer sufficient to maintain the systems. Most libraries were able to automate because they were successful in applying for funds, but these sources do not provide for operating costs and the budgets provided by the authorities are no longer large enough to cover these costs, either. It is definitely necessary for libraries to obtain budgets large enough to securely cover and at least maintain the results achieved so far. It would be desirable to be able to apply for grants that would cover operating costs as well.

Results of Automation. In the third group of questions, I was interested in the results of automation from the perspectives of both the staff and the customers. The answers given to these questions directly relate to our basic question of what qualitative changes were wrought by automation.

In most libraries, the change in work processes appeared in organizational tasks. Because the introduction of the various systems into the libraries usually began with the cataloging module, traditional catalog building was the first activity to cease. Naturally, a certain amount of parallelism was present everywhere for some period of time, with both manual and automated cataloging going on simultaneously, but the libraries are increasingly trying to eliminate manual work processes. New tasks appeared alongside the traditional ones, such as retrospective cataloging, bar-coding, equipping books with security stripes, matching collection data to records taken from other databases, the use of authority control, archiving, and regularly (each day before closing, for example) saving all work done on computers throughout the library for data protection reasons.

Supplying overdue notices and placing holds on books have become much more efficient in the area of circulation. One of the definite results of automation is that work processes have become more transparent and they have ceased to be separate from each other.

Regarding the changes in working conditions, almost everybody mentioned the increase in time spent in front of computer screens and, along with it, an increase in eye complaints. In certain places, staff rooms have become more crowded because of the workstations that are placed there. Working conditions were made more difficult by the fact that staff had to learn new skills and the libraries could not increase their workforce to meet the demands of the new tasks; actually, the general tendency in this time period was one of downsizing for libraries.

It is generally true, of the changes in staff attitudes, that as a result of automation everyone's work became more visible, for everyone now uses the same database. This, though, caused tension at first in certain individuals but it forced staff to work in a more disciplined way and more accurately. The change in staff attitudes is visible through the extent that staff members value each other's work more than before and rely on each other during critical times. Their intellectual horizons have widened; new tasks also mean new opportunities and they encourage closer cooperation between individual staff members and other libraries as well. The novelty of the situation and the fact that people feel more "modern" have had a good effect on everybody. One of the participants in the survey said that staff members are definitely more self-confident, that they have become more open toward professional questions, and that they have started to take a more active part in the life of the professional community.

The libraries' attempts at automation were also positively received by patrons, especially so because it provided them with a number of new services. In the case of academic libraries, it has become possible to download catalogs onto the local network, to keep a record of the publications a library holds, to supply images along with bibliographical items, and to forward search hits via e-mail. It has become possible to forward and receive interlibrary loan requests through the network, and the reservation service has become wider in scope and more reliable. A number of libraries are able to offer Internet access to their patrons and only the computers themselves and the lack of space set limits. The public libraries are planning the development of a number of local and regional services on the basis of the opportunities made possible by the systems.

It was evident from the answers that the libraries have conducted major promotional campaigns and are continuing to do so to raise awareness of their new systems and services. These include the use of informational publications that are available at the library and on the network as well, informational leaflets, more staff being placed at reference desks, patron training, demonstrations, and courses. It is worthwhile to note one of the responses to this question: The library's new system did not require any large-scale promotion because reader interest was already greater than what library staff could easily handle.

Future Needs. Concerning future tasks, libraries would like to continue the development of their system and their services. Every single library pinpointed as its greatest problem its inability to finance the costs necessary to develop, maintain, and run its system. Libraries are also facing difficulties because of the prices of rented telephone lines. Staff members need further training in professional matters, information science, and computer technology, and new demands have surfaced for changing the librarian's basic education.

Conclusion

We can draw the following conclusions from the answers to the survey. Automation has changed the operations of the library and the integrated computer system has also integrated the work flow. It is probably not an overstatement to say that it has "integrated" staff members as well—that is, it brought them closer to each other. The work of departments working quite separately from each other also became more integrated. In other words, the walls that were isolating each task group in the library have broken down and cooperation has developed between these groups, but their group consciousness has not been lost.

Automation has made it possible, or will make it possible in the future, to introduce services which unquestionably increase the range of patron-oriented services, for they make it possible more and more to adjust the services to individual needs. It is also noteworthy that computers also enable patrons to search the Internet for themselves, to search for what they need and to choose for themselves from the available data. Based on all of the above, we can say that the survey supported our working hypothesis that automation unquestionably contributes to the improvement of the quality of library work.

In conclusion, the libraries surveyed made it their primary task to continually develop their services as extensively as they could. It is evident from their responses that the automation of the library meant a renewal for both patrons and staff. It is not new challenges that pose difficulties but an insufficient financial basis, which delays work and makes it more difficult.

Appendix 35.1 Questionnaire on Automation

1. The reasons for automation:

   1.1 Why did you choose this system?
   1.2 How did you find out about this system?
   1.3 What were your professional reasons for automation?
   1.4 What user needs did you base your decision on?
       a. from the perspective of your staff members, librarians;
       b. from the perspective of your users.

2. The circumstances of automation:

   2.1 How did you prepare for the introduction of the system?
   2.2 What were the different steps in introducing the system?
   2.3 What kind of training did the staff receive?
   2.4 How did the staff welcome the introduction of the system and the system itself?
   2.5 Do you have a computer expert in your library?
   2.6 How do you guarantee the conditions of operation?
   2.7 How do you carry the tasks of a system manager?

3. The results of automation:

   3.1 From the perspective of the staff:
   3.1.1 How did the library's work processes change, and what changes did you have to implement?
   3.1.2 How did working conditions change?
   3.1.3 How did staff attitudes change?
   3.1.4 Did you change anything in the software?
   3.1.5 Do you have the source program?

   3.2 From the perspective of the customers:
   3.2.1 How did your service system change?
   3.2.2 What new services did you introduce?
   3.2.3 How did your environment and your customers receive the changes?
   3.2.4 What did you do to raise the awareness of the new system among your customers?

4. Further tasks:

4.1 How do you promote the system among your customers?
4.2 What are the costs of maintaining the system?
    a. costs of operation and upgrading;
    b. from the perspective of staff members and new staff?
4.3 Do you have any other new ideas?

Appendix 35.2 Addresses of Libraries Surveyed

Central Library of Budapest University of Economic Sciences
    H - 1093 Budapest, Közraktár u. 18/20.
Central Library of the University of Veterinary Science
    H - 1078 Budapest, István u. 2.
City Library, Miskolc
    H - 3530 Miskolc, Mindszent tér 2.
Hungarian Academy of Fine Arts Library
    H - 1062 Budapest, Andrássy u. 69/71.
József Katona Library, Kecskemét
    H - 6000 Kecskemét, Piaristák tere 8.
Library and Information Center of the Technical University of Budapest
    H - 1111 Budapest, Budafoki út 4.
Library of the Hungarian Academy of Sciences
    H - 1051 Budapest, Arany János u. 1.
University and National Library
    H - 4010 Debrecen, Egyetem tér 1.

Appendix 35.3 Statistical Data for Libraries Surveyed, 1996

Name of Library	Collection (number of items)	OPAC (items)	Number of Registered Users	Number of Loans	Number of Staff Members	
					Librarians	Information People
Central Library of Budapest University of Economic Sciences	493,468	234,162	15,387	98,845	28	6
Central Library of the University of Veterinary Science	127,134	51,240	1,301	4,962	6	3
City Library, Miskolc	370,318	25,852	7,859	305,886	34	5
Hungarian Academy of Fine Arts Library	56,654	12,000	1,107	26,002	5	1
József Katona Library, Kecskemét	449,297	195,640	24,026	212,368	64	1
Library and Information Center of the Technical University of Budapest	700,000	123,095	24,003	71,443	49	2
Library of the Hungarian Academy of Sciences	2,067,514	150,000	11,650	14,000	65	2
University and National Library, Deprecen	3,888,075	135,317	7,705	61,234	77	5